Utsira

Norway

Farm and Family History

1521–1995

JOSTEIN AUSTRHEIM

Utsira

Norway

Farm and Family History

1521–1995

Translated by Johannes Christoffersen

Edited by Virginia Stover

Foreword by Jan Sjåvik

Heron Run Press
Kenmore, WA
USA

The publisher thanks Jan Sjåvik, Professor of Scandinavian Studies, University of Washington, Seattle, for writing the Foreword for this book.

Revised March 2013.
(This edition contains a few updates and corrections.)

Published by Heron Run Press
Kenmore, WA
2012

ISBN 978-0-615-59837-6

Visit Heron Run Press website at www.HeronRunPress.com

This book is a translation and update of *Utsira, Gard og slekt* by Jostein Austrheim, published in Norway by Utsira Kommune in 1995.

Book cover photo and all other photos, maps and charts in this book are reprinted with the written permission of the author or copyright owner.

Printed in the United States of America

Contents

Foreword

It seems like family has always mattered a lot to Norwegians. Life in pre-industrial rural Norwegian society was strongly influenced by the extended family, which affected not only social and economic relations but also the identity of the individual. A person's social position depended far more on what kind of family he or she had been born into than by whatever individual accomplishments the person might have. This made for both social stability and a strong sense of identity, but it also meant that it was not easy for an individual to significantly alter his or her position in life.

When your extended family is of such paramount importance, you will naturally be inclined to know as much as possible about your ancestors and other relatives. In pre-industrial Norway this knowledge was transmitted orally as well as through direct contact with members of the extended family, or *ætt*. Some individuals were of course better than others at holding onto and transmitting this kind of traditional oral knowledge, much as some people in cultures based on writing are more interested in intellectual pursuits.

While reading and writing skills were taught in some families during the medieval period, it was only in the 1700s that Norway saw the beginnings of a system of public education. While rudimentary at first, schooling gradually became both more widely available and of increasingly better quality, and by the second half of the 1800s some young men of rural origins even managed to get university degrees. Others became teachers, as did many women as well, especially toward the end of the 1800s. By the time we get into the 20th century, becoming a teacher was a common way for talented rural youths to make their way in the world. Frequently, these men and women also served as leaders in their local communities, including as members of the local farm history commission.

The farm history or *bygdebok* holds a very special place in Norwegian life, and it is squarely placed in the written culture that replaced the oral culture of pre-industrial rural Norway. But it is equally the case that the concerns of promoters and authors of farm histories are similar to those who kept up the knowledge of who was related to whom, and how, in traditional Norwegian society. Additionally, the modern *bygdebok* has a memorial function: like an ancient *bautastein* (memorial stone), it stands as a visible reminder of past generations.

Such works of local history as *bygdebøker* began appearing in Norway shortly after 1910 and could, in addition to genealogy, also deal with other aspects of local life. It is fair to say, though, that the most common form of the *bygdebok* is a record of who owned the various farms and sub-farms, how the land was valued and taxed, and who lived on and worked the land. A typical farm history deals with one or more local communities and is organized by farms and the various families that lived on those farms; not included are the landless, such as servants, boarders, and cottagers who did not possess cultivable land. This, too, is a reflection of what life was like in pre-industrial Norway, as these people received less respect and generally had fewer descendants than those of greater fortune, including better family connections and better health. There is a certain irony in this, however, as the egalitarianism of contemporary Norway, where the local *bygdebok* is usually published under the auspices of local government, nevertheless in certain ways reflects the class distinctions of the past. I should hasten to add that Utsira—perhaps because of its size—seems to be a place where all members of the community mattered, regardless of social or economic status.

A separate municipality (*kommune*), Utsira is a small island off the coast in Rogaland County and today has a population of slightly more than 200 people. The population has been cut roughly in half since 1950. Its main road is slightly less than two miles in length, and it takes a little more than an hour to reach the mainland by boat. The weather can be brutal at times, especially during the winter, but the landscape is impressive and the bird life spectacular. Evidence of human presence has been found from as far back as the Stone Age.

The credit for this Utsira *bygdebok* belongs to Jostein Austrheim, a member of the local community, whose talent and commitment cannot be questioned. It is also very much to the credit of the translator and editor that this excellent farm and family history now appears in English translation.

Jan Sjåvik
Professor of Scandinavian Studies
University of Washington, Seattle
March, 2012

Editor's Note

I first came upon the book *Utsira, Gard og slekt* by Jostein Austrheim in Norway in October 2000 when visiting the island of Utsira with the hope of finding relatives of my maternal great–grandfather. I found them, thanks to a photo in that book — a photo that I had often seen as a child when visiting my grandmother — of the parents (presumably) of her father, Knut Mathias Johnson. The photo (of John Mathias and Petronelle Johnsen, p. 316) also led ultimately to this translation.

I brought the book back to the states with me in 2004 and proceeded to show it to various friends and family members. Everyone enjoyed looking at the fascinating old photos in the book, but no one could read the Norwegian text, so two years ago I decided I was going to translate it. Of course, I couldn't do it on my own, so I placed an ad for a Norwegian translator. After a number of responses, I found someone who lived just a few miles away from me. Johannes Christoffersen was not a professional translator, but a retired engineer originally from Norway. He was looking for a "project" and the idea of translating a Norwegian family history book interested him, so I showed him the book and he agreed to work with me.

Almost all of our collaboration on this project has been via email. Johannes would translate a few pages, send them to me by email attachment, I would send them back to him after editing, he would approve them or make corrections and shoot them back to me, page after page. He would also collaborate with Jostein, the author, via email, when he came across a particularly difficult old Norwegian word or phrase. When it got to be too much work (I was also teaching almost full–time), I would forward some of the newly translated pages to my brother Ed Stover, who had agreed to help out, for editing. It took about a year and a half to complete the initial translation and editing of the book, then another few months or so to format, tweak and polish before going to press.

The whole process from beginning to end has been a very rewarding experience. However, it was truly a joint effort and I need to acknowledge the rest of the team.

I want to thank my brother, Ed, whose advice and assistance in editing these pages have been invaluable. His many years' experience as a career journalist and a writer has made the sometimes tedious process of page–by–page editing much easier. Ed also wrote the book summary on the back of the dust jacket. He didn't want to share the credits on the title page, but just to be acknowledged, so here it is — thanks, Ed.

I wish to thank the author, Jostein Austrheim, whose assistance and support of this translation have been unwavering. He was behind this project primarily so his relatives in Alberta, Canada would finally be able to read his book in English. I hope they enjoy it.

I would like to thank the translator, Johannes Christoffersen. His insight into the quirks of the west coast Norwegian written language and his lyrical and expressive writing style have helped to bring alive, for the first time in English, those old Norse records, articles, and anecdotes of the past. Thank you, Johannes, for agreeing to translate this book.

In addition, many thanks to Jolinda Fernhout for her expert technical assistance with the intricacies of Word pagination.

The footnotes in this book were written by the editor, and the research for footnote 48 was done by both the editor and translator. The Notes were written by the author Jostein Austrheim and appeared in the original book, with the exception of Notes 34 and 35, written by the translator and editor, respectively. Some additional information, updates, and photos for some family members, especially those who emigrated, which were received too late to appear in the first edition, have also been added. The Index, which appeared in the Norwegian edition, is alphabetized by first name, rather than last. For more on Norwegian naming customs, go to http://www.norwayheritage.com/norwegian-names.htm.

In this translation, the extra Norwegian vowels *ø,* pronounced like the *u* in British "burn" *(bu:n), å,* like the *o* in British "lord," *æ,* like the *a* in "mad," have been retained or have been replaced with the commonly excepted substitute, *oe, aa,* and *ae*, respectively, especially where this spelling has been used in Norwegian – American names. Also, note that the letters "j" and often "g" (if before i or j or at the end of some words) are pronounced like the vowel *y* in "yes." See website http://wikitravel.org/en/Norwegian_phrasebook for more on Norwegian pronunciation.

Finally, those who wish to purchase a copy of this book, or who are simply interested, may go to www.heronrunpress.com. Click on "tourist brochure" for more about Utsira (scroll down for English). Go to http://digitalarkivet.uib.no /sab/howto.html for a Norwegian emigration history and for links to trace their own ancestors.

Virginia Stover
Editor

A Note from the Translator

I was intrigued by the project of translating the book about Utsira, one of the outer islands along the Norwegian west coast, when it was brought to my attention, and the prospect of learning about life on this remote island.

As the translator I have tried to stay as close to the original text as possible and avoid temptations to strengthen or color descriptions of certain events in the book, as they are described in a very straightforward and down–to–earth way, probably typical for the people there and the times. I have particularly enjoyed the time capsules from old newspaper clippings and excerpts from old records (often written in old, very formal Norwegian language and sometimes spelled phonetically), as well as the extraordinary portraits throughout the book of the people who carved out a living on Utsira.

In this process I have enjoyed and benefited from the assistance of Jostein Austrheim, the author, who helped me, with his insight and historical knowledge, in the translation of words and expressions in the old clippings that I had not been able to identify or find in any dictionaries.

Finally, I have enjoyed working with Virginia, who was the driving force in making this book available to English–speaking descendants from Utsira and others interested in Norwegian history and culture. She has helped me to bring my "Norwegian/English" into proper English, as only a teacher can.

Johannes Christoffersen
Translator

Utsira Scottish cows. Photo by Johannes Christoffersen, 2011.

A Note from the Author

It is 16 years since *Utsira – Gard og slekt* was completed and published. For me, as an amateur historian, it was a challenge to collect and write all the information needed to create this book. This while simultaneously working as a full–time farmer made it even harder, but by means of great interest and help from others on the island, I was able to complete the project. I remember well the last weeks before the manuscript was to be sent to the printer — I went with my camera and tripod to some of the homes on the island to photograph the big family portraits hanging on their walls.

Over the years we have mailed copies of the book to our relatives in the USA and Canada and some have obtained a copy when visiting Utsira. We were well aware of the language barrier for our English–speaking relatives. Only being able to read the names and dates, without understanding all the other information given in the book, lessened the experience of knowing our ancestors better. Early last year when first told of the plan to translate the book, we were overjoyed by the news, and also relieved because we had only a few copies left of the first edition. Now, with the work completed, I want to congratulate the editor, Virginia Stover, and the translator, Johannes Christoffersen, on the work they have done to make this project happen, especially Virginia for her decision to do this translation. I think there are very few, if any, translated versions of Norwegian farm and family–history books (*bygdebøker*).

I and others in the last years, by means of more and more tools on the web, have gathered new information relating to many of those who emigrated. As this is a translated edition, most of this information is not added here, but eventually will be saved in a database open for the reader and others to play a part. For now, the reader can find out more about Utsira at http://www.utsira.kommune.no (click on "tourist information in English").

Jostein Austrheim
Author

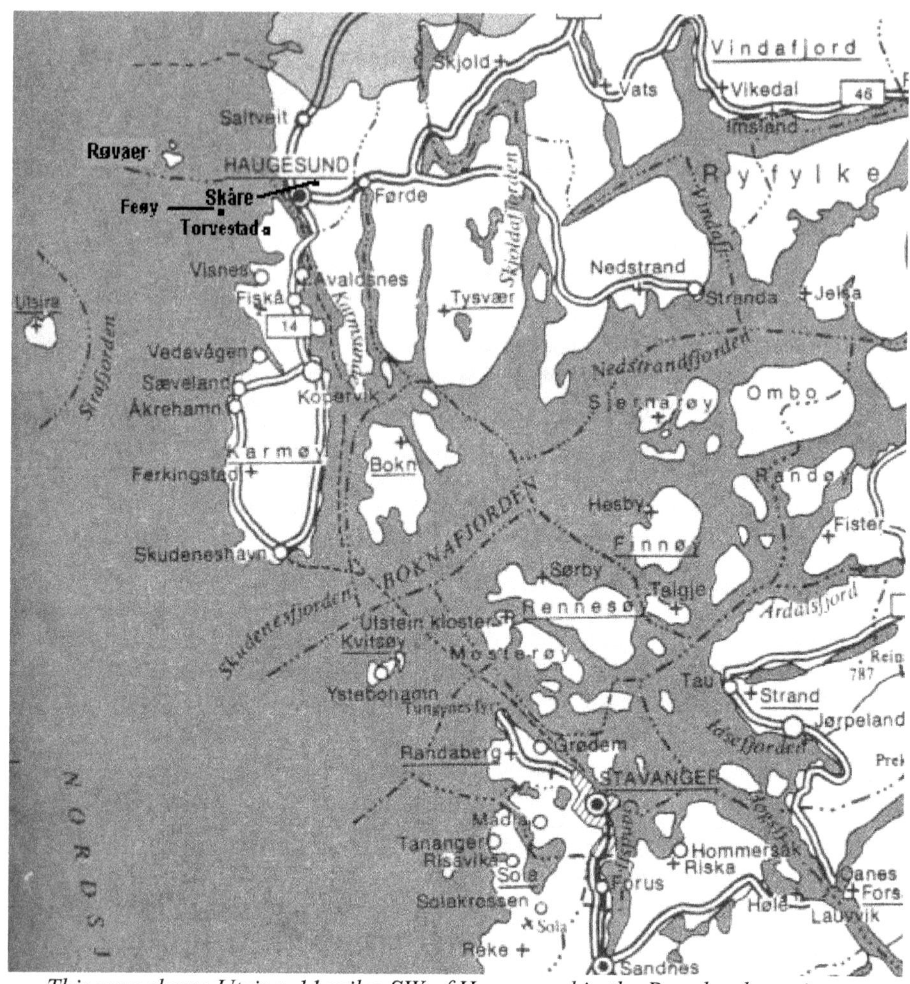

This map shows Utsira, 11 miles SW of Haugesund in the Rogaland province of southwest Norway.

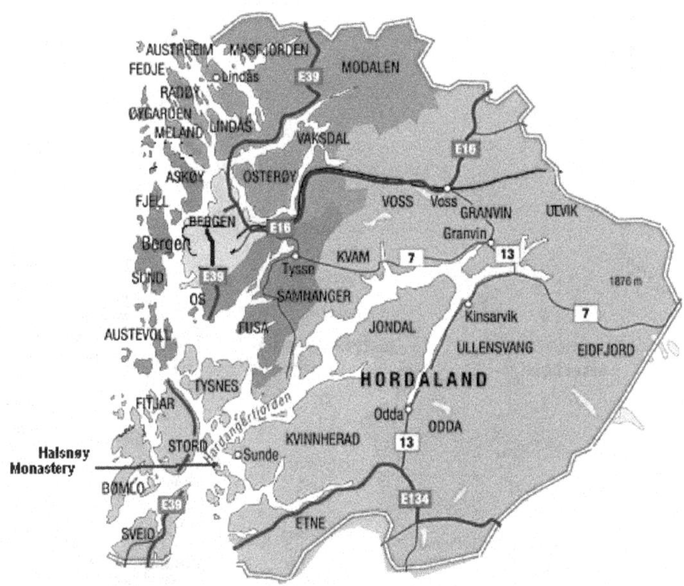

The map above, the province of Hordaland, shows the location of Halsnøy Monastery in the south. Rogaland province below (south of Hordaland) shows the location of Utsira relative to the mainland and Stavanger to the south.

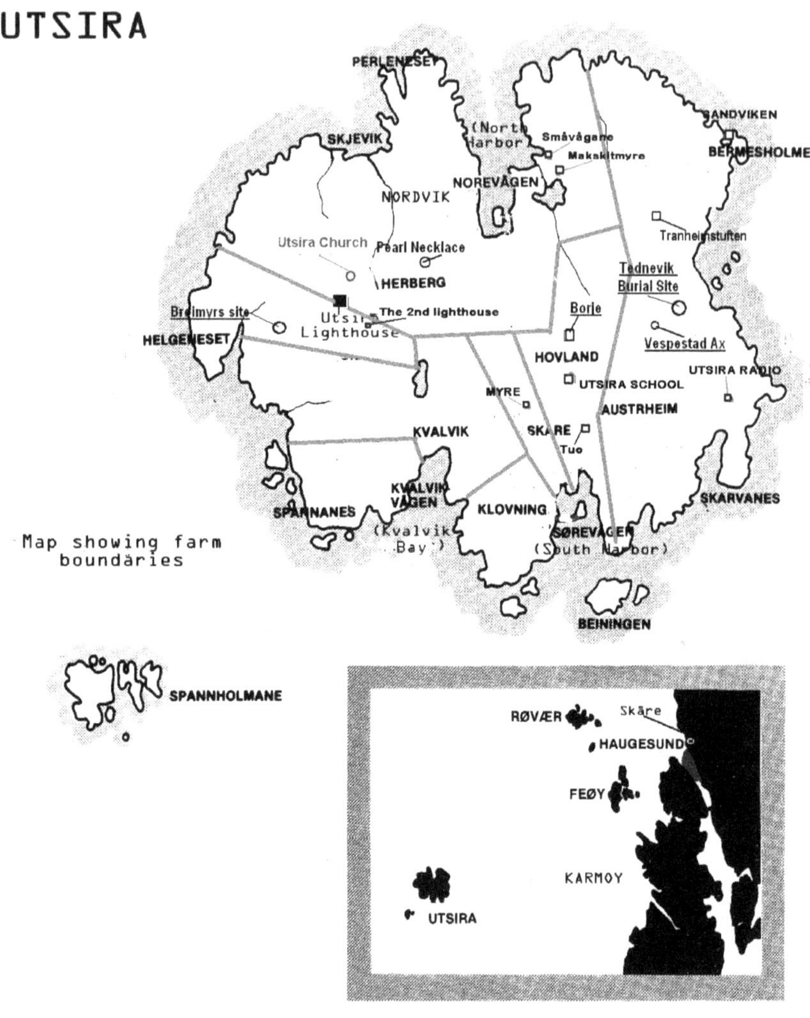

Map of Utsira showing farm boundaries and place names. Inset: Utsira relative to the island of Karmøy and Haugesund on the mainland.

Utsira
Norway

Farm and Family History

1521–1995

Utsira Harbor. Photo by Kjell Strand, 2004.

Preface

Torvestad and Utsira[1] belonged in the past to Avaldsnes judicial district in the province of Ryfylke. Torvestad along with Utsira and Skåre[2] eventually became a separate judicial district in 1837. Haugesund was incorporated in 1855 and in 1881 the district was again divided so that Skåre became a township and Torvestad and Utsira became a separate municipality. On June 1, 1924, Utsira became its own municipality, but stayed part of Torvestad church parish. This arrangement is still in effect.

The local municipal council consisted of 12 representatives and 3 of those were elected to the presidency. At the second municipal election in 1925, a surprising development came about: 11 women and only one man were voted into the local government. This was coined the "Petticoat Council" and became big news not only in Norway, but also abroad. This had not happened before, at least not in Europe.

Mayors in Utsira :

1924–1925: Sivert Helgesen
1926–1928: Åsa Helgesen
1929–1931: Sivert Helgesen
1932: Mathias Larsen
1932–1940: Gudmund Klovning
1946–1951: Thorvald Austrheim
1952–1959: Tore Nordvik
1960–1975: Sverre Klovning
1976–1979: Hersleb Helgesen
1980–1991: Torbjørn Rasmussen
1992– : Reidar Klovning

---

[1] **Utsira** is pronounced "oot – seer – rah."

[2] **Skåre** is on the mainland, now part of Haugesund, and **Skare** is the farm Skare on Utsira. The vowel sounds are prounounced differently, but both with two syllables ("skoh–ray" and "skah – ray," respectively).

Utsira district government voted on June 18, 1952 for their first Book Commission consisting of: Thoralf Kvalvik, Chairman, Hersleb Helgesen and Svend Klovning. Now, more than 40 years later, the farm and family history for Utsira can finally be presented. When the book was published in 1995, the Book Commission consisted of the following members:

Oystein Haugland, Chairman
Arnstein Eek, Secretary
Sverre Klovning, Jostein Austrheim and Johannes G. Klovning.

The Book Commission is also planning to publish a book about the general history of Utsira.[3] In this connection, we are very interested in contacting people who may have knowledge of old pictures, etc., from Utsira which may be useful in this research.

The main committee for cultural affairs has been the Book Commission leaders and the book is financed by the Utsira Municipality.

The Book Commission wishes to acknowledge and thank everyone who has contributed and made possible the publishing of this book.

Utsira, September 1995.

Utsira Book Commission, 1995. Front from left: Johannes G. Klovning and Jostein Austrheim. Back row from left: Oystein Haugland, Sverre Klovning and Arnstein Eek.

[3] The *History of Utsira* book was published in Norway in May 2000. It contained corrections to this book that have been included herein where possible.

Introduction

Farm and family history for Utsira is structured in the same manner as the books written about Karmøy.[4] Today's system with farm number and farmer number, in use since 1886, is also used as it has been done through the ages, in an effort to make it easier to see the continuity. Everybody who has managed a particular farm is identified with the farm number, example: "Farmer 1–4"[5] where "1" is the farm number, and "4" is the farmer no. 4. All others are listed as "tenant farmer." [6] The year indication to the right shows the period the individual ran the farm or when he occupied the property. We have tried to include as many as possible of those who have lived on Utsira from the earliest periods where written records existed to the present. Unfortunately, there has not been time to include data on some newcomers, particularly teachers, and those who have worked at Utsira Lighthouse and Utsira Radio over the years.

The most important sources used are church records from 1753 – 1925, public records showing property transactions from 1725 – 1875, local community records (to 1822 and some miscellaneous records 1840 – 1870), electoral records, census records, district financial records 1600 – 1645, deposit books and deposit records. Examination of these records has been done to some degree on location, but some

---

[4] Karmøy is a large island just off the mainland near Haugesund, Norway.

[5] *Farmer 1–4* means "farm section no. 1, farmer no. 4." In this English translation, we have (in most cases) used "farm" or "farmer" in place of the abbreviations used in the book (for example, Norwegian "Bnr." meaning *bruksnummer* or farm section–user number) to identify a particular farm section/farmer number.

[6] *Tenant farmer* (Norwegian *andre oppsittere,* or "second tenants") *3–5* means "tenant farm no. 3, tenant farmer no. 5." Farm numbers can also refer to place, especially when indicating where the bride came from.

have also been made available through photocopying and the generous loan of microfilm records from various libraries. The books on Sveio, Tysvaer and particularly Karmøy have been very helpful in reconstructing the immigration and emigration history. Several family history books and *Norges Bebyggelse* ("Norwegian Homes") have also been utilized along with old newspapers from the period 1834 – 1935.

Words such as "maybe," "perhaps," and "possibly" are often used in descriptions of before 1753, when we did not have the benefit of church records to support our research and because the writings before that period are very limited. We feel it is better to present what is apparently the case, in our opinion, and let future research confirm or disprove the statements. The written material is also sometimes not completely reliable. This applies particularly to the period before 1800.

With only six farms in the municipality, we have the opportunity to include more information on each family than is normally possible in local history books. This applies especially to writings and follow–up stories that often provide important data. These writings provide details about fishing equipment and boats, etc., used by the individuals. Fishing has, perhaps to a greater extent than in neighboring communities, been the main source of income, even though they did have farms also. In places where no work description is indicated, one can assume that fishing was the source of income. The fishing activities on Utsira are an extensive part of the history of the civilization on Utsira, a book that will be finished in the not too distant future.

Abbreviations and Terms[7]

Al.	– cubit (*alen)* 1 alen = 62.75cm = approx. 25 inches
A.O.	– tenant farmer (*andre oppsittere* or "second tenants")
a.u.o.	– of unknown origin
bnr.	– farmer or farm (*bruksnummer* – literal translation: "user number," refers to farm section or farmer)

[7] These Norwegian abbreviations and their meanings were included in the original Norwegian text of the book and we include them here with the English translation as a reference along with a few additional terms. In this translation most abbreviations are spelled out in English, for clarity, with the exception of some Norwegian monetary or measurement terms that are frequently used, such as, "sk." for skilling, "rdl." for riksdaler, mrk. for merker, "v.tf," "v.dr.f." or "v. dried fish" for våger of dried fish, "kr." for kroner and "Sp." for Speciedaler.

bp.	– bismerpound *(bismerpund):* 1 våger = 3 bismerpound = 72 merker = 18.52 kg.
dat.	– date or dated (*datert*)
d.	– dead (*død)*
dl.	– monetary unit from 1838–86 (*skylddaler)*
dp.	– baptized (*døpt)*
e.	– widow (*enke)*
e.m.	– widower (*enkemann)*
f.	– born (*født)*
gl.	– old (*gammel)*
g.m.	– married to (*gift med)*
grl.	– buried (*gravlagt)*
hj.br.	– pursuant to a letter (*hjemmelsbrev.)*
mål	– (*mål åker)* 1 mål = 1 dekar = 1000 sq. meters = ¼ acre)
mrk.	– merker – *merker fiskevekt* or fish weight. (1 våg = 72 merker = 18.52 kg. = 39.5 lbs. (Often property was valued and rent was paid using these units.)[8]
nr.	– number (*nummer)*
pd.	– pound (*pund, bismerpund, fiskevekt, 1 pund* (1 pound) = 24 merker)
rdl.(rbdl.)	– riksdaler (*riksbankdaler)* – monetary unit before 1813: 1 rdl. = 4 ort = 96 sk.[9]
sk.(s.)	– shilling or schilling (*skilling)* – before 1813: 1 rdl.= 4 ort = 96 sk.; 1816–75: 1 Spd. = 5 ort = 120 sk.; after 1876: 1 Spd. = 4 kroner
sk.	– *skyld* debt – ”guilt” – to owe money or a debt, also tax or rent on a farm
SK.	– separated or divorced; signs (*skilt)*

---

[8] In Norway's barter economy, the taxes were set in terms of what the farm produced. Along the coast the taxes might be levied in the value of the fish; in the mountains, butter. In actuality the farmer usually did not deliver tanned hides, fish or butter to the official, but rather the currency obtained from the sale of such. – wiki.familysearch.org.

[9] Multiplying by 100 gives an approximate equivalent in Norwegian kroner today; by 15, in US dollars; by 10, pounds sterling. For more on Norwegian currency, the reader can go to en.wikipedia.org/wiki/Norwegian_speciedaler and wiki.familysearch.org/en/Norwegian_Currency.

sk.m.	– new currency or "skyldsetting" from 1886 (*skyldmark)*
s.m.	– live–in partner, unmarried (*samboer med)*
Spd.	– monetary unit 1816–75 (*Speciedaler)* – 1 Spd. = 120 sk. = 5 ort; from 1876: 1 Spd. = 4 kroner
sk.p.	– *skålpund* – grain weight just under ½ kg. – approx. 1 lb.
skp.	– *skjepper* (1 skjepper = 20 liters or 20.13 quarts or 1/2 bushel)
sp.	– *spann (spand)* or "grain bucket" (*kornvekt)* – weight unit used for grain: 1 span = 30 merker = 7.72 kg
t.(tdr.)	– *tønne(r=* more than one*)* barrel: 1 barrel grain = 144 potter = 139.4 liters, 1 fishbarrel *(fisketønne)* = 120 potter = 115.8 liters
tf.	– dried fish (*tørrfisk)* – Property rental was often paid with a certain amount (*våger)* of dried fish or the monetary equivalent.
tv.	– twin (*tvilling)*
u.	– under or below *(under)*
u.e.	– outside marriage; illegitimate (*utenfor ekteskap)*
utv.	– emigrated (*utvandret)*
v.	– våger fishweight (*fiskevekt,* 1 våg = 3 bismerpund = 72 merker = 18.52 kg.)
v.s.u.	– ultimate fate unknown or further information unknown (*videre skjebne ukjent)*
v.tf. (v.dr.f.)	– våger dried fish (*våger torrfisk)* – old monetary unit vager of dried fish; often used for paying property rental: 1 våg = 18 ½ kg. = around 40 lbs.

Utsira

The Oldest Period.[10]

The few findings from the Stone Age that have been recorded on the island of Utsira, among them an ax found in Kvalvik in 1911 and a stone ax of the "Vespestad type" found in Austramarka in 1948, tell us that people lived here before 1000 – 2000 BC, but they were possibly only visitors from the mainland at that time. At Austrheim and Klovning there are traces of settlements from the Stone Age.

It is difficult to say with any degree of certainty when people first settled on Utsira. After the excavations by Jan Petersen in Vestramarka and Austramarka (western and eastern areas of the island) in 1929–1933, it was confirmed that in any case the island was settled from the Migration Period, from the year 400 AD and later. The farm names, "Austrheim" and "Hovland," themselves indicate that this is true, in the same way the hill "Børje" at Hovland does. [11]

The "pearl" necklace that Åsa and Sivert Helgesen found in 1932–33 is probably the most valuable find on the island. It dates back to the 8th century AD and most likely came from across the North Sea. It consists of 40 beads of glass, most of them blue, one of amber and two

---

[10] Jan Petersen (1887–1967). Director of the Stavanger Museum, Norway. Data retrieved is from Jan Petersen's manuscript detailing his excavations at Utsira in 1929–33. In the Local History Archive, Stavanger Museum, Norway. (See Note 1.)

[11] Place names of Germanic origin date back to The Migration Period, also called the Barbarian Invasions or German *Völkerwanderung* (wandering of the peoples), which was a period of human migration that occurred roughly between 300 and 700 AD in Europe, after the fall of the Roman Empire. wikipedia.org/wiki/Migration_Period.

Brøimyrs site, the remains of a settlement from the Migration Period in the western part of the island of Utsira.

of quartz. A piece of a single–edged sword with a narrow blade was also found and dates from the same period. This was given to Stavanger Museum in 1917 by Mr. K. Bing of Bergen.

The youngest homesteads, Tranheimstuften in Austramarka (eastern Utsira) and the homestead near Måkskitemyre, date back to the Viking Age, approximately 900 AD. The smallest homestead in the area of Småvågane on the east side of Nordvik Bay is possibly younger, probably from the Middle Ages, 1300 AD.

Utsira is mentioned briefly in *Snorre Sagaer* (the Icelandic Sagas) a couple of times.[12] Apart from that, the island is mostly in the dark during the Middle Ages, with the exception of when the island on June 17, 1247, was visited by Cardinal Wilhelm of Sabina[13] and his

---

[12] Snorri Sturluson's Sagas of the Norwegian kings. *Heimskringla* is the best known of Old Norse kings' sagas, written in Old Norse in Iceland by the poet and historian Snorri Sturluson around 1230 AD. wikipedia.org/wiki/Snorri_Sturluson.

[13]On 29 July, 1247, Cardinal Wilhelm of Sabina crowned King Håkon Håkonsson at Bergen. Cardinal Wilhelm (William of Modena 1184 – 1251),

One of two burial sites at Tednevik in the eastern part of the island from the late medieval or early Viking age.

entourage. He came to Norway to crown Håkon Håkonsen[14] that summer and first landed on Utsira where he sent an advanced message to the king announcing his imminent arrival in Bergen.

In 1897 a local pilot, Bertel Helgesen, Nordvik, told this to Nils Okland: *The first Christian minister who came to Norway landed first on Sira. He came on a sailing vessel and anchored up in the bay of Nordvikvågen. At that time there were 12 fishermen homes on Sira.* [15]

That there were 12 families on the island sounds reasonable, and is probably correct. It is more difficult to believe that the "first Christian minister" first set foot in Norway on Utsira, as many communities along the coast make the same claim.

---

was an Italian clergyman and papal diplomat. newadvent.org/cathen/16009b.htm.

[14]In 1247 Håkon Håkonsson was recognized by the Pope, who sent Cardinal William of Sabina to Bergen to crown him. wikipedia.org/wiki/HaakonIV.

[15]Økland, Nils, "Utsira in the Norwegian National Story," Karmsund Yearbook Award, 1951–55, Karmsund Folk Museum, p. 83–85. (See Note 2.)

Who all those people were who lived on the island during the hundreds of years between 400 and 1500 AD, we will never know. For the first time in 1521 do we learn the names of those who occupied the farms on the island. All five farms (Klovning became a farm in its own right more than 100 years later) were then productive farms, something that may indicate that the great "Black Plague"[16] in 1349 did not affect Utsira as much as in many other places. They fared probably worse during later plagues, in the middle of the 1640s, when we learn through county reports that the island was ravaged with infectious disease (leprosy) and that the inhabitants suffered from hunger and poverty, which exempted them from all tax responsibilities.[17]

Ownership

At one point during the Middle Ages, Utsira became the property of the Halsnøy Monastery.[18] This could have been as a result of a gift or that the island was actually purchased by the monastery. The monastery was founded in the late 1100s and was part of the Augustine Movement.[19] After the Reformation[20] the cloister estate became a part

---

[16] Black Death, 1348 to 1350, killed up to 60 percent of Europe's population causing religious, social and economic upheaval. eyewitnesstohistory.com/plague.htm.

[17] From the District Financial Records of 1646, Stavanger, Norway. (Note 3.)

[18] The cloister on Utsira was a part of the Halsnøy Monastery, an Augustinian monastery located on the island of Halsnøy just north of present day Haugesund; possibly a branch of Halsnøy Abbey near Bergen. wikipedia.org/wiki/Halsnoy_Abbey.

[19] Takes its name from St. Augustine (born in 354 AD in Roman Africa) whose teachings influenced the development of Christianity and the founding of monasteries throughout western Europe during the Middle Ages. en.wikipedia.org/wiki/Augustine_of_Hippo.

[20] The Protestant Reformation, a European Christian reform movement that established Protestantism as a part of contemporary Christianity, began in 1517, when Martin Luther published *The Ninety-five Theses*, and concluded in 1648 with the Treaty of Westphalia, which ended years of religious wars. theopedia.com/Protestant_Reformation.

of the Hardanger district. It was subsequently sold during the 1700s and the farms on Utsira were first offered for sale in 1727. At the time no one was interested.

The lowest prices were recorded as:

Nordvik:	100 rdl.	Kvalvik:	40 rdl.
Spanne:	20 rdl.	Skare:	30 rdl.
Klovning:	10 rdl.	Hovland:	30 rdl.
Austrheim:	60 rdl.		

In 1744 – 45 there was again an auction of the cloister properties and in the first round the bailiff Andreas Heiberg and the dean P. Schrøder got the bid. Schrøder got the Skare, Klovning and Spanne properties, while Heiberg got the rest of the properties at the minimum prices listed (below) in parentheses:

Nordvik:	120 rdl (100)	Kvalvik:	54 rdl. (40)
Spanne:	42 rdl. (16)	Skare:	60 rdl. (50)
Klovning:	38 rdl. (18)	Hovland:	82 rdl. (60)
Austrheim:	150 rdl. (100)		

In the meantime Peder Vallentinsen put in a bid on all the land estates owned by Halsnøy monastery in the Stavanger area. The offer was accepted at 9000 rdl., according to a deed dated Jan. 20, 1746. Peder Vallentinsen (1692 – 1761) was council chairman and commerce–assessor in Stavanger and owned many farmsteads in Rogaland and was the richest man around Stavanger at that time. His second wife, Anna Wilhelmine Bredahl administered the farms after her husband died. After her death in 1784, the farms were inherited by her children, in–laws and grandchildren:

Nordvik:	Peder Vallentinsen Forman, Bergen	– 480 rdl.
Hovland:	Peder Vallentinsen Forman, Bergen	– 150 rdl.
Kvalvik:	Justice Vallentinsen, Bergen	– 150 rdl.
Skare:	Justice Vallentinsen, Bergen	– 150 rdl.
Klovning:	Captain Arnoldus von Krogh, Nyvold	– 95 rdl.
Austrheim:	Hans B. Forman, Bergen	– 375 rdl.

Peder Vallentinsen got Kvalvik and Skare after the death of Justice Vallentin Christian Vallentinsen in Sept. 1787. He bought Klovning for 125 rdl. from von Krogh on May 3, 1789. After Peder's death in 1792 Hans B. Forman became the owner of all the farmsteads on

Utsira. We include below some biographical notes about Hans B. Forman:[21]

Hans Berendtsen Forman was born Nov. 18, 1739, died July 11, 1822. He was the son of Modesta Hansdatter Forman and Berendt Madstzen Forman, a merchant in Bergen.

He was married the first time on Aug. 14, 1764 to **Johanne Benedicte Vallentinsen**, born Aug. 19, 1746, died Feb. 20, 1775, daughter of Anna Wilhelmine Bredahl and Peder Vallentinsen, council chairman in Stavanger.

Painting of Hans B. Forman. On the backside of the painting, it says: "Hans Berentsen Forman – Born 18th November 1739, Acting Commerce–Assessor, Mayor and First–Secretary, Bergen Supreme Court, Owner of Utsira and the Utsira Church."

Second marriage on Sept. 24, 1781 to widow **Birgithe Meyer**, born May 16, 1744, died Feb. 2, 1801, daughter of merchant Peter Lexau and Catharina Møller, Bergen, widow of parish priest Paul Meyer.

---

[21] See Note 4.

Children in first marriage:

a. Modesta Berentine, born Oct. 6, 1765, married in 1791 to Henrik Jansen Fasmer (1766 – 1836), Consul General of Holland, owner of Alvoen near Bergen and businessman.
b. Peder Vallentinsen, born Dec. 8, 1766, died on Utsira Aug. 27, 1792, became owner of the farms on Utsira (except Austrheim). He was buried under the church altar on Utsira.
c. Anna Wilhelmine, born Mar. 11, 1768, married in 1794 to Jacob Christian Friedrrich Dahm (1767 – 1809), merchant in Bergen. Their son Johan Julius, became the next owner of the island of Utsira.
d. Karen Elizabeth, born Mar. 12, 1770, died unmarried May 11, 1822.
e. Berendt, born Aug. 16, 1772, died Sept. 27, 1772.

Public Announcement:
Aside from the proclamation done by me, the undersigned on September 24th, this is read to the appropriate courts in Bergen, Stavanger and Ungvoldsnes, that I hereby let it be known that upon the death on August 27 of my only son Hans B. Valentinsen Forman on the island of Utsire in the jurisdiction of Ryfylke, I hereby confirm that all creditors with legitimate claims will be settled by me to the extend the law will allow.
Bergen, December 1st, 1792

H. B. Forman
Acting Council Assessor and
Council Secretary.

Newspaper announcement from "The Address Register newspaper in Bergen", Dec. 1, 1792:

Hans was a student from 1759, finished his finals in philosophy in 1760, and received his Bachelor of Law in 1762. The same year he became deputy chancellor–assessor and vice council chairman. From 1763 he was vice mayor and he became court counsel from Oct. 1774. In 1807 he said goodbye to his career and settled on his estate Kristinegård in Sandviken.

Hans B. Forman was very much engaged in improvements and further developments of the farms at Utsira. He offered a number of books to be loaned to the general public on various subjects such as grain cultivation, potato growing and sheep farming. In the lease papers, he encouraged farmers to abandon traditional methods and crop-growing customs, which he was convinced hindered initiative and productive development. He also considered settling on the island, according to one mortgage letter; however, it never materialized. It was his grandchild, Johan J. Dahm, when he took over as the owner of Utsira, who moved out and settled there. See Farm no. 2, Skare.

Table of planting and harvesting for grain and potatoes on Utsira:

Year	Grain sown	Potatoes planted	Grain harvested	Potatoes harvested
1668	18	–	–	–
1703	28	–	–	–
1712	28.5	–	–	–
1723	23	–	111.5	–
1802	48	–	268	–
1822	–	–	486	172
1845	105	34.5	–	–
1866	134.3	72.7	822	560
1875	133.1	82.7	–	–
1945	86.9	54.1	–	–

Figures for 1945 are in acres or number of barrels. In 1822 the yield on Skare was projected and included in the total.

Table of livestock, houses and resident population on Utsira:

Year	Horses	Cattle	Sheep	Houses	Inhabitants
1668	–	66	–	–	–
1703	9	69	x	–	–
1712	8	71	x	–	–
1723	5	53	21	–	–
1758	–	–	–	25	111
1801–02	20	81	60	27	134
1822	34	115	180	–	–
1845	31	105	260	38	249
1866	32	129	422	65	394
1875	27	109	450	62	363
1900	–	–	–	67	355
1929	26	139	403	–	–
1949	30	159	389	–	393
1959	16	136	271	–	399
1969	4	102	192	–	–
1974	1	70	216	–	–

The overview of livestock from 1657–1658, in the records of the so–called cattle tax, hardly provides an accurate image regarding the number of livestock for each the farmers on the island then, but the following is stated:

Austrheim:	2 cows and 1 calf	Skare:	2 cows
Hovland:	1 cow	Nordvik:	1 cow
Kvalvik:	1 cow and 1 calf	Klovning:	1 cow

Parti av Nordvik Havn. Utsire.

Postcard from 1919 of Nordvik harbor seen from the east.

Nordvik

Before 1824:	Registration no. 15, annual tax liability 6 v.tf.
1824 – 1851:	Reg. no. 54, Serial No. 229–235, tax 16 dl. 17 sk.
1851 – 1886:	Reg. no. 64, Serial No. 322–334, tax 16 dl, 4 ort 18 sk.
1886 – :	Farm no. 26, tax 28 marks 76 ore

Nordvik was the largest farm on Utsira until 1743, when either one or two farmers cultivated the farm. Around 1800 this was increased to four, and in 1830 there were eight separate farms at Nordvik. Later in 1950, records show that 19 farms were in operation at Nordvik.

Around 1600, there were two unregistered settlements at Nordvik: Støren, the largest one in western Nordvik, and the other, Espehaugen, in eastern Nordvik. From approximately 1750 until about 1780, two smaller settlements were established on Nordvik.

According to the Land Register of 1668:[22]

> Utsiiere, an island 3 miles[23] from the mainland out in the ocean belonging to Halsnøy Cloister, with several farms paying tax to the King's treasury. One of the farms in Nordvik, farm no. 15, 6 våger dried fish (annual tax), providing fields for farming and pastures, sowing of 6 barrels grain, providing sufficient feed for 20 cows, enough fuel (peat) and cooking facilities for life sustenance, good for tax of 1-1/2 pound of grain, 4 goat hides for local defenses, 6 buckets of grain for the church, and 12 skillings in cash contributions.

[22] From the 1640s the annual land tax was dependent on the land rent. In 1665, Norway got its first land register (Norwegian: *matrikkel*), with an annual land rent that reflected the value of the production of the farm, based on expected returns in agriculture. wikipedia.org/wiki/Taxation_in_Norway #Middle_Ages.

[23] From 1889 the Norwegian "mil" equals 6.2 miles or 10 kilometers, but earlier it had different values. Utsira is actually 18 km. or about 11 miles SW from the closest port, Haugesund. See wikipedia.org/wiki/Scandinavian_mile.

Previous pages: Aerial view of Utsira. Nordvik harbor entrance in the foreground (Telemark Aircraft Co. 1954).

Public sale of the western pastures and forests was done in 1863, and the farmed fields were sold in 1876 – 1879.

Table showing planting and harvesting of grain and potatoes:

Year	Grain sown	Potatoes planted	Grain harvested	Potatoes harvested
1668	6	–	–	–
1703	8	–	–	–
1712	8	–	–	–
1723	5	–	–	–
1802	15	–	73	–
1822	–	–	145	60
1845	36	11	–	–
1866	48	27	305	211
1875	50	32	–	–
1945	35	19	–	–

The numbers for 1822 are estimated, as the source for this information is lost. For the year 1945 the published data are listed in dekar and barrels.

Table below indicates farm animals, homes and inhabitants:

Year	Horses	Cows	Sheep	Homes	Inhabitants
1668	–	20	–	–	–
1703	1	18	x	–	–
1712	1	19	x	–	–
1723	2	15	16	–	–
1758	–	–	–	7	33
1801–02	4	21	32	7	42
1822	10	34	50	–	–
1845	10	34	92	12	79
1866	10	48	123	20	106
1875	10	43	188	18	106
1900	–	–	–	20	108

Farmers

From around 1500 to the first part of 1600 we have only sporadic names, as it was impossible to determine an exact sequence of the active farmers. The sources before 1700 are furthermore very sparse.

View showing Nordvikvågen (Nordvik Bay) from Beite. Photo by P. O. Ottesen 1907.

The very first actual recording (for Utsira) of probate material dates to around 1725.

1. **Erik.** 1521
He is one of the two active farmers from 1521.

2. **Sjur.** 1521

3. **Lars.** 1563
He is listed as the farmer of all of Nordvik in 1563. He is listed as paying 1 daler in tax, the same as the other farmers on the island. He has two hired hands, Anbjorn, who pays 1/2 daler and Torstein who pays 1 ort in taxes.

4. **Mikkel.** – 1629.
It looks like Mikkel is farming 2/3 of the farm, according to tax records. Mikkel's widow continues working the farm until 1638.

5. **Ole Sjursen.** 1604 – 1634
Ole appears then to farm the remaining 1/3 of the Nordvik farm. He is listed in the tax records as "struggled and spent" until 1639.

6. **Peder.** 1631 –
Peder is working as much of the farm as Ole Sjursen.

7. **Nils.** 1637 –
In 1637 Nils pays 1/2 rdl. 16 sk. for a 3-year lease. He is then receiving 4 pd. fish from the farm. The same year he is listed as "hired hand" at "half salary."

8. **Lars.** 1638 –
Tax records state that Lars took over the farming after the death of the widow of Mikkel.

9. **Sigurd.** 1634 – 1641
Sigurd is a tenant farmer of a smaller part of the estate or is a hired hand, as are:

10. **Sjur.** 1641–1643
11. **Hans.** 1643 –
12. **Anders.** – 1658

Farm No. 1

1. **Jens Pedersen.** – 1683
Born around 1622, perhaps the son of Peder Austrheim.

Jens is at first a farmer together with Anders (no. 12 above), but from 1659 he is farming the entire Nordvik estate by himself. We do not know the name of his wife, but she was buried below the chancel under the church around 1713.[24]

Known children:

a. Peder, born around 1647.
b. Barbro, married to the next farmer.

Jens is mentioned in the court records on a couple of occasions. In 1663 he takes Simen and Asbjorn Hovland to court for not returning a sail he had lent them on an earlier occasion. In 1668 he is fined for a fistfight with Sjur Austrheim during that Christmas. On the second occasion a brother of Jens is mentioned.

---

[24] See Note 5.

2. **Anders Thomassen.** 1683 – 1710

Born around 1650 on Osnes, died Mar. 21, 1725 on Ytraland. His mother's name was Kirsten Andersdatter.

Married in first marriage around 1683 to **Barbro Jensdatter**, died after 1705, probably daughter of the previous farmer.

Married in second marriage to **Margrethe Olsdatter**, further information unknown.

Children from first marriage:

a. Karen, born around 1683, married to Claus Anbjornsen, farmer no. 4.
b. Mette, married in 1718 to Salomon A. Ahasverussen, Saevik in Åkra.
c. Barbro, born around 1696, married to Torres Sveinsen, Ytraland.

On May 16th 1683 Anders was cited in court at Eide in Bomlo by the bailiff Johan Frimand for letting his bride appear without the customary silver crown, and because she was pregnant:

> Anders Norvig appeared, and could not disprove that his wife was pregnant under her belt at the time she was a bride, and denied that she did not have a crown in silver, while she had pearls in her hair which actually belonged to Mattias Bugges' girlfriend, and wore a tiny silver necklace around her neck. For this crime as well as cohabiting with his woman too early, the court fined him in total 7 riksdaler.

The same year he was cited along with Johannes Hovland on a misdemeanor against another citizen, Jacob Brinchmand.

Anders was in good shape financially and also owned some real estate on Karmøy. In 1699 he purchased the farm, Saevik, from Nils Knutsen Steinsnes in Skåre. In 1705 he bought 2 pounds of grain from Søren Nilsen Sandberg in Torvestad for 144 rdl. (riksdaler), and in 1707 he bought 1–1/2 pounds of grain in Ytraland from Lars Meland, Avaldsnes.

In 1703 he earns 3 våger, 2 pounds tf. (dried fish) in commission in Nordvik. His financial condition is considered good, the houses on his property are also in good condition, and he "owes nothing to Frimand nor to anyone else." He sows 5 barrels oats and feeds 7 cows, 3 calves and some sheep.

Around 1710 he moves to Ytraland on Karmøy, but he is still receiving 2 pd.tf. from Nordvik for a few years more. In 1715 a tenant,

Lars, is appointed to run the farm at Nordvik. Lars is only mentioned this one time.

When the estate was settled after Anders' death in 1725, it was estimated at the full 355 riksdaler. The daughter Karen receives 1 pd. 1–1/2 spann grain in Torvestad, approximately a value of 76 rdl. 2 ort.

3. **Ole (Olsen ?).** – around 1698

Ole has possibly used up the 1–1/2 våger, 1 pd.tf., which the next farmer customarily receives in 1700. He is mentioned in military records from 1688, and also in a correspondence with the county in 1696, when several farmers ask to be excused from meeting with the County Board, Sunn–Hordaland,[25] which was also granted.

4. **Claus Anbjornsen.** 1700 – 1729

Born around 1670, son of Anbjorn Nilsen and Magdalena Clausdatter Torvestad.

Married to **Karen (Kari) Andersdatter**, born around 1683, died 1768, daughter of Barbro and Anders Thomassen, farm no. 1–2.

Children:

a. Barbro born 1705, married to Jørgen Thorsen, farm no 15–1 here.
b. Jens, born Jan. 1707, married 1748 to Bertha Danielsdatter, farm no. 17–1.
c. Malene, further information unknown.
d. Mette, born 1718, married to Kristoffer Ommundsen, Munkejord.
e. Karen, born 1724, married to Knut Danielsen, Hinderaker.

On May 19, 1700 Claus got a lease contract worth 1–1/2 v.tf. in Nordvik. In 1703 his financial condition is described as "fairly good" and also the buildings on the property were in fairly good condition (only around 3 ort in repair). He owes 7 riksdaler and 1–1/2 barrels cod on the lease obtained in 1700. It is recorded he also sows 3 barrels of oats, feeds 6 cows, 2 calves and some sheep. Two of the cows are leased. In 1711 he pays the "shoe–tax" (it is not explained what this is) for himself, his wife and 3 children with 30 skillings. He has a handyman (Ole Olsen) at an annual salary of 1 riksdaler and a housekeeper at 1-1/2 riksdaler.

In 1712 he spends 4 våger 2–1/2 pd.tf. from the farm and his financial condition is described again as "fairly good." The repair of the buildings is estimated to cost the full amount of 5 rdl. He has still not paid the 7 rdl. for the lease in 1700 and also owes 3 rdl. for lease of

[25] Stavanger County Archives, Section 86, Supplement (Note 6).

the fields for 1708. To someone else he owes 3 or 4 rdl., which he borrowed to pay taxes and other expenses.

He sows 7 to 8 barrels of oats, feeds 13 to 14 cows, 5 to 6 calves, 1 horse and . . . *some sheep, but exactly how many could not be determined, as they are scattered across the island.*

In 1721 the cost of repair of the barn will cost 2 ort 8 sk., but otherwise the buildings are in good condition. He has no debt and does not owe anyone anything, and the fields appear well taken care of.

The Land Register indicates the following in 1723:

> 6 våger (around 100 kg.) dried fish (annual tax). A small mill belongs to this farm. The farm is in poor shape. Claus Anbiornsen is not present during the sheriff's assessment: Sows 5 barrels grain, harvests 24 barrels, feeds 2 horses, 15 cows and 16 sheep.

The value of the estate after Claus on August 31, 1725 is 297 rdl. 12 sk. The following is left for the heirs:

> Cash 17–3–16, real estate in Torvestad (27–3/4 sp. grain) 83–1–0, gold and silver 19–3–16, large copper kettle 10–0–0, boathouses 6–0–0 and 3–2–0, food storehouse 3–0–0, boat with sail 10–0–0, 2 four–oar boats 2–3–0, 6 herring nets 2–0–0, 25 cows and 1 calf 59–3–0, 2 bulls 5–0–0, 2 horses 8–0–0, 40 sheep 13–1–8, 20 lambs 1–2–10, 8 "unborn" calves 10–0–0, 6 goats 2–2–0, 2 cows 0–1–0, 1 ram 3–1–0 and 14 barrels grain 10–3–16.

5. **Rasmus Abrahamsen.** 1729 – 1736
Born around 1708 at Klovning, son of Abraham Olsen, tenant farmer no. 2, Klovning.

Possibly married to **Karen Andersdatter**, the widow of the previous farmer.

Rasmus is listed in the military records of 1734, where it says he is a pilot and resident farmer at Nordvik. In 1735 the widow on Nordvik is listed with a note, "arrears on Royal contribution," which indicates that Rasmus must be deceased.

No known children.

6. **Paul Knutsen.** 1737 – 1740
Married to **Karen Andersdatter**, widow of previous farmer.

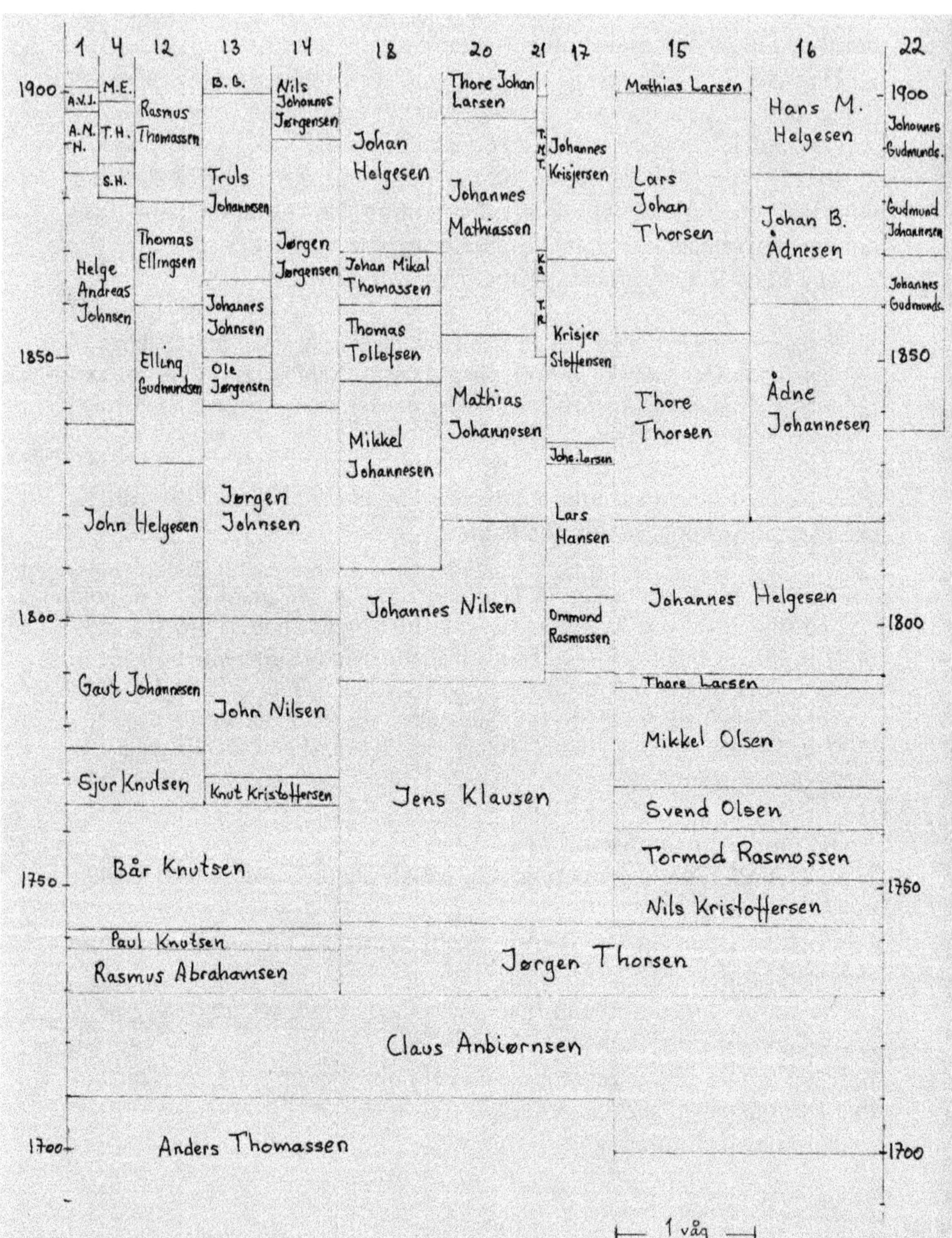

Table of farmers for Nordvik, 1700–1900. (Farm numbers are across the top of the table.)

There is no further information about him, other than a legal notification about his lease of 2 v.tf. at Nordvik in 1737. By 1740 he must be deceased, as the widow at Nordvik is listed with arrears on a Royal contribution.

No known children.

7. **Bår Knutsen.** 1742 – 1765

Born about 1716, buried Oct. 6, 1765, possibly brother of previous farmer (son of Knut Olsen, farmer no. 4 – 5, Austrheim?).

Around 1742 he married **Karen Andersdatter**, widow of previous farmer. Karen died in Dec. 1768, and in March the next year there was a record of settlement of her estate.

The estate was estimated at 95 rdl., of which 59–2–5 is in cash or coins: 4-1/2 English kroner and 3 Danish kroner for 5–3–0, a tiled heating stove 7–0–0, 9 lobster pots 0–1–12 and 1 cow 4–0–0.

8. **Sjur Knutsen.** 1765–1775

Born around 1745, buried July 16, 1775, son of Berta Knutsdatter and Knut Sjursen, tenant farmer no. 15, Nordvik.

Married Oct. 6, 1767, to **Lisbeth Tollefsdatter,** born 1746, died Oct. 17, 1814, daughter of Ingeborg and Tolleiv Rasmussen, tenant farmer no. 14, Nordvik.

Children:

a. Bår, baptized Oct. 23, 1768, confirmed Oct. 9, 1786.
b. Tollef, baptized Jan. 29, 1771, married in 1795 to Ingeborg Gudmundsdatter, farm no. 2–3, Austrheim.
c. Knut, baptized Nov. 7, 1773, married in 1801 to Berta Gudmundsdatter, farm no. 5–4, Austrheim.

A lease of 1 v.tf. in Nordvik from Sjur is dated Sept. 6, 1765. In the estate settlement after Sjur's death in 1775, the amount of 82–1–8 rdl. is indicated, of which 60–1–16 is designated for distribution among the heirs. The estate is listed as follows:

> Silver and tin 7–2–8, 3 herring nets 2–2–0, 2 old herring nets 0–2–16, 1 old four–oar boat without sail 1–0–0, boat with sail 4–2–0, 1 millhouse with tools and equipment 4–0–0, small boathouse 1–2–0, 1 small silver brandy bowl 1–0–0, 1 large trough for cattle 4–2–0, 1 broken tiled heating stove 7–0–0, 1 baking board 1–0–0, 4 cows 14–3–0, 1 gray mare 4–2–0, 4 barrels oats 3–0–0, 5 v. dried ling cod 5–0–0, 2 v. dried cod 1–2–0.

9. **Gaut Johannesen.** 1776 – 1802
Baptized Feb. 9, 1755, died Mar. 23, 1825, son of Johannes Askildsen Dale and Tyrid Gautsdatter Kalland.

Married first on June 30, 1776, to **Lisbeth Tollefsdatter**, widow of the previous farmer.

Second marriage was on Mar. 31, 1816, to **Marthe Trondsdatter Hemmingstad.**

Children in first marriage:

a. Ingeborg, baptized Mar. 15, 1777, married 1800 to John Helgesen, next farmer.
b. Tyrid, baptized Apr. 2, 1780, married 1800 to Hans Hansen Håvåsen, Rossabo.
c. Martha Elisabeth, baptized Dec. 16, 1782, married 1803 to Lars Hansen, 17 –3 Nordvik.
d. Eli. baptized Apr. 18, 1786, buried Oct. 8, 1786.
e. Sjur, baptized June 7, 1789, married in 1808 to Tyrid Olsdatter Vikse.

On February 29, 1776, Gaut receives an approved lease contract amounting to 1 v.tf in Nordvik from Anna Wilhelmina Bredahl, widow of Counselor Peder Vallentinsen, in Stavanger.

In 1802 he sows 3 barrels of grain and harvests 15 barrels. He feeds 1 horse, 5 cows, 1 calf and 10 sheep. There is sufficient fuel (in the form of peat) and summer feed including mill capacity (same as other farms in Nordvik). Part of the farm is also a cottage for Rasmus Tollefsen, with an income of 48 sk. for 3 work days.

10. **John Helgesen.** 1802 – 1837
Born 1778, died Mar. 24, 1860, son of Helge Bårsen and Ragna Rasmusdatter at the cottage allotment, Reinen, at Nordre–Våge in Sveio.

First married on Mar. 30, 1800, to **Ingeborg Gautsdatter**, baptized Mar. 15, 1777, buried Oct. 18, 1807, daughter of the previous farmer.

Second marriage on Oct. 2, 1808, to **Anne Malene Olsdatter**, baptized Aug. 19, 1781, died Jan. 4, 1849, daughter of Ole Osmundsen and Malene Johannesdatter Stange.

Children in 2nd marriage:

a. *Ingeborg* Oline, baptized Feb. 3, 1809, married 1825 to Johannes Johannesen, farm no. 6–6, Austrheim.
b. Ragna Serine, baptized Jan. 5, 1811, married 1830 to Elling Gudmundsen, farm no.12–1, Nordvik.

Aerial view of Nordvik. Farm no. 1 in background in the middle of the picture. Telemark Aircraft Co., 1954.

c. Anne Malene, baptized May 30, 1813, died Apr. 2, 1877; she lived in 1865 at Skare and in 1875 at Tuo.
d. Helge Andreas, Jan. 22, 1816, became next farmer.
e. Elisabeth Karoline, July 16, 1818, married in 1839 to Job Rasmussen, no. 7–9, Hovland.
f. John Mathias, born Mar. 29, 1821, died June 27, 1894, married in 1843 to Petronelle Knutsdatter Kvalvik, farm no. 3–1, Skare.

John obtained a lease contract of 1 v.tf. on Aug. 31, 1802, from Hans B. Forman in Bergen, on conditions negotiated during Forman's visit to Utsira in July 1802. The conditions were based on the father–in–law Gaut be allowed to run half the farm as long as he desired, and after that receive benefits such as 6 barrels of oats, feed for 2 cows and a patch for growing potatoes.

In 1830 he bought half the farm (1/2 v.tf.) from J. Dahm for 125 Spd. Elling Gudmundsen, his son–in–law, inherited the other half.

In the years 1800 and 1808, John was in charge of the school on Utsira.

In 1822–23 the executor of the H.B. Forman estate demanded a value assessment of the farms at Utsira (except Skare). The following is recorded among other things about John's farm:

> The farm was then inspected and evaluated and the various buildings were identified as follows: One old cottage with kitchen and an attached room with turf roof, One storage room with turf roof and a logged barn and a sheltered storage area covered with turf in reasonable condition, 1 stone laundry building with turf roof. – The soil is good and an area with peat for fuel on the eastern part is somewhat depleted. The farm yields approx. 27 – 28 barrels of grain, 10 – 12 barrels of strawberries and feeds 6 cows, 1 calf, 2 horses and 4 – 6 sheep. Within the boundaries a cottage exists which is leased to Tollef Tollefsen and his wife as long as they live and which corresponds to 18 days of work annually. A mill belongs to the estate with sufficient capacity for own consumption.

The estate was assessed in 1823 to 220 Spd., not including the cottage.

11. **Helge Andreas Johnsen.** 1837 – 1884
Baptized Jan. 22, 1816, died July 7, 1884, son of previous farmer.

Married Sept. 29, 1835, to **Valborg Tollefsdatter**, baptized July 9, 1809, died July 30, 1896, daughter of Ingeborg and Tollef Sjursen, farmer no. 2 – 3 Austrheim.

Children:

a. Hansine, born Jan. 2, 1836, died Aug. 18, 1836.
b. Sjur, born Sept. 29, 1837, married 1868 to Anne Marthe Koubkje Jørgensdatter, farm no. 4 – 1, Nordvik.
c. Johan, born June 12, 1840, married 1864 to Karoline Thomasdatter, farm no. 18 – 5, Nordvik.
d. Tollef, born Oct. 9, 1842, married 1880 to Eli Knudiane Larsdatter, farm no. 4 – 2, Nordvik.
e. Hans Mathias, born Aug. 3, 1845, married 1879 to Lovise Marie Tollefsdatter, Kvalvik, farm no. 16 – 3, Nordvik.
f. Anne Malene, born Aug. 30, 1849, became next user of the farm.
g. Andreas *Bertel*, born Aug. 28, 1853, married 1878 to Berta Karine Knutsdatter, Veim, tenant farm no. 39, Nordvik.

Lease to Helge Andreas from his father was 1/2 v.tf. and half of the small holding called Esphaugen was dated May 20, 1837, for 220 Spd. and a pension contract. New tax liability was 1 dl. 4 ort, 2 sk. In the description of the new pension contract the following is mentioned:

> 12 v. oats, feed for 1 cow, 1–1/2 cans of cod liver oil and the "use of a piece of indigent field on the eastern side of the bay and a small piece of

field located at Espehoug, a little piece at the old house, as well as the other half of a field called Oungnaa; it is assessed for 5 years to 70 Spd.

In 1866 the whole estate was assessed to 535 Spd. There were 41 mål fields and pastures at 329 Spd., pasture for 82 Spd., peat for 30 Spd., and land rights for 28 Spd. Yield estimated at 27–1/2 barrels of oats, 5 barrels of barley and 18-1/2 barrels of potatoes. The livestock on Dec. 31, 1865, consisted of 1 horse, 4 cows, 10 sheep and 2 pigs.

Helge Andreas was a skilled fisherman and earned the nickname "King of the Herring" (*Sildakongen*).[26] In the years 1865 to 1870 he built himself a large main house of 2 stories, 10.3 x 7.8 meters. In the fire insurance document in 1869 it says the house is new, but not finished and assessed to 710 Spd. In 1880 half of the estate (farm no. 4) is deeded to his son Sjur and in 1884 the other half is deeded to his daughter Anne Malene.

12. **Anne Malene Helgesen.** 1884 – 1895

Born Aug. 30, 1849, died Feb. 20, 1912, daughter of the previous farmer. Unmarried.

In the mortgage document dated Mar. 29, 1884, and the deed dated Apr. 18, 1884, the father on his deathbed gave the property to his daughter Anne Malene for the amount of 1600 kr. (noted in the loan document).

13. **Andreas Valnum Helgesen.** 1896 – 1902

He is listed in the census of 1900 as a tenant on the farm and his family lives on the second floor in the main building. See farm no. 18–6.

14. **Hans Mathias Helgesen.** 1903 – 1912

He receives the deed for farm no. 1 and 9 for 3000 kroner in 1905. For some years he runs these farms and the farm in west Nordvik, farm no. 16.

15. **Mikal Eriksen** 1912 – 1928

He acquires the deed for this property at auction for 5000 kr. in 1922. See farm no. 4.

16. **Mikal Mikalsen.** 1929 – 1964

---

[26] "Rogaland Fishing History," 1933, page 303. (Note 7)

Born Dec. 25, 1907, died May 26, 1964, son of the previous farmer. In 1929 he acquires the deed to the property at an auction for 4100 kroner.

Unmarried.

The farm has since been run as an additional farm. The property was taken over in 1979 by Anna Jonassen and Mikal Åse, Sandnes.

Farm no. 4. From farm no. 1 in 1880

1. **Sjur (Sivert) Helgesen.** 1880 – 1886
Born Sept. 29, 1837, died Mar. 12, 1882 son of Valborg and Helge Andreas Johnsen, farmer no. 1 – 11b, Nordvik.

Sjur Helgesen (1837–1882) and wife Malene (1857–1928).

First marriage May 17, 1868, to **Anne Marthe Koubkje Jørgensdatter**, born Aug. 17, 1845, died Mar. 29, 1876, daughter of Bolette Koubkje and Jørgen Jørgensen, farmer no. 14–1 b, and widow of Thomas Ellingsen.

Married the 2nd time on May 12, 1879, to ***Malene*** **Mikkeline Johannesdatter**, born May 6, 1857, died June 11, 1928, daughter of Anne Marthe Ådnesdatter and Johannes Johannesen, tenant farmer no. 29b, Nordvik, later farm no. 2 – 2, Klovning.

Children in first marriage:

a. Thomas, born Mar. 11, 1869, emigrated to S. Dakota, USA in March 1888.

Children in 2nd marriage:

b. Anne Marie, born July 22, 1879, married in 1898 to Mikal Eriksen, farm no. 3.

Sjur was a farmer for a few years on farm no. 12, before he received the deed from his father to this farm, 1.16 sk.m., for 1600 kroner, followed by an old age pension for 300 kroner.

Sjur was a marine pilot and lost his life while piloting a ship to Bergen. Karmsund newspaper on Mar. 18, 1882 reports:

> In a Bergen newspaper it was reported that the shipwreck near Selbjorn's fjord is confirmed to be the barkentine "Flora" of Bergen skippered by Captain Hilt and which left St. Ydes on the 15th last month with a load of salt. Several bodies were found all with life vests. We have also been informed from Utsira that the ship received pilot assistance from Utsira Sunday evening and that also the body of Sjur Helgesen has been recovered. –*Karmsundposten*, 18 March 1882.

In July the same year the main house with inventory was auctioned off. The farm was left to his son Thomas. Among the miscellaneous items are various fishing equipment, some boats, boathouses and a share in a larger fishing vessel, a good lathe and some carpenter tools. In 1874 a logged main building with tiled roof is assessed to 410 Spd. Malene married again in 1886 to the widower Johan Mathias Ellingsen, Skare.

2. **Tollef Helgesen.** 1886 – 1898

Born Oct. 9, 1842, died Jan. 18, 1924, brother of the last farmer.

Married on Aug. 27, 1880, to **Eli Knudiane Larsdatter**, born July 5, 1860, died Feb. 2, 1924, daughter of Marta Serine and Lars Knutsen, Nodland in Avaldsnes, later Kvala in Skåre.

Children:

a. Laura Marie, born Feb. 12, 1881, died Nov. 1922, emigrated to USA in 1905 and there married Charles Hausken.
b. Andreas Valnum, born Oct. 29, 1882, married widow Anne Bertine Pettersen (maiden name, Kallevik), Haugesund.
c. Sigvald Amandius, born July 7, 1885, died 1943, emigrated to USA in 1905 and married Stella Thorn.
d. Tillie Elise, born Sept. 12, 1887, emigrated to USA in 1905, married Frank Glitner.

e. *Julie* Amanda, born Dec. 25, 1889, died in 1949, married Henrik Ivers, organ builder in Bergen. Julie became a real estate broker in Haugesund, spent much time in the 1920s collecting information on the so–called "Dutch Inheritance."[27]
f. Hanna Serine Dagmar, born Mar. 10, 1892, married to Robert Ablett, emigrated to USA in 1929.
g. Pauline Alvilde, born Jan. 23, 1896, married to Martin Leonard Høie, Haugesund.
h. Martin Nikolai, born Apr. 5, 1898, emigrated to Minnesota, USA in 1915, married Anna Hanson in 1924.
i. Agnes Hermane, born Feb. 14, 1900, died Feb. 22, 1900.

Tollef built himself a house and operated a general store from 1879 to approximately 1891. His new house was 10.5 x 7.5 meters, roofed and covered with tile and assessed in 1879 to 2160 kroner.

In 1894 Tollef got the deed to farms no. 4 and 8 from Thomas Sjursen, but in 1897 he passed the deed over to Sjur Helgesen's daughter Anne Marie.

The family moved in 1904 to Haugesund, where Tollef bought a farm on Rossabø, but he still worked as a fisherman out of Utsira for several years. The main house, farm no. 3, was deeded over to Hersleb Helgesen.

Mikal Eriksen (1874–1928) and his wife Anne Marie (1879–1946).

3. **Mikal Eriksen**. 1898 – 1931

Born Apr. 12, 1874, died Feb. 4, 1928, son of Anna Martha and Erik Eriksen, farm no. 1 – 9 g, Skare.

---

[27] See Note 34.

Map of east Nordvik. ("Bnr." means farm or farmer).

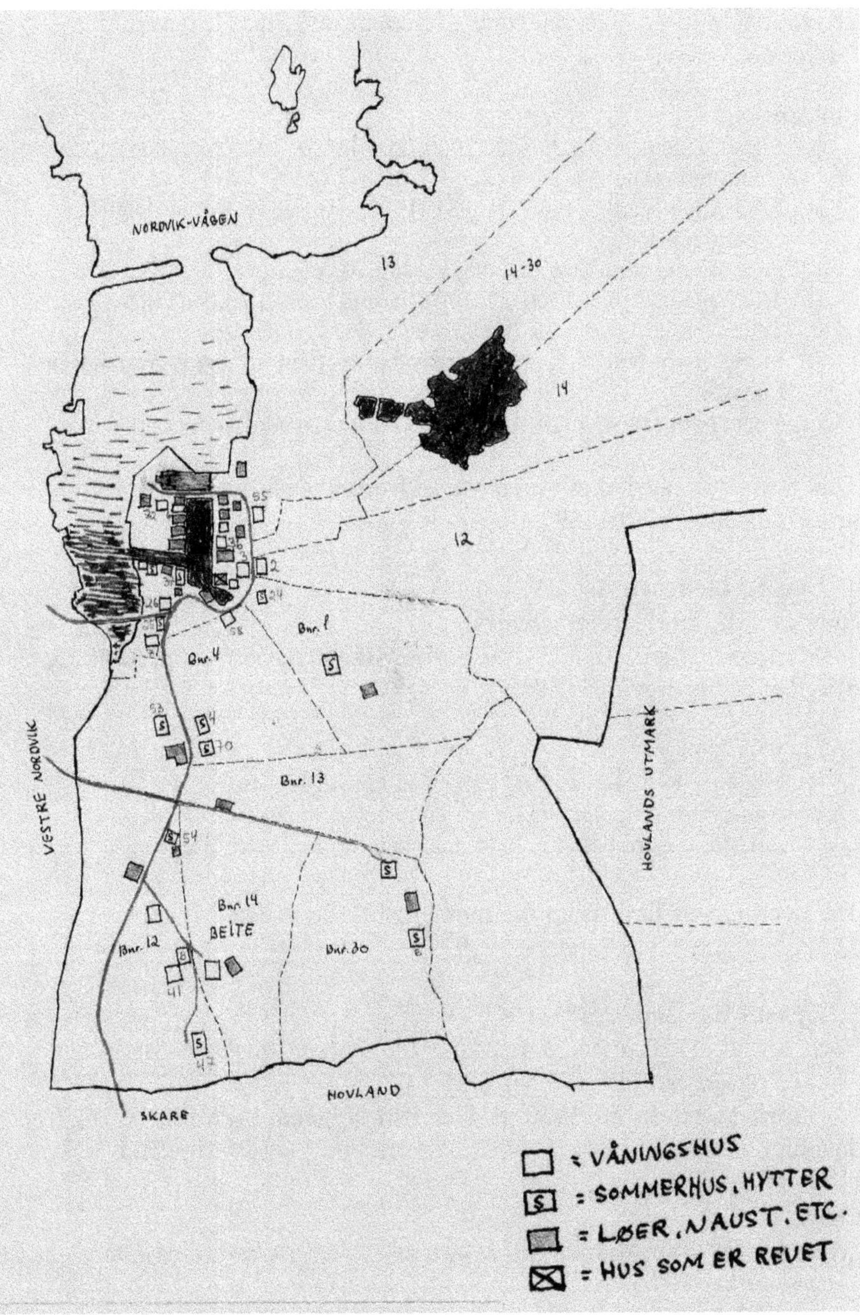

Key: 1– Main farmhouses, 2– Summer houses, cabins, 3– Barns, sheds, etc. 4– Buildings now torn down.

Married May 9, 1898 to **Anne Marie Sjursdatter**, born July 22, 1879, died Mar. 9, 1946, daughter of Malene and Sjur Helgesen, farmer no. 1 here.

Children:

a. *Signe* Malene, born July 2, 1900, married in 1925 to Johan Nilsen, tenant farmer no. 55, Nordvik.
b. Erna Anne Martha, born Dec. 31, 1902, married to Kasper Helleberg, Ølberg, Kleppe.
c. *Sofie* Juline, born Aug. 9, 1905, became next farmer.
d. *Mikal* Magnus, born Dec. 25, 1907, farmer no. 1–16 and no. 6 here.
e. Telma, born Mar. 26, 1912, unmarried, lived on Karmøy.
f. Mety, born Nov. 16, 1915, married in 1944 to Olaf Osmundsen Fikstveit.
g. Ernst, born Jan. 4, 1920, married to Gunfrid Nygård, farmer no. 5 here.

This farm was deeded to Anne Marie from Tollef Helgesen for 2400 kroner, dated Aug. 20, 1897.

4. **Svein Martinsen Åse.** 1931–1938
Born Jan. 22, 1907, from Sandnes.

Married on Jan. 10, 1931, to **Sofie Mikalsen,** born Aug. 9, 1905, daughter of the previous farmer.

Children:

a. Magnus, born Mar. 20, 1931, married to Kari Jonassen.
b. Anna, born Aug. 22, 1933, married to Jonas Jonassen.
c. Jan Mikal, born Feb. 12, 1936, married to Bjorg Marit Berge.

The deed to this farm from the mother to Sofie is dated June 6, 1928. The family moved to Sandnes in 1938.

5. **Ernst Mikalsen.** 1938 – 1941
Born Jan. 4, 1920, died Mar. 24, 1976, the son of Anne Marie and Mikal Eriksen, farmer no. 3 here.

Married on Apr. 22, 1950, to **Gunfrid Nygård,** born July 8, 1927, daughter of Tilla and Jakob Nygård, farmer no. 1 – 16b, Hovland.

Children:

a. Jostein, born May 21, 1953, married to Ingjerd Skeie, lives on Håvik, Karmøy.
b. Mary Elise, born July 11, 1957, lives in Haugesund.

The deed to Ernst from Sofie Åse is dated June 16, 1938. The family moved to Viken, Torvestad in 1957.

6. **Mikal Mikalsen.** 1942 – 1964
Mikal has been running this farm together with farmer no. 1.

The farm has since been used as an additional farm. The estate was taken over by Magnar Nilsen in 1957.

Farm no. 12. From farm no. 1 in 1830

1. **Elling Gudmundsen. 1830 – 1860**
Baptized Jan. 8, 1807, died July 11, 1859, son of Bertha Anbjornsdatter and Gudmund Thomassen, farmer no.3 – 2 o, Austrheim.

Married Aug. 26, 1830, to **Ragna Serine Johnsdatter**, baptized Jan. 5, 1811, died Mar. 6, 1898, daughter of Anna Malene and John Helgesen, farmer no. 1 – 10 b, Nordvik.

Children:

a. Thomas, born Sept. 21, 1830, became next farmer.
b. Berta Malene, born Jan. 30, 1833, married 1854 to Gudmund Anbjornsen, farmer no. 3 – 6, Austrheim.
c. Berta Gurine, born Aug. 27, 1835, died July 11, 1859, see below.
d. John Mathias, born July 1, 1838, married 1866 to Martha Olava Mikkelsdatter, farmer no. 2–6, Skare.
e. Anna Martha, born Apr. 23, 1841, married in 1861 to Erik Eriksen, farmer no. 1–9, Skare.
f. Asseline, born Aug. 26, 1845, died Aug. 26, 1846.
g. Asseline, born Dec. 8, 1847, married 1869 to Knut Hansen, farmer no. 5 – 6, Austrheim.
h. Elling, born Apr. 15, 1851, married 1892 to Juliane Teodora Tormodsdatter, farm no. 38, Nordvik.
i. Gunhilde Oline, born June 12, 1854, married 1872 to Mathias Jobsen, farmer no. 10– 2, Hovland.

Elling received the deed from Johan Dahm, 1/2 v.tf., the part which his father–in–law John Helgesen had used before, for 125 Spd. on May 24, 1830, plus old age pension valued for 5 years at 70 Spd. (See Helge A. Johnsen, farmer no. 1). Settlement of the estate was done June 30th the same year.

In 1845 a total of 12 persons lived on the farm including the cottage, and 1/2 barrel of barley, 4 barrels of oats and 1–1/2 barrels of potatoes were planted. The livestock consisted of 1 horse, 4 cows, 10 sheep and 1 pig.

Elling bought farm no. 2 at Skare from his brother Rasmus in 1849 with a lease contract.

Elling and his daughter Berta Gurine and five others from Utsira perished on a trip back from Bergen after shopping in preparation for the planned wedding party for Bertha Gurine and Johannes Johannesen Skåren. The boat capsized and only one onboard was saved. This was Jobiane Rasmusdatter Tuen.[28]

At the estate settlement after Elling's death in 1860, the farm was deeded to the son Thomas and was assessed to 560 Spd. The farm on Skare was deeded to son Mathias and assessed to 400 Spd., farm equipment, 16 Spd., livestock 40 Spd., 11 "bulk" (about 275 fathoms) seine fishing nets 80 Spd., and storage sheds for 50 Spd.

2. **Thomas Ellingsen.** 1860 – 1868

Born Sept. 21, 1830, died Apr. 9, 1867, son of previous farmer.

First married on May 8, 1853, to **Jobiane Rasmusdatter**, born Mar. 21, 1831, died Apr. 15, 1861, daughter of Jobiane Jobsdatter and Rasmus Tollefsen, farmer no. 7 – 7 h, Hovland.

Married the second time on May 25, 1862, to **Berthe Karine Thoresdatter,** born Oct. 20, 1823, died Oct. 22, 1862, daughter of Anne Kristine Johannesdatter and Thore Thorsen, farmer no. 15–8 b, Nordvik, and widow of Tollef Rasmussen Nordvik, farmer no. 21.

Married the third time on Aug. 30, 1863, to **Anne Marthe Koubkje Jørgensdatter,** born Aug. 17, 1845, died Mar. 29, 1876, daughter of Bolette Koubkje Larsdatter and Jørgen Jørgensen, farmer no. 14–1 b, Nordvik.

Children in 1st marriage:

a. Berthe Serine, born May 18, 1853, married in 1873 to Lars Aslaksen, farmer no. 4 here.
b. Rasmus, born Dec. 12, 1854, married in 1880 to Berthe Gurine Johannesdatter, farmer no. 5 here.

Children in 3rd marriage:

---

[28] *Stavanger County Gazette*, Monday, August 1, 1859. According to the article, it was "another example of the sorry effects of hard liquor." (Note 8)

c. Bolette Karine (Kaia), born Apr. 4, 1865, emigrated to Mobile, Alabama, USA, and there she married Christopher Schavland, the oldest son of lighthouse keeper Ole Schavland.

Proof of ownership of the estate after the father was issued to Thomas in the amount of 560 Spd. on Aug. 22, 1860.

In 1866 the farm of 44 mål, 11 acres was assessed to 353 Spd., pasture, 82 Spd., and peat and land usage is the same as farmer no. 1. Livestock consist of 1 horse, 4 cows, and 1 pig. The entire farm is assessed to 555 Spd.

3. **Sjur Helgesen**, 1868 – 1879
He was married in 1868 to **Anne Marthe,** the widow of the last farmer. In 1875 they are using part of this farm for growing oats, sowing 1/2 barrel oats, planting 1/2 barrel potatoes and feeding 2 cows and 8 sheep. See farmer no. 4, Nordvik.

4. **Lars Aslaksen.** 1874 – 1877
Born 1839, son of Anna Marthe Rasmusdatter and Aslak Larsen, Midt–Eide, Avaldsnes.

Married on Sept. 28, 1873, to **Berthe Serine Thomasdatter**, born May 18, 1853, daughter of farmer no. 2 here.

Children:

a. Thomas Job Elius, born 1874, died 1875.
b. Albert Martin, born June 4, 1876, married to Berta Kirstine Gudmundsdatter, lived in Midt–Eide, Avaldsnes.
c. Tomas Jabinius, born 1878.
d. Elling Severin, born 1881
e. Kornelius, born 1885.

Lars was tenant farmer on part of the farm a few years before the family moved to Midt–Eide, Avaldsnes and took over the farm there.

In 1875 he owned 1 cow, 5 sheep and a pig.

5. **Rasmus Thomassen.** 1874 – 1912.
Born Dec. 12, 1854, died Jan. 18, 1913, son of farmer no. 2 here.

Married on Sept. 18, 1880, to **Berthe Gurine Johanessen**, born July 22, 1859, died Nov. 16, 1946, daughter of Anne Marthe Ådnesdatter and Ole Johannes Johannessen, farmer no. 29, Nordvik, and farmer no. 2 – 2, Klovning.

The Rasmus Thomassen family at Beite 1903. Back row from left: Mikal, Thomas, Julie, and Sivert. In the middle: Rasmus (1854 – 1913) and Gurine (1859 – 1946). Front row from left: Mathias, Gunda, Amanda, Berner, Inga and Gina.

Children:

a. Thomas, born July 24, 1881, became next farmer.
b. *Sivert* Johannes, born June 5, 1883, died Sept. 14, 1904. He drowned in Sira Fjord on his way home from Haugesund.[29]
c. *Julia* Amalia, born Dec. 18, 1884, buried in 1905, married to Elling Knutsen, farmer no. 21, Austrheim.
d. Adolf *Mikal*, born Dec. 7, 1885, married in 1914 to Tilla Gurine Mathiasdatter, farmer no. 49, Nordvik.
e. *Regine* Bertine, born Mar. 30, 1889, married in 1915 to Johan Valnumsen, farmer no. 18 – 9, Nordvik.
f. Johannes, born Mar. 10, 1891, married Emma Eriksen Skare, emigrated to USA.

---

[29] From *Haugesund Avis* newspaper, Sept. 15, 1904 (Note 9).

g. Milla *Amanda*, born June 11, 1893, married to Elmer Helgesen, Haugesund, farmer no. 61, Nordvik.
h. Erna *Gunda* Berthe, born July 11, 1895, Married to Fred Frettevik, emigrated to USA.
i. *Inga* Serine, born July 30, 1897, married in 1920 to Mikal Ellingsen, farmer no. 3 – 8, Austrheim.
j. Mathias, born Oct. 18, 1899, married in 1929 to Martha Helgesen, farmer no. 56, Nordvik.
k. Julius *Berner*, born June 2, 1902, died Mar. 18, 1954. He also had a farm here.

Proof of ownership is dated May 11, 1868, after settlement of the estate of his father in the amount of 500 Spd. In 1875 he feeds 1 horse, 2 cows and 8 sheep. He plants 3/4 barrel rye, 2 barrels oats and 3–1/2 barrels potatoes (together with Lars Aslaksen).

The main building, 14 x 6.7 meters, framed and logged, lined with boards and tiled roof, was in 1879 assessed to 1030 kroner. The barn, 18 x 7 meters, with one detached utility shed, 6.7 x 4.8 meters, and a smaller shed were assessed to 460 kroner. In 1928 the main house was separated and became farm no. 47, Beite, which was taken over by Amanda and Berner Rasmussen, and from 1970, Bjarne Eldholm.

Rasmus became a marine pilot around 1879.

6. **Thomas Rasmussen.** 1812 – 1962
Born July 24, 1881, died May 30, 1962, son of previous farmer.

Married on May 10, 1922, to **Laura Lovise Ellingsen**, born Dec. 21, 1896, died Mar. 22, 1971, daughter of Astrid and Elling Gudmundsen, farmer no. 3 – 7 c, Austrheim.

Children:

a. Rasmus, born May 9, 1923, the next farmer.
b. *Erling* Aleksander, born Aug. 29, 1928, married to Eli Dahl from Stord, lived in Haugesund.

Property deeded from his father in the amount of 1800 kroner on Sept. 22, 1912. A new dwelling house was built in 1912.

7. **Rasmus Rasmussen.** 1952 –
Born May 9, 1923, son of previous farmer.

Married on June 22, 1957, to **Laila Vik**, born May 6, 1932, from Jondal in Hardanger.

Children:

a. Torleif, born July 7, 1958, married 1982 to Elisabeth Blix, lives in Røyksund.
b. Hildegunn, born June 7, 1962, married in 1991 to Arnstein Eek, farmer no. 44, Hovland.

Rasmus took over the farm in 1963 and build a new utility building in 1960.

Farm no. 13. from farm no. 1 in 1765

1. **Knut Kristoffersen**, 1764 – 1771

Born around 1745, buried June 30, 1771, son of Elisabeth Knutsdatter and Kristoffer Knutsen, farmer no. 12, Nordvik.

Married on Oct. 7, 1765, to **Margrete Jørgensdatter**, born around 1737, died July 2, 1823, daughter of Barbro Klausdatter and Jørgen Thorsen, farmer no. 15–1 c, Nordvik.

Children:

a. Bår, baptised Jan. 10, 1767, buried Mar. 22, 1767, 8 days old.
b. Berthe, baptized Mar. 28, 1786, married in 1786 to Bent Bentsen, Vestre in Skåre, many descendants on Utsira.
c. Knut, born in May 1771, buried Nov. 23, 1771, 6 months old.

In 1765 farm no. 1 was divided between Knut Kristoffersen and Sjur Knutsen, and Knut officially registered his lease contract of 1 v.tf. on Sept. 6, 1765.

In the estate settlement after Knut in 1771, the estate was valued at 83–3–10. Debt and other expenses totaled 30–1–8 including burial expenses of 10–0–0.2. Annual salary to a farmhand 4–1–8, repair and upkeep on the houses 5–0–0. Among the items in the settlement were:

> 3 cows 11–2–0, calf 1–1–0, bull calf 0–2–0, 1 mare 0–3–0, 3 barrels of oats 3–2–0, 1 tiled heating stove 5–0–0, spring herring fishing net 1–2–8, large herring fishing net 0–2–0, fishing boat with sail 2–1–6, lobster pots 0–3–8, 10 v. ling cod 10–0–0, 1 silver pot 8–0–0, 1 large kettle 2–0–0, 1 baking board 1–1–0 and 1 blue woolen shirt with 13 silver buttons 1–3–0.

2. **John Nilsen.** 1772–1801

Born approx. 1750, died on July 20, 1804, son of Eli Danielsdatter and Nils Johnsen, Visnes, Karmøy.

Married on June 28, 1772, to **Margete Jørgensdatter**, widow of previous farmer.

Children:

a. Eli, baptised Dec. 3, 1772, married in 1812 to Daniel Jensen Osthus, Åkra on Karmøy.
b. Jørgen, baptized Jan. 22, 1777, became next farmer.
c. Nils, baptized July 23, 1780, married in 1780 to Kari Oline Olsdatter, farmer no. 2 – 5, Kvalvik.

Lease contract to John for 1 v.tf. was issued on Dec. 2, 1771, by A. W. Bredahl in Stavanger.

In the settlement of John in 1805 the estate was valued at 207 rdl., of which 99–3–14 (riksdaler–ort–skilling) is left over to share among the heirs. Compensation for the burial expenses to the widow is 30 rdl. and wedding expenses to the two unmarried children, 60 rdl. Among miscellaneous items in the settlement were:

> 3 cows, "Skantrej," "Dyrkolla" and "Brunkolla," 27–2–0, 1 gray calf 7–0–0, 1 horse 7–2–0, 2–1/2 barrels oats 3–3–0, 1 cast–iron stove in the living room, 5–2–0, iron tools 6–1–6, misc. kitchen utensils made of wood 7–3–8, silver in the amount 8–3–8, brass, tin, copperware 5–3–4, *a house covered with tiles with a tiled heating stove on a vacant lot* and assessed to 44–0–0, a logged house for drying on a vacant lot, 4–0–0, 3 herring nets, 1–1–16, lobster pots, 2–2–0, a four–oar fishing boat with sail, 6–0–0, an eight–oar fishing boat, specially equipped for sailing including all rigging and a small anchor and 2 fishing lines, 26–0–0, 1 logged boat house 10–0–0.1, sheds with lean–to, 8–0–0, misc. sheds, 4–0–0. 1 blue feather–filled comforter 4–0–0, bedding material, 5–2–0, 1 old damask vest with 16 silver buttons, 1–0–8, and other clothing, 10–1–16.

3. **Jørgen Johnsen.** 1801 – 1841
Baptized Jan. 22, 1777, died Mar. 25, 1841, son of previous farmer.

Married on Mar. 28, 1802, to **Bertha Olsdatter**, baptized Nov. 16, 1799, died Nov. 9, 1830, daughter of Mari Knutsdatter and Ole Olsen, farmer no. 2 – 3 d, Kvalvik.

Married the second time on Sept. 21, 1831, to **Anne Malene Pedersdatter**, baptized Sept. 23, 1792, died July 27, 1845, daughter of Melene Rasmusdatter, and Peder Johannesen, Osner, Torvestad. (Peder was the grandson to Petter Olsen, Skare.)

Children in first marriage:

a. Ola, baptized Aug. 23, 1802, buried Oct. 16, 1803, 1 year old.
b. John, baptized Feb. 1, 1806, died between 1832 and 1841.

Construction of harbor at Nordvik, July 1869. Photo: N. Bing, Riksantikvaren.

c. Berthe Marie, baptized July 9, 1808, married in 1829 to Johannes Larsen, farmer no. 17 – 4, Nordvik.
d. Ole, baptized Oct. 6. 1811, became next farmer.
e. Margrete, baptized Aug. 11, 1814, married in 1846 to Daniel Johnsen, farm no. 26, Nordvik.
f. Jørgen, born July 8, 1818, married in 1842 to Bolette Koubkje Larsdatter, farmer no. 14 – 1, Nordvik.
g. Mikkel, born Apr. 24, 1822, married in 1845 to Lavine Nicoline Larsdatter, farm no. 2– 1, Hovland.

Children in 2nd marriage:

h. John Bendik, born Nov. 11, 1832, died approx. 1868, had 1 child, Jonette Bendikke, born April 12, 1851, with Berthe Hansdatter, Austrheim. Oct. 4, 1872: *Estate settlement after the disappearance of John Bendix Jørgensen, Nordvik* (Settlement sought on Oct. 31, 1868.).

Jørgen obtained a lease contract in the amount of 1 v.tf. from Forman in Bergen on July 16th, 1801, on the condition he assist his parents with

6 barrels of oats, 1 barrel of rye, 1/2 barrel of potatoes and feed for 3 cows and 6 sheep.

In 1802 he planted 4 barrels yielding 16 barrels of grain and he feeds 1 horse, 5 cows, 2 calves and 6 sheep, and the farm is assessed to 160 riksdaler.

In 1822 the buildings on the farm are described as:

> The main dwelling house consisted of a large living room with kitchen in fairly good shape. A storage house with a roof covered with turf and a smaller storage house also covered with turf, and also a logged cow stable with manure trap with a roof covered with birch bark at the end of the house, and a shed also covered with turf. These houses are old but still useful anyway.

The farm yields 30 barrels of grain and 10 to 12 barrels of potatoes, the livestock consists of 6 cows, 1 calf, 2 horses and 8 to 10 sheep. The farm is assessed in 1823 to 250 Spd. In the estate settlement after Bertha in 1832 the entire estate assets are valued at 1002 Spd. 3 ort, of which the farm makes up for 440 Spd. Among the items the following are listed:

> 2 cast–iron stoves 13–0–0, one living room clock with case 8–0–0, 1 4–oar boat with oars and sail 12–0–0, 1 old storage house 18 x 7 alen (alen = approx. 0.6 meter) 10–0–0, a house on empty lot with tile roof 50–0–0, 1 small 4–oar boat with sail 5–0–0, 1 herring seine net, 10 fathoms long and 5–1/2 fathoms deep 24–0–0,. 1 small sloop with boom 40–0–0, 1 new shed (20 x 8 alen) covered with birch bark 30–0–0, 1 four–oar boat with sail and associated equipment 2–2–12, 20 lobster pots with associated equipment 2–3–8.1, 1 outside mill with housing and equipment 25–0–0, 6 coalfish nets 14–0–0, 4 spring herring nets 5–0–12, 6 dozen empty barrels 15–0–0, 16 barrels salt 25–3–0, gold in the amount of 14–2–12, 1 silver mug 64 lod (approx. 2 lbs.) 44–4–0, other silverware 25–2–12, 7 cows 52–0–0, 1 oxen 4–3–12, and 2 horses 16–0–0.

On June 1st 1829, J. Dahm sells the first parcels of the farm to the users, among others, Jørgen. He gets the parcel with the dwelling including associated rights for 260 Spd.

In the settlement after Jørgen's death in 1841, the total assets are estimated to 550 Spd. and at the auction on June 24 miscellaneous items are sold for 751–4–1, and in cash 111–1–0. The farm is then divided between the two sons, Ole and Jørgen. The formalities were carried out on July 2, 1841.

4. **Ole Jørgensen.** 1841 – 1850

Baptized Oct. 6, 1811, died Sept. 30, 1845, son of previous farmer.

Married on July 11, 1837, to **Marthe Karine Larsdatter**, baptized Jan. 30, 1814, died Dec. 19, 1874, daughter of Anne Martha and Lars Thorsen, Storesund in Torvestad.

Children:

a. Berthe Mallene, born July 8, 1839, married in 1864 to Truls M. Johannesen, farmer no. 6.here.
b. Anna Martha, born Feb. 20, 1842, died Dec. 6, 1842.
c. Anne Martha, born Apr. 6, 1843, died Feb. 26, 1870.

The mortgage to Ole in the settlement after his father's death is in the amount of 275 Spd. and is dated Oct. 8, 1841. New property tax is 1 daler, 4 ort and 3 skilling.

Ole was at first the farmer at no. 6, Austrheim, which he bought in 1832. When the estate was divided in 1841, 6 parcels were divided in two: Stemhaug, Hjemmemyren, Rasfestemstykket, Voldestykket, Sigestykket and Sjabråtet. Ole gets Nordåkeren and half of upper Stemflekket, Jørgen gets Søråkeren and Abrahamflekket, while upper and North Trae, Svinetrae, Sveiven, Eastern Stem, including the mill, the kelp beach, and the lots for the sheds, become common areas. In 1845 he plants 1/4 barrels of barley, 3 barrels oats and 1 barrel of potatoes and feeds 1 horse, 3 cows and 8 sheep.

In the settlement after Ole's death in 1851 there are assets valued at 880–4–16 Spd., of which this farm is estimated at 425 Spd. and the farm at Austrheim at 250 Spd. His widow gets the farm at Austrheim, while the grand–daughter Berthe Malene gets the farm here. Among misc. items, the following could be noted:

> 1 four–oar boat with sail 3–0–0, 1/10 share of four–oar boat 0–2–12, 1/8 share of four–oar boat 0–0–7, 1/3 of fishing vessel for net fishing with sail and associated equipment, 9–0–0, 1/10 of another fishing vessel for net fishing with equipment, 3–0–0, 2 "balker" (around 56 fathoms) spring herring seine nets with accessories and 1/10 of a tarp, small anchor and lines 12–0–0, 1/8 share in a large seine net with associated equipment 4–0–0, 1/8 share in a small cast net with accessories 2–2–12, 5 pollock nets 2–2–12, 3 spring herring nets 0–4–18, 1 coal fish net 1–0–0, 1 boathouse clad with boards and tile roof 30–0–0, 1 pair of binoculars 5–0–0, 1/2 share in plow, 1–0–0.4, 4 cows 30–0–0, 1 calf 0–4–0 and a horse 8–0–0.

5. **Johannes Johnsen.** 1850 – 1864

Married in 1850 to the widow of previous farmer. See farmer no. 6, Austrheim.

6. **Truls M. Johannesen.** 1864 – 1900
Born Feb. 26, 1830, died Sept. 7, 1899, son of Ingeborg Oline and Johannes Johannesen, farmer no. 6 – 6 c, Austrheim.

Married on Sept. 18, 1864, to **Berthe Malene Olsdatter**, born July 8, 1839, died Mar. 29, 1878, daughter of farmer no. 4 here.

Children:

a. Caroline Vegner, born May 8, 1865, died May 24, 1884.
b. Ida Josefine, born Jan. 24, 1867, became next farmer.
c. Berthe Malene, born Apr. 9, 1869, died Aug. 17, 1869.
d. Anne Marthea Jonette, born Apr. 16, 1871, died Sept. 14, 1898.
e. Lavine Kristine, born Nov. 14, 1875, married in 1903 to Ole Nordhus, farmer no. 21 – 5, Nordvik.

Mortgage to Berthe Malene in the settlement after the father in the amount of 425 Spd. is dated Feb. 13, 1852.

In 1866 there are 42 mål (approx. 10.5 acres) of meadows and fields belonging to the farm, which is estimated at 324 Spd. Grazing, peat and pasture are the same as on farm no. 1. Annual harvest is 21 barrels of oats, 6 barrels of barley, 18 barrels of potatoes and 38 skålpund hay (about 38 lbs.). The entire farm is estimated at 545 Spd. The livestock consist of 1 horse, 4 cows, 11 sheep and 1 pig.

7. **A. Bertel Gudmundsen.** 1900 – 1936.
Born Sept. 26, 1854, died Feb. 4, 1938, son of Berthe Malene and Gudmund Anbjornsen, farmer no. 3 – 6a, Austrheim.

Married on May 9, 1889, to **Ida Josefine Trulsdatter**, born Jan. 24, 1867, died Oct. 14, 1943, daughter of previous farmer.

Children outside marriage with Berthe Karoline Johannesdatter, Hovland:

a. Josefine, born Feb. 21, 1882, died Oct. 27, 1887.
b. Kristine, born Nov. 8, 1884, died Mar. 6, 1885.

Children:

c. Tilly Bertine, born Oct. 13, 1889, married to Hagbart Gabrielsen, lived at Sevland, Karmøy.
d. Gustav Berner, born July 29, 1891, died May 3, 1912.
e. Kasper Wlhelm, born Oct. 1, 1893, married to Anne Martha Johannesdatter, Mannes, Åkra, tenant farmer no. 51, Nordvik.
f. Amanda Sigfrida, born June 29, 1895, married in 1817 to Johan Hansen, tenant farmer no. 22, Nordvik.
g. Alvilde Juline, born Apr. 15, 1898, married in 1923 to Klaus Wegner Løvland, tenant farmer no. 52, Nordvik.

h. Thorval Johan, born Mar. 4, 1901, died July 3, 1921.
i. Adolf Martin, born May 2, 1903, became next farmer.
j. Oluf Mikael, born Jan. 10, 1906, died Mar. 14, 1911.
k. Gunda Sigfryda Amalie, born Dec. 17, 1909, died Nov. 4, 1911.
l. Gunda Sigfryda, born June 15, 1912, married in 1940 to the widower Aslak Miljeteig, tenant farmer no. 66, Nordvik.

The deed transferred to Bertel from Ida Josefine's sister Lavina as the only heir of the farm, tax liability 2.75 sk.m., in the amount of 2,500 kr., is dated May 3, 1900.

Bertel was a seaman for many years before he took over the farm here.

Bertel Gudmundsen Leite.

Bertel Gudmundsen Leite.

"Haugesunds Avis" newspaper, 20 Sept. 1934.

See article below.

The oldest inhabitant on Norway's most outer island.

Among all my friends out there on the island furthest out, there is one who I cherish most to visit with. This is – Bertel Gudmundsen Leite in Nordvaagen. I have on many occasions mentioned my friend Bertel Leite, but now I would like to again "put him on the spot," as on Saturday the 22nd this month, he turns 80 – and on top of that he is Utsira's oldest inhabitant.

Bertel was born on Utsira and has lived there all his days. In his youth, however, he did spend a few years abroad, something he is very proud of, as he sailed the proud schooner "Lesseps" of Haugesund. Owned by Hans J. Olsen, Lesseps was a sharp sailing ship and left all other sailing vessels they encountered on the high seas struggling behind, according to Bertel. Such a sailing ship as Lesseps – would be difficult to find again.

Bertel Leite, however, gave up sailing the seas around the world and settled as a fisherman and farmer on the island where he was born. In all his days, the courageous Bertel pursued all challenges that came his way in work and life with vigor, which he still does at the age of 80. He also cuts the hay alone, as always.

Throughout the years he experienced a lot on land and at sea including many dangerous situations. Ages ago, he sailed a cargo of grain to the mill together with another Utsira'er. The cargo was bagged and stowed in the hold, and halfway between Utsira and Urter the vessel filled with water and capsized. Bertel and his buddy climbed up on the keel and rode the capsized vessel for hours in heavy seas before anybody came to assistance. Bertel did not want to lose his valuable cargo and with help from the rescuers, he (righted) the vessel and sailed around in the heavy seas to pick up the floating bags to bring the cargo back to Utsira.

Also, some years ago on one of his trips to Ostmarken to look for ocean shrimp from the cliffs, he slipped and fell on the slippery rocks and landed on a ledge on the steep cliff facing the ocean. It is difficult to tell how long he lay injured on the ledge, however, many hours later he managed to climb back up and came crawling home with an injured back. Bertel was laid up in bed and a doctor was summoned. He was not very happy when told that his injuries were serious and was told to stay in bed for at least three months.

Bertel has received many public acknowledgements for honorable deeds. In his living room there is a framed document from the German Government acknowledging his participation in saving "Pylos's" crew on a stormy night in January 1920, and somewhere in a drawer there is a box with a medal he received on that occasion. Whether he still has intact the 500 kroner he received as a reward from Carnegie's Hero's Fund, I cannot say.

He is a typical example of the strength and stamina of our coastal population. He is quick in response and forceful in actions and words, and his wit and satire can be hard–hitting. However, he is also pleasant and comforting, and this is how I came to know him.

I remember particularly well a meeting with him eight years ago, when the large "Inheritance from Holland" became an issue on everybody's mind and became a topic of conversation everywhere. One day as I came along the road I found Bertel harvesting the fields (with his scythe). As I walk by he says, "I suppose you are good at calculations? …Listen,… from the Dutch inheritance[30] we are supposed to get for this area, a good part is supposed to go to Sira … and I am also an heir. So, sit down and take notes."

I took the numbers he gave me and started to multiply, divide and subtract according to his instructions, and came up with a conclusion that Utsira should receive 2 million kroner, if Bertel's assumptions were correct.

"That is a lot of money," Bertel says thoughtfully.

"Yes, but it is very doubtful that anybody gets anything out of this," I tell him. "I doubt if you will get rich on this inheritance, Bertel."

"Oh, no, just so," Bertel replies phlegmatically, his quaint accent propelled to power again. And then he takes his scythe, splits off a stalk, leans onto his scythe – with zeal and bright mood. "It is probably best to stick with what you have. It's the daily work that bears the fruit." — and that's Bertel Gudmundsen's philosophy in life.

By Ola Nordmann.
Haugesund Avis 20 September 1934.

[30] A fortune allegedly inherited from Holland by two Scottish girls who had been rescued off the west coast near Utsira and who remained in Norway until they died. (See Note 34).

From left: Thomas T. Helgesen, Karsten Vestre and Adolf Bertelsen.

8. **Adolf Bertelsen.** 1936 –1974
Born May 2, 1903, died July 3, 1974, son of previous user.

Married on Mar. 3, 1948, to **Dina Malene Davidsen,** Saeverud, born Feb. 26, 1904, died May 5, 1979, daughter of Gjertrud and Olai Davidsen, Bremnes.

The deed to Adolf from his parents in the amount of 5000 kr. is dated May 26, 1936. The old main building on the farm was taken over by the sisters Alvilde and Sigfryda (farm no. 53) and Adolf built himself a new main dwelling house, approx. 50 square meters in 1936.

In 1957 the livestock consisted of 3 cows, a calf, a horse and 20 sheep.

9. **Tor–Bjørn Miljeteig.** 1975 –
Born Jan. 9, 1942, son of Sigfryda and Aslak Miljeteig, tenant farmer no. 66, Nordvik.

The farm was taken over by Tor–Bjorn in 1991; he built himself a new work shed in 1989.

Farm no. 14. From farm no. 13 in 1841. Beite

1. **Jørgen Jørgensen.** 1841 – 1892
Born July 8, 1818, died Jan. 19, 1893, son of Bertha Olsdatter and Jørgen Johnsen, farmer no.13 – 3 f, Nordvik.

First marriage on July 3, 1842, to **Bolette Koubkje Larsdatter**, born Nov. 4, 1817, died May 24, 1849, daughter of Anne Martha and Lars Thorsen, Storesund.

Second marriage on June 24, 1852, to **Kirsti Johannesdatter**, born Feb. 3, 1822, died Feb. 19, 1854, daughter of Martha Lisbet Mathiasdatter and Johannes Knutsen, Gunnarshaug, Torvestad.

Third marriage on May 15, 1859, to **Elisabeth Johnsdatter**, born June 4, 1820, died Jan. 15, 1902, daughter of Berthe Kirstine Johannesdatter, Nordvik and John Ommundsen Skare.

Children in first marriage:

a. Jorgine Berentine, born June 11, 1843, married to Kristian Simonsen, farmer no. 21–2. Nordvik.
b. Anne Marthe Koubkje, born Aug. 17, 1845, married in 1863 to widower Thomas Ellingsen, farmer no. 12–2, Nordvik.
c. Jørgen Olai, born Feb. 28, 1848, died Aug. 26, 1868.

Children in second marriage:

d. Johannes, born Aug. 19, 1852, died Nov. 5, 1872.

Children in third marriage:

e. Nils Johannes, born July 18, 1859, became next farmer.
f. Martin Mikal, born May 14, 1861, married in 1890 to Berthe Sylfestdatter, farmer no. 4–10, Austrheim.

Proof of ownership to Jørgen after the settlement of the father's estate in the amount of 275 Spd. is dated Oct. 8, 1841, new debt is listed as 1 daler, 4 ort and 2 skillings.

In the settlement after Bolette in 1849 the estate is assessed at 500 Spd. Among the miscellaneous items for 331 Spd. are listed:

> 5 cows 32–2–12, 2 horses 22–0–0, 1/2 plow 1–2–12, 2 ovens 6–2–12, 1 small boat house 30–0–0, 4 barrels spring herring 6–2–0, 30 lobster pots 3–0–0, 1/6 fishing boat 2–0–0, 1/10 fishing boat 4–0–0, 1/3 fishing boat 10–0–0, 1/8 four–oar boat 0–0–12, 1 four–oar boat 8–2–12, 1/10 herring fishing net 8–0–0, 1/8 fishing net 8–1–0, 2 "bulk" (50 fathoms) herring seine nets 8–0–0, 4 spring herring nets 2–0–6, 2 misc. fishing nets 1–2–12, gold 5–4–14 and silver 5–3–18.

The estate after Kirsti was settled in 1859. At that time the estate was valued at 1252 Spd. of which the farm was estimated to 500 Spd., as it was estimated 10 years earlier; while the farm at Austrheim, which Jørgen bought from his brother Mikkel in 1851, was assessed to 270 Spd. Among misc. items, valued at 312 Spd. total, are livestock at 72 Spd., misc. boating equipment at 75 Spd. and salt herring at 85 Spd.

In 1866 there are 61–1/2 mål of fields estimated at 349 Spd. including pastures, peat and meadows comprising Farm no. 1. Annual yields are estimated to 24 barrels of oats, 5 barrels of rye, 18 barrels of potatoes and 42 skålpund (approx. 20 lbs.) hay. The entire farm is estimated at 565 Spd. The livestock consist of 1 horse, 4 cows, 15 sheep, and 1 pig. Ten years later there are 1 horse, 1 oxen, 4 cows, 1 calf, 24 sheep and 2 pigs.

The main dwelling here is a 13.8 x 6.4 meter logged house with basement, clad with boards and covered with a tiled roof. In 1874 it was assessed to 460 Spd. The barn, 18.2 x 6.4 meters, and outside storage house, 12.4 x 2.7 meters, were assessed to 120 Spd.

Kathrine Gudmundsdatter Beite (1861–1899).

2. **Nils Johannes Jørgensen.** 1892 – 1901

Born July 19, 1859, died Apr. 12, 1901, son of the last farmer.

Married on Aug. 6, 1882 to **Ingeborg Kathrine Gudmundsdatter**, born Sept. 1, 1861, died Nov. 5, 1899, daughter of Kari Oline and Gudmund Knutsen, farmer no. 1–8 h, Austrheim.

Children:

a. Elida Karoline, born May 17, 1884, married to Ole Brekne, lived on Lista.
b. Jørgen Olai Berner, born Aug. 13, 1887, farmer no. 4 here.
c. Gudmund, born May 25, 1891, emigrated to Camrose, Alberta, Canada, and there married Nelly Lyseng.
d. Julia Minda, born Dec. 4, 1893, died Apr. 1, 1905.

e. Nelly Kristine, born Feb. 18, 1897, emigrated to USA.

The property deed to Nils Johannes from the father in the amount of 1600 kr. followed with an old age pension of 1100 kr. is dated Nov. 22, 1892, tax liability sk.m. 2.91.

Kristian Jakobsen (1865–1909) and Anne Martha (1879–1965).

3. **Kristian Jakobsen,** 1902 – 1911
Born Sept. 12, 1865, died Nov. 30, 1909, son of Gurine Johannesdatter and Jakob Kristiansen, tenant farmer no. 11, Klovning.

Married on Nov. 4, 1900 to **Anne Martha Larsdatter**, born Feb. 28, 1879, died in 1965, daughter of Elene Ånensdatter and Lars Nilsen (Kvalvik) Vikse in Skåre.

Children:

a. Johan Georg, born Apr. 3, 1902, married in 1931 to Birgit from Bremnes, lives in Haugesund. Johan worked with Haugesund newspaper for many years, and from 1953 he was the general manager. He has written several books, the last one *Vester Ute* ("Out West"), published in 1993.
b. Kristense Amanda, born Mar. 31, 1904, married to Torleif Saetre, lives in Haugesund.
c. Lovise Karoline, born Jan. 29, 1908, married to Truls Hagland.

Anne Martha's adopted daughter:

d. Martea, born Mar. 5, 1911, married Ole Vikse in Sveio. Martea's biological mother was Marthe Elisabeth Gautsdatter Klovning.

Anne Martha and Kristian worked the farm here until Jørgen (farmer no. 4 here) became old enough to take over.

Kristian worked 12 years as crew onboard the mail boat owned by Hans Knut Eriksen, before he started to work for the harbor master. He was injured during work on the breakwater construction project in Sorvågen.

Anne Martha and the children moved to her dad's farm in Viksmarka in 1911. They later used Vikse as their family name.

Wedding picture of Jørgen and Anna Nilsen

4. **Jørgen O. B. Nilsen.** 1908 – 1950. Born Aug. 13, 1887, died Feb. 5, 1937, son of farmer no. 2 above.

Married to **Anna Serine Aslaksdatter**, born Nov. 10, 1890, died Feb. 23, 1961, daughter of Marta Larsdatter and Aslak Orjansen, Skålnes in Åkrafjorden.

Children:

a. Nelly *Kristine*, born Sept. 20, 1909, married to Elias Bjelland, tenant farmer no. 59, Nordvik.
b. Adolf, born Jan. 15, 1912, next farmer.
c. *Arne* Julius, born Sept. 9, 1918, married in 1949 to Målfrid Klovning, tenant farmer no. 33, Klovning.

The deed to Jørgen after the estate settlement from the parents is in the amount of 3000 kr. and is dated Dec. 16, 1903.

In 1904 the farm was divided in two and half of the farm went to Thomas Johansen. The debt on this part was 1.41 sk.m.

The main dwelling house on farm no. 14 in 1903. In front of the house from left:Elida Karoline, Nelly Kristine, Kristian Jakobsen, Anne Martha holding her son Johan, Julia Minda, Jørgen and Ingvald J. Klovning.

5. **Adolf Nilsen.** 1950 – 1985

Born Jan. 15, 1912, died Nov. 18, 1985, son of previous farmer.

Married on Sept. 16, 1939 to **Astrid Haugseth**, born July 12, 1918, daughter of Gunda and Petter Haugseth, farmer no. 13–1b, Austrheim.

Children:

a. Arthur Johannes, born Apr. 13, 1942, married in 1964 to Marit Klovning, tenant no 80, Nordvik.
b. Svein Bjarne, born Oct. 30, 1944, married to Ingrid Brekke, lives in Kopervik.
c. Ella Alice, born Mar. 27, 1948, married in 1967 to Nils Terje Rasmussen, lives in Haugesund.
d. Geir, born Sept. 30, 1960, married to Mai Synnøve Floysvik, Sandnes.

Adolf took over the estate in 1960. The livestock on the farm consist of 2 cows and a calf.

The farm was used in later years as a supplementary farm and was taken over by Jostein Nilsen in 1992.

Farm no. 15, West Nordvik. From farm no. 1 in 1729

1. **Jørgen Thorsen.** 1729 – 1742
Born around 1710, died in 1740, son of Marita Knutsdatter and Thore Jonsen, Grønningen, Torvestad.

Married around 1729 to **Barbro Klausdatter,** born around 1705, daughter of Karen and Klaus Anbjornsen, farmer no. 1 – 4b, Nordvik.

Children:

a. Martha, born around 1730. died on Aug. 16, 1773.
b. Malene, born around 1734, married in 1760 to Tolleiv Knutsen, Saevik.
c. Margrethe, born around 1737, married in 1765 to Knut Kristoffersen, farmer no. 13 – 1, Nordvik.
d. Jørgensine, born around 1739, married in 1768 to Ludvig Larsen, Feoy.

Lease contract dated Mar. 26, 1729 is issued to Jørgen in the amount (3 v. 1 bp. 12 mrk. tf. or around 55 kg. dried fish for the entire "Western Nordvik."

According to local records, the following is stated:

> At the annual spring council meeting Jørgen was summoned to explain the circumstances as to why his wife Barbro gave birth to their child too early. Jørgen did not show up, but Johannes Gundershaug attended the meeting on behalf of Jørgen and explained that the child was born approximately 41 weeks after the wedding. However, he was presented with certification from the minister E. Leganger to the contrary and had to pay a fine of 3 riksdaler, 1 ort and 12 skilling.

On the 26th of March 1740 the Jørgen estate is settled. The net worth of the estate is 32–3–17 riksdaler, of which 1–3–20 is in cash, 9 riksdaler in real estate and the rest in miscellaneous items. The guardians of the children are Lars Brekke and Thomas Nordbo.

2. **Nils Kristoffersen.** 1743 – 1752
Born around 1720, from Stangeland.

Married in 1743 to **Barbro Klausdatter,** widow of previous farmer.

Children:

a. Berthe, born around 1744, married in 1767 to the widower Ole Knutsen, farmer no. 6 – 2, Austrheim.
b. Klaus, born around 1748, married in 1772 to Mari Andersdatter. Lived on Vedoy, Akra. Klaus was raised by his uncle, Jens Klausen, farmer no. 17-1, Nordvik.

Lease to Nils for this property in the amount of 3/4 v.tf. was issued from the bailiff A. Heiberg on Dec. 31, 1743.

The following is mentioned is the county records:

> During the local government summer session on 7 July 1745, Nils was cited for several infractions by the local bailiff Anders Heiberg. Barbro had again been premature in childbirth, but Nils presented his draft papers for military service dated Oct. 12, 1740, and consequently escaped further punishment after paying Barbro's fine of 1 riksdaler and 12 skilling. His other infractions were not resolved that easily. It turned out that, as a married man, he also had a child with a "loose" woman by the name of Trude Olsdatter. Nils admitted guilt, and Trude admitted that she had met an Osmund Vikingstad and told him she was so poor that she did not own the clothes she was wearing, and also admitted guilt. Nils was sentenced by the court to transfer all his fortune to the King's treasury on Dec. 2, 1744. Also, Trude was sentenced to pay a fine of 12 lod silver or, "for lack of funds, . . . to suffer on her body . . . "

Finally, Nils was cited for brawling in the fall of 1744, but the case was dismissed for lack of evidence and witnesses.

Also, the following is incident is recorded:

> Approximately 14 days after Easter in 1750, there was an engagement party at Bår Knutsen's home in Nordvik. (This was possibly a party celebrating the engagement between Tormod Rasmussen and Marta Knutsdatter.). Nils was also there, together with several others. Nils got loud and yelled at Askild Larsen Haugland, and when his old mother–in–law, Karen, came in to try to calm him down, he also yelled at her and grabbed her by the shoulders and put her up on a table. Ole (Abrahamsen) tried to help her, and he is also yelled at and is pulled by the hair. Several of the guests assembled by the door, and when Nils tried to leave the room, he stabbed John Klovning and cut him across the face with a knife. The people who witnessed this are Ole Abrahamsen, who was hired to cater the party, Elling Austrheim, and Anders Hovland. Later, the same year, the parties agree that Nils should pay John Klovning his medical expenses and for time lost to heal his wounds. Nils still had to pay an additional fine of 6 riksdaler and 3 ort to the King's treasury.

Around 1752 the family moved to Munkejord, Åkra.

Pedlehåyen, to the left is farm no. 16 and farm no. 15 is to the right. In the foreground is the foundation to the main dwelling of Tordis and John Larsen, farm no. 75, which is being built. Photo by Telemark Aircraft Co. in 1954.

3. **Tormod Rasmussen. 1752 – 1760**
Born around 1728, died 1759, son of Guri Larsdatter and Rasmus Tormodsen, farmer no. 7 – 4a, Hovland.

Married in 1751 to **Martha Kristine Knutsdatter** born around 1728, (buried July 6, 1800?). Her sisters were Berta, married to Knut Sjursen tenant farmer no. 15, Nordvik; Ingeborg, married to Henrik Mathiassen Vormedal (estate settlement after her death, June 23, 1781); Elisabeth, married to Kristoffer Knutsen, tenant farmer no. 12, Nordvik; and Malene, married to Anders Pedersen farmer no. 1–7, Hovland.

Children:

a. Rasmus, baptized Aug. 6, 1756, estate settlement Apr. 10, 1781.
b. Malene, baptized May 23, 1759, married in 1783 to Tore Larsen, farmer no. 6 here.

Because the court record book was missing for the period 1751 to 1760, there is no record of Tormod's lease.

The estate settlement after Tormod's death was carried out in 1760. At that time the two children received all miscellaneous items valued at 38–2–20 riksdaler. The children's guardians were Thomas Skare and Elling Austrheim.

4. **Svend Olsen.** 1761 – 1768
Born around 1731, died December 1767, son of Anna Svendsdatter and Ole Abrahamsen, tenant farmer no. 11c. Nordvik.

Married on Feb. 6, 1761 to **Martha Kristine Knutsdatter**, widow of previous farmer.

Children:

a. Anna, baptized May 2, 1761, buried Sept. 27, 1761, 10 weeks old.
b. Anna, baptized June 16, 1762, buried Sept. 30, 1781.
c. Tormod, baptized May 1, 1765, buried Nov. 23, 1771.
d. Malene, baptized Jan. 15, 1768, buried Nov. 23, 1771.

Lease contract to Svend in the amount of 1–3/4 v.tf. issued Jan. 5, 1761 by county executive Vallentinsen in Stavanger.

The county records in the period 1755 – 58 indicate that both farms in western Nordvik had a tax liability in the amount of 2 v.tf., and this amount is changed in subsequent evaluations.

The estate of Svend is settled in 1768. Assets are estimated to 76–1–18 rdl., expenses and debt amount to 46–1–8, of which 12 rdl. is due John Klovning and 4 rdl. is due to the handyman Ole Paulsen. Among misc. items are:

> 5 cows 17–0–0, 3 calves 5–2–0, 2 horses 7–0–0, 3 barrels of oats 4–0–0, part ownership in mill with tools 4–0–0, 1 tiled heating stove 2–2–0, 1/3 of a boat and boathouse 13–0–0, 1 four–oar boat with sail 2–0–0, 1 shed for same 2–0–0 and 3 spring herring fishing nets 2–0–0.

5. **Mikkel Olsen.** 1768 – 1787
Born approx. 1731, died Oct. 16, 1787, son of Synnøve Mikkelsdatter and Ole Larsen, Stor – Hagland in Skåre.

Married on July 12, 1769 to **Martha Kristine Knutsdatter**, widow of previous farmer.

Children:

a. Svend, born 1769, buried Nov. 23, 1771.

Lease contract to Mikkel in the amount of 2 v.tf. issued by Mrs. Vallentinsen on Sept. 13, 1768.

Mikkel perished at sea in the Rovaer area together with his brother Ole Kvalvik, and on Oct. 31, 1787, his estate was settled. As he did not have any heirs, the estate went to his mother Synnøve, who died and was buried on Utsira on July 5, 1795, at the age of 90. Subsequently, her brother Ole Kvalvik's children, the sister Ingeborg, half–brother

Lars St. Hagland, half–sister Kari Bjelland and the youngest half–sister Anne Strøm, Sveio, and his children and grandchildren inherited the estate. The cash value of the estate amounted to 142–1–22 rdl. Among the misc. items were:

> 7 cows 30–0–0, 1 calf 2–0–0, 3 horses 9–1–0, 5 sheep 2–1–16, 1 ram 0–2–0, 17 barrels of oats 18–1–16, 1 old outside mill with housing 3–0–0, 1 cast-iron kettle 2–2–0, 1 blue embroidered jacket with 24 silver buttons 3–0–0. 1 large cast–iron stove 6–0–0, 1 small house with kitchen build on empty lot 8–0–0, 1 six–oar boat with sail and equipment 6–0–0, 1 four–oar boat with sail 2–2–16, 1 small four–oar boat without sail 1–0–16, 1 shed near the water 6–0–0, 8 spring herring fishing nets 4–0–16, 32 lobster pots 2–2–16 and silver for 4–3–0.

In 1787 Johannes Johannesen, Berthe Thomasdatter and Lisbet Andersdatter were servants on the farm.

6. **Thore Larsen.** 1788 – 1789
Born around 1749, buried Feb. 8, 1789, son of Lars Larsen, Storesund, Torvestad.

Married on June 14, 1783 to **Malene Tormodsdatter**, baptized May 23, 1759, died Dec. 20, 1843, daughter of farmer no. 3 here.

Malene's child outside marriage with Søren Sjursen:

a. Tormod, baptized Aug. 7, 1779, married in 1815 to Berthe Malene Bendtsdatter, tenant farmer no. 24, Nordvik.

Children:

b. Marta Kristine, baptized Oct. 19, 1783, married in 1807 to Ole Kristoffersen Bo, Torvestad.
c. Kari, baptized July 17. 1785, married in 1813 to Mikkel Johannesen, farmer no. 18–2, Nordvik.
d. Lars, baptized Apr. 1, 1787, married in 1813 to Anne Marthe Nilsdatter. They lived in Storesund, Torvestad. Two of their daughters were married to the two brothers Ole and Jørgen Jørgensen, Nordvik.
e. Tore, baptized Feb. 8, 1789, farmer no. 8 here.

Lease contract to Thore in the amount of 2 v.tf. was issued by Peder Valentin Forman in Bergen (assessor H.B. Forman's son) on July 9, 1788, on the condition he supplied Martha Kristine, the widow of the former farmer, with 4 barrels of oats, 1/2 barrel of barley and feed for 2 cows annually.

Thore was a schoolmaster in Torvestad and lived in Storesund before the family moved to Utsira in 1788, but Thore had already died the same winter.

In the estate settlement after his death on Feb. 27, 1789, the cash value is 98 riksdaler, from which was subtracted 2–2–0 in servant's wages to Johannes Helgesen (next farmer) and 10 riksdaler to the widow after the burial. Among other items the following were listed:

> 3 cows 15–2–0, 2 calves 6–0–0, 1 sheep, 3 rams and 1 ram lamb 2–1–12, 6 barrels of grain 6–0–0, 1 large stove 7–0–0, silver worth 6–1–0, 6 old spring herring fishing nets 2–2–0, 1 old large herring fishing net 0–2–0, 2 old longliners 0–1–8, 20 lobster pots 1–2–16, 1 four–oar boat with old sail 2–0–0, 1 goose–feather comforter 4–2–0, 1 home–woven comforter filled with animal hair 1–2–16, 1 blue waistcoat with trousers 4–2–0.

7. **Johannes Helgesen.** 1789 – 1819
Baptized Mar. 26, 1757, died Apr. 2, 1839, son of Martha Olsdatter and Helge Knutsen, Rossebø in Skare.

Married on Mar. 25, 1790, to **Malene Tormodsdatter**, widow of previous farmer.

Children:

a. Anne Marta, baptized July 11, 1790, married in 1824 to Johannes Gudmundsen, farmer no. 22–1, Nordvik.
b. Oline, baptized Sept. 30, 1792, married in 1819 to Ådne Johannesen, farmer no. 16 – 1, Nordvik.
c. Berta Malene, baptized Oct. 25, 1795, died June 7, 1818.
d. Ellen, baptized Nov. 4, 1797, buried Mar. 17, 1804.
e. Sofie Hansine, baptized Oct. 17, 1802, married in 1821 to Mathias Johannesen, farmer no. 20 – 1, Nordvik.
f. Helene, baptized Apr. 4, 1807, buried July 11, 1807, 1–1/2 month old.

Lease to Johannes in the amount of 2 våger dried fish is issued by Peder V. Forman on Dec. 8, 1789, on condition of taking responsibility for Martha Kristine's descendants.

Before Johannes leased the farm he was schoolmaster at the Utsira school.

In 1802 he sows 4 barrels of grain and harvests 20 barrels and feeds 1 horse, 5 cows and 6 sheep. The entire farm is assessed at 160 riksdaler.

In 1819 the farm is divided between the son–in–law Ådne and his stepson Thore.

8. **Thore Thorsen.** 1819 – 1854

Baptized Feb. 8, 1789, died Dec. 8, 1872, son of farmer no. 6 here.

Married on July 15, 1821, to **Anne Kirstine Johannesdatter**, baptized Feb. 18, 1795, died Jan. 24, 1861, daughter of Anna Karine Ådnesdatter and Johannes Ambjornsen, tenant farmer no. 13b, Nordvik.

Children:

a. Berthe Malene, born Sept. 18, 1821, married in 1851 to Johannes Mathiassen, farmer no. 20–2, Nordvik.
b. Berte Karine, born Oct. 20, 1823, married in 1849 to Tollev Rasmussen, farmer no. 21–1, Nordvik.
c. Torine, born Mar. 19, 1826, married in 1850 to Ole Bardsen, farmer no. 2–6, Kvalvik.
d. Marte Kristine, born Mar. 11, 1829, married in 1859 to widower Johannes Mathiassen, who was previously married to her sister above.
e. Lars Johan, born June 9, 1833, next farmer.
f. Thore Mikal, born Sept. 20, 1838, married in 1862 to Marthe Kristine Jansdatter, farm no 21–3, Nordvik.

Lease to Thore in the amount of 1 våger dried fish was issued on July 5, 1819 by Assessor Forman in Bergen, and the following was awarded to Malene and Johannes:

> 3–1/2 barrel oats, 1/2 barrel pure barley, feed for 1 cow and 4 sheep, half of what is required of fuel and light and including the following fields: *The largest hill south of an area called "Kringlen," a small parcel on the southern part of the so–called northern Skurvedahl and western Stølsviigen, and grazing for 1 pig.*

The old age pension was assessed to 130 Spd. for 15 years. Included in the estate was half of the deserted cottage that was previously used by Amund Reiersen.

In 1822 the farm was described as follows:

> Half of a very old cabin with one small room and kitchen covered with sod, half of an old barn and storage shed and a stable also covered with sod. Included in this farm is half of a mill. The quality of the farmland is fairly good with some clay, but contains enough peat fuel for own consumption. The farm yields annually 15 barrels of grain, 6 barrels of potatoes, feeds 4 cows, 6 to 8 sheep and 1 horse.

In 1823 The farm was assessed to 125 Spd.

A few years later Thore built himself a new main dwelling house, as we see in 1828 in the following note in the mortgage register.

Approval. According to the owner's approval, Thore Thorsen, Nordvik has built a house on the part of the farm that he leased on 5 July in the year 1819 and which is deemed to be his true property. – Utsire, Nov 21, 1827. J. Dahm.

On Dec. 27, 1838, Thore bought the entire farm from J. Dahm for 300 Spd.

Thore was schoolmaster for a few years before he got married. In 1845 the livestock consisted of 1 horse, 4 cows, 12 sheep and 1 pig.

Lars Johan Thorsen (1833–1886) and wife Marthe Kristine Mathiasdatter (1838 – 1910)

9. **Lars Johan Thorsen.** 1854 – 1900

Born June 9, 1833, died Mar. 13, 1886, son of previous farmer.

Married on July 6, 1862, to **Marthe Kristine Mathiasdatter**, born June 24, 1838, died July 27, 1910, daughter of Sofie Hansine and Mathias Johannesen, farmer no. 20 – 1 h, Nordvik.

Children:

a. Marthe Karine, born Oct. 30, 1862, died Sept. 22, 1889.
b. Anna *Sophie*, born Aug. 22, 1865, died in 1944 in Piedmont, CA, married in 1893 in Oakland, CA to Waldemar Andreas Schmidt from Visby in Denmark, lived in Oakland, CA.

c. Berthe Malene, born June 10, 1867, married to Ole Tobias Olsen, farmer no. 2 – 8, Kvalvik.
d. Mathias, born May 23, 1869, next farmer.
e. Karen Kristijanne, born Nov. 6, 1871, emigrated to USA in 1893, died in Oakland, CA in 1942, unmarried, used the name Jennie Thorsen.
f. *Thore* Johan, born May 23, 1874, farmer no. 20–3, Nordvik.
g. Johan *Mikal*, born Feb. 6, 1877, died in 1936 in Newark, CA, married in 1905 in Stavanger to Bergljot Hoff Svensen from Porsgrunn, lived in Stavanger–Bergen– Floro, emigrated to Oakland, CA in 1912.
h. *Tomine* Josefine, born July 11, 1881, married in 1899 to Olaf A. Skjelde, farmer no. 16 – 4, Nordvik.

The deed to Johan in the amount of 1 våger dried fish or 2 d. 1 sk. from the father for 350 Spd. dated May 22, 1854, and other assets consisting of 5 barrels of grain and the use of 2 outfields of grain, Langeflekket field and the largest field south of Haugen, feed and pasture for 2 cows and 8 sheep, 2 cords of peat, 1 cord birch wood and 2 cans of cod liver oil, the total of which to be available for 5 years and valued to 75 Spd.

In 1856 Lars built a new barn for hay storage and cows, and in 1866 he built a new main dwelling house, 13.8 x 6.9 meters, with logs and clad with boards and tiled roof. The house was assessed in 1867 to 680 Spd. The house, which Lars' father built nearby in 1827, was moved and became approximately half of the new house.

In 1866 49–1/2 mål (approx. 12 acres) of fields and pastures are assessed to 360 Spd. There are pastures for 92 Spd., peat for 110 Spd., land rights for 40 Spd. and beach access for 43 Spd. The farm yields annually 26 barrels oats, 5 barrels barley and 24 barrels of potatoes. The entire farm is assessed to 655 Spd. The livestock consists of 1 horse, 5 cows, 17 sheep and 1 pig.

10. **Mathias Larsen.** 1900 – 1940

Born May 23, 1869, died Mar. 29, 1933, son of previous farmer.

Married on July 4, 1901, to **Stine Johnsdatter**, born Oct. 24, 1877, died Aug. 6, 1951, daughter of Randi Johnsdatter and John Holgersen, Upper Kvinesland in Tysvaer.

Children:

a. *Marthe* Kristine, born June 16, 1902, married in 1937 to Sverre L. Horgen, tenant farmer no. 57, Nordvik

From the left: Mathias Larsen, Thomas Kvalvik and Sivert Helgesen.

b. *Tore* Johan, born Mar. 20, 1904, next farmer.
c. Randi, born Sept. 11, 1906, married in 1937 to Johan P. Klovning, tenant farmer no. 64, Nordvik.
d. *Janna* Karine, born July 15, 1909, married in 1933 to Hellik B. Tobiasen, Upper Kvinesland in Tysvaer.
e. *Jon* Kvinesland, born Apr. 23, 1911, married in 1936 to Tordis Kvalvik, farmer no. 75 –1, Nordvik.
f. Laura, born Aug. 22, 1918, married in 1938 to Leif Ostensen, tenant farmer no. 65, Nordvik.
g. Josefine Regine, born Oct. 30, 1920, married in 1947 to Johannes M. Solsvik, tenant farmer no. 73, Nordvik.

The deed to Mathias from the mother in the amount of 3200 kr. and old age pension for 800 kroner is dated May 13, 1903, tax liability 3.39 sk.m. (skyldmark).

Mathias was mayor on Utsira in 1932.

Mathias Larsen (1869–1933) and Stine Johnsdatter (1877–1951) with son Tore, born 1904.

11. **Tore J. Larsen** 1940–1974
Born Mar. 20, 1904, died Nov. 9, 1982, son of last farmer.

Married Oct. 26, 1921, to **Ellen Tobiasdatter Sørhus**, born June 2, 1902, died Oct. 13, 1952, daughter of Anne Martha Laurine and Tobias Sørhus, tenant farmer no. 23 i, Klovning.

Children:

a. Mathias, born Dec. 16, 1921, married to Sigrund Solvag, tenant farmer no. 71, Nordvik.
b. Tobias, born Oct. 18, 1923, married in 1948 to Målfrid Mathiasen, tenant farmer no. 69, Nordvik.
c. Tormod, born Nov. 10, 1926, married in 1949 to Marit Ugland, lives in Kristiansand.
d. Sigurd, born May 12, 1936, next farmer.

Tore took over the farm in 1951 and in 1957 the farm consisted of 2 cows, 4 calves, a horse and 15 sheep.

Tore was mayor on Utsira from 1952–1959.

Tore Larsen (1904–1982) and his wife Ellen Sørhus (1902–1952) in 1945.

12. **Sigurd Nordvik.** 1975 – 1990
Born May 12, 1936, son of previous farmer.
Married on June 3, 1972, to **Jorun Braathen**, born Nov. 18, 1951 in Hurum.

Children:
a. Jostein, born Nov. 18, 1972.
b. Havard, born Aug. 7, 1975.

They took over the farm here in 1975 and from 1990 it was farmed as additional acreage. In 1977 they built a new main dwelling house.
Jorun is a teacher at Utsira Children and Youth School.

Farm no. 16. From farmer no. 15 in 1819

1. **Ådne Johannesen.** 1819–1861
Baptized Sept. 30, 1792, died July 29, 1877, son of Anna Karine and Johannes Ambjornsen, tenant farmer no. 13 a, Nordvik.
Married on Apr. 18, 1819, to **Oline Johannesdatter,** baptized Sept. 30, 1792, died Nov. 11, 1875, daughter of Malene Tormodsdatter and Johannes Helgesen, farmer no. 15 – 7 b, Nordvik.

Children:
a. Ambjorn Lorens, born May 25, 1819, died July 11, 1859, perished during a shipwreck on the way home from Bergen with six others from Utsira.
b. Berta Malene, born Mar. 4, 1821, died Mar. 5, 1821.
c. Malene Mikkeline, born Apr. 29, 1822, died Oct. 19, 1855. She was disabled and paralyzed from the neck down and was confined at home in 1843.
d. Johan Bendix, born Aug. 21, 1824, became next farmer.
e. Anne Marta, born June 29, 1828, married in 1854 to Ole Johannes Johannesen, tenant farmer no. 29, Nordvik and farmer no. 2 – 2, Klovning.
f. Mette Karine, born Oct. 14, 1831, died Nov. 1, 1855.
g. Johannes, born July 3, 1835, married in 1864 to Anne Pedersdatter, Vikshaland, tenant farmer no. 28, Nordvik.

Lease issued to Ådne in the amount of 1 våger dried fish by H. B. Forman in Bergen on July 5, 1819, and old age pension to his in–laws (see Thore Thoresen, at farm no. 15).

At the time of the assessment in 1822–23, Ådne and Thore Thoresen have joint ownership of the houses, and they are described under farmer no. 15. Ådne bought the farm from J. Dahm for 300 Spd. on Dec. 27, 1838.

In 1845 he feeds 1 horse, 4 cows, 12 sheep and 1 pig.

Ådne built a main dwelling and a boathouse at "Sildeberget." The main dwelling and half of the boathouse were sold to his son Johannes in 1865.

Lisebeth Karine Eriksdatter (1831–1919) photographed in her later years when she lived at the "Bolle–house."

2. **Johan B. Ådnesen.** 1861 – 1884.
Born Aug. 21, 1824, died Mar. 17, 1907, son of previous farmer.

Married on Oct. 16, 1853, to **Lisebeth Karine Eriksdatter**, born Aug. 5, 1831, died Nov. 28, 1919, daughter of Torborg and Erik Svendsen, farmer no. 1 – 8 a, Skare.

Children:

a. Johan Michael, born May 9, 1858. died Apr. 20, 1872.

The deed to Johan on the property from the father in the amount of 350 Spd. (Speciedaler) is dated Apr. 30, 1861. There is a debt in the amount of 2 daler, 5 skilling. Exempt from the sale is Ådne's new house and half of the boathouse. Here is an excerpt from the pension agreement with the parents:

> 4 barrels of oats at 8 buckets per barrel, 1/2 barrel of rye at 10 buckets per barrel, free use of 2 fields, one called "Kringlan" and the other called "Tommeland" with enough manure, winter feed and summer grazing for 2 cows, and also for 12 sheep, if they have that many. It is expected that they also let their cows graze where they have kept the rest of the cows during the summer. I reserve the right to let my own cows graze there in the summer season. Furthermore, they may use an area called Rauhaug for peat fuel. I will also arrange for a supply of birch wood and 2 cans cod liver oil transported to their home free of charge.

This pension agreement was assessed to 150 Spd. for 5 years.

In 1866 the farm is 43–1/2 mål (approx. 150 acres) including fields and meadows valued to 362 Spd. Pastures, peat and the beach is considered part of farm no. 15. The farm yields 30 barrels of oats, 6 barrels of barley and 24 barrels of potatoes. The entire farm is assessed to 660 Spd.

The livestock consist of 1 horse, 6 cows, 22 sheep and 1 pig.

In 1861 he agreed to let Ole Johannes Johannesen build a house on the "Storetre." Johannes later bought farm no. 2 at Klovning and moved there.

3. **Hans Mathias Helgesen.** 1884–1908
Born Aug. 3, 1845, died 1928, son of Valborg and Helge Andreas Johnsen, farmer no. 1–11 e, Nordvik.

From "Haugesunds Avis" newspaper, Jan 4, 1908.

Farm for sale on Utsira
Farm, capable of feeding 7 – 8 cows, horse and approx. 30 sheep, with new main dwelling and new barn, large and easily accessed outfields, potentially useful coastline for building lots and boathouses and part ownership in a salmon fishing area for sale. Please contact Hans M. Helgesen, Utsira.

Married in first marriage on May 17, 1879, to **Lovise Marie Tollefsdatter**, born May 14, 1859, died Feb. 22, 1880, daughter of Torborg Eline and Tollef Knutsen, farmer no. 1–4 b, Kvalvik.

Married in second marriage on July 24, 1883, to **Elida Lovise Mikalsdatter**, born Jan. 19, 1863, died Dec. 22, 1937, daughter of Thala Sophie and Svend Mikael Larsen, farmer no. 4–5 b, Klovning.

Children in first marriage:

a. Lovise Marie, born Feb. 16, 1880, died Apr. 2, 1880.

Children in second marriage:

b. *Helge* Andreas Wallum, born Feb. 8, 1884, married in 1921 to widow Marie Ormset, maiden name Bjercke. Lived in Haugesund and Oslo.
c. *Lydia* Amanda, born Sept. 23, 1885, emigrated to USA in 1905, married in 1907 to Arnt Olsen Kvalvik. Lived in Oakland, California.
d. *Milla* Sofie, born Sept. 21, 1887, moved to California in 1907, married in 1911 to Philip Edward Kaneen.
e. *Sigfried* Otilia, born June 14, 1889, moved to California in 1930.

f. *Hjalmar* Ludolf Olaus, born Aug. 19, 1891, married in 1911 to Constance Elisabeth Kristiansdatter, Kallevik, lived on Garstol in Skåre.
g. *Herman* Mathias Emil. born Mar. 18, 1894, died Nov. 7, 1908.
h. *Hagerup* Alfred Mikal. born Dec. 14, 1895, moved to Chicago, USA in 1925.
i. *Thala*, born Mar. 24, 1898, married in 1945 to John Stange, lived in Oslo.
j. Lauritz *Alexander*. born June 11, 1900, lived in Haugesund. He was a telegraph communications manager.
k. Edward *Korner*, born Mar. 19, 1903, married in 1932 to Anny Leigvold, Stavanger. Korner was a missionary priest.
l. *Agnes* Othelie, born Aug. 22, 1905, was an officer in The Salvation Army.

The deed to Hans Mathias on this farm from Johan, indicating a potential tax revenue of 3.42 skyldmark or 342 ore (cent), for 2800 kroner, and an old age contract of 800 kroner, is dated May 27, 1884.[31]

They built their main dwelling house on this farm in about 1885. It was taken out of the estate in 1943 and was designated farm no. 65, Nordheim, and taken over by Olav Skjelde in 1948.

From 1902 he also managed farm no. 1 in East Nordvik, which he bought in 1905. In 1908 he bought a farm in Gard, Skåre and moved there with his family.

4. **Olav A. Skjelde.** 1908 – 1940

Born June 1, 1874, died Nov. 4, 1927, from Voss.

Married on Oct. 7, 1899 to ***Tomine* Josefine Larsdatter**, born July 11, 1881, died Nov. 28, 1957, daughter of Marthe Kristine and Lars Johan Thorsen, farmer no. 15 – 9 h, Nordvik.

Children:

a. Lars Johan, born Nov. 25, 1898, died Nov. 26, 1898.
b. Marie, born Nov. 24, 1899, married to Reidar Nordås, Utsira Radio no. 6.
c. Kristine, born Apr. 23, 1901, died 1981, married in 1920 to Sigvart Gabrielsen, lived in Mattingsdal, Ogna.
d. Martha, born May 4, 1904, married to Hans Hansen Austevik, Avaldsnes.
e. Andreas, born Dec. 30, 1909, became next farmer.

---

[31] Included in this deed is also an agreement to provide for the parents, valued at 800 kr. over 5 years, which was customary in such transactions and corresponds to today's social security. Such agreements were paid in the form of pasture rights for livestock, free fuel, supplies or services.

Olav A. Skjelde (1874–1927) and his wife Tomine Larsdatter (1881–1957).

f. Kaja (Kari), born June 17, 1911, died Aug. 14, 1951, worked as a cabin attendant at sea. Perished in M/S Bess shipwreck in the North Sea.
g. Lars, born Nov. 8, 1913, married in 1940 to Olga Valnumsen, tenant farmer no. 63, Nordvik.
h. Olav, born Dec. 13, 1915, married in 1943 to Alvhild Konstanse Solvåg, farmer no. 62–1, Nordvik.

Auction deed dated July 19, 1908, is issued to Olav in the amount of 10,150 kroner.

Olav ran a country general store and bakery in Nordvik from 1898.

5. **Andreas Skjelde.** 1940 – 1992
Born Dec. 30, 1909, died June 18, 1993, son of previous farmer.

Married on Sept. 19, 1933, to **Solveig Helgesen**, born Dec. 17, 1909, daughter of Åsa and Sivert Helgesen, farmer no. 32, Nordvik.

Children:

a. Trygg–Olav, born Dec. 15, 1934, married to Else Marie Jess, lives in Hafrsfjord.
b. Ar–Stein, born Feb. 27, 1937, married in 1995 to Karen Marie Holberg. Ar–Stein also has a farm here.

c. Aud Sigrid, born Apr. 8, 1940, married to Ommund Vorre, lives in Avaldsnes.
d. Odd Gunnar, born Feb. 5, 1943, married to Else Margrethe Ragnhildstveidt, Eikeland, lives in Halandsdalen.

Farm no. 17. From farm no. 15 in 1743

1. **Jens Klausen.** 1743 – 1790

Born 1707, buried July 11, 1790, son of Karen Andersdatter and Klaus Anbjornsen, farmer no. 1 – 4 a, Nordvik.

Married on June 24, 1748, in Avaldsnes to **Berta Danielsdatter**, born around 1725, buried July 6, 1800, daughter of Synnøve Knutsdatter and Daniel Sjursen, Visnes on Karmøy.

No children, but one foster son:

a. Klaus, born around 1748, son of Barbro and Nils Kristoffersen, farmer no. 15-2, Nordvik.

In 1743 western Nordvik was split between Jens Klausen and Nils Kristoffersen, and Jens' lease contract of 1 3/4 våger dried fish (later increased to 2 våger) is issued by Andreas Heiberg on Mar. 1, 1743.

As Jens and Berta did not have children, they established a trust in 1770 where the longest living received 3/4 of the estate.

In 1784 he makes an agreement with Johannes Nilsen that he will take over part of the farm (farm no. 18) for 1–1/2 v.tf., also agreeing to work for the 1/2 v.tf., part of which Jens and his wife reserved for themselves, and also including the right to collect as much peat for fuel as they need.

The estate of Jens was settled in 1790. The assessed value of the estate was 248–2–9 rdl., and all expenses and debt amounted to 54–1–18 rdl., of which 16 rdl. was awarded to the widow to cover the funeral expenses, 9 rdl. for the burial plot inside the church near the altar, and 2–3–4 rdl. for Martha Knutsdatter as a servant salary. Among the estate items the following is mentioned:

> 10 sp.k. annual land taxes in Torvestad 80–0–0, in cash 60–0–0 (19 rdl. in "orte" coins, 16 daler in Dutch currency, and 23 rdl. in banknotes), silver for 14–1–4, 1 pair of gold buttons 6–0–0, 4 cows and 1 calf 24–0–0, 2 rams, 2 sheep and 2 goats 2–1–8, 1 cattle trough 3–2–0, 1 mill house with tools 4–0–0, 3 old spring herring fishing nets 0–1–8, 1 cast–iron stove 8–0–0, 1 embroidered waistcoat with 22 silver buttons 2–2–0, and one blue wool waistcoat with 24 silver buttons 4–2–0.

2. **Ommund Rasmussen.** 1791 – 1804
Born 1747, died June 4, 1832, son of Malene Johannesdatter and Rasmus Ommundsen, South–Våge in Sveio. (Ommund is John Helgesen's uncle, farmer no. 1 here.)

Married first time on Apr. 3, 1791, to **Berta Danielsdatter**, widow of the previous farmer.

Married in second marriage on Mar. 15, 1801, to **Anna Rasmusdatter,** baptized Jan. 4, 1781, daughter of Dorte Andersdatter and Rasmus Tollevsen, tenant farmer no. 17 a, Nordvik.

Children in second marriage:

a. Berta Malene, baptized Nov. 18, 1801, married to Mathias Andreassen, Hellevik, Avaldsnes.
b. Anne Dorte, baptized June 3, 1805, married in 1829 to Hans Paulsen Skyllingstad, Torvestad.
c. Johanne Marie, baptized Mar. 26, 1815, married in 1846 to Gabriel Mikkelsen Torvestad.
d. Simon, baptized June 23, 1816, married in 1834 to Sara Oline Pettersdatter. Lived in Torvestad.
e. Ole Andreas, born June 1, 1819, died on Feb. 4, 1821.

Lease contract to Ommund in the amount of 1/2 v.tf. (våger dried fish) was issued by Peder Valentin Forman in Bergen on Dec. 14, 1790.

In 1802 he sows 1 barrel grain and harvests 7 barrels. He feeds 2 cows and 4 sheep and the farm is assessed at 60 rdl.

In 1803 he moves to the cotter's farm called Kalven on Feoy, where the 4 youngest of the children are born. On the next farmer's lease contract it indicates that Ommund left the farm on Nordvik without canceling his lease and giving notice to the owner. This farm is then named "Flagra– farm."

3. **Lars Hansen.** 1804 – 1831
Baptized June 21, 1778, died Nov. 20, 1829, son of Marta Larsdatter and Hans Larsen, Gard in Skåre.

Married on Oct. 17, 1803, to **Martha Elisabeth Gautsdatter**, baptized Dec. 16, 1782, died Aug. 16, 1837, daughter of Lisbeth Tollefsdatter and Gaut Johannesen, farmer no. 1 – 9c, Nordvik.

Children:

a. Anne Marte, baptized Jan. 22, 1805, married in 1823 to Asbjorn Gudmundsen, farmer no. 2–2, Skare and later farmer no. 3 – 4, Austrheim.

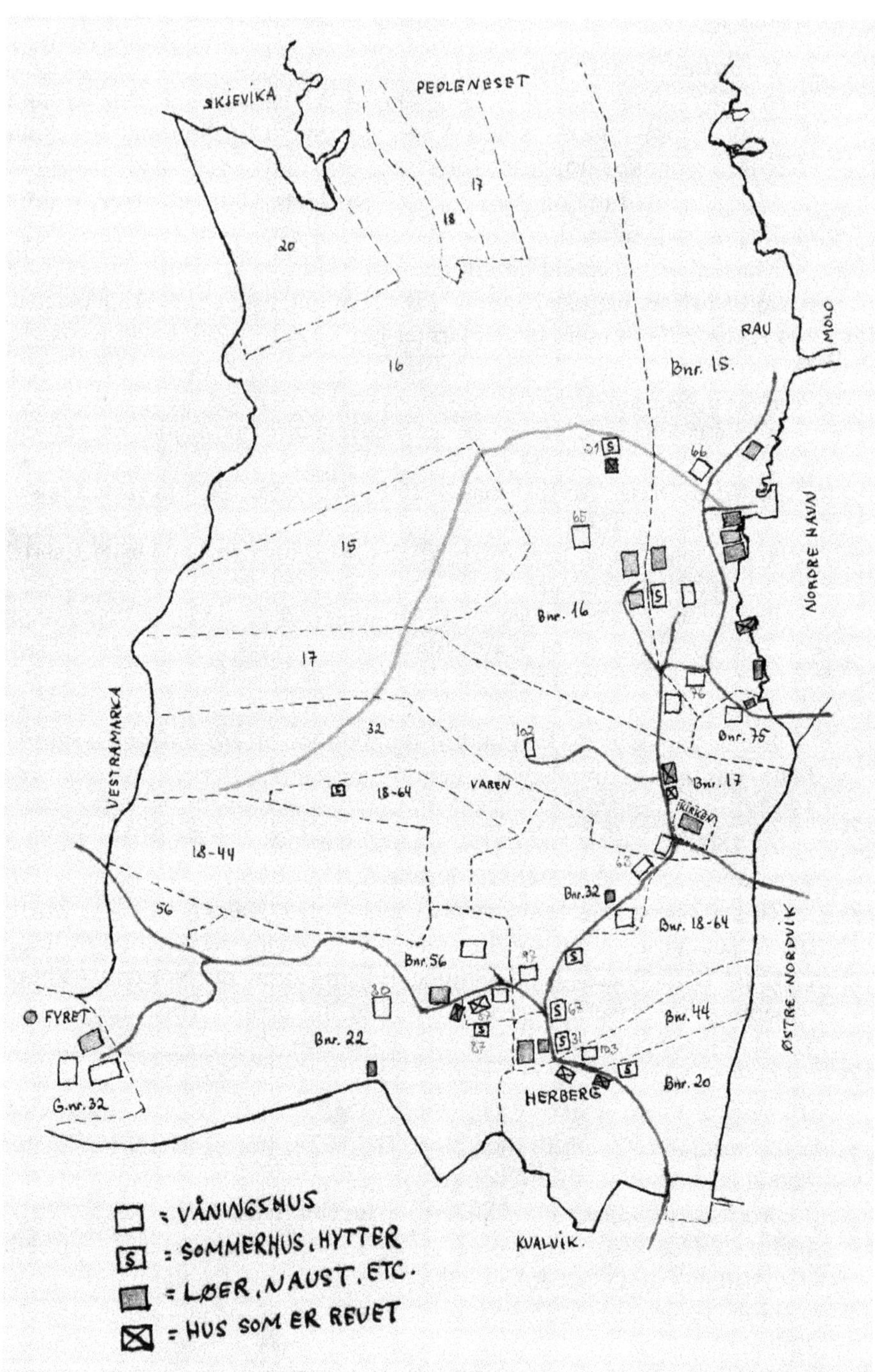

Map of west Nordvik. Key (from top): 1– Main farmhouses, 2– Summer houses, cabins, 3– Barns, sheds, 4– Buildings now torn down.

b. Johannes, baptized May 1, 1807, next farmer.
c. Gundela, baptized Oct. 6, 1810, married to Helge Ådnesen, Hauge in Skåre.
d. Elisabeth, baptized Sept. 17, 1813, died Feb. 4, 1886, was a servant for many years until her death at farm no. 2, Klovning.
e. Hansine, baptized Jan. 27, 1817, married in 1845 to Ole Mikal Kristiansen, Hausken. Lived in Dale in Torvestad.
f. Sivert, born May 26, 1820, died June 19, 1820.
g. Gaut Mathias, born Feb. 14, 1822, married in 1852 to Berthe Eline Jørgensdatter, farm no. 2–1, Klovning.
h. Ingeborg Kirstine, born May 19, 1825, married in 1842 to Ole Knutsen, tenant farmer no. 29, Austrheim.

On July 14, 1804, assessor Forman in Bergen issued a lease contract in the amount of 1/2 v.tf. on the so–called Flagra farm to marine pilot Lars Hansen Gard. In lease money he pays 40 rdl. From the lease contract it appears that previous farmers Jens Klausen and Johannes Nilsen used most of the property as a common area between themselves, but that the main part of the pasture on the northern part of Seio, Barne field, 2 smaller fields and the southern Kirkegangs field were split between them in terms of debt (contracts dated July 13, 1787 and Nov. 15, 1784).

In 1822 the buildings on the farm are described as follows:

> A living room where a kitchen and a closet are separated with a divider and a storage area and a small lean–to all under one roof covered with peat and bark and also a cooking shed with peat roof. The houses are in usable condition.

Annual yield of the farm is 14 barrels of grain and 10 – 12 barrels of potatoes. The farm can feed 1 horse, 3 cows and 6 – 8 sheep. The farm is assessed at 110 Spd. During an auction the inventory after Martha Elisabeth's death in 1837 was sold for 74–1–13 Spd. Left to be split between the heirs is 33 Spd.

4. **Johannes Larsen.** 1832 – 1834
Baptized May 1, 1807, died Dec. 4, 1832, son of last farmer.

Married on Aug. 30, 1829, to **Marie Jørgensdatter**, baptized July 9, 1808, died Nov. 18, 1876, daughter of Bertha Olsdatter and Jørgen Johnsen, farmer no. 13–3 c, Nordvik.

Children:

a. Lars, born Mar. 24, 1831, died Jan. 14, 1904. No children. Lars was a sailor. In 1875 he lived in Heroy, Nordland. There he married Gunnhild Ellingsdatter in 1876. In 1881 they emigrated to USA and settled in Gibraltar, Door County, Wisconsin. In 1884 he bought 40 acres there for $210 in section 17.

The lease contract between Johannes and J. Dahm in the amount of 1/2 v.tf. is dated May 21, 1832. Annually he is required to pay 5 Spd. and 1 bp. fish. In the contract to provide for old age assistance to the mother he is obligated to provide, among others, the following items:

> 12 våger oats, 4 bushels clean grain, feed for 1 cow, 3 sheep, 2 cords of peat, 3 cans cod liver oil, free milling of the mother's grain and the use of the following fields: Nylaenden, Barneflaekket, Skudflaekket and part of the field around the dwelling house.

The value of this additional pension contract for 5 years is estimated to 70 Spd.

Johannes perished on the Sirafjorden on the way home from Karmsund, and the estate after him was settled in 1833 at an estimated value of 135–1–14 Spd. Among the misc. items the following are mentioned:

> 1 horse 10–0–0, 2 cows 14–0–0, 2 sheep with lamb 3–0–0, 1 cattle trough 3–0–0, 1 outside mill with associated equipment 12–0–0, 1 boathouse 2–2–12, 1 old boat without sail 2–2–12, 1 large four–oared boat without sail and jib 7–0–0, 2 new pollock nets 4–2–12, 4 spring herring fishing nets 4–4–12, 10 lobster pots 1–0–0, 1 French pocket watch with silver chain 6–0–0 and silver for 6–3–0.

AGED SETTLER OF JUDDVILLE DROPS DEAD LAST WEEK

Funeral Held From Juddville Swedish Lutheran Church Saturday—No Relatives Nearby

EGG HARBOR—On Wednesday of last week, Ole Christjohnson, one of the oldest settlers of Door county, passed away at the age of 74, having been born in Norway in 1851. Mr. Christjohnson had no warning of death, for as he came into the house, where he and his wife reside alone, after working all day, he sat down in a chair and passed away before assistance could be secured.

Examination by Dr. H. F. Eames revealed the fact that the deceased died of heart failure. The home being set considerable distance from any neighbors and Mrs. Christjohnson's aged and invalid condition being such as it was made it very difficult for her to get any word to others so they might come and give assistance, it was only after several attempts that Mrs. Christjohnson was able to muster up courage and strength to go to a neighbor and notify them of her husband's condition.

Mr. Christjohnson was a very noted character in all of Juddville, where he has lived the past 48 years or more. No children were born to the couple, which also had no relatives living in these parts of the county.

The funeral was held from the Juddville Sweedish Lutheran church at 1 o'clock Saturday afternoon and interment was at the Juddville cemetery, The Rev. Beisaas of Ellison Bay officiated.

Clipping from "Door County Advocate," Wisconsin newspaper, approx. Jan. 19, 1925; left: tombstone in St. Paul's Cemetery, Gibraltar, Wisconsin.

6. **Krisjer Steffensen.** 1834 – 1868.

Baptized Nov. 3, 1805, died Mar. 6, 1890, son of Berte Malene Reiersdatter and Steffen Steffensen, Tornes in Skåre.

Married on July 6, 1834 to **Berte Marie Jørgensdatter,** widow of last farmer. (Anna Malene, a sister of Krisjer, was the mother of Malene, their son Ole Johannes's wife (See below.).

Children:

a. Johannes, born Jan. 7, 1835, next farmer.
b. Jørgen Kristian, born Feb. 22, 1838, married in 1863 to Berthe Kristine Rasmusdatter, Storesund, Torvestad. Bought farm at Sakkestad in Skåre and moved there.
c. Bertha Malene, born Aug. 18, 1841, married in 1864 to Torres Thorsen, tenant farmer no. 30, Nordvik.
d. Endre Stefanus, born Sept. 27, 1844. He died as a passenger on the *S/S Undine*, May 14, 1871, of meningitis, while emigrating to Florida, USA.
e. Marthe Marie, born Apr. 8, 1847, married in 1868 to Kristoffer Tostensen, tenant farmer no. 36, Nordvik.
f. Ole Johannes, born Dec. (Nov.?) 15, 1851, emigrated to USA around 1876, where he married his cousin Berthe Malene Jorgensdatter in Wisconsin, Dec. 12, 1894, in a Moravian ceremony. Ole bought 80 acres for $317 in 1886, at Gibraltar, Door County, Wisconsin, in the same section as his half–brother, Lars (See under farm no. 4 above.). Ole died Jan 14, 1925 and Malene died March 22, 1933 in Poulsbo, WA (see article right). No children.

Clipping from the "Door County Advocate," Wisconsin, Mar. 1933.

Former Resident Buried Last Week

Juddville — Funeral services were held at the Juddville church last week Wednesday afternoon for Mrs. Ole J. Christianson, former resident, who died at the Ebenezer Old Folks' home at Poulsbo, Washington, of old age complications. The Rev. C. O. Anderson officiated.

Pallbearers were Art Witallison, Charles Anderson, John Haltug, Jack Hanson, Christ Hanson and John Peterson. Burial was at the Juddville cemetery.

Mrs. Christianson, whose maiden name was Malinda Jorgenson, was born in Norway, daughter of Mr. and Mrs. Knut Jorgenson, and came alone to this country in 1880. After living in Illinois, North Dakota and Minnesota for a number of years, she came to Wisconsin where she was married to Ole J. Christianson and settled at Juddville where the couple lived about 35 years. Mr. Christianson died in 1925, and Mrs. Christianson went to Astoria, Oregon, about a year later. About five years ago she wen to Poulsbo.

Surviving are one brother and two nieces in Minnesota; one nephew in Oregon, and one niece and one nephew in Norway.

The Christians once owned the farm on which Mrs. Teodore Peterson now resides. The place was sold when Mrs. Christianson went west.

Johannes Krisjersen (1835 – 1920 and his wife Berthe Serine (1842 – 1880).

The deed to Krisjer from J. Dahm for the so–called Flagrahaug farm, in the amount of 1/2 v.tf. for 200 Spd. is dated May 24, 1834.

In 1866 the farm of 34 mål (approx 120 acres) is estimated at 232 Spd. Pastures are estimated at 46 Spd., available peat 83 Spd. and easements 29 Spd. Annual yield is 22 barrels oats, 5 barrels of barley, 16 barrels of potatoes, 27 skp.[32] hay. The entire farm is assessed to 420 Spd. The livestock consists of 1 horse, 4 cows, 10 sheep and 1 pig.

6. **Johannes Krisjersen.** 1868 – 1910
Born Jan. 7, 1835, died Oct. 16, 1920, son of previous farmer.

Married on Nov. 10, 1867 to **Berthe Serine Thorsdatter**, born Oct. 16, 1842, died Jan. 2, 1880, daughter of Marta Elisabet Torresdatter and Thore Kristoffersen, Våge in Avaldsnes.

Children:

a. Theresia Elisabeth, born Apr. 6, 1868, emigrated to Nebraska, USA in 1888, married to Ole G. Oss.
b. Endre Michael Kristian Vegner, born Nov. 13, 1871, next farmer.
c. Bertha Olava, born Oct. 21, 1875, died Apr. 18, 1876.

The deed to Johannes from the father on this farm, tax liability 1 dl. 2 ort 16 sk., for which he paid 450 Spd., followed by an old age pension

[32] skalpund – "bowl pound" – a grain weight just under 1/2 kg. or around 1 lb.

agreement of 140 Spd., is dated July 9, 1868. Among the items listed in the agreement with the parents, the following can be mentioned:

> 4 barrels of oats, free use of the field "Ladehaugsflekket," feed for 1 cow and 4 sheep, 1 cord peat and 1 cord birch wood, 2 cans of cod liver oil and free board "until suitable old age living arrangements have been found, for which a lot on the southern portion of the so–called "Barneflekket" is made available."

In 1875 he feeds 1 horse, 2 cows, 15 sheep and 1 pig, while his father feeds 1 cow and 6 sheep. He plants 1 barrel barley, 4–1/2 barrel oats and 3 barrels of potatoes, while the father on his retirement plot plants 1/4 barrel of barley, 3/4 barrel of oats and 3/4 barrel of potatoes.

The main log dwelling house here, 13.3 x 7 meters, with basement lined with boards and covered with roof tiles is assessed in 1880 to 1260 kroner. The barn, 12.7 x 6.3 meters with log–built area for the cows is assessed to 720 kroner.

An older sister of Berthe Serine, Martha Elisabeth, worked here as a housekeeper for many years until she died in 1886.

A new mortgage on the farm was obtained in 1886 in the amount of 2.17 sk.m. (taxes owed in new marks, the "skyldmark" – from 1886).

7. **Michael Johannesen.** 1910 – 1944.

Born Nov. 13, 1871, died May 6, 1940, son of the last farmer.

Married on Apr. 17, 1919, to **Kaia Johannesen,** born Feb. 6, 1889, died Jan. 18, 1944, daughter of Marta Larsdatter and Aslak Orjansen, Skålnes in Skanevik and widow of Johannes Johannesen Herberg on farm no. 20.

Children:

a. Berta Serine, born July 18, 1919, died Dec. 14, 1919.
b. Berta, born Oct. 26, 1920, married in 1940 to Konrad Ostrem, farmer no. 20–7, Nordvik.
c. Johannes, born Oct. 26, 1922, next farmer.

The deed to Michael from Therese Elisabeth as the sole heir in the amount of 1600 kroner is dated Oct. 26, 1921.

Michael worked this farm together with the Herberg farm no. 20.

8. **Johannes Johannesen.** 1944 – 1972

Born Oct. 26, 1922, died July 14, 1960, son of previous farmer.

Married on Apr. 2, 1947 to **Julia Austrheim**, born Nov. 1, 1919, daughter of Julie and Konrad Knutsen, farmer no. 1 – 10 h, Austrheim.

Children:

a. Vigdis Kari. Born June 12, 1948, married in 1967 to Jan Jensen, now separated and living in Tønsberg.
b. Kåre Jan, born May 30, 1951, married to Kari Gunderstad, lives in Bleikmyr, Haugesund.

The farm was used as an additional farm and was taken over in recent years by Kåre Jan Johannesen.

Farm no. 18. Herberg. From farm no. 17 in 1784

1. **Johannes Nilsen.** 1784 – 1810

Born 1752, died Apr. 4, 1815, son of Eli Danielsdatter and Nils Johnsen, Visnes, Karmøy.

Married on Aug. 16, 1783 to **Kari Mikkelsdatter**, baptized Sept. 18, 1763, died Oct. 25, 1833, daughter of Randi Olsdatter and Mikkel Mathiassen, farm no. 2 – 1 a, Austrheim.

Children:

a. Nils, baptized Apr. 17, 1784, married to Ingeborg Elisabet Jensdatter, lived in Vårå, Avaldsnes.
b. Mikkel, baptized Oct. 8, 1785, became next farmer.
c. Ole, baptized Mar. 2, 1788, died Aug. 25, 1838.
d. Jon, baptized May 5, 1790, married in 1816 to Helga Nilsdatter, lived in Kolstø, Avaldsnes.
e. Mathias, baptized Feb. 18, 1792, married in 1821 to Sofie Hansine Johannesdatter, farm no. 20–1, Nordvik.
f. Mikkel, baptized June 29, 1794, buried Sept. 21, 1794, 12 weeks old.
g. Daniel, baptized Jan. 18, 1795, married in 1826 to Kari Oline Jakobsdatter, farm no. 4–9, Austrheim.
h. Johannes, baptized June 30, 1799, married in 1825 to Ingeborg Oline Johnsdatter, farm no. 6–6, Austrheim.
i. Hans Sakarias, baptized July 4, 1802, married in 1825 to Valborg Knutsdatter, farm no. 5–5, Austrheim.

According to the contract dated Nov. 15, 1784, 1–1/2 v.tf. of the farm is left to Johannes from Jens Clausen on the condition that Jens can continue to farm the remaining 1/2 v.tf. portion which Jens reserved for himself and can harvest what he needs of peat.

On May 1, 1788 Johannes is awarded by Peder Vallentin in Bergen a lease contract issued on the 1–1/2 v.tf. share of the farm.

Herberg on the left with the lighthouses in the background. North of the church "the Leversen house" can be seen which was torn down in 1950. Photo: P. O. Ottesen 1907

In 1802 he plants 3 barrels of grain and harvests 15 barrels. He feeds 1 horse, 4 cows and 6 sheep, and the entire farm is assessed at 156 Spd.

In the estate settlement after Johannes in 1815 the estate is valued at 447 rbdl. (riksbankdaler) or approx. 44 Spd. Expenses and debt amounts to 156 rbdl., of which 60 rbdl. is paid for burial expenses and 50 rbdl. covers upkeep on the houses. Among miscellaneous items the following are also mentioned (amounts listed in rbdl.):

> 4 cows 185–0–0, 2 horses, of which one is over 20 years old, 18–0–0, 1 outside mill with housing and misc. equipment 84–0–0, 1 cast–iron stove 25–0–0 and 1 old four–oar boat without sail 16–0–0.

2. **Mikkel Johannesen.** 1810 – 1846

Baptized Oct. 8, 1785, died Feb. 20, 1864, son of the previous farmer.

Married on Apr. 5, 1813 to **Kari Thorsdatter,** baptized July 17, 1785, died Dec. 3, 1845, daughter of Malene Tormodsdatter and Thore Larsen, farmer no. 15–6 b, Nordvik.

Children:

a. Berthe Malene, born Apr. 11, 1822, next farmer.

Lease contract to Mikkel on the 1–1/2 v.tf. section was issued by H. B. Foreman on Sept. 1, 1810, and the old age commitment to the parents as follows:

> . . . seven barrels of oats at 4 våger per barrel, 1/2 barrel barley, feed for two cows and use of the sections of the land called "Brøkken" and "Toskskjaerebaekken" for farming and other utilization as long as Johannes Nielsen and his wife Karen Mikkelsdatter live, but only half of that, when one of the parents dies.

He pays 45 rdl in lease money. In 1819 he leases half of farm no. 20 to his brother Mathias including the existing buildings. Mikkel and Kari built their own main dwelling house below the main courtyard and lived there. In the lease contract between Mikkel and Mathias, Mikkel reserves the right to use half of the other buildings on the farm, however, maintenance shall be Mathias' responsibility in addition to half of the burden to care for the mother's old age requirements. In case Mikkel desires to relinquish the rest of the 3/4 v.tf. share in the farm (to one of the brothers), Mathias shall be obligated to let the next farmer take over half of the buildings, while Mikkel and Kari continue to use the house they live in into their old age.

In 1823 the farm is assessed to 95 Spd. A description of the houses and the annual yield is not available.

In 1838 he buys the farm from J. Dahm for 300 Spd., the deed is dated Dec. 27, 1838, debt is 2 pounds 6 merker or 3/4 v.tf.

On the farm in 1845 he plants 1/2 barrel barley, 4 barrels oats and 1–1/2 barrels potatoes. The livestock consist of 1 horse, 4 cows, 12 sheep and 1 pig.

3. **Thomas Tollefsen.** 1846 – 1860.
Baptized May 8, 1814, died Feb. 23, 1859, son of Ingeborg Gudmundsdatter and Tollef Sjursen, farmer no. 2 – 3 h, Austrheim.

Married on Jan. 17, 1839, to **Berthe Malene Mikkelsdatter,** born Apr. 11, 1822, died Oct. 23, 1891, daughter of previous farmer.

Children:
a. Johan *Mikal*, born Feb. 15, 1839, next farmer.
b. *Bolette* Karine, born July 1, 1840, married in 1869 to Andreas Larsen, Fjeld in Vingers parish.
c. Tollef, born Feb. 10, 1842, married in 1867 to Maren Helene Knutsdatter, tenant farm no. 32, Nordvik.
d. Ingeborg Kristine, born Mar. 26, 1844, died Nov. 22, 1853.
e. Berte Karine, born Mar. 26, 1846.

f. Caroline, born Apr. 28, 1847, married in 1864 to Johan Helgesen, farmer no. 5, here.
g. Berthe *Helgesine*, born Mar. 22, 1849, married in 1870 to John Bendik Mathiassen, farmer no. 3 – 2, Skare.
h. Severine, born Dec. 20, 1851, died Sept. 29, 1869, was blind.
i. Ingeborg Kristine, born Feb. 8, 1855, died July 3, 1871, was blind.
j. Thomas, born Sept. 11, 1857, died Nov. 10, 1872.

The deed to Thomas from Mikkel in the amount of 300 Spd. is dated Sept. 25, 1846, debt is 1 dl. 2 ort. 16 sk. Old age contract for 5 years is valued at 100 Spd. consisting of 5 barrels of oats, 1/2 barrel barley, a section of a field yielding 1/2 barrel of potatoes, feed for 1 cow and 6 sheep, 1 cord peat and 1 cord birch wood and 2 cans of cod liver oil.

At the estate settlement after Thomas in 1861, the farm was assessed at 700 Spd. and deeded over to the son Johan Mikal. The estate contained 50 Spd. in cash and miscellaneous items in the amount of 357 Spd. 36 sk., consisting of :

> Livestock 57–0–0, farm tools and equipment 11–0–36, carpenter tools 10–0–0, 1 wood–burning stove 10–0–0, 4 dozen barrels 16–0–0, 11 "balker" (275 fathoms) seine fishing nets 88–0–0, 8 mackerel nets 16–0–0, 3 herring nets 6–0–0, 1 coal fish and 1 pollock fishing net 4–0–0, 2/3 of a large fishing boat 66–0–0, 1 four–oar fishing boat with sail 4–0–0, 1 loom with accessories 7–0–0 and 1 living room clock with casing 4–0–0.

It is said that Thomas built a new dwelling house here around 1850.

Johan Mikal and Magel Serine Herberg

4. **Johan Mikal Thomassen (Herberg).** 1861 – 1870
Born Feb. 15, 1839, died in 1919, son of last farmer.

Married in 1863 to **Magel Serine Thorsdatter,** born Dec. 24, 1845, died 1935, daughter of Kristine Pedersdatter and Thor Olsen, Kalsto in Avaldsnes.

Children:

a. Thomas, born Sept. 20, 1864, emigrated to Minnesota, USA, married in 1887 to Anette Bergsven.
b. *Theresa* Kirstine, born Nov. 27, 1866, emigrated to N. Dakota, USA, married to Halvor B. Rover (born 1854 in Rovaer) in 1888. Theresa lived to 105 and lived for many years in San Diego, California.
c. Olaf Michael, born Jan. 8, 1869, emigrated to USA, married Marie Magdahl.
d. Berta Malina (Lina), born June 25, 1872, married in 1894 in USA to George Adelbert Tripp.
e. Albert, born Feb. 5, 1875, married in 1899 to Inga Mathilde Martinsen in USA. Lived in Minnesota.
f. Edward, born June 8, 1879, married in USA to Karen Petrina Thomson, born 1879 in Mosvigen, Norway.
g. Thorolf, born Nov. 29, 1882.
h. Olga, born July 4, 1884, married in USA in 1920 to John J. Johnsen. Lived in Hallstad, Minnesota.
i. Fridthjof Wilhelm, born Oct. 3, 1885, died in 1909.
j. Herbert Gerhard, born Dec. 9, 1890, married in USA to Gina Fosses.

Power of attorney dated May 15, 1861, to Johan Mikal in the estate settlement after the father and old age contract for his mother dated Aug. 17, 1868, in the amount of 5–1/2 barrels of oats, 1/2 barrel of barley, 2 fields named "Traeflekket" and "Vaneflek," *including the dwelling house plot which Mikkel Johannesen has used and 15 paces from each corner used as a garden*, feed for 1 cow and 5 sheep, 1 cord birch wood and 2 cans of cod liver oil.

In 1866 the farm has 52 mål fields and pastures valued to 364 Spd. There are pastures for 72 Spd., peat for 100 Spd. and easements for 29 Spd. Annual yield is 28 barrels of oats, 5 barrels of barley, 30 barrels of potatoes and 41 skp. hay. The entire farm is assessed at 650 Spd. The livestock consists of 1 horse, 6 cows, 12 sheep and 1 pig.

The main dwelling house here is 9.4 x 5.5 meters, log–built, lined with boards and roofed with tiles, and was assessed in 1867 to 300 Spd. There is a basement under half of the house and a porch on the western wall. The hay–barn, 20.4 x 9.4 meters was assessed at 120 Spd. and an outhouse, 7.8 x 4.7 meters, was assessed to 20 Spd.

In 1870 the father sold the farm and left for USA with his family. The trip across the Atlantic took 6 weeks and 2 days. They lived the first year in Faribault, Minnesota, but in 1871 they moved to North Dakota (Herberg Township, Traill County), homesteaded, and were among the first settlers there.

In 1916 they moved to Halstad, Minnesota.

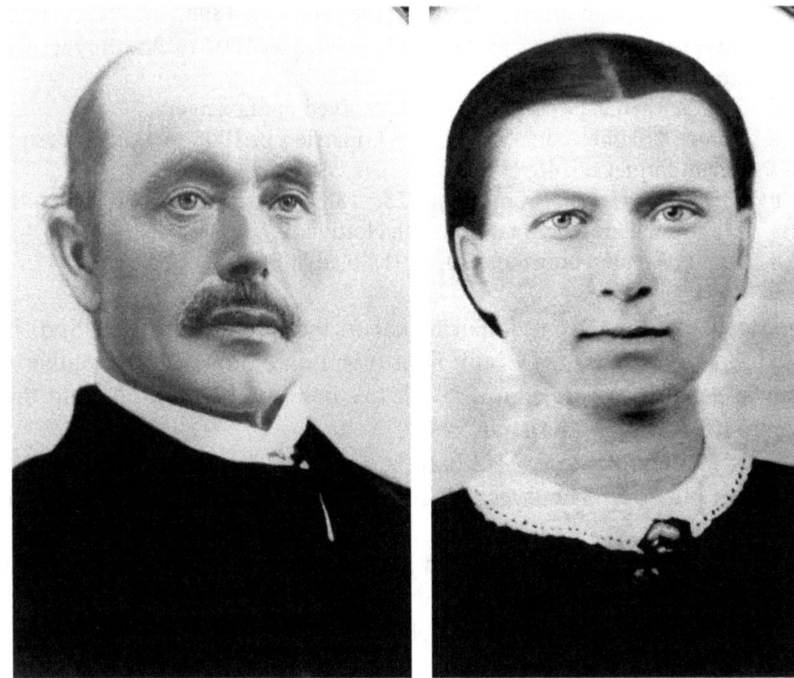

Johan Helgesen (1840–1913) and Karoline Thomasdatter (1847–1903).

5. **Johan Helgesen.** 1870 – 1909.
Born June 19, 1840, died June 9, 1913, son of Valborg and Helge Andreas Johnsen, farmer no. 1 – 11 c, Nordvik.

Married on May 22, 1864, to **Karoline Thomasdatter,** born Apr. 28, 1847, died Apr. 11, 1903, daughter of farmer no. 3 here.

Children:

a. Ida *Tomine*, born Feb. 1, 1865, married in 1884 to Knut Gudmundsen, farmer no. 1 – 9, Austrheim.
b. Andreas *Vallum*, born Dec. 28, 1866, next farmer.
c. Hanna Kristine, born Feb. 22, 1869, died Mar. 23, 1889.
d. Berthe *Mathilde*, born June 10, 1871, married in 1893 to Lars M. Mikalsen, farmer no. 4–6, Klovning.
e. Gamalie Helene (Lene), born May 15, 1873, married on Sept. 20, 1890 to Oystein Larsen Rullestad, Utsira School no. 13.
f. Elise Sofie (Lisa), born June 5, 1875, married in 1900 to Peder S. Klovning, tenant farmer no. 44, Nordvik.
g. *Thomas* Johan, born May 7, 1877, married in 1903 to Ragna Serine Eriksdatter, farmer no. 30 – 1, Nordvik.
h. Johan Kristian, born May 12, 1879, married in 1900 to Gina Mathiasdatter, tenant farmer no. 43, Nordvik.

i. *Lovise* Marie, born June 13, 1881, died June 25, 1898.
j. *Sivert* Martin, born Apr. 24, 1883, married in 1907 to Åsa Roynesdal, farmer no. 32–1, Nordvik.
k. Minda Theresia, born Apr. 23, 1885, lived in Stavanger.
l. *Laura* Kristine, born May 9, 1887, married in 1908 to Daniel Vestre, tenant farmer no. 48, Nordvik.
m. *Hersleb* Kristian, born Sept. 28, 1889, married in 1910 to Julie Mathiasdatter, tenant farm no. 50. Nordvik.
n. Hanna Amalie, born June 20, 1891, lived in Stavanger.

The deed to Johan from Johan Mikal in the amount of 1000 Spd. is dated Apr. 11, 1870. They built their own home on part of the father's farm in eastern Nordvik farm no. 2, tax liability 13 ore). He sold the farm to his son Johan Kristian in 1902.

In 1875 they planted 1–1/2 barrels of barley, 4 barrels of oats and 4 barrels of potatoes. The livestock consists of 1 horse, 3 cows, 1 calf, 11 sheep and 1 pig.

In 1907 he subdivides the farm and gives a part, farm no. 32, to his son Sivert.

An obituary in the *Haugesund Avis* newspaper, dated 11 June, 1913 reads:

Obituary

A well–known Utsira man, master seiner Johan Helgesen has passed away, 73 years old. The deceased was one of the best known master seiners on Utsira – a man whose words were heard often among the island's population. The deceased was strongly religious and participated much in religious life. He involved himself in many community activities. Three sons have inherited their father's skill and involvement as master seiners.

6. **A. Valnum Helgesen.** 1909 – 1940
Born Dec. 28, 1866, died July 9, 1942, son of last farmer.

Married in his first marriage on Oct. 16, 1892, to **Olga Mathilde Johannesdatter**, born Jan. 14, 1872, died Apr. 6, 1910, daughter of Eli Kristine and Johannes Rasmussen, tenant farmer no. 14c, Klovning.

Married in his second marriage on Nov. 3, 1912, to **Anna Ellingsdatter**, born Aug. 30, 1874, died Dec. 29, 1918, daughter of Anna Helene Torbjornsdatter and Elling Olsen, Sandve in Skudenes.

Children in first marriage:
a. *Johan* Kristian, born June 24, 1893, farmer no. 9 here.
b. Johannes, born Apr. 14, 1895, died Apr. 16, 1895.

Valnum Helgesen (1866-1942) and Olga Johannesdatter (1872-1910) with children Jenny, born 1896, Johan, born 1893 and Lovise, born 1899.

c. Jenny Kristine, born Sept. 7, 1896, emigrated to USA, married in 1925 to Oscar Nilsen (tenant farm no. 41 c, Nordvik), lived in Brooklyn.
d. *Lovise* Marie, born July 12, 1899, married in 1919 to Trygve Skåren, farmer no. 22 – 4, Nordvik.
e. Hanna Malene, born Nov. 24, 1901, died Feb. 7, 1912.
f. Andreas Valnum, born Feb. 25, 1905, died Mar. 9, 1907.
g. Andreas Valnum, born Dec. 16, 1907, died Aug. 23, 1925.
h. Olga Mathilde, born Aug. 6, 1909, died Dec. 18, 1917.

Children in second marriage:
i. Elling, born Aug. 5, 1913, next farmer.
j. Hersleb Mikal, born Feb. 15, 1916, died Dec. 24, 1916.

The deed to Valnum from the father on this farm is in the amount of 3000 kr. with a tax estimate of 3.00 sk.m. (skyldmark) and an old age agreement with the parents of 1000 kr., and is dated May 4, 1909.

They build a main dwelling on the farm in 1903. The second story on Hiljen's main house in eastern Nordvik was moved here. The old main dwelling was separated from the estate in 1907 and was renamed

"Lilleherberget" (the small lodge) and re–established as farm no. 31. Laura and Daniel Vestre took over this house in 1920.

7. **Elling Valnumsen.** 1941 – 1945
Born Aug. 5, 1913, died Oct. 29, 1995, son of last farmer.

Married on May 28, 1939, to **Pauline Hansdatter Veastad,** from Vikebygd, born Apr. 13, 1911.

Children:

a. Anna Valborg, born Apr. 26, 1940, married to Asmund Våge, lives in Fordesfjorden.
b. *Harald* Arvid, born Aug. 7, 1942, married in 1965 to Anne Marie Skjold, Sauda, lives in Avaldsnes.
c. *Trygve* Olav, born July 3, 1945, married to Kirsten Fossmark, lives in Stavanger.
d. *Edith* Pauline, born Mar. 22, 1948, married to Ola Dvergsnes, lives in Aksdal.
e. Svein Einar, born Dec. 29, 1950, married to Signe Boliva Johnsen, lives in Sauda.

Elling ran the farm during the war (WWII), half of it from 1943, when his brother Johan came home from the USA. Half the farm was separated from the estate and became farm no. 64 in 1943.

The main dwelling house was separated from the estate in 1946 and became farm no. 67.

Elling was the municipal treasurer and secretary for the county council from 1958, and became head of the board of assessement in 1947. They moved to Vikebygd.

8. **Rasmus Johansen.** 1943 – 1945
Born July 14, 1918, died Nov. 9, 1945, son of next farmer.

Rasmus was a seaman and perished at sea in the M/S "Skåre" shipwreck.

9. **Johan Valnumsen.** 1946 – 1967
Born June 24, 1893, died Dec. 5, 1967, son of farmer no. 6 here.

Married on May 16, 1915, to **Regine Bertine Rasmusdatter**, born Mar. 30, 1889, died Sept. 28, 1967, daughter of Gurine and Rasmus Thomassen, farmer no. 12–5 e, Nordvik.

Children:

a. Olga Matilde, born Aug. 4, 1915. married in 1940 to Lars Skjelde, farmer no. 11 here.
b. Rasmus, born July 14, 1918, last farmer.

View of Nordvik from the southwest. Telemark Aircraft Co., 1954.

c. Johan Georg, born June 25, 1921, next farmer.

Johan took over the farm here and farm no. 64 in 1946. From 1925 he lived and worked as a fisherman in Seattle, USA for many years. In 1939 a new main dwelling was built on the farm.

The livestock consisted in 1957 of 2 cows, 3 calves and 27 sheep.

10. **Johan Georg Johannesen.** 1967 – 1979
Born June 25, 1921, died Sept. 4, 1979, son of last farmer.

Married on Sept. 23, 1956, to **Gerd Kristense Klovning,** born Dec. 2, 1932, died June 8, 1967, daughter of Marie and Johannes Klovning, farmer no. 2 – 4 b, Klovning.

Children:

a. *Johannes* Tor Geir, born Mar. 26, 1959, married to Elisabeth Rasmussen, lives in Royksund.
b. Gunvor, born Aug. 20, 1963, married to Sveinung Larsen, lives in Stavanger.

11. **Lars Skjelde.** 1980 – 1990.

Lars ran the farm for these years, see under tenant farmer no. 63, Nordvik. The farm was taken over by Oddleif Skjelde in 1984.

Farm no. 20, Herberg. From farm no. 18 in 1819

1. **Mathias Johannesen.** 1819 – 1855
Baptized Aug. 12, 1792, died July 11, 1859, son of Eli Danielsdatter and Johannes Nilsen, farmer no. 18 – 1 e, Nordvik.

Married on Oct. 11, 1821, to **Sofie Hansine Johannesdatter**, baptized Oct. 17, 1802, died Apr. 22, 1845, daughter of Malene Tormodsdatter and Johannes Helgesen, farmer no. 15 – 7 e, Nordvik.

Children:

a. Johannes, born July 31, 1822, next farmer.
b. Martha Malena, born July 23, 1824, died Dec. 18, 1904, she was a housekeeper for Lars Johan Thorsen, Pedle–haugen for over 40 years.
c. Jan, born May 31, 1826, had one daughter: Laurine Teodora, born Jan. 17, 1848, outside marriage with Marthe Marie Torstendatter, Stavanger.
d. Karen Kristine, born Sept. 30, 1828.
e. Tormod, born June 15, 1830, married in 1855 to Anne Marthe Johannesdatter, tenant farmer no. 31, Nordvik.
f. Berthe Helene, born Mar. 26, 1832, died Jan. 30, 1907, lived at home and was a housekeeper on the farm.
g. Anne *Martha*, born Feb. 10, 1835, died Aug. 13, 1888, was also a housekeeper at the Lars Johan Thorsen residence.
h. Martha Kristine, born May 19, 1838, married Lars Johan Thorsen in 1862, farmer no. 15–9, Nordvik (Pedle–Haugen)
i. Johan *Mathias*, born Aug. 5, 1840, married Kathrine Osmundsdatter in 1864, tenant farmer no. 27, Nordvik.

Lease contract issued to Mathias in the amount of 3/4 v.tf. by H. B. Forman in Bergen on Aug. 15, 1819, and a contract with the brother Mikal, see farm no. 18.

Similar to farm no. 18, we also miss here the description of the houses and the annual yield from 1822, but the farm is assessed to 115 Spd.

In 1845 he plants 1/4 barrel of barley, 3 barrels of oats and 1 barrel of potatoes. The livestock consists of 1 horse, 4 cows, 6 sheep and 1 pig.

In estate settlement after Sofie Hansine's death in 1845 the estate is worth 98–2–8 Spd. and debt and expenses amount to 44–4–14. Among miscellaneous items the following can be mentioned:

> 4 cows 28–2–12, 2 horses 8–0–0, 1/2 of a mill with mill housing 6–0–0, 1 cast–iron stove 4–0–0, 1 living room clock 8–0–0. 1/2 boat shed 1–1–0, 1 four–oar fishing boat with sail 6–0–0, 3 herring fishing nets 3–2–0, 1 pollock fishing net 1–1–0, 40 lobster pots 2–4–0 and silverware 3–0–12.

Mathias and six others from Utsira perished when their boat capsized on their way home from Bergen.

2. **Johannes Mathiassen.** 1855–1896
Born July 31, 1822, died Aug. 11, 1900, son of previous farmer.

Married in 1st marriage on Apr. 7, 1851, to **Berthe Malene Thoresdatter**, born Sept. 18, 1821, died May 11, 1852, daughter of Anne Kristine and Thore Thorsen, farmer no. 15–8 a, Nordvik.

Married in 2nd marriage on July 6, 1854 to **Martha Elina Henriksdatter,** born May 28, 1821, died Jan. 23, 1857, daughter of Berta Pedersdatter and Henrik Johannesen, Skjølingstad, Torvestad.

Married in 3rd marriage on Dec. 6, 1859 to **Martha Kristine Thoresdatter**, born Mar. 11, 1829, died Nov. 29, 1860, daughter of Anne Kristine and Thore Thorsen, farmer no. 15–8 d, Nordvik. Sister of Berthe Malene above.

Married in 4th marriage on July 6, 1865 to **Åsa Kristine Bårdsdatter,** born May 13, 1841, died July 14, 1882, daughter of Eli Oline and Bård Ommundsen, Saebø, Torvest.

Married in 5th marriage on Aug. 18, 1889 to **Sofie Hansine Tormodsdatter,** born Dec. 17, 1855, died Feb. 26, 1896, daughter of Anne Marthe and Tormod Mathiassen, tenant farmer no. 31, Nordvik.

Children in 5th marriage:

a. Åsa Birgitte, born Nov. 18, 1889, died Dec. 3, 1904.
b. *Johannes* Magnus, born Feb. 27, 1892, farmer no. 5 here.
c. Sofie Amanda, born June 29, 1894, died Dec. 24, 1895.

The deed to Johannes from J. Dahm in the amount of 300 Spd. is dated June 1, 1842, taxable at 1 dl. 2 ort and with an old age pension to his father of 5 barrels of oats, 1/2 barrel of barley, 2 cords of peat, feed for 1 cow and 6 sheep and the use of the field called "Skjolden." The pension to his father is estimated at 130 Spd.

In 1866 the farm with 40 mål of meadows and fields is assessed at 312 Spd. There are pastures for 67 Spd., peat for 100 Spd. and easements for 29 Spd. Annual yield is 25 barrels of oats, 16 barrels of potatoes and 38 skp. hay. The entire farm is worth 585 Spd. The livestock consist of 1 horse, 5 cows, 12 sheep and 1 pig.

3. **Thore Johan Larsen.** 1896 – 1903
Born May 23, 1874, died Apr. 4, 1903, son of Marthe Kristine and Lars Johan Thorsen, farmer no. 15 – 9 f, Nordvik.

Unmarried.

The deed to Thore from Johannes in the amount of 2500 kr. is dated July 6, 1896, tax assessement of 3.01 sk.m. and old age contract of 700 kr. with the following clause:

> The contributor is obligated, if the receiver should die, to support his now living children, with food, clothing and raise these children as was required of the father and mother, as best he is able to do and be responsible for their welfare, until they are 15 years of age.

4. **Lars Karlsen.** 1903 – 1908
Born June 20, 1867, son of Martha Larsdatter and Karl Nilsen, Davoy, Askoy.

Married to **Pauline Hansine Nilsdatter**, born April 20, 1870, died Apr. 3, 1908 on Utsira, daughter of Grethe Pedersdatter and Nils Nilsen, Follesoy, Askoy.

No records on file.

5. **Johannes Johannesen.** 1909 – 1919
Born Feb. 27, 1892, died Jan. 24, 1917, son of farmer no. 2 here.

Married in 1915 to **Kaia Aslaksdatter**, born Feb. 6, 1889, died Jan. 18, 1944, daughter of Marta Larsdatter and Aslak Orjansen Skålnes, Skanevik.

Children:

a. Martha *Sofie*, born Feb. 19, 1916, married in 1941 to Henrik Arnold Olavsen Landa, moved to Eikeland in Vats.

The deed to Johannes from Thore Larsen's heirs for 3000 kr. is dated Nov. 17, 1908

6. **Mikal Johannesen.** 1919 – 1943.
Born Nov. 13, 1871, died May 6, 1940, farmer no. 17-7, Nordvik.

Married on Apr. 17, 1919, to **Kaia Johannesen,** widow of last farmer.

The children are listed under farmer no. 17.

Johannes Johannesen (1892 – 1917) and Kaia Aslaksdatter (1889 – 1944)

Kaia and Mikal ran the farm together with farmer no. 17, but in 1921 this farm was divided, and farm no. 44 was separated and became Jørgen Nilsen's farm.

7. **Konrad Østrem.** 1943 – 1974
Born Mar. 6, 1918, son of Julie and Konrad Knutsen, farmer no. 1 – 10 g, Austrheim.

Married on Sept. 15, 1940, to **Berta Johannesen,** born Oct. 26, 1920, died Apr. 7, 1984, daughter of last farmer.

Children:

a. Gerd Johanna, born Mar. 29, 1941, married in 1961 to Tor Ellingsen, Austrheim, moved to Haugesund.
b. Kåre Magne, born Apr. 2, 1944, moved to Haugesund.
c. Berit Kjellaug, born June 15, 1949, died Feb. 18, 1950.
d. Kjell Bodvar, born Dec. 21, 1950, married to May Helen, moved to Haugesund.

Konrad inherited the farm in 1943, and a new main dwelling was built in 1951. The family moved to Haugesund.

The farm was later worked as an additional farm. The farm is since taken over by Kåre Magne Ostrem.

Farm no. 21 Naesset (Nordhus). From farm no. 20 in 1850

1. Tollef Rasmussen. 1850 – 1864

Born Mar. 1, 1822, died Jan. 12, 1860, son of Jobiane Jobsdatter and Rasmus Tollefsen, farmer no. 7 – 7 e, Hovland.

Married on Oct. 8, 1849, to **Berthe Karine Thoresdatter,** born Oct. 20, 1823, died Oct. 22, 1862, daughter of Anne Kirstine Johannesdatter and Thore Thorsen, farmer no. 15– 8 b, Nordvik.

No children.

The farm is sold to Tollef from Johannes Mathiassen for 100 Spd. on May 24, 1850. In the contract it is noted that the transaction concerns two separate pieces of land and that the buyer does not have the right to cut peat and can feed only one cow from it.

Division of the property and tax assessment was conducted in 1853 and tax was assessed to 6 mrk. dried fish or 16 sk. in new tax obligation. (Mentioned here are: Skarven, Fladbjerget, Josabjerget).

Berthe Karine was married second time in 1862 to widower Thomas Ellingsen Beite.

2. Kristian Simonsen. 1865 – 1871

Born Oct. 23, 1842, son of Anna Johnsdatter And Simon Kristiansen, Svinakleiv at Skjold.

Married in first marriage on April 2, 1865, to **Jorgine *Berentine* Jørgensdatter,** born June 11, 1844, died in 1882, daughter of Bolette Koubkje Larsdatter and Jørgen Jørgensen, farmer no. 14–1 a, Nordvik.

Married in second marriage in 1885 to **Sophia Staveteig**.

Children first marriage:

a. *Boletha* Kristine, born Aug. 8, 1866, married in 1891 to Thomas Gudmundsen Ostrem. (son of Gudmund Knutsen Austrheim)
b. Thomine Gurine (*Minnie*), born Mar. 28, 1868, married in 1887 to Jahn Andreas Thorsen, 4 children, lived in S. Dakota. Jahn Andreas married second time to Marie Olsdatter Randen (See page 96). Minnie and children moved back to Newman Grove, Nebraska.
c. Jørgen Olai (George), born May 4, 1870, married in 1899 to Hannah Vikse.
d. Elisabeth, born and died 1871, one day old.
e. Anne Serine, born 1872, died Dec. 25, 1873 in Nebraska.
f. Anna, born Nov. 14, 1875, married to Halvor Halvorsen.
g. Simon, born Mar. 27, 1877, married to Kanutta Vaage.
h. *Kristian* Johannes, born Sept. 14, 1879, married to Anna Carlsen.

Children in 2nd marriage:

i. Bernthina (Tina) born Mar. 26, 1886, married in 1907 to George Vaage.

The title to Kristian from the heirs of Tollef Rasmussen in the amount of 200 Spd. is dated Aug. 17, 1865. Included in the purchase is the still–standing storage building.

In 1866 there is 9 mål (approx 36 acres) of meadows in the estate of estimated value of 35 Spd. and pastures for 10 Spd. Annual yield is 3-1/2 barrels of oats, 8 barrels of potatoes and 6 skp. (1 skp. = >1/2 kg. = about 1 lb.) hay. The entire farm's estimated worth is 65 Spd. Livestock consist of 1 cow, 3 sheep and 1 pig.

Kristian Simonsen and Berentine, Boletha and Minnie.

The main dwelling here is a 7.8 x 5.3 meter frame house clad with boards and roofed with tiles, and in 1868 its worth was estimated at 200 Spd. A tenant house, 10.6 x 5 meters, was assessed at 50 Spd. The house was just north of the Nordhus dwelling.

The Simonsen family traveled in April 1871 from Stavanger with the frigate "Undine" to the USA. One of the passengers on that ship was Jørgen B. (George) Hovland. Altogether there were 385 passengers onboard, the trip took 5 weeks and enroute in the Newfoundland area, they hit an iceberg. The crew managed to save the ship and they finally arrived in Quebec on June 5th.

The first years they lived in Columbus, Wisconsin. In 1873 they moved together with four other families further west to Wisner, Nebraska, where they settled. In addition to farming, Kristian and his brother–in–law, Nils Wick, started a freight–forwarding company and carried freight between the populated areas of Columbus and Newman Grove, Nebraska.[33]

3. **Thore Mikal Thorsen.** 1871 – 1899
Born Sept. 20, 1838, died Jan. 19, 1899, son of Anne Kristine and Thore Thorsen, farmer no. 15 – 8 f, Nordvik.

Married on Mar. 27, 1862, to **Marthe Kristine Jansdatter,** born Feb. 22, 1839, died July 3, 1924, in Los Angeles, CA, daughter of Anna Kristine Olsdatter and Jan Berdinius Halvorsen, Nord–Velde in Avaldsnes. (Thore Mikal and Anna Kristine were cousins.)

Children:

a. Jahn Andreas, born May 30, 1862 in Avaldsnes, married in 1887 to Minnie Simonsen (See page 94); married second time in 1907 in Seattle, WA to Marie Olsdatter Randen. Lived in Los Angeles, CA.
b. Thore, born Feb. 8, 1864, died Mar. 10, 1864.
c. Berthe Karine, born Apr. 30, 1865, died May 23, 1865.
d. Teodor, born Jan. 1, 1867, emigrated to USA in 1884, died in Seattle in 1925.
e. Olava Christine, born Sept. 16, 1870, emigrated to USA in 1887, died in 1901 on Ellis Island.
f. *Michael* Christian, born Feb. 17, 1873, died in 1945, emigrated to USA in 1893 where he married Ågot (Agnes) Marie Frantzen. Lived in Los Angeles.
g. Berthe Karine, born Oct. 17, 1874, died in 1944, married in 1904 to Adolph Ben Tennesen, lived in Los Angeles.
h. Berthe Mallene, born July 24, 1877, died in 1974 in Alhambra, California.
i. Anne Serine, born May 10, 1880, married Laerum, died in 1962 in Alhambra.

Thore Mikal's son with Ingeborg Karine Johannesdatter Klovning:

j. Carl Johan, born July 5, 1859, died Dec. 28, 1924, married Elisabeth Jane Planciers in Cardiff (Wales). He was a sailor.

---

[33] See Note 10.

The lease contract to Thore Mikal from Thomas Ellingsen Beite on the building lot where the Karine and Tollef Rasmussen house is situated includes a condition that Mikal was required to work three days per year, one day in each season. The lease is dated Sept. 29, 1863.

In 1875 he plants 1/3 barrels of barley, 1/2 barrels of oats, 1 barrel of potatoes, and feeds 1 cow and 3 sheep.

In addition to fishing and farm activities, Thore Mikal also had a shoe repair shop.

After Thore Mikal's death the rest of the family left for Los Angeles, California, USA.

4. **Karoline Rasmusdatter Oppen.** 1899 – 1903

Born Apr. 22, 1848, died Dec. 7, 1921, widow of lighthouse attendant Lars Peder Knoph Oppen, (See under tenant farmer no. 19, Skare.)

Auction title to Johannes Johannesen Klovning on this farm for 1050 kr., tax assessment of 0.35 sk.m., dated Feb. 26, 1901.

5. **Ole Johan Nordhus.** 1903 – 1954.

Born July 27, 1874, died Sept. 19, 1954, son outside the marriage of previous farmer (Karoline above) and Johan Nyman Mikalsen Hovland.

Married on July 14, 1903, to **Lavine Kristine Trulsdatter** born Nov. 14, 1875, died Dec. 25, 1929, daughter of Berthe Malene and Truls M. Johannesen, farmer no. 13 – 6 e, Nordvik.

Children:

a. Toralf Berner, born Sept. 15, 1903, died Mar. 26, 1924.
b. *Petra* Karoline, born Dec. 22, 1906, married in 1926 to Aslak Miljeteig, tenant farmer no. 66, Nordvik.
c. Otille Kristine, born June 29, 1909, married in 1940 to Torjus Johannesen Kvandal, Skanevik.
d. John, born Oct. 1, 1913, next farmer.

6. **John Nordhus.** 1954 – 1964

Born Oct. 2, 1913, died Oct. 9, 1966, son of last farmer.

Married in 1945 to **Olga Gustava Nilsen**, born in 1917.

Children:

a. *Olaug* Johanne, born Aug. 19, 1946, died Apr. 18, 1995, lived in Haugesund.

The farm was combined with farm no. 16 in 1964.

Farm no. 22. Skåren. The earlier settlement called Stølen.

1. Johannes Gudmundsen. 1836 – 1877
Baptized Apr. 25, 1797, died Aug. 24, 1881, son of Berta Anbjornsdatter and Gudmund Thomassen, farmer no. 3 – 2 k. Austrheim.

Married in first marriage on Mar. 27, 1824, to **Anne Marthe Johannesdatter**, baptized July 11, 1790, died Feb. 17, 1828, daughter of Malene Tormodsdatter and Johannes Helgesen, farmer no. 15 – 7 a, Nordvik.

Married in second marriage on Oct. 5, 1829, to **Mette Kristine Johannesdatter**, baptized Mar. 30, 1800, daughter of Anna Karine Ådnesdatter and Johannes Ambjornsen, tenant farmer no. 13 d. Nordvik (Stølen settlement).

Children in first marriage:

a. Anne Marta, born Dec. 18, 1829, married in 1855 to Tormod Mathiassen, tenant farmer no. 31, Nordvik.
b. Anne Karine, born Jan. 26, 1831, died Feb. 18, 1838.
c. Johannes, born Oct. 17, 1833, died July 11, 1859, perished when capsizing in sailboat on the way home from Bergen, together with his fiancé Berthe Gurine Ellingsdatter and five others from Utsira.
d. Gudmund, born Feb. 2, 1842, next farmer.

The inheritance documents to Johannes Gudmundsen from J. Dahm on this estate by Johannes Ambjornsen (his father–in–law in 2nd marriage), regarding the Stølen property in the amount of 200 Spd., dated Oct. 30, 1836, includes the condition that he continues to fulfill the work requirements of three days annually on farms no. 18 and 20, as long as the now–living farmers and their wives are alive, and after that he pays the new owners an annual amount of 1 Spd.

Johannes lived approximately 16 years on the Skår farm in Stangeland, until in 1829 he moved to Utsira and settled here.

In 1866 the 27 mål acre farm and its fields are assessed to 227 Spd. There are pastures for 35 Spd. and peat for 60 Spd. The annual yield is 18 barrels of oats, 6 barrels barley, 20 barrels of potatoes and 26 skp. hay. The entire farm is assessed for 320 Spd.

The livestock consists of 1 horse, 3 cows, 9 sheep and 1 pig.

Gudmund Johannesen Skåren (1842–1876).

2. **Gudmund Johannesen**. 1865 – 1876
Born Feb. 2, 1842, died Oct. 5, 1876, son of last farmer.

Married on Oct. 14, 1860, to **Marthe Susanne Larsdatter,** born July 9, 1840, died Dec. 5, 1906, daughter of Dortea Maria Nilsdatter and Lars Toresen, Nedre–Hauge, Torvestad.

Children:

a. Mette *Marie*, born Mar. 15, 1861, died in 1939, she was a children's home manager in Kristiania (Oslo).
b. Berthe *Karine*, born Oct. 15, 1862, married in 1895 to Tore Johannes Torresen, farmer no. 1 – 15, Hovland.
c. *Johannes* Gurnelius, born Oct. 11, 1864, next farmer.

Gudmund started during the end of the 1860s to work on the harbor projects in Nord and Sorevågen, and also for some time as a diver. Later he was hired as the harbormaster.

Gudmund farmed half of the farm together with his father. In 1875 they plant 7/8 barrels of barley, 2–1/2 barrels of oats and 2–1/2 barrels of potatoes and feed 1 horse, 2 cows, 1 calf, 14 sheep and 1 pig.

Thomine (1871-1940) and Johannes Gudmundsen (1864-1950).

3. **Johannes Gudmundsen.** 1877 – 1937
Born Oct. 11, 1864, died June 24, 1950, son of last farmer.

Married on May 14, 1893, to **Thomine Kathrine Tollefsdatter**, born July 23, 1871, died Apr. 30, 1940, daughter of Torborg Eline Eriksdatter and Tollef Knutsen, farmer no. 1 – 4 g, Kvalvik.

Children:

a. *Gunda* Marthine Sofie, born Feb. 21, 1894, died 1959, married in 1919 to Martin Nag, from Strand in Ryfylke, lived in Stavanger.
b. *Lovise* Marie, born May 14, 1895, died in 1967, married in 1916 to Per Leite from Strand in Ryfylke, lived in Stavanger.
c. Johannes *Trygve*, born Nov. 26, 1896, next farmer.
d. *Tilla* Torbara Elene, born Aug. 18, 1898, married to Jakob Olsen Nygård, farmer no. 1 – 16, Hovland.
e. Jenny Margot Kristine, born May 10, 1900, died July 3, 1901.
f. *Edvard* Jenius, born Mar. 6, 1902, died 1985, moved to USA, married.
g. Knut Kristian, born Mar. 6, 1904, died Apr. 11, 1930, perished fishing for lobster, see under tenant farmer no. 30, Skare.
h. Mette *Marie*, born Dec. 27, 1905, married to Samuel Isaksen, was a hospital nurse and lived in Oslo.

Family home on farm no. 22 in 1907. From left: Karine Hovland, Marie Skåren, Gunda, Lovisa, Marie, Tilla, Trygve, Edvard, Thomine and Johannes Gudmundsen.

i. Elias, born Aug. 5, 1907, emigrated to USA, married to Harriet.
j. Martha, born Nov. 5, 1910, married in 1942 to Karsten Vestre, tenant farmer no. 68, Nordvik.
k. Elisabeth, Aug. 25, 1912, married in 1931 to Hjalmar Ellingsen, tenant farmer no. 25, Austrheim.
l. Gudmund,, born Feb. 1, 1914, married in 1933 to Hanna Helgesen, farm no. 56 – 1, Nordvik.
m. Lars, born Feb. 20, 1916, died Apr. 11, 1930, perished at sea during lobster fishing with his brother Knut Kristian.

Lease contract to Johannes from the grandfather dated Aug. 23, 1877 and title after the grandfather Johannes in the amount of 1750 kr. is dated July 29, 1882, tax liability 1.63 sk.m.

Johannes was reserve assistant on Utsira Lighthouse in the years 1914 – 1934.

In 1937 part of the farm was excluded from the son Gudmund's property, farm no. 56, sk.m. 0.25. The old farm house dwelling, excluded from the farm in 1938, farm no. 57, is now torn down.

Trygve Skåren in America in the 1960s. From left: Trygve Skarren, Thomas Bendiksen, Konrad Bendiksen and Elias Skåren.

4. **Trygve Skår.** 1937 – 1952
Born Nov. 26, 1896, died May 27, 1972, son of last farmer.

Married Nov. 13, 1919, to **Lovise Helgesen**, born July 12, 1899, died Sept. 14, 1977, daughter of Olga Mathilde and A. Valnum Helgesen, farmer 18–6 d, Nordvik.

Children:

a. Johannes, born Dec. 20, 1919, next farmer.
b. Vilhelm, born July 29, 1922, married Magnhild K. Karlsen, Stavanger.
c. Torleiv, born Jan. 16, 1924, died Apr. 17, 1925.
d. Lars, born Apr. 4, 1933, married to Bjorghild Hilseth, lives in Haugesund.

The deed to Trygve from the father on this farm is dated Oct. 16, 1937. A new main dwelling was built in 1929, separated from the estate in 1961 and was designated farm no. 87, Fagerheim.

Trygve was a commercial sailor.

5. **Johannes Skår,** 1952 – 1987
Born Dec. 20, 1919, son of last farmer.

Married on Sept. 15, 1945, to **Gurine Rasmussen**, born Jan. 14, 1915, daughter of Tilla Gurine Mathiasdatter and Mikal Rasmussen, tenant farmer no. 49, Nordvik.

Children:

a. Leiv Terje, born Feb. 16, 1946, married to Anne Pettersen, lives in Haugesund.
b. Tormod, born Jan. 6, 1948, married to Sissel Vivaas, lives in Hafrsfjord.
c. Jon Reidar, born Apr. 10, 1950, lives in Stavanger.
d. Asbjorn, born June 6, 1951, married to Kari Grinde, lives in Aksdal.

They built a new main dwelling house here, farm no. 80, Vestheim, in 1954.
Johannes took over the farm in 1962. The old barn was destroyed by fire in 1978. The farm was later used as an additional farm and is owned by the sons.

Farm no. 30, from farm no. 14 in 1904

1. **Thomas J. Helgesen.** 1904 – 1950

Born May 7, 1877, died Feb. 15, 1927, son of Karoline and Johan Helgesen, farm no. 18 – 5 g, Nordvik.

Married on June 6, 1903, to **Ragna *Serine* Eriksdatter** born Oct. 1, 1881, died Oct. 16, 1964, daughter of Anne Marthe Ellingsdatter and Erik Eriksen, farm no. 1 – 9 j, Skare.

Children:

a. Johan Kristian, born Apr. 5, 1904.
b. Erika Anne *Martha*, born July 7, 1905, married in 1929 to Mathias Rasmussen, tenant farmer no. 56, Nordvik.
c. *Thomas* Sverre, born June 1, 1907, next farmer,
d. Karoline, born Jan. 11, 1909, married to Mikal Kvalvik, farmer no. 2 – 9, Kvalvik.
e. *Erik* Ludolf, born Oct. 26, 1911, married to Anna Nilsen., lives in Haugesund.
f. Helge, born Dec. 14, 1914, married to Jenny Helgesen, lives in Torvestad.
g. Lindy, born Nov. 12, 1916, married in 1945 to Halvor Jakobsen, tenant farmer no. 67, Nordvik.
h. Hersleb, born Sept. 10, 1918, married to Edel Marie Nilsen, lives in Torvestad.

From the wedding of Serine and Thomas J. Helgesen in June 1903.

Serine (1881–1964) and Thomas J. Helgesen (1877–1927).

i. *Lovise* Marie, born Apr. 13, 1921, married in 1956 to Hersleb Helgesen, tenant farmer no. 77, Nordvik.
j. *Leif* Karsten, born May 11, 1923, married to Margit J. Laugaland, lives in Skudesneshavn

The deed in the amount of 1800 kr. to Thomas from Jørgen Nilsen on this farm is dated July 1904. The tax on this property is 1.40 sk.m. A new main dwelling and barn is built in 1906.

2. **Thomas Helgesen,** 1950 – 1975.

Born June 1, 1907, died Mar. 15, 1978, son of last farmer.

Married on May 10, 1952, to **Lava Lie Nesse**, born Mar. 2, 1923, daughter of Anna and Ole Lie in Sveio.

Children:

a. Tor Leif, born Mar. 27, 1954, married Bodil Jensen, tenant farmer no. 47, Hovland.
b. Sigurd Thomas, born Nov. 30, 1955, married Claudia Guargena, lives in Stavanger.
c. Olav Arne, born Mar. 24, 1957, lives in Bergen.
d. Arvid, born July 23, 1958, married to Åse Marit Eike, lives in Haugesund.
e. Solfrid, born Mar. 20, 1960, married to Terje Overland, lives in Haugesund.

The farm was later run as an additional farm.

Farm no. 32. From farm no. 18 in 1907
Farm no. 46. From farm no. 44 in 1922

1. **Sivert M. Helgesen.** 1907 – 1942

Born Apr. 24, 1883, died Nov. 30, 1941, son of Karoline and Johan Helgesen, farm no. 18 – 5 j, Nordvik.

Married on June 23, 1907, to Åsa Olsdatter Roynesdal, born Feb. 11, 1877, died Apr. 29, 1968, from Bjelland near Mandal.

Children:

a. Karoline, born Apr. 25, 1908, married in 1936 to John G. Jansen, lived in Fordesfjorden.
b. Solveig, born Dec. 17, 1909. married in 1933 to Andreas Skjelde, farm no. 16 – 5, Nordvik.

Sivert Helgesen (1883 – 1941) and Åsa Roynesdal (1877 – 1968).

c. Johan, born Aug. 30, 1911, married in 1933 to Berta Malene Bendiksen, farm no. 3 – 4, Skare.
d. Olav, born July 10, 1913, married in 1941 to Klara Pedersdatter. Hellvik, tenant farmer no. 47, Skare.
e. Sigurd, born Feb. 5, 1915, married in 1940 to Edna Johannsdatter Melbo, lives in Langevag, Alesund.
f. Lovise, born Feb. 9, 1917, married in 1946 to Martin Johannesen Midtun, lives in Trengereid.
g. Thomas, born Jan. 18, 1920, next farmer.
h. Arne, born Dec. 22, 1921, married in 1949 to Oddlaug Gronmyr, lives in Langevag, Alesund.

The deed to Sivert from the father on farm no. 32, on Roynesdal, tax liability 0.30 sk.m., is dated May 18, 1908. The deed to Sivert from Jørgen Nilsen and his wife on farm no. 46, Solberg, tax liability of 0.48 sk.m., is dated Apr. 19, 1929. They built a new main dwelling house in 1909.

Sivert became Utsira's first chairman in the period 1924 – 1925 and in the period 1929 – 1931. Åsa became Norway's first chairwoman and served the period 1926 – 1928. She came to Utsira as a midwife in

1903, a service that she performed until 1942. She was recognized by the king as an outstanding public servant for her services.

2. **Thomas Helgesen.** 1943 –
Born Jan. 18, 1920, son of last farmer.
Married on May 9, 1942, to **Gina Theresia Haugland**, born Sept. 19, 1920, daughter of Benny and Severin Haugland, Utsira Lighthouse no. 9.

Children:
a. Tor Geir, born Oct. 29, 1920, lives in Fosen, Royksund.

Thomas took over the farm in 1943.

Farm no. 44. From Farm no. 20 in 1921

1. **Jørgen Nilsen.** 1924 – 1937
The deed to Jørgen from Kaia Johannesen on farm no. 44, listing tax liability of 1.47 sk.m. is dated Jan. 12, 1924. This farm was worked together with farm no. 14.
The estate was taken over by Jostein Nilsen in 1992.

Farm no. 56. From Farm no. 22 in 1937

1. **Gudmund Skåren.** 1937 – 1975
Born Feb. 1, 1914, son of Thomine and Johannes Gudmundsen, farm no. 22 – 3 l, Nordvik.
Married on May 4, 1933, to **Hanna Helgesen,** born Oct. 18, 1915, daughter of Gina and Johan Kristian Helgesen, tenant farmer no. 43, Nordvik.

Children:

a. *Gerhard* Torfred, born Sept. 29, 1933, married in 1957 to Kjellaug Hansen, farmer no. 1—17, Hovland.
b. *Reidun* Kristine, born May 26, 1937, married in 1956 to Oystein Haugland, tenant farmer no. 76, Nordvik.
c. *Gunnbjorn* Herman, born Dec. 13, 1939, next farmer.
d. Bjorg Irene, born Nov. 2, 1944, married in 1962 to Torbjorn Rasmussen, farmer no. 7 – 13, Hovland.

Farm no. 22 and 56 in the foreground. The pasture is in the background to the left. Photo by Telemark Aircraft Co., 1954.

The deed to Gudmund from his father on this farm lists the tax liability as 0.28 sk.m. and is dated Oct. 15, 1937. They built a new main dwelling in 1938.

2. **Gunnbjorn Skåren. 1975 –**
Born Dec. 13, 1939**,** son of the previous farmer.

Married on July 25, 1970, to **Kari Pedersen**, born Apr. 13, 1944, from Stangaland, Karmøy.

Children:

a. Bente, born Nov. 9, 1971.
b. Hanne Grete, born Apr. 8, 1973.
c. Gudmund, born Dec. 26, 1978.

They built a new main dwelling house here in 1972 and a new farm house in 1980. Kari has been the school principal at Utsira Children and Youth School since 1987.

Farm no. 62, from Farm no. 16 in 1942

1. **Olav Skjelde.** 1942 – 1960

Born Dec. 13, 1915, died Apr. 26, 1959, son of Tomine and Olav A. Skjelde, farmer no. 16 – 4 h, Nordvik.

Married on June 12, 1943, to **Alfhild Konstanse Solvag**, born Mar. 7, 1918, died Apr. 30, 1995, from Selje.

Children:

a. *Odd* Torbjorn, born May 30, 1945, married and lives on Torvestad.
b. *Arne* Henrik, born Sept. 24, 1948.

The deed to Olav from his mother on this farm lists a tax liability of 1.14 sk.m. in 1942. The main dwelling on farm no. 65, Nordheim, was taken over by them in 1948 (built by Hans M. Helgesen around 1885).

The farm was merged with farm no. 16 in 1964.

Farm no. 64, from Farm no. 18 in 1943

1. **Johan Valnumsen.** 1946 –

This farm, listed with a tax liability of 1.48 sk.m., was worked together with farm no. 18 and was taken over by Gunvor and Johannes Johannesen in 1980.

Farm no. 75, from Farm no. 15 in 1950

1. **John Larsen.** 1950 – 1992

Born Apr. 23, 1911, died Sept. 17, 1994, son of Stine and Mathias Larsen, farmer no. 15 — 10 c, Nordvik.

Married on Nov. 18, 1936, to **Tordis Kvalvik,** born Apr. 24, 1913, daughter of Astrid and Ludvig Kvalvik, tenant farmer no. 72 a., Nordvik.

Children:

a. *Bjorg* Modgunn, born Feb. 25, 1939, married to Hugo Austevik, lives in Havik, Karmøy.
b. *Steinar* Mathias, born Feb. 8, 1944, married to Margot Toskedal, lives in Avaldsnes.
c. Aud, born Sept. 8, 1949, married to Jan Hessvik, lives in Svelgen.

They took over part of the farm from the father and assumed a tax liability of 0.25 sk.m. A new main dwelling was built in 1954 – 55.

The farm was later worked as an additional farm and eventually taken over by Bjorg, Steinar and Aud in 1988.

Tenant Farmers

In the years between 1750 and 1785, there were four settlements in Nordvik: Stølen, Esphaugen, Kleven and a place under farm no. 15. The largest one of these was Stølen (later designated as farm no. 22. In the years before 1750, it is difficult to identify the correct tenant farmers with specific farms.

1. **(Mikkel).**

In a number of military records and censuses dating from 1664, we found three sons of Mikkel:

a. Knut Mikkelsen Skare, born around 1644, mentioned in two registers in 1664 and 1669.
b. Erik Mikkelsen Ostrem, born around 1645. In 1664, he is listed as a handyman in Gronningen and in a record from 1680 it states: *Erich Michelsen Østrim has served for ten years.*
c. Mikkel Mikkelsen Nordvik, born around 1646. In 1664 he is listed as a servant at Landanes and in a record from 1673 he is listed as a crew member on the warship "Gyldenløve."

2. **Jarar.** 1664

Born around 1624 and is mentioned in the 1664 census as a cottager on Nordvik.

3. **Lars (Bjornsen).** 1675

In the court records in 1675, he is mentioned as "Lars huusmand (cottager)." This may be the Lars Bjornsen who was born around 1648 and who is mentioned in military records from 1665 – 1669 and who in 1664 is listed as a servant at Austrheim.

4. **Halvor Knutsen.** 1669
Born around 1652. He is only mentioned in some military record in 1669.

5. **Anders Larsen.** 1681 – 1683
Born around 1664. He is mentioned in several military records in the period 1681 – 1683.

6. **Knut Kristoffersen.** 1689 – 1696
Born around 1672. He is also mentioned in several military records in the period 1691 – 1696.

7. **Tore Jensen.** 1696 – 1702
Born around 1665 at Torvestad. He is listed in a 1701 census as a cottager or caretaker in Nordvik, and in 1706 in the same position in Feoy.

Children:

a. Thomas, born in 1697 on Utsira, farmer no. 10 here.

8. **Ole Hansen.** 1703 – 1711
Born around 1677 at Klovning. In the military census in 1706, Ole is listed as the only cottager in Nordvik. In 1714, it appears that he has moved to Klovning.

9. **Tore.** 1712 – 1734
He is mentioned as a cottager in Nordvik in 1712 and 1734. It could possibly be the same person as number 7 above.

10. **Thomas Toresen.** 1719 – 1734
Born around 1697, died in 1740, possibly the son of Tore Jensen, no. 7 above. Thomas is mentioned in the court records of 1719 and 1724, when he was cited for drunkenness in the church. From the middle of the 1730s Thomas is mentioned as a cottager in the settlement called "Hestavikja" (Horse Bay) at Sund in Stangeland, where he had the following children:

a. Hans, born 1734, possibly moved to Ferkingstad, farm no. 25.
b. Brita, born 1736, died in 1743.

Photo from summer 1870 when work on the harbor was completed. Photo: Heritage

Stølen, cottage farm

11. **Ole Abrahamsen.** 1728 – 1773
Born in 1703, buried Mar. 25, 1770, son of Abraham Olsen, tenant farmer no. 2, Klovning. Married to **Anna Svendsdatter,** born 1700, buried July 16, 1775. Origin unknown.

Children:

a. Trua, born 1728, married to Paul Bårsen, tenant farmer no. 15, Hovland.
b. Berte, born 1730, married in 1754 to Johannes Pedersen, farm no. 5 – 2, Austrheim.
c. Svend, born 1731, married in 1761 to Marta Kristine Knutsdatter, farm no. 15 – 4, Nordvik.
d. Abraham, born in 1743, buried on Mar. 25, 1773.

In the military records from 1734, the following is written about Ole:

> Born in Utsira subparish, married and lives at Sire, 31 years old, has no farm, lives in a cottage in Norvig, makes a living from fishing.

In the estate settlement after Ole's death in 1770, listed worth is in the amount of 12–3–8 rdl. Particular items in the estate are listed as follows: *an old stone building with storage, barn and cooking shed at 6–0–0 and a black cow 4–0–0.*

The name "Stølen" was used on the (Johannes Gudmundsen) farm as late as the census in 1865, later the name "Skåren" was used. The place was part of farm no. 17, 18 and 20, and the cottagers were required to compensate the farmers with an annual fee of 48 sk. and three work days per season.

12. **Kristoffer Knutsen.** 1774 – 1790
Born 1718, of unknown origin.

Married to **Elisabet Knutsdatter,** born in 1720, buried June 7, 1789, sister of Martha Kristine on farm no. 15 – 3, Nordvik, see here for further reference.

Children:

a. Knut, born 1745, married in 1765 to Margrete Jørgensdatter, farm no. 13 – 1, Nordvik.
b. Johannes, born in 1748, married in 1777 to Bertha Jørgensdatter, tenant farmer no. 7, Klovning
c. Bår, born 1755.
d. Berthe, born 1766.

The family lived at a place called "Dalen under Utvik" in Avaldsnes before they came to Nordvik. All the children were born there.

In the estate settlement after the death of Elisabet in 1790 is listed a small house with kitchen for 2 rdl. and an iron stove for 3 rdl.

13. **Johannes Ambiørnsen.** 1790 – 1836
Baptized Oct. 11, 1766, died Sept. 9, 1834, son of Anna Johannesdatter and Ambjorn Rasmussen, farmer no. 7 – 5 e, Hovland.

Married on June 26, 1791, to **Anna Karine Ådnesdatter,** baptized Jan. 16, 1773, died May 27, 1846, daughter of Mette Kristine Johannesdatter and Ådne Helgesen, tenant farmer no. 23 a, Nordvik.

Children:

a. Ådne, baptized Sept. 30, 1792, married in 1819 to Oline Johannesdatter, farmer no. 16 – 1, Nordvik.
b. Anna Kristine, baptized Feb. 18, 1795, married in 1821 to Tore Toresen, farmer no. 15 – 8, Nordvik.
c. Berta, baptized Oct. 1, 1797, buried June 30, 1799.

d. Mette Kristine, baptized Mar. 30, 1800, married in 1829 to widower Johannes Gudmundsen, farmer no. 22 – 1, Nordvik, next farmer here.
e. Marta Serine, baptized May 1, 1803, married in 1803 to Tollef Gudmundsen, tenant farmer no. 12, Skare.
f. Thomas Galtung, baptized Jan. 29, 1807, buried July 11, 1907.
g. Berta Kristine, baptized July 23, 1808, married in 1834 to widower Johannes Knutsen, farmer no. 4 – 3, Klovning.
h. Guriana, baptized Apr. 12, 1812, married in 1836 to Rasmus Gudmundsen, farmer no. 2 – 5, Skare.

The place in 1823 was assessed at 50 Spd. It is recorded that it was able to feed 2 cows and 1 horse and could yield 12 barrels of grain.

Espehaugen, cottage farm

14. **Tolleiv Rasmussen.** 1740

Born around 1715, died around 1780, son of Ramus Rasmussen Spanne.

Married in 1st marriage to **Ingeborg Danielsdatter,** baptized Sept. 19, 1717, buried Nov. 15, 1761, daughter of Synove Knutsdatter and Daniel Sjursen, Visnes.

Married in 2nd marriage in 1762 to **Siri Johannesdatter,** born around 1738, daughter of Anna Larsdatter and Johannes Hansen, Nedre – Hauge.

Children in 1st marriage:

a. Daniel, born in 1741, married to Malena Osmundsdatter, Aksdal.
b. Lisbet, born 1746, married in 1767 to Sjur Knutsen., farmer no. 1 – 8, Nordvik.
c. Synnøve, born 1751, died 1782.
d. Rasmus, baptized Jan. 18, 1756, farmer no. 17 below here.

Children in 2nd marriage:

e. Tollef, baptized June 10, 1764, married in 1799 to Anna Knutsdatter, Nedre – Hauge, lived in Hauske.
f. Johannes, baptized Nov. 23, 1766.
g. Hans, baptized Feb. 14, 1769, married in 1797 to Magel Olsdatter Dale.
h. Peder, baptized Feb. 2, 1772, married to Mangela Olsdatter Forland, lived in "Beite under Utvik."
i. Ingeborg, baptized Nov. 12, 1775.

Tollef and Ingeborg lived in Nordvik a few years before they moved to Spanne, Torvestad.

15. **Knut Sjursen.** 1741 – 1775
Born around 1708, buried on Mar. 25, 1786, son of Sjur Knutsen, tenant farmer no. 11 a, Hovland.

Married to **Berta Knutsdatter,** born around 1712, buried on July 10, 1785, sister of Martha Kristine at farm no. 15 – 3, Nordvik, see there for further reference.

Children:

a. Maren (*Mari*), born 1743, married in 1771 to Ole Olsen, farm no. 2 – 3, Kvalvik.
b. Sjur, born in 1746, married in 1767 to Lisbeth Tollefsdatter, farm no. 1 – 8, Nordvik.
c. Malene, born 1749, married in 1768 to widower Ole Knutsen, farm no. 6 – 2, Austrheim.
d. Elisabet, born 1751, next farmer.
e. Berte, baptized May 25, 1757, buried on Oct. 14, 1758.

In the estate settlement after Berta's death in 1785 the estate's cash value is close to 25 Spd., but only 16 skillings is left between the heirs. Of odds and ends the following items can be mentioned:

> Buildings 8–0–0, one old six–oar boat in disrepair 1–1–8, 1 cast–iron stove 0–2–16, 1 four–oar boat 0–3–8, 1 small outside hand–mill with housing 3–0–0, 1 cow 4–2–0 and 1 stoneware kettle 2–1–8.

16. **Kristen Bårsen.** 1776 – 1795
Born 1751, buried July 11, 1790, son of Berte Sjursdatter and Bård Olsen, Nordre – Våge in Sveio.

Married on Sept. 28, 1776, to **Elisabet Knutsdatter**, born 1751, died Feb. 26, 1810, daughter of last tenant farmer.

Children:

a. Sjur, baptized Apr. 30, 1777, buried Mar. 23, 1779.
b. Berta, baptized Apr. 2, 1780, buried June 26, 1796.
c. Mari, baptized Apr. 1783, buried Mar. 25, 1784.
d. Berta, baptized July 10, 1785. She had a son, Kristen, tenant farmer no. 21, Kvalvik, with John Johannesen Klovning, and a son Soren, tenant farmer no. 16, Skare, with Nils Olsen Skyllingstad.
e. Mari, baptized Feb. 8, 1789, buried July 11, 1790.

In 1776 Kristen got a contract to work the place, "Osthaugen," with Anne W. Bredahl in Stavanger, when Knut and Berta due to old age and sickness were no longer able to run the farm.

The estate is settled after Kristen's death in 1790. The estate is worth 8 rdl. 2 ort, but the debt was greater so nothing was left to the heirs.

Elisabet was married in her second marriage to Rasmus Tollevsen, see below.

17. **Rasmus Tollevsen**. 1795 – 1820.
Baptized Jan. 18, 1756, died Jan. 18, 1828, son of Ingeborg and Tolleiv, no. 14 above.

Married in 1st marriage on Sept. 24, 1780, to **Dorte Andersdatter**, baptized Mar. 14, 1756, buried Dec. 10, 1786, daughter of Anders Olsen Veste.

Married in 2nd marriage on Sept. 21, 1794, to **Elisabet Knutsdatter**, widow of last tenant farmer.

Married in 3rd marriage on Oct. 16, 1814, to **Ingeborg Ambjørnsdatter,** baptized Feb. 6, 1770, died Mar. 7, 1854, daughter of Anna Johannesdatter and Anbjorn Rasmussen, farmer no. 7 – 5 g, Hovland.

Children in first marriage:

a. Anna, baptized Jan. 4, 1781, married in 1801 to Ommund Rasmussen, farmer no. 17–2, Nordvik.
b. Ingeborg, baptized Sept. 23, 1783, married in 1819 to widower Hans Jonsen, tenant farmer no. 17, Hovland.
c. Dorte Kristine, baptized Oct. 4, 1795, buried Mar. 20, 1796.

The estate was settled after Elisabet in 1810, with the estate's cash value at over 42 rdl., and 10 rdl. was left for the heirs. The following buildings and equipment are listed:

> 1 log building with kitchen and sheltered storage 16–0–0, 1 small log barn 3–2–0, 1 cow "Graasia" 14–0–0, 1 broken stove 1–0–0 and 1 fishing net for herring 2–2–0.

18. **Tollef Tollefsen.** 1820 – 1874
Baptized Jan. 18, 1801, died Nov. 25, 1873, son outside marriage of Ingeborg Anbjornsdatter and Tollef Tollefsen, Hovland (they were step–siblings).

Married on June 29, 1823, to **Ingeborg Andersdatter,** baptized Feb. 5, 1798, died Feb. 4, 1875, daughter of Martha Paulsdatter and Andres Knutsen, farmer no. 1 – 8 i, Hovland.

Children:

a. Anne Ingeborg, born Jan. 30, 1824, died Apr. 11, 1855.
b. Andreas, born Nov. 20, 1827, married to Anna Marta Hansdatter, lived on Nedre Liknes, Karmøy.
c. Rasmus, born May 27, 1831, died Nov. 13, 1831.

In 1823 it is recorded that Tollef must contribute 18 days work to the farmer John Helgesen of farm no. 1. The farm feeds 1 cow and yields 5 barrels of grain, and is being taxed 20 Spd.

In 1865 Tollef has lifestock consisting of 2 cows, 6 sheep and 1 pig. He plants 1/4 barrels of barley, 1–3/4 barrels of oats and 3/4 barrels of potatoes.

Kleven, cottage farm, under farm no. 13 and 14

19. **Hans Pedersen.** 1736 – 1774

Born around 1705, buried July 5, 1778, origin unknown.

Married in 1st. marriage to **Agnethe (Anne) Johnsdatter**, born around 1708, buried Nov. 1, 1753, possibly daughter of John Johannesen, farm no. 1–6, Hovland.

Married in 2nd. marriage on July 3, 1756, to **Maren Hansdatter**, born around 1717, buried Oct. 14, 1758, origin unknown.

Married in 3rd. marriage on Apr. 8, 1759, to **Anna Andersdatter,** born around 1710, buried on Sept. 30, 1781, origin unknown.

Children in 1st marriage:

a. Knut, born in 1735, married in 1754 to widow Ingeborg Olsdatter, lived on Hasseloy, Haugesund.
b. John, born in 1739, buried on Oct. 14, 1758.
c. Ole, born in 1744, buried on Mar. 25, 1778.
d. Anna, born 1750, next tenant farmer.

From Haugesund newspaper, July 22, 1929 (following article)*: Johan Dahm received fisheries profits during the years 1845 to 1868, and from his records it appears that spring herring fishing on Utsira varied drastically from year to year. The year 1859 must have been an extraordinary year, referred to as "Sturtfiske" meaning a smashing season, as Dahm referred in his books to "very large catches." In the years 1860 – 1868 very small catches are indicated except in 1862 when he is paid 150 Spd. in compensation.*

A stormy night on the sea off Sira 70 years ago.

More than 100,000 barrels of herring were lost, and the damage amounted to more than 1 million kroner.

O. Indrehus has written a series of excellent articles about the herring fisheries and we are pleased to include this story:

There were signs indicating excellent herring fishing already before Christmas 1859, and the Utsira fishermen had several indications of this situation early on. News of this came from Kvitsoy and Espevaer, but the herring did not really arrive before mid February. In addition, storms and bad weather dominated the entire month of January and the early part of February. However, as soon as the weather let up, one could see the big whales float out there like an archipelago along the coast. Never had experienced fishermen seen signs like this before. Around the 20th of February the fishermen were preparing for their trip back home, and the people from the southern part of the country came as far as Tananger. However, there the weather conditions around the southernmost and exposed part, Jaeren, forbade further sailing. For the fourth time this year, and now in huge quantities, the herring came to Utsira, and local people caught immediately 10,000 barrels. The next day, the herring reached Aakra, Veavaag, Røvaer, Haugesund and Sletta and everywhere in huge numbers. Messages and telegrams recalled all fishermen. Day and night, fully loaded vessels, fishing nets and catches around points and bays continued, and every available fishing net that could be found anywhere was used and filled with herring. In Osnesgavlen there were fishing nets thrown out as far as one could see, and it became a task just to find a vacant place to set the net. Everything now became joy and pleasure everywhere – herring and money. Around the new business area, Haugesund, there was now also extreme activity. The boat houses were finished and prepared for use. People were hired for gutting and salting and the processing plants buzzed with activity. Noise from the machinery and winches filled the air night and day. There was nothing else of interest in this world, except spring herring.

Then, in the afternoon on the 22nd of February the sky in the west and northwest became threatening with shades of blue, yellow and green, and in the evening the weather broke out in a full scale hurricane stirring up heavy seas from the northwest, a storm which even real old people today can remember and tell about.

The storm caused a colossal amount of damage on buildings and equipment particularly in places like Sletten, Espevaer, Rovaer and even in places around Haugesund in varying degrees. Fishing nets in the sea were torn to shreds and in some places thrown way inland. The storm caused more damage to equipment and the herring harvest than had ever been experienced in the herring fisheries. Conservatively, 100,000 barrels of herring were lost. If one counts catches lost due to the storm, the loss according to the prices at the time could have amounted to over 250,000 Spd. (1 million kroner). In addition material damage to fishing nets, equipment and boats amounted to several thousand Spd.

After the storm, the pattern of herring behavior changed and schools of herring appeared to be split up and the fisheries became sporadic. The herring started to appear in narrow straits and bays, for example, "Aalfjord was filled with herring."

Around this time the "Skudenes fisheries" changed to "Haugesund fisheries" in the southern district. The price was good, around 6 to 12 kroner per barrel.
O. Indrehus, Haugesunds Avis, 22 July 1929.

In the estate settlement after Agnethe (Anne) in 1754, each of the children Knut, John and Ole receive 1 1/2 rdl. Anna is not mentioned in the estate settlement.

In 1774 he relinquishes his place for the benefit of his son–in–law Hans, under protest from John Nilsen, who feels he was next in line to run the farm.

20. **Hans Hansen.** 1774–1782

Born around 1750, buried on Nov. 1, 1829, origin unknown.

Married on July 1, 1770, to **Anna Hansdatter,** born in 1750, died Nov. 15, 1824, daughter of last tenant farmer.

Children:

a. John, baptized Sept. 30, 1770, buried Nov. 23, 1771.
b. Maren Agnethe, baptized May 17, 1772, buried 1799, married to widower Johannes Johannesen, Tveit, outer Sveio.
c. John, baptized June 3, 1775, married in 1805 to widow Mari Steffensdatter, Hokla below Tveit, outer Sveio.
d. Ole, baptized May 2, 1778, lives in 1801 in Nordvik, further history unknown.
e. Anna, baptized Mar. 25, 1781, died Mar. 17, 1855.
f. Hans Knut, baptized Dec. 18, 1784, tenant farmer no. 19, Hovland.
g. Margrethe, baptized Sept. 7, 1788, died Oct. 10, 1841.
h. Anna Karine, born 1792, died Jan. 21, 1864.
i. Hans, baptized Feb. 7, 1796, married in 1823 to Barbro Olufsdatter Opheim, tenant farmer no. 19, Kvalvik.
j. Marte Kirstine, baptized June 16, 1798, married in 1821 to Hans Kristensen, tenant farmer no. 20, Hovland.

In a 1776 Hans publishes his contract dated Aug. 24, 1774 as manager of the farm "Kleven" after his in–laws.

In about 1782 the family moves into the small holding called "Tiphaugen" below Hovland and establishes their home there. Hence "Kleven" is then left largely unoccupied, but is used by the tenant John Nilsen.

The cottage farm belonging to Farm no. 15.

21. **Amund Reiersen.** 1748 – 1787

Born around 1722, son of Gunhild Olsdatter and Reier Ommundsen, tenant farmer no. 13 b, Hovland.

Married to **Ellen Olsdatter,** born around 1713, buried Mar. 25, 1798, origin unknown, possibly widow of Johannes.

Children:

a. Ole, mentioned in some military records in May 1762.
b. Johannes, born in 1750, buried Mar. 25, 1770.
c. Anna, baptized Nov. 8, 1753, buried Oct. 14, 1758.

At the end of the 1780s, this settlement is left deserted, but is used by the tenant in farm no. 15.

22. **Paul Jakobsen.** 1760 – 1770.
Born around 1690, buried Oct. 6, 1765, origin unknown.

Married in 1762 to **Johanna Omundsdatter,** born around 1715, buried Mar. 23, 1771, daughter of Omund Ellingsen Beite, below Utvik, Avaldsnes.

These people are listed in the tax register as cottagers under the category "poor."

23. **Ådne Helgesen.** 1772 – 1799
Born around 1725, buried Mar. 20, 1796, son of Karen Ådnesdatter and Helge Sjursen, Orpetvedt in Skåre.

Married on Dec. 15, 1765, to **Mette Kristine Johannesdatter,** born around 1746, buried on Oct. 27, 1799, daughter of Anne Olavsdatter and Johannes Jørgensen Galtung, Feoy.

Children:

a. Anna Karine, baptized Jan. 16, 1773, married in 1791 to Johannes Ambjornsen, tenant farmer no. 13, Nordvik.

Ådne was schoolmaster on Utsira from 1772 to around 1780.

24. **Tormod Sorensen.** 1800 – 1816
Baptized Aug. 7, 1779, died Apr. 20, 1816, son outside marriage of Malene Tormodsdatter, Nordvik, and Soren Sjursen.

Married on Oct. 16, 1815, to **Berte Malene Bentsdatter,** baptized Aug. 17, 1790, died June 20, 1856, daughter of Berte and Bent Bentsen, Vestre in Skåre.

No children.

In the estate settlement after Tormod in 1817 for 41 Spd., the following assets are listed:

1 new spring herring fishing net 2–0–0, 1 pair of Dutch silver buttons 1–1–0, 1 jacket and trousers 2–3–0, 1 pair of boots 2–2–0, 3 dozen building logs 8–0–0, 1 padlocked locker with ornamental fittings 1–0–0, 1 tool bench 1–0–0 and miscellaneous carpenter tools 10–2–2.

Judging from the above items, one can assume that Tormod was in the process of building himself a house. Malene moved to her brother Knut's house in Kvalvik.

25. **Rasmus Gudmundsen.** 1836 – 1843
Was a marine pilot and lived in Nordvik a few years before he bought Farm no. 2 at Skare, see farmer no. 5 there.

26. **Daniel Johnsen.** 1848 – 1872
Born on Feb. 14, 1821, died Sept. 1, 1899, son of John Hansen Skogland in Skåre.

Married in 1st marriage on July 5, 1846, to **Margrete Jørgensdatter,** baptized Aug. 11, 1814, died Dec. 22, 1866, daughter of Bertha Olsdatter and Jørgen Johnsen, farmer no. 13 – 3 e, Nordvik.

Married in 2nd marriage on Nov. 10, 1867, to **Gurine Kristine Sivertsdatter,** born around 1833, daughter of Sivert Knutsen, Egenes in Stavanger.

From the "Chatfield News," Chatfield, Minnesota, Oct. 23, 1941.

BROTHERS MEET FIRST TIME IN HALF CENTURY

Luverne—When Martin Johnson, Lismore, arrived in Seattle, Washington, recently he met his brother, Ole C. Wagner, whom he had not seen for 55 years. In 1886 Martin left the family home in Utsire Island, three miles off the coast of Norway to come to America; fourteen years later Ole came to this country. Only occasional letters during the past five and one-half decades have kept the brothers in touch with each other. The reason the names of the men fail to reveal their relationship is because Mr. Ole Wagner changed his name to avoid being confused with another Ole Johnson.

Children in 1st marriage:

a. Berthe Malene, born Sept. 11, 1846, married in 1868 to Jørgen Andreas Johannesen Våge, Fosen, Avaldsnes, tenant farmer no. 34, Nordvik.
b. Jørgen, born and died June 10, 1848.

Children in 2nd marriage:

c. Daniel Martin, born Aug. 14, 1868, emigrated to USA in 1886, married Lizzi (Louise) Hildahl. He was a railroad worker in Lismore, Nobles County, Minnesota.
d. Sivert Johan Vegner, born Jan. 11, 1871, emigrated to USA, married Lena W. Hildahl, lived in Lake Park, Iowa and Albany, New York.
e. Anne Ragnhilde Berthea, born July 7, 1874, emigrated in 1898, married to George Johnson, lived in the Palouse area, E. Washington.

f. Ole Cornelius Vegner, born Feb. 19, 1880. He and his mother Gurine Kristine emigrated to USA in July 1900. Ole C. Wagner lived in Ballard, WA, and worked in the fishing industry; married to Anna Martha.

The family lived on farm no. 14, Beite, in "Tappadal," until 1872 when they settled at their seaside home, "Tappanaustet" which it was later named, in Tuevågen. The lease contract to this property from Jørgen Jørgensen is dated Aug. 30, 1865.

Their home at Beite, a frame–built house, 9.5 x 5.5 meters, with tiled roof, was assessed in 1867 at 210 Spd. The seaside house in Tuevågen with 3 rooms upstairs, 10.8 x 5.8 meters, was fire–insured for 700 kroner.

After Daniel died in 1899, his widow Gurine Kristine emigrated to USA with her son Ole (see above).

From Haugesund newspaper dated 6 July 1894.

From Utsire:

Mr. Publisher:

Please allow me through your honorable paper to express my deepest appreciation and thanks for all the friendliness and help which has been shown me after that fateful day, when I was crippled for life with the unavoidable consequence that one of my legs had to be amputated.

Specially, the Utsire congregation, who unselfishly arranged a collection day for my benefit resulting in nearly 100 kr., I have now therefore the pleasure of being able to arrange for an artificial leg and therefore look forward to a much better future. The Utsire congregation has done a good deed, which I believe is well worth making public.

Let He who loves all happy donors richly reward all who gave to this fund with happiness and blessings, in Jesus' name.

Utsire, 4th July 1894

Daniel Johnsen Hovland.

27. **J. Mathias Mathiassen.** 1864 – 1869

Born Aug. 5, 1840, son of Sofie Hansine and Mathias Johannesen, farmer no. 20 – 1 i, Nordvik.

Married on Sept. 18, 1864, to **Inger *Kathrine* Osmundsdatter,** born 1845, daughter of Osmund Hansen, Feigedahl.

Children:

a. Martha Sofie, born June 2, 1865.
b. Jan Teodor, born Oct. 11, 1868.
c. Knut, born in 1880.
d. Karin, born in 1883.

The family lived in the main dwelling on farm no. 15 with Lars Johan Thorsen. They built soon after a new house on leased ground here and sold the house in 1872 to Osmund Hansen Dalen for 100 Spd. They moved to Haugesund in 1869.

28. **Johannes Ådnesen.** 1864 – 1866
Born July 3, 1835, son of Oline and Ådne Johannesen, farmer no. 16 – 1 g, Nordvik.

Married on Aug. 7, 1864, to **Anne Pedersdatter,** born June 7, 1843, daughter of Eli Serine and Peder Torbjornsen, Vikshaland, Torvestad. Anne and Thala Pedersdatter were half sisters.

One child born on Utsira:

a. Laurits Johan, born Nov. 30, 1865, emigrated to USA.

The family lived a couple of years on Utsira before they moved to Vikshaland and took over the farm.

29. **Ole Johannes Johannesen.** 1854 – 1876
Born June 13, 1827, died Jan. 13, 1891, son of Ingeborg Oline Johnsdatter and Johannes Johannesen, farmer no. 6 – 6 b, Austrheim.

Married on Sept. 24, 1854, to **Anne Marthe Ådnesdatter,** born June 29, 1828, died Aug. 31, 1895, daughter of Oline and Ådne Johannesen, farmer no. 16– 1 e. Nordvik.

Children:

a. *Martin* Mikal. Born Nov. 22, 1855, married in 1891 to Thala Sofie Mikalsdatter, tenant farm no. 34, Klovning
b. *Malene* Mikkeline, born July 6, 1857, married in 1879 to widower Sjur Helgesen, farmer no. 4 – 1, Nordvik.
c. Berthe Gurine, born July 22, 1859, married in 1880 to Rasmus Thomassen, farmer no. 12 – 5, Nordvik.
d. Ase Oline, born May 8, 1861, married in 1886 to Elling Eriksen, farmer no. 1 – 10, Skare.
e. Anne Marthe *Laurine*, born Mar. 6, 1863, married in 1885 to Tobias Johannesen Sørhus, tenant farmer no. 23, Klovning.
f. Johannes, born Sept. 29, 1865, married in 1894 to Thala Sofie Mikalsdatter, farmer no. 2 – 3, Klovning.

Ole Johannes was a marine pilot, in 1861 he receives a lease for a house lot in "Storatrae" from Johan Bendik Ådnesen. The house is then already built, and for the title he pays 5 Spd. and a contribution of 3 days of labor annually.

In 1876 he buys farm no. 2 at Klovning and moves there.

30. **Torres Thorsen.** 1864 – 1909.
Born in 1839, died on Feb. 2, 1891, son of Marta Elisabet Torresdatter and Thore Kristoffersen, Våge in Avaldsnes.

Married on Aug. 25, 1864, to **Berthe Malene Krisjersdatter,** born Aug. 18, 1841, died Mar. 21, 1909, daughter of Berte Marie Jørgensdatter And Kristjer Stephensen, farmer no. 17–5 c, Nordvik.

Children:

a. Thore, born and died on Jan. 12, 1866
b. *Thore* Johannes, born Apr. 27, 1869, married in 1895 to Berthe Karine Gudmundsdatter, farmer no. 1 – 15, Hovland.
c. Endre Mikal Christian Vegner, born May 1, 1872, died June 21, 1884.
d. Peder Jacob, born Nov. 26, 1875, died Feb. 21, 1882.

In 1875 the they live on farm no. 16, have 3 sheep and plant no crops. From Bendik Ådnesen they received a lease contract on a lot south–east of the house Ole Thorsen Kalsto built in the so–called "Rau" in Nordvigvaag. The lease is dated Mar. 21, 1867 and was paid with 6 Spd. plus 1–0–60 Spd. in annual rent.

In 1900 the widow Berthe Malene sold the house to her nephew, Mikal Johannesen Nordvik for 200 kroner, with the right to live there (during her lifetime).

31. **Tormod Mathiassen.** 1855 – 1874.
Born June 15, 1830, died Oct. 7, 1867, son of Sofie Hansine and Mathias Johannesen, farm no. 20 – 1 e, Nordvik.

Married on Sept. 30, 1855, to **Anne Marthe Johannesdatter,** born Dec. 8, 1829, died Feb. 21, 1874, daughter of Mette Kristine and Johannes Gudmundsen, farm no. 22 – 1 a, Nordvik.

Children:

a. Sophie Hansine, born Dec. 29, 1855, married in 1889 to widower Johannes Mathiassen (her uncle), farm no. 20 – 2, Nordvik.
b. Anne Karine, born Dec. 29, 1855, died Sept. 20, 1856.
c. Johannes, born Mar. 31, 1858, died Jan. 28, 1881. In the 1875 census he is listed as living with Johannes Gudmundsen on farm no. 22. It notes that he, in the summers of 1874 and 1875, worked as cook on the sloop "Dykkeren" (the Diver) owned by the Harbor Authority.
d. Martha Kristine, born Aug. 25, 1860, died Dec. 17, 1870.
e. Mette Karine, born June 5, 1863, died Jan. 4, 1887.
f. Jonette Marie, born Mar. 19, 1865, married in 1886 to Mons Larsen, tenant farmer no. 40, Nordvik.

g. Juliane Theodore, born Mar. 19, 1865, married in 1892 to Elling Ellingsen, tenant farmer no. 38, Nordvik.

Tormod received the lease contract on a house lot, 20 x 20 alen (1 alen = approx. 25 inches), in Myre from his brother Johannes in 1865. The house was then already built.

32. **Tollef Thomassen (Herberg).** 1867 – 1871
Born Feb. 10, 1842, died Sept. 15, 1907, son of Berthe Malene and Thomas Tollefsen, farm no. 18 – 3 c, Nordvik.

Married on Aug. 21, 1867, to **Maren Helene Knutsdatter,** born Aug. 18, 1849, died Aug. 8, 1905, daughter of Knut Erekim, Goa at Randaberg.

Children:

a. Thomas, born Dec. 6, 1867, died June 30, 1871.
b. Lava Elisa, born Feb. 25, 1870, married to Thomas Tilly.
c. Tomine Bergitta (Minnie Herberg), born Aug. 26, 1872, died 1950, married to O. H. Lewis.
d. Thomas.
e. Jennie, married to William Hendricks.
f. Theresa Maria, born Sept. 28, 1878, married to William M. Pelkey.
g. Eilert, born May 20, 1880, married to Juliet Qellette.
h. Rueben, born Aug. 1, 1882, lived in Montana.
i. Lillian.
j. Ralph, born Oct. 6, 1886 died in 1914.
k. May, born Feb. 19, 1890.

Tollef was a seaman when he lived on Utsira. In 1871 he emigrated to USA, where he worked as a blacksmith and inventor.

In 1857 Tollef was hired by the minister as a substitute teacher for 1/2 year on Utsira when he was 15 years old, until Knut Knutsen Åsen took over the position.

33. **Even Kristian Evensen.** 1863 – 1883
Born in Drammen in 1815, unmarried. Even worked as assistant to lighthouse attendant Eyde. His domicile was according to the 1875 census "the northern lighthouse."

34. **Jørgen Andreas Johannesen.** 1868 – 1870
Born in 1840, son of Gunla Gregersdatter and Johan Jonsen, Våga, Fosen in Avaldsnes.

Married on May 17, 1868, to **Berthe Malene Danielsdatter** born Aug. 11, 1846, daughter of Margrete Jørgensdatter and Daniel Johnsen, tenant farmer no, 26, Nordvik.

Children born on Utsira:
  a. Berthe Margrethe, born Mar. 20, 1869.

The family emigrated in 1870 on the ship "Iris."

35. **Andreas Larsen Fjeld.** 1869 – 1871
Born in 1834, son of Lars Guldbrandsen, Fjeld in Vingers parish district.

Married on Nov. 21, 1869, to **Bolette Karine Thomasdatter,** born July 1, 1840, daughter of Berthe Malene and Thomas Tollefsen, farm no. 18 – 3 b, Nordvik.

Children:
  a. Thomas Ludvig, born July 6, 1870, married in 1895 to Ingeborg M. K. Sakkariassen.
  b. Mikal, born Sept. 27, 1875, unmarried.
  c. Ebba, born Aug. 20, 1876, married in 1899 to Ole Rasmussen Ryan, shoemaker in Haugesund.

The family moved to Haugesund.

36. **Kristoffer Torstensen.** 1868 – 1871.
Born 1845, died in January 1875, son of Bronla Serine and Torstein Kristoffersen, Kallevik in Avaldsnes.

Married on Mar. 29, 1868, to **Berthe Marie Kristjersdatter,** born Apr. 3, 1847, died Feb. 16, 1918, daughter of Berte Marie and Kristjer Stephensen, farm no. 17– 5 e. Nordvik.

Children:
  a. Torstein Severin, born Mar. 8, 1869, emigrated to USA and worked as railroad worker and fisherman, lived in Putnam County, Florida.
  b. Stine Kristine Marie Wegner, born in 1872, married to Nils Pedersen, tenant farmer no. 41, Nordvik.
  c. Ole Johannes, born Aug. 31, 1875.

The family lived alternating between Kallevik, Nordvik and Visnes, where Kristoffer worked in the copper mines from March 1871 until he died, except for the 8 weeks in 1873 when he worked for Olsen's mining company.

After her husband died Berthe Marie went home to her father.

37. **Bolla Kirstine Rasmusdatter** 1870 – 1941
Born Oct. 29, 1843, died in Jan. 11, 1941, daughter of Marta Kirstina Sorensdatter and Rasmus Nilsen, Vikingstad.

Unmarried.

Bolla Kirstine served many years at the house of Johan Bendik Ådnesen on farm no. 16, Nordvik. The house where she lived was named after her.

38. **Elling Ellingsen.** 1892 – 1945
Born Apr. 15, 1851, died on July 22, 1930, son of Ragna Serine and Elling Gudmundsen, farm no. 12 – 1 g, Nordvik.

Married in 1st marriage on Oct. 16, 1892, to **Juliane Teodora Tormodsdatter**, born Mar. 19, 1865, died on Feb. 15, 1894, daughter of Anne Marthe and Tormod Mathiassen, tenant farmer no. 31, Nordvik.

Married in 2nd marriage on Apr. 10, 1896, to **Anna *Kathrine* Jobsdatter,** born Apr. 8, 1860, died Aug. 10, 1945, daughter of Karoline Elisabeth and Job Rasmussen, farm no. 7 – 9 i, Hovland.

Children in 1st marriage:

a. Julie Teodore, born Feb. 9, 1894, died May 6, 1894.

Children in 2nd marriage:

b. Elling Berner, born May 18, 1897, died Mar. 1, 1898.
c. Elin Bertine, born and died June 19, 1898.
d. Johan *Kristian*, born Dec. 2, 1899, died Mar. 24, 1953, unmarried.

Their main dwelling house was built on leased property on farm no. 12, possibly built by his brother, Thomas, as a farmhouse around 1850.

39. **Andreas *Bertel* Helgesen.** 1878 – 1900
Born Aug. 28, 1853, died Apr. 8, 1912, son of Valborg and Helge Andreas Johnsen, farm no. 1 – 11 g, Nordvik.

Married on Sept. 25, 1878, to **Berta Karine Knutsdatter,** born May 9, 1852, died Dec. 17, 1935, daughter of Knut Andersen Veim.

Children:

a. Kamilla Berthea, born July 14, 1880, married in 1915 to Leonard Andersen from Sweden.
b. Severine, born Oct. 16, 1882, unmarried, lived in Haugesund.
c. Helge Andreas Vallum, born Aug. 7, 1884, married in 1912 to Olava Johannesen Haugland from Valestrand.
d Adolf Berner, born May 30, 1886, married in 1917 to Sara Claudine from Bergen.

The Andreas Bertel Helgesen family around 1902. In the first row from left: Bertel (1853–1912), Hersleb born 1891, Lindy born in 1897 and Berta Karine (1852–1935). Back row from the left: Severine born 1882, Kamilla born 1880, Helge born 1884, Kristian born 1888 and Adolf born 1886.

e Kristian, born Dec. 13, 1888, unmarried, lived in Haugesund.
f. Hersleb, born July 9, 1891, married in 1919 to Gunhild Marie Hausken, Haugesund.
g. Elise Marie Konstance, born May 17, 1894, died Apr. 18, 1902.
h. Klara Sofie *Lindy*, born Nov. 24, 1897, married to widower Johannes Hovda, Haugesund.

Andreas Bertel was marine pilot on Utsira, They built the main dwelling on farm no. 6 in 1885, which was taken over by Lisa and Peder Klovning in 1900.

In 1900 Bertel became the harbor pilot in Haugesund and the family settled there.

40. **Mons Larsen Vikoren.** 1886 – 1939
Born in March 1858, died on Apr. 13, 1939, from Vik in Sogn.

Married in 1st marriage on Mar. 12, 1886, to **Jonette Marie Tormodsdatter,** born Mar. 19, 1865, died on Dec. 26, 1895, daughter of Anne Marthe Johannesdatter and Tormod Mathiassen, tenant farmer no. 31, Nordvik.

Married in 2nd marriage on Apr. 4, 1901, to **Thora Johanne Thoresdatter,** born Sept. 24, 1877, died July 11, 1919, daughter outside marriage of Severine Halvorsdatter And Thore Johannes Johannesen, Austrheim.

Children in first marriage:

a. Thomine Amalie, born Sept. 23, 1886, died Feb. 19, 1887.
b. Thomine Amalie, born June 25, 1888, emigrated to USA in 1907, married Karl Ludvig Johansen, lived in Oakland, Calif.
c. Lars Elias, born May 28, 1891.
d. Jenny Kristine, born Nov. 21, 1893, died Apr. 4, 1895.

Children in 2nd marriage:

e. Jenny Marie, born Sept. 5, 1902, married in 1921 to Rasmus Hoidal, Utsira Lighthouse no. 21.
f. Hans Severin, born Nov. 14, 1904, emigrated to USA.
g. Johannes, born Jan. 6, 1907, died May 9, 1914.
h. Martha, born Apr. 20, 1909, died July 11, 1919.
i. Johannes, born Aug. 12, 1914, died July 11, 1919.
j. Tilla Elisabeth, born May 26, 1917, died Sept. 26, 1917.

Thora's son outside her marriage, with Elling Haugland:

k. Elling Jobinius, born 1889, died 1917.

They built a main dwelling house here on farm no. 14, from 1901 farm no. 25, Vestre Hoelen, in 1895. The estate was taken over by Jenny Marie and Rasmus Hoidal in 1934, and in 1946 by Laura and Leif Ostensen.

Mons was a businessman in Haugesund before he came to Utsira. Thora and the two youngest children perished under tragic circumstances in the summer of 1919.

41. **Nils Karl Martinius Pedersen Finvig.** 1894 – 1897
Born July 10, 1871 in Borgund, Sunnmøre, died July 2, 1905.

Married to **Marie Kristine Kristoffersdatter,** born 1872, daughter of Berthe Marie and Kristoffersdatter and Kristoffer Torstensen, tenant farmer no. 36 b. Nordvik.

Children:

a. Kristian Bernhart, born June 27, 1894, died Jan. 14, 1895.
b. Klara Marie Vegner, born Oct. 21, 1895, died July 6, 1896.

c. Peder *Oskar*, born in 1897, emigrated to USA, married in 1925 to Jenny Kristine Vadnumsen. Their daughter was Ester Rasmussen. Lived in Brooklyn, NY.
d. Karl Martin Wegner, born Nov. 2, 1905, died Sept. 26, 1908.

Marie Kristine's twins born in Bergen:
e. Kristoffer, born Jan. 29, 1912.
f. Marie, born Jan. 29, 1912.

Nils was a commercial seaman, and the family traveled from Utsira to Alesund in 1897. Maria and the two children moved back to Utsira in 1906, and in 1911 she moved to Bergen.

42. **Thore J. Torresen.** 1895 – 1904
He and his family lived at Nordvik then bought farm no. 1 on Hovland.

43. **Johan Kristian Helgesen.** 1900 – 1958.
Born May 12, 1879, died Jan. 19, 1954, son of Karoline and Johan Helgesen, farm no. 18 – 5 h, Nordvik.

Married on Oct. 25, 1900, to **Regine (Gina) Mathiasdatter,** born July 10, 1879, died Apr. 25, 1958, daughter of Gunhilde Oline and Mathias Jobsen, farm no. 10 – 2 c, Hovland.

Children:
a. Johan Kristian, born Oct. 25, 1901, married in 1948 to Marie Magnusdatter Grannaes. He perished without trace with his fishing boat "Stjerna."
b. *Marie* Gunhilde, born Aug. 25, 1904, married in 1926 to Johannes Johannesen, farm no. 2 – 3, Klovning.
c. *Juline* Kristense Regine, born Jan. 19, 1908, married in 1936 to Bjorn Ommundsen, Våg in Skjold.
d. Helge Wilhelm, born May 7, 1910, died Oct. 17, 1911.
e. Hanna Vilhelmine, born Oct. 18, 1911, married in 1933 to Gudmund Skåren, farm no. 56 – 1, Nordvik.

Johan Kristian was a seiner. They built a main dwelling house on farm no. 2 in 1900. He took over the farm from the father in 1902.

44. **Peder Klovning.** 1900 – 1964
Born June 24, 1872, died June 7, 1959. son of Thala Sofie and Svend Mikael Larsen, farm no. 4 – 5 h, Klovning.

Married on Apr. 24, 1900, to Elise **Sofie (Lisa) Johansdatter**, born June 5, 1875, died Aug. 2, 1964, daughter of Karoline and Johan Helgesen, farm no 18 – 5 f. Nordvik.

The family of Johan Kristian Helgesen in 1919. From left: Johan Kristian (1879 – 1954), Marie born 1904, Juline born 1908, Hanna born 1911 and Gina (1879 – 1958).

Children:

a. Tala, born Dec. 31, 1902, tenant farmer no. 70, Nordvik.
b. Karoline, born Apr. 24, 1904, died Nov. 29, 1904.
c. Johan, born May 30, 1906, married in 1937 to Randi Larsen, tenant farmer no. 64. Nordvik.
d. Karoline, born Nov. 27, 1912, married in 1936 to Mathias Hansen, farm no. 4 – 13, Austrheim.

Besides fishing, Peder together with his brother ran a wholesale fishing operation buying and selling fish. They took over the main dwelling here, farm no. 24, Nordmandiet, from Bertil Helgesen in 1900.

45 a. **Soren Juell.** 1901
He was the first baker working with Olav Skjelde, about 6 months before the fisheries started in 1901. He was from Arendal.

45 b. **Carl Amundsen.** 1902
From Haugesund, he was also a baker working for Skjelde after Juell. He started in 1903 at the business location on Risoy.

Peder and Elise Klovning in front of their home around 1915. Gina Jobsen Helgesen to the left.

46. **Ole Sorensen Roynesdal.** – 1938
Born June 24, 1852, died Apr. 22, 1938, from Bjelland near Mandal. His daughter was Åsa, born in 1877, married to Sivert Helgesen. Ole was among other things a shoemaker and church caretaker.

47. **Rasmus Leversen.** 1906 – 1937
Born Oct. 2, 1858, died in 1939, son of Astrid Kittelsdatter Rokking and Levard Eivindsen, under Rorheim at Ombo in Ryfylke.

Unmarried.

Rasmus was a baker, first in Haugesund, and from 1906 he was a baker working for Olav Skjelde at Utsira.

48. **Daniel O. Vestre** 1908 – 1971
Born Oct. 26, 1882, died on July 25, 1971, son of Sigrid and Ole Vestre in Skjold.

Married in 1st marriage on Nov. 26, 1908, to **Laura Kristine Helgesen**, born May 9, 1887, died Nov. 26, 1922, daughter of Karoline and Johan Helgesen, farm no. 18 – 5 l, Nordvik.

Laura Helgesen (1887 – 1922) and Daniel O. Vestre (1882 – 1971).

Married in 2nd marriage to **Lovise Ellingsen,** born Apr. 2, 1887, died Apr. 1, 1966, daughter of Mallene and Mathias Ellingsen, farm no. 2 – 6 d, Skare.

Children:

a. *Sigrunn* Oline, born Apr. 10, 1910, married in 1937 to Trygve Klovning, farm no. 8 – 2, Klovning.
b. Johan *Karsten*, born July 9, 1912, married in 1942 to Martha Skåren, tenant farmer no. 68, Nordvik.
c. Arne, born Oct. 24, 1916, died Jan. 15, 1917.
d. Agnes, born Sept. 21, 1918, married to Ingvald Svendsen, Haugesund.

Children in 2nd marriage:

a. Laura, born Dec. 16, 1926, married to Rasmus Martinsen, Stavanger.

Daniel was a carpenter and built many houses on Utsira. They lived in the old main dwelling on farm no 18. This was separated from the farm in 1907 and became farm no. 31, "Lilleherberget," which was taken over in 1989 by Ovind Vestre.

49. **Mikal Rasmussen.** 1914 – 1965
Born Dec. 7, 1886, died Mar. 16, 1941, son of Gurine and Rasmus Thomassen, farm no. 12 – 5 d, Nordvik.

Married on May 12, 1914, to ***Tilla*** **Gurine Mathiasdatter,** born Oct. 27, 1890, died Aug. 24, 1965, daughter of Malene and Mathias Ellingsen, farm no. 2 – 6 f, Skare.

From the wedding of Tilla and Mikal Rasmussen Beite in 1914.

Children:

a. Ragna *Gurine*, born Jan. 14, 1915, married to Johannes Skår, farm no. 22– 4, Nordvik.
b. Mathias, born May 23, 1916, married in 1940 to Ester Nilsen, tenant farmer no. 62, Nordvik.
c. Sivert, born July 13, 1820, took over the farm in 1962.

Mikal became a full–time marine pilot in 1910, and they built a main dwelling here, farm no. 41, Beite in 1919.

50. **Hersleb Helgesen.** 1910 – 1974
Born Sept. 28, 1889, died Jan. 20, 1965, son of Karoline and Johan Helgesen, farm no. 18 – 5 m, Nordvik.

Married on May 7, 1910, to **Julie Mathiasdatter,** born Oct. 30, 1888, died Sept. 13, 1974, daughter of Malene and Mathias Ellingsen, farm no. 2 – 6 e, Skare.

The Hersleb Helgesen family in 1952. In the back from the left: Julia, Hanna, Malene, Hersleb, Lovise and Martha. In from the left: Laura, Julie, Hersleb and Karoline.

Children:

a. Jenny *Karoline*, born Feb. 6, 1911, married in 1938 to Einar Martin Valler, Balke Island, Toten.
b. Milla *Malene*, born July 4, 1912, married in 1930 to Birger Nilsen, tenant farmer no. 58, Nordvik
c. *Lovise* Marie, born June 14, 1914, married in 1941 to Mandy Antony Hemmingstad, Tysvaer.
d. Anna *Martha*, born Mar. 9, 1916, married to Johannes Selvåg.
e. Hersleb Julius, born Sept. 11, 1917, died Oct. 28, 1917.
f. *Julia* Helene, born Nov. 14, 1918, married in 1940 to Fritz Aspen, Utsira Lighthouse no. 37.
g. *Hanna* Kristine, born July 18, 1920, married to Laurits Kristian Hemmingstad, lives in Haugesund.
h. *Hersleb* Julius, born Feb. 23, 1922, married in 1956 to Lovise M. Nordvik, tenant farmer no. 77, Nordvik.
i. Laura, born May 20, 1924, married in 1951 to Leif Tobias Hansen, tenant farmer no. 38, Hovland.

Hersleb became one of the best known seiners at Utsira. They took over the main dwelling house on the farm in 1910, farm no 3.

51. **Kasper Bertelsen.** 1918 – 1923
Born Oct. 1, 1893, son of Ida Josefine and Bertel Gudmundsen, farm no. 13 – 7 e, Nordvik.

Married to **Anne Martha Kristoffersen**, born in 1899, daughter of Berta Gurine and Johan Kristoffersen, Mannes, Akra.

Children born on Utsira:

a. Gustav Berner, born Apr. 30, 1919, is a coastal marine pilot, married and lives in Kopervik.
b. Berta Johanna, born Feb. 14, 1922.

The family moved to Karmøy.

52. **Klaus W. Løvland.** 1923 – 1963.
Born Jan. 6, 1890, son of Sofie and Mons Lovland, Tysvaer.

Married on June 15, 1923, to **Alvilde J. Bertelsdatter,** born Apr. 15, 1898, died Mar. 6, 1963, daughter of Ida Josefine and Bertel Gudmundsen, farm no. 13 – 7 g, Nordvik.

Children:

a. Mathias Sigurd, born Jan. 9, 1924, married in 1958 to Ragnhild Hermansen, tenant farmer no. 78, Nordvik.

53. **Emil Storesund.** 1920 – 1922
Born Nov. 10, 1894, died in 1960, son of Anna Pedersdatter and Peder Jakob Johnsen, Storesund.

Married to **Endrine Kringeland,** from Skjold.

Emil became the first manager of the general wholesale company on Utsira. He left that company in 1922 and started a general food store in Haugesund.

54. **Selmer Hop.** 1922
He was the general manager of the general wholesale company from the spring of 1922 until it ended in bankruptcy in the fall the same year.

55. **Johan Nilsen.** 1925 – 1972
Born July 6, 1901, son of Jonette and Martin Nilsen, tenant farmer no. 20, Austrheim.

From the Signe and Johan Nilsen wedding in 1925. In the back row from left: Julie Lervik, Knut Lervik, Sofie Eriksen Åse, Elling Ellingsen, Martha Eriksen, Lars Nilsen, Milla Nilsen, Mikal Eriksen and Birger Nilsen. In the middle row from left: Lovise Vestre, Mikal Eriksen, Signe and Johan, Martin Nilsen and Sofie Helgesen. In the front row from left: Dagny Veste, Signe Thomassen, Telma Eriksen, Juline, Martine and Emma Eriksen.

Married on Apr. 23, 1925, to **Signe Eriksen**, born July 2, 1900, daughter of Anne Marie and Mikal Eriksen, farm no. 4 – 3 a, Nordvik.

Children:

a. Mikal, born Mar. 2, 1928, married in 1952 to Aslaug Miljeteig, tenant farmer no. 75, Nordvik.
b. John *Magnar*, born Aug. 16, 1936, married in 1957 to Martha Johanna Sventsen, tenant farm no. 79, Nordvik.

Johan was substitute lighthouse attendant on Utsira lighthouse in the period 1946 – 1965. They built a main dwelling here, farm no. 70, Soltun, in 1949.

56. **Mathias Rasmussen**. 1929 – 1978
Born Oct. 18, 1929, died in 1993, son of Berthe Gurine and Rasmus Thomassen, farm no. 12 – 5 j, Nordvik.

Married on May 19, 1929, to **Anne *Martha* Helgesen,** born July 7, 1905, died in 1987, daughter of Ragna Serine and Thomas J. Nordvik, farm no. 30 – 1 b, Nordvik.

Children:

a. *Gudrun* Ranveig, born Mar. 15, 1930, married to Jan Furuvald, Slemmestad in Royken municipality.
b. *Sigurd* Torstein, born Aug. 26, 1933, married in 1956 to Johanne Theodora Bua, tenant farmer no. 82, Nordvik.
c. Else *Margot*, born Sept. 26, 1940, married to Arne Innbjo, lives in Haugesund.

They built their main dwelling here on farm no. 37, Havnestykket, in 1932. Taken over in 1975 by the son Sigurd. They later lived in Stavanger at Aksnes from 1975 and in Vormedal from 1985.

57. **Sverre L. Horgen.** 1937 – 1951.
Born Jan. 17, 1902 in Austevold.

Married on May 15, 1937, to ***Marta* Kirstine Nordvik**, born June 16, 1902, daughter of Stine and Mathias Larsen, farm no. 15 – 10 a, Nordvik.

Children:

a. Sigrid, born July 30, 1939, lives in Haugesund.
b. Magnbjorg, born Jan. 7, 1941, married to Magne Kjellesvik, lives in Haugesund.
c. Modstein, born May 26, 1942, married to Ellen from Stavanger, lives in Avaldsnes.

They built their home here on farm no. 66, Nordheim, in 1947. The farm was taken over in 1950 by Randi and Johan P. Klovning. In 1951 the family moved to Haugesund.

58. **Birger Nilsen**. 1930
Born July 16, 1910, son of Jonetta and Martin Nilsen, tenant farmer no. 20, Austrheim.

Married on May 24, 1930, to **Malene Nordvik,** born July 4, 1912, died Jan. 26, 1986, daughter of Julie and Hersleb Helgesen, tenant farmer no. 50 b, Nordvik.

Children:

a. *Magnus* Johannes, born Sept. 3, 1930, married to Jenny Birkenes, lives in Haugesund.
b. Herman Julius, born Aug. 16, 1931, died Apr. 9, 1932.
c. *Birgit* Malene, born Sept. 27, 1934, married to Frank Kristiansen, lives in Haugesund.
d. Herdis Johanne, born Aug. 14, 1938, died Feb. 3, 1942.
e. Sigfried Kjellaug, born May 27, 1940, married to Agnar Hole, lived in Haugesund.
f. Herdis Helene, born June 22, 1943, married to Reidar Serdal, lives in Aksdal.

They built their home here on farm no. 58, Sjahaug in 1939.

59. **Elias Bjelland**. 1931 – 1935.
Born Aug. 6, 1908, from Skanevik.
Married Oct. 25, 1931, to **Nelly *Kristine* Nilsen,** born Sept. 20, 1909, daughter of Anna and Jørgen Nilsen, farm no. 14 – 4 a, Nordvik.

Children:

a. *Torjus* Martin, born Feb. 10, 1932, married to Gerd Solberg, lives in Drammen.
b. *Anna* Johanna, born Sept. 13, 1934, married to Villhelm Steen, lives at Mo in Rana.
c. Jørgen, married to Torill Grønnskog, lives in Drammen.

They moved to Kinsarvik.

60. **Martin Skålnes.** 1942
Born Sept. 24, 1904, died June 26, 1980, son of Gurina and Torgeir Skålnes, Akrafjorden, Skanevik.
Married on Sept. 17, 1933, to **Laura Austrheim**, born Mar. 31, 1913, daughter of Julie and Konrad Knutsen, farm no. 1 – 10 d, Austrheim.

Children:

a. Konrad Johannes, born Dec. 15, 1933, married in 1972 to Bjorg Wang–Johannesen from Oslo, tenant farmer no. 81, Nordvik.
b. Gerhard, born Mar. 14, 1937, took over the farm in 1986.
c. Liv *Margit*, born Apr. 4, 1944, married in 1966 to Einar Sande, Randaberg.

They lived at Austrheim and in the "Leversen house" until in 1951 they built their own home here on farm no. 71, Sandvik.

In front of the old farmhouse on farm no. 12 (now farm no. 47) in 1961. From left: Gina Valnumsen, Lovise Rasmussen, Johan Valnumsen, Inga Ellingsen, Elmer Helgesen, Amanda Helgesen, Ellen Austrheim with Ronnie Ellingsen (in her arms) and Solvi Austrheim, Mathias Rasmussen, Anne–Solveig Furuvald and Martha Rasmussen.

61. **Elmer Helgesen.** 1956 – 1965
Born ?, died Jan. 25, 1973, from Haugesund.

Married to **Amanda Rasmusdatter Helgesen**, born June 11, 1893, died 198x, daughter of Berthe Gurine and Rasmus Thomassen, farm no. 12 – 5 g, Nordvik.

No children.

Elmer and Amanda lived many years in USA. They took over the old farm house on farm no. 12 and it was named farm no. 47, Beite. Later, they lived in Haugesund. The estate was in 1970 taken over by Bjarne Eldholm.

61. **Mathias M. Rasmussen**. 1940 – 1974
Born May 23, 1916, died Aug. 30, 1971, son of Tilla Gurine and Mikal Rasmussen, tenant farmer no. 49 b, Nordvik.

Married on Aug. 3, 1940, to **Ester Nilsen Herberg**, born Apr. 7, 1920 in Oslo, daughter of Jenny Valnumsen Herberg and Oskar Nilsen.

Children:

a. Tor Malvin, born Dec. 31, 1940, married to Randi Ingulvsen, lives in Kopervik
b. *Solfrid* Johanne, born Apr. 12, 1943, married to Kjell R. Thingvold, lives in Stavanger.
c. *Marit* Elise, born May 24, 1948, married in 1968 to Rasmus Skjelde, lives in Kopervik.

The house here, farm no. 36, Ospetre, was built originally as a sea shanty in 1938, was converted in 1938 to a home, adding a second story. The farm was taken over in 1988 by Greta Karin Hermansen from Haugesund.

63. **Lars Skjelde.** 1940 –
Born Nov. 8, 1913, died May 18, 1990, son of Tomine and Olav Skjelde, farm no 16 – 4 g, Nordvik.

Married on Aug. 20, 1940 to **Olga Valnumsen,** born Aug. 4, 1915, daughter of Gina and Johan Valnumsen, farm no 18 – 9 a, Nordvik.

Children:

a. Olaug *Turid,* born June 4, 1941, married to Reidar Hausken, Torvestad.
b. *Kari* Reidun, born July 23, 1944, married to Sten Oddvar Ludvigsen, lives in Kopervik.
c. Rasmus, born June 23, 1946, married in 1968 to Marit Elise Rasmussen, lives in Kopervik.
d. Oddleiv, born July 11, 1951, married Feb. 28, 1996 to Senayda Layos from Cebu City, Phillipines, lives in Karmøy.

The main dwelling here, farm no. 26, Skjelde, was built around 1900 by Olav Skjelde and later taken over by Olga and Lars Skjelde in 1946.

64. **Johan P. Klovning.** 1937 –
Born May 30, 1906, died on July 15, 1980, son of Lisa and Peder Klovning, tenant farmer no. 44 c, Nordvik.

Married on Apr. 24, 1937, to **Randi Larsen**, born Sept. 11, 1906, daughter of Stine and Mathias Larsen, farm no. 15 – 0 c, Nordvik.

Children:

a. Elfrid Sigrun, born May 29, 1940, married to Georg K. Georgsen, lives in Veavågen.
b. *Marit* Solveig, born Nov. 11, 1943, married in 1964 to Arthur Nilsen, tenant farmer no. 80, Nordvik.

From the wedding of Sigfryda and Aslak Miljeteig in 1940. From the left: Juline, Severine, Bjorg, Bjorn Vag, Aslak and Sigfryda, Bertel Hansen, John Nordhus, Andreas Miljeteig, Martha Braskott, Amanda Hansen and Alvilde Løvland.

c. John Reidar, born Mar. 20, 1949, married to Gerd I. Rasmussen. Lives in Frakkagjerd.

They took over the main dwelling here on farm no. 66, Nordheim after Marta and Sverre Horgen in 1950.

65. **Leif Ostensen.** 1936 – 1968
Born Mar. 4, 1915, son of Marie and Lauritz Ostensen, Skudeneshavn.

Married on Oct. 1, 1938, to **Laura Larsen**, born Aug. 22, 1918, daughter of Stine and Mathias Larsen, farm no. 15 – 10 f, Nordvik.

Children:

a. Margot, born Aug. 31, 1939, died Dec. 8, 1939.

b. Bjarne, born Sept. 10, 1942, married to Karin Fosen, lives in Avaldsnes.
c. *Steinar* Magne, born Feb. 3, 1946, married to Ellen Tjosvold, lives in Akrehamn.
d. Oystein, born Apr. 17, 1952, married to Astri Mikalsen, lives in Haugesund.

Leif was a baker on Utsira from 1936, when he built a combined bakery and home, farm no. 54, Solheim. In 1946 they took over the main dwelling on the farm from Jenny Marie and Rasmus Hoidal, farm no. 25, Vestre Holen.

66. **Aslak Miljeteig.** 1926 – 1990
Born June 26, 1899, died Mar. 19, 1957, son of Margrethe and Orjan Miljeteig, Akrafjorden, Skanevik.

Married in first marriage to **Petra Karoline Nordhus,** born Dec. 22, 1905, died Feb. 22, 1927, daughter of Lavine Kristine and Ole Johan Nordhus, farm no. 21–5 b, Nordvik

Married in 2nd marriage on May 2, 1940, to **Sigfryda Gudmundsen**, born June 15, 1912, died Nov. 11, 1990, daughter of Ida Josefine and Bertel Gudmundsen, farm no. 13– 7 l, Nordvik.

Children in 1st. marriage:
a. *Arne* Kristoffer, born May 27, 1926, died April 1956.

Children in 2nd marriage:
b. *Tor Bjorn* Oyvind, born Jan. 9, 1942, farm no. 13 – 9, Nordvik.
c. *Inger* Marie, born Dec. 3, 1944, married to Torstein Gronningen, Torvestad.
d. *Aud* Solbjorg, born Nov. 20, 1950, married Edvin Skjollingstad, lives in Torvestad.

Aslak built his home here, farm no. 55, Nordvåg, in 1938.

67. **Halvard Johan Jacobsen,** 1945 – 1950
Born Oct. 29, 1905, from Bua in Sveio.

Married on Sept. 7, 1945, to **Lindy Helgesen,** born Nov. 12, 1916, daughter of Serine and Thomas Helgesen, farm no. 30 – 1 h, Nordvik.

Children:
a. Gunvor Jorunn, born July 1, 1946, married to Ottar Midtgaard, lives in Eike, Fordesfjorden.
b. Solveig Johanna, born Apr. 21, 1949, married to Trygve Haugsgjerd.

They moved to Skre, Fordesfjorden in 1950.

From the herring fisheries in 1948: From left: Unknown, Arne Nilsen, Tobias Nordvik, Edvard Kvalvik, Mathias Nordvik, Tore L. Nordvik and Thomas Austrheim (all from Utsira).

68. **Karsten Vestre.** 1942 –
Born July 9, 1912, died Dec. 25, 1995, son of Laura and Daniel Vestre, tenant farmer 48 b, Nordvik.

Married on Aug. 15, 1942, to **Martha Skåren,** born Nov. 5, 1910, daughter of Tomine and Johannes Skåren, farm no. 22 – 3 j, Nordvik.

Children:

a. Torleiv, born Jan. 20, 1944. Torleiv also has a farm here.
b. Dagfinn Jostein, born June 3, 1945, married to Solveig Årekol, lives in Fordesfjorden, Tysvaer.
c. Joanne Margrethe, born May 7, 1949, married to Arne I. Hammersand, lives in Gandal.
d. Oyvind Arne, born Aug. 7, 1953, married to Mary Anne Rasmussen, lives in Haugesund.

They built their home here, farm no. 72, Sjaneset, in 1954. Martha was a midwife on Utsira in 1942 – 54.

69. **Tobias Nordvik.** 1948 –
Born Oct. 18, 1923, died Sept. 2, 1972, son of Ellen and Tore Larsen, farm no. 15 – 11 b, Nordvik.

Married on Apr. 24, 1948, to **Malfrid Myre,** born Feb. 17, 1925, daughter of Laura and Mikal Mathiassen Myre, farm no. 2 – 7 e, Skare.

Children:

a. *Elfrid* Torun, born Mar. 10, 1949, died Jan. 31, 1973.
b. Linmar, born Nov. 25, 1950, married in 1972 to Astrid Lillian Kvalvik, lives in Kleppe, Bryne.
c. Tore Mikal, born July, 30, 1954, died May 8, 1976.
d. Margrethe, born Jan. 10, 1956, lives in Tananger, Sola.

Their built their home here, farm no. 76, Sjonar, in 1950.

70. **Tala P. Klovning.** 1960 – 1984
Born Dec. 31, 1902, died Dec. 8, 1984, daughter of Lisa and Peder Klovning, tenant farm no. 44 a, Nordvik.

Unmarried.

Tala was a trained chef (garde manger) and ran a pension here in her home (where she was born).

The place, farm no. 24, Normandiet, was in 1987 taken over by Johan and Nils Fredrik Jansen.

71. **Mathias Nordvik.** 1948 – 1954
Born Dec. 16, 1921, died Feb. 14, 1968, son of Ellen and Tore Larsen, farm no. 15 – 11 a, Nordvik.

Married to **Sigrun Solvåg,** born May 5, 1923, from Selje.

Children:

a. Torill Elin, born Dec. 25, 1948, married to Sigmund Stenersen, lives in Bergen.
b. Henrik Arnvid, born July 7, 1953, married to Gunhild Hosto, lives in Torvestad.
c. Oystein, born Dec. 27, 1954, married to Synnøve Lunde, lives in Haugesund.
d. Egil, born Sept. 17, 1960, married to Liv Reidun, lives in Skre, Fordesfjorden.

They lived later in Torvestad.

72 a. **Ludvig J. Kvalvik.** 1917 – 1954.
Born Aug. 1, 1886, died June 21, 1954, son of Martha and Job Tollefsen, tenant farmer no. 30, Kvalvik.

Married in 1911 to **Astrid Eriksen,** born Sept. 22, 1894, died Nov. 22, 1951, daughter of Anna and Kristen Eriksen, Akra.

Children:

a. *Tordis* Kristine, born Apr. 24, 1913, married in 1936 to John Larsen, farm no 75 – 1, Nordvik.
b. Jon Meier, born Oct. 28, 1917, died July 31, 1996, took over the home in Kvalvik, farm no. 12, Fagerheim, in 1954.
c. *Anna* Lovise, born July 1, 1920, married in 1943 to Ola L. Rossbo, Skåre.
d. Karsten, born Dec. 27, 1921, next tenant farmer.
e. Edvin, born July 13, 1928, married in 1961 to Borgny Elise Kvalvik, moved to Valevåg, Sveio.

As did his father and grandfather, Ludvig worked for the Port Authority. They built their home here, farm no. 6, in 1917.

72. **Karsten Kvalvik.** 1951 –
Born Dec. 27, 1921, son of previous tenant farmer.

Married on Apr. 14, 1951, to **Judit Klovning,** born Nov. 1, 1930, daughter of Marie and Johannes Klovning, farm no. 2 – 4 a, Klovning.

Children;

a. *Astrid* Lillian, born May 13, 1952, married in 1972 to Linmar Nordvik, lives in Kleppe, Bryne.
b. *Johannes* Olgeir, born Feb. 27, 1956, married to Liv Salamonsen, lives in Avaldsnes.

They took over the farm here in 1954.

73. **Johannes M. Solsvik.** 1947 – 1948
Born Nov. 28, 1915 in Fjell.

Married on Apr. 13, 1947, to **Josefine Regine Larsen,** born Oct. 30, 1920, daughter of Stine and Mathias Larsen, farm no. 15 – 10 g, Nordvik.

Children born on Utsira:

a. Roald Olav, born Jan. 13, 1948, married to Sandra from England, lives in Vormedal.

They lived in Bolle House and later in Haugesund, Brattholmen and Avaldsnes.

74. **Åsmund Faremo.** 1950 – 1956

Born Apr. 10, 1925 in Bygland, married **Gunhild**, born 1927.

Operated a general store in Nordevågen in these years, and this store was taken over by Lovise and Hersleb Helgesen.

Children:

a. Birgit, born June 20, 1951.

75. **Mikal Nilsen.** 1952 – 1975

Born Mar. 2, 1928, died in 1976, son of Signe and Johan Nilsen, tenant farmer no. 55 a, Nordvik.

Married on June 21, 1952, to **Aslaug Miljeteig,** born Apr. 26, 1928, daughter of Hjordis and Andreas Miljeteig, tenant farmer no. 25 b, Skare.

Children:

a. Arne Henry, born May 28, 1953.
b. *Magne* Jostein, born Apr. 27, 1958, died Dec. 30, 1977, perished in the "Emly" shipwreck.
c. Sissel, born Aug. 27, 1960, married to Nabil Saoula, lives in Vedavagen.
d. Ase Marian, born July 1, 1965, married to Henrik Kristoffersen.

The family moved to Vedavagen, their home there on farm no. 70, Soltun, which was taken over by Knut Andreas Bentsen in 1975.

76. **Oystein Haugland.** 1956 –

Born June 1, 1929, son of Benny and Severin Haugland, Utsira Lighthouse no. 9 d.

Married on Dec. 8, 1956, to **Reidun Skåren,** born May 26, 1937, daughter of Hanna and Gudmund Skåren, farm no. 56 – 1 b, Nordvik

Children:

a. Heidi Synnøve, born Feb. 15, 1958, married in 1989 to Edgar Pettersen, lives in Haugesund.
b. Gunn Hilde, born Aug. 29, 1962, married in 1987 to Bjarne Austrheim, farm no. 3 – 10, Austrheim.
c. Raymond, born Aug. 8, 1964, married in 1986 to Ingrid Ellingsen, lives in Algard.

Oystein was a radio telegraph operator, and from 1971 he became a lighthouse keeper at Utsira Lighthouse, and from 1990 he was lighthouse manager. They took over the main dwelling, Varden, on farm no. 63, after Benny and Severin Haugland in 1975.

The Norevågen harbor the summer of 1870 when the harbor project was finished. Photo by N. Bing, Heritage.

77. **Hersleb Helgesen.** 1956 – 1990.
Born Feb. 23, 1922, son of Julie and Hersleb Helgesen, tenant farmer no. 50 h, Nordvik.

Married on Sept. 20, 1956, to **Lovise M. Helgesen,** born Apr. 13, 1921, daughter of Serine and Thomas Helgesen, farm no. 30 – 1 j, Nordvik.

Lovise and Hersleb ran the general store in Nordvagen from 1956.

Hersleb was the mayor on Utsira in 1976 – 1979. They moved to Haugesund in 1990.

78. **Mathias Løvland.** 1958 – 198x
Born Jan. 9, 1924, son of Alvilde and Klaus V. Lovland, tenant farmer no. 52 – a, Nordvik.

Married on June 21, 1958, to **Ragnhild Hermansen**, born Apr. 2, 1918, from Voss.

Children:

a. *Annette* Julie, born Feb. 10, 1964, married to Daniel Danielsen, lives in Kopervik.

They moved to Kopervik.

79. **Magnar Nilsen.** 1957 – 1970.
Born Aug. 16, 1936, died Dec. 30, 1977, son of Signe and Johan Nilsen, tenant farmer no. 55 b, Nordvik.

Married on Apr. 6, 1957, to **Martha Johanna Sventsen**, born Dec. 1, 1936, from Vedavågen.

Children:

a. John Sigve, born July 23, 1957, married to Toril Lygre.
b. Oddny Elen, born Mar. 6, 1960, married to Walter Taranger.
c. Margareth, born June 22, 1962, married to Steinar Bjorgheim
d. May Britt, born Apr. 21, 1971

The family moved to Vedavagen. Magnar perished in the "Emly" shipwreck.

80. **Arthur Nilsen.** 1964 –
Born Apr. 13, 1942, son of Astrid and Adolf Nilsen, farm no. 14 – 5 a. Nordvik.

Married in 1964 to **Marit Klovning,** born Nov. 11, 1943, daughter of Randi and Johan P. Klovning, tenant farmer no. 64 b, Nordvik.

Children:

a. Arve, born Jan. 9, 1965, married to Siv Torunn Vaage, lives in Rubbestadneset, Bomlo.
b. Jarle, born Sept. 22, 1966, lives in Stavanger.

Arthur is a marine pilot, and they built a home here, farm no. 103, Vestli, in 1975.

81. **Johannes Skålnes.** 1972 –
Born Dec. 15, 1933, son of Laura and Martin Skålnes, tenant farmer no. 60 a, Nordvik.

Married on July 22, 1972, to **Bjorg Wang – Johannesen**, from Oslo, born Oct. 8, 1946.

Children:

a. Jens, born Aug. 8, 1973.
b. Gry, born Aug. 1, 1977.

They built their home, Varatun, here, farm no. 102 in 1974. Bjorg is a teacher at Utsira Children and Youth school.

82. **Sigurd Rasmussen.** 1974 – 1977
Born Aug. 26, 1933, son of Martha and Mathias Thomassen, tenant farmer no. 56 b, Nordvik.

Married in 1956 to **Johanne Theodora Bua,** born May 30, 1936, daughter of Theodora and Jakob Bua, in Sveio.

Children:

a. Mary Anne, born Sept. 10, 1958, married to Oyvind Vestre, lives in Haugesund.
b. Ruth Irene, born July 25, 1961, married to Lino Egidio Lubiana. She is a missionary in Croatia.
c. Freddy, born Mar. 22, 1967, married to Synnøve Nymark, lives in Haugesund.

Sigurd started out as a marine pilot on Utsira in 1974, and they lived earlier in their lives in Stavanger. Lives now on Vormedal.

83. **Tor Arild Bakke**. 1978 – 1984
Born in 1951 in Sokndal, married in 1973 to **Anne Tove**, born 1953 in Stavanger. Their son is Tom Atle, born Apr. 19, 1977. Tor Arild was secretary on the Utsira County Board and office manager there. Later on they moved to Haegebostad, Vest–Agder.

84. **Arne Mo,** chief administrative officer at Utsira, 1989 – 1990.

85. **Marie Solberg,** born May 17, 1949, from Mykja on Karmøy, chief administrative officer on Utsira from 1991.

Austrheim

Before 1824:	Reg. no. 33, tax 5 v.tf.
1824 – 1851:	Reg. no. 55, serial no. 242–247, tax 9 dl. 1 ort 18 sk.
1851–1886:	Reg. no. 65, serial no. 335–340, tax 9–1–8.
1886:	Farm no. 27, tax 13 mark 12 ore.

At Austrheim there is only one farmer until 1650, then two, and until 1700 there were three farmers. From 1761 there were six farms into our century (20th C.).

At Austrheim there was only one unregistered homestead, "Skarvanes," which was deserted even as early as 1710. Except for Anders Knutsen's place at "Lynghilder, farm no. 5, in the period 1768 – 92, there were no unregistered homesteads at Austrheim.

Official settlements of Austrheim properties were held in 1889 and the outfields and meadows were settled in the period 1895–1898.

Austramarka was a common outfield for Austrheim, Hovland and eastern Nordvik, until 1839 when this piece was divided among the farms.

Recorded in the Land Registry of 1668:

Ostrimb (Austrheim), 5 våger fish, acceptable grain fields and sufficient peat for fuel for domestic needs, sowing 5 barrels of grain: enough to feed 16 cows, potential to pay: 5 baskets of grain, 3 goat hides and 3 calf hides for local defenses, 5 buckets grain to the church, and 10 sk. in cash contributions.

Austrheim from the air, farm no. 1 and 2 in the foreground and no. 3 in the back and to right in the back, farm no 5. Photo by Telemark Aircraft Co., 1954.

Table: Overview of planted crops and yields for grain and potatoes:

Year	Grain sown	Potatoes planted	Grain Yield	Potato Yield
1668	5	–	–	–
1703	7	–	–	–
1712	7	–	–	–
1723	7	–	34	–
1802	11	–	67	–
1822	–	–	105	49
1845	21	7	–	–
1866	22	12	144	86
1875	21	11	–	–
1945	13	9	–	–

The numbers for 1945 are in dekar, otherwise in barrels.

Table: Overview of livestock, homes and inhabitants:

Year	Horses	Cows	Calves	Homes	Inhabitants
1668	–	16	–	–	–
1703	3	19	x	–	–
1712	3	19	x	–	–
1723	1	13	5	–	–
1758	–	–	–	5	22
1801–02	6	21	10	7	27
1822	8	27	46	–	–
1845	6	21	40	6	50
1866	6	21	53	10	74
1875	4	19	54	7	40
1900	–	–	–	8	46

Farmers

1. **Torgils**. 1521
He is the only farmer at Austrheim mentioned in 1521.

2. **Peder.** 1563
He also farms the entirety of Austrheim by himself.

3. **Peder.** 1600 – 1645
Peder is mentioned in the county records from 1603 and up to 1643. In this period he is the only farmer at Austrheim.

Possible children listed as:

a. Hans, born around 1614, next farmer.
b. Jens, born around 1622, farmer no 1 –1, Nordvik.
c. Jens, mentioned in the records in 1668.
d. Nils, born around 1634, tenant farmer no. 6, Austrheim.

Farm no. 1.

1. **Hans Pedersen.** 1646 – 1688

Born around 1614, possibly the son of the last farmer.

His possible children could be:

a. Peder, born around 1644.
b. John, born around 1656.
c. Ole, born around 1664, next farmer.

2. **Ole Hansen.** 1688 – 1695

Born around 1664, died around 1694, possibly son of last farmer.

Married to **Ingeborg Olsdatter,** died in 1725, estate settled Nov. 4, 1725, further history unknown.

Children:

a. Knut, born 1688, married in second marriage to Gjoa Ellingsdatter, farmer no. 4 – 5, Austrheim.
b. Hans, born 1691, died between 1707 – 1725.
c. Marte, mentioned in the settlement after her mother in 1725 and listed as unmarried.

Ole is mentioned in several military records in the period 1681 – 1690. Ingeborg married the 2nd time to the next farmer Tormod Rasmussen.

3. **Tormod Rasmussen.** 1695 – 1724

Born around 1667, died 1724, son of Rasmus Hausken, Torvestad.

Married in 1695 to **Ingeborg Olsdatter**, widow of last farmer.

Children:

a. Ole, born in 1697, next farmer.
b. Rasmus, born 1704, married to Guri Larsdatter, farmer no 7 – 4, Hovland.

Tormod registered the lease contract on the property in 1705 listing the worth as 2 v.tf. dated May 7, 1695.

In 1708 Tormod split the 2 v.tf. lease after the death of Lars Jakobsen on farm no. 4, with his step son, Knut, and the farm from then on is 3 v.tf.

Tormod's financial condition was in 1703 described as "tenuous." However, the houses on the farm are in reasonable state and in no need of immediate repair. He plants 3 barrels of oats, feeds 4 cows, 2 calves, 1 horse and some sheep. He owns all the livestock and has no debt to J. Frimand, but *owes others – 4 rdl. for bread grain.*

In 1712 his financial condition is described in the same manner, but he receives 1 rdl. in compensation for repair of the houses, plants 3 to 4 barrels of oats, feeds 6 to 7 cows, 2 – 3 calves and some sheep, all which he owns himself. He now owes 9 rdl. to cloister manager J. Frimand.

In 1721 he is free of debt and the fields and meadows are in "good condition," but he has to repair his barn at the cost of 2 ort.

In 1723 the farm is listed as follows:

> Tormod's farm, 3 våger, sowing 3–1/2 barrels grain yielding 18 barrels, feeds 1 horse, 5 cows, 5 calves.

In the estate settlement after Ingeborg in 1724 the assets are listed as 29–3–20 rdl.

Before the distribution to the heirs, Rasmus receives 11 rdl. as a wedding gift. Among various items the following are mentioned:

> 2–1/2 barrels of grain, a smokehouse on an empty lot 7–0–0, 3 cows, 1 calf 8–2–0 and miscellaneous clothing 10–1–16.

Tormod was church trustee in the period 1707 – 1713.

4. **Ole Tormodsen.** 1724 – 1748

Born 1697, died in 1745, son of last farmer.

Married in 1724 to **Randi Larsdatter**, born in 1702, buried on Mar. 31, 1765, daughter of Berthe and Lars Johannesen, farmer no. 1 – 3 c. Skare.

Known children:

a. Randi, born 1733, married in 1762 to Mikkel Mathiassen, farmer no. 2 – 1, Austrheim.

Ole's lease contract in the amount of 2–1/2 v.tf. is dated May 15, 1724. The same day his half brother, Knut, signs a lease on the rest of the farm in the amount of 1/2 v.tf.

There is a settlement after Ole in May 1746. Randi inherits 3–1–1 rdl., guardian for Randi is her mother's father, Lars Skare.

Randi was married in her 2nd marriage to the next farmer, Elling Johannesen.

5. **Elling Johannesen.** 1749 – 1792
Born in 1720, buried on July 10, 1785, son of Johannes Ellingsen, tenant farmer no. 10 a, Kvalvik.

Married first in 1749 to **Randi Larsdatter**, widow of last farmer.

Second marriage Jan. 9, 1766, to **Gjoa Johannesdatter**, born 1747, died Jan. 18, 1825, daughter of Berta and Johannes Pettersen, Osnes.

Children:

a. Randi, baptized June 29, 1766, married in 1806 to Kristen Eriksen, Hauge in Skåre.
b. Berta, baptized Nov. 22, 1767, married in 1817 to Jørgen Andersen Klovning, lived at Storesund in Torvestad.
c. Marta, baptized Aug. 19, 1769, lived on Hasseloy 1801–1806.
d. Johannes, baptized Mar. 25, 1773, married in 1795 to Dorte Bårdsdatter, lived in Vollsvik, Fosen in Avaldsnes.
e. Elling, baptized Mar. 15, 1775.
f. Rasmus, baptized Apr. 30, 1777, buried Mar. 25, 1781.
g. Ole, baptized Oct. 12, 1779, buried Nov. 22, 1788 at Osnes.
h. Rasmus, baptized Sept. 1, 1782, married in 1805 to Eli Johannesdatter, Hagland, lived in Storesund in Torvestad.
i. Guri, born Oct. 18, 1785, buried Mar. 25, 1786.

Lease contract to Elling in the amount of 2–1/2 v.tf. is dated Nov. 23, 1749.

In 1761, half of the farm, farm no. 2, was taken out of the estate for Mikkel Mathiassen.

In the estate settlement after Elling in July 1786, the estate assets are 31 rdl., while the debt and expenses is 36 rdl., so there is nothing left for the heirs. The debt, expenses and tax for 1785 represents 3–0–0, annual land lease is 2–0–11, repair on the houses 4–0–0 and estate settlement costs 5–1–4. Among misc. items, the following are mentioned:

> 3 barrels of oats 4–0–0, 1 cow and 1 calf 5–2–0, 1 mare 5–0–0, 1 iron stove 7–0–0, 1 large kettle 3–0–0, 1 old four–oar boat 0–3–8 and 2 spring herring fishing nets 1–1–8.

Gjoa was married the second time in 1802 to John Johnsen, Storesund in Torvestad.

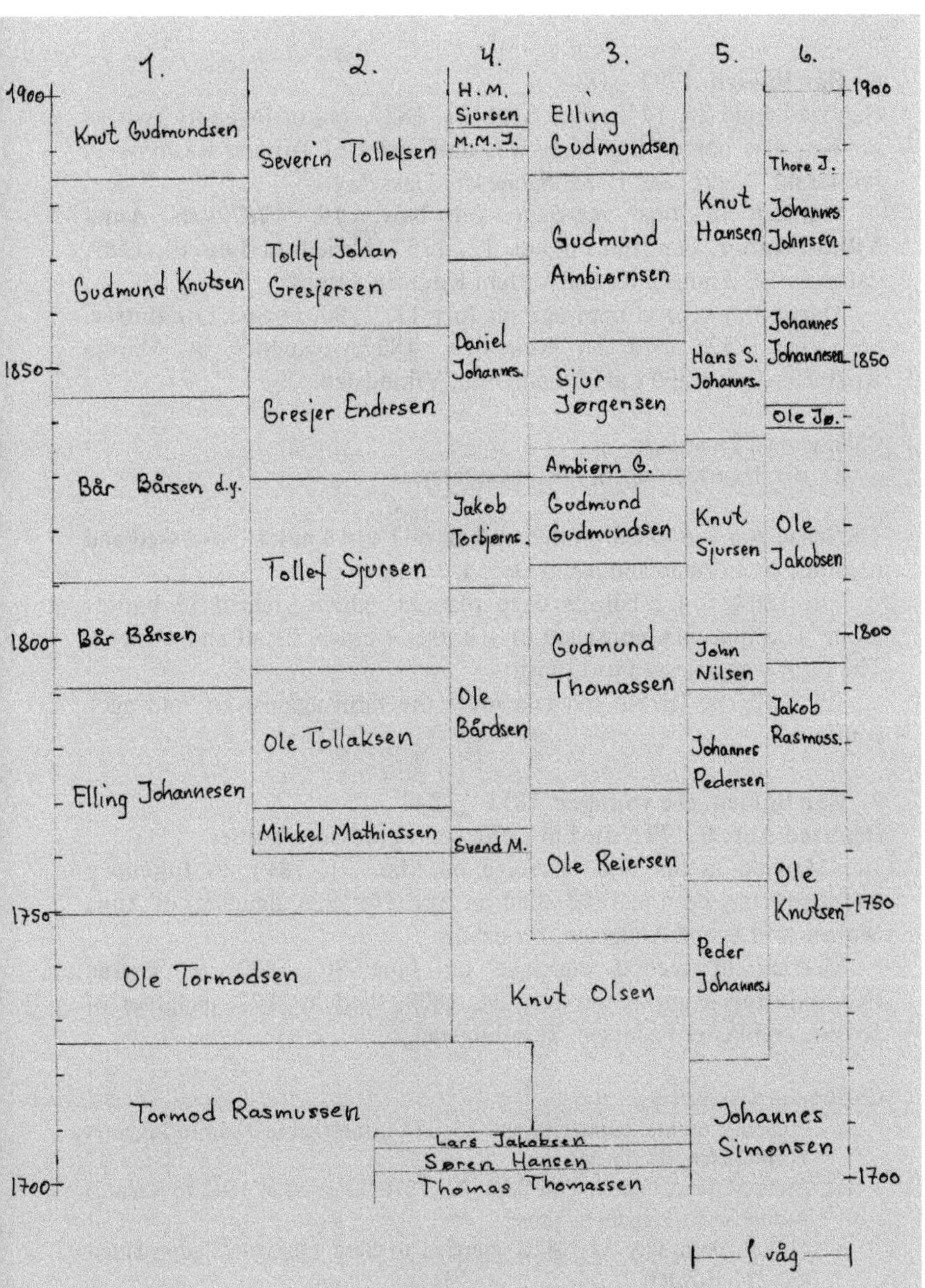

Table of farmers for Austrheim, 1700–1900.

6. **Bår Bårsen.** 1792 – 1811
Baptized June 20, 1756, died Sept. 21, 1827, son of Ingeborg (whose mother, also named Ingeborg, was half–sister of Tormod Rasmussen, farmer no. 3 here) and Bår Johannesen, Hasseloy.

Married in first marriage on Nov. 15, 1787, to **Anna Villumsdatter,** baptized on Jan. 17, 1757, buried on July 19, 1789, daughter Eli Knutsdatter and Villum Knutsen, Osnes.

Married in second marriage on July 11, 1790, to **Siri Larsdatter,** born in 1752, died on Mar. 19, 1827, daughter of Martha Kristoffersdatter and Lars Johannesen, Vikingstad.

Children in 2nd marriage:

a. Bår, baptized Aug. 6, 1791, next farmer.

The lease is given to Bår in the amount of 1 v. 18 mrk.tf., assessed and recorded by Forman and dated Dec. 4, 1792.

In 1802, 2 1/2 barrels were planted, which yielded 15 barrels grain. The livestock consisted of 1 horse, 4 cows, 1 calf and 4 sheep. The farm was assessed to 130 rdl.

In 1811 he let his son take over the farm against an "old age" contract.

7. **Bår Bårsen, the younger**. 1811 – 1844
Baptized Aug. 6, 1791, died in 1870, son of previous farmer.

Married in his first marriage on Mar. 31, 1814, to **Ingeborg Svendsdatter,** born in 1792, died on Apr. 14, 1826, daughter of Anna Malene and Svend Andersen, Kvalavåg.

Married in second marriage on June 30, 1827, to **Torine Pedersdatter,** baptized on July 24, 1803, died in 1877, daughter of Jensine and Peder Pedersen, Skjollingstad.

Children in first marriage:

a. Ingeborg Serine, baptized Sept. 13, 1814, married in 1848 to Ingebret Torbjornsen, Kvalavåg.
b. Anne Malene, baptized on Sept. 22, 1816, married in 1842 to Rasmus Amundsen, Stoggdal in Skåre.
c. Torkel, born July 11, 1820, married to Sara Elisabeth Pedersdatter, lived on Rovaer.
d. Anna Andersina, born Mar. 9, 1823, married in 1841 to Johannes Andersen, Kvalavåg.
e. Jakob Jansen, born Sept. 25, 1825, died Dec. 1, 1859 at Rovaer.

Children in 2nd marriage:

f. Ingeborg Katrine, born Apr. 3, 1828, married in 1857 to Ola Olsen, Kvalavåg.
g. Jan Henrik, born Aug. 2, 1830, died 1851.
h. Svend, born June 16, 1833, died on June 20, 1835.
i. Karen Jensine, born Nov. 15, 1835, died Sept. 3, 1836.
j. Karen Jensine, born Mar. 29, 1838, married in 1859 to Svein Olsen, Kolsto.
k. Martha Serine, born May 3, 1841, married in 1868 to Anders Omundsen, Kvalavåg.
l. Bår, born Feb. 25, 1844, died in 1848.

The lease contract to Bår in the amount of 1 v. 18 mrk.tf. from Forman is dated Sept. 20, 1811. He paid 50 rdl. in rent and his contribution to his parents' pension fund was estimated to 50 rdl as follows:

> 6 barrels of oats at 4 våger per barrel, feed for 2 cows, 3 to 4 sheep and a piece of a field called "Big Peat at Gunhild's Hill" plus a small parcel of meadows near the houses . . .

In 1822 the buildings were described as follows:

> 1 old house with kitchen covered with peat (dried sod or turf), 1 new building with logged barn, covered with peat. 1 little storage house with peat roof, 1 small old stable with peat roof, 1 old smokehouse covered with peat.

The farm has an annual yield of 20 barrels of grain and 10 to 12 barrels of potatoes, he feeds 5 cows, 1 calf, 2 horses and 6 to 8 sheep. The farm was in 1823 assessed at 150 Spd.

In the estate settlement after Ingeborg in 1827 there were assets totaling 92–1–14 Spd. Among the items listed were:

> 1 red–spotted horse, 13 years old 5–0–0, 1 black–spotted cow called "Søndrej," 10 years old 5–0–0, 1 coal–black calf called "Svartsia," 3 years old 5–1–0, 1 coal–black cow called "Dagros," 3 years old 6–2–12, 1 coal–black cow called "Svartsia," 10 years old 5–2–12, 1 wooden storage shed with hide–covered roof 5–0–0, 1 large cattle trough (1/2–barrel capacity) 4–0–0, 1 bread–baking board 1–3–0, 1 green and white rose–embroidered silk damask shirt with green leather trim 1–1–0, 1 blue homespun shirt and jacket 1–0–0, 1 clothing locker with lock and decorative hinges 2–0–0, 1 long locker painted red with 2 compartments and marked "B.B.S.O. 1816" 0–1–0, 2 spring herring nets with accessories 1–3–0, 1 pollock fishing net with accessories 0–4–0, 14 lobster pots 0–3–12 and 1 old four–oar boat without sail 1–0–0.

In 1831 Bår bought the farm from J. Dahm for 220 Spd. and the deed is dated May 18, 1831. In 1844 he sold it to Gudmund Knutsen, and the family moved to Kvalavåg, Karmøy.

8. **Gudmund Knutsen.** 1844 – 1885
Baptized Oct. 20, 1813, died on Apr. 4, 1896, son of Berta Gudmundsdatter and Knut Sjursen, farmer no. 5 – 4 f, Austrheim.

Married on June 26, 1845, to **Kari Oline Nilsdatter,** born Oct. 22, 1825, died Nov. 12, 1877, daughter of Anne Marte Johnsdatter and Nils Johnsen, farmer no. 2 – 5 a, Kvalvik.

Children:

a. Berthe Eline, born Mar. 1, 1846, married in 1866 to Tollak Johan Andersen, Kolsto.
b. Nils, born Dec. 13, 1847, died Dec. 14, 1848.
c. Anne Marthe, born Dec. 28, 1848, died May 21, 1884.
d. Johanne Margrethe, born June 22, 1851, died Aug. 9, 1852.
e. Johanne Margrethe, born May 4, 1853, married in 1877 to Erik Brynjulvsen Evanger, Eggeboneset.
f. *Gunhilde* Oline, born Apr. 3, 1856, emigrated to USA in 1886, there married in 1887 to Hans Hansen.
g. Knut, born Feb. 18, 1859, became next farmer.
h. Ingeborg *Cathrine*, born Sept. 1, 1861, married in 1882 to Nils Johannes Jørgensen, farmer no. 14 – 2, Nordvik.
i. Nils Johan, born Aug. 28, 1864, was a merchant seaman, drowned near New York around 1890. He had a daughter Berthe Amanda, born Mar. 3, 1888 to Valborg Eline Gautsdatter.
j. Gudmund, born July 1, 1867, married to Andrea Ingebrigtsen, worked as a shoemaker in Haugesund. He was nicknamed "Halte–Gudmund" (Limping Gudmund).
k. Thomas, born July 2, 1870, emigrated to USA in 1886, there in 1891 married Boletha Simonsen, daughter of Kristian Simonsen, farmer no. 21 – 2, Nordvik.[34]

The deed to Gudmund from Bår Bårsen on this farm, tax liability 1 v. 18 mrk.tf. or 2 d. 9 sk., for 700 Spd. is dated May 22, 1844. In addition he had to contribute an equivalent of 55 Spd. over 5 years to the "old age pension" of Torine and Bår as mentioned in the following contract:

> . . . 3 barrels of oats per weight, 5 våger barley, will help board and feed 10 sheep in the winter, without being responsible for accidents, 2 barrels of potatoes and 2 cans of cod liver oil. Should any of the sheep become ill

[34] See Note 11.

or in danger of spreading any disease to others, they will themselves be responsible for making arrangements for removal and all damage.

In 1866 the farm was 47 mål (about 11 acres) of fields and meadows valued to 331 Spd. There are pastures for 106 Spd. and income from adjacent fishing rights, 71 Spd. Annual yield from the farm is 22 barrels of oats, 8 barrels of barley, 24 barrels of potatoes and 34 Skp. hay. The entire farm is assessed at 575 Spd.

The livestock consists of 1 horse, 5 cows, 15 sheep and 1 pig.

The main dwelling is 9.4 x 7.8 meters, logged with basement, lined with boards and covered with tiles and was assessed in 1868 at 400 Spd. The barn, 17.9 x 6.3 meters, is assessed at 150 Spd.

9. **Knut Gudmundsen.** 1885 – 1909

Born Feb. 18, 1859, died July 22, 1899, son of the last farmer.

Married on Aug. 16, 1884, to **Ida *Thomine* Johansdatter,** born Feb. 1, 1865, died Sept. 5, 1954, daughter of Karoline and Johan Helgesen, farmer no. 18 – 5 a, Nordvik.

Knut Gudmundsen (1859–1899) and Thomine Johansdatter (1865–1954).

Children:

a. Gudmund *Konrad*, born May 25, 1885, next farmer.
b. *Johan* Kadolf, born June 11, 1886, died Nov. 17, 1902.
c. August, Aug. 17, 1888, married in 1925 to Amanda Tobiasdatter, farmer no. 4 – 13, Hovland.
d. *Thomas* Berner, born Mar. 30, 1890, died Oct. 28, 1915.

e. *Hanna* Kristine, born Aug. 5, 1892, married in 1916 to Peter Jensen Enevold, tenant farmer no. 48, Skare.
f. Nelly *Juline*, born Feb. 18, 1895, emigrated to USA, married in 1925 to Andrew Christophersen Brattesto, lived in Havre, Montana.
g. Konstanse Tomine, born Sept. 27, 1897, died Feb. 12, 1900.
h. Lovise Marie, born Jan. 13, 1900, died Jan. 14, 1912.

The deed to Knut from the father for 2000 kroner and an old age pension agreement, is dated Apr. 16, 1895, with tax liability of 2.97 sk.m.

Thomine was married the second time in 1909 to widower Elling Eriksen, farmer no. 1 – 10, Skare.

10. **Konrad Knutsen.** 1909 – 1940

Born May 25, 1885, died Feb. 26, 1929, son of last farmer.

Married on May 25, 1907, to ***Julie*** **Kristine Sørhus**, born July 22, 1886, died Apr. 10, 1956, daughter of Anna Martha Laurine and Tobias Sørhus, tenant farmer no. 23 a., Klovning.

Bridal couple 1907. Konrad Knutsen (1885 – 1929) and Julie Sørhus (1886 – 1956).

Children:

a. Knut *Thorvald*, born Oct. 9, 1907, next farmer.
b. Laura Lovise, born Sept. 4, 1909, died Nov. 4, 1912.
c. Tobias, born Sept. 27, 1911, farmer no. 16 – 1, Austrheim.

d. *Laura* Lovise, born Mar. 31, 1913, married in 1933 to Martin Skålnes, tenant farmer no. 60, Nordvik.
e. *Lovise* Marie, born Dec. 7, 1914, died Jan. 7, 1991.
f. *Thomas* Berner, born May 16, 1916, died Dec. 4, 1952.
g. *Konrad* Julius, born Mar. 6, 1918, married in 1940 to Berta Johannesen, farm no. 20 – 7, Nordvik.
h. *Julia* Kristine, born Nov. 1, 1919, married in 1947 to Johannes Johannesen, farmer no. 17 – 8, Nordvik.
i. Johan, born Apr. 3, 1922, married in 1953 to Inger Hertås, tenant farmer no. 28, Austrheim.

From "Haugesund Avis" newspaper, 9 March 1927.

A Pioneer, – Konrad K. Austrheim from Utsira.

We knew that on the outer island of Utsira there were skillful seamen, and it is reasonable to think so, but "Utsira–lites" were also outstanding and capable farmers.

Particularly in the Sira valley there are quite a few especially well–managed and productive farms.

And one of Utsira's most successful pioneers is Konrad K. Austrheim.

He took over his father's farm 20 years ago and, as well known as he was a hard–working, effective farmer, it did not take many years before he more than tripled the yield of the farm.

He is now feeding 8 cows and 1 horse after having scarcely been able to feed 4 cows when he took over the farm.

He harvests more potatoes than he needs for his own consumption leaving some for sale on the market.

Of grain he produced quite a lot of barley. "Sirabyggen" (Sira barley) has been well known for years as giving outstanding yields, more than any other place in the entire country. – The steady gentle breeze there seems to encourage the growth of sturdy stalks supporting a heavy load of good barley.

Traditionally, thrashing has been carried out with American methods for over 20 years. There are 2 automatic machines available with built–in engines with electrical ignition capable of thrashing 100 barrels of pure grain per day, finished and bagged, ready for shipment.

The pioneer, K. Austrheim has worked the farm's fields and continues to break new ground in the outfields. He has drained water–soaked wetland by digging thousands of meters of draining ditches. All the houses on the farm have been rebuilt or improved.

The "Sira–lite" has a good life here and also has another enormous workplace: the ocean around it!

But the women still do not participate in the conquest of the sea.

The Sira–lites have always been a vigilant group open to everything around them on land and at sea.

– by Torfeus jr.

Julie and Konrad K. Austrheim's children in front of their house in 1926. In the back from the left: Lovise, Tobias and Thorvald. In the first row from the left: Laura, Konrad, Julia, Johan and Thomas.

The deed to Konrad from Thomine and Elling Eriksen in the amount of 3734 kr. and an old age contract is dated Nov. 1912. Tax assessment was 1.96 sk.m. One–third of the farm (farm no. 8) was in 1912 deeded out to his brother, August.

11. **Thorvald Austrheim,** 1940 – 1974
Born Oct. 9, 1907, died Oct. 8, 1979, son of previous farmer.

Married on June 24, 1950, to **Emma Ellingsen,** born Aug. 15, 1918, daughter of Julie and Elling Knutsen, tenant farmer no. 21 f., Austrheim.

Children:

a. *Konrad* Johannes, born Aug. 14, 1951, married in 1981 to Ann Helene Ramstad, lives in Frakkagjerd, Fordesfjorden.
b. Elling *Jostein*, born July 11, 1953, next farmer.

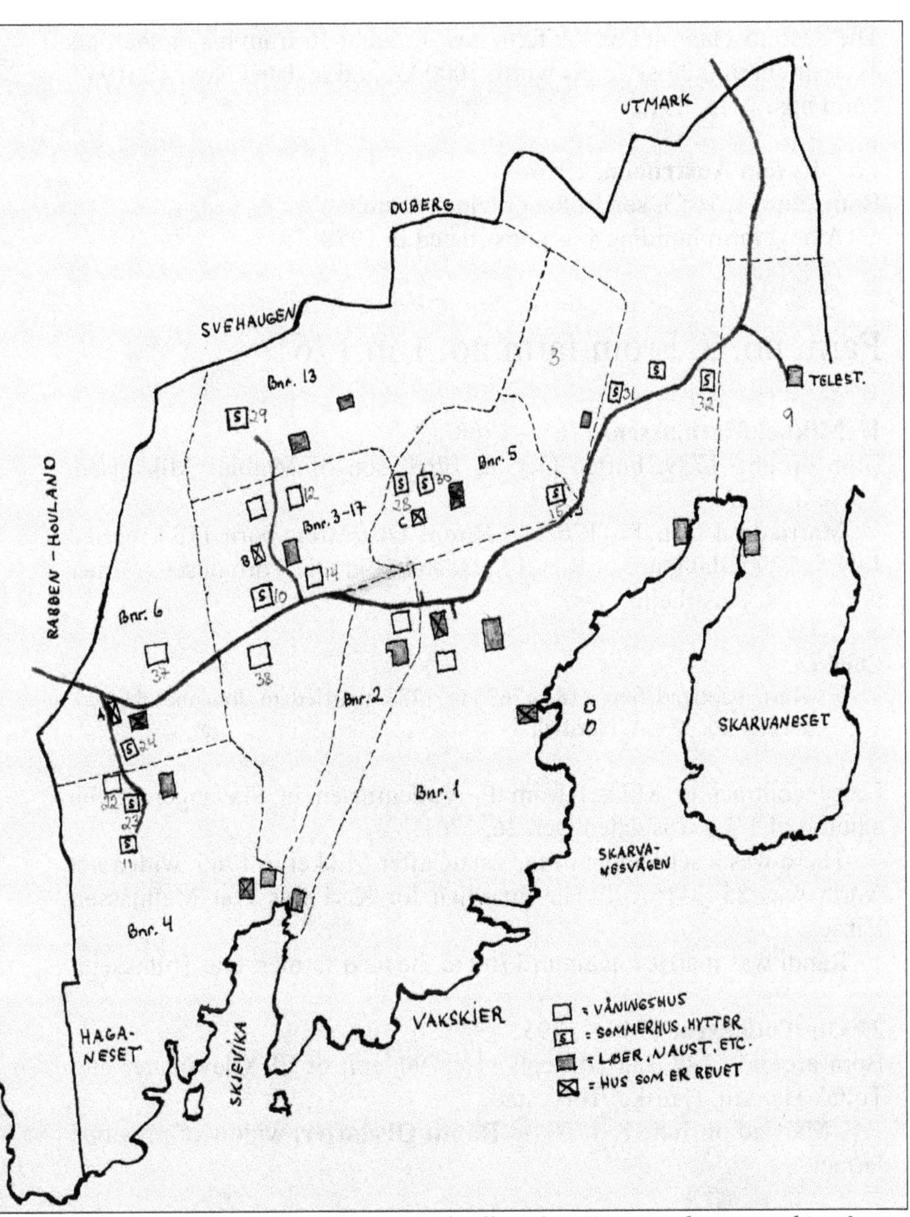

Map of Austrheim. Key: 1 – Main dwelling 2 – Vacation homes, cabins 3 – Hay and misc. storage sheds. 4 –Houses that have been torn down. (Bnr. means farm or farmer.)

The deed to Thorvald on the farm nos. 1, 8 and 16 from his mother, tax assessment of 2.27 sk.m., is worth 7000 kr. and is dated Nov. 12, 1947. Farm nos. 7, 18, 19,

12. **Jostein Austrheim.** 1974—
Born July 11, 1953, son of the previous farmer.
A new farm building was constructed in 1978–79.

Farm no. 2. From farm no. 1 in 1761

1. Mikkel Mathiassen. 1761 – 1768
Born around 1739, buried Oct. 6, 1765, son of Mathias Mikkelsen, Vikse in Skåre.

Married on Oct. 17, 1762, to **Randi Olsdatter,** born 1733, buried July 5, 1795, daughter of Randi Larsdatter and Ole Tormodsen, farmer no. 1 – 4 a, Austrheim.

Children:

a. Kari, baptized Sept. 18, 1763, in 1783 married to Johannes Nilsen, farmer no. 18 – 1, Nordvik.

Lease contract to Mikkel from P. Vallentinsen in Stavanger in the amount of 1/4 v.tf is dated Oct. 26, 1761.

There was a settlement of the estate after Mikkel in 1765, with a net worth was 25–1–15 rdl. The guardian for Kari was Ivar Mathiassen Vikse.

Randi was married again in 1769 to the next farmer, Ole Tollaksen.

2. **Ole Tollaksen.** 1768 – 1795
Born around 1747, buried Sept. 11, 1790, son of Eli Olavsdatter and Tollak Hansen, Hauske, Torvestad.

Married on June 8, 1769, to **Randi Olsdatter,** widow of previous farmer.

Children:

a. Mette, baptized July 1, 1769, buried Sept. 29, 1769.
b. Mette, baptized Oct. 7, 1770, buried Mar. 29, 1772.
c. Mikkel, baptized Dec. 26, 1772, buried Sept. 26, 1784.
d. Eli (Ellis), born in 1777, mentioned in 1795, further information unknown.
e. Ole, baptized Jan. 30, 1780, buried Apr. 6, 1794.

Lease contract to Ole in the amount of 1–1/4 v.tf. is dated Oct. 29, 1768. In July 1795 Randi's estate was registered. From the estate's assets of 51–1–6 rdl., 24–2–18 rdl. was withheld to cover debt and expenses as well as 20 rdl. dowry to the youngest daughter Eli. Among miscellaneous items in the estate were:

> 14 rdl. in cash (income from the year's crop), 1 silver wine carafe 0–2–16, 1 silver ring 0–2–0, 1 iron stove 4–2–0, 1 light–red cow called "Blegrei" 6–2–0, 1 gray heifer 5–2–0, 1 white mare 6–0–0, 1 old boat 3–0–0, 1 old four–oar boat without sail 0–2–0 and 1 large herring fishing net 1–0–16.

3. **Tollef Sjursen.** 1795 – 1829
Baptized Jan. 29, 1771, died Mar. 16, 1851, son of Lisbeth Tollefsdatter and Sjur Knutsen, farmer no. 1 – 8 b, Nordvik.

Married on July 5, 1795, to **Ingeborg Gudmundsdatter,** baptized June 19, 1774, died Jan. 16, 1863, daughter of Valborg Olsdatter and Gudmund Thomassen, farmer no. 3 – 2 b, Austrheim.

Children:

a. Sjur, born in 1796, buried June 26, 1796, 3 months old.
b. Berte, baptized Feb. 27, 1797, married in 1824 to Helge Endresen, Gard in Skåre.
c. Valborg, baptized Dec. 23, 1799, buried Mar. 30, 1800.
d. Elisabet, baptized May 22, 1802, next farmer.
e. Sjur, baptized Nov. 24, 1806, married in 1832 to Berthe Gurine Danielsdatter, tenant farm no. 30, Austrheim.
f. Valborg, baptized July 9, 1809, married in 1835 to Helge Andreas Johnsen, farm no. 1 – 11, Nordvik.
g. Gudmund, baptized Mar. 14, 1812, married in 1838 to Anne Rasmusdatter, farm no. 10 – 1, Hovland.
h. Thomas, baptized May 8, 1814, married in 1839 to Berthe Malene Mikkelsdatter farm no. 18 – 3, Nordvik.

In the lease contract to Tollef in the amount of 1 v. 18 mrk.tf., dated Mar. 23, 1795, there is a notation that Randi due to her age had to relinquish the farm to the bachelor Tollef Sjursen against an old age contract, however, she had already died the same year.

In 1802 he plants 1-1/2 barrels grain and harvests 14 barrels, and feeds 1 horse, 4 cows and 1 calf.

In 1822 the houses on the farm were described as follows:

> 2 old cabins with a kitchen between them under a peat-covered (turf) roof, 1 new storage shed with a logged barn and a main shed covered with turf.

The annual crop is 20 barrels of grain, 10 to 12 barrels of potatoes, and the farm feeds 5 cows, 2 horses and 7 to 8 sheep.

In 1823 the farm was assessed to 170 Spd.

In 1851 the estate was settled again after the death of Tollef Sjursen. Among misc. items the following is mentioned:

> 2 herring fishing nets 2–4–0, 2 pollock fishing nets 1–0–0, 23 lobster pots 3–0–8, 1 shed 1–2–12, 1 4–oar boat 2–2–12, 1 oven 0–2–12, 1 large locker 0–3–0, sermon book 0–4–0, 1 psalm book, 0–2–0, 1 pillow with feathers 0–3–0, 1 rug 0–2–12, 1 blue jacket, trousers and a vest 1–2–12 and 1 leather jacket 0–2–12.

4. **Gresjar Endresen.** 1829 – 1857

Baptized Dec. 3, 1797, died July 23, 1859, son of Endre Andersen, Gronhaug in Skåre.

Married on Aug. 19, 1826, to **Elisabet Tollefsdatter**, baptized May 22, 1802, died Jan. 27, 1851, daughter of previous farmer.

Children:

a. Tollef Johan, born July 29, 1831, next farmer.
b. Endre, born Sept. 11, 1835, married in 1859 to Berta Gurine Jensdatter, lived Osnes, Torvestad.

The deed to Gresjar from J. Dahm, in the amount of 1 v. 18 mrk.tf, for 200 Spd., is dated Sept. 26, 1829.

Old age contract for his in–laws is estimated to be worth 70 Spd for 5 years and consists of the following:

> 4-1/2 barrels of oats in the field, care and good shelter in winter and summer for 1 cow and 4 sheep; a part of the field called Rochen is available for their use; furthermore they will enjoy free housing, including peat fuel for heating and lighting, which they however must harvest themselves as long they are able to.

In 1845 he planted 1/2 barrel of barley, 4 barrels of oats and 1–1/2 barrels potatoes. The livestock consisted of 1 horse, 5 cows, 10 sheep and 1 pig.

5. **Tollef Johan Gresjersen.** 1857 – 1878.

Born July 29, 1831, died Apr. 26, 1872, son of previous farmer.

Married on Sept. 14, 1856, to **Berte Serine Jensdatter,** born Nov. 21, 1837, died July 21, 1914, daughter of Ingeborg Endresdatter and Jens Johnsen, Stava in Skåre.

An old photo of the main dwelling house on farm no. 2, Austrheim. Around 1869. The photographer could be N. Bing, an engineer who worked on the harbor project in 1870. He had his family with him and the two girls with hats in the foreground could be his daughters. The others are probably Serine and Tollef (sitting on the stairs in front of the house) and the children.

Children:

a. Kristian Lauritz, born Feb. 8, 1857, died May 22, 1877.
b. *Severin* Johan, born Aug. 20, 1859, next farmer.
c. Elisabeth *Kristine*, born Dec. 11, 1861, married in 1883 to Lauritz Johan Knutsen Åsen. Emigrated to California in USA.
d. Jens Johan, born Apr. 12, 1864, died Apr. 10, 1866.
e. Jens *Johan*, born Apr. 5, 1866, married in 1896 to Berta Gurine Mathiasdatter Hauge, lived in Haugesund.
f. Berthe Helene, born June 21, 1868, died July 29, 1886.
g. *Tomine* Johanne Bertine Serine, born Apr. 12, 1872, married in 1891 to Svend Magnus Gaard.

Severin Tollefsen (1859–1925).

The deed to Tollef from his father for 700 Spd. is dated Mar. 14, 1857, including old age contract, which for 5 years is estimated to be worth 100 Spd. The three boathouses that he owned, he kept for himself.

In the beginning of the 1860s Tollef built a new main dwelling house on the farm. The old house was sold to Lars Ambjornsen and moved to Aksteberg on farm no. 6.

In 1866 the farm consists of 40 mål fields (about 10 acres) and meadows valued at 319 Spd. There are also pastures for another 106 Spd. and 71 Spd. in income from fishing rights. Annual crops are 22 barrels of oats, 8 barrels of barley, 16 barrels of potatoes and 30 skp. of hay. The entire farm is estimated worth 565 Spd. The livestock consists of 1 horse, 5 cows, 6 sheep and 1 pig.

Tollef was in good shape, in the settlement after him in 1873 the estate is worth in total 1997 Spd. The farm with the house on it and the boat shed in Skjeviken was assessed to 500 Spd. The boathouse in Skarvanesvågen was estimated at 120 Spd., and miscellaneous items, 421 Spd., various amounts owed them, 466 Spd., and 489 Spd. in a savings account.

6. **Severin Tollefsen.** 1878 – 1935
Born Aug. 20, 1859, died Apr. 27, 1925, son of previous farmer.

Married on July 8, 1890, to **Synnøve Mikalsdatter,** born Apr. 22, 1864, died Oct. 20, 1946, daughter of Thala Sofie Pedersdatter and Svend Mikael Larsen, farmer no. 4 – 5 d, Klovning.

Children:

a. Tilli Serine, born May 6, 1892, died May 7, 1892.
b. Tandrup Mikal, born Oct. 3, 1894, died Oct. 12, 1894.
c. *Thoralf* Berner, born Mar. 10, 1897, next farmer.

The proof of ownership of the farm to Severin after the estate settlement of his father, tax liability 2 dl. 9 sk., listing a new tax obligation of 2.91 sk.m., valued at 500 Spd., is dated Jan. 10, 1873. In 1878 he signs an old age contract with his mother for 5 years estimated to be worth 780 kroner:

> 16 v. of oats, 5 v. barley, feed for 1 cow, 4 sheep, and a pasture near the farm called "Nasetraet," including *the use of two eastern rooms below the attic and also the southern part of the attic – including the two small rooms on both sides under the slanting ceiling . . .*

In 1914 he sold part of the estate, farm no. 9, with a tax commitment of 0.40 sk.m., to the Telegraph Authority who the same year started to construct a building for their activities.

7. **Toralf Austrheim** 1922 – 1944.
Born Mar. 10, 1897. died Aug. 23, 1925, son of previous farmer.
Married on Aug. 17, 1919, to **Kristine Hovland,** born Aug. 8, 1894, died July 17, 1948, daughter of Katrine and Elling Mathiassen, farmer no. 2 –2 b, Hovland.

Children:

a. Sigfred *Severin,* born Sept. 27, 1921, next farmer.
b. *Elling* Karsten, born Jan. 1, 1924, married in 1952 to Astrid Ellingsen, farm no. 3 – 9. Austrheim.

Thoralf, together with Mikal and Elling Ellingsen, built in 1918–19 a motor fishing boat called "Utsire" (later named "Utholm") which they later for some years put in service between Utsira and Haugesund.

The farm was divided in 1942, farm no. 17, with a tax responsibility of 1.25, and one part was turned over to Elling Austrheim.

8. **Severin Austrheim,** 1944 – 1989.
Born Sept. 27, 1921, son of previous farmer.
Married on Nov. 4, 1949, to **Ellen Ellingsen,** born Mar. 15, 1931, died Dec. 17, 1990, daughter of Inga and Mikal Ellingsen, farm no. 3 – 8 e, Austrheim.

Children:

a. Tor Kare, born Oct. 16, 1951, married in 1976 to Anne Jorun Fjelland on Halsnoy in Kvinnherad, lives in Kopervik.
b. Unbaptized boy, born Nov. 30, 1955, died Dec. 14, 1955

c. Svein Inge, born Aug. 19, 1957, married in 1987 to Wenche Klovning, lives in Fordesfjorden.
d. Solvi, born Mar. 30, 1959, married in 1988 to Kelvin Davies, lives in Bristol, England.

The deed to Severin from Synnøve on this farm with a tax assessement of 1.26, is dated June 10, 1944. Half of the farm, farm no. 17, is then split out to his brother, Elling.

The livestock consisted in 1956 of 2 cows, 1 calf and 10 sheep.

The farm is later utilized as a supplementary farm.

Farm no. 3. Leito. From farm no. 4 in 1744

1. Ole Reiersen. 1744 – 1772
Born around 1720, died on Nov. 5, 1766, son of Gudhild Olsdatter and Reier Ommundsen, tenant farmer no. 13 a, Hovland.

Married in first marriage around 1743 to **Valborg Knutsdatter,** born around 1722, died around 1751, daughter of Gjoa Ellingsdatter and Knut Olsen, farmer no. 4 – 5 d, Austrheim.

Married in second marriage on Jan. 6, 1754, to **Berthe Hansdatter,** born in 1714, buried on Mar. 29, 1795, daughter of Asseline Hansdatter and Hans Rasmussen, Landanes in Avaldsnes.

Children in first marriage:

a. Berte, born 1743, buried on Mar. 22, 1767, there is an estate settlement after her in March 1767. She was a maidservant on the farm Vikse in Skåre, her assets were 18–0–21 rdl.
b. Gjoa, born 1747, married in 1768 to Anders Knutsen, tenant farmer no. 9. Austrheim.
c. Ole born in 1749, married in 1775 to Malene Oddsdatter, tenant farmer no. 14, Kvalvik.

Children in second marriage:

d. Valborg, baptized Feb. 3, 1756, next farmer.

Lease contract to Ole in the amount of 1 v.tf. is dated Mar. 27, 1744.

According to local records, at Easter 1740, Valborg had to report to the minister at the church to answer to rumors on the island that she had lied about giving birth to a child. She has to appear in court and she receives the death penalty. However, as was customary in such cases, she was pardoned. The King's pardon was dated in Copenhagen, Dec. 15, 1741. She was jailed for 743 days, from May 10, 1740 until

A group of youths at Austrheim in 1947. In front from left: Tobias Austrheim, Ellen Austrheim, Kristine Haugseth and Johan Austrheim. In the back from left: Knut Ellingsen, Astrid Austrheim, Johannes Nilsen, Rasmus Ellingsen and Thomas Austrheim.

May 22, 1742. The father of the child, Ole Reiersen, was sentenced to either a fine of 12 rdl. or corporal punishment. It is assumed that he received the last option, as he did not own more than the clothes he wore.

In 1767 there was an estate settlement after Ole. Among items in the estate, estimated worth 114–3–8 rdl,, the following is listed:

> Cash 38–3–0, 1 four–oar boat with sail 2–2–0, 1 four–oar boat without sail 1–3–0, 4 spring herring fishing nets 2–3–0, 19 lobster pots 1–2–14, 1 shed 5–0–0, 2 v. dried fish 1–1–18, 1 cast iron stove 6–0–0, 4 barrels of seed (grain) 4–0–0, 3 containers (ea. approx. 10 gallons) with beer 0–1–16, 1 half–barrel (approx. 15–1/2 gal.) beer 0–1–8, 1 white mare 3–2–0, 1 brown mare 1–2–0, 5 cows 18–0–0, 10 sheep 3–1–8, 1 embroidered vest with 8 silver buttons 1–0–0 and 1 blue waistcoat with 18 silver buttons 2–2–0.

2. **Gudmund Thomassen.** 1772 – 1814.
Baptized Oct. 31, 1755, died June 2, 1832, son of Ingeborg Larsdatter and Thomas
Johannesen, farmer no. 1 – 4 b, Skare

Married in 1st marriage on Mar. 9, 1773, to **Valborg Olsdatter,** baptized Feb. 3, 1756, buried July 1, 1787, daughter of previous farmer.

Married in 2nd marriage Feb. 8, 1789, to **Berta Ambjornsdatter,** baptized July 2, 1768, died Jan. 5, 1823, daughter of Anna Johannesdatter and Ambjorn Rasmussen, farm no. 7 – 5 f, Hovland.

Children in 1st marriage:

a. Ole, baptized Mar. 25, 1773, buried June 27, 1773.
b. Ingeborg, baptized June 19, 1774, married in 1795 to Tollef Sjursen, farm no. 2 – 3, Austrheim.
c. Berte, baptized Jan. 22, 1777, married in 1801 to Knut Sjursen, farm no. 5 – 4, Austrheim.
d. Marta, baptized Sept. 5, 1779, buried Apr. 2, 1780.
e. Ole, baptized Aug. 26, 1780, buried Sept. 24, 1780.
f. Thomas, baptized Sept. 30, 1781, became a seaman. In 1834 he lives at Skippergaten 77, Fredrikshavn, Denmark. He is then a fisherman and his wife is Maren Larsdatter, born in 1803.
g. Ole, baptized Apr. 24, 1784, married in 1810 to Gjoa Andersdatter, farm no. 1 – 9, Hovland.

Children 2nd marriage:

h. Valborg, baptized Apr. 18, 1790, buried June 26, 1796.
i. Ambjorn, baptized Jan. 21, 1792, farmer no. 4 here.
j. Gudmund, baptized Nov. 2, 1793, next farmer.
k. Johannes, baptized Apr. 25, 1797, married in 1824 to Anne Marthe Johannesdatter, farm no. 22 – 1, Nordvik.
l. Lars, baptized June 30, 1799, married in 1819 to Ella Eline Knutsdatter, lived on Feoy, later tenant farmer no. 52, Skare.
m. Valborg, baptized Feb. 10, 1802, married in 1824 to Jørgen Johnsen, farm no. 1 – 8, Klovning.
n. Tollef, baptized Apr. 15, 1804, married in 1830 to Marta Serine Johannesdatter, tenant farm no. 12, Skare.
o. Elling, baptized Jan. 8, 1807, married in 1830 to Ragna Serine Johnsdatter, farm no. 12 – 1, Nordvik.
p. Anne Marte, baptized Apr. 23, 1809, buried June 29, 1816.
q. Rasmus, baptized Oct. 16, 1814, married in 1836 to Guri Johannesdatter, farm no. 2 –5, Skare.

Lease contract to Gudmund in the amount of 1 v.tf. is issued by A. W. Bredahl in Stavanger on Oct. 28, 1772.

In 1802 2 1/2 barrels of seed was planted which yielded 14 barrels of grain. The livestock consisted of 1 horse, 4 cows and 1 calf. The farm was assessed to 130 rdl.

There was a settlement after Valborg in 1787, the estate was then estimated to 86–3–22 rdl. When expenses and debt were settled, there was 26 rdl. left for the heirs. The following items were also left:

> 1 shed near *Schare Soen* (South Skare) 2–0–0, 1 small shed 2–0–0, 1 six–oar boat with sail and misc. equipment 5–0–0, 24 lobster pots 2–0–0, 2 four–oar boats 2–0–0, 5 spring herring fishing nets 2–3–8, 1 small fishing net 3–0–0, 1 black horse 2–0–0, 1 black mare, 14 years old 2–2–0, 4 cows (Skionrey, Hiertrey, Rødsia and Knoprey) and 1 calf 20–2–22, 1 60–liter cattle trough 2–2–0, 1 outside mill in mill house with associated equipment 4–0–0, 6 barrels of oats 9–0–0, 1 small stove 5– 2–0, 1 blue striped feather–filled pillow 1–0–0, 1 green, gathered Bayes–skirt 0–1–2, 1 wool waistcoat with red sleeves and 17 silver buttons 1–0–4, 1 book called *Brochmann's Book of Sermons* 1–0–0, 1 silver spoon with a twisted shaft 1–0–8, 1 silver spoon with the initial "W" 1–0–0, 1 silver spoon engraved with the initials G.T.S. 0–3–8, and 1 silver cord (for decorating uniforms) with needle 1–0–0.

In 1814 he turns the farm over to his son, Gudmund, on the conditions that he can continue to run half the farm, and that he have after that an arrangement that he will have:

> . . . an area that yields 6 barrels of oats and a field called "East Kringla" for growing potatoes and feed for 2 cows and 6 sheep.

There was also an estate settlement after Gudmund. He left some miscellaneous items valued at 42–3–12 Spd., a cottage without kitchen, roofed with peat, 16 Spd., and various people owed him 50–3–6 Spd.

3. **Gudmund Gudmundsen.** 1814 – 1829
Baptized Nov. 2, 1793, died Apr. 30, 1828, son of previous farmer.

Married in 1815 to **Tyri Johannesdatter,** baptized July 6, 1788, daughter of Åsa Johannesdatter and Johannes Johannesen, south Eikje in Avaldsnes.

Children:

a. Anne Marte, baptized June 20, 1817, buried Dec. 2, 1817.
b. Johannes, born Mar. 30, 1820, died June 10, 1841, drowned near Feoy.

Lease contract to Gudmund in the amount 1 v.tf is issued by H. B. Forman on Oct. 25, 1814, on the same conditions outlined under the previous farmer.

In 1822 the houses on the farm were described as follows:

> 1 cottage covered with turf, 1 logged barn and shed under roof covered with turf. These buildings are in usable condition. Half of a mill also belongs to this farm.

Annual crop is 24 barrels of grain and 10 to 12 barrels of potatoes, the farm can feed 6 cows, 1 calf, 1 horse and 10 – 12 sheep. The farm was in 1823 assessed to 150 Spd., and included in the farm is an abandoned settlement.

In 1828 there was an estate settlement after Gudmund. Among the estate's assets valued at 79–3–6 Spd., the following items are mentioned:

> Cash (receipts for sale of 3 cows) 23–0–0, 1 pale–colored mare 12–0–0, 1 cattle trough 5–2–12, 1 baking board 0–4–0, 1 iron–built scale 1–0–0, 1 small turf–covered cottage 4–0–0, 1 small smokehouse 2–0–0, 1 pair of weaving tools 3–0–0, 1 steel weaving tool 0–4–0 and 1 empty Swedish tar barrel 0–1–12.

Tyri got married on Nov. 5, 1829 to widower Hans Knut Olsen, lower Hauge in Torvestad.

4. **Ambjorn Gudmundsen.** 1829 – 1834
Baptized Jan. 21, 1792, died Jan. 16, 1834, brother of previous farmer.

Married on Apr. 13, 1823, to **Anne Marte Larsdatter,** baptized Jan. 22, 1805, died Jan. 15, 1873, daughter of Martha Elisabeth Gautsdatter and Lars Hansen, farm no. 17 – 3 a, Nordvik.

Children:

a. Berta Karine, born July 2, 1824, died Feb. 2, 1825.
b. Gudmund, born Nov. 30, 1826, farmer no. 6 here.
c. Lars, born Mar. 15, 1829, married in 1860 to I. Karine Jensdatter, tenant farm no. 12, Austrheim,
d. Berta Gurine, born Dec. 28, 1831, married in 1862 to Tollef Johan Tollefsen, tenant farmer no. 13, Skare.
e. Anbjor Eline, born Feb. 21, 1834, married in 1866 to widower Sjur Knutsen, tenant farmer no. 26, Hovland.

The deed to Ambjorn from J. Dahm in the amount of 200 Spd. is dated June 1, 1829, and the old age contract with Tyri, until she possibly got married to a farmer,
consisted of 1 barrel of oats, feed for 1 cow and 3 sheep. This contract covering 5 years was worth 50 Spd.

Ambjorn was the tenant farmer on farm no. 2, Skare (Myre), from 1822 until he took over the farm here on Austrheim after his brother. To the old age contract to Tyri, *Mr. J. Dahm on Utsire out of the goodness in his heart contributes as long as her father–in–law Gudmund Thomassen lives, one barrel of oats.*

In the estate settlement after Ambjorn in 1834 the farm is assessed to 200 Spd., and there are a few misc. items worth 92–2–20 Spd. that are divided among the heirs. Among others the following items are listed:

> 2 cows and 1 heifer (Brunrei and Salrei) 15–0–0, 1 white–spotted horse, 28 years old 3–0–0, 1 white horse, 26 years old 2–0–0, 1 kettle 3–0–0, 1/2 outside mill with housing and accessories 6–0–0, 1 old stove 4–0–0, 1 old boat shed covered with slabs 2–2–12, 1 new 4–oar sailboat with fittings 3–0–0, 1 old 4–oar sailboat 2–0–0, 1/2 of new 4–oar boat w/out sails and equipment 5–0–0, 3 spring herring fishing nets 1–3–0, 18 lobster pots 0–4–12, 1 blue–striped feather-filled comforter, bedspread and pillow 5–2–14, 1 locker with lock and nameplate engraved "A.G.S.O 1816" 1–2–12, and a pair of silver pins 1–0–0.

Anne Marte got married a second time in 1835 to Sjur Jørgensen, next farmer.

5. **Sjur Jørgensen** 1835 – 1854.
Baptized Dec. 8, 1793, died Feb. 4, 1847, son of Jørgen Stole in Skåre.

Married on Sept. 29, 1835, to. **Anne Marte Larsdatter** widow of previous farmer.

Children:

a. Marthe Elisabeth, born July 27, 1837, married in 1861 to Gudmund Johan Rasmussen, tenant farmer no. 11, Austrheim.
b. Jørgen Johan, born May 4, 1840, emigrated to USA.
c. Hans Mathias, born Jan. 20, 1844, married in 1882 to Severine Halvorsdatter, farm no. 4 – 11, Austrheim.

Sjur's children with Malene Bentsdatter, Nordvik:

d. Margrethe Elisabet, born Sept. 13, 1819, married in 1850 to Johannes Johannesen, Osthus in Åkra.

The probate deed for Anne Marte on this farm is assessed to 200 Spd. and is dated Sept. 6, 1834

The farm in 1845 planted 1/2 barrel of barley, 4 barrels of oats and 1/2 barrel of potatoes. The livestock consist of 1 horse, 5 cows, 6 sheep and 1 pig.

In the estate settlement after Sjur in 1848 there were miscellaneous items for a total value of 119–0–20 Spd., among which were:

> 1 cow "Malik" 9–0–0, 1 cow "Plomrei" 8–0–0. 1 cow "Nølrei" 7–2–12, 1 cow "Skjenrei" 6–0–0, 1 red mare 10–0–0, 1/2 mill 3–2–12, 1 stove 3–0–0, 1 four–oar boat 4–0–0, part owner in seiner 21–0–0, 36 lobster pots 3–3–0.

6. **Gudmund Ambjornsen**. 1854 – 1885
Born Nov. 30, 1826, died Dec. 31, 1884, son of farmer no. 4 here.

Married on Mar. 27, 1854 to **Berthe Malene Ellingsdatter,** born Jan. 30, 1833, died Oct. 17, 1916, daughter of Ragna Serine Johnsdatter and Elling Gudmundsen, farm no. 12 – 1 b. Nordvik.

Children:

a. Anbjorn *Bertel,* born Sept. 26, 1854, married in 1889 to Ida Josefine Trulsdatter, farm no.13 – 7, Nordvik.
b. Berthe Serine, born Aug. 6, 1856, died Jan. 2, 1861.
c. Anna Martha, born and died Feb. 26, 1859.
d. *Elling* Severin, born Aug. 20, 1860, next farmer.
e. *Anton* Martin, born Feb. 17, 1863, died June 16, 1895.
f. Berthe Serine, born Jan. 26, 1865, died Aug. 3, 1880.
g. Gurine Amalie, born Nov. 1, 1870, married in 1894 to Rasmus Johan Jobsen, farmer no. 7 – 10, Hovland.

The deed to Gudmund on the settlement after Sjur Jørgensen is dated Sept. 7, 1848 in the amount of 200 Spd. In 1854 he took over the farm against an old age pension contract. Gudmund's contract with his mother included the following: 3 barrels of oats, 1 cord of peat, 1/2 cord of birch wood, 1 can of cod liver oil, feed for 1 cow and 3 sheep, free use of 2 fields – "Skudeflekket" and "Lille–Storetrae," the cultivated field "Storehaugen," and free unlimited use of the northern living room. This contract was estimated at 75 Spd.

In 1866 the 43 mål fields and meadows were estimated to be worth 340 Spd. There were pastures for 72 Spd. and fishing rights income for 32 Spd.

Annual yield is 24 barrels of oats, 8 barrels of barley, 18 barrels of potatoes and 30 skp. hay. The entire farm was estimated to be worth 520 Spd.

Clipping from Haugesund Avis newspaper, Nov. 19, 1927. (next page)

When the Grain Security Law shall be put into Real Life at Utsira.

The Farmers Party's big action item – and the farmer's "life raft" – The Grain Treaty, surely secured many votes at the election this fall – aside from the arguments concerning the law regarding debt write–offs. Both large and small farmers are now mobilizing and maneuvering to be in their best possible position to enjoy benefits from government subsidies for what they eat of grain in the form of flour. More and more districts are so fortunate to have farms that have access to mills, and many actually have their own mills. And now it is important to get the milling industry into full operation. On Karmøy we have Fiskaa Mill, where according to reliable sources, I have been informed runs night and day and 2 additional people have been hired – the unemployment situation in Avaldsnes has thus been significantly improved thanks to the Grain Treaty. The situation is not as good on Utsira. Here, not even one mill is in operation. For the Sira farmer the transportation of the grain to the mill is both cumbersome and comparatively expensive.

In all communal and business–related questions concerning Sira, I always consult with my old friend, Bertel Gudmundsen Leite. He always gives me straight forward and sincere advice. When I visited Sira a couple of days ago, I asked Bertel, who owns a good size farm in Nordvaagen, how he liked "The Grain Treaty"?

He replied (in dialect): "Yes, now I will tell you about a miracle. First, I have to tell you that 11 farmers on Sira have bought a thrashing machine driven with a gasoline engine. It then occurred to me that we must also be able to run the mill with such an engine, since the transportation of the grain to the mill is so prohibitively expensive. We did not, however, have drying facilities, but we did get the gasoline engine hooked up to the mill and were able grind the grain. However, we milled and we milled..... the entire day and filled the fuel tank by the buckets and after a day's work we finally produced a half a sack of flour. This had cost us 12 kr. to do, with 8 kr. for only the fuel. I have calculated – and correct me if I am wrong – that if each farmer on Sira had a gasoline engine for his thrashing machine and he thrashed flour for his own consumption and received a (grain) subsidy, there would have to be 13 months in the year to break even. Yes, there are many funny things the Big Shots in the Government invent sometimes. I don't believe the Sira–ites will benefit any more from the new Grain Law than they benefited from the so–called 'Dutch Inheritance' – you remember last year you calculated that 2 million kr. would be paid to us on Sira from this inheritance.... No, Sir...." — Bertel is shaking his head. He is probably right in both cases.

I have spoken.
- Ola Nordmann.

Elling Gudmundsen (1860 – 1942) and Astrid Mikalsdatter (1870 – 1950).

The livestock consisted of 1 horse, 4 cows, 10 sheep and 1 pig.

7. **Elling Gudmundsen.** 1885 – 1930.
Born Aug. 20, 1860, died Jan. 29, 1942, son of previous farmer.

Married on Apr. 6, 1891, to **Astrid Mikalsdatter,** born Jan. 20, 1870, died Oct. 10, 1950, daughter of Thala Sophie and Svend Mikael Larsen, farmer no. 4 – 5 g, Klovning.

Children:

a. *Gunda* Marie Sigfryda, born Jan. 19, 1894, married in 1916 to Petter Haugseth, farmer no. 13–1, Austrheim.
b. Svend *Mikal* Trygve, born Mar. 14, 1895, next farmer.

c. Laura *Lovise,* born Dec. 21 1896, married in 1922 to Thomas Rasmussen, farmer no. 12 – 6, Nordvik.
d. Amanda *Martine,* born Apr. 18, 1899, married in 1st marriage to Rønning, lived in Haugesund.
e. *Elling* Severin Alexander, born Jan. 1, 1902. married to Bergliot Johannsen, tenant farm no. 26, Austrheim.
f. Olav *Hjalmar,* born Jan. 16, 1906, married in 1931 to Elisabeth Skåren, tenant farm no. 25, Austrheim.
g. Alv Bernard, born Mar. 21, 1908, died June 7, 1908.

The deed to Elling from his mother on this farm lists a tax assessement of 2.69 sk.m., for 2000 kr. and an old age contract dated Apr. 15, 1885.

In 1934 half of farm no. 13 was taken over by Petter Haugseth.

Mikal Ellingsen (1895 – 1962) in uniform about 1920

8. **Mikal Ellingsen.** 1930 – 1956

Born Mar. 14, 1895, died Dec. 25, 1962, son of previous farmer.

Married on May 16, 1920, to **Inga Serine Rasmusdatter,** born July 30, 1897, died Dec. 11, 1973, daughter of Berthe Gurine and Rasmus Thomassen, farmer no. 12–5 i, Nordvik.

Children:

a. *Astrid* Ella, born Sept. 25, 1921. next farmer.
b. *Rasmus* Bernhard, born June 11, 1923, took over the estate here in 1972.
c. *Borghild* Gurine, born Feb. 18, 1926, married to Erling Hellesø, lives in Laksevåg near Bergen.

d. Solveig, born Sept. 15, 1929, lives in Oslo.
e. Ellen, born Mar. 15, 1931, married in 1949 to Severin Austrheim, farmer no. 2 – 8, Austrheim.
f. *Trygg* Sverre, born July 16, 1938, married to Solbjorg Gjertsen, lives in Algard.

The deed to Mikal with a tax assessment of 1.30 sk.m. is dated Apr. 18, 1941.

The old main dwelling was in 1934 taken out of the estate and became farm no. 12, Fjellhaug, and taken over by Hjalmar Ellingsen. Inga and Mikal built themselves a new house here, farm no. 14, Nedrebo, in 1935.

Mikal together with his cousin Thoralf and his brother Elling built themselves a motorized fishing smack in 1918–19 named "Utsire" (later renamed "Utholm") which they put in service between Utsira and Haugesund.

Mikal and Rasmus bought "Sirahav" in 1955 to carry freight, in the first few years, to Iceland. They sold it in 1963.

9. **Elling Austrheim.** 1956 – 1989
Born Jan. 1, 1924, son of Kristine and Thoralf Austrheim, farmer no. 2 – 7 b, Austrheim.

Married on Sept. 13, 1952, to **Astrid Ellingsen,** born Sept. 25, 1921, daughter of the previous farmer.

Children:
a. *Magne* Ingolf, born Mar. 26, 1955.
b. *Toralf* Kristian, born Apr. 29, 1957, married in 1979 to Irene Klovning, tenant farmer No. 35, Klovning.
c. *Anny* Elise, born Feb. 14, 1959, no. 10 b, below.
d. Bjarne, born June 27, 1961, next farmer.
e. Jan, born Nov. 15, 1966, died Jan. 29, 1985.

Elling farmed, in addition to his own farm here, farm no. 17, with a tax assessment of 17 sk.m., which was taken out of farm no. 2 in 1942. The livestock at the farm in 1956 consisted of 3 cows, 4 calves, 1 horse, 2 pigs and 15 sheep. In 1957 they built a new main dwelling on the farm. A new barn was built in 1982.

Photo of Utsira ferry and schedules, from Haugesund Avis, July 1922.

Haugesund Motorship Company:
To Sonhordaland.
Tuesday 12:00 noon
Thursday 2 p.m.
to Tysvaer and Skjold.
Wednesday 4:30 p.m.
Saturday 2:00 p.m.
To Askrehavn and Utsire:
Tuesday 12:00 noon
Friday 2:00 p.m.
To Faeo, Rovaer and Utsire:
Wednesday 5:00 p.m.
Saturday 5:00 p.m.
To Kopervik and Stavanger:
Monday 7:00 a.m.
Thursday 7 a.m.
D. Stakland.

Motor Ferry "Utsire"
To Utsire:
Every Thursday and Saturday at 4 p.m.
From Utsire to Haugesund:
Every Thursday and Saturday at 8 a.m.
Tickets: Birger Pedersen & Son

10 a. **Bjarne Austrheim.** 1989 –
Born June 27, 1961, son of previous farmer.

Married on Jan. 10, 1987, to **Gunn Hilde Haugland,** born Aug. 29, 1962, daughter of Reidun and Oystein Haugland, tenant farmer no. 76 b, Nordvik.

Children:
a. Christine, born June 27, 1987
b. Håkon, born Jan. 28, 1989
c. Oystein, born Sept. 24, 1990.

Bjarne and Gunn Hilde took over the farm here in 1992, Bjarne works offshore, Gunn Hilde is a nurse. They built a main dwelling here, farm No. 37, "Utsikten," in 1889.

10 b. **Sigbjorn Hoiland.** 1989 –
Born Nov. 15, 1960, came from Stavanger.
Married to **Anny Austrheim,** born Feb. 14, 1959, daughter of farmer No. 9.

Children:
a. Jan Kristoffer, born Apr. 14, 1989
b. Viktoria, born Nov. 8, 1992.

Anny is the post office clerk, and they built a main dwelling here in 1989, farm no. 38, Hoiland.

Farm No. 4

1. **Sjur Andersen**. 1655 – 1690
Born around 1628, of unknown origin.
Sjur's wife in 1681 is known as **Guri Olsdatter**. They were cited in court that year for giving birth to a child before they were properly married, but did not have to pay the fine since Utsira was then under the jurisdiction of Sunn–Hordaland.
We do not know any names of children.
According to court records, Sjur was cited in court several times. In 1663 he cut Hans Hovland on the head with a knife in church during a funeral for the daughter of Jens Nordvik. He explained it was not done on purpose, as he was only trying to cut some chewing tobacco and the knife slipped in his hand. He was sentenced to pay for a wax candle in the church, valued at 1/2 rdl., and to the cloister he had to provide 1 våger of good quality dried fish.
See also Simon Torkelsen, farm No. 4, Hovland.
Sjur farmed half of Austrheim, 2 1/2 v.tf.

2. **Thomas Thomassen.**1690 – 1702

Born around 1656, son of Kirsten Andersdatter and Thomas Osnes, Torvestad.

Apparently married to the widow of the previous farmer.

In 1706 Thomas is listed as a tenant on Feoy.

3. **Soren Hansen.** 1702 – 1706

Died in 1703, from "Nordlandene."

Possibly married to (name unknown), daughter of farmer no. 1 here, Sjur Andersen.

Soren had 2 sons from a previous marriage:

a. Soren, born in 1696, further history unknown.

b. Hans, born in 1697, further history unknown.

In 1703, Soren's widow is listed as manager of the farm, 2 v.tf. Her financial condition is listed as "poor and miserable," but the houses on the farm are in good condition, only 3 ort in upkeep expenses.

She planted 3 barrels of oats and fed 6 cows, 2 calves, 1 horse and some sheep. She owns all the animals, but has a large debt. To the cloister leader, J. Frimand, she owes 7 rdl., 2 v. 1 lb. clip fish for Soren's first lease in 1702. She also owes others as much as 35 rdl.

4. **Lars Jakobsen.** 1706 – 1708

Born around 1683 in Aske County.

Married in 1706 to (name unknown), widow of last farmer.

No known children.

During 1704 – 1706, Lars was paid 8 rdl. to install a new roof on the church. He is also part of the group who assisted in saving the *Arendal* ship that nearly perished in a storm off Utsira.

5. **Knut Olsen.** 1708 – 1760

Born in 1688, buried on Oct. 12, 1760, son of Ingeborg Olsdatter and Ole Hansen, farm no. 1 – 2 a, Austrheim.

Possibly married in first marriage in 1708 to (name unknown), widow of previous farmer.

Married in second marriage to **Gjoa Ellingsdatter,** who died around 1745, possibly the daughter of Elling Hansen, farmer no. 2—1, Kvalvik.

Married in third marriage to **Anna Andersdatter,** born around 1708, buried on Sept. 30, 1781, of unknown origin.

Children in first marriage (a and c not confirmed):

a. Ole, born around 1709, married around 1732 to the widow Anna Eriksdatter, farm no. 6 – 2, Austrheim.
b. Berta, born around 1714, married to Johannes Pettersen Osnes, Torvestad (son of Petter Olsen, Skare).[35]
c. Bår, born in 1716, married around 1742 to the widow Karen Andersdatter, farm no. 1 – 7, Nordvik.

Children in second marriage:
d. Valborg, born around 1722, married to Ole Reiersen, farm no. 3 – 1, Austrheim.

Knut leased the property in 1708. He renewed the lease for 1 v.tf. on Dec. 23, 1720, and for 1/2 v.tf. on May 15, 1724.

In 1712, his financial condition is described as "poor." Maintenance expenses on his houses is assessed at 3 ort. He grows 1–1/2 barrels of oats and feeds 4 cows, 1 calf, 1 horse and some sheep. Of these he personally owns only 1 cow and 1 calf. He owes Frimand 4 rdl. for the lease in 1708, and to others 1 rdl.

In 1721, he is in better condition, and all the houses are in good shape without any assessed maintenance costs, and he does not owe anything to anybody.

In 1723, he plants 1 1/2 barrels and harvests 8 barrels of grain. The livestock consists of 4 cows.

In 1744, he relinquishes 2/3 of the farm, 1 v.tf. to his son–in–law, Ole Reiersen, farmer no. 3.

6. **Svend Mathiassen.** 1761 – 1764
Born in 1742, buried on Mar. 24, 1763, son of Mathias Mikkelsen, Vikse in Skåre.

Married on July 5, 1761, to **Anna Ellingsdatter,** born 1741, buried Mar. 12, 1769, daughter of Berta Ellingsdatter and Elling Knutsen, farmer no. 2 – 2 b, Kvalvik.

Children:
a. Mathias, born 1762, buried on June 9, 1771.

Lease contract to Svend on 1/2 v.tf. is dated Mar. 30, 1761.

Anne was married in second marriage to Ole Bardsen, next farmer.

7. **Ole Bårdsen.** 1764 – 1809

[35] See Note 12.

From the spring herring fisheries outside Haugesund in 1900. Photo by: K. Knudsen. University Library in Bergen.

Born around 1741, died on Nov. 27, 1800, son of Ingeborg Rasmusdatter and Bard Olsen, N. Våge in Sveio.

Married in first marriage on Oct. 7, 1764, to **Anne Ellingsdatter,** widow of previous farmer.

Married in second marriage on Sept. 27, 1769 to **Kari Villumsdatter,** born around 1749, buried on Apr. 14, 1810, daughter of Eli Knutsdatter and Villum Knutsen, Osnes.

Children in first marriage:

a. Svend, baptized on June 8, 1766, buried on Oct. 8, 1785.

Children in 2nd marriage:

b. Anna, baptized Dec. 22, 1771, next farmer.
c. Eli, baptized Nov. 2, 1775, also the next farmer.
d. Bård, baptized Mar. 25, 1778, buried Mar. 25, 1779.
e. Ingeborg, baptized May 19, 1781, married in 1808 to Elias Olsen Skeie.
f. Kari Olina, baptized Nov. 19, 1786, buried Mar. 28, 1787.

Lease contract to Ole on 1/2 v.tf. is dated Feb. 3, 1764.

In the settlement after Anne's death in 1769, the estate is worth 27–3–22 rdl. but expenses and debt represent an equal amount, so there is nothing left for the heirs. The following misc. items are mentioned:

> 1 white, horned cow 3–0–0.1, 1 bluish cow 5–0–0, 1 red mare 3–0–0, 2 rams 1–0–0, 1 kettle 1–1–8, 1 locker with lock 0–3–0, 1 four–oar boat with sail 2–2–0, 1/10 part in 8–oar boat with sail 2–0–0 and 1 spring herring fishing net 0–2–0.

Servants on the farm are at that time Eli Villumsdatter and Kirsten Bårdsen.

In 1802 there is 1–1/2 barrels of grain sown, which yields 8 barrels. The livestock consists of 1 horse, 2 cows and 2 sheep. The farm was then valued at 60 rdl.

There is also an estate settlement after Ole's death in 1801, and approx. 8 rdl. is left for the heirs out of the estate's estimated worth of 28–3–8 rdl.

8. **Jakob Torbjornsen.** 1809 – 1829
Baptized Apr. 17, 1773, died Jan. 1, 1848, son of Malene Halvorsdatter and Torbjorn Monsen, tenant farmer no. 10 a, Skare.

Married in 1st marriage on Oct. 4, 1801, to **Anna Olsdatter,** baptized Dec. 22, 1771, died Apr. 6, 1815, daughter of previous farmer.

Married in 2nd marriage on Apr. 13, 1818, to **Eli Olsdatter**, baptized on Nov. 2, 1775, died Nov. 16, 1846, daughter of previous farmer.

Children 1st. marriage:

a. Kari Oline, baptized July 4, 1802, next farmer.
b. Torbjorn, baptized May 19, 1805, buried June 29, 1816.
c. Anne Malene, baptized Sept. 29, 1810, next farmer.
d. Ole, baptized Apr. 4, 1813, married in 1840 to Oline Eliasdatter, Vikene. They were unregistered farmers at Uratre near Kalstø, Avaldsnes.

Children in 2nd marriage:

e. Anne Marte, born Sept. 23, 1819, died Mar. 16, 1826.

Lease contract to Jacob on 1/2 v.tf is issued by the assessor Forman on Mar. 16, 1809, against 25 rdl. in lease money and an old age contract to his in–laws consisting of free rent, light and heating, 2 barrels of grain and feed for 1 cow.

In 1822 the houses on the farm are described as follows:

> One old cottage with kitchen and covered with peat. One newly built storage house with an attached lean–to also covered with peat. Half of a mill house also belongs to this farm.

Annual crop was 12 – 14 barrels of grain and 2 – 3 barrels of potatoes. The livestock consists of 2 cows, 1 calf, 1 horse and 4 – 6 sheep.

The entire farm was in 1823 estimated to 60 Spd.

In the estate settlement after Anna's death in 1815 the following items were presented (amounts in rbdl. – *riksbankdaler*):

> 1 10–year old mare 50–0–0, 1 cow "Dyrej" 50–0–0, 1 cow "Mautrej" 15 years old 40–0–0, 1 four–oar boat without sail 10–0–0, 1 iron stove 25–0–0, 1 spinning wheel 6–0–0.

9. **Daniel Johannesen.** 1829 – 1868
Baptized on Jan. 18, 1795, died Apr. 7, 1868, son of Kari Mikkelsdatter and Johannes Nilsen, farm no. 18– 1 g, Nordvik.

Married in 1st marriage on Sept. 16, 1826 to **Kari Oline Jakobsdatter,** baptized July 4, 1802, died Aug. 31, 1846, daughter of previous farmer.

Married in 2nd marriage on July 1, 1849, to **Anne Malene Jakobsdatter,** baptized Sept. 29, 1810, died July 30, 1879, daughter of previous farmer.

Children in 1st marriage:

a. Anne Marte, born Mar. 2, 1827, married in 1854 to Lars Thorbjornsen, Kvalavåg, Avaldsnes.
b. Johannes, born Nov. 10, 1828, in 1865 it is recorded that he is unmarried and is a commercial seaman.
c. Karen Eline, born Dec. 12, 1830, married in 1861 to Knut Hansen, farmer no. 5–6, Austrheim.
d. Randi Karine, born Jan. 13, 1833, married in 1859 to Jon Kristian Hansen, Kalsto in Avaldsnes.
e. Jakob, born Jan. 6, 1836, married around 186x to Ingeborg Katrine Nilsdatter, tenant farmer no. 15. Austrheim.
f. Ingeborg Oline, born June 12, 1839, married in 1864 to Askild Hansen, Kalsto in Avaldsnes.
g. Kari Oline, born July 4, 1846.

Children in 2nd marriage:

h. Anne Malene, born Apr. 7, 1849, died Apr. 10, 1849.

i. John, born May 1, 1850, died May 15, 1850.
j. Nils Daniel, born Nov. 18, 1851, married Berentine, lived in Bergen in 1884. He was a sailor.
k. Hans Zakarias, born Oct. 15, 1856, married in 1884 to Jacobine Andrea Bergesen from Vanse, lived in Bergen.

Tenant farming contract to Daniel from J. Dahm in the amount of 1/2 v. or 36 mrk. tf. is for over 40 years and is dated Sept. 21, 1829.

He pays in annual rent to the owner 4 Spd., 1 bp.tf and 4 workdays. To his parents–in–law he offers an old age contract that for 5 years was valued at 50 Spd.:

> 2–1/2 barrels of oats and 1/2 barrel pure grain, free use of the field called "Skutflekket", including the right to use it as pasture winter and summer for 1 cow; and finally free lodging and a can of cod liver oil including required peat as long as it can be harvested.

The estate after Kari Oline's death is in 1847 worth 68 Spd., debt and expenses is 31–3–0 Spd. Among misc. items listed:

> 1 cow "Bollrei" 15 years–old 7–0–0, 1 cow "Salrei" 8–0–0, 1 sheep 1–0–0, ½ of a mill (outside) with housing 8–0–0, 2 "balker" (50 fathoms) new herring seine nets with associated equipment 20–0–0, 1 bp. 8 mrk. fishing line 1–2–12, 2 herring fishing nets 0–4–12, 1 four–oar boat with sails 1–2–12, 25 lobster pots 3–0–10. 1 short 2–barrel container 0–4–0, 1 large clothes locker 0–4–0, 1 blue and red–trimmed comforter 3–0–0, 1 blue and red–trimmed pillow 1–2–12, 1 80–liter cattle trough 1–2–12.

In 1866 the farm consists of 23 mål of fields and meadows valued at 207 Spd. There are pastures for 50 Spd. and fishing rights income potential for 12 Spd.

Annual crop yield is 14 barrels of oats, 3 barrels of barley and 8 barrels of potatoes. The entire farm is assessed at 295 Spd.

The livestock consists of 1 horse, 1 cow, 8 sheep, and 1 pig.

In 1842 J. Dahm sold this farm to Mikkel Jørgensen, then at Nordvik, later at Hovland, for 200 Spd. Nine years later Mikkel sold the farm to his brother, Jørgen Jørgensen, for 270 Spd.

In the years between 1870 and 1890, this farm was unoccupied but used by Jørgen Jørgensen, Nordvik. The old farmhouse was, before it was separated from the main farm in 1888, located on farm no. 3, Leito, and was moved and joined with the barn here.

10. **Martin Mikal Jørgensen.** 1890 – 1893

Born May 14, 1861, died Dec. 13, 1892, son of Elisabeth Johnsdatter and Jørgen Jørgensen, farmer no. 14 – 1 f, Nordvik.

Married in 1890 to **Berthe Sylfestdatter**, born 1857, died Jan. 24, 1894, daughter of Sylfest Sylfestsen, Feoy.

Children:

a. Mikkeline, born and died on Jan. 22, 1891.

Further information missing from records.

Hans Mathias Sjursen (1844–1913) and Severin Halvorsdatter (1856–1933).

11. **Hans Mathias Sjursen.** 1893 – 1914

Born Jan. 20, 1844, died July 8, 1913, son of Anne Marthe Larsdatter and Sjur Jørgensen, farmer no. 3 – 5 c, Austrhiem.

Married on Mar. 26, 1882, to **Severine Halvorsdatter,** born Mar. 9, 1856, died Aug. 21, 1933, daughter (outside marriage) of Bertha Hansdatter, Austrheim and Halvor Halvorsen, Tinn in Telemark.

Children:

a. Hans *Severin*, born Aug. 13, 1882, next farmer.
b. Anna Martha, born July 26, 1885, married in 1907 to Peder Olai Andreassen, tenant farmer no. 34, Hovland.
c. *Berthe* Victoria, born Aug. 10, 1888, married to Johan Hovland, lived in Bakaroyne in Haugesund.
d. Jørgen *Johan*, born July 19, 1890, married in 1917 to Amanda Bertelsdatter, tenant farmer no. 22, Austrheim.
e. Sigvald, born July 28, 1893, was a commercial seaman and lived in Seattle, USA, died there on Nov. 3, 1922. He also would hunt and fish during the winter season in Kenai, Alaska.
f. Alfred, born Oct. 11, 1896, married in 1924 to Minda Sørhus, tenant farmer no. 35, Hovland.

The deed to Hans Mathias on this farm – tax assessed at sk.m. 1.53, from Jørgen Jørgensen, Nordvik for 2200 kroner and an old age contract (1 cord birch wood and 10 hectoliters coal) is dated Jan. 5, 1893.

Hans Mathias worked many years as a bricklayer and diver for the port authority.

From *Haugesund Avis*, Jan 16th,1908.

Smack for Sale:
A former pilot "smack" boat used in pilot service, approx. 12 years old, a "Hvaleroe" model with capacity for approx. 70 maal herring and excellent sailing characteristics and suitable for mackerel fishing.
Available for quick sale.
H. Hansen, Utsire.

12. **Severin Hansen.** 1914 – 1945
Born Aug. 13, 1882, died June 6, 1926, son of previous farmer.

Married on Apr. 10, 1908, to **Elisabeth M. Johnsdatter,** born July 17, 1887, died Feb. 5, 1966, daughter of Randi Johnsdatter, and John Holgersen, Upper Kvinnesland in Tysvaer.

Children:

a. Hans *Mathias*, born Sept. 26, 1908, next farmer.
b. *John* Kvinnesland, born June 24, 1910, married in 1952 to Lindy Klovning, tenant farmer no. 17, Klovning.
c. Severine, born June 22, 1912, married to Petter Pedersen, Stavanger.
d. Randi, born Dec. 24, 1915, married to Nils Melkevik, Fordesfjorden.
e. *Josefine* Regine, born Mar. 29, 1917, married to Erling Rossavik, Helle.
f. *Sigvald* Emil, born Aug. 25, 1920, tenant farmer no. 31, Austrheim.
g. Hanne Sofie, born Oct.5, 1922, married to Alf Thorkildsen, Stavanger.
h. Elisabeth, born Oct. 5, 1922, lives in Håvik.
i. Sverre, born May 27, 1925, married to Helga, lives in Stavanger.

The deed to Severin from the mother in the amount of 1400 kroner, and an old age contract for 5 years valued at 350 kroner, is dated Nov. 19, 1914.

They built a new main dwelling here in 1907, and this was taken out of the estate in 1953 and was designated farm no. 23, Solheim, and taken over in 1967 by Severine Pedersen and Elisabeth Hansen.

13. **Mathias Hansen.** 1945 – 1978
Born Sept. 26, 1908, died Sept. 7, 1992. son of previous farmer.

Married on Apr. 19, 1936, to **Karoline Klovning**, born Nov. 27, 1912, died May 14, 1942, daughter of Lisa and Peder Klovning, tenant farmer no. 44 d, Nordvik.

Children:

a. *Einar* Sigurd, born Feb. 7, 1937, twin, married to Helga Jaatun, lives in Kopervik.
b. Solveig *Elbjorg*, born Feb. 7, 1937, twin, married in 1960 to Johannes Klovning, farmer no. 2 – 5, Klovning.
c. Målfrid. born Jan. 16, 1939, twin, married in 1958 to Sigvald A, Hansen, tenant farmer no. 41, Hovland.
d. Kjellaug, born Jan. 16, 1939, twin, married in 1957 to Gerhard Skåren, farmer no.1 – 17, Hovland.

They took over the house after Jonette and Martin Nilsen (which was built on leased property), and it was separated from the estate in 1934 and designated farm no. 11, Solheim. It was taken over in 1993 by Eli Solfrid Rovik.

14. **Målfrid and Sigvald A. Hansen.** 1974 –
They took over the estate in 1973 and run the farm at this time. See under "Tenant Farm no. 41, Hovland."

Farm no. 5. Lynghilder. From farm no. 6 in 1722

1. **Peder Johannesen.** 1722 – 1754
Born around 1687, buried Mar. 9, 1755, son of Johannes Simonsen, farmer no. 6 – 1. Austrheim.

Married to **Anbjor Torsdatter,** buried Apr. 8, 1764, *84 years old* (In 1758 she is listed in records as 60 years old.) Of unknown origin.

Children:

a. Johannes, born around 1723, next farmer.
b. Anders, born around 1726, married to Malene Knutsdatter, farm no. 1 – 7, Hovland.

Peder got half of his father's farm, and his lease contract was in the amount of 1/2 v.tf. and is dated Mar. 6, 1722.

2. **Johannes Pedersen.** 1754 – 1790
Born around 1723, buried July 11, 1790, son of previous farmer.

Married in 1st. marriage on Nov. 14, 1754, to **Berta Olsdatter,** born around 1730, buried June 23, 1765, daughter of Anna Svendsdatter and Ole Abrahamsen, tenant farmer no. 11 b, Nordvik.

Married in 2nd marriage on June 29, 1766, to **Anna Knutsdatter,** born around 1725, buried May 25, 1788, of unknown origin.

Children in 1st marriage:

a. Berta, baptized Apr. 18, 1755, confirmed in 1775, further history unknown.
b. Anne, baptized Jan. 13, 1757, next farmer.
c. Peder, Aug. 15, 1759, buried Nov. 23, 1771.
d. Anbjor, baptized Sept. 20, 1761, buried Mar. 29, 1762.
e. Anbjor, born Feb. 1764, died in 1770.

Children in 2nd marriage :

f. Siri, baptized May 16, 1773, further history unknown.

As the county register of the 1750s is lost, we have not been able to find the lease contract to Johannes.

In the settlement after Berta's death in 1765 the estate was valued at 8–3–12 rdl. and divided among the 4 children.

3. **John Nilsen.** 1790 – 1800.

Born in 1765, buried on Mar. 25, 1803 from Torvestad.

Married on Oct. 23, 1784, to **Anna Johannesdatter,** baptized Jan. 13, 1757, died Apr. 29, 1842, daughter of previous farmer.

Children:

a. Berta, baptized on Dec. 26, 1784, buried Apr. 3, 1791.
b. Nils, baptized Sept. 23, 1787, buried Apr. 3, 1791.
c. Kari, baptized Oct. 3, 1790, buried Apr. 3, 1791.
d. Berta, baptized July 8, 1792, buried July 3, 1815.

Lease contract to John in the amount of 1 bp. 12 mrk. (1/2 våger) tf. issued by Hans B. Forman on June 15, 1793.

In the military records from 1784 John is listed as: *Joen Nielsen Torvestad in Utsire, 20 years old.*

In the next farmer's lease contract, it is recorded that John had to relinquish the farm due to illness. The family could continue to use the older buildings on the farm that were located directly east of the main courtyard on farm no. 6 at "Hopse," while the next farmer, Knut Sjursen, possibly built a new courtyard with buildings at Lynghilder.

4. **Knut Sjursen.** 1800 – 1836

Baptized Nov. 7, 1773, died Dec. 17, 1840, son of Lisbeth Tollefsdatter and Sjur Knutsen, farmer no. 1 – 8 c, Nordvik.

Married on Mar. 25, 1801, to **Berta Gudmundsdatter,** baptized Jan. 22, 1777, died Sept. 13, 1822, daughter of Valborg Olsdatter and Gudmund Thomassen, farmer no. 3 – 2 c, Austrheim.

Children:

a. Bår, baptized Aug. 30, 1801, buried Oct. 4, 1801.
b. Bår, baptized Aug. 29, 1802, died Apr. 28, 1837.
c. Valborg, baptized June 26, 1805, next farmer.
d. Ingeborg, baptized July 22, 1808, buried June 29, 1811.
e. Ingeborg, baptized Apr. 11, 1811, married in 1835 to Jakob Jonsen, tenant farmer no. 31, Austrheim.
f. Gudmund, baptized Oct. 20, 1813, married in 1845 to Kari Oline Nilsdatter, farmer no. 1 – 8, Austrheim.
g. Ole, baptized on Aug. 4, 1816, married in 1842 to Ingeborg Kristine Larsdatter,, tenant farm no. 29, Austrheim.
h. Sjur, born Mar. 18, 1819, married in 1848 to Anne Marthe Jonsdatter., tenant farm no. 26, Hovland.

Lease contract to Knut in the amount of 1 bp.18 mrk. t.f. issued by Hans B. Forman on Oct. 9, 1800.

In 1802 the livestock consisted of 1 horse, 2 cows and 2 sheep. He planted 1–1/4 barrels of grain and harvested 8 barrels. The farm is valued at 60 rdl.

In 1822 the houses on the farm are described as follows:

> 1 cabin with sleeping room at one end and a kitchen between them under one roof covered with peat and bark; storage area and paneled barn for the livestock and attached shed for the manure at the end of the barn – everything under one roof covered with peat and bark.

Annual yield was then 12 barrels of grain and 6 barrels of potatoes, while the livestock consisted of 3 cows, 1 horse and 6 sheep. The farm was in 1823 was assessed at 70 Spd.

In the estate settlement in 1823 after Berta died there are assets worth 155 Spd. to be divided among the heirs. The following items are listed:

> 1 iron stove 6–0–0, 1 boat shed covered with peat 16–0–0, 1 large 8–oar boat with new main sail, 2 jibs and associated equipment 30–0–0, 1 4–oar boat with main and jib 5–0–0, 20 lobster pots 2–0–0, 2 spring herring fishing nets with associated equipment 2–2–0, 1 net (for containment of the herring in the water) with boom and accessories (for controlling and

Aerial photo over farm no. 5, Lynghilder. In the background is the house where among others Martin and Nils Johannes Nilsen grew up. Photo by Telemark Aircraft Co., 1954.

handling the net in the seas) 2–0–0, 1 gray horse, 3–1/2 years old, 9–0–0, 1 brown, horned cow "Mondrey" with a lame foot 4–0–0, 1 brown, horned cow "Lovrey," 10 years old 8–2–12, 1 red, blue and white–striped comforter with feather fill 3–2–0, 1 blue–striped comforter with feather fill 2–1–12, 2 pillows with feather fill 2–0–0, 1 red–striped feather bed 3–0–0, 3 gold rings 7–0–0, 3 silver spoons 3–2–0, 1 silver carafe with 5 decorative gold–plated leaves 2–0–0, and 1 white locker with lock and iron reinforcements 2–0–0.

5. **Hans Sakarias Johannesen,** 1836 – 1858
Baptized July 4, 1802, died Dec. 14, 1853, son of Kari Mikkelsdatter and Johannes Nilsen, farm no. 18 – 1 i, Nordvik.

Married on Sept. 18, 1825 to **Valborg Knutsdatter,** baptized June 26, 1805, died Dec. 13, 1880, daughter of previous farmer.

Children:

a. Berta, born Dec. 17, 1825. She had a daughter, Severine, born Mar. 9, 1856, outside marriage with Halvor Halvorsen, Tinn in Telemark.
b. Johannes, born Mar. 16, 1828, died July 12, 1855. There was a settlement after his death in 1857. From the estate's assets valued at 51–3–6 Spd. there was left 13–1–16 Spd. to the heirs. Besides 15 Spd. in cash, he owned among other things one–twelfth share in a fishing net system valued at 15 Spd.
c. Knut, born Feb. 16, 1831, next farmer.
d. Karen Juliane, born Dec. 24, 1833, married in 1860 to Nils Nilsen, tenant farmer no. 10, Austrheim.
e. Hansine, born Jan. 11, 1837, married in 1866 to Lars Tormodsen, tenant farmer no. 16, Austrheim.
f. Inger Oline, born June 15, 1840, married in 1869 to Tormod Tormodsen, tenant farmer no. 17, Austrheim.
g. Ellen Elisabeth, born Mar. 10, 1843, married in 1865 to Torkel Torkelsen, Ose in Etne. Lived in Rovaer.
h. Severine Bertine, born Apr. 8, 1847, lived in Bergen.
i. Thomas Sakarias, born Dec. 3, 1849, married to Mathilde Kristine Møller, Høllen in Sogne. Thomas worked as a mason with The Port Authority, and settled in Sogne. He died in 1889.

The deed to Hans Sakarias in the amount of 36 mrk. or one–half v.tf. issued by J. Dahm for 100 Spd. is dated May 17, 1831.

In 1836 he wrote an old age contract with his father–in–law, Knut:

> *3 barrels of oats and one–half barrel of barley in acreage, 1 cow and 4 sheep in full care both winter and summer and full use of the field called Hoberg Field.*

The contract for 5 years was valued at 66 Spd.

In 1845 there was planted one–quarter barrel of barley and 2–1/2 barrels of oats and 1 barrel of potatoes. The livestock consisted of 1 horse, 2 cows and 6 sheep. Hans Sakarias was then the only registered full–time marine pilot on Utsira.

He left assets worth 350 Spd. of which the farm represented 200 Spd. There was 129 Spd. left for the heirs. Among the misc. items left:

> 2/15 of a seine fishing operation 24–0–0, 1 old boat shed 10–0–0. 18 lobster pots 1–2–0, 2 spring herring fishing nets 2–2–0, 1 coalfish net 3–0–0, 1 pair of binoculars 4–0–0, 1 bakery stove with kettle 6–0–0, 2 bp. 15 mrk. feathers 7–2–8, 1 cow "Netrei" 10–0–0, 1 cow "Ringros" 9–0–0, 1 dun–colored mare 14–0–0, 3 sheep 3–3–0 and 26–0–0 in cash.

6. **Knut Hansen,** 1858 – 1910

Born Feb. 16, 1831, died Jan. 14, 1893, son of previous farmer.

Married in first marriage on Aug. 11, 1861, to **Karen Eline Danielsdatter,** born Dec. 12, 1830, died Sept. 21, 1862, daughter of Kari Oline and Daniel Johannesen, farm no. 4 – 9 c, Austrheim.

Asseline Ellingsdatter (1847–1924) around 1880.

Married in 2nd marriage on Aug. 1, 1869 to **Asseline Ellingsdatter,** born Dec. 8, 1847, died Mar. 23, 1924, daughter of Ragna Serine and Elling Gudmundsen, farmer no. 12 – 1 g, Nordvik.

Children in first marriage:

a. Magdalene Caroline, born July 13, 1862, died Mar. 31, 1864.

Children in 2nd marriage:

b. Hans Cornelius, born Apr. 25, 1871, died June 27, 1872.
c. *Hans* Cornelius, born July 6, 1873, next farmer.
d. *Elling* Teodor, born Sept. 14, 1876, married in 1905 to Julie Rasmussen, tenant farm no. 21, Austrheim.
e. *Hanna* Elisabeth, born Oct. 13, 1879, married in 1900 to Thomas Eriksen, farmer no. 6 – 1, Skare.
f. Berthe *Serine*, born Oct. 7, 1882, married in 1902 to Martin Eriksen, farmer no. 5 – 1, Skare.
g. Knut, born Jan. 21, 1886, died Jan. 22, 1888.

Official title of the ownership of the farm to Knut indicates tax assessment of 1.43 sk. m. in the settlement dated Oct. 12, 1857 after his father's death.

In 1866 the 22 mål of fields and meadows on the farm is assessed at 186 Spd. There are pastures valued at 57 Spd. and fishing rights income for 12 Spd. Annual crop yield is 12 barrels of oats, 4 barrels of barley, 10 barrels of potatoes and 20 skp. hay. The entire farm is assessed at 275 Spd.

The livestock consists of 1 horse, 2 cows, 17 sheep and 1 pig.

7. **Hans Knutsen.** 1910 – 1939

Born July 6, 1873, died July 31, 1941, son of previous farmer.

Unmarried.

The deed to Hans from the other heirs in the amount of 1000 kroner is dated Dec. 29, 1926.

Hans built himself a new main dwelling here in 1907. This was taken out of the farm in 1969 and became farm no. 30, taken over by Knut Ellingsen. From 1992 Ann Helen and Konrad Austrheim own the farm.

8. **Rasmus Ellingsen.** 1939 – 1957

Born May 2, 1916, died June 19, 1993, son of Julie and Elling Knutsen, tenant farmer no. 21 e, Austrheim.

Married on July 6, 1957, to the widow **Jenny Jacobsdatter Steensnaes,** born Apr. 4, 1922, from Haugesund.

The deed to Rasmus from Hans Knutsen in the amount of 3000 kroner is dated Feb. 2, 1939.

Rasmus was a carpenter aside from fishing and managing the farm. He moved to Haugesund when he got married.

9. **Laurits Nernes.** 1957 – 1960

Born Jan. 18, 1908, died in 1977, from Skånevik, Etne.

Married on June 4, 1938, to **Klara Ellingsen,** born July 9, 1908, died in 1987, daughter of Julie and Elling Knutsen, tenant farmer no. 21 b, Austrheim.

Children:

a. Edith, born Jan. 15, 1939, married in 1959 to Erling Grindheim, Etne.
b. Leif Kare, born Nov. 28, 1950, married in 1977 to Randi Skeie, lives in Havik, Karmøy.

Laurits was a carpenter and construction worker. They lived in Etne before they came to Utsira. The family moved to Viken, Torvestad.

The farm has since been worked as a supplementary farm, and was in 1970 taken over by Konrad J. Austrheim.

Farm no. 6. Smaie. From farm no. 4 in 1696

1. **Johannes Simonsen.** 1696 – 1732
Born around 1659, died between 1728 and 1732, of unknown origin (possibly the son of Simon Torkelsen, Hovland)

Possibly married in first marriage to (first name?) **Pedersdatter**.

Married in second marriage to **Anna Eriksdatter,** born around 1677, buried on Sept. 28, 1766, of unknown origin.

Known children:

a. Peder, born around 1688, married to Anbior Torsdatter, farm no. 5 – 1, Austrheim.

Johannes leased (the farm) for 1 v.tf. in 1696. The lease contract was not officially published.

In 1722 he leased half of the farm to his son Peder for 1/2 v.tf., farm no. 5.

In 1703 his financial condition is described as "poor," but the houses on the farm were without any claim to the tenant for disrepair. He planted 1–1/2 barrel of oats and feeds 4 cows, 1 calf, 1 horse and some sheep, and he was the sole owner of all the animals. He owed the cloister steward Mr. Frimand 2 rdl. for the first lease contract in 1696, 2–1/2 rdl. for land lease in 1702 and 4 pd. clip fish. He also owed others 6 rdl.

In 1712 his financial condition was described as "marginally good," while the claims for tenant repair on the houses amounted to 1 rdl. Farm production and livestock remained as described in 1703. He owed 2 rdl. to the heirs of Frimand and also 0–1–8 rdl. in "1/4 money"[36] to the cloister for the year 1710.

In 1721 he was free of any debt, but repairs on the houses would amount to 4–1–2, of which 3 rdl. would be required to build a new barn.

2. **Ole Knutsen.** 1732 – 1772
Born around 1709, buried on Mar. 29, 1772, possibly son of Knut Olsen, farmer no. 4 – 5 a, Austrheim.

---

[36] A surcharge of 1 mark silver was imposed in 1307 by the Court of Borgarting, then it was imposed on the whole country in 1604, and in 1687 it was set to 1/4 of the land rent, "4th the money," due and payable if the land rent was not paid by Christmas Eve. – from the *Norwegian Historical Encyclopedia.*

Married in 1st marriage around 1732 to **Anna Eriksdatter,** widow of previous farmer.

Married in 2nd marriage on May 14, 1767, to **Berta Nilsdatter** born around 1744, died July 21, 1767, daughter of Barbro Klausdatter and Nils Kristoffersen, farmer no. 15 – 2 a, Nordvik.

Married in 3rd marriage on Sept. 25, 1768, to **Malene Knutsdatter,** born in 1749, buried Oct. 3, 1790, daughter of Berta Knutsdatter and Knut Sjursen, tenant farmer no. 15 c, Nordvik.

Children in 3rd marriage:

a. Anna, baptized Dec. 19, 1770, married in 1794 to Karl Asbjornsen, tenant farmer no. 13, Kvalvik.

Lease to Ole in the amount of 1/2 v.tf. is dated Mar. 18, 1732.

Ole was a regular marine pilot and in 1741 he and Elling Knutsen Kvalvik registered their pilot logs, dated Dec. 2, 1740.

In the estate settlement after Berta in 1768 there are assets worth 81 rdl., but debts and expenses amounted to an equal amount, so there was nothing left for the heirs. The following misc. items are listed:

> 1/2 of a six–oar boat with sail 5–1–0, 1 four–oar boat with sail 2–1–0, 6 spring herring fishing nets 3–1–0, 6 lobster pots 0–2–0, 1 tiled heating stove 5–0–0, 1 shed 3–1–0, 3 cows and 1 calf 12–1–16, 1 old dun–colored mare 1–0–16, 1 brown mare 5–1–0, 5 silver spoons and 1 silver brandy goblet 7–0–0, 3 kettles 4–2–0 and 1 down bed 2–0–16.

3. **Jakob Rasmussen.** 1772 – 1794

Born around 1750, son of Synnøve Paulsdatter and Rasmus Johannesen, Vikse in Skåre (Jakob and Ommund Rasmussen, farm no. 17, Nordvik, were cousins).

Married in 1st marriage on June 27, 1773, to **Malene Knutsdatter,** widow of previous farmer.

Married in 2nd marriage on Oct. 10, 1792, to **Siri Sakariasdatter,** born in 1724, buried Apr. 14, 1793, daughter of Brynhild Tjerandsdatter and Sakarias Pedersen, Blikra in Vats, and widow of Ole Olsen Stange, and before that, widow of Nils Nilsen, Aurdal in Vats.

Married in 3rd marriage to **Johanna Larsdatter,** born in 1750, widow of Ola Kjellsen, Adland in Akra.

Children in 1st marriage:

The main dwelling house on farm no. 6, "Smaie", the way it looked in 1932. Photo by: Robert Kloster, Historic Museum in Bergen.

a. Ole, baptized Nov. 7, 1773, next farmer.
b. Synnøve, baptized Nov. 2, 1775, married, moved to Bokn.
c. Berta, baptized Dec. 4, 1777.
d. Eli, baptized Sept. 30, 1781, died before 1790.
e. Eli, baptized Feb. 7, 1783, married in 1821 to Tore Olsen, Saevland.
f. Malene, baptized Aug. 14, 1785, buried Feb. 8, 1789.
g. Mikkel, baptized June 21, 1788, married to Gjertrud Eliasdatter, farmed the Adland farm in Akra.

Lease contract to Jakob in the amount of 1/2 v.tf. is dated Oct. 8, 1772.

Malene's estate with assets to 74–2–18 rdl. was settled in 1790 and the remaining 60–2–0 rdl. was divided among the heirs. Among misc. items left:

> 4 cows (Morchrej, Sondrej, Laprej and Livrej) 22–0–0, 1 black mare with foal 5–0–0, 1 tiled heating stove 6–0–0, 1 old six–oar boat with sail and associated equipment 4–2–0, 1 four–oar boat with sail 3–2–0.

Siri was first married to Nils Nilsen from Aurdal in Vats. They moved later to the farm Krabbetveit in Tysvaer. They owned this farm, and also for a while the church in Tysvaer. When Siri's estate was settled in January 1793, it was the grandson Nils as well as Jakob who were the heirs. The estate's assets were then 222–3–11 rdl., and left to the heirs after settlement was 157 rdl. Among misc. items left the following is listed:

> Silver items 53–2–16, among them a silver carafe 44–2–0, 1 copper kettle 9–3–2, gold 9–0–0, 2 tiled heating stoves 10–2–0, 30 lobster pots 1–1–0, 1 herring fishing net 0–3–8, 1 four–oar boat with sail and an old six–oar boat 4–3–0, bed sheets 14–1–0, 2 cows (Hoprej and Laprej), 1 heifer, 1 calf and a pig 20–3–0, 1 brown horse 3–2–0, 1 mill with housing 3–2–0, 5 barrels of oats 7–2–0, 15 v. of oatmeal 7–2–0, flat bread for 1–2–16 and 9 bushels salt for 1–2–0.

Jakob moved in 1794 to Adland, Akra on Karmøy and took over the farm there with his third wife.

4. **Ole Jakobsen.** 1794 – 1838

Baptized on Nov. 7, 1773, son of previous farmer.

Married to **Anne Marie Olsdatter,** born 1772, daughter of Johanna Larsdatter and Ola Kjellsen, Adland in Akra.

Children:

a. Malene, baptized Aug. 3, 1795, married in 1819 to Hans Andersen Bo. They lived in Meland, Avaldsnes.
b. Johanne, baptized on Dec. 9, 1798, married in 1824 to Peder Osmundsen Osthus, lived in Havik, Avaldsnes.
c. Berta Karine, baptized Mar. 28, 1802, buried June 30, 1816.
d. Rasmus, baptized Mar. 4, 1806, died Dec. 12, 1825.
e. Anna Elisabet, baptized July 28, 1811, married in 1835 to Tonnes Olsen, Akra.
f. Juliane Marie, baptized Jan. 5, 1814, moved in with parents in Kvalavåg in 1840.

Lease contract to Ole in the amount of 1/2 v.tf. issued by Hans B. Forman is dated June 12, 1794.

Ole was schoolmaster at Utsira for a few years from 1790.

In 1802 he planted 1–1/4 barrels and harvested 8 barrels of grain. The livestock consisted of 1 horse, 2 cows and 2 sheep.

In 1822 the houses on the farm were described as follows:

> 1 living room with a side room and kitchen under peat–covered roof. 1 storage shed with a brick–built barn with attached dung bin under peat–covered roof.

Annual crop was then 16 barrels of grain and 6 barrels of potatoes. There was feed for 3 cows, 1 horse and 10 sheep, a small pasture and an insufficient supply of peat fuel for heating.

The farm was assessed in 1823 at 75 Spd.

In 1838 he relinquished the farm to the owner, Ole Jørgensen Nordvik, against an old age contract. The family moved in 1840 to Kvalavåg, Karmøy.

5. **Ole Jørgensen.** 1838 – 1843
Baptized Oct. 6, 1811, son of Berthe Olsdatter and Jørgen Johnsen, farmer no. 13 – 3 d, Nordvik.

Ole bought this farm from J. Dahm on May 22, 1832 for 180 Spd., after it first had been offered to Ole Jakobsen.

In 1838 Ole Jakobsen again relinquished the farm and accepted an old age contract instead, which for 5 years was assessed to be worth 80 Spd:

> 4 barrels of well–grown oats, 4 bushels barley, free use of a field called Skevikeflekket, including necessary manure, and feed for 4 sheep, winter and summer, and also 3 Spd. in cash.

In 1841 Ole took over half of farm no. 13, Nordvik. See more about Ole and the family there.

6. **Johannes Johannesen.** 1843 – 1864
Baptized on June 30, 1799, died on Sept. 14, 1861, son of Kari Mikkelsdatter and Johannes Nilsen, farm no. 18 – 1 h, Nordvik.

Married on July 9, 1825, to Ingeborg Oline Johnsdatter, baptized Feb. 3, 1809, died Jan. 18, 1892, daughter of Anne Malene Olsdatter and John Helgesen, farm no. 1-10a, Nordvik.

Children:

a. Ole Hansen, born Nov. 14, 1825, died Apr. 22, 1826.
b. Ole Johannes, born June 13, 1827, married in 1854 to Anne Marthe Ådnesdatter, tenant farmer no. 29, Nordvik, later farm no. 2 – 2, Klovning.
c. Truls Mathias, born Feb. 26, 1830, married in 1864 to Berthe Malene Olsdatter, farm no. 13 – 6, Nordvik.
d. Berthe Karoline, born Feb. 8, 1841, died on Dec. 27, 1848.
e. John Christian, born Nov. 29, 1842, died Dec. 11, 1842.
f. John Christian, born June 5, 1845.
g. Berthe Karoline, born Nov. 11, 1849, tenant farmer no. 32, Hovland.

Lease contract to Johannes from Ole Jørgensen on this farm in the amount 1/2 v.tf. is dated May 18, 1843.

On this farm in 1845 there is planted 1/4 barrel of barley, 2 barrels of oats and 1 barrel of potatoes. The livestock consisted of 1 horse, 2 cows, 6 sheep and 1 pig.

The family lived on Torvestad until in 1843 they leased the farm on Utsira.

In the settlement after Johannes in 1864 there were miscellaneous items in the estate worth 72 Spd. 66 sk., part ownership in the main dwelling worth 65 Spd., and a bank account in the amount of 111 Spd. Among various items the following are mentioned:

> 2 cows ("Brunsia" and "Sjovrei") 25–0–0, 1 dun–colored horse 8–0–0, 3 "balker" (75 fathoms) seine nets with accessories 21–0–0, 2 coal fish nets 1–0–56, 28 lobster pots 5–0–72, and 1 four–oar boat with sail 4–0–0.

In 1865 Ingeborg, daughter Karoline, and son John Christian lived on farm no. 7, Hovland.

7. **Johannes Johnsen.** 1864 – 1900
Born Sept. 28, 1825, died Feb. 17, 1900, son of Anne Andersdatter and John Johannesen, tenant farmer no. 8 f, Klovning.

Married on Apr. 21, 1850, to **Martha Karine Larsdatter,** baptized Jan. 30, 1814, died Dec. 19, 1874, daughter of Anne Martha Nilsdatter and Lars Thorsen Storesund, Torvestad, and widow of Ole Jørgensen Nordvik.

Children:

a. Lars Olai, born Aug. 27, 1850, died Dec. 11, 1872.
b. Jonetta, born May 13, 1853, died Jan. 28, 1871.
c. Bolette Malene, born Aug. 8, 1855, married to Nils Daniel Danielsen, Avaldsnes. They lived on Risoy, Haugesund.
d. Thore Johannes, born July 26, 1860, next farmer.

Johannes's child outside marriage with Ingeborg Karine Johannesdatter, Klovning:

e. Johan *Ingvald*, born Sept. 7, 1876, married in 1919 to Hanna Marie Hansen, tenant farmer no. 26, Klovning.

Marthe Karine owned the title dated July 24, 1851 on this farm, with tax assessment of 1.59 sk.m., at the time of the settlement after Ole Jørgensen, Nordvik.

Martha Karine and Johannes farmed farm no. 13 at Nordvik in the period 1850 – 1864.

In 1866 the farm consisted of 24 mål of meadows and fields and was assessed to 212 Spd. There were also pastures worth 50 Spd. and fishing rights income worth 12 Spd. The entire farm was assessed at 305 Spd. Annual crop yield was 15 barrels of oats, 4 barrels of barley, 10 barrels of potatoes and 20 skp. of hay.

In 1865 the livestock consisted of 1 horse, 2 cows, 6 sheep and 1 pig, while 10 years later he was the only farmer on Utsira that saw the benefits in raising goats. He then raised 11 goats along with 3 cows.

In the settlement after Martha Karine in 1876 the estate's assets were 803 Spd., after debts and expenses were paid, there was 473 Spd. left to the heirs. The farm was then assessed at 360 Spd. and left for son Thore Johannes.

8. **Thore Johannesen.** 1885 – 1888
Born July 26, 1860. died Apr. 8, 1888, son of previous farmer.

Married on May 5, 1885, to **Berthe Mallene Jobsdatter (Madlo),** born Mar. 27, 1850, died Jan. 26, 1929, daughter of Karoline Johnsdatter and Job Rasmussen, farmer no. 7 – 9 e, Hovland.

Children:

a. Lars Johannes, born June 8, 1885, farmer no. 1 – 14, Hovland.

Thore's children with Severine Halvorsdatter, Austrheim:

b. Thora Johanne, born Sept. 24, 1877, married in 1901 to Mons Larsen, tenant farmer no. 40, Nordvik.

The title on this farm owned by Thore is dated Jan. 11, 1876. The farm has a tax assessment of 1.59 sk.m. and is valued at 360 Spd.

In 1900 Berthe and her son Lars Johannes lived on Tuo, with her brother Rasmus Jobsen. The old dwelling was torn down in the 1930s.

Job Rasmussen Tuo, born 1883.

9. **Job Rasmussen.** 1915 – 1920
Born Mar. 11, 1883, son of Kristine Mathiasdatter and Rasmus Jobsen, farmer no. 7 – 10 b, Hovland.

Unmarried.

Job bought this farm in an auction for 1060 kroner. He emigrated to the USA and died there.

10. a. **Gustav Rasmussen.** 1920 – 1970
Born Mar. 19, 1896, died on July 22, 1976, son of Gurine Gudmundsdatter and Rasmus Jobsen, farmer no 7 – 10 d, Hovland.
Unmarried.

10. b. **Kristine Rasmussen.** 1920 – 1970
Born Sept. 11, 1894, died Feb. 16, 1974, sister of previous farmer.
Unmarried.

Kristine and Gustav took over the farm here and also the farm no. 18, Hovland.

The farm here is later used as additional fields, and the estate was in 1978 taken over by Torbjorn Rasmussen.

Farm no. 8. from farm no. 1 in 1912

1. **August Knutsen.** 1912 – 1922

The deed to August from Elling and Thomine Eriksen on this farm, with a tax potential of sk.m. 0.98, for 1266 kroner, and an old age contract, is dated Nov. 1912.

In 1922 he sold the farm, to his brother Konrad on the main farm, for 3000 kroner. They lived a few years in the "Oliver House" in Kvalvik, before they bought farm no. 4 on Hovland in 1928 and moved there. See more on this family there.

Farm no. 9. Rovaretre. From farm no. 2 in 1914

1. **Televerket (Radio and Telegraph Corp.).** 1914 –

They bought this estate, tax assessment 0.40 sk.m., from Severin Tollefsen for 4,157.25 kroner in Sept. 1914, and is where Utsira Radio was built.

Farm no. 13, From farm no. 3 in 1934

1. **Petter Haugseth.** 1934 – 1973

Born Sept. 4, 1895, died Apr. 21, 1987, son of Karoline and Bernt Haugseth, Sykkylven.

Married on Oct. 8, 1916, to **Gunda Gudmundsen,** born Jan. 19, 1894, died Jan. 26, 1977, daughter of Astrid and Elling Gudmundsen, farm no. 3 – 7 a. Austrheim.

Children:

a. *Bernhard* Konrad, born July 4, 1917, married in 1st marriage to Martha Johannesen, Feoy, and in 2nd marriage to Perdy, lives in Sykkylven.
b. *Astrid* Edel, born July 12, 1918, married in 1939 to Adolf Nilsen, farmer no. 14–5, Nordvik.
c. *Elling* Severin, born June 3, 1920, married in 1949 to Kristine Thorsen, tenant farm no. 27, Austrheim.

The deed to Petter on this farm, tax assessment sk.m. 1.32, from Elling Gudmundsen is dated Nov. 12, 1934.

They built themselves a main dwelling here in 1926, farm no. 10, Haugset, later taken over by Trygg Ellingsen. In 1956 the livestock consisted of 2 cows, a calf, a horse and 17 sheep. Petter worked for a number of years (1925–32) in America.

2. **Einar Hansen.** 1973 –
Born Feb. 7, 1937, son of Karoline and Mathias Hansen, farm no. 4 – 13 at Austrheim.

Married to **Helga Jaatun**, born Nov. 23, 1937.

Children:

a. Jorun Sofie, born Oct. 10, 1961, married to Egil Skaara.
b. Kari Helene, born July 13, 1963, married to Edgar Opsal.
c. Elisabeth, born Apr. 30, 1968, married to Geir Egil Hovring.

Einar took over the farm here in 1973 and the main dwelling after Kristine and Elling Haugseth in 1972. They live in Kopervik.

Farm no. 16. From farm no. 1 in 1936

1. **Tobias Austrheim.** 1936 – 1955
Born Sept. 27, 1911, died Sept. 25, 1955, son of Julie and Konrad Knutsen, farm no. 1 – 10 c, Austrheim.

Unmarried.

Tobias made arrangements for separating this farm from the entire Tranheim farm, with an estimated tax liability of 0.44 sk.m., and turning it over to his brother Thorvald in 1947.

Farm no. 17. From farm no. 2 in 1942

1. **Elling Austrheim.** 1942 –
   See farm no. 3 here.
   Elling took over half the farm from his father in 1942.

Farm no. 18. From Farm no. 1 in 1944

1. **Tobias Austrheim.** 1944 – 1955

See farm no. 16 here.

The deed to Tobias on this farm, "Utgarden," with an estimated tax liability of 0.60 sk.m., from his mother for 4,000 kr. is dated Sept. 26, 1953.

The farm was consolidated with farm no. 1 in 1960.

Tenant farmers

1. **Lars (Laurits).** 1606

He is only mentioned that year in the county records.

2. **Jakob.** 1629 – 1633

He is mentioned as living at Austrheim in the above years. It may be the same man who from 1634 is listed as the farmer at Kvalvik.

3. **Anbjorn.** 1634 – 1638

He is referred to as a cottager at Austrheim in 1635–38, in 1634 as a servant.

4. **Anders.** 1643 – 1644

The last two years where they list actual names in the county financial records lists Anders as a cotter or tenant.

Along with the farmers and their sons in numbers 5, 6 and 7, the following three tenants, nos. 5, 6 and 7, are mentioned in the church census from 1664 in connection with Austrheim:

5. **Laurits (Lars) Bjørnsen.** 1664

Born around 1648, listed under "servants and sons of farmers" in the 1664 census. He is also mentioned in two military records from 1665 and 1669. This may be the same person listed as tenant farmer no. 3, Nordvik.

6. **Nils Pedersen.** 1664
Born around 1634, possibly the son of Peder, farmer no. 3 here. Nils is recorded as serving in the military several different times from 1657 – 58 and is listed as: *Nils P. Skare.*

7. **Anders Lauritsen.** – 1664
He is listed as a tenant. He may be the same person as no. 4 above.

8. **Knut Jensen.** 1692 – 1707
Born around 1674 in Torvestad.

Children:

a. Hans, born in 1697 at Austrheim. Further information is unknown.

Knut is listed in the naval records from 1706 as: *Knut, a cotter*[37] *at Scharwenes rooming house, is ill.*

In 1711 there are no tenants or other residents besides the farmers at Austrheim.

9. **Anders Knutsen.** 1768 – 1792
Born around 1750, died Sept. 12, 1817, son of Knut (Knutsen?) and Siri Andersdatter, who in 1758 lived in Saebo, Torvestad.

Married first on July 24, 1768, to **Gjoa Olsdatter,** born 1747, buried June 23, 1782, daughter of Valborg Knutsdatter and Ole Reiersen, farmer no. 3 – 1 b, Austrheim.

Married the second time on Apr. 4, 1783, to **Martha Paulsdatter,** baptized May 16, 1758, died Apr. 24, 1824, daughter of Trua Olsdatter and Paul Bardsen, tenant farmer no. 15 e, Hovland.

Children from first marriage:

a. Ole, baptized July 2, 1768, buried Nov. 23, 1771.
b. Knut, baptized Sept. 1, 1770, buried Nov. 23, 1771.
c. Berta, baptized Aug. 17, 1772, buried Mar. 30, 1800.
d. Siri, baptized Jan. 16, 1775, buried July 16, 1775.

---

[37] The Norwegian word h*uusman*, used in the 18th C. translates as a cottager or cotter – someone who is a tenant, and probably works for a landowner for his lodging.

e. Berthe, born in 1779, she was 40 years old and unmarried when her father's estate was settled in 1819.
f. Siri, baptized June 18, 1780, buried July 19, 1789.

Children from second marriage:

g. Gjoa, baptized Aug. 6, 1783, married in 1810 to Ole Gudmundsen, farmer no. 1 – 9, Hovland.
h. Knut, baptized Sept. 7, 1788, buried Apr. 6, 1805.
i. Anna, baptized July 8, 1792, married in 1818 to John Johannesen, tenant farmer no. 18, Klovning.
j. Ingeborg, baptized Feb. 5, 1798, married in 1823 to Tollef Tollefsen, tenant farmer no. 18., Nordvik.

Anders was the last cotter farmer at Austrheim. The houses were located on farm no. 5, Lynghyller.

In the estate settlement after Gjoa in 1782, there were assets worth 82–2–18 rdl., from which debt and expenses of 18–0–16 rdl. were subtracted. Items listed were:

> 1 cow 3–0–0, 2 v. clip fish 3–2–0, 1 six–oar boat with sails 12–0–0, 1 old four–oar boat with sail 1–2–0, 28 lobster pots 1–3–0, 5 herring fishing nets 3–0–16, 1 on–site house with kitchen, living room and covered entrance 26–0–0, silver for 1–3–16, and an old tiled heating stove 6–0–0.

In 1792, the family moved to Hovland and took over the farm there.

10. **Nils Nilsen.** 1860 – 1923
Born Jan. 15, 1836, died Apr. 3, 1864, son of Anne Marte Johnsdatter and Nils Johnsen, farmer no. 2 – 5 f, Kvalvik.

Married on Mar. 26, 1860, to **Karen Juliane Hansdatter,** born Dec. 24, 1833, died Mar. 10, 1923, daughter of Valborg Knutsdatter and Hans Sakarias Johannesen, farmer no. 5 – 5 d, Austrheim.

Karen Juliane Hansdatter (1833 – 1923).

Children:

a. *Nils* Johannes, born Apr. 9, 1860, married in 1887 to Ingeborg Tollefsdatter, tenant farmer no. 19, Austrheim.
b. Hans Sakarias, born Jan. 16, 1862, died 1952, immigrated to Nebraska, USA, married in 1892 to Marta Johnsen from Sveio.
c. Nils *Martin*, born June 29, 1864., married in 1900 to Jonette Sjursdatter, tenant farmer no. 20, Austrheim.

The family lived on farm no. 1, in the house that today is a vacation cabin to Johan Austrheim's family.

11. **Gudmund J. Rasmussen**, 1861 – 1866
Born May 26, 1837, died May 9, 1885, son of Guri Johannesdatter and Rasmus Gudmundsen, farm no. 2 – 5 a, Skare.

Married on Mar. 24, 1861, to **Marthe Elisabeth Sjursdatter,** born July 27, 1837, died Mar. 6, 1890, daughter of Anne Marte Larsdatter and Sjur Jørgensen, farm no. 3 – 5 a, Austrheim.

Children:

a. Anna Maria, born Apr. 4, 1861, married in 1883 to Hans Knut Eriksen, tenant farmer no. 20, Skare.
b. Rasmus Johan, born Oct. 18, 1863, died Oct. 5, 1883, *perished at sea in Nordbotten after falling from the rigging on board the "Patria" from Stavanger.*
c. Guriane, born Jan. 2, 1866, married in 1886 to Nils Andreas Larsen, Akra, Karmøy.
d. Jørgen Johan, born Apr. 4, 1868.
e. Lars Tobias, born Oct. 1, 1881.

The family lived later at Klovning and Kvalvik, and in the 1880s at Skare. Gudmund was killed in a mining accident on the harbor construction project in Sorevågen.

12. **Lars Ambjornsen.** 1860 – 1884
Born Mar. 15, 1829, died Oct. 21, 1879, son of Anne Marte Larsdatter and Ambjorn Gudmundsen, farmer no. 3 – 4 c, Austrheim.

Married May 13, 1860, to **Ingeborg *Karine* Jensdatter** (Karino Agsteberg), born in 1839, died Jan. 3, 1930, daughter of Jens Johnsen, Stave in Skåre.

They had one foster–daughter:

a. Anbjor *Elene (Lene),* born May 10, 1874, daughter of Berthe Gurine and Tollef Johan Tollefsen, tenant farmer no. 13. She married Johannes Tollefsen, Hausken.

The main dwelling here, 10 x 6.3 meters, frame and log with basement and clad with boards and roofed with tiles, was in 1868 assessed at 200 Spd. They bought the old dwelling from Tollef Gresjersen and moved it to Agsteberg in the early 1860's. The house was then on leased ground at farm no. 6, but in 1956 it was separated from that estate and became farm no. 24, Aksteberg, owned by Bertel Hansen.

Lars was a marine pilot and fisherman. Karine got married in her second marriage to widower Svend Mikal Eriksen, next tenant.

13. **Svend Mikal Eriksen.** 1885 – 1930
Born Jan. 24, 1839, died Nov. 14, 1909, son of Torborg Hans–Knutsdatter and Erik Svendsen, farmer no. 1 – 8 d, Skare.

Married the second time on Mar. 29, 1885, to **Karine Jensdatter,** widow of previous farmer. No children.

Svend Mikal had been married before in Stavanger and worked as a ship's captain.

14. **Ole Andreas Olsen.** 1863 – 1870
Born in 1836, died before 1875, he was from Bergen, and his father was Sjur Olsen.

Married on May 17, 1863, to **Berthe Jakobsdatter,** born Oct. 3, 1839, daughter of Ingeborg Knutsdatter and Jakob Johnsen, tenant farmer no. 31, Austrheim.

Children:

a. Sivert Fredrik, born Aug. 26, 1863.
b. Jakob Elias, born Mar. 22, 1865, married in 1910 to Larsine Martine Larsen.
c. Johan Arent, born Apr. 10, 1867.
d. Ole Berrendt, born Sept. 17, 1869.
e. Julius.
f. Ida, born 1873.

The lease to Ole Andreas on one lot, "the Beitene," from Gudmund Knutsen, is dated May 1, 1865. The house on that lot is the one that, among others, Mathias Hansen lived in later (farm no. 11, Solheim).

Ole was a shoemaker, and later apparently also a diver. The family moved to Bergen in 1870.

15. **Jakob Danielsen.** 1863 – 1870
Born Jan. 1, 1836. died in 1901, son of Kari Oline Jakobsdatter and Daniel Johannesen, farmer no. 4 – 9 e, Austrheim.

Married in 186x to **Ingeborg Katrine Nilsdatter,** born in 1840, died in 1889, daughter of Elisabet Katrine Olsdatter and Nils Abrahamsen, Kalsto, Karmøy, originally from Fjellberg in Sunnhordaland.

Children:
a. Magel Serine, born Sept. 30, 1863.
b. Johannes, born Nov. 30, 1865.
c. Nils Daniel, born June 25, 1868, immigrated to USA in 1888, married in 1913 to Janne Emalie Knutsen.
d. Ola, born and died in 1871.
e. Ola, born 1873.
f. Kornelius, born in 1875, married in 1901 to Ovidia Josefine Osmundsdatter Våra.
g. Elisabet Katrine, born 1878, married to Bertil Ask.
h. Janna Elida, born 1881.
i. Inger Oline, born in 1885.

The lease to Jakob on a house lot, 28 x 14 alen situated at "the new area" (Lynghilder) from Knut Hansen is dated May 2, 1865. This house is understood to have been moved to Rabben, farm no. 10, Hovland.

The house, 7.5 x 6.6 meters, frame built and with logs, with a basement and clad with boards and roofed with tiles, was in 1869 assessed at 200 Spd.

The family moved to Kalsto, Karmøy in 1870.

16. **Lars Tormodsen.** 1866 – 1870

Born in 1833, died Jan. 21, 1919 in Kristiansund, and was from Birkeland in Vikedal.

Married on July 8, 1866, to **Hansine Hansdatter,** born Jan. 11, 1837, died in 1871(?), daughter of Valborg Knutsdatter and Hans Sakarias Johannesen, farmer no. 5 – 5 e, Austrheim. After Hansine's death, Lars remarried Anne from Valdres.

Children (from 1st marriage):
a. Tormod *Johan,* born Oct. 9, 1866, married Inger Anne Kristoffersdatter in 1891. He was a sailor.
b. Hans Sakarias *Wallum* (W. Tormodsen), born Apr. 23, 1869, married Engel Marie Karlson in 1895, 5 children. Wallum was a "fish discards man," both in Norway and Scotland. He founded the insurance company *Nordlys* in Bodø. They lived a few years in Grimsby, England and Kristiansund, before they moved to Bodø in 1913.
c. Hansine Lovise, born in 1871, died Mar. 4, 1873.

d. Zacharias, emigrated to USA.

Lars moved to Haugesund in July 1870, then lived in Bergen a few years before he in October 1876 moved to Kristiansund.

17. **Tormod Tormodsen.** 1869 – 1872
Born in 1832 and came from Birkeland in Vikedal.

Married Oct. 30, 1869, to **Inger Oline Hansdatter,** born June 15, 1840, daughter of Valborg Knutsdatter and Hans S. Johannesen, farmer no. 5 – 5 f, Austrheim.

Children:

a. Thomine Chathrine, born Sept. 3, 1871, died before 1875.
b. Konrad, born 1873.
c. Hans, born 1880.
d. Alfred, born 1882.

The family moved to Bergen. Tormod was a diver.

18. **Gaut Mathias Larsen.** 1876 – 1900
See farm no. 2, Klovning.

Gaut Mathias owned the house and lived on farm no. 4. In 1900, the daughter Valborg Helene lived there with her daughter, Berta Amanda.

19. **Nils Johannes Nilsen.** 1887 – 1932
Born Apr. 9, 1860, died Sept. 14, 1903, son of Karen Juliane and Nils Nilsen, tenant farmer no. 10 a, Austrheim.

Married on Aug. 7, 1887, to **Ingeborg Oline Tollefsdatter,** born Jan. 29, 1858, died Mar. 17, 1932, daughter of Berthe Jakobsdatter and Tollef Amundsen, tenant farmer no. 29 at Kvalvik.

Children:

a. Nils Kornelius, born Apr. 6, 1888, died Jan. 24, 1893.
b. Tilla Bertine, born Jan. 11, 1890, married in 1911 to Enes E. Rossebø, Skåre.
c. *Hanna* Virginie, born Dec. 19, 1891, married 192x to Kato Larsen, Bergen.
d. *Nils* Kornelius, born Dec. 6, 1894, died June 1, 1970, also had a farm here.
e. *Milla* Gunhilde, born Aug. 21, 1897. She and Nils took over the main house, farm no. 15, Austhus, following Tobias Austrheim. Milla moved to Haugesund in 1970, and died in 1978.

Family of Martin Nilsen around 1930. From left Juline, Birger, Martin, Signe, Jonette, Martine and Lars.

The family lived in the house that was later taken over by Johan Austrheim as a vacation home.

20. **Martin Nilsen.** 1900 – 1943
Born June 29, 1864, died Sept. 24, 1947, son of Karen Juliane and Nils Nilsen, tenant farmer no. 10 c, Austrheim.

Married on Nov. 4, 1900, to ***Jonette*** **Katrine Sjursdatter**, born Mar. 19, 1865, died Apr. 19, 1956, daughter of Anne Marthe Ådnesdatter and Sjur Olsen, farmer no. 3 – 2 b, Kvalvik.

Children:

a. Nils *Johan,* born July 6, 1901, married in 1925 to Signe Eriksen, tenant farmer no. 55, Nordvik.
b. *Signe* Anne Martha, born Dec. 20, 1902, married in 1943 to Erik Thomassen, farmer no. 6 – 2, Skare.
c. *Martine* Jonette, born July 2, 1905, married in 1931 to Aastein Thomassen, tenant farmer no. 32, Skare.
d. Nelly *Juline*, born July 2, 1905, married in 1931 to J. Stener Bendiksen, tenant farmer no. 24, Skare.

The Elling Knutsen family in 1926. From left: Rasmus, Gurine, Klara, Ragna, Marie, Julie, Elling, Knut, Sivert and Emma.

e. *Lars* Johannes, born May 5, 1907, married in 1931 to Gurine Austrheim, tenant farmer no. 24, Austrheim.
f. Olav *Birger*, born July 16, 1910, married in 1930 to Malene Helgesen, tenant farmer no. 58, Nordvik.

Jonette's daughter with Elling Mathiassen:

g. Julie Kristine, born Jan. 20, 1887, married to Knut M. L. Lervik, tenant farmer no. 39, Skare.

The family lived and owned a house here on farm no. 4. This house was later taken over by Mathias Hansen, farm no. 11, Solheim.

21. **Elling Knutsen.** 1905 – 1950

Born Sept. 14, 1876, died Mar. 29, 1936, son of Asseline and Knut Hansen, farmer no. 5 – 6 d, Austrheim.

Married on July 14, 1905, to **Julie Amalie Rasmusdatter,** born Dec. 18, 1884, died Oct. 2, 1950, daughter of Gurine and Rasmus Thomassen, farm no. 12 – 5 c, Nordvik.

Children:

a. *Sivert* Johannes, born Feb. 21, 1906, died Mar. 2, 1982.
b. *Klara* Asseline, born July 9, 1908, married in 1938 to Laurits Nernes, farmer no. 5 – 9, Austrheim.
c. Berthe *Gurine*, born Dec. 25, 1910, married in 1931 to Lars Nilsen, tenant farmer no. 24, Austrheim.
d. Ragna, born July 5, 1913, died Apr. 5, 1933.
e. Rasmus, born May 2, 1916, married in 1957 to widow Jenny Selle Steensnaes, farm no. 5 – 8. Austrheim.
f. *Emma* Juline, born Aug. 15, 1918, married in 1950 to Thorvald Austrheim, farm no. 1 – 11, Austrheim.
g. *Knut* Andreas, born Jan. 16, 1921, died Nov. 30, 1991. Knut also had a farm here.
h. Anne *Marie*, born Dec. 18, 1923, married in 1949 to Trygve Gravelsaeter, Stødle, Etne.

The main dwelling house here was built in 1903 on leased property. This is now farm no. 28 and is used as a summer home. It was taken over in 1982 by Anne Marie Gravelsaeter.

22. **J. Johan Hansen.** 1917 – 1975

Born July 19, 1890, died Aug. 30, 1934, son of Severine and Hans Mathias Sjursen, farm no. 4 – 11 d, Austrheim.

Married July 25, 1917, to **Amanda S. Gudmundsen,** born June 29, 1895, died Apr. 24, 1978, daughter of Ida Josefine and Bertel Gudmundsen, farm no. 13 – 7 f, Nordvik.

Children:

a. Severine, born Sept. 26, 1917, married in 1948 to Martin Endressen, Berøy in Moster.
b. *Bertel* Ambjorn, born Aug. 29, 1918, died Apr. 29, 1979. He also had a farm here.
c. Hans Mathias, born May 22, 1920, died Apr. 2, 1923.
d. *Thorvald* Johan, born Oct. 31, 1922, died Aug. 3, 1944.
e. *Hanne* Marie, born Feb. 28, 1924, died Jan. 19, 1939.

Johan took over the main house after Karine Eriksen (Aksteberg). This house was taken out of the estate in 1956 and is now farm no. 24 and a summer vacation house. It was taken over in 1979 by Severine Berøy.

23. **Alfred Hansen.** 1924 – 1926
They lived for a while on farm no. 1, Austrheim. See tenant farmer Hovland.

24. **Lars Nilsen.** 1931 – 1950
Born May 5, 1907, son of Jonette and Martin Nilsen, tenant farmer no. 20 e, Austrheim.

Married May 2, 1931, to **Gurine Austrheim,** born Dec. 25, 1910, daughter of Julie and Elling Knutsen, tenant farmer no. 21 c, Austrheim.

Children:

a. Martinius *Johannes*, born Aug. 30, 1931, married in 1954 to Tordis Lillesund, Torvestad.
b. *Judit* Eline, born Apr. 23, 1933, married in 1953 to Andreas Haaland, Torvestad.
c. Liv *Gunhild*, born May 19, 1937, married in 1959 to Ivar Åse, lives in Haugesund.
d. Harald. born Aug. 19, 1946, married in 1968 to Johanna Marie Vinnes (Mia), lives in Storesund, Torvestad.

The main dwelling here was built in 1937, farm no. 15, Austhus.

The family moved to Viken, Torvestad during the summer of 1950. The estate was taken over by Tobias Austrheim, and later by Nils Nilsen. The house is today used as a summer house and is owned by Trygve Nordvik.

25. **Hjalmar Ellingsen.** 1930 – 1993
Born Jan. 16,1906, died May 3, 1991, son of Astrid and Elling Gudmundsen, farm no. 3 – 7 f, Austrheim.

Married Apr. 29, 1931, to **Elisabeth Skåren,** born Aug. 28, 1912, daughter of Thomine and Johannes Gudmundsen, farm no. 22 – 3 k, Nordvik.

Children:

a. *Henry* Edvin, born Aug. 30, 1931, married to Aud Eriksen, lives in Haugesund.
b. *Tor* Jostein, born May 18, 1935, died in 1982. Married in 1961 to Gerd Østrem, lived in Haugesund.
c. *Audny* Elise, born Aug. 17, 1937, lives in Haugesund.

d. *Kirsten* Lovise, born Sept. 2, 1940, married in 1963 to Eivind Hammer, lives in Sveio.
e. *Berit* Margit, born May 16, 1947, married to Olav Vikshåland, Torvestad. Divorced and married again to Magnus Juvik, now living in Kopervik.
f. Elling, born Apr. 21, 1948, took over the estate in 1989, married in 1996 to Florenda Layos from Cebu City, Philippines.

The main dwelling here is the old farmhouse on farm no. 3, now farm no. 12, Fjellhaug.

26. **Elling Ellingsen.** 1928 – 1935
Born Jan. 1, 1902, son of Astrid and Elling Gudmundsen, farm no. 3–7 e, Austrheim.

Married to **Bergliot Johannesen,** born Nov. 1, 1906, daughter of Karin and Kasper Johannesen, Torvestad.

Children:
a. *Else* Bergliot, born Aug. 16, 1929, married to Mathias Kristiansen, Torvestad.
b. *Karine* Alise, born Mar. 21, 1933.

The family moved to Feoy.

27. **Elling Haugseth.** 1960 – 1972
Born June 3, 1920, died June 20, 1975, son of Gunda and Petter Haugseth, farm no. 13 – 1 c, Austrheim.

Married on July 30, 1949, to **Kristine Thorsen,** born May 28, 1929, daughter of Olga and Gaut Thorsen, tenant farmer no. 34 a, Skare.

Children:
a. Per Svein, born Feb. 14, 1951, married to Bente Tjøsvold, lives in Håvik, Karmøy.
b. Gerd *Oddgunn*, born Sept. 22, 1956, lives with Ricardo Allende in Torvestad.

Elling worked on a pilot boat. The main dwelling here was built in 1960, farm no. 29, Skogtun; taken over by Einar Hansen in 1972.

The family moved to Karmøy.

28. **Johan Austrheim.** 1953 – 1957
Born Apr. 3, 1922, son of Julie and Konrad Knutsen, farm no. 1 – 10 i, Austrheim.

Married Dec. 12, 1953, to **Inger Hertas,** born Feb. 2, 1928, came from Olve in Kvinnherad.

Children:

a. *Turid* Bodil, born May 27, 1954, married in 1974 to Kjell Morten Tungland, lives in Sandnes.
b. *Mary* Irene, born Mar. 21, 1956, married in 1975 to Odd Magne Berheim, lives in Sandnes.
c. Gunn, born Dec. 15, 1960, lives in Høgstad, Sandnes.
d. May Britt, born Mar. 8, 1964, married in 1981 to Rolf Skare, tenant farmer no. 51, Skare.

The family moved to Hogstad near Sandnes in 1957.

29. **Ole Knutsen.** 1836 – 1843
Baptized Aug. 4, 1816, son of Bertha Gudmundsdatter and Knut Sjursen, farmer no. 5 – 4 g, Austrheim.

Married July 3, 1842, to **Ingeborg Kirstine Larsdatter,** born May 19, 1825, daughter of Martha Elisabeth Gautsdatter, and Lars Hansen, farmer no. 17 – 3 h, Nordvik.

Children:

a. Marthe Lisbeth, born Sept. 29, 1842, married first in 1860 to Bryngel Rovaer, and married the second time in 1867 to Thomas Forde, emigrated to N. Dakota, USA.
b. Bertha, born in 1844, married to Truls Gaard.
c. Hansine, born in 1847.
d. Knut, born in 1851.
e. Johannes, born in 1853.
f. Kirstine, born in 1855.
g. Gunla, born in 1858.
h. Marthe, born in 1860.
i. Laurense, born in 1863.

Most of these children emigrated to the USA.

Ole was schoolmaster on Utsira from 1836 – 1840. In 1843 the family moved to Sundfør in Skjold. According to the teacher Torbjørn Elleflådt (born in 1868), "Sir–Ola" was a master storyteller.[38]

30. **Sjur Tollefsen.** 1829 – 1833
Baptized Nov. 24, 1806, died Jan. 4, 1837, son of Ingeborg Gudmundsdatter and Tollef Sjursen, farmer no. 2 – 3 e, Austrheim.

---

[38] See Note 13.

Married July 16, 1832, to **Berthe Gurine Danielsdatter,** born 1807, died Nov. 1, 1855, daughter of Daniel Bårdsen and Brita Kristensdatter Tunge, from Utvik in Avaldsnes.

Children:

a. Berthe Kristine, born Mar. 22, 1835, married to the widower Nils Thomassen, tenant farmer no. 18, Klovning.

Sjur was schoolmaster on Utsira from 1829 – 1833. After he was married they moved to Gahre in Skåre. Gurine was married a second time in 1838 to Ole Karlsen, Kvalvik (farm no. 3 – 1).

31. **Jakob Jonsen.** 1836 – 1840
Born 1794, died in 1841, came from Haraldseide in Tysvaer.

Married first on July 12, 1829, to **Martha Serine Karlsdatter,** baptized Oct. 17, 1802, died Sept. 16, 1829, daughter of Anna Olsdatter and Karl Asbjornsen, tenant farmer no. 13 d, Kvalvik.

Married again on Nov. 1, 1835, to **Ingeborg Knutsdatter,** baptized Apr. 11, 1811, died Apr. 15, 1871, daughter of Bertha Gudmundsdatter and Knut Sjursen, farmer no. 5 – 4 e, Austrheim.

Children from second marriage:

a. Marthe Serine, born Feb. 13, 1836.
b. Knut Mathias, born Jan. 28, 1838, died Mar. 9, 1838.
c. Berthe, born Oct. 3, 1839, married in 1863 to Ole Andreas Olsen, tenant farm no. 14, Austrheim.
d. Jakob, born in 1842, died Mar. 20, 1902.

Ingeborg's daughter with Ole Karlsen Kvalvik:

e. Ingeborg, born May 20, 1832, married in 1860 to barrel maker Ole Olsen, who lived on Risoy.

Jakob worked as a carpenter when he lived on Utsira. In 1840 he moved to Sunfor in Skjold. Ingeborg and son Jakob lived on Austrheim in 1865. She was then a widow and is listed as a poorhouse lodger.

32. **Sigvald Hansen.** 1940 –
Born Aug. 25, 1920, son of Elisabeth and Severin Hansen, farm no. 4 – 12 f, Austrheim.

In 1968 Sigvald built a new home here on farm no. 22, Sorheim.

Hovland (Haugland)

Before 1824:	Reg. no. 49, tax liability 2 v. tf.
1824 – 1851:	Reg. no. 56, serial no. 237 – 241, tax 9 dl. 12 sk.
1851 – 1886:	Reg. no. 66, serial no. 341 – 346, tax 4–4–3 dl.
1886 –:	Farm no. 28, tax liability 13 mark 80 ore.

Hovland is a common farm name in this district. The name normally indicates that the land is near a temple or other religious institution, but may also indicate that the property lies on a ridge or elevated ground. The western part of Hovland borders on Skare, to the north on Nordvik, and to the east on Austrheim. The southern part of Hovland, farm no. 7, "Tuo," is listed in the church records from 1706 – 1724 as a separate individual farm.

The farm name is spelled in the above manner ("Hovland") in 1521, and in 1606: "Hoffland," in 1610: "Houffland," and in 1661 and 1723: "Hougland."

The following is from the public records of 1668:

> Hougland, 2 våger dried fish, acceptable grain fields for domestic needs, while meadows and pastures are marginal, but peat supply is sufficient for domestic fuel requirements, 2 barrels of grain is planted and sufficient feed is available for 9 head of cattle. It is estimated that the farm can pay taxes as follows: 2 wetter grain, 1 goat hide for local defenses, 2 buckets of grain for the church and 4 skillings in cash contributions.

At Hovland there were two farmers working the farm during most of the 16th century. Except for a short period of time around 1700, when there were four farmers, three farmers worked the farm most of the time up to 1849. In 1930 the number of farms increased to seven.

There were two settlements at Hovland, the largest one was "Dahlen" listed under farm no. 1 and the other was "Tiphaugen" listed under farm no. 4. A third settlement is listed in the 1758 census under

Aerial photo taken from Yrefjellet showing Hovland. "The Old School" seen to the left and "Skarshoien" with the "Pilot Cottage" to the right. Photo by: Robert Kloster in 1932 and made available by the Historical Museum in Bergen.

Tuo (Hans Hansen), but this settlement should probably be listed under Skare.

Public separation of some of Hovland's cultivated land (farm no. 2 and 4) was carried out in 1871–72 and for cultivated and uncultivated land 1928 – 29.

Table showing planted and harvested crops of grain and potatoes:

Year	Grain planted	Potatoes planted	Grain harvested	Potatoes harvested
1668	2	–	–	–
1703	5	–	–	–
1712	5.5	–	–	–
1723	3.5	17	–	
1802	7.5	–	42	–
1822	–	–	89	21
1845	16	5	–	
1866	20	11	116	79
1875	17	13.5	–	–
1945	10.5	5	–	–

For 1945 the numbers are shown in dekars and barrels.

Table showing livestock, homes and inhabitants:

Year	Horses	Cows	Calves	Homes	Inhabitants
1668	–	9	–	–	–
1703	2	12	x	–	–
1712	1	12	x	–	–
1723	1	8	–	–	–
1758	–	–	–	6	29
1801–02	3	15	0	5	30
1822	7	21	19	–	–
1845	4	16	22	5	30
1866	5	19	45	11	61
1875	4	12	78	13	67
1900	–	–	–	9	39

Farmers

1. **Nils.** 1521
He is mentioned in the tax register from 1521.

2. **Erlend.** 1563

He is also mentioned in the tax register from 1563.

3. **Knut.** – 1625
Knut is mentioned in the county records up to and including 1615. From 1618 to 1625 he is listed as a widower at Hovland. At the Avaldsnes quarterly council meeting in 1620 Knut Hovland's heirs are cited for owing unpaid taxes.

4. **Mogens (Mons).** 1616 – 1643
Mogens pays 3 rdl. in a first lease contract. In 1616, he spends 2 pound 8 mrk. dried fish from the farm (approx 1/3 of the farm's assets). In 1630 he is listed in bad condition financially and *poor*.

Farm no. 1

1. **Anders Nilsen.** 1626 – 1661
Anders pays 8 rdl. in a first lease contract in 1626. He spends 4 pd.16 mrk. dried fish or approximately 2/3 of the farms assets.

2. **Hans Olsen.** 1661 – 1664
Born around 1634. Hans is mentioned in the census in 1664, but in the church records the same year only the next farmer is mentioned.

3. **Ingebret Hansen.** 1664 – 1670
Born around 1642, possibly son of Hans Ingebretsen, farmer no. 1 – 2, Klovning.

4. **Johannes Hansen.** 1670 – 1703.
Born around 1650, lives at Hovland in 1711, but is not mentioned there in the 1707 census.

His children may be:

a. Hans, born around 1677, farm no. 4 – 2, Hovland.
b. Jon, born around 1679, farmer no. 6 here.
c. Name unknown, possibly married to Ingvald Halvorsen, next farmer.
d. Magdalena, born around 1686, married to Hans Korneliussen, farmer no. 4 – 3, Hovland.

Johannes is mentioned for the first time in the military records from 1673, and is then the only tenant farmer at Hovland. In 1683 he was cited in Bømlo court together with Anders Nordvik for assault on Jakob Bringmand.

In 1703 he spent 1 pd. 20 mrk. dried fish of the farm's assets, and his financial condition was described as poor and repair on the buildings was 2 ort. Together with his son Hans, he planted 1 barrel of oats and fed 2 cows, 1 calf, 1 horse and some sheep. He did not own the livestock himself, but leased them from others. He still had not paid the 6 rdl. for the brawl fines that he owed from 20 years earlier.

In 1714 he was among a number of others who received a salvaging bonus (7 ort.) for rescuing items from a shipwreck in 1707.

5. **Ingvald Halvorsen.** – 1715

Born around 1650 in Bergenhus county.

Ingvald was possibly married to a daughter of previous farmer.

Known Children:

a. Hans, born in 1701, further information unknown.
b. Ingvald, born 1710, mentioned in 1734.
c. Ole, born in 1714, mentioned in 1734.

Stepson:

d. Ole Hansen, born 1676 at Klovning, tenant farmer no. 8, Nordvik.

Ingvald spent 2 pound 20 merker dried fish of the farm's assets; from 1700, only 1 pound dried fish.

His financial condition was described in 1703 as poor, but the buildings on the farm were in good condition with about 2 ort estimated for repairs. He planted 1/2 barrel of oats and fed 1 cow, 1 calf and some sheep, all of which he owned. He does not owe anything to the cloister manager Frimand, but to others he owes 6 rdl. for bread grain.

The next time we again hear about Ingvald, his financial condition is worse. In a report from 1712 listing the farmers of Halsnoy Cloister, it is recorded:

> He is in miserable condition; cost of repair of his buildings is estimated at 2 ort, he plants 1–1/2 barrels of oats, feeds 1 cow, 1 calf and some sheep and does not own a single animal.

He also owes a large debt to Mikkel Eeg of 15 – 16 rdl. Mikkel was a citizen of Stavanger and did, among other things, some business with Utsira. Ingvald was also among those who received a salvaging bonus for the Arendal ship that was shipwrecked off Utsira, but he is not listed among the farmers on Hovland in the tax collector's records in 1715.

6. **Jon Johannesen.** 1704 – 1750
Born around 1679, buried on Mar. 23, 1754, possibly son of Johannes Hansen, farmer no. 4 above. The name of his wife is unknown.

The children are possibly:

a. Anna (Agnete), born 1708, married to Hans Pedersen, tenant farmer no. 19, Nordvik.
b. Ole, born 1707, mentioned in the military records from 1734.

Jon spent 1 pd. 20 mrk. dried fish of the farm's assets. Between 1720 and 1730, two other tenant farmers at Hovland hold equal amounts of the assets: 2 pd. 20 mrk., but later Jon's farm is worth 1 pound 16 merker dried fish.

The houses on the farm must have been situated at Tuo. In the written records Jon is listed in connection with this farm until 1731. From the 1750s it is only Anbjorn Rasmussen who is listed under Tuo.

Jon served in the Navy and was perhaps the only one from Utsira who served during the Great Nordic War.[39]

In 1712 his financial condition was described as poor and it was estimated that 1 rdl. 2 ort would be required to repair his houses. He planted 1 barrel of oats and fed 2 cows, 2 calves, 1 horse and some sheep, and he owned the livestock. When he was away for his military service with the Navy, there was no one at home who could answer questions about what he owed.

In 1721 many of the buildings on the farm needed repairs estimated to 1 rdl., 2 ort, 8 sk., and he already had a debt of 4 rdl.

In 1723 he planted 1 barrel of oats and harvested 5 barrels. The livestock consisted of 2 cows.

7. **Anders Pedersen.** 1750 – 1792
Born in 1726, buried Mar. 25, 1787, son of Anbjør Torsdatter and Peder Johannesen, farm no. 5 – 1 b, Austrheim.

Married in 1st marriage to **Malene Knutsdatter,** born 1723, died Oct. 1767, sister of Marthe Kristine at farm no. 15 – 3, Nordvik.

---

[39] Also called the "Great Northern War," 1700-1721, it was a conflict between Denmark-Norway, and its allies, and the Swedish Empire, ending with a defeat for Sweden. See http://en.wikipedia.org/wiki/Great_Northern_War.

Married in 2nd marriage on Sept. 21, 1768, to **Ingeborg Knutsdatter,** born in 1747, buried June 7, 1789, daughter of Knut and Siri Andersdatter Osnes.

Children in 1st. marriage:

a. Marthe, born 1753, buried July 2, 1753, lived only 3 days.
b. Malene, baptized Apr. 16, 1754, died before 1758.
c. Peder, baptized Aug. 14, 1755, buried Mar. 28, 1756.
d. Peder, baptized Feb. 2, 1757, in 1787 he is a commercial seaman "shipping out of Copenhagen." Died before 1819.
e. Malene, baptized Jan. 14, 1760, died childless before 1819.
f. Ambjor, baptized Oct. 7, 1762, buried July 10, 1785.
g. Elisabet, baptized Dec. 22, 1765, died Aug. 13, 1819. She was a servant at Kvalvik and earlier, in the household of the senior marine pilot in Kopervik, among others.

Children in 2nd marriage:

h. Malene, baptized Jan. 19, 1769; in 1819, as a widow, lived in Bergen.
i. Siri, baptized Jan. 15, 1771, buried June 7, 1789.
j. Agnete, baptized Oct. 18, 1772, buried Apr. 16, 1813.
k. Anders, baptized Nov. 12, 1774, buried Mar. 25, 1779.
l. Gunvor, baptized Jan. 9, 1778, buried Dec. 21, 1794.
m. Anders, baptized Sept. 9, 1780, tenant farmer no. 15, Kvalvik.
n. Berta, baptized Feb. 4, 1783, buried Mar. 30, 1800.

The lease contract to Anders is dated Apr. 20, 1750 in the amount of 2 bp. 20 mrk. dried fish. It is also recorded in the tax records in 1755–66 that the debt on the farm is 1 bp. 16 mrk. dried fish with an additional 2 pds. for each of the three tenants working the farm at Hovland.

From 1770 and later Anders is listed in the financial records as a permanent marine pilot.

In the settlement after Malene's death in 1768 the estate's assets are 82 rdl. 3 ort. There is 54 rdl. left to be split among the heirs. The funeral costs are 8 rdl. Among the items left are the following:

> 2 horses 7–0–0, 3 cows and 1 heifer 14–3–0, 2 rams 1–0–0, 1 tiled heating stove 6–2–0, smithy tools 3–3–0, 3 kettles 3–3–0, 3 barrels oats 4–0–0, silverware 6–0–0, 3 spring herring nets 2–1–0, 10 lobster pots 0–3–8, a 4-oar boat with sail 3–0–0, 1/3 share in a fully rigged boat 10–0–0, 1/3 share in a fishing shed 3–0–0, and 1/3 share in a mill 2–0–0.

At the settlement after Anders' death in 1787 there were assets in the amount of 34 rdl., but outstanding debt and expenses amounted to 37 rdl., so there was nothing left to the heirs.

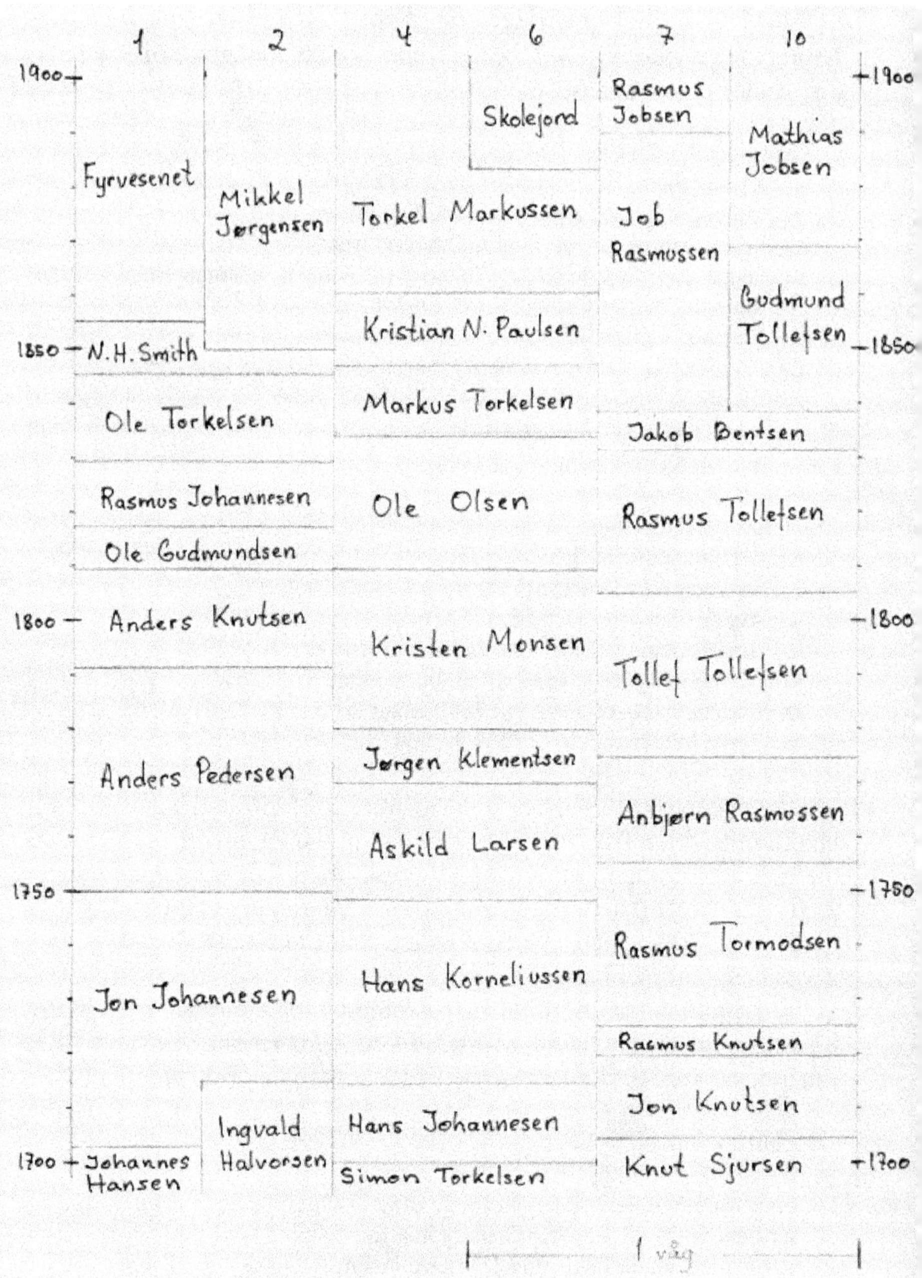

Table of farmers at Hovland from 1700 – 1900 (farm numbers across the top).

8. **Anders Knutsen.** 1792 – 1809
See under tenant farm no. 9, Austrheim.

Anders was the brother of Ingeborg (above). He was issued a lease contract in the amount of 2 bp. 8 mrk. dried fish by Forman in Bergen on Mar. 22, 1793.

The family lived as renters at Lynghilder, belonging to farm no 5, Austrheim, before they leased here.

In 1802 the farm planted 2–1/2 barrels of grain and harvested 14 barrels. The livestock consisted of 1 horse, 3 cows and 2 calves. The farm was estimated to be worth 120 riksdaler.

There was a settlement after Anders in 1819. Expenses and debt were larger than the assets, so there was nothing left to the heirs. Among the items left were:

> 1 cabin, with kitchen at one end and a small lean–to on the other, 20–0–0, 1 cow "Snørej" 6–0–0, 1 small iron stove 5–0–0, 4 spring herring fishing nets 2–0–12 and 16 lobster pots 1–0–8.

9. **Ole Gudmundsen.** 1809 – 1817
Baptized on Apr. 24, 1784, died Mar. 8, 1816, son of Valborg Olsdatter and Gudmund Thomassen, farmer no. 3 – 2 g, Austrheim.

Married on Jan. 20, 1810, to **Gjoa Andersdatter,** baptized Aug. 6, 1783, died May 20, 1875, daughter of previous farmer (tenant farmer no. 9 g, Austrheim).

Children:

a. Marta, baptized May 26, 1810, married in 1830 to Lars Mikkelsen, tenant farmer no. 22, Hovland.
b. Knut, baptized Apr. 18, 1812, married in 1865 to Serine Jørgensdatter (Strilo), tenant farm no. 24, Hovland.
c. Gudmund, baptized Dec. 11, 1814, buried June 30, 1816.

Lease contract to Ole in the amount of 2 bp. 8 mrk. dried fish is dated June 7, 1809 and is issued by assessor Forman in Bergen. Ole also had to contribute to his in–laws in an old age contract with, among other items, 5 barrels of oats, feed for 2 cows and part of a field near Skarshaugen. He also had to prepare a 28 x 28 alen field and provide enough peat for fuel. The farm had the following buildings: The main dwelling, cow–stable, barn, shed and boathouse.

There was a settlement after Ole's death in 1816. Among the assets amounting to 74–1–13 Spd., there were 56 Spd. left for the heirs. The following items were left:

2 horses 13–1–0, 3 cows ("Rødsia", "Plomrej" and "Snorej") and 1 calf 15–0–0, 1 stove 3–0–0, 1 cattle trough 3–0–0, 1 new boathouse 5–3–0, 1 old four–oar boat with old sail 4–3–0, 1/2 share in a herring fishing boat with sail 5–3–0, 12 lobster pots 0–2–0, 1 spring herring fishing net 1–2–12.

Gjoa married in 2nd marriage in 1817 to Rasmus Johannesen, next farmer.

10. **Rasmus Johannesen.** 1817 – 1829
Baptized Aug. 15, 1790. died Sept. 22, 1825, son of Synnøve Olavsdatter and Johannes Rasmussen, Vikingstad.

Married on Apr. 13, 1817, to **Gjoa Andersdatter,** widow of previous farmer.

Children:

a. Oline, baptized July 2, 1817, buried Dec. 29,1817.
b. Ole Andreas, born Apr. 7, 1819, married in 1845 to Guri Larsdatter, lived at Aksdal in Tysvaer.
c. Johannes, born Jan. 21, 1821, married in 1848 to Mette Kristine Larsdatter, Ovrebo, Vikingstad.
d. Synnøve, born May 30, 1823.
e. Ingeborg Serine ("Gjoa–Serino"), born Sept. 13, 1825, died May 27, 1912. She was a servant for many years at the home of Helge Andreas Johnsen, Nordvik.

The lease contract to Rasmus in the amount of 2 bp. 8 mrk. t.f. is dated Mar. 25, 1817 and is issued by Forman in Bergen, and the old age contract to his in–laws is similar to the one from the previous farmer.

In 1822 the houses on the farm were described as follows:

An old cabin with living room and kitchen, with peat–covered roof. 1 storage shed with a paneled cow stable in usable condition with a concrete manure bin attached.

As in most of the farms at Hovland there is still available peat for fuel for a few more years, and included with the farm is one-third of a mill close to the landing area for boats in Austramarka.

The farm yields annually 20 to 22 barrels of grain and 6 to 8 barrels of potatoes. It feeds 5 cows, 2 horses and 6 to 8 sheep. There is also a fenced–in homestead lot rented out to Hans Johnsen.

The entire farm is in 1823 assessed to 150 Spd.

There was a settlement after Rasmus in 1826. The estate had assets for 62–2–22 Spd., but there was only 7–2–18 Spd. left to be divided among the heirs. Among the estate's assets the following items are listed:

> Fishing equipment and a boat 13–3–4, 3 cows ("Makrej" 7 years old, "Rødsia" 9 years old and "Romrej" 10 years old) and 1 calf 18–0–0, 2 horses 13–0–0 and 1/2 share in a mill with housing and associated equipment 4–0–0.

11. **Ole Torkelsen.** 1829 – 1845
Born Apr. 22, 1798, son of Anne Olsdatter and Torkel Olsen, renter at Thornes in Opdahl, Tysnes.

Married on Oct. 5, 1829, to **Anna Kristine Paulsdatter,** born in 1790, daughter of Berta Asbjornsdatter and Paul Paulsen, Landa in Avaldsnes, and widow of Kornelius Olsen, Stange.

Children:

a. Torkel, born Aug. 23, 1830, married in 1857 to Johanna Marie Jokumsdatter. Lived in Ovre–Risdal, Skudesnes.

Ole bought this farm with a 2 bp. dried fish tax potential from Johan Dahm June 1, 1829 for 200 Spd. In the contract it is noted that the rights to grazing and other usages of the Beiningen share of the property be ceased.

The family moved to upper Risdal in Skudesnes.

12. **Nikolai Hansen Smith.** 1846 – 1855
See further information under Utsira Lighthouse.

Nikolai Smith was the first lighthouse manager for the new lighthouses on Utsira. He suggested to the director of lighthouses that the government should buy the property, which was then for sale. When this proposal was rejected, he bought the property himself.

The deed to Nikolai from Ole Torkelsen with a tax liability of 2 bp. dried fish is dated Dec. 15, 1845 for 1000 Spd. This transaction was later taken to court, as Nikolai felt he had paid too much. The tax liability on the deed had been changed by Ole's son, Torkel, from 2 to 3 bp. The case, however, was settled out of court after several meetings.

In 1849 he sold half of the farm, farm no. 2, to Mikkel Jørgensen.

13. **The Lighthouse Authority.** 1855 – 1903

The deed to the Lighthouse Authority from N. Smith for 850 Spd. is dated May 16, 1855.

The farm did not then have a main dwelling, and was used by the Lighthouse Authority and the manager.

In 1866 the farm consisted of 43 mål acres of fields and meadows assessed at 292 Spd. Annual yield was 13 barrels of oats, 12 barrels of potatoes and 38 skp. hay. In addition there were fields and pastures worth 79 Spd., peat for 20 Spd. and income from general fishing activities, 9 Spd. The entire farm was estimated to have a value of 420 Spd.

In 1865, the livestock consisted of 1 horse, 4 cows and 1 pig.

14. **Lars Thorsen.** 1903 – 1905

Born June 8, 1885, died May 10, 1906, son of Berthe Mallene and Thore Johannesen, farm no. 6 – 8 a, Austrheim.

Unmarried.

Lars leased the farm from the Lighthouse Authority in 1903. The contract was not published.

15. **Thore Torresen.** 1905 – 1927

Born in April 27, 1869, son of Berthe Malene and Torres Thorsen, tenant farmer no. 30 b, Nordvik.

Married on Oct. 27, 1895, to **Berthe *Karine* Gudmundsdatter**, born Oct. 15, 1863, died Aug. 2, 1918, daughter of Marthe Susanne and Gudmund Johannesen, farmer no. 22 – 2 b, Nordvik.

Children:

a. Tilla, born Dec. 13, 1896, died Dec. 19, 1896.
b. *Thorvald* Bernhard Kristian, born Dec. 3, 1900, married in 1925 to Anna Johannesen, Skudesnes.
c. Gunvald, born Dec. 31, 1902, died July 30, 1924.
d. Tilla, born Aug. 11, 1906, died Mar. 26, 1907.

The deed to Thore from the Department of Defense for 2700 kr. is dated Aug. 10, 1904. Estimated tax liability is listed as 2.18 sk.m. The main dwelling here was built in 1905. It could have been the old house belonging to his parents, which stood at Rau but moved here to Hovland. The house was expanded in 1948 by the next farmer. The family moved to Stava, Skudesnes in 1927.

Karine and Thore Torresen together with Gunda and Martin Nag among others in front of the main dwelling at farm no. 1 in 1918.

16. **Jakob Olai Nygård.** 1927 – 1963
Born Jan. 10, 1894, died Mar. 24, 1949, son of Ola O. Gautun and Ragnhild Nygård, Glamo in Skanevik.

Married to **Tilla Skåren,** born Aug. 18, 1898, died in 1989, daughter of Thomine and Johannes Gudmundsen, farmer no. 22 – 3 d, Nordvik.

Children:

a. Ragnar, born Oct. 19, 1922, died in 1974, married in 1953 to Inga Ingvaldsen from Tau, Strand in Ryfylke.
b. Gunnfrid, born July 8, 1927, married in 1950 to Ernst Mikalsen, farmer no. 4 – 5, Nordvik.
c. Einar, born Apr. 21, 1933.
d. Torleiv, born Aug. 26, 1940.

The deed to Jakob from Thore Torresen is dated Mar. 31, 1927 in the amount of 8,000 kroner.

"The General Store" belonging to J. O. Nygård around 1930. Standing in the doorway is Tilla Nygård.

Jakob took over a wholesale business in Nordvågen in 1922 and ran a grocery store there until he died. This store was taken over by Åsmund Faremo in 1950. The family moved later to Haugesund.

17. **Gerhard Skåren.** 1964 –
Born Sept. 29, 1933, son of Hanna and Gudmund Skåren, farmer no. 56 – 1 a, Nordvik.

Married on May 25, 1957, to **Kjellaug Hansen**, born Jan. 16, 1939, daughter of Karoline and Mathias Hansen, farmer no. 4 – 13 d, Austrheim.

Children:

a. *Margaret* Karoline, born July 22, 1958, married to Bjorn Eldhuset, lives in Haugesund.
b. *Gunnvor* Helen, born May 31, 1961, married to Johan Mindresundet, lives in Leirvik, Stord.
c. Kjell Gerhard, born Jan. 26, 1967. Kjell also had a farm here.

Gerhard took over the farm in 1964. He worked as lighthouse assistant at Utsira Lighthouse. They built a new main dwelling here in 1982.

Farm No 2. From farm No. 1 in 1849

1. **Mikkel Jørgensen,** 1849 – 1907

Born Apr. 24, 1822, died Aug. 21, 1909, son of Bertha Olsdatter and Jørgen Johnsen, farmer no. 13 – 3 g, Nordvik.

Married June 29, 1845, to ***Lavine* Nicoline Larsdatter,** born 1821, died Feb. 8, 1901, from Melkevik on Hitra.

Children:

a. Lars Martinius, born Apr. 8, 1845, married in 1869 to Berthe Malene Mathiasdatter, tenant farm no. 28, Hovland.
b. Jørgen Bertel (George), born Sept. 20, 1846, died in 1930, was a sailor and settled in Nebraska, USA. There he married Dorthea Simonsen in 1876. He became, among other things, a deputy sheriff, trader and farmer.[40]
c. Martha Olava, born May 6, 1849, married in 1866 to John Mathias Ellingsen, farmer no. 2 – 6, Skare.
d. Ole Mikal, born Apr. 4, 1851, died Nov. 29, 1871.
e. Johan Nyman, born Dec. 23, 1854, died Aug. 16, 1878. He had a son, Ole Johan, born July 27, 1874 (to farm no. 21, Nordvik), with Karoline Rasmusdatter, Skare. She later married Oppen.
f. Lovise Amalie, born Apr. 1, 1859, died Nov. 17, 1867.

The deed to Mikkel from Lighthouse Steward N. Smith for 1 bp. dried fish, dated May 16, 1849 for 500 Spd. (tax 1 dl. 2 ort 19 sk.).

Mikkel served as First–Assistant (Deputy Manager) at Utsira Lighthouse for more than 45 years, from May 1, 1853 to Oct. 18, 1898, when he retired at the age of 76. Besides Kristian Paulsen, Hovland, he is the one who has served the longest at Utsira Lighthouse.

In 1865, the farm consisted of 34.5 mål fields and meadows, estimated worth 270 Spd. Annual crop yield was 17 barrels of oats, 3 barrels of barley, 15 barrels of potatoes and 27 skp. of hay. In addition,

> **Mikkel Jørgensen** has left his position as deputy lighthouse keeper at the Utsire Light House on the 18th of this month. He was born in 1822 and was hired as First Assistant on May 1, 1853 at Utsire Light House and has without interruption worked this position during a time span of 46 years. He has during his long service served under five lighthouse keepers and from all of them he has received the highest praise for his conscientious recognition of his duties. Even though he is now 77 years old he is still going strong doing his part of the daily chores with considerable vigor and interest. (*Stavanger Amtstid.* 21 Oct. 1898)

[40] See Note 14.

Mikkel Jørgensen (1822 – 1909) and Lavine Nicoline Larsdatter (1821 – 1901).

there was peat for 16 Spd. and fishing rights income of 9 Spd. The farm was assessed at 404 Spd.

The livestock on the farm in 1865 consisted of 1 horse, 2 cows, 10 sheep and 1 pig. Ten years later the livestock had almost doubled: 2 horses, 3 cows, 21 sheep and 1 pig.

George B. Hovland

Notice

I would like to inform my friends, that we, undersigned, are here from USA and have had a wonderful trip here visiting families and friends, but will be traveling back to America on first of August. If anyone wishes to travel to USA on the same ship, you can buy tickets from me by writing to Utsire. Address:

Geo. B. Hovland,
Utsire.
Chr. Simonsen.
Simon Christiansen.

Notice, Karmsund newspaper, June 8, 1882. According to George Hovland's report a total of 35 persons, all from Utsira, went with them to USA.

2. **Elling Mathiassen.** 1907 – 1927

Born Mar. 2, 1869, died Oct. 26, 1918, son of Martha Olava Mikkelsdatter and J. Mathias Ellingsen, farm no. 2 – 6 b. Skare.

Married July 5, 1891, to **A. Kathrine Mathiasdatter,** born Jan. 18, 1864, died Apr. 27, 1927, daughter of Petronelle Knutsdatter and John Mathias Johnsen, farm no. 3 – 1 i, Skare.

Children:

a. *Milla* Otelie Lovise, born Sept. 20, 1891, married to Johan Mathias Rasmussen, farmer no. 7 – 11, Hovland.
b. Berthe *Kristine*, born Aug. 8, 1894, married in 1919 to Toralf Austrheim, farmer no. 2 – 7, Austrheim.
c. Johan *Mathias*, born Mar. 3, 1901, next farmer.
d. Mikael, born Mar. 5, 1903, died Apr. 12, 1967, became a commercial seaman. Mikael also had a farm here.

Elling's child with Jonette Sjursdatter Kvalvik:

e. Julie Kristine, born Jan. 20, 1887, married Knut M. L. Lervik, tenant farmer no. 39, Skare.

The deed to Elling from Mikkel on this farm, with a tax assessment of sk.m. 2.14, and farm no. 5, "Yrebrekko," sk. m 0.47, in the amount of 2,580 kr. plus services for 250 kr., is dated Nov. 14, 1907.

3. **Mathias Hovland.** 1927 – 1975
Born Mar. 3, 1901, died Jan. 1, 1985, son of previous farmer.

Married on Jan. 28, 1928, to **Sofie Rasmussen,** born Mar. 5, 1903, died Apr. 25, 1994, daughter of Gurine Amalie Gudmundsdatter and Rasmus Jobsen, farmer no. 7 – 10 f, Hovland.

Children:

a. *Margit* Sofie, born Aug. 16, 1938, married to Ragnar Floysvik, lives in Sandnes.

The deed to Mathias from the other heirs is dated Dec. 28, 1927.

The livestock on the farm consisted in 1956 of 3 cows, a calf, a horse and 10 sheep. The farm was later used as an additional farming area. The estate was eventually taken over by Margit Floysvik in 1975.

Farm No. 4

1. **Simon Torkelsen.** 1650 – 1700
Born around 1622, died sometime between 1684 and 1700.

Elling Mathiassen Hovland (1869 – 1918) and Kathrine Mathiasdatter (1864 – 1927).

His children are possibly:

a. Johannes, born around 1659, farm no. 6 – 1, Austrheim.
b. Jakob, born around 1664, tenant farmer no. 6, Hovland.

Simon possibly took over the farm after Mogens, as he farmed one–third of Hovland, the same as Mogens (2 bp. 8 mrk. dried fish).

Simon is mentioned in the county records several times. On May 29, 1663, Cloister Steward Friman's deputy, Hans Hansen, district recorder Jakob Buch and council members from Foyno in Sunnhordaland, went to Utsira to conduct a council meeting.

Simon, together with Sjur Austrheim, were cited for causing the drowning of Anders Skare's servant. This happened 1–1/2 years earlier, when they both were battling to be the first to reach a ship from Kristiansand to pilot it to port. Asbjorn Skare's boat arrived first and he managed to climb on board. Soon after, Sjur and Simon's boat arrived alongside the vessel, but Sjur did not manage to latch onto the ship, so that his boat, due to the moving vessel, hit Asbjorn's boat and both boats capsized and Simon and his servant fell into the water. Sjur managed to climb on board again:

> . . . and the servant hanging on to Simon, both still in the water. Simon managed to at last climb on to the keel with the servant, but did not manage to hold on and both fell back in the water and under the water. The servant still hung on to Simon's foot as he could feel. Simon finally managed to climb on board, but the servant disappeared in the sea.

Judge Hansen felt that Simon and Sjur did not have any business being on the vessel as the ship already had a pilot on board. After some deliberation, the parties came to an agreement with the result that Simon and Sjur had to pay two barrels of cod products or 6 rdl. in cash.

The following year, Simon had to pay a fine of 1 rdl. for refusing to provide transportation home from Utsira for the judge and his deputy.

The last time we find references to Simon in the county records is in November 1684, when he is in the Stavanger business logs, listed as having been there selling four barrels of coalfish and one barrel of haddock for 28 sk.

2. **Hans Johannesen.** 1700 – 1714
Born around 1677, died around 1714, possibly the son of Johannes Hansen, farmer no. 1 – 4 a, Hovland.

Children:

a. Ole, born around 1702, further information is unknown.
b. Hans, born around 1707, married in his second marriage in 1759 to Siri Torsdatter, tenant farm no. 16, Hovland.
c. Marthe, married around 1735 to Knut Andersen, tenant farmer no. 14, Hovland.
d. Johannes, born around 1711, married to Bertha Andersdatter, lived in Stange, Torvestad.

Hans received a first lease contract in 1700 for this farm, 2pd. 20 mrk. dried fish.

In 1703 his financial condition is described as poor, but the houses that he used together with his father are in good condition. He planted 1–1/2 barrels of oats and fed 2 cows, 1 calf and some sheep. Of these, he owned only the cow, the rest he leased. He owed Friman 4 rdl. for the first lease in 1700, 2 rdl. in rent, and 3 rdl. 3 ort to others for *grain-corn.*

In 1712, he is in somewhat better financial condition. However, according to a district judge, Hans:

. . . did not show any proof of a lease contract in 1710 for the homestead, and then again in 1711 when he was using the farm, the county sheriff Claus Nordbø confirmed that no proof of a lease contract existed, but Borch, on behalf of the tax assessors, demanded that he pay 1 rdl., 4 ort and 1 s. for the year 1710. To Michel Eeg he was in great debt, but how much he could not tell.

3. **Hans Korneliussen.** 1715 – 1747

The settlement report after him dated Mar. 26, 1740 is of unknown origin.

Married to **Magdalena Johannesdatter,** born around 1687, buried Oct. 6, 1765, possibly the daughter of Johannes Hansen, farmer no. 1 – 4 d, Hovland.

Children:

a. Johannes, born around 1715. In the seamen records from 1734 it is stated about Johannes: *born in Utsira subparish, married and lives at Håland, 19 years of age, farms half a "laup," is a pilot, not away at sea.* He is not mentioned under Håland in the Torvestad book.
b. Hans.
c. Marthe.
d. Ingeborg, born around 1718, next farmer.
e. Mallene, born around 1724, married to Knut Ivarsen, Stange.

Hans got his lease contract renewed, 2 bp. 20 mrk. dried fish on Dec. 23, 1720.

During the survey in 1721 of Utsira by the district recorder his farm was also surveyed. It was concluded that the houses were in need of repair at an estimated cost of 3 ort 4 sk.. and among other things the barn needed 3 v. bark. Meadows and fields were in good condition and he had a debt of 6 rdl.

In 1723, he planted 1–1/4 barrels of grain and harvested 6 barrels. The livestock consisted of 1 horse and 3 cows.

4. **Askild Larsen (Thorsen?).** 1748 – 1770

Born around 1720, buried Sept. 28, 1766. of unknown origin.

Married around 1748 to **Ingeborg Hansdatter,** born around 1718, buried Mar. 25, 1787, daughter of the previous farmer.

Children:

a. Guri, born 1748, buried Oct. 14, 1758.
b. Marta, born 1751, married in 1775 to Kristen Monsen, farm no. 6 here.

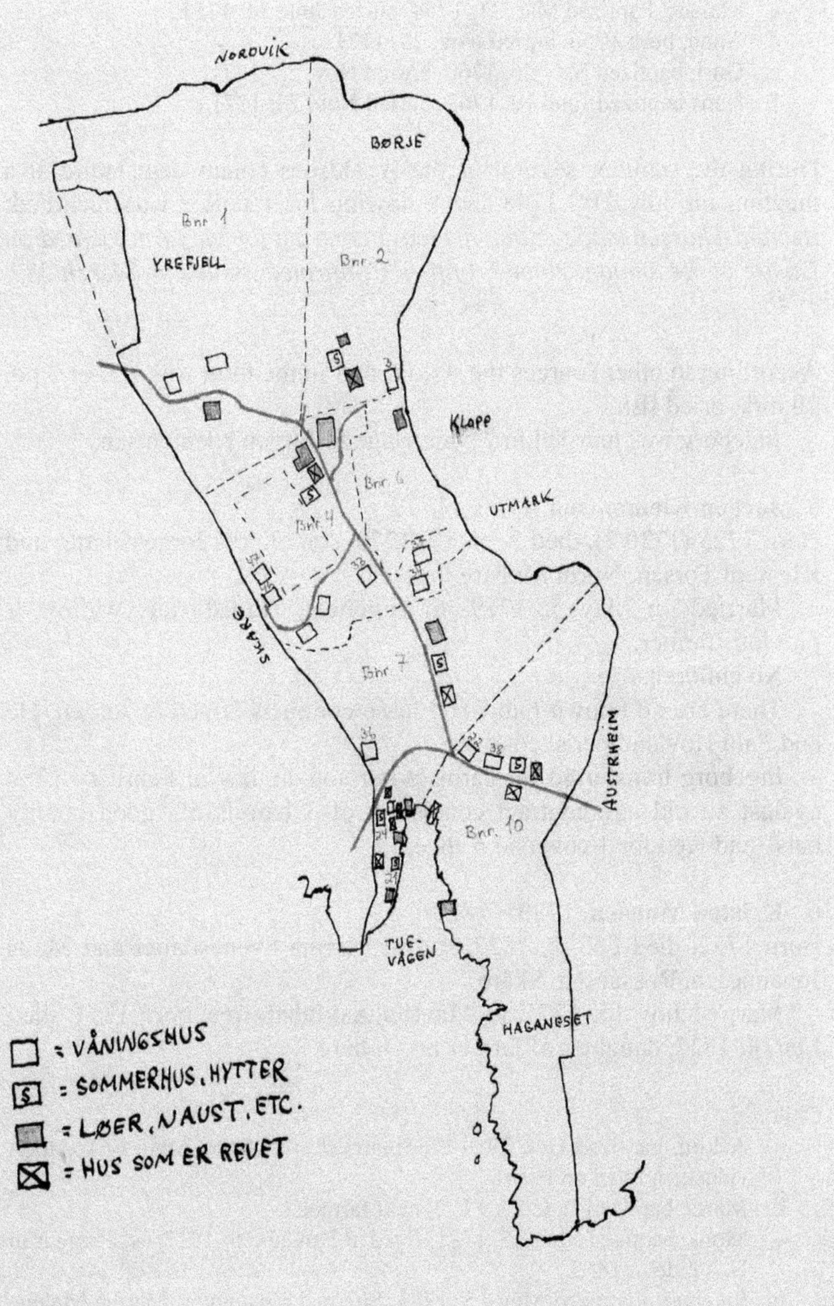

Map of Hovland. Key: 1– Main farmhouses, 2– Summer houses, cabins, 3– Barns, sheds, 4– Buildings now torn down

c. Malene, baptized Mar. 31, 1754, buried June 24, 1754.
d. Anna, born 1756, buried Nov. 23, 1771.
e. Guri, baptized May 26, 1760. buried Nov. 23, 1771.
f. Hans baptized June 19, 1763, buried Nov. 23, 1771.

During the summer session of the Avaldsnes county legislature at a meeting on July 20th 1748 the following brief notice was recorded: *Aschild Thorsen made public his lease contract for the farm located on Udsire in the amount 20 mrk. of fish. Confirmed, issued on March 28th, 1748.*

According to other sources the Askild part in the farm was 1/3, or 2 pd. 20 mrk. dried fish.

Ingeborg was married in 2nd marriage to Jørgen Klementsen.

5. **Jørgen Klementsen.** 1770 – 1779

Born 1725 (1730 ?), died Sept. 19, 1779, son of Alis Jørgensdatter and Klement Torsen, North Molstre in Sveio.

Married on May 5, 1769, to **Ingeborg Hansdatter**, widow of previous farmer.

No children.

There are no known published lease contracts issued to Jørgen. He and Paul Hovland perished at sea.

Ingeborg transferred the farm to her son–in–law in February 1780 against an old age contract consisting of 3 barrels of "good quality oats" and feed for 1 cow and 6 sheep.

6. **Kristen Monsen.** 1780 – 1809

Born 1752, died Feb. 2, 1827, son of Martha Svendsdatter and Mons Johannesen, Rossabo in Skåre.

Married July 15, 1775, to **Martha Askildsdatter,** born 1751, died Mar. 4, 1827, daughter of farmer no. 4, here.

Children:

a. Askild, baptized Oct. 29, 1776, married in 1810 to Anna Eriksdatter, Hausken, lived on Feoy.
b. Marta, baptized June 27, 1779, next farmer.
c. Mons, baptized Mar. 25, 1781, lived at Hovland in 1827, as a beggar in N. Velde in 1865.
d. Ingeborg, baptized May 15, 1783. She had a daughter, Martha Malene born on July 13, 1821, with Nils Nilsen Gard. She lived with her brother Askild on Feoy and died there in 1852.

e. Johannes, baptized Apr. 30, 1785, died between 1801 – 1827.
f. Hans, baptized Feb. 8, 1789, married in 1821 to Marta Kirstine Hansdatter, tenant farm no. 20, Hovland.
g. Svend, baptized Apr. 1, 1792, married in 1823 to Kari Ommundsdatter, lived in Skeie, Avaldsnes.
h. Anna Malene, baptized Aug. 25, 1794, buried Oct. 2, 1796.

Lease contract to Kristen in the amount of 1 v. 8 mrk. dried fish is dated Feb. 29, 1780.

In 1802, 2–1/2 barrels of grain were planted and 14 barrels were harvested. The livestock consisted of 1 horse, 3 cows and 2 calves. The farm was estimated to be worth 130 rdl.

Kristen is mentioned in the county records a couple of times. During the wedding festivities in the fall of 1777 at Klovning, when Bertha Jørgensdatter and Johannes Kristoffersen got married, a fight broke out between Kristen, Anders Kristoffersen and Gudmund Thomassen. After a number of court hearings and many witness reports, Anders and Gudmund were fined 6 lods silver or 9 rdl., and 6 rdl. in court expenses and 2 rdl. for the poor.

In 1786 he took his neighbor Tollef Tollefsen to court accusing him of breaking down the door to the mill, which they owned together, and using up all the water, so there was nothing left when Kristen went to mill his own flour. The following year we find this entry in the county records:

> . . . in as much as this mill over the years has been used to mutual benefit of the part owners: including the widow of Anders Pedersen Hovland, Ingeborg Knudsdatter, who also has enjoyed users rights of the mill according to the 1/3 part ownership agreement. The utilization of the mill shall alternate evenly between the part owners. In situations when somebody may not have sufficient water to grind his meal, one shall in a friendly way help each other to carry out the grinding operation with available water. The case was resolved when Tollev Hovland agreed to pay the plaintiff's estimated costs of 3 rdl. 1 ort, whereupon all parties were satisfied and the dispute was resolved…

In the fall of 1798 he was himself cited in court by his neighbors, Anders Knutsen and Henrik Thomassen Kvalvik, for threatening them with both ax and knife, but also here it looks like the case was settled out of court.

In the settlement after Kristen and Martha in 1827, the estate listed assets in the amount of 88–2–16 Spd. After the estate was settled there was 57 Spd. left to be divided among the heirs. Among misc. items mentioned are:

Misc. clothing, tablecloths, etc. 22–4–0, 2 rings and a necklace in gold 12–2–12, misc. silverware 13–2–0, bedding 5–4–12, 3 lockers with locks and ornamental reinforcements 4–2–12, 99 fathoms of cable rope 2–1–18, misc. yarn 2–1–12, 1 four–oar boat with sail 5–0–0.

7. **Ole Olsen.** 1809 – 1835

Baptized Apr. 3, 1785, died Dec. 3, 1844, son of Malene Oddsdatter and Ole Olsen, tenant farmer no. 14 d, Kvalvik.

Married Oct. 8, 1809, to **Martha Kristensdatter,** baptized June 27, 1779, died Feb. 5, 1850, daughter of previous farmer.

Children:

a. Anne Marta, baptized Mar. 4, 1810, married in 1833 to Simon Jonsen Nap, lived in Stange and Torvestad.
b. Oline, baptized Mar. 15, 1812, married in 1843 to Hans Larsen, tenant at Vikse in Skåre.
c. *Guri* Malene, baptized May 8, 1814, died in 1892, married to Jan Kristoffersen, Sveio.
d. Malene, baptized Sept. 16, 1816, died Sept. 15, 1838. She had a son, Sjur Mathias, born Aug. 17, 1838, with Sjur Knutsen, Austrheim.
e. Ole, born Mar. 12, 1818, married in 1842 to Kristine Larsdatter, Vikse, was a tenant at Vikse in Skåre.
f. Kristian, born Nov. 18, 1820, married in 1841 to Elisabeth Larsdatter, Vikse and tenant at Vikse in Skåre.
g. Berta, born Oct. 23, 1822, died Nov. 1, 1824.

The lease contract to Ole in the amount of 1 v. 8 mrk. dried fish is issued by the assessor Forman on Apr. 1, 1809. (It is noted in the records that according to the loan requirements the fee the farmers had to pay to the landowners for this farm was 2 bp. tf.). Also, that:

> . . . he is using Christen Monsen's farm until all the neighbors are committed to giving up the damaging common utilization of the fields, and that his part is completely separated from the neighbors' parcels, and making sure that free access to the individual farms and houses is available without having to trespass on any of the others' parcels anytime throughout the year.

He provides old–age pension to his in–laws, among other things, consisting of: 5–1/2 barrels of oats based on 8 spann in each barrel, 1/2 barrel of pure grain and feed for both winter and summer for 2 cows.

In 1822 the houses on the farm were described as follows:

Arial photo taken in 1954. In the foreground farm no. 4, to the right "The Old School " and behind it farm no. 2. Photo by Telemark Aircraft Co.

> 2 old houses with kitchen under roof covered with turf, 1 old storage building with peat roof, 1 old cow stable with attached manure shed covered with turf roof, and a separate mill house belonging to the 1/3 part-ownerships.

Annual crop yield was 26 barrels of grain, and 4–6 barrels of potatoes, while the livestock consisted of 2 horses, 6 cows and 4–6 sheep. The farm was in 1823 assessed to 150 Spd.

In the settlement after Ole in 1845 the estate's contents were sold at an auction taking in 76–4–7 Spd. Left to the heirs was 29–2–10 Spd.

In 1834 he gave up the farm, against an old age contract with the owner, Jan Dahm.

8. **Jan Henrik Fasmer Dahm.** 1834 – 1835

Born June 24, 1802, drowned near Skudenes in 1834, son of Anna W. Forman and Jakob C. F. Dahm, businessman in Bergen.

Married Apr. 12, 1830, on Askoy to **Christiane Ovidia Orning,** born in 1777, died May 1, 1837 in Bergen, daughter of Ovidia Magdalene (Helene) Tonning and Christian Orning, Innvik in Nordfjord.

No children.

The deed to Jan from his brother, Johan, with a tax assessment of 2 bp. dried fish, for 200 Spd. is dated Sept. 8, 1831. The purchase did not include the 1/3 of "Beiningen" which also actually belonged to the farm, and Johan demanded summer pasturing for 1 cow at "Yrebekken."

Jan lived on Utsira from 1829 and was registered as a trader when he got married in 1830. He took over the farm in 1834 against an old age contract with Ole and Martha, consisting of among other items, the following:

> 12 v. oats, feed for 1 cow in both summer and winter and including usage of two smaller parcels, "Buetrae" and "Christine–trae."

9. **Markus Torkelsen.** 1835 – 1847

Baptized Feb. 2, 1806, buried in the main cathedral in Bergen Aug. 24, 1842, son of Eli Johnsdatter and Torkel Bjørnsen in Torvestad.

Married Apr. 3, 1834, to **Gunhilde Kristiansdatter,** baptized Jan. 10, 1831, died in 1903, daughter of Mette Marie Mathiasdatter and Kristian Hansen, Hausken.

Children:

a. Torkel, born June 7, 1834 in Dale, farmer no. 11 here.
b. Matias, born Feb. 18, 1836. died Feb. 28, 1836.
c. Eli Kristine, born July 9, 1837, died July 13, 1837.
d. Jon Kristian, born Feb. 7, 1839, died May 20, 1845.
e. Eli Kristine, born Feb. 6, 1841, died Feb. 29, 1844.
f. Girl not baptized, died Nov. 29, 1852.

The deed to Markus from J. Dahm, tax assessed 2 bp. dried fish, on 780 Spd. is dated May 17, 1835.

In 1845 the farm planted 4 barrels of oats, 1/2 barrel of barley and 1–1/2 barrels of potatoes. The livestock consisted of 1 horse, 5 cows, 6 sheep and 1 pig.

Markus and his farmhand were killed in an accident when they one day (Thursday, August 11 in 1842) were in the process of picking up some lumber on another part of the island in a rowing boat. On the way back with the fully loaded boat, the boat capsized, and even though they managed to right the boat, they lost the oars and drifted away from the shore, and 8 days later they were found by some fishermen outside Bergen.

There was an estate settlement after Markus in 1846. The farm was turned over to his son Torkel for an assessed amount of 650 Spd.

Among the misc. items left worth 203 Spd. 3 ort, the following items are mentioned:

> 1 spotted mare 18–0–0, 3 cows ("Sortsia", "Hoprei" and "Braadrei") 22–0–0, 1 oxen 4–2–12, 1 iron plow 1–4–0, 1 iron harrow 0–4–12, 1 stove 6–0–0, 1/2 share in a mill house 5–0–0, 12 balker (300 fathoms) herring seine nets of which 4 are old 29–3–0, 5 balker (125 fathoms) smaller types of herring seine 8–0–0, 37 lobster pots 3–3–12, 3 spring herring fishing nets 1–1–0, 6 cans with tar in a barrel 0–3–12 and 1 wharfside shed 50–0–0.

Gunhilde got married the second time in 1847 to Kristian Nikolai Paulsen.

10. **Kristian N. Paulsen,** 1847 – 1861
Born in 1814 in Sponeviken, Drammen, died June 8, 1898.
Married Mar. 27, 1847, to **Gunhilde Kristiansdatter,** widow of previous farmer.

Children:

a. Marte Antonette, born June 8, 1846. died in hospital in Oslo, Jan. 8, 1860.
b. Marianne, born Oct. 18, 1847, died July 31, 1925 in Haugesund, married in 1874 to Gudmund Helgesen, Aksnes, lived in Visnes, Karmøy.
c. Severine Marie, born Jan. 6, 1849, married in 1872 to Tollak Ådesen, Stensnes, lived in Visnes, Karmøy.
d. Kristine Nicoline, born Dec. 14, 1850, married in 1884 to Abraham Johannes Larsen, Norem, lived in Visnes in the 1880's, later Haugesund.
e. Andreas Richard Meider, born June 24, 1852.
f. Gustav Adolph. born July 30, 1854.

Kristian was lighthouse keeper assistant on Utsira Lighthouse from 1844 to 1890, and is along with Mikkel Jørgensen one of those who worked longest at Utsira Lighthouses.

In 1861 they gave up the farm to Torkel Markussen against an old age contract consisting of:

> 18 v. oats, 2–1/2 barrels barley, feed for 2 cows, 1 cord birch firewood, free use of the southern half of a parcel called "Anen," and the grass field on "Krinetrae," usage of the eastern half of the main dwelling, half of the boathouse in Tjuevågen and the mill, including the northern laundry house.

11. **Torkel Markussen.** 1861 – 1906.

Born June 7, 1834, died Feb. 22, 1903, son of farmer no. 9 here.

Married in 1st marriage on Mar. 24, 1861, to **Anne Hedvig Olsdatter,** born May 12, 1838, died Apr. 12, 1877, daughter of Marta Lisbet Toresdatter and Olav Larsen, Nedre Hauge, Torvestad.

Married in 2nd marriage on Oct. 30, 1879, to **Anne *Gurine* Endredatter,** born Jan. 10, 1854, died Oct. 31, 1925, daughter of Anne Gurine Osmundsdatter and Endre Sjursen, Røvaer.

Children in 1st marriage:

a. Markus, born Oct. 11, 1862, never married, lived with Ingvald and Olga from 1911 to 1926, after that on Klepp.
b. Ole Christian, born Feb. 21, 1864.
c. John Mathias, born May 28, 1866, died June 22, 1867.
d. Gunhilde Elisabeth, born June 4, 1868.
e. Martha Kristine, born Oct. 11, 1870.
f. John Mathias, born Apr. 22, 1873, emigrated to USA in 1886.
g. Andreas Nicolaus, born Oct. 5, 1875.
h. Helvig Antonette, born Apr. 4, 1877, died Oct. 10, 1877.

Children in 2nd marriage:

i. Osmund Nikolai, born Dec. 26, 1879, died Oct. 9, 1897.
j. Helvig Antonette, born Jan. 20, 1882, died Feb. 2, 1885.
k. Elen Marie, born May 31, 1884.
l. *Ingvald* Adolf Bertinius, born Dec. 15, 1886, next farmer.
m. Helvik Antonette, born Oct. 23, 1889.
n. Kristian Gunvald, born Apr. 26, 1892.
o. Bertha Knutiane, born Apr. 21, 1894.

The settlement after Torkel is dated Nov. 14, 1846, for an assessed amount of 650 Spd., and a title to the estate for an amount of 2100 kr. after Anne Helvig is dated Dec. 1, 1879.

The farm consisted in 1866 of 51 mål of fields assessed to 426 Spd., and meadows and pastures valued at 227 Spd. Annual crop yield was 28 barrels of oats, 4 barrels of barley and 16 barrels of potatoes. The farm also had peat valued at 30 Spd. and income from fishing rights for 19 Spd. The entire farm was assessed to 785 Spd.

The livestock consisted of 1 horse, 6 cows, 11 sheep and 1 pig.

In 1868 he sold part of the farm, Yrebekken, tax potential sk.m. 0.47, to Mikkel Jørgensen Hovland and Mathias Ellingsen Skare for 400 Spd.

In 1884 he sold half of what was left to Utsira board of education for 1600 kroners.

12. **Ingvald Torkelsen.** 1906 – 1928.
Born Dec. 15, 1886, son of previous farmer.

Newspaper clipping from "Haugesund News", April 21, 1928.

Auction – Utsira.
Thursday, April 26 at 11:00 am, there will be — due to leaving for USA – an auction at the Olga Hovland place, Utsira. of household goods, farm equipment, mackerel fishing nets, a horse, 2 cows, 8 sheep, 30 chickens and more.
The real estate with house and boathouse will also be sold.
—Sheriff Lunde.

Married Aug. 3, 1910, to **Olga Gabrielsdatter,** born 1888, daughter of Anna Johanne Osmundsdatter and J. Gabriel Olsen, Mannes in Åkra.

Children:
a. Tordis Gunhilde, born May 15, 1911, died Feb. 14, 1914.
b. Adolf George, born Nov. 10, 1912.
c. Johan Gabriel, born Dec. 31, 1914, twin.
d. Osmund Nikolai, born Dec. 31, 1914, twin.
e. Ingolf Villiam, born Apr. 8, 1917, died Nov. 23, 1918.
f. Tordis Antonette, born Apr. 6, 1920, married Arthur Larsen, lived in Brooklyn, NY.
g. Ingrid Oline, born Dec. 3, 1923, married Robert Larsen.

The deed to Ingvald on this farm, with a tax burden of sk.m. 1.79. from his mother, Anne Gurine, is dated Nov. 10, 1906 in the amount of 800 kroner plus old–age contract.
The family emigrated to USA in 1928.

13. **August Knutsen.** 1928 – 1960
Born Aug. 17, 1888, died July 23, 1956. son of Tomine and Knut Gudmundsen, farmer no 1 – 9 c, Austrheim.
Married Aug. 23, 1925, to **Amanda Tobiasdatter,** born Mar. 25, 1896, died Aug. 9, 1964, daughter of Berthe Malene and Tobias Olsen, farm no. 2 – 8 d, Kvalvik.

Children:
a. Knut Torleiv, born Jan. 27, 1927, died Aug. 8, 1946.
b. *Mildrid* Torborg, born Jan. 27, 1928, lives in Stavanger.
c. *Liv* Konstanse, born Oct. 4, 1929, lives in Stavanger.

The family of August Knutsen in 1937. Last row from left: Jardar, Amanda, August and Knut. In front from the left: Liv, Audny, Mildrid, Trygve and Odd.

d. *Trygve* Mikal, born Feb. 26, 1931, died Jan. 16, 1947.
e. *Audny* Amalie. born Sept. 5, 1932, lives in Tau.
f. *Odd* Tobias, born Mar. 28, 1935, married in 1964 to Grethe Fjostheim, lives in Tau.
g. Torfinn *Jardar,* born July 21, 1936, lives in Forus, Stavanger.

The deed to August from Ingvald and Olga on farm no. 4 and 14 is dated May 29, 1928 in the amount of 3500 kroner. August was chief municipal treasurer for Utsira from 1933 until his death.

A large part of the farm was sold in 1977 to Utsira municipality as a football field and for home sites.

The school grounds, farm no. 6, with the island's first schoolhouse built in 1859 – 61. Photo: Telemark Aircraft Co. 1954.

Farm no. 6, Breidablikk, From farm no. 4 in 1884, and Farm no. 3, Schoolhouse, from farm no. 2 in 1865.

Utsira board of education bought part of Torkel Markussen's estate in 1884 (with a tax burden of sk.m. 1.80) for school facilities. This was confirmed in use at least until the 1920s. It was later leased out for a variety of other purposes, among others to Valnum Jørgensen, Klovning, and from 1967 to Lars Bentsen.

1. **Lars Bentsen.** 1954 – 1984.

Born Jan. 6, 1914, died May 16, 1992, son of Inger and Peder Bentsen, Osnes.

Married in 1946 to **Martha Hausken,** born Feb. 29, 1920, daughter of Kristiane and Knut K. Hausken, Torvestad.

Children:

a. Inger, born Feb. 21, 1947, married in 1966 to Sigve Oritsland (died in 1985) lives at Dale, Torvestad.
b. Knut Andreas, born Feb. 2, 1953, married in 1978 to Heidi Hemnes from Akra, lives in Hauskevågen, Torvestad.
c. *Kristi* Anne Benedikte, born Dec. 14, 1956, married in 1974 to Oyvind Selsas, lives on Karmøy.
d. Gjertrud, born Mar. 6, 1961, married in 1982 to Per Steffen Hinderaker, lives in Kopervik.

They managed the schoolhouse grounds here from 1967, later they also managed farm no. 2. Martha was a midwife on Utsira from 1954. They moved to Hauskevagen in 1984.

Farm no 7. Tuo.

1. **Knut Sjursen (Jonsen?)** 1675 – 1704.
Born around 1630 (1640?), died around 1704.

It appears that his sons were:

a. Sjur, born 1666, tenant farmer no 11, Hovland.
b. Anders, born 1676, tenant farmer no. 4, Klovning.
c. Jon, born 1681, next farmer.
d. Knut, born 1683. In 1706 he is a sergeant and lives on Hasseloy
e. Rasmus, born 1690, farmer no. 3 here.

It is not confirmed if this Knut is the same person who in 1664 is 20 years old and a sailor (a "Jack") serving the local defense on Nordvik. In the settlement after Jon Andersen Skjollingstad in 1675, we see that he is among those owing money to the estate: "*Knud Tueaa Zire (Knut, Tuo, Utsira), 8 ort.*"

In 1703 his financial situation was described as poor, but the houses on the farm were in good condition, only 3 ort required in tenant repair. He plants 2 barrels of oats and feeds 2 cows, 1 calf, some sheep and 1 horse, of these he owns 2 cows. He owes the landlord, Mr. Friman, 24 sk. and 3 rdl. to others.

2. **Jon Knutsen.** 1704 – 1720.
Born in 1681, died between 1715 and 1719, son of previous farmer.

Married to **Randi,** of unknown origin.

They had no children in 1711.

In 1712 he spent 2 bp. 20 mrk. dried fish of the farm's assets, and his financial condition was described as bad. One riksdaler was required in repairs of the buildings on the farm. His plantings and livestock were similar to his neighbor, Hans Johannesen. For the most part he owned the livestock himself. He owed taxes and fees for 1711 and: *. . . in addition he owes Mr. Michel Eeg money, but how much, he is not able to account for.*

Jon is also mentioned in the county records in 1714, when he is among many others who received compensation of 7 ort for participating in saving items during a shipwreck in 1707.

3. **Rasmus Knutsen.** 1720 – 1723
Born in 1690, died in 1723, brother of previous farmer. Possibly married to the widow of the previous farmer.

No known children.

In 1721 he had to spend 1–3–20 rdl. in repair of the houses on the farm. "True Rasmussen," as the succeeding tenant, was listed as owing 9 rdl. on the lease and 3 rdl. to others, but the fields and meadows were in good shape and solidly his without any restrictions.

In 1723 he planted 1–1/4 barrels and harvested 6 barrels of grain, and was feeding 3 cows.

4. **Rasmus Tormodsen.** 1724 – 1755
Born 1704, died 1733, son of Ingeborg Olsdatter, and Tormod Rasmussen, farmer no. 1 – 3 b, Austrheim.

Married to **Guri Larsdatter,** born 1704, buried June 29, 1766, daughter of Berthe Anbjornsdatter, and Lars Johannesen, farmer no. 1 – 3 d, Skare.

Children:

a. Tormod, born 1728, married around 1751 to Martha Kristine Knutsdatter, farmer no. 15–3, Nordvik.
b. Anbjorn, born 1729, next farmer.
c. Lars, further information is unknown.

Lease contract to Rasmus in the amount of 2 pd. 20 mrk. dried fish is issued by county clerk Ole Larsen Jan. 12, 1724.

"Tuo," farm no. 7, in 1932. Photo by Robert Kloster, Historic Museum in Bergen.

On Sept. 30, 1733 there was an estate settlement after the deceased Rasmus Tormodsen. The estate's assets were worth 48–2–0 rdl., but debt and expenses were only 1–2–0 rdl. Among the items left were:

> 7 cows and 1 heifer (of which 5 were black–, 2 red– and 1 gray–sided, all with horns) 19–3–0, 1 horse 2–2–0, 1 oxen 1–0–12, 6 sheep 2–0–0, 3 kettles 2–2–12, bedding 4–2–0, 1 locker 0–1–8, 1 four–oar boat with sail 1–0–0, part ownership in 6–oar boat 1–0–0 and cash 12–3–14.

Ole (Tormodsen) Austrheim was guardian for Tormod, and the grandfather Lars (Johannesen) Skare was the guardian for Anbjorn, and Johannes (Larsen) Gunnarshaug for Lars.

5. **Anbjorn Rasmussen.** 1756 – 1775
Born 1729, died Nov. 4, 1773, son of previous farmer.

His first marriage was on June 19, 1757, to **Kari Mathiasdatter,** born 1735, buried Apr. 8, 1759, daughter of Anna Iversdatter and Mathias Mikkelsen, Vikse in Skåre.

He married the second time in Sept. 28, 1761, to **Anna Johannesdatter**, born 1745, daughter of Berta Knutsdatter and

Johannes Pettersen, Osnes. (Berta's father, Knut Olsen Austrheim, and Anbjorn's father, were half–brothers.)[41]

Children in first marriage :

a. Rasmus, baptized Aug. 20, 1757, died Nov. 4, 1773.
b. Mathias, born Sept. 1758. In 1781 he served in the army. Further information is unknown.

Children in second marriage:

c. Kari, baptized Oct. 18, 1761, married in 1791 to Hans Jonsen, tenant farmer no. 17, Hovland.
d. Guro, baptized Oct. 7, 1764, buried Nov. 23, 1771.
e. Johannes, baptized Oct. 11, 1766, married in 1791 to Anna Karine Ådnesdatter, tenant farmer no. 13, Nordvik.
f. Berta, baptized July 2, 1768, married in 1789 to widower Gudmund Thomassen, farmer no. 3 – 2, Austrheim.
g. Ingeborg, baptized Jan. 6, 1770, married in 1814 to widower Rasmus Tollefsen, tenant farmer no. 17, Nordvik.
h. Tormod, born 1771, buried Nov. 23, 1771, 8 days old.
i. Guro, baptized Nov. 9, 1772, married in 1814 to Johannes Knutsen, farmer no. 4 – 3, Klovning.
j. Anna, baptized July 17, 1774, buried Mar. 25, 1779, estate settled in 1781.

As the county records for the period 1751 to 1761 have been lost, we do not have the lease contract to Anbjorn.

Anbjorn and his son, Rasmus, perished at sea, but only Anbjorn was found later. At the estate settlement in March 1774, the estate's assets were valued to 114–0–10 rdl., of which 19–1–20 rdl. were Rasmus' current cash containment from the estate settlement after the death of his mother, Kari. in 1759. Debt and expenses amounted to 20–1–8 rdl. The following items among others were left:

> Anbjorn's working clothes 8–2–16, 5 cows and 1 heifer 21–2–16, 1 brown and 1 gray mare 7–3–0. 3 rams 1–2–0, 3 spring herring nets and 1 mature herring fishing net 3–0–16, some lobster pots 1–1–0, one–third share in a "Somands" fishing boat with associated equipment 3–0–0, one–third share in a seiner net 2–0–0, 1 four–oar boat with sail 2–2–0, some dried fish 1–2–0, 1 brandy glass and 4 silver spoons 5–2–0, 4 lockers with locks 2–2–16, 1 iron stove 4–0–0, 1 baking board 0–3–8, 1 large kettle 3–0–0, one–third share in outside mill with associated equipment 0–3–0, 2 feather pillows 1–1–8, and 1 blue–striped undershirt with 18 silver buttons 1–3–16.

[41] See Note 12.

In the years between 1700 and 1750, the farmers here are not registered with the farm name of Tuo, however, Jon Johannesen, on farm no. 1, is. This possibly means that Anbjorn built new farm houses here in the 1750's, while Jon's successor Anders Pedersen built a new compound further north on Hovland.

Anna got married the second time to Tollef Tollefsen.

6. **Tollef Tollefsen.** 1775 – 1805
Born in 1750, buried Oct. 16, 1803, son of Anna Olsdatter and Tollef Johannesen, Storesund in Torvestad.

Married on Sept. 16, 1775, to **Anna Johannesdatter,** widow of previous farmer.

Children:

a. Anbjorn, baptized Aug. 29, 1778, buried June 30, 1799.
b. Tollef, baptized Feb. 23, 1780, married in 1802 to Margretha Bardsdatter, Snik. Tollef had one son, Tollef, baptized Jan. 18, 1801, with his half–sister, Ingeborg. For this, he was sentenced to death, but was pardoned by the king in Copenhagen on the condition that they ever after had to live 40 kilometers apart.
c. Rasmus, baptized Nov. 24, 1781, next farmer.

The lease contract to Tollef in the amount of 20 mrk. dried fish (including the amount of previous debt of 2 bp. 20 mrk.) was issued by Anna W. Bredahl in Stavanger on Jan. 5, 1775.

In 1802 he planted 2–1/2 barrels and harvested 14 barrels of grain. The livestock consisted of 1 horse, 3 cows and 2 calves. The grain sown and harvested and the amount of livestock are similar to the other three tenant farmers at Hovland. The farm was assessed at 110 Spd.

7. **Rasmus Tollefsen.** 1805 – 1832
Baptized Nov. 24, 1781, died Feb. 20, 1832, son of previous farmer.

He married July 8, 1810, to **Jobiane Jobsdatter,** baptized Jan. 27, 1788, died June 13, 1865, daughter of Ingeborg Tollefsdatter, Storesund in Torvestad and Job Fredriksen, Lillesund in Torvestad.

Children:

a. Ingeborg Oline, baptized Mar. 15, 1812, married in 1830 to Jakob Bentsen, next farmer and tenant farmer no. 22, Kvalvik.
b. Anna, baptized Sept. 3, 1814, married in 1838 to Gudmund Tollefsen Rabben, farmer no. 10 – 1, Hovland.
c. Job, baptized Aug. 19, 1817, farmer no. 9 here.

d. Berte Karine, born Sept. 27, 1819, married in 1852 to Sjur Knutsen, tenant farmer no. 26, Hovland.
e. Tollef, born Mar. 1, 1822, married in 1849 to Berthe Karine Thoresdatter, farmer no. 21 – 1, Nordvik.
f. Gundele, born Sept. 5, 1825, died Dec. 20, 1838. There was an estate settlement after her in 1839. Her fortune was then 60–3–15 Spd.
g. Anne Marte, born Feb. 21, 1827, married in 1849 to Saebjorn Knutsen Birkeland, tenant farmer no.. 20, Kvalvik.
h. Jobiana, born Mar. 21, 1831, married in 1853 to Thomas Ellingsen, farmer no. 12 – 2, Nordvik.

Lease contract to Rasmus from the assessor Forman in the amount of 2 bp. dried fish is dated July 14, 1805. He paid 35 rdl. in lease money and had to contribute an old age pension of 3–1/2 barrels of oats and 1/2 barrel of grain, including feed for 2 cows, to his mother Anna Johannesdatter.

In 1822 the houses on the farm were described as follows:

> One main dwelling with 2 small living rooms and a room with kitchen lined with boards and covered with peat, one shed covered with peat (turf) roof, one new concrete laundry shed covered with peat roof, and a logged cow stable barn with peat roof, all in good condition.

The farm yields annually 28 barrels of grain and 8–10 barrels of potatoes and can feed 6–7 cows, 2 horses and 6–8 sheep. The farm was in 1823 assessed at 220 Spd.

On Sept. 26, 1829 Rasmus bought the farm from J. Dahm for 250 Spd. In the deed it is noted that the historic "grazing and user privileges" of the adjacent border properties of Beiningen are cancelled.

In the estate settlement after the death of Rasmus in 1836, the farm was assessed at 400 Spd. Among the miscellaneous items left in the estate, the following are mentioned:

> 2 horses, 6 and 15 years old 18–0–0, 6 cows and 2 calves (Netrej, Salrej. Sortsia, Hoprej,, Taesia, Brandeko, Skjønrej and Skautrej) 54–2–12, 1 outside mill with housing and associated equipment 17–0–0, 1 tiled heating stove 10–0–0, 1 boat shed with peat roof 4–0–0, 1 logged shed for food 6–0–0, 1 fishing shed 1–2–12, 1 four–oar boat with main sail and jib 6–0–0, 1 new 6–oar boat with main sail and jib and other associated equipment 15–0–0, 5 herring fishing nets 3–1–12, 4 coalfish fishing nets 3–3–0, 20 lobster pots 0–2–12, 1 gold–flowered comforter with down fill 5–0–0, 1 newly painted locker with ornamental reinforcements and lock with letters marked "E.S. 1779" 1–0–0, and miscellaneous silverware, among them a vest pocket watch 7–2–0.

8. **Jakob Bentsen.** 1832 – 1837
He was a tenant farmer for a few years until Job was old enough to take over the farm. They then moved to Kvalvik, tenant farmer no. 22.

9. **Job Rasmussen.** 1838 – 1890
Baptized Aug. 19, 1817, died Oct. 24, 1890, son of farmer no. 7 here.

He married on June 30, 1839, to **Karoline Elisabeth Johnsdatter,** born July 16, 1818, died Oct. 21, 1906, daughter of Anne Malene Olsdatter and John Helgesen, farmer no. 1 – 10 e, Nordvik.

Children:

a. Gundela Oline, born Oct. 11, 1839, married 1858 to school teacher Ole Reinertsen Agdesten, Stord.
b. Rasmus Johan, born Mar. 10, 1842, died Aug. 7, 1846.
c. Berte Gurine, born June 2, 1844, married 1867 to widower Konrad Severin Ånensen, tenant farmer no. 25, Hovland.
d. Mathias, born Apr. 28, 1846, married 1872 to Gunhilde Oline Ellingsdatter,, farmer no. 10–2, Hovland.
e. Berthe Malene, born Mar. 27, 1850, married 1885 to Thore Johannes Johannesen, farmer no. 6 – 8, Austrheim.
f. Rasmus Johan, born Oct. 21, 1852, next farmer.
g. Truls Johannes, born Oct. 3, 1855, died Mar. 9, 1859.
h. Anna Chatrine, born July 17, 1858, died Mar. 7, 1859.
i. Anna Chatrine, born Apr. 8, 1860, married 1896 to widower Elling Ellingsen, tenant farmer no. 38, Nordvik.
j. *Truls* Johannes, born Mar. 20, 1864, married to Guriane Johannesdatter, tenant farm no. 15, Klovning.

The estate settlement statement to Job amounted to 2 bp. dried fish for 400 Spd. The transaction is dated Feb. 8. 1836. The old age compensation to his mother consisted among other things of:

> . . . 5 barrels of oats and 1 barrel of barley, including use of the field " Stor Resestykket," feed for 2 cows and 6 sheep, however, the sheep should not have access to the 2 fenced–in fields "Smahaugerne" and "Hagenes."

Half of this commitment was on account of Gudmund Tollefsen Rabben who leased half of the farm from Job.

In 1865 the farm consisted of 34 mål fields and meadows valued at 298 Spd. and outfields at 50 Spd. Annual yield was 18 barrels of oats, 5 barrels barley and 16 barrels of potatoes. There was peat at 20 Spd. and fishing rights income of 75 Spd. The entire farm was assessed at

505 Spd. The livestock consisted of 1 horse, 3 cows, 20 sheep and 1 pig.

When Gudmund Rabben died he also took over the use of farm no. 10 against an old age contract to his widow, Anne Rasmusdatter:

> 14 barrels of oats, 1–1/2 barrels barley, 1/3 of the field "Outer Rabbestykket" or 1–1/2 barrels of potatoes, 1/2 cord of good peat and 1 cord of birch wood, feed for 1 cow and 4 sheep or 1 can of "freshly milked milk" every day. The contract was valued at 20 Spd. annually.

The main dwelling of the farm, and which is standing there today, was possibly built in 1852.

Kristine Mathiasdatter Tuo (1854 – 1884)

10. **Rasmus J. Jobsen.** 1890 – 1929
Born Oct. 21, 1852, died Mar. 11, 1938, son of previous farmer.

He married first on Sept. 6, 1879, to **Kristine Mathiasdatter,** born Nov. 3, 1854, died Apr. 14, 1884, daughter of Petronelle Knutsdatter and John Mathias Johnsen, farmer no. 3 – 1 e, Skare.

He married the second time on Apr. 15, 1894, to ***Gurine* Amalie Gudmundsdatter,** born Nov. 1, 1870, died Feb. 12, 1912, daughter of Berthe Malene Ellingsdatter and Gudmund Ambjornsen, farmer no. 3 – 6 g, Austrheim.

Children in 1st marriage:
a. *Johan* Mathias, born June 24, 1880, next farmer.
b. Job, born Mar. 11, 1883, farmer no. 6 – 9, Austrheim.

Children in 2nd marriage:
c. Julie *Kristine*, born Sept. 11, 1894, farmer no. 18 – 1, Hovland.
d. *Gustav* Adolf, born Mar. 19, 1896, farmer no. 18 – 1, Hovland.
e. *Elling* Konow, born Jan. 30, 1899, farmer no. 12, here.
f. *Sofie* Amalie, born Mar. 5, 1903, married in 1928 to Mathias Hovland, farmer no. 2 – 3, Hovland.

The deed to Rasmus from the father on this farm with a tax liability of 2.53 sk. m., for 1400 kr. and an old age contract of 500 kr., is dated Apr. 19, 1890.

Gurine Gudmundsdatter (1870–1912) and Rasmus Jobsen Tuo (1852–1938).

In 1929 the farm was divided between Johan and Gustav Rasmussen.

11. **Johan Rasmussen.** 1929 – 1948
Born June 24, 1880, died Feb. 20, 1941, son of previous farmer.

Married to **Milla Ellingsdatter,** born Sept. 20, 1891, died Mar. 31, 1955, daughter of Kathrine Mathiasdatter and Elling Mathiassen, farmer no. 2 – 2 a, Hovland. (She ran the farm after her husband died.)

Children:

a. Anne Kristine, born May 9, 1929, died June 18, 1977. She managed the post office from 1956 until she died. She also had her own farm here.

The deed to Johan from his father on half the farm, with a tax liability of 1.20 sk. m., is dated May 25, 1929.

A new cow stable and barn were built in 1937.

12. **Elling Rasmussen.** 1948 – 1973
Born Jan. 30, 1899, died Apr. 5, 1961. He was a brother of the previous farmer.

Married on Dec. 11, 1928, to **Methie Tobiasdatter,** born July 20, 1900, died Dec. 24, 1981, daughter of Berthe Malene Larsdatter and Ole Tobias Olsen, farmer no. 2 – 8 f, Kvalvik. (Methie ran the farm after her husband died until 1973.)

Children:

a. Rolf Gunnar, born Feb. 10, 1934, married in 1968 to Lucy from Singapore. He perished in the "Buckom Island" shipwreck in 1977.
b. Torbjorn, born Dec. 16, 1936, next farmer.
c. Magnhild, born Sept. 11, 1938, married in 1960 to Oddvar Holgersen, Stangeland.
d. Bodil, born Sept. 10, 1941, married in 1963 to Reidar Odland, North Kvinnesland in Tysvaer.
e. Leiv Modolf, born May 11, 1943, twin, married in 1968 to Signe Saetre, Moi, lives in Sola.
f. *Arna* Elise, born May 11, 1943, twin, married in 1969 to Jakob Rygg, lives in Skudesneshavn.

Elling took over the farm in 1948. Before the war he sailed as a first mate in international trade. He later became crew member on a pilot vessel.

13. **Torbjorn Rasmussen.** 1974 –
Born Dec. 16, 1936, son of previous farmer.

He married on July 15, 1962, to **Bjorg Irene Skåren,** born Nov. 2, 1944, daughter of Hanna and Gudmund Skåren, farmer no. 56 – 1 d, Nordvik.

Children:

a. *Edgar* Modolf, born Apr. 10, 1963, married in 1987 to Helga Rasmussen, Rovaer.
b. Geir Helge, born Mar. 1, 1966.
c. Trude Irene, born July 30, 1969. Trude also has a farm here.

Torbjorn took over the farm here in 1974 and farm no. 18 in 1975. From 1977 he was hired as a lighthouse operator at Utsira Lighthouse. He was Mayor of Utsira in the period 1980 – 91. Bjorg is the manager of Utsira Island Library.

They built themselves a new main dwelling on farm no. 36, Soltun, in 1966.

Farm No. 10. Rabben. From farm No. 7 in 1838.

1. **Gudmund Tollefsen,** 1838 – 1866
Baptized Mar. 14, 1812, died Apr. 5, 1865, son of Ingeborg Gudmundsdatter and Tollef Sjursen, farm no. 2 – 3 g, Austrheim.

Married on June 25, 1838, to **Anne Rasmusdatter,** baptized Sept. 3, 1814, died Jan. 2, 1892, daughter of Jobiane and Rasmus Tollefsen, farmer no. 7 – 7 b, Hovland.

Children:

a. Gundela, born Jan. 26, 1839, married in 1863 to Konrad Severin Anensen, tenant farmer no. 25, Hovland.
b. Sjur, born Oct. 6, 1840, died July 2, 1867.
c. Rasmus, born Apr. 9, 1842, died Apr. 17, 1867.
d. Tollef, born Apr. 3, 1845, died May 28, 1854.
e. Berthe Malene, born Feb. 14, 1848, died Nov. 28, 1865.

They had one adopted son:

f. Nils Jørgen (Nelson George), born Mar. 28, 1852, died Oct. 12, 1940 in USA, son of Kristi Samsonsdatter and Mathias Damsen, Sørvåg, Avalsnes, Karmøy. According to Martin Ulvestad (p. 233 and 821), he emigrated in 1869; one of the first Norwegians in western Oklahoma. He was a farmer and ran a store in Sayre, Roger Mills, later Beckham Co. Married 2 or 3 times; in 1910 and 1930, his wife's name is Sarah.[42]

The lease contract to Gudmund in the amount of 1 bp. dried fish from Job Rasmussen is dated Sept. 22, 1838, including agreement to provide half of it to his mother–in–law, Jobiane.

In 1865 the farm consisted of 35 mål fields and meadows valued at 316 Spd. and outfields for another 50 Spd. Peat and fishing rights were valued at 20 and 75 Spd. Annual crop was 22 barrels of oats, 6 barrels of barley and 20 barrels of potatoes. The total value was 535 Spd.

The livestock consisted of 1 horse, 3 cows, 16 sheep and 1 pig.

Gudmund and four of his children died of TB in the summer of 1867. Anne gave up the farm in 1866 against an old age contract from

Mathias Jobsen (1846 – 1910) and Gunhilde Ellingsdatter (1854 – 1939).

[42] See Note 35.

Job Rasmussen, who ran the farm (see above), in addition to farm no. 7 for a few years until Mathias Jobsen took over. Their house is supposed to have stood where there is a garden today.

2. **Mathias Jobsen.** 1872 – 1906

Born Apr. 28, 1846, died May 2, 1910, son of Karoline Elisabeth Johnsdatter, and Job Rasmussen, farmer no. 7 – 9 d, Hovland.

Married June 23, 1872, to **Gunhilde Oline (Golno) Ellingsdatter,** born June 12, 1854, died Feb. 27, 1939, daughter of Ragna Serine Johnsdatter and Elling Gudmundsen, farmer no. 12 – 1 i, Nordvik.

Children:

a. *Elling* Jobinius, born Nov. 18, 1873, next farmer.
b. *Elisabeth* Caroline, born Aug. 2, 1876, married in 1898 to Bendik Tollefsen, farmer no. 4 – 1, Kvalvik.
c. *Regine* Severine, born July 10, 1879, married in 1900 to Johan Kristian Helgesen, tenant farmer no. 43, Nordvik.
d. Berthe *Gurine,* born Apr. 22, 1882, married in 1905 to Svend Klovning, farmer no. 8 – 1, Klovning.

The deed to Mathias on this farm, with a potential tax liability of 2.75 sk.m., from the father is dated Apr. 19, 1890 and is in the amount of 1200 kr. plus an old age contract.

In 1875 they planted 4 barrels of oats, 1 barrel of barley and 4 barrels of potatoes. The livestock consisted of 1 cow, 1 calf, 10 sheep and 1 pig.

Mathias was treasurer for the Utsira parish council for many years. According to common knowledge they apparently bought Jakob Danielsen Austrheim's house around 1870 and rebuilt the house here, south of the road. It was eventually torn down in 1960.

3. **Elling Haugland.** 1906 – 1958.

Born Nov. 18, 1873, died Sept. 3, 1954, son of previous farmer.

He was married July 13, 1902, to **Gunhilde Katrine (Kaia) Kristoffersdatter**, born Dec. 31, 1877, died Jan. 19, 1973, daughter of Gunhilde Oline Johannesdatter and Kristoffer Danielsen, tenant farmer no. 9, Klovning.

Children:

a. *Klara* Juline, born June 3, 1903, married in 1932 to Olaf Thorsen, Saevlandsvik. She died July 6, 1934. Their daughter was Klara Liadal, born July 6, 1934.
b. Marie Gunhilde, born Oct. 19, 1905, married in 1935 to Elias B. Kvalvik, tenant farmer no. 37, Hovland.

At "Rabben" around 1950. In front: Elling and Kaia Haugland. In the back from left: Tilla Bendiksen, Gurine Klovning, Svend Klovning, Mathie Rasmussen, Elling Rasmussen, Marie Kvalvik, Mathias Haugland, Klara Liadal, Lindy Hansen and Ågot Torstal

c. *Emma* Katrine, born Sept. 11, 1909, died 1993, married in USA to Matt. Steinsvik, Ferkingstad. They lived in Seattle, WA.
d. Mathias, born May 8, 1908. died Apr. 15, 1909.
e. Mathias, Nov. 11, 1911, died Dec. 9, 1911.
f. Jon *Mathias*, born Aug. 8, 1917, next farmer.

Elling's son outside marriage with Thora Thoresdatter:
g. Elling Jobinius, born 1898, died 1917.

The deed to Elling on the farm, with a tax liability of 2.72 sk.m., from the parents is dated Nov. 23, 1906.

Elling was a full–time marine pilot from July 9, 1912 until he retired.[43]

A new main dwelling house was built in 1902, and a new farm house was built in 1920.

4. **Mathias Haugland.** 1948 – 1970
Born Aug. 8, 1917, died Dec. 2, 1990, son of previous farmer.

Unmarried.

The livestock consisted in 1956 of 3 cows, 1 calf, 1 horse and 11 sheep.

---

[43] According to *Haugesund Avis*, Nov. 18, 1933, and the Christmas issue, 1934. (Note 16).

In recent times the farm has been utilized as an additional farm. The estate was divided in 1994 and taken over by Torbjorn Rasmussen and Jostein Austrheim. The main dwelling was separated from the estate and taken over by Klara Liadal.

Farm no. 18. From farm no. 7 in 1929

1. **Gustav Rasmussen.** 1929 – 1970
Born Mar. 19, 1896, died July 22, 1976, son of Gurine and Rasmus Jobsen, farm no. 7 – 10 d, Hovland.

Unmarried.

The deed to Gustav from his father on this farm, with a tax liability of 1.19 sk.m., is dated Apr. 15, 1929.

Gustav farmed this farm and farm no. 6 (Smaoie), Austrheim, together with his sister:

2. **Kristine Haugland,** born Sept. 11, 1894, died Feb. 16, 1974. Unmarried.

This farm is later managed together with farm no 7.

Tenant farmers

1. **Helge.** 1622 – 1627
He is mentioned in the county records in the years above.

2. **Peder.** 1637 – 1639
Peder is mentioned in the county records in 1637 – 38. Peder's widow is mentioned as "impoverished" in 1639.

3. **Ole.** 1629 – 1633.
Ole is described as "impoverished" in the above years.
4. **Hans.** 1640 – 1643
Hans is mentioned in the county records during the above years.

5. **Asbjorn Jonsen.** 1664
Born in 1627, he is listed as a tenant in the minister's census from 1664.

6. **Jakob Simonsen.** 1682 –

Born in 1664, possibly a son of Simon Torkelsen, farmer no 4 – 1, Hovland. He is only mentioned in two military records from 1682–83.

His son may possibly be:

a. Anders, born 1689 at Hovland. In 1706 he is listed as a servant at Visnes, Karmøy.

7. **Mats Sjursen.** 1682 –

Born in 1664. He is also mentioned in two military records from 1682–83.

8. **Jon Nilsen.** 1683 –

Born in 1666, and he is also mentioned in two military records from 1682 – 83.

9. **Nils Olsen.** – 1701

Born in 1645. He is mistakenly listed as a tenant under Austrheim in the 1701 census. Further information about him is unknown.

10. **Ole Olsen.** 1706 –

Born 1688, tenant farmer no. 7, Skare. Ole is a handyman on farm no. 4 here in 1706 and is also mentioned in 1710.

11. **Sjur Knutsen.** 1706 –

Born in 1666, son of Knut Sjursen, farm no. 7 – 1 a, Hovland.

Known children:

a. Lars, born 1704, next tenant farmer.
b. Knut, born 1708, married to Berta Knutsdatter, tenant farmer no. 15, Nordvik.
c. Hans, born 1712. In the years 1734 – 35 he lives on Skare.

In 1706 Sjur lives with his brother, Jon, on farm no. 7 here. In 1711 he pays 24 sk. in "shoe tax" for himself, his wife and 2 children.

12. **Lars Sjursen.** 1734

Born 1704, son of previous tenant farmer.

In one of the military records from 1734 we can see that Lars is married and lives at Hovland. No records were found of his wife's name or the names of any children.

13. **Reier Amundsen.** – 1785

Born in 1690, buried Mar. 23, 1771, from Hardanger.

Married in 1st marriage to **Gunhild Olsdatter,** born in 1696, buried July 1, 1759. She is of unknown origin.

Married in 2nd marriage on July 13, 1760 to **Siri Andersdatter,** born in 1708, buried Oct. 8, 1785, widow of Knut (Knutsen, Saebo?), mother of Anders Knutsen on farm no. 1, Hovland.

Children in 1st marriage:

a. Ole, born 1720, married to Valborg Knutsdatter, farm no. 3 – 1, Austrheim.
b. Amund, born 1722, married to Ellen Olsdatter, tenant farmer no. 21, Nordvik.
c. Martha, born 1725, buried Jan. 21, 1761.

In 1734 Reier is listed as tenant at Tuo, and that he owes 2 ort 16 sk. on a lease from Halsnoy Cloister. He is later listed as tenant on farm no. 1, Hovland.

There was a settlement after Reier's death in 1771. In the estate there were miscellaneous items worth 27–3–10 rdl. and debt and expenses amounted to 10–2–8 rdl. Among the miscellaneous items listed are:

> 1 four– and 1 six–oar boat with sail 3–2–0, 3 spring herring fishing nets 2–0–0, 10 lobster pots 0–1–16, 1 cow 3–0–0, 1 iron stove 1–0–0, and the houses on the lot 9–0–0.

14. **Knut Andersen** 1736 –

Born 1711, son of Anders Knutsen, tenant farmer no. 4 a, Klovning.

Married 1735 to **Martha Hansdatter,** settlement Sept. 23, 1750, daughter of Hans Johannesen, farmer no. 4 – 2 d, Hovland.

Children:

a. Gjertrud, born 1736, buried July 17, 1774.
b. Guri, further information is unknown.

In the settlement records after Martha's death in 1750, both daughters inherit 2 ort and 4 sk. Guardian for the daughters was their uncle Johannes Stange.

15. **Paul Bårdsen** 1758 – 1790

Born 1726, died Sept. 19, 1779, son of Bard Olsen, North Vage in Sveio.

Sheep shearing on the Tuemarka around 1930. From left: Emma Haugland, Gustav R. Haugland, Klara Haugland, Marie Kvalvik, Kaia Haugland and Gunhilde Haugland.

Married in 1749 to **Trua Olsdatter,** born 1728, buried July 1, 1798, daughter of Anna Svendsdatter and Ole Abrahamsen, tenant farmer no. 11 a, Nordvik.

Children:

a. Amund, born 1749, married in 1774 to Malene Jonsdatter, tenant farm no. 11, Skare.
b. Ole, born 1751, registered in Skåre in 1769, further history unknown.
c. Ingeborg, born 1752, buried June 29, 1777, possibly named after Paul's mother.
d. Anna, born 1754, buried Oct. 14, 1758.
e. Marta, born May 16, 1758, married in 1783 to widower Anders Knutsen, farmer no. 1– 8, Hovland.
f. Knut, born 1763, buried Mar. 22, 1767.
g. Berte, baptized Oct. 6, 1765, buried Sept. 30, 1792.
h. Svend, baptized Nov. 7, 1773, buried Mar. 25, 1774.

Paul was a farmer on North Vage in Sveio before the family moved to Utsira in 1758, and he became a tenant on farm no. 1 here. He is erroneously listed under Austrheim in the 1758 census. Paul had two half–brothers who became Sira–ites: Ole Bardsen Austrheim and Kristen Bardsen Nordvik, aside from his nephew John Helgesen Nordvik.

Paul and Jørgen Hovland perished at sea.

Settlement under farm no. 7, Tuo.

16. **Hans Hansen.** – 1799.
Born 1707?, records show him buried June 30, 1799, at 96 years old. He is listed as 36 years of age in 1758. He is perhaps the son of Hans Johannesen, farm no. 4 – 2 b, Hovland.

Married in 1st marriage to (unknown).

Married in 2nd marriage on Apr. 8, 1759, to **Siri Torsdatter (Gundersdatter),** born 1708, buried Mar. 25, 1770. In 1758 she was housekeeper living on Salhuset in Bo, Torvestad.

Married in 3rd marriage on Oct. 2, 1770, to **Eli Olsdatter** born 1712, buried Mar. 25, 1798. Her origins are unknown.

Sara Hansdatter, born 1730, buried Apr. 8, 1784, may possibly be a daughter of Hans from his first marriage. In 1758 she was listed as a tenant living in the Salhuset on the Bo farm, Torvestad.

The Dahlen settlement under farm no. 1 and 2.

17. **Hans Johnsen.** 1791 – 1849
Baptized Sept. 3, 1767, died May 4, 1849, son of Berta Andersdatter and Jon Jørgensen, farm no. 1 – 6 g, Klovning.

Married in 1st marriage June 13, 1791, to **Kari Anbjornsdatter,** baptized Oct. 18, 1761, died Dec. 12, 1818, daughter of Anna Johannesdatter and Anbjorn Rasmussen, farm no. 7 – 5 c, Hovland.

Married in 2nd marriage Dec. 3, 1819, to **Ingeborg Rasmusdatter,** baptized Sept. 23, 1783, died Aug. 22, 1856, daughter of Dorte Andersdatter and Rasmus Tollefsen, tenant farmer no. 17 b, Nordvik.

Children 1st marriage:

a. Anbjorn, baptized Oct. 29, 1791, married to widow Marta Torsteinsdatter on the settlement Nygård under the Birkeland farm in Sveio.
b. Jon, baptized Dec. 6, 1794, buried Mar. 29, 1795.
c. Jon, baptized June 18, 1797, married 1818 to Anne Olsdatter, Vikse, Skogland in Skåre. Their son was Daniel Johnsen Nordvik.

Children in 2nd marriage:

d. Kari, born Mar. 25, 1820, married 1849 to Hans Jonsen, Skogland in Skåre, They lived also for a period on Hovland.

In 1823 this settlement was assessed to 30 Spd. The livestock consisted of 2 cows, and 1 horse, and yearly crop yield was 10–12 barrels of grain.

There was a settlement in 1850 following Hans' death. Misc. items were sold at an auction in October the year before for 38–1–7 Spd. The buildings on the place were described as follows: *A main dwelling built with logs with a shed at one end and an outside storage at the other end estimated at 8–0–0 including a cow stable with concrete base estimated at 2–0–0*, which was taken over by the widow. There was 13–4–5 Spd. left to be divided among the heirs.

Settlement Tiphaugen, under farm no. 4 and 6.

18. **Hans Hansen.** 1782 – 1822
See also under tenant farm no. 20, Nordvik.
Hans was tenant on the Kleven place in eastern Nordvik from 1774 – 82, before he and his family moved to Hovland.
His son Hans Knut became the next tenant farmer on the place.

19. **Hans Knut Hansen,** 1822 – 1828
Baptized Dec. 18, 1784, died Dec. 4, 1828, son of previous tenant farmer.

Unmarried.

In 1823 his place was assessed to 15 Spd. He fed 1 cow and harvested each year 3 barrels of grain.

20. **Hans Kristensen.** 1821 – 1825.
Baptized Feb. 8, 1789, died in 1877, son of Marta Askildsdatter and Kristen Monsen, farmer no. 4 – 6 f, Hovland.

Married in 1st marriage to **Marta Kirstine Hansdatter,** baptized June 16, 1798, died Nov. 24, 1822, daughter of Anna Hansdatter and Hans Hansen, tenant farmer no. 20 j, Nordvik.

Children:

a. Hans Ole, born Dec. 5, 1821, died June 29, 1845

Hans moved to Neset belonging to Kalstø in Avaldsnes, where he was married in his 2nd marriage in 1825 to Margrete Eliasdatter (1803 – 1877). They had 8 children.

In 1823 there was an estate settlement after the death of Marta Kirstine. From the estate's assets of 49 Spd., 28 Spd. was deducted to cover debt and expenses. Among the miscellaneous items left, the following are mentioned:

> 1 logged storage house covered with peat and lined with boards 10–0–0, 2 herring fishing nets with associated equipment 1–0–0, 1 old four–oar boat 1–0–0, 1 red mare, 6–years old, 6–0–0, 2 sheep with lambs 2–0–0, 1 clothing locker with lock and ornamental reinforcements 2–2–12, 1 silver–plated nameplate marked "M.C.H.D." 0–2–0 and 1 silver–plated filigree broach 0–1–0.

21. **Jakob Bentsen.** 1830 – 1837.
See also tenant farmer no. 22, Kvalvik.

Jakob and Ingeborg were tenant farmers for a few years at farm no. 7, and are also mentioned here, before they moved to Kvalvik.

22. **Lars Mikkelsen.** 1830 – 1834.
Birth date unknown. Came from Kleppe in Tysvaer.

Married Oct. 4, 1830, to **Marthe Olsdatter,** baptized May 26, 1810, daughter of Gjoa Andersdatter and Ole Gudmundsen, farmer no. 1 – 9 a, Hovland.

Children born on Utsira:

a. Kristine Oline, born Feb. 11, 1831, married to Tollef Tollefsen, Hoyland.

The family moved to Nodland, Tysvaer, in June 1834.

23. **Johannes Olsen.** 1862 – 1909
Born 1828, died Feb. 23, 1880, son of Margrete Johannesdatter, and Ola Johannesen, Kvalvagnes, at Nonsli in Sveio.

Married in 1861 to **Jorgine Nilsdatter,** born in 1835, died Jan. 3, 1917 in Haugesund, daughter of Inger Andersdatter and Nils Nilsen, Vårå in Avaldsnes.

Children:

a. Nils Olai, born in 1860 and lived in Sveio. He and Johannes Johannesen Dalastein perished in Sirafjord on their way to Haugesund with a boat load of herring on Mar. 10, 1890.
b. Elise Margrete, born Aug. 29, 1863, died 1936, lived in Haugesund.
c. Lars Christian, born Mar. 27, 1866, died Oct. 27, 1885 in the hospital in Stavanger.
d. Ole Johannes, born Feb. 6, 1869, died Oct. 30, 1887. He fell overboard from a ship from Stavanger in the Baltic Sea.

e. Anna *Ragnhilde*, born Dec. 12, 1871, moved to Haugesund and married Samson Underhaug, from Strandebarm.
f. Eli Marthea, born Feb. 17, 1875, moved to Haugesund, married in 1899 to Martines Jensen.
g. Olga Josefine, born Jan. 10, 1878, moved to Haugesund, had one daughter: Nelly, born July 29, 1898.

Johannes is listed in 1875 as a day worker on farms carrying out miscellaneous chores and also as a fisherman. Their home was sold in 1910 for 8 kroner. It was located to the north and west of Marit and Arne O. Klovning's home. In 1900 Jorgine lived alone here and made a living from her chicken farm. She moved later to Haugesund.

24. **Knut Olsen.** 1852 – 1900.
Baptized Apr. 18, 1812, died Nov. 16, 1881, son of Gjoa Andersdatter, and Ole Gudmundsen, farm no. 1 – 9 b, Hovland.

Married July 2, 1865, to **Serine Jørgensdatter,** born in 1823, died Aug. 25, 1900, daughter of Jørgen Amundsen, Sund Church district in Hordaland.

No children.

Knut became blind at the age of 22. He and his mother, Gjoa lived at Austrheim until 1852, when they moved to Hovland.

An interesting description of Serine is given in an article in the publication *Rogaland Fishing*:

> A woman lived at Utsira who took her turn at sea in the fishing boat along with the men. This was the well–known "Strilo" from Sund County near Bergen. She came to Utsira together with the lighthouse tender Eide for whom she worked as a housekeeper. Her Christian name was Serina, and that is all the neighbors knew about her. She got married to one they called the "Blind Knut", and their only income came from fishing. They managed very well. She came with her "Knut" to sea. When they were out fishing for cod or lingcod, she did all the rowing and maneuvering while he was fishing. They also trawled for pollock and coal fish and fished for lobster.
>
> Their catch was processed and salted and dried, as it was not possible to sell fresh fish at the market in those days. With only manual fishing lines they managed to fish so much fish that they had to hire young boys to help them dry all the fish.
>
> Strilo used to work as a maid in fine homes. She was godmother to the minister Solheim in Stavanger and he always went to visit Strilo when he came to Utsira. Her husband died many years before her, but she managed very well without help from anybody until she died.

Serine died when she was walking along the beach collecting wood for burning.

25. **Konrad Severin Ånensen.** 1863 – 1916
Born 1842 in Kristiansand, died Aug. 24, 1882.

Married in 1st marriage on Nov. 9, 1863, to **Gunhilde Gudmundsdatter,** born Jan. 26, 1839. died July 27, 1866, daughter of Anne Rasmusdatter and Gudmund Tollefsen, farmer no. 10 – 1 a, Hovland.

Married in 2nd marriage to **Berthe Gurine Jobsdatter,** born June 2, 1844, died Apr. 10, 1916, daughter of Karoline Elisabeth Johnsdatter and Job Rasmussen, farmer no. 7 – 9 c, Hovland.

Children in 1st marriage:

a. Berthe Karine, born May 31, 1863, died Mar. 29, 1864.
b. Gudmund, born Apr. 23, 1866, died July 19, 1866.

Konrad Severin Ånensen (1842–1882)and Berthe Gurine Jobsdatter (1844–1916).

Children in 2nd marriage:

c. Gunhilde Amalie, born Oct. 9, 1868, emigrated to USA in 1889, married in 1890 to Gustav Danielsen, farmer in Potlatch, Idaho. She moved to Palouse City, WA, after the death of her husband and her youngest daughter Anna in 1922.
d. Mette *Marthea*, born Aug. 14, 1870, died July 1, 1917, emigrated to USA in 1887, married widower George B. Hovland in Newman Grove, NE. They later divorced, and Marthea remarried and moved to Newport, Oregon where she and her husband ran the Abby Hotel.
e. Elisabeth Julia (*Julia Lisa*), born Oct. 5, 1872, emigrated to USA in 1888, married Elliot, lived in Seattle, WA.
f. Berthea Karine, born June 5, 1875, married in 1894 to Johannes Olsen, tenant farmer no. 32, Kvalvik.
g. *Regine* Severine, born Nov. 27, 1877, married in 1894 to Thomas Bendiksen, farmer no 3 – 3, Skare.

Konrad obtained the deed to two lots from Job Rasmussen on Aug. 31, 1865.The main dwelling was occupied by Geir Helge Rasmussen today, while the other was a smithy when Konrad was the island's smith. The house, 7.5m x 6m, a frame house and logs, with basement and lined with boards and covered with a tile roof, was in 1869 assessed at 230 Spd. The smithy, 5 x 4.4 meters, was estimated to be worth 30 Spd. According to the 1900 census Berthe Gurine made a living at that time as a seamstress.

26. **Sjur Knutsen (Sjur Kvarkaneset). 1850 – 1884**
Born Mar. 18, 1819, died Aug. 16, 1884, son of Berta Gudmundsdatter and Knut Sjursen, farmer no. 5 – 4 h, Austrheim.

Married in 1st marriage on July 2, 1848, to **Anne Marthe Johnsdatter,** baptized Feb. 19, 1806, died Dec. 2, 1849, daughter of Oline Johannesdatter and Jon Larsen, Dale on Torvestad, and widow of Nils Johnsen, Kvalvik.

Married in 2nd marriage on Apr. 5, 1852, to **Berthe Karine Rasmusdatter,** born Sept. 27, 1819, died Sept. 24, 1862, daughter of Jobiane Jobsdatter and Rasmus Tollefsen, farmer no. 7 – 7 d, Hovland.

Third marriage, May 27, 1865, to **Anbjorg Eline Anbjornsdatter,** born Feb. 21, 1834, died Jan. 16, 1873, daughter of Anne Marte Larsdatter and Ambjorn Gudmundsen, no. 3 – 4 e, Austrheim.

Sjur's children with Malene Olsdatter Haugland:

a. Sjur Mathias, born Aug. 17, 1838, married in 1865 to Kristine Elisabeth Henriksdatter, Haraldseide in Skjold. He lived in Haugesund in 1900 running his own house–painting business.

Children in 2nd marriage:

a. Rasmus, born Mar. 5, 1852.
c. Anne Marthe, born Mar. 23, 1854, died June 12, 1857.
d. Knut Mathias, born June 4, 1856, emigrated to USA in 1888. According to the Martin Ulvestad book (page 821), he was a farmer at Newman Grove, Madison Co, Nebraska.[44]
e. Bertel Martin, born July 7, 1858, died Mar. 29, 1865.
f. Anne Martha, born Sept. 24, 1860. died July 17, 1867.

Children in 3rd Marriage:

g. Berthe Karine, born Aug. 4, 1866, married in 1886 to Ole Endresen, tenant farmer no. 30, Hovland. She emigrated to USA with half–brother Knut Mathias (See above.) in 1888.

---

[44] See Note 35.

Photo from 1930. View towards "Kvarkaneset." In the background "Smuget" (The Alley) and "Stareberget" (farm no. 6 and 4 at Austrheim).

h. Bertel Martin, born May 30, 1868, died July 5, 1871.
i. Anne Marthe, born July 16, 1870, died Dec. 11, 1871.

The lease to Sjur on the lot, 23 x 12 alen, is dated May 1, 1865 for 5 Spd. and annual fee 60 sk. The house, 10.7 x 7m, built with logs and lined with boards, with a basement and covered with a tiled roof, was assessed at 1700 kroner in 1878. His two–story boathouse, 7.5 x 7.2 meters, was assessed at 250 kroner. The house must then have been new, as it is mentioned that his old sea shed (assessed in 1866 at 120 Spd.) was torn down, and some of the materials were used to build the new one. Today only the foundation is left of the old main dwelling.

27. **Bernt Tonnessen.** 1872 – 1876
Born 1833, died Feb. 12, 1918, son of Tonnes Larsen, Naes County in Flekkefjord.

Married May 30, 1872, to **Berthe Kristine Johannesdatter,** born Mar. 15, 1838, daughter of Berta Kristine Johannesdatter and Johannes Knutsen, farm no. 4 – 3 d, Klovning.

Berthe Kristine's children with Gudmund Jørgensen Klovning:

a. Gudmund, born July 2, 1864.

Bernt and Berthe Kristine had two stillborn children in 1872 and 1875.

The family lived on farm no. 10, Rabben. Bernt was a crew member on one of the government–owned harbor maintenance vessels. They moved to Haugesund.

He later worked as a cooper.

28. **Lars M. Mikalsen Hovland.** 1869–1882 Born Apr. 8, 1845, died June 14, 1924, in Newman Grove, NB (See article right.), son of Lavine Nicoline Larsdatter and Mikkel Jørgensen, farm no. 2 – 1 a, Hovland.

Married June 20, 1869, to **Berthe Malene Mathiasdatter,** born June 30, 1849, died Sept. 11, 1891, daughter of Petronelle and John Mathias Johnsen, farm no. 3–1c, Skare.[45]

Married 2nd time June 9, 1895, to **Serina Ness Hanson**, born (?), died June 3, 1921, in Newman Grove, Nebraska.

Sons of Lars Hovland: (from left) Christian, George, and Johnny (Ole) , (front) Laurits, 1905.

June 18 1924

LARS M. HOVELAND PASSES AWAY

The death of Lars M. Hoveland, who has been failing for a number of months occurred last Saturday morning at his residence in Newman Grove. He suffered from a stroke of apoplexy over a year ago from which he never recovered.

Mr. Hoveland was one of the first settlers in this community, coming forty-two years ago and making his home here ever since with the exception of two years.

Funeral services were held at the Trinity church yesterday, Rev. O. C. Hellekson officiating and interment was made in the Free church cemetery.

Obituary

Lars M. Hovland was born on the island of Ursira, Norway, April 8, 1845, his parents being Mikal and Lavina Hovland. He was baptized and confirmed in the Lutheran church on Ursira and remained a lifelong member of the Lutheran faith.

In 1869 he was united in holy wedlock with Bertha Malinda Johnson and together they came to Newman Grove 42 years ago and here the deceased has made his home ever since, except about two and a half years which he spent with his children in Canada. His wedded life was blessed with 8 children, of whom one is dead. His first wife died on September 11, 1891. On June 9, 1895, he was married to Serina Ness Hanson and they lived happily together till she died June 8, 1921.

Mr. Hovland has been hard of hearing since he was a boy. On February 12, 1923, he sustained a stroke of apoplexy from which he never fully recovered. He returned to Newman Grove last winter but his health has continued to fail and he passed away quietly on Saturday morning, June 14, being at the time of his death 79 years, 2 months and 6 days of age.

Mr. Hovland leaves to mourn his departure, seven children as follows: Lauritz Mikal, Paulina Marie Johnson, Ludvig Johan and Mandius George, all of Holden, Alberta, Canada; Mrs. Christina Amelia Heckt, Bloomfield, Nebr., Christian Louis, and Johannes Olaf, both of Atlee, Canada. He is also survived by one brother, George Hovland of Ames, Iowa. Mrs. Heckt, John and the brother George were present at the funeral. He is also survived by eighteen grandchildren and 2 great grandchildren. He also leaves a host of friends who long will cherish his memory.

Mr. Hovland has for many years been a member of the Trinity Lutheran church and we trust he obtained a blessed end and entered into the rest of the saints.

[45] Lars' wife, Berthe Malene Mathiasdatter, is the sister of Knut Mathias Johnsen, who emigrated to the USA in 1875 (See p. 315-316).

Yard in front of farm no. 2, Hovland. Photo taken in 1907 when Lars was home on a visit. From left, probably Mikkel Jorgensen, Lars' father, Lars, unknown, to the right: Serina(?).

Children:

a. Laurits Mikal (*Lewis*), born Feb. 20, 1870, died June 9, 1954, married Augusta Emelia Seaberg in 1897, 8 children, lived (from 1904) in Palmer District, Holden, Alberta, Canada.
b. Pauline Marie (*Lena*), born Aug. 11, 1872, died June 20, 1958, married Gust Johnson in 1897, 3 children.
c. Oluf Johannes, born July 20, 1875, died Nov. 17, 1887.
d. *Ludvig* Johan, born Sept. 21, 1877, died Apr. 18, 1971, married Augusta Bransmo Robertson in 1907, 6 children.
e. *Kristine* Amalie, born April 10, 1880, died Nov. 1967, married Cornelius Heckt in 1907, 2 children.
f. *George* Mikal, born 1883, died 1959, unmarried.
g. Christian Lewis (*Christ*), born June 27, 1885, died Dec. 10, 1974, married to Gunda Marie Forre in 1923, 3 children.
h. Olaf Johannes (*Johnny*), born Nov. 30, 1887, died July 23, 1951, unmarried.

The family lived in the house northeast of the main dwelling on farm no. 2 here. In July 1882 they emigrated to Nebraska, USA.

29. **Daniel Johnsen.** 1873 – 1899.
See tenant farm no. 26, Nordvik.

Daniel and his family lived in Tappanausted in Tuevagen on farm no. 10 in those years.

30. **Ole Endresen.** 1886 – 1888.
Born 1856, died before March 1888, son of Guri Andrine Olsdatter and Endre Korneliussen, North Vage in Sveio.

Married April 28,1886, to **Berthe Karine Sjursdatter,** born Aug. 4, 1866, daughter of tenant farmer no. 26, see previous entry here.

Children:

a. Sofie Amalie, born Oct. 16, 1886, emigrated to USA.

Ole worked with the Harbor Authority. After Ole's death in 1888, Berthe Karine and their daughter Sofie emigrated to the USA together with her half–brother Knut Mathias Sjursen.

31. **Johannes Olsen.** 1894 – 1902
See tenant farmer no. 32, Kvalvik.

Johannes and Berthe Karine lived on farm no. 7, with his mother, before they purchased their home and moved to Kvalvik.

32. **Karoline Johannesdatter ("Smago")** 1865 – 1925
Born Nov. 11, 1849, died April 21, 1930, daughter of Ingeborg Oline Johannesdatter and Johannes Johannesen, farm no. 6 – 6 g, Austrheim.

Unmarried.

Karoline and her mother Ingeborg (1809 – 1892) lived in the house directly south of the main dwelling on farm no. 7, Tuo. Only the foundation is left today. They made a living spinning, weaving and knitting.

33. **Truls J. Jobsen.** 189x — 1914
See under tenant farmer no. 15, Klovning.

Truls and Janna lived on farm no. 7 here during this period, before they took over the house at Klovning, farm no. 9, Sorheim (Trulsahuset). They took in a boarder in 1900, **Marta Bru,** from Rennesoy, a midwife on Utsira before Åsa Helgesen came to the island in 1903.

34. **Peder Olai Andreassen Barane.** 1907 – 1912
Born in 1880, son of Mette Gurine Torgjersdatter and Ole Andreas Olsen, Oldereide on Moster.

Married Oct. 25, 1907, to **Anne Marta Hansdatter,** born July 26, 1885, daughter of Severine Halvorsdatter and Hans Mathias Sjursen, farmer no. 4 – 11 b, Austrheim.

Children:

a. Adolf Mikal, born April 17, 1908, died in 1935.
b. Hans Severin, born Dec. 21, 1909, died in 1931.
c. *Petra* Marie, born Aug. 18, 1911, married to Jakob Endressen, Baeroy on Moster.
d. Olga, born 1913, died 1931.
e. Benny Borghild, born 1916, died 1931.
f. Anna, born 1918, married to Lars J. Mathiassen, Haugesund.
g. Sigurd, born 1922, married to Laura Helene Johansdatter, Baeroy on Moster
h. Johannes, born 1925, unmarried.
i. Sverre, born 1930, died 1931.

They lived at Kvarkaneset. In 1912, they moved to Baeroy on Moster. The house was sold and they moved to Roykesund.

35. **Alfred Hansen.** 1934 – 1987

Born Oct. 11, 1896, died March 18, 1992, son of Severine Halvorsdatter and Hans Mathias Sjursen, farm no. 4 – 11 f, Austrheim.

Married on May 2, 1924, to **Minda Sørhus,** born June 20, 1892, died June 17, 1971, daughter of Anne Martha Laurine Johannesdatter and Tobias Sørhus, tenant farmer no. 23 d, Klovning.

Children:

a. Margit *Solveig*, born Aug. 19, 1924, lives in Sandnes.
b. Leiv *Tobias,* born Feb. 7, 1926, married in 1951 to Laura Helgesen, tenant farmer no. 38, Hovland.
c. *Alf* Magne, born Oct. 27, 1927, married in 1954 to Sigrunn Klovning, tenant farmer no. 40, Hovland.
d. Sigvald. born Aug. 24, 1929, married in 1958 to Malfrid Hansen, tenant farmer no. 41, Hovland.
e. Agna Laurine, born June 18, 1933, died Oct. 21, 1933.
f. Agnar, born Sept. 6, 1934, married to Bjorg from Fredrikstad, lives in Sandnes.
g. *Else* Birgit, born Nov. 21, 1937, lives in Sandnes.

Alfred built a house at Kvarkaneset, farm no. 21, Fjellberg, in 1936.

36. **Valnum Klovning.** 1944 – 1992

Born July 5, 1908, died Jan. 17, 1970, son of Laura and Valnum Jørgensen, tenant farmer no. 21 c, Klovning.

Married Sept. 19, 1934, to **Lovise Klovning,** born April 8, 1902, died March 1, 1992, daughter of Thala and Johannes Klovning, farm no. 2 – 3 d, Klovning.

Children:

a. Svanhild, born July 9, 1932, married in 1952 to Tobias Hansen, tenant farmer no. 37, Kvalvik.
b. *Viktor* Leidulf, born Feb. 5, 1935, died 1989, married to Marit Soyland, Buoy, lives in Stavanger.
c. *Jenny* Solbjorg Bergny, born Feb. 27, 1944, married to Torbjorn Hatlevik, lives on Espevaer.

Besides fishing, Valnum worked for a period for the Harbor Authority. He started to build his new house at Kvarkeneset, farm no. 24, Valderhaug, during the war.

37. **Elias B. Kvalvik.** 1939 – 1955
Born July 27, 1907, son of Lisa and Bendik Tollefsen, farm no. 4 – 1 f, Kvalvik.

Married May 7, 1935, to **Marie Gunhilde Haugland,** born Oct. 19. 1905, daughter of Kaia and Elling Haugland, farm no. 10 – 3 b. Hovland.

Children:
a. *Leiv* Bjarne, born April 1, 1938, is marine pilot, married to Borgny, lives in Skudeneshavn.
b. Egil *Kare*, born May 7, 1940, is a marine pilot, married to Else, lives in Kopervik.
c. *Magne* Elias, born July 16, 1942, is a marine pilot, married to Torill, lives at Beiningen, Skudesneshavn.
d. *Eva* Klara Juline, born Oct. 6, 1944, married to Frode Toje, MD, Drobak.
e. *Torodd* Kasper, born May 26, 1948, died in 1985, married to Reidun, lives in Kopervik.
f. May Lise.

Elias was a first mate and later a marine pilot on Utsira. The family moved in 1955 to Skudeneshavn.

38. **Tobias Hansen.** 1951 –
Born Feb. 7, 1926, son of Minda and Alfred Hansen, tenant farmer no. 35 b, Hovland.

Married June 30, 1951, to **Laura Helgesen,** born May 26, 1924, died April 27, 1993, daughter of Julie and Hersleb Helgesen, tenant farmer no. 50 i, Nordvik.

Children:
a. *Arnvid* Modstein, born April 2, 1953, married in 1976 to Liv Pedersen, tenant farmer no. 43, Hovland.

From spring herring fisheries outside Sørvågen around 1910. Photo by A. P. Wallevik, Hardanger Folk Museum, Utne.

b. *Helga* Jorunn, born Jan. 13, 1958, married in 1987 to Torger Lund from Steinkjer, lives in Sandnes.

They built themselves a house here on farm no. 22, Bakken, in 1956.

39. **Ivar Amundsen.** 1948 – 1951
Born June 12, 1918, son of Martha and Jørgen Amundsen, Skjold.
Married to **Serine Eriksen,** born July 17, 1921, daughter of Serine and Martin Eriksen, farm no. 5 – 1 j, Skare.

Children:

a. Edvin, born Sept. 5, 1947, moved in with Ellen, lives in Skjoldavik.
b. *Jan* Gunnar, born Oct. 7, 1948, married to Jorunn, lives in Skjoldavik.
c. *Vigdis* Irene, born Nov. 24, 1950, married to Lars Huseby, lives in Forde in Sveio.
d. Froydis, born April 3, 1953, married to Bernt Huseby, lives in Forde in Sveio.

Ivar worked for the Harbor Authority. They lived a few years here before they built their home and moved to Skjold.

40. **Alf Hansen.** 1954 –
Born Oct. 27, 1927. son of Minda and Alfred Hansen, tenant farmer no. 35 c, Hovland.

Married April 11, 1954, to **Sigrunn Klovning**, born Aug. 14, 1934, daughter of Marie and Johannes Klovning, farm no. 2 — 4 c, Klovning.

Children:

a. Judith *Torill* Marie, born May 29, 1955, married in 1976 to Torodd Nilsen, tenant farmer no. 49, Skare.
b. *Alvin* Magnar, born Aug. 21, 1959, married to Jorunn Georgsen, lives in Kopervik.
c. Alf Johannes, born April 5, 1962, married to Ann Karin Floysvik, lives in Sandnes.
d. *Gerd* Kristense, born July 24, 1967, lives in Haugesund. She also has a farm here.

They made their home here, farm no. 33, Soltun, in 1958.

42. **Sigvald A. Hansen.** 1958 –
Born Aug. 24, 1929, son of Minda and Alfred Hansen, tenant farmer no. 35 d, Hovland.

Married Sept. 20, 1958, to **Malfrid Hansen**, born Jan. 16, 1939, daughter of Karoline and Mathias Hansen, farm no. 4 – 13 c, Austrheim.

Children:

a. Egil, born April 17, 1960, twin, married to Laila Gautesen, lives in Haugesund.
b. Torunn, born April 17, 1960, twin, died Dec. 20, 1960.

Sigvald built himself a house here, farm no. 34, Granli, in 1963.

43. **Arne O. Klovning.** 1977 –
Born Sept. 20, 1951, son of Laurine and John Klovning, tenant farmer no. 28 b, Klovning.

Married July 10, 1976, to **Marit Eide,** born April 13, 1955, from Haugesund.

Children:

a. Anders, born July 19, 1977.
b. Arne, born Feb. 3, 1980.
c. Marte Eide, born Oct. 13, 1983.

Arne was a carpenter. They built themselves a house here on farm no. 37, Hovland. Marit is listed as a teacher at Utsira Children and Youth School.

43. **Arnvid Hansen.** 1976 – 1990
Born April 2, 1953, son of Laura and Tobias Hansen, tenant farmer no. 38 a, Hovland.

Married Sept. 4, 1976, to **Liv Pedersen Kolås,** born April 24, 1954, from Volda.

Children:

a. Tommy, born May 19, 1974.
b. Anita, born Aug. 31, 1977.
c. Solveig Elise, born June 9, 1980.
d. Tone Lillian, born Nov. 3, 1982.

Arnvid was captain on board the M/S "Utsira" from 1979 until they moved to Orsta in 1990. He is now a marine coastal pilot on the "Hurtigruten" (coastal ferry) between Bergen and Kirkenes.

Their house on farm no. 38, "Arnheim," built in 1976, was taken over by Unni and Wilhelm Magne Klovning in 1987.

44. **Arnstein Eek.** 1988 –
Born Sept. 3, 1962, came from Sparbu in North Trondelag.

Married June 7, 1991, to **Hildegunn Rasmussen,** born June 7, 1962, daughter of Laila and Rasmus Rasmussen, farm no. 12 – 7 b, Nordvik.

Children:

a. Guro, born June 26, 1992.
b. Gunnar, born June 7, 1995.

Arnstein has worked for Utsira municipality as a consultant and case worker since 1988.

45. **Kenneth Klovning.** 1990 –
Born Jan.3, 1971, son of Åsta Klovning and Oystein Andersen.

Married July 19, 1991, to **Kari Johnsrud,** born Nov. 3, 1972, daughter of Aslaug and Kåre Johan Johnsrud, Veim in Fordesfjorden.

Children:

a. Ken Roger, born May 30, 1991.
b. Silje, born Aug. 15, 1994.

They built their home on farm no. 47, in 1990. Kenneth works for the Norwegian Coast Guard.

46. **Bjorn J. Sandmo.** 1988 –
Born April 22, 1963, came from Roan in South Trondelag.
Married July 19, 1991, to **Wenche Klovning,** born Oct. 19, 1969, daughter of Asta Klovning and Oystein Andersen.

Children:
a. Ole Jørgen, born Dec. 18, 1988.
b. Benjamin, born Feb. 19, 1991.

Bjorn was general manager of Sildakongen, before he in 1995 began fishing with his own boat. Wenche works in a nursery school. They built their home on farm no. 46, in 1990.

47. **Wilhelm *Magne* Klovning.** 1984 –
Born March 7, 1944, son of Mathilde Mortensen, Stavanger.
Married in 1992 to **Unni Sunde,** born Dec. 30, 1952, and came from Stavanger.

Children:
a. Merete Ånestad, born Dec. 31, 1966.
b. Ane Kristine, born May 15, 1974.
c. Remi, born Dec. 18, 1982.
d. Jan Magne, born Nov. 22, 1985.

Magne sailed as a cook from 1962 – 78. In addition to his fishing activities, he and Unni ran a cafe at Siratun. They took over farm no. 38, Arnheim, from Liv and Arnvid Hansen in 1987.

48. **Gunn Ellingsen.** 1980 – 1983
Came from Stavanger and worked as manager of the Social Security in this period.

49. **Håkon Fredly.** 1983 – 1984
Came from Vigeland, Lindesnes, was manager for the Social Security system for one year.

50. **Tor Leif Helgesen.** 1980 – 1982
Born March 27, 1954, son of Lava and Thomas Helgesen, farm no. 30 – 2 a, Nordvik.
Married to **Bodil Jensen,** born March 14, 1954.

Children:

a. Karianne.

Tor Leif was hired as chief municipal treasurer after Elling Valnumsen in 1980, and in 1982 worked in the same position in Tysvaer County.

51. **Britt Lochting.** 1983 – 1987
Came from Oslo and was chief municipal treasurer on Utsira 1983 – 87.

52. **Magnus Skare.** 1985 – 1989
Born July 27, 1926, son of Åsa Oline and Adolf Ellingsen, farm no. 1 – 11 h, Skare.

Married Nov. 15, 1952, to **Jorunn Margit Thomassen,** born Feb. 20, 1934, daughter of Marthine and Astein Thomassen, tenant farmer no. 32 b, Skare.

Children:

a. Jane Marit, born Nov. 30, 1959, married to Tore Martinsen, lives on Sevlandsvik, Karmøy.
b. Linda, born Dec. 22, 1969, lives with Helge Hustvedt in Stavanger.

Magnus was Utsira's first chief administrative officer. Earlier he was principal at Sund School on Karmøy. Jorunn was general manager of Siratun. They live in Akrehamn.

53. **Atle Grimsby.** 1992 –
Born Apr. 23, 1965 and came from Flekkefjord.

Atle was hired as an environmental consultant for Utsira municipality in June 1992.

Skare farmland stretches from Sørevågen north over Siradalen towards Nordvik. Telemark Aircraft Co. photo, 1954.

Skare

Before 1824:	Reg. no. 48, tax between 2 and 2 2/3 v.tf.
In 1824–1851:	Reg. no. 57, serial no. 248 a–b, tax 4 dl. 4 ort 16 sk.
In 1851–1886:	Reg. no. 67, no. 347 – 349, tax 4 dl. 4 ort 11 sk.
In 1886:	Farm no. 29, tax 9 mark 54 ore.

Skare[46] is a wide, elongated farm situated between Klovning and Kvalvik in the western part (of the island), with Nordvik to the north and Hovland to the east. The name itself implies a gap or a dip in the terrain between two hills.

Except for two brief periods, there was only one farmer at Skare until 1822, when J. Dahm came to Utsira and settled on the northern half of Skare called Myre. Between 1845 and 1912 there were 3 farmers – and later 5.

There was only one unregistered settlement at Skare, "Myren," which was left unattended around early 1800. Tollef Gudmundsen later obtained title to a place called "Ambores" which is the area where Siratun is today.

When we look at the table below, we see that the number of houses is almost doubled in the period between 1875 to 1900.

A note in the official Land Register in 1668 indicates:

> Schaere (Skare), tax 2 våger dried fish, doubtfully suitable fields for growing grain, but sufficient to provide peat for fuel, sowing 2 barrels grain to feed 8 head of cattle, expected to be sufficient to pay tax — 2 wetter (approx. 75 kg) grain and 4 calf hides for local defenses, contributions to the church — 2 buckets (15 kg) grain, and misc. fees of 4 sk. in cash.

---

[46] Skare should not be confused with Skåre, now a part of Haugesund.

Table listing crops planted and harvested for grain and potatoes:

Year	Grain planted	Potatoes planted	Grain harvested	Potatoes harvested
1668	2	–	–	–
1703	3	–	–	–
1712	3	–	–	–
1723	3	–	15	–
1802	5	–	30	–
1845	10.5	4.5	–	–
1866	15	9	86	68
1875	17	9.5	–	–
1945	12	7	–	–

Figures for 1945 indicate number of dekars, otherwise, the figures indicate number of barrels.

Table listing livestock, homes and inhabitants.

Year	Horses	Cattle	Sheep	Homes	Inhabitants
1668	–	8	–	–	–
1703	1	8	x	–	–
1712	1	8	x	–	–
1723	–	7	–	–	–
1758	–	–	–	2	9
1801–02	2	8	6	2	14
1845	4	12	28	4(5)	29
1866	4	13	35	7	39
1875	4	11	47	6	38
1900	–	–	–	11	72

Farmers

1. **Jon.** 1521
He is the first person for whom we know the name of those living at Skare.

2. **Olaf.** 1563
He is mentioned in the tax records for this year.

3. **Sjur.** 1603–1625
Sjur is mentioned in the county records as late as 1624.

View from Skarshaugen over Sørrevågen around 1948.

4. **Steffen Larsen.** 1617–1664

Born in 1584 (1594?), Steffen is mentioned in the county records for the first time in 1617, and was probably the first farmer together with Sjur and later Anders. In 1661 he spent 2 bp. dried fish.[47] or 1/3 share of the farm.

5. **Anders Larsen.** 1626 – 1663
Born around 1604, Anders paid 7 rdl. in the first lease in 1626. In the church census in 1664 he is listed as a cotter on Austrheim. He farmed 2/3 of the farm.

Farm no. 1, Haugen (Håien)

1. **Anders Rasmussen.** 1664 – 1670

---

[47] About 12 kg. or 26.5 lbs. (2 bismerpund of dried fish) or equivalent in tangible assets (such as land) or currency. See page 10, Abbreviations.

Born in 1629, he is also mentioned in the church census in 1664. There is also on this farm a Jon Rasmussen, born 1630, listed under "jacks and crofters." He could possibly be a brother of Anders.

2. **Johannes Larsen.** 1671 – 1692
Born around 1652, he is also mentioned in the military records from 1669. In 1673 he is listed as the sole farmer at Skare.

His son is possibly:

a. Lars, born 1675, next farmer.

3. **Lars Johannesen.** 1692 – 1749
Born 1675, buried July 13, 1760, possibly son of previous farmer.

Married to **Berthe Anbjornsdatter,** born 1672, buried July 2, 1756, possibly daughter of Magdalena Klausdatter and Anbjorn Nilsen, Torvestad.

In 1711 he paid a "shoe tax" for himself, his wife and 6 children. Of the children, the following names are known:

a. Johannes, born 1698, married in 1729 to Marita Larsdatter, lived at Gunnarshaug, Torvestad.
b. Malene, born around 1700, died in 1746, married to Jørgen Jonsen, farmer no. 1 – 5, Klovning.
c. Randi, born 1701, married to Ole Tormodsen, farmer no. 1 – 4, Austrheim.
d. Guri, born 1705, married to Rasmus Tormodsen, farmer no. 7 – 4, Hovland.
e. Ingeborg, born 1714, next farmer.

In one military record from 1692 Lars is registered as a farmer at Skare, his renewed lease contract is then in the amount of 2 v. 2 pd. dried fish and is dated Dec. 23, 1720.

In 1703 his financial condition is described as good, however, he had to commit to 1 rdl., 1 ort in repair and upkeep on the houses. He planted 3 barrels of oats and fed 6 cows, 2 calves and some sheep and 1 horse. The animals he owned himself. He owed nothing to the cloister proprietor Mr. Friman, but had other debt in the amount of 3 riksdalers.

Nine years later his financial condition is described as " not especially good": The repair of the houses would amount to 3 riksdalers, while his farming and livestock appeared to be as in 1703.

In 1721 the cloister, after inspection of the property, described Lars' farm as follows: *Lars and all his houses are found in good shape, no repair needs to be done, fields and meadows are in good shape, and he does not owe anything.*

In 1749 he turns half of the farm over to his son–in–law, Thomas, and probably the remaining half before 1755, but no lease letter was found, as the court records for this period are lost.

4. **Thomas Johannesen.** 1749 – 1790

Born 1724, buried Oct. 8, 1786, son of Johannes Ellingsen, tenant farmer no. 10 b, Kvalvik.

Married in 1st marriage in 1749 to **Ingeborg Larsdatter,** born 1714, buried Mar. 12, 1769, daughter of previous farmer.

Married in 2nd marriage on Oct. 2, 1770 to his cousin **Berta Ellingsdatter,** born in 1747, buried July 11, 1790, daughter of Berta Ellingsdatter, and Elling Knutsen, farmer no. 2 – 2 d. Kvalvik.

Children in 1st marriage:

a. Marta, born 1750, next farmer.
b. Gudmund, baptized Oct. 31, 1755, married in 1773 to Valborg Olsdatter, farm no. 3 – 2, Austrheim.

> With all due respect and according to the Royal generous order dated July 5th it is hereby officially announced and confirmed that 16 men from the island of Utsira in Stavanger County on the 23rd of last month found a small one–masted ship drifting on the open sea 10 kilometers off the coast with nobody onboard. On this ship in the cabin they found a red flag with a white/grey horse imprinted on it. – After the ship was successfully brought into the island of Utsira, it was discovered that the ship had 160 crates of indigo which had been loaded onboard in London on October 1st the same year. – When this cargo will be auctioned off (in case the government itself has decided not to take care of disposing of this cargo) shall be announced in both Bergen and Kristiansand weekly publishings.
> *Egersunden*, Nov. 14, 1808. U. W. Koren, County Executive, Stavanger County.

From the "Kristiansand Adressekontoirs" newspaper, "Notices," dated 25 Nov. 1808:[48]

---

48 The "flag with the white/gray horse imprinted on it" mentioned in the Notice resembles the logo for the finest and rarest Scotch whisky "White Horse." If the flag indicates there was also a cargo of whiskey onboard, it apparently was never reported to authorities. The logo pictured here was the actual logo on the White Horse Cellar Inn, Edinburgh, which can be traced back to 1742 to a distillery on the island of Islay just off the west coast of Scotland. whisky.com/brands/white_horse_brand.html.

Children in 2nd marriage:

c. Berta, baptized June 28, 1771, buried Mar. 30, 1800.
d. Ingeborg, baptized Nov. 10, 1773, married in 1813 to Johannes Galtung Jonsen, Vikingstad.
e. Marta, baptized Sept. 28, 1776, in 1801 she lives on Vikingstad.
f. Elling, baptized Apr. 2, 1780, buried June 18, 1780.
g. Gundela, baptized June 24, 1781, buried Sept. 27, 1782.
h. Lars, baptized June 30, 1783, died May 28, 1809 in Kristiansand, He was in the Navy. In the estate settlement after his death in 1809, there was besides 11 rdl., a locker with clothing, etc., including 90 rdl. in cash. This 90 rdl. was what he received the same winter when he sold his share in the compensation for the "DE VROUW ALBERDINE" salvage operation.[49]

Lease contract to Thomas in the amount of 1 v. 1 pd. dried fish in Skare, is issued by P. Vallentinsen in Stavanger on Nov. 23, 1749. From 1755 he also farmed the other half of the farm.

The settlement after Ingeborg in 1769 shows that they were in good financial shape. From the assets of the estate listed as 170–0–14 rdl., 35–2–0 is deducted, of which 12 rdl. is for the funeral. Among misc. items left, the following is mentioned:

> 6 cows, 2 young cows and 4 calves 29– 1–0, 1 old black horse and 1 gray mare 5–2–0, 4 sheep and 1 lamb 1–2–0, 3 kettles 2–2–8, 1/2 of outside mill 3–0–0, 5 barrels of oats 5–3–8, 1 tiled heating stove in "new living room" 7–2–0, 1 small stove in the living room 5–0–0, 1/3 share in an eight–oar boat with sail 2–0–0, 1/2 share in a small "seat–boat" 0–3–0, 1 four–oar boat with sail and one without sail 5–0–0, 2 spring herring fishing nets 1–2–0, 24 lobster pots 2–0–0, cash 39–0–0, misc. silverware 10–0–2, 6 pillows 3–2–16, misc. clothing, etc. 22–0–8, and the deceased's daily clothing 9–1–0.

Eighteen years later there is a settlement after Thomas, and at that time there is nothing left to the heirs. Debt and expenses amounted to more than the 107 rdls. left in the estate.

5. **Kornelius Johannesen.** 1769 – 1771
Born 1739, died Feb. 25, 1771, son of Berta Andersdatter and Johannes Hansen, Stange in Torvestad.

Married on Jan. 3, 1770, to **Marta Thomasdatter,** born 1750, buried Nov. 23, 1771, daughter of previous farmer.

---

[49] (see Note 18.).

Children:

a. Ingeborg, baptized Sept. 30, 1770, married to Joachim Johannesen, Molbrekke in Skåre.

Lease contract to Kornelius in the amount of 4 pd. dried fish is dated Aug. 28, 1769.

Marta and Kornelius did not get to run the farm on Skare very long. Kornelius and his neighbor, Jakob Torkelsen, perished at sea and only Kornelius was later recovered. They left behind them 123 rdl. in assets from which 25 rdl. were taken out to cover debt and expenses. Among the items left are the following listed:

> 4 cows and 3 calves 30–2–0m, 1 mare 2–0–0, 2 rams, 2 sheep and 2 lambs 2–0–0, 2 pigs 1–2–0, 1 four–oar boat with sail 2–0–0, 2 spring herring fishing nets 1–2–8, 20 lobster pots 1–2–16, 1 tiled heating stove 5–0–0, 1 barrel of oats 1–1–8, 1 gold ring and a pair of gold buttons 10–2–0, misc. silverware 6–2–8, cash 3–1–12, 1 blue waistcoat with 24 silver buttons 3–0–0, and a blue damask vest 12–0–0.

Thomas Johannesen took over that half of the farm at Skare so that he could continue to farm the entire farm as before; reference lease contract dated Sept. 2, 1771.

6. **Elias Nilsen.** 1790 – 1809

Born 1748, died June 4, 1830, son of Marta Eriksdatter and Nils Eliasen, Saebø, Torvestad.

Married on July 25, 1767, to **Elisabeth Nilsdatter,** born 1744, buried June 28, 1806, of unknown origin.

Children: (all, except Dortea are born on Saebø)

a. Erik, baptized Oct. 4, 1767, confirmed in 1783, further history unknown.
b. Nils, baptized Dec. 27, 1768, buried Aug. 28, 1771.
c. Jon, baptized Oct. 20, 1770, buried Dec. 27, 1785.
d. Nils, baptized Mar. 22, 1772, buried Feb. 24, 1782.
e. Marta, baptized Mar. 27, 1774, married in 1801 to widower Svend Knutsen, Torvestad.
f. Elias, baptized Sept. 21, 1777, married in 1804 to Åsa Eliasdatter, Skjøllingstad.
g. Dortea, baptized Sept. 19, 1779, buried Feb. 1, 1786.
h. Elisabeth, baptized June 17, 1781, next farmer.
i. Synnøve, baptized Feb. 8, 1784, twin, buried Feb. 1, 1786.
j. Barbro, baptized Feb. 8, 1784, twin, buried Feb. 1, 1786

k. Dortea, baptized Jan. 15, 1790, married in 1810 to Elias Knutsen, Vikshåland.

The lease contract to Elias in the amount of 2 2/3 v. dried fish for Skare (the entire farm) was issued by Peder Valentin Foreman in Bergen on June 28, 1791 (should be 1790) on condition, among other things, that a main dwelling, barn and associated outhouses should be built on the property for the widow Berta Ellingsdatter, however, she died the same year. In the lease contract it is also stated that from 1787, the harvesting of peat on the western side of the property should be regulated.

Before Elias and his family came to Utsira, they ran a farm on Saebo.

In 1802 he sowed 5 barrels of grain and harvested 30 barrels. The livestock consisted of 2 horses, 5 cows, 3 calves and 6 sheep. The farm was assessed at 240 rdl.

In the estate settlement after Lisbeth in 1806, there were assets worth 123 rdl. Debt and expenses amounted to 40 rdl., of which the funeral expenses came to 20 rdl. Among misc. items left are mentioned:

> 1 cow "Brunsia" 12–0–0, 4 calves 9–1–0, 1 brown horse 16–0–0, 1 small pig 2–0–0, 5 barrels of oats 6–0–0, 1 tiled heating stove 4–2–0, 1 six–oar boat 6–0–0, 1 four–oar boat with sail 2–0–0, 1 boat shed 3–0–0, 40 lobster pots 5–0–0, 1 small herring fishing net 0–1–12, and a green and red bedspread 4–2–0.

7. **Svend Eliasen.** 1805 – 1840

Baptized Sept. 26, 1773, died Dec. 27, 1848, son of Eli Knutsdatter and Elias Danielsen, Vikshåland.

Married July 6, 1805, to **Elisabeth Eliasdatter**, baptized June 17, 1781, died Mar. 12, 1852, daughter of previous farmer.

Children:

a. Erik, baptized Oct. 27, 1805, next farmer.
b. Elisabeth, baptized Aug. 22, 1807, buried July 2, 1815.
c. Elisabeth, baptized May 11, 1809, married in 1835 to Lars Olsen, farm no. 4 – 4, Klovning.
d. Elias, baptized Sept. 6, 1812, buried July 2, 1815.
e. Eli, baptized May 7, 1815, married in 1851 to Osmund Osmundsen, Adland.
f. Elias, baptized June 23, 1817, buried Oct. 27, 1817.
g. Elias, born June 21, 1819, died June 22, 1822.
h. Anna, born Apr. 23, 1824, died July 30, 1824.

i. Anna, born Oct. 24, 1825, married in 1853 to Erik Eliassen, Vikshaland.

Lease contract to Sven in the amount 2 2/3 v. dried fish issued by H.B. Foreman on Jan. 7, 1807 and again in May 20, 1809 with a note that according to the loan agreement the outstanding amount is 2 v. dried fish. Mr. Foreman reserved the right to the use of the northern half of the estate for himself (as did the previous farmer until 1809):

> . . . the southern part of the Skare farm which is south of the "Tremanstuen" and the southern point of Skare land according to the chart. However, the northern part of the farm from the aforementioned "Tremanstuen" and the southern part of Skare land is reserved for the owner himself in case he desires to build, live or use part of it. Furthermore, Svend Eliasen should be agreeable to relinquish any special rights in order to accommodate everybody concerned to have access to necessary fields around their houses to grow required food or feed anytime of the year. All shorelines must be kept open to anybody, so that access to the sea and fishing activities can go on unhindered, even to the extent that they can be permitted to build a shed or other facilities to accommodate their activities.

He paid 90 rdl. for this lease plus an old age contract to his father–in–law consisting of: 4 barrels of oats, feed for 2 cows and 6 sheep, use of the field called "Storehatten" for potatoes and grain. The value of this contract was estimated to be 31 rdl. per year.

Before Svend came to Utsira he was farming on Vikshaland.

When J. Dahm bought the farm in 1822, Svend relinquished the northern part of the farm, Farm no. 2, to him according to an agreement dated Jan. 1, 1823, which among other conditions stipulated the following:

1. J. Dahm must on an annual basis provide 4 barrels of oats, feed for 1 cow and the use of the field called "Kirkeflekken," starting at a time when Svend relinquishes his rights to "Håjen."
3. J. Dahm takes over the old age contract to Elias Nilsen.
4. In case J. Dahm should not "against expectations" feel comfortable with the arrangements and life on the island, he is obligated to deliver the farm back to Svend in the condition described in the lease contract of 1809.
6. Svend agrees to make half of the main dwelling, the barn and storage available to J. Dahm from May 3, 1822.

In the deed to J. Dahm it is mentioned that this agreement was already made in 1821.

There was an estate settlement after Svend Eliassen in 1849. Part of the estate consisted of miscellaneous items that were sold at an auction for 142 Spd. In addition, there was 1 cow "Hoprei" at 10–2–12, 1 cow "Knaprei" for 8–2–12 Spd. and a house assessed at 25 Spd.

8. **Erik Svendsen.** 1840 – 1862

Baptized Oct. 27, 1805, died Aug. 10, 1868, son of previous farmer.

Married on June 27, 1830, to **Torborg Hans–Knutsdatter,** baptized Dec. 3, 1809, died Jan. 16, 1874, daughter of Kari Halvorsdatter and Hans Knut Olsen, Lower Hauge, Torvestad.

Children:

a. Elisabet Karine, born Aug. 5, 1831, married in 1853 to Johan Bendik Ådnesen, farm no. 16 – 2, Nordvik.
b. Torborg Eline, born Nov. 18, 1833, married in 1856 to Tollef Knutsen, farm no. 1 – 4, Kvalvik.
c. Erik, born Sept. 17, 1836, next farmer.
d. Svend Mikal, born Jan. 24, 1839, married in 2nd marriage in 1885 to Karine Agsteberg, tenant farm no. 13, Austrheim.
e. Hans Knut, born May 18, 1842, married in 1883 to Anne Marie Gudmundsdatter, tenant farm no. 20, Skare.
f. Elias, born Dec. 3, 1844, died May 27, 1867.
g. Nils Johan, born Feb. 27, 1848, married in 1880 to Anne Kristine Larsdatter, tenant farm no. 18, Skare.
h. Oline Theodora, born Jan. 11, 1851, married in 1882 to Hans Emanuel Andreassen, Bo at Torvestad.

The deed to Erik for the southern half of Skare with tax liability of 2 dl. 2 ort 8 sk., from J. Dahm for 340 Spd. is dated Mar. 18, 1840. The seller reserved the right to half of the fishing income ("landslot" = 3%) due to this particular farm as long as he and his wife live – including *free grazing for his geese anywhere.*

He furthermore had to agree to support the parents' old age as follows:

> 5 barrels of oats, 1/2 barrel of barley, feed in both winter and summer for 2 sows and 6 sheep, and the use of the field called "Store–hatten."

This contract was estimated to be worth 100 Spd. over 5 years.

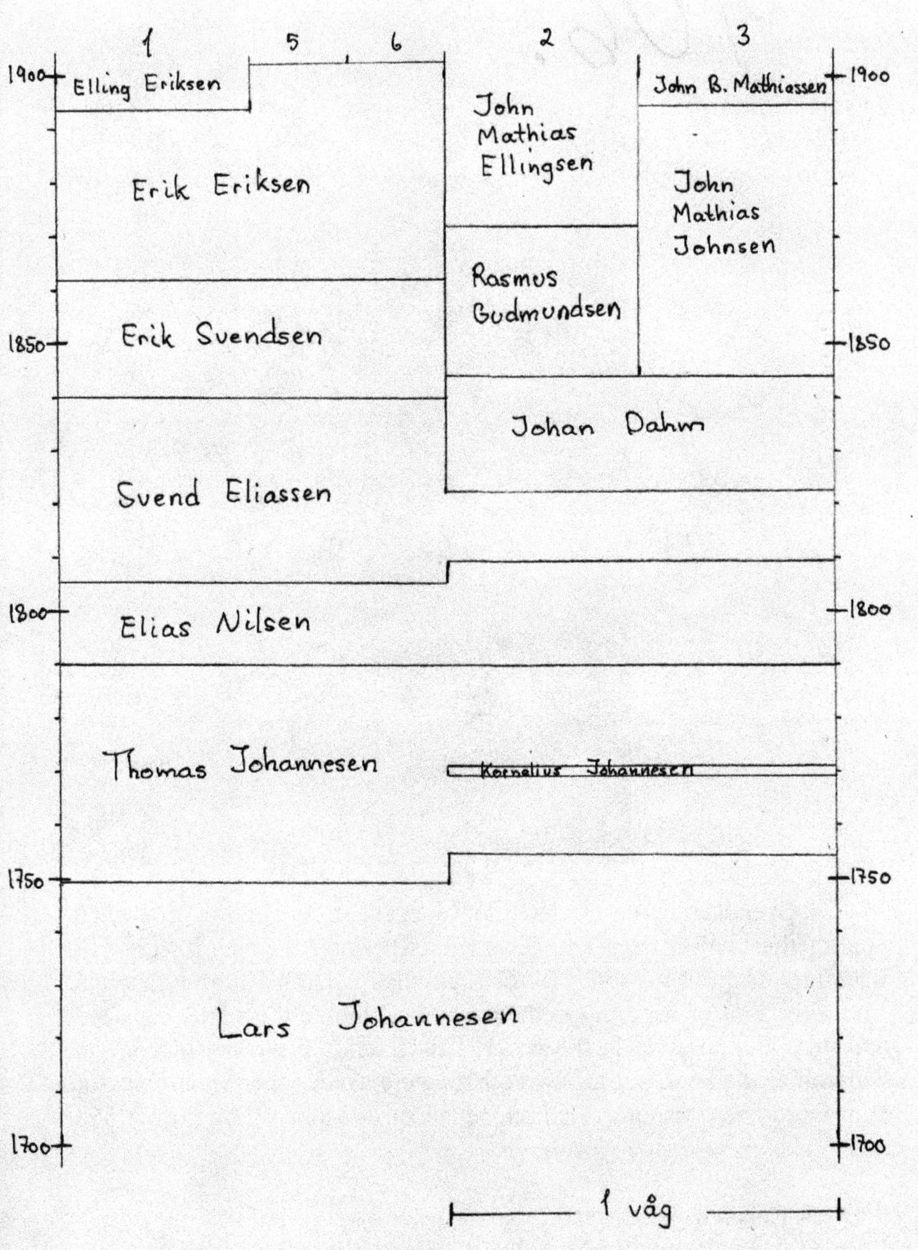

Table of farmers for Skare, 1700 – 1900. (Across top are farm numbers.)

Erik Eriksen (1836 – 1923) and Anne Marthe Ellingsdatter (1841 – 1911).

Erik Svendsen was a marine pilot by occupation. He drowned when he, together with his servant, Elias Knutsen, and Johannes Johannesen Klovning, had put his son, Erik Eriksen, also a marine pilot, onboard a ship to be piloted ashore. On their way back home their boat capsized and they all ended up in the water. Erik Svendsen did not manage to hang on to the keel, but the two others were saved when their calls for help were heard ashore. This happened on a Monday Aug. 10, 1868 near Vakskjaer outside Austrheim.[50]

9. **Erik Eriksen.** 1862 – 1912
Born Sept. 17, 1836, died Mar. 23, 1923, son of previous farmer.

---

[50] Stavanger newspapers *Amtstidende* and *Adresseavis*, Sept. 3, 1868 (See Note 19).

The children of Anne Marthe and Erik Eriksen Skare. Front from the left: Elling born 1862 and Tobias born 1869. In the back from left: Thomas born 1871, Serine born 1881, Kaia born 1865, Mikal born 1874, Elius born 1867 and Martin born 1876.

Married on Aug. 11, 1861, to **Anne Marthe Ellingsdatter**, born Apr. 23, 1841, died Nov. 1, 1911, daughter of Ragna Serine Johnsdatter and Elling Gudmundsen, farm no. 12 – 1 e, Nordvik.

Children:

a. *Elling* Severin, born Mar. 18, 1862, next farmer.
b. Gudmund, born and died May 6, 1864.
c. Hanna Cathrine (Kaia), born Mar. 24, 1865, married in 1884 to Peder Jakob Jonsen Helgeland, tenant farmer no. 22, Skare.
d. Elius Theodor, born Apr. 11, 1867, emigrated to USA in 1886.
e. Erik *Tobias*, born June 11, 1869, married to Marie Kristine Bentsen, tenant farm no. 21, Skare.
f. Thomas, born June 23, 1871, married in 1900 to Hanna Elisabeth Knutsdatter, farm no. 6 – 1, Skare.
g. Johan *Mikal*, born Apr. 12, 1874, married in 1898 to Anne Marie Sjursdatter, farm no. 4 – 3, Nordvik.
h. *Martin* Gurinius, born Aug. 13, 1876, married in 1902 to Berthe Serine Knutsdatter, farm no. 5 – 1, Skare.
i. Svend Ludolf, born Jan. 12, 1879, died Feb. 12, 1885.
j. Ragna *Serine*, born Oct. 1, 1881, married in 1903 to Thomas J. Helgesen, farm no. 30 – 1, Nordvik.

The deed to Erik from his father for this farm, with a tax liability of 2 dl. 2 ort 5 sk. or 4.90 sk. mark, is dated May 1862 for 500 Spd., plus an old age contract which among other obligations consists of 5 barrels of oats, 1 barrel of barley, use of the field called "Storehatt," for feed for 2 cows and 8 sheep and grazing for 1 pig.

The farm consisted in 1865 of 65 mål fields and meadows estimated to be worth 598 Spd., outfield for 100, peat for 60 and fishing rights income worth 39 Spd. Annual yield was 32 barrels of oats, 10 barrels of barley and 30 barrels of potatoes. The livestock consisted of 2 horses, 7 cows, 18 sheep and 1 pig.

The farm was estimated to be worth 990 Spd.

The main dwelling here is 13.5 x 6.6 meters logged and lined with boards and covered with tiles and was in 1868 assessed at 470 Spd. There was a lean–to on the eastern side and 2 chimneys. The hay storage barn, 16.6 x 7.5 meters, and an addition on the western side, 4.7 x 2.5 meters, were assessed to 230 Spd. There was also an outhouse, 14.4 x 5.6 meters, which was assessed to 50 Spd.

Erik was perhaps one of the best known marine pilots at Utsira. He was full–time pilot from 1867 to 1905.[51]

In 1912 he split the farm between his 3 sons, in such a way that Elling got half the farm and Thomas and Martin got the other half between them.

Ragna Serine Eriksdatter, when she was confirmed on December 1, 1895. The note in her report card from school: "Outstanding."

10. **Elling Eriksen** 1893 – 1912

Born Mar. 18, 1862, died Aug. 15, 1932, son of previous farmer.

Married in 1st marriage on Mar. 13, 1886, to **Åsa Oline Johannesdatter,** born May 8, 1861, died Jan. 26, 1906, daughter of Anne Marthe Ådnesdatter and Ole Johannes Johannesen, tenant

[51] "Stavangeren," Aug. 21, 1880, and "Haugesunds Avis," Mar. 24, 1923 (Note 20).

farmer no. 29 d, Nordvik, later farm no. 2 – 2, Klovning.

Married in 2nd marriage on Mar. 23, 1909, to widow **Thomine Johansdatter,** born Feb. 1, 1865, died Sept. 5, 1954, daughter of Karoline and Johan Helgesen, farm no. 18 – 5 a, Nordvik, and widow of Knut Gudmundsen, Austrheim.

Children in 1st marriage:

a. Johan *Adolf*, born May 22, 1886, next farmer.
b. Elin Anne Martha, born Feb. 18, 1888, died Mar. 7, 1888.
c. *Eminda* Amalie, born July 22, 1889, died Feb. 26, 1916.
d. *Sigfryda* Oline, born Mar. 17, 1891, died May 31, 1913.
e. Milla *Martine*, born Feb. 24, 1893, died young.
f. Sofie *Lovise*, born Jan. 4, 1895, died May 19, 1967, married to Elius Svendsen, Vorrå, Avaldsnes.
g. *Emma* Theoline, born May 25, 1897, died May 12, 1967, moved to her sister's on Stangeland.
h. Anne *Marta*, born Aug. 6, 1899, moved to Stangeland.
i. *Dagny* Marie, born Oct. 17, 1901, married in 1935 to Johannes Veste, lived on Skåre.

Children in 2nd marriage:

j. Jenny Konstanse. born Apr. 13, 1911, died in 1913.

Elling Eriksen (1862–1932) and Åsa Oline Johannesdatter (1861–1906).

The deed to Elling from his father for this farm indicates a tax liability of sk.m. 2.45 and is dated Aug. 8, 1912 in the amount of 4000 kr. plus an old age contract for the parents.

Elling was a full time marine pilot from Oct. 6, 1886 until the summer of 1912, when he was hired as a harbor pilot in Haugesund.

The family of Adolf Ellingsen Skare around 1926.

He continued to work as a harbor pilot in Haugesund until Jan. 1, 1928 and then moved back to Utsira that year.[52]

They built a new house on the farm no. 14, "Solbakken" in 1927. The estate was later taken over by Sverre Klovning in 1974.

11. **Adolf Ellingsen.** 1912 – 1957

Born May 22, 1886, died Oct. 23, 1962, son of previous farmer.

Married on May 27, 1911 to **Åsa Oline Tobiasdatter,** born May 30, 1888, died Nov. 7, 1957, daughter of Anne Martha Laurine and Tobias Sørhus, tenant farmer no. 23 b. Klovning.

Children:

a. Åsa Oline, born Feb. 16, 1912, married in 1935 to Svend Klovning, tenant farmer no. 27, Klovning.
b. Sigfrida, born July 16, 1913, married in 1944 to Ole Klovning, tenant farmer no. 22, Klovning.
c. *Elling* Martinius, born May 6, 1915, next farmer.
d. Laurine, born Oct. 27, 1917, died Nov. 13, 1918.
e. Tobias, born May 7, 1919, married in 1943 to Hanna Eriksen, tenant farmer no. 43, Skare.

---

[52] *Haugesund Avis* newspaper, Mar. 18, 1927, Jan. 4, 1928 and Mar. 18, 1932 (Note 21).

The old farmhouse, at Farm no. 1 in 1903.

f. Adolf, born July 5, 1921, married in 1953 to Reidun Jakobsen, tenant farm no. 45, Skare.
g. Laurine, born Feb. 27, 1923, married in 1948 to John Karsten Klovning, tenant farmer no. 28, Klovning.
h. *Magnus* Andreas, born July 27, 1926, married in 1952 to Jorunn.

The deed to Adolf from the father on this farm indicates a tax liability of 2.45 sk.m., for 4000 kr. and is dated Oct. 1, 1925. They took over the main dwelling on farm no. 16, "Krossen," after Hanna Helgeland in 1910.

12. **Elling Skare.** 1957 – 1980

Born May 6, 1915, died Dec. 17, 1962, son of previous farmer.

Married on May 16, 1942, to **Lindy Eriksen,** born Nov. 20, 1914, daughter of Hanna and Thomas Eriksen, farm no. 6 – 1 h, Skare.

Children:

a. *Harry* Thomas, born Mar. 6, 1943, a marine pilot, married to Gerd Pedersen, lives in Stavanger.
b. *Odd* Arne, born Aug. 11, 1944, next farmer.
c. Leif Erling, born Dec. 11, 1946, died Apr. 3, 1947.
d. Liv Eidis, born Aug. 18, 1948, married to Edvard Sørensen, lives in Vedavågen.
e. *Eli* Lovise, born July 1, 1950, married in 1970 to Jonas Bjarne Hansen, lives in Sandnes.

The livestock on the farm in 1956 consisted of a horse, 4 cows, 20 sheep and some chickens. They built a new main dwelling in 1962.

13. **Odd Skare.** 1980 –
Born Aug. 11, 1944, son of previous farmer.

Married on Aug. 13, 1966, to **Sigrid Johanna Hauge,** born on Apr. 5, 1944, from Bremanger.

Children:

a. *Egil* Arne, born June, 6 1967, married to Norunn Hauge, tenant farm no. 41, Kvalvik.
b. Siv Åse, born Feb. 9, 1971, died Feb. 11, 1971.
c. Frode, born Mar. 31, 1972.
d. Linn–Irene, born Nov. 27, 1978.

Odd is skipper on the ferry M/S "Utsira." He took over the farm here in 1985. Sigrid works at Sildakongen. They built their main dwelling here in 1972.

Johan Julius Albertus Dahm (1796–1872).

Farm no. 2. Myre. From farm no. 1 in 1822

1. **Johan J. A. Dahm.** 1822 – 1843
Born Sept. 21, 1796, died on Mar. 4, 1872, son of Anna Wilhelmine Hansdatter Forman and Jacob Christian Friedrich Dahm, businessman in Bergen.

Married at Alvoen on Mar. 30, 1824, to **Margrethe Munthe,** born Jan. 7, 1777, died Oct. 21, 1866, daughter of Inger Maria Hanning and Gerhard Munthe, Outer Kroken, Luster in Sogn. One brother of Margrethe, Ole Hanning Munthe (born 1778) died on Utsira on Dec. 7, 1830.

No children.

The deed to Johan from his mother's father H. B. Forman on the entire farm Skare, dated Apr. 15, 1822 was in the amount of 500 Spd. and an agreement with Svend Eliasen was in force from May 3, 1822. From the same date an agreement between Dahm and Anbjorn Gudmundsen is also made.

Johan Dahm came to Utsira and settled on his newly purchased estate at Skare. His house, named "Dahmshaab" (Dahm's Hope) was situated approximately where Utsira School is today. He received a special Royal permission to operate a business starting January 1824.

He built a seaside cabin, 10.8 x 7.4, where he ran a ship chandler operation and a beer saloon and where he also sold hard liquor. The foundation to this house is still visible today. He was one of the very few (in Kopervik) who at that time had an official business license in the area between Bergen and Stavanger.

In March 1824 he bought the rest of the farms at Utsira and the church for 1600 Spd. from the estate of H. B. Forman. From 1829 and later, he sold the farms to the farmers who ran them.

Johan had a close relationship with his relative, Fasmer, who owned the Alvoen paper plant near Bergen. From the book *Alvøen og Fasmerslekten* (Alvoen and the Fasmer Family), we quote the following:

> . . . he [Dahm] was very well educated and prepared to go the usual route of business, but he settled soon with his wife on his newly purchased estate on the outermost edge of the island in Ryfylke Sea. They lived at Skare on Utsira, in a large house that for many years was named "Dahmhuset" (The Dahm House). From there he operated seiners, running a ship owner business and trading companies and was one of the very few who had an official business license in the Haugesund area in those days, and he had a good income from herring when the herring fishing was good. The young couple were city–folk, but they thrived and got along well with the island folk and became part of the local population. "The Dahmmen" (The Dahm–guy), as he was called, sort of ruled in a fatherly way the six square–kilometer Utsira with three hundred subjects as an informal, unofficial king. And as a Sira–ite said: "Dahmmen is such an unusually outstanding guy."
>
> He was closely knit with strong bonds to his kinsman and benefactor at Alvoen. And Fasmer had much pleasure from his extended "branch" and the fatherly relationship to Utsira, as the patriarch in Alvoen.

Photo from 1930. The house on the left at the intersection is what is left of J. Dahm's place. The house in the middle of the picture is farm no. 3.

In 1838 Dahm bought a sloop called "Selma" for 420 Spd. and on April 15, 1843, he came sailing to Alvoen with all his belongings. He arrived at "Mathopen," where to his astonishment he found a new house Fasmer had built for them. It was a pleasant place, which it continued to be as was described in a song dedicated to the couple at their silver anniversary on March 30th 1849.

Only one time later in the next near almost 30 years did he again visit Utsira, and at that time he was greatly honored as the "Good old Dahmen." But he held on to the church until 1864, when he finally sold it. And he continued to receive a pension until 1868. After his wife's passing in 1866 he moved from his home "Mathopen" to Alvoen and lived with Fasmer. And there he passed away on March 4th, 1872.[53]

2. **Anbjorn Gudmundsen.** 1822 – 1829
See Farm no. 3 – 4, Austrheim.

Anbjorn had an agreement with J. Dahm regarding a 10–year lease of "the northern half of the farm, commonly referred to as "Myren," starting from May 3, 1822 and dated Jan. 2, 1823. Johan Dahm agreed

[53] Jonas Dahl's novel *Cargador Sahl* from 1898 gives a nice picture of Dahm and the Sira folk. See also article in the *Haugesunds Avis* newspaper, Feb. 3, 1930 and Feb. 24, 1931 (Note 22).

to repair and restore the outhouses and a barn, while Anbjorn had to build a main dwelling himself.

J. Dahm bought 2 cows and 1 horse as livestock, and Anbjorn turned over the same amount when he left the farm, and he had to provide his own tools and equipment. All crops and produce from the farm were divided equally between the tenant farmer and the owner.

Anbjorn took over farm no. 3 at Austrheim in 1829 after his brother died.

It appears J. Dahm let tenant farmers run the farm until he moved away from the island, but there are no public records or announcements of such arrangements. Based on church records, however, it can be concluded that the farm was run by tenant farmers for the next two years.

3. **Tollef Gudmundsen.** 1831 – 1836
See tenant farm no. 12, Skare.

Tollef is listed as the tenant farmer at Skare during these years. He later got the deed for the "Ambøres" place from J. Dahm.

4. **Lars Olsen.** 1839 – 1842
See Farm no. 4 – 4, Klovning.

Lars came to Utsira with J. Dahm as a farmhand before he became a tenant farmer.

5. **Rasmus Gudmundsen.** 1843 – 1872
Baptized Oct. 16, 1814, died Jan. 21, 1890, son of Berta Ambjornsdatter and Gudmund Thomassen, farm no. 3 – 2 q, Austrheim (The youngest of "the 18 at Leito").

Married July 10, 1836, to **Guri Johannesdatter**, baptized Apr. 12, 1812, died Jan. 11, 1892, daughter of Anna Karine Ådnesdatter and Johannes Ambjornsen, tenant farmer no. 13 h., Nordvik.

Children:

a. Gudmund Johan, born May 26, 1837, married in 1861 to Marthe Elisabeth Sjursdatter, tenant farm, no. 11, Austrheim.
b. Berthe Karine, born June 2, 1839, died June 4, 1844.
c. Johannes, born July 16, 1841, married in 1863 to Eli Kristine Ommundsdatter, tenant farm no. 14, Klovning.
d. Berthe Karine, born Dec. 4, 1843, died Jan. 6, 1847.
e. Mette Kristine, born Aug. 22, 1847, married in 1868 to Gudmund Jørgensen, farm no. 1 – 10, Klovning.

f. Karoline, born Apr. 22, 1848, married in 1885 to Lars Peder Knoph Oppen, tenant farmer no. 19, Skare.
g. Berthe Gurine, born Sept. 10, 1849, married in 1871 to Jørgen Jørgensen, tenant farmer no. 20, Klovning.
h. Thomas, born July 24, 1851, died Feb. 22, 1853.
i. Thomasine, born Mar. 16, 1853, married in 1878 to Johannes Johannesen, tenant farmer no. 17, Skare.
j. Anne Marthe, born Mar. 22, 1854, died July 7, 1854.
k. Lars Tobias, born Jan. 3, 1857, died Nov. 29, 1861.

The deed on the farm issued by J. Dahm to Rasmus indicates a tax liability of 1/2 v. dried fish or 1 dl. 1 ort 3 sk., for 600 Spd., which is dated Apr. 10, 1845. It is noted in the documents that the purchase does not include Beiningen and "Nøsterne."

In 1848 there was a settlement between Rasmus and John M. Johnsen, where Rasmus got the northern part of the farm.

The year after Rasmus sold his part to his brother, Elling Gudmundsen Nordvik, against a 30–year contract dated May 16, 1849 for 5 Spd. annual rent.

The farm had 40 mål of fields and meadows in 1865, valued at 289 Spd. In addition there were land areas worth 50 Spd., peat for 30 and fishing rights income of 3 Spd. Annual yield was 18 barrels of oats, 6 barrels of barley and 20 barrels of potatoes. The farm was assessed at a total at 420 Spd. The livestock consisted of 1 horse, 3 cows, 16 sheep and 1 pig.

On Sept 1, 1872 he received an old–age contract from the owner John Mathias Ellingsen, consisting of: full use of the field "Steinflekket," 1 barrel of oats and 1/2 barrel of barley per year, 1 cord of birch wood, feed for 4 sheep and milk from one cow which Rasmus must milk himself every second day. This contract was estimated to be worth 100 Spd. for 5 years.

6. **John Mathias Ellingsen.** 1873 – 1919
Born July 1, 1838, died July 26, 1922, son of Ragna Serine Johnsdatter and Elling Gudmundsen, farm no. 12 – 1 d, Nordvik.

Married first on May 27, 1866, to **Martha Olava Mikkelsdatter,** born May 6, 1849, died Jan. 6, 1885, daughter of Lavine Nicoline Larsdatter and Mikkel Jørgensen, farm no. 2 – 1 c, Hovland.

Married the second time on June 26, 1886, to the widow ***Malene*** **Mikkeline Johannesdatter** (widow of Sjur Helgesen Nordvik), born July 6, 1857, died June 11, 1928, daughter of Anne Marthe Ådnesdatter and Ole Johannes Johannesen, tenant farmer no. 29 b, Nordvik, and later farmer no. 2 – 2, Klovning.

Children in first marriage:

a. Lovise Gurine, born Dec. 14, 1866, married in 1884 to Thore Mikal Olsen, tenant farm no. 27, Kvalvik.
b. Elling, born Mar. 2, 1869, married in 1891 to Kathrine Mathiasdatter, farm no. 2 – 2, Hovland.
c. Michal, born Aug. 4, 1871, died Nov. 17, 1892.

Children in second marriage:

d. Martha *Lovise,* born Apr. 2, 1887, married to the widower Daniel Vestre, tenant farm no. 48, Nordvik.
e. Sofie *Julie* Amalie, born Oct. 30, 1888, married in 1910 to Hersleb Helgesen, tenant farmer no. 50, Nordvik.
f. *Tilla* Gurine, born Oct. 27, 1890, married in 1914 to Mikal Rasmussen, tenant farmer no. 49, Nordvik.
g. Mikal, born Nov. 5, 1892, next farmer.
h. Martine, born Nov. 21, 1894, tenant farmer no. 30, Skare.

The title of the farm was issued to John Mathias on Aug. 22, 1860 after the settlement of his father's estate indicating a tax liability of new sk. 2 marks 30 cents (ore) for 400 Spd., and included an old–age contract to the previous farmer dated Sept. 25, 1872.

In 1875 it is recorded that 1 barrel of barley and 4 barrels of oats were sown and 3 barrels of potatoes were planted, while the livestock consisted of 2 horses, 3 cows, 13 sheep and 1 pig.

The main dwelling here consisted of a logged 10.2 x 6.9 m. house clad with boards and a basement and which was covered with a tile roof. There was a lean–to shed on the eastern side. In 1878 it was assessed at 2270 kr. The hay storage building was 12.5 x 6.7 m., and a brick laundry house was 10 x 5.6 m., which were assessed at 380 kroner.

John Mathias was a full–time marine pilot from the beginning of the 1870's.

7. **Mikal Mathiassen Myre.** 1919 – 1961

Born Nov. 5, 1892, died Jan. 20, 1961, son of previous farmer.

Married on June 18, 1916, to **Laura Tobiasdatter,** born Sept. 1, 1893, died Sept. 25, 1973, daughter of Malene and Tobias Olsen, farm no. 2 – 8 c, Kvalvik.

Children:

a. Malene, born Dec. 12, 1916, died Jan. 20, 1934.
b. Mathias, born Mar. 13, 1918, died Nov. 30, 1918.
c. Mathias, born Oct. 9, 1919, died in 1979, married to Helene Svendsen, lived in Stavanger.

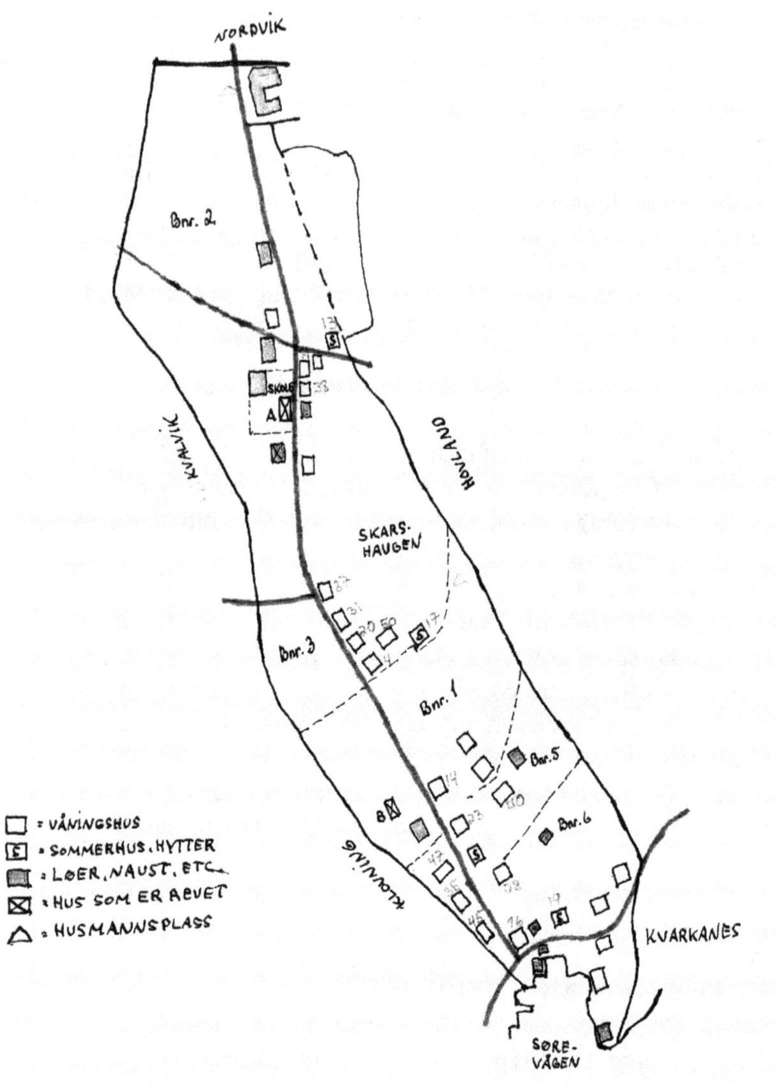

Map of Skare

Key (from top): 1– Main farmhouses, 2– Summer houses, cabins, 3– Barns, sheds, 4– Buildings now torn down, 5– Cotter homes, houses for hired hands.

John Mathias Ellingsen (1838 – 1922) and Martha Olava Mikkelsdatter, born May 6, 1849, died Jan. 6, 1885.

d. Tobias, born July 15, 1921, next farmer.
e. Malfrid, born Feb. 17, 1925, married in 1948 to Tobias Nordvik, tenant farmer no. 69, Nordvik.

The deed to Mikal from his father on farm no. 2 indicates a tax liability of sk. m. 2.23, for 4,000 kr. plus an old–age contract to his parents and is dated 08–11–1919. They built a new main dwelling in 1923.

8. **Tobias Mathiassen.** 1961 – 1985
Born July 15, 1921, died Oct. 24, 1992, son of the previous farmer.
Married on Dec. 29, 1948, to **Anna Hovland,** born May 24, 1912, died Sept. 19, 1984, daughter of Karine and Johannes Hovland, Sauda.

Children:
a. *Lodvar* Mikal, born Aug. 12, 1949, next farmer.

Tobias managed farm no. 3 here from 1951, and took over the farm in 1962.
A new barn was built on the farm in 1977.

Bridal couple in 1916. Mikal Mathiassen Myre (1892 – 1961 and Laura Tobiasdatter (1893 – 1973).

9. **Lodvar Mathiassen.** 1970 –
Born Aug. 12, 1949, son of last farmer.

Married on July 15, 1972, to ***Aslaug*** **Oline Hansen,** born May 24, 1953, daughter of Johanne Kristine and Kristian Hansen, Skåre, Haugesund.

Children:

a. Tor Arne, born July 30, 1973. Tor Arne also had a farm here.
b. Jan Kristian, born Jan. 23, 1976. He also had a farm here.
c. Inger Johanne, born May 21, 1979.

Lodvar has worked offshore since 1985. Aslaug works at Siratun nursing home.

On the west side of Yrefjell mountain around 1924. From the left: Marie Bakke Smith, Olga Kvalvik, Edvard Kvalvik, Laura Mathiassen, Amanda Knutsen, unknown, Lovise Vestre, Mikal Rasmussen with son Sivert, Martine Ellingsen, Mathias Myre Skare and Mikal Myre.

Farm no. 3. Myre. From Farm no. 2 in 1845

1. **John Mathias Johnsen.** 1845 – 1894

Born Mar. 29, 1821, died June 29, 1895, son of Anne Malene Olsdatter and John Helgesen, farmer no. 1 – 10 f, Nordvik.

Married on Apr. 10, 1843, to **Petronelle Knutsdatter,** born Oct. 5, 1820, died Sept. 7, 1898. daughter of Kristine Tollefsdatter and Knut Bentsen, farmer no. 1 – 2 b, Kvalvik.

Children:

a. John Bendiks, born July 29, 1843, next farmer.
b. Knut Mathias, born Apr. 10, 1847, died Aug. 19, 1849, drowned in the water well.
c. Berthe Malene, born June 30, 1849, married in 1869 to Lars Martinius Mikalsen (Hovland), tenant farmer no. 28, Hovland.
d. *Knut* Mathias, born Dec. 18, 1851, emigrated to Minnesota, USA in 1875. In 1882 he married Margit Sanderson, born Aug. 26, 1859 in Ål, Buskerud, Norway, daughter of Sven and Åse Sandersen, who emigrated to USA in 1864.

John Mathias Johnsen (1821 – 1894) and Petronelle Knutsdatter (1820–1898).

Knut and Margit lived in Adrian, MN, Sheldon, IA, and later, Palmer, WA. In 1904, the family moved to Holden, Alberta to homestead. Children: Annette *(Nettie)*, born 1883, Samuel *(Sam)*, born 1885, and Clara, born 1890. Knut was a railroad foreman and farmer.[54]

e. Christiane, born Nov. 3, 1854, married in 1879 to Rasmus Jobsen, farmer no. 7 – 10, Hovland.
f. Lovise Marie, born Dec. 28, 1857, died May 11, 1884.
g. John Mathias, born July 19, 1859, died Aug. 2, 1859.
h. Johannes, born Aug. 16, 1860, died Jan. 21, 1873.
i. Anne *Kathrine*, born Jan. 18, 1864, married in 1891 to Elling Mathiassen, farmer no. 2 – 2, Hovland.

The deed to John Mathias from J. Dahm on this farm, tax 1 dl. 1 ort 3 sk., for 600 Spd. is dated Apr. 10, 1845. The purchase did not include

---

[54] Knut Mathias Johnsen moved his family in 1904 to homestead in Alberta, following Ludwig Hovland from Utsira, to the Wetaskiwin area. Knut's daughter Annette (Nettie) Pitherina (the Editor's grandmother), stayed behind in WA state, married Albert Amundson, and settled in Sunnyside, WA where they raised their family and founded (along with Albert's father Ole) Amundson Hardware Co., which operated as a family business until 1984.

Beiningen and "Nosterne." In 1848 it was decided to divide the property and determine the tax assessment on this farm as well as Rasmus' farm.

The farm in 1865 consists of 43 mål (about 10–3/4 acres) and fields and meadows are assessed to 320 Spd. There are outfields for 50 Spd., peat for 30 Spd. and easements for 3 Spd. Annual yield is estimated to 20 barrels of oats, 4 barrels of barley and 18 barrels of potatoes. The estimated value of the entire farm is 440 Spd.

The livestock consisted of 1 horse, 3 cows, 9 sheep and 1 pig.

The main dwelling was built here around 1845, and was modernized in 1949.

2. **John Bendik Mathiassen.** 1894 – 1906

Born July 24, 1843, died Apr. 10, 1908, son of last farmer.

Married on Mar. 27, 1870 to **Berthe *Helgesine* Thomasdatter,** born Mar. 22, 1849, died Nov. 29, 1929, daughter of Berthe Malene Mikkelsdatter and Thomas Tollefsen, farmer no. 18 – 3 g, Nordvik.

Berthe Helgesine "Sino" Thomasdatter ("Sino in Myre") (1849–1929).

Children:

a. Thomas, born July 30, 1871, next farmer.

b. *Johan* Mathias, born May 14, 1878, married in 1905 to Anna Sofie Mikalsdatter, tenant farm no. 23, Skare.

c. *Kasper* Ludolf Mikal, born Nov. 6, 1888, married in 1923 to Tilla T. Kvalvik, tenant farm no. 28, Skare.

The deed issued by the father to Bendik on this farm indicates a tax liability of sk.m. 2.34 at 1600 kroner plus old age contract and is dated Aug. 13,1894.

3. **Thomas Bendiksen.** 1906 – 1939

Born July 30, 1871, died Jan. 25, 1946, son of previous farmer.

Married on Aug. 12, 1894 to **Regine Severine (Gina) Konradsdatter,** born Nov. 27, 1877, died Apr. 19, 1939, daughter of

Photo from 1930. In the back row from left: Tilla Bendiksen, Gina Bendiksen, Thomas Bendiksen, Benny Haugland, Lene Helgesen and Karoline Valler. In front row from left: Bjarne Haugland, Ågot Tørsdal, Gina Helgesen, Anna H. Hansen and Ragna Nygård.

Berthe Gurine Jobsdatter and Konrad Severin Anensen, tenant farmer no. 25 g, Hovland.

Children:

a. *Konrad* Bernhard, born Mar. 17, 1895, married in 1922 to Sarah Eamor, emigrated to Canada.
b. *Benny* Hilma Sigfrid, born Feb. 19, 1899, married in 1920 to Severin Haugland, Utsira Lighthouse no. 9.
c. *Thomas* Georg, born Oct. 11, 1902, married in 1930 to Dorothea Bolinger, emigrated to California, USA.
d. *Julie* Karoline, born Aug. 18, 1905, married in 1930 to Olaf Hoff.
e. Berta Malene (Lene), born June 10, 1909, next farmer.

The deed issued by the father in the amount of 1400 kr. plus old age contract is dated Sept. 22, 1906.

4. **Johan Helgesen.** 1939 – 1951

Hay harvesting in Myre around 1930.

Born Aug. 30, 1911, son of Åsa and Sivert Helgesen, farm no. 32 and 46 – 1 c, Nordvik.

Married on July 1, 1933 to **Berta Malene (Lene),** born June 10, 1909, daughter of previous farmer.

Children:

a. Åsta Modgunn, born Nov. 2, 1934, married to Magne Kirkhus, lives in Døle, Førdesfjorden.
b. John Bodvar, born Mar. 2, 1937, married to Sigfrid Eline Eliassen, lives in Spannhelgeland.

The deed in the amount of 8000 kroner to Johan from Thomas on this farm indicated a tax liability of sk.m. 2.15 and is dated Aug. 14, 1939.

The family moved to Skre in Fordesfjorden in 1951 and moved later to Haugesund.

5. **Tobias Mathiassen.** 1951 – 1985
See under farm no. 2 here.

Tobias bought this farm in 1951, and from 1961 he also managed farm no. 2 here. Both of these farms are now taken over by Lodvar Mathiassen.

Farm no. 5. From Farm no. 1 in 1912.

1. **Martin Eriksen.** 1909 – 1945
Born Aug. 13,1876, died Mar. 19, 1931, son of Anne Martha and Erik Eriksen, farm no, 1 – 9 h, Skare.

Married on Oct. 19, 1902 to **Serine Knutsdatter,** born Oct. 7, 1882, died June 28, 1967, daughter of Asseline and Knut Hansen, farm no. 5 – 6 f, Austrheim.

Serine Knutsdatter Eriksen and Bertha Hovland, born Hansen. approx. 1950.

Children:

a. *Erik* Aleksander, born Mar. 21, 1903, died Apr. 22, 1936. He was a pilot ship crew member and died from carbon dioxide poisoning onboard the pilot ship in Stavanger. Erik also had a farm here.
b. *Klara* Aseline, born Jan. 23, 1905, married in 1932 to Arnt M. Halvorsen Bakken, Førland in Tysvaer.
c. *Martin* Berner, born Dec. 16, 1906, next farmer.
d. Sven *Ludolf*, born Feb. 3, 1909, married in 1950 to Brita Grindheim, tenant farm no. 54, Skare.
e. *Hilma* Charlotte, born Apr. 1, 1911, married to Olaf Henry Garberg, lived in Skjold–Liverpool–Arendal–Haugesund.
f. Anne Martha, born July 18, 1913, died Apr. 13, 1979. She had a farm here.
g. *Elling* Sigurd, born July 23, 1915, died Oct. 1, 1979. Elling also had a farm here.
h. *Eminda* Martine, born June 9, 1917, married to Larseus Skogen, lives in Tysvaer.
i. Kaia, born June 3, 1919, died Jan. 11, 1965.
j. Berta *Serina,* born July 17, 1921, married to Ivar Amundsen, tenant farmer no. 39. Hovland.

k. Valborg, born Nov. 5, 1923, married in 1954 to Hans Knut Hansen, tenant farmer no. 46, Skare.
l. Toralf, born Apr. 1, 1926. Toralf also had a farm here.

The deed dated Aug. 8, 1912 issued to Martin from the father on this farm indicates a tax liability of sk.m. 1.22 and is in the amount of 1030 kroner.

They built their main dwelling here in 1905, farm no. 8, and in 1991 it was taken over by Roald Hansen.

2. **Martin Martinsen.** 1945 – 1975
Born Dec. 16, 1906, died Nov. 1, 1984, son of the previous farmer.
Unmarried.

3. **Hans Knut Hansen.** 1976 –
See under tenant farm no. 46, Skare.

Hans Knut and Valborg took over the farm here in 1980. The farm has been farmed as additional acreage in recent times.

Farm no. 6. From farm no. 1 in 1912

1. **Thomas Eriksen.** 1912 – 1943
Born June 23, 1871. died April 24, 1947, son of Anne Martha and Erik Eriksen, farm no. 1– 9 f, Skare.

Married June 24, 1900 to **Hanna Knutsdatter,** born Oct. 13, 1879, died Feb. 13, 1939, daughter of Asseline and Knut Hansen, farm no. 5 – 6 e, Austrheim.

Children:

a. *Erik* Alfred Martin, born Jan. 30, 1901, next farmer.
b. *Konrad* Alexander, born Nov. 20, 1902, died Oct. 4, 1954. He sailed many years as steward, married to Alma Iversen from Eidsvoll.
c. *Petra* Kathrine, born Oct. 21, 1904, married to Peder Olav Bjork.
d. Elling Severin *Åstein,* born Aug. 18, 1906, married in 1931 to Marthine Nilsen, tenant farm no. 32, Skare.
e. *Thomas* Herman, born Oct. 9, 1908. died May 21, 1983. Thomas also had a farm here.
f. *Elmer* Sverre, born Apr. 11, 1911, died Mar. 18, 1964. Elmer also had a farm here.

g. *Hjalmar* Clarence, born Feb. 17, 1913, married in 1940 to Jenny Sjursen, tenant farm no. 37. Skare.
h. *Lindy* Anne Marthe, born Nov. 20, 1914, married in 1942 to Elling Skare, farm no. 1 – 12, Skare.
i. *Hanna* Asseline, born Feb. 25, 1917, married in 1943 to Tobias Skare, tenant farmer no. 43, Skare.
j. *Sigfryda* Oline, born Mar. 19, 1919. She also had a farm here.
k. *Knut* Hagerup, born Jan. 9, 1922, died Nov. 18, 1991.
l. Sigurd, born Apr. 29, 1923, died Oct. 14, 1928.

Thomas Eriksen (1871–1946) and Hanna Knutsdatter (1879–1939).

Thomas' pilot vessel "Parat," photo around 1930

Two brothers enjoy retirement in the 1970's. From left: Erik Thomassen (1901 – 1983) and Thomas Thomassen (1908 – 1983).

The deed dated Aug. 8, 1912 to Thomas from his father for the farm for 980 kroner, indicates a tax liability of sk.m. 1.20,

Thomas was a full–time marine pilot on Utsira from 1906 to 1935. They built their main dwelling on farm no. 29, "Skarhaug," in 1908. The estate was taken over by Sigfryda Eriksen in 1948.

2. **Erik Thomassen.** 1943 – 1974
Born Jan. 30, 1901, died May 27, 1983, son of previous farmer.

Married on July 31, 1943 to **Signe Nilsen,** born Dec. 20, 1902, died Jan. 16, 1991, daughter of Jonette and Martin Nilsen, tenant farm no. 20 b, Austrheim.

Children:

a. Turid Hanna Elisabeth, born July 11, 1944, next farmer.

Erik was, as his father, grandfather and great–grandfather, a full–time marine pilot on Utsira, from Apr. 1, 1938 until retirement age.

They built their main dwelling on the farm in 1951.

3. **Harald Eriksen.** 1974 – 1990
Born Jan. 21, 1937, came from Valestrand in Sveio.

Married on June 1, 1963 to **Turid Thomassen**, born July 11, 1944, daughter of previous farmer.

Children:

a. *Eirik* Sigbjorn, born Apr. 10, 1964, lives in Sveio.
b. *Ingvar* Edmund, born July 5, 1967, took over the farm in 1994.
c. Tove Helen, born Oct. 17, 1969, tenant farmer no. 56, Skare.
d. Evelyn, born Feb. 14, 1977.
e. Marlin, born Feb. 24, 1982.

Turid and Harald took over the farm in 1974. Harald is pilot boat crew. They moved to Koppervik in 1990.

Tenant farmers

1. **Valtin (Valtug).** 1606 – 1607
He is mentioned in the county records in Stavanger for above years, under "impoverished farmhands and crofters."

2. **Torkel.** 1606 – 1607
He is mentioned in the same place and period as the previous tenant.

3. **Gudmund.** 1610 – 1636
Same as above for these years.

4. **Sigurd.** 1626 – 1628
He is also mentioned in the above records for these years with a name only.

5. **Peder.** 1638
He is only mentioned by name in this year.

6.a. **Asbjorn Andersen.** – 1664
He was a tenant at Skare and paid 2 ort in basic rent in 1661. He is also mentioned in the county records in 1663, see under Simon Torkelsen, farm no. 4, Hovland.

His son is possibly:

a. Mogens, born 1644, and is listed in the church census from 1664 as a farm hand at Hovland.

Asbjorn is listed as a tenant in the tax collector records from 1664, but not in the church records the same year. However, there is:

6.b. **Steffen Johannesen,** born around 1594, listed as tenant here, but in the county records from 1726 we find the following note under Skare: *. . . concerning the tenant Asbjorn, however, he has not lived on the farm in the last 50 years nor has any one else taken his place.*

7. **Ole Skare.** 1670 – 1690
We know about two sons of Ole both born at Skare:

a. Hans, born 1674, in 1706 he lived at Moksheim, where he was a seaman.
b. Ole, born 1688, tenant farmer no. 10, Hovland.

Skarshaugen, cotter homestead

8. **Petter Olsen.** 1697 – 1715
Born 1671 in Holland.
We do not know the name of his wife (Anna?).

Known children:

a. Simon, born in 1702, the military records from 1734 lists the following about Simon: *born on Utsira island, married and lives at Egrene, part of Stange, 30 years old.* He is not mentioned in the book about Torvestad.
b. Johannes, born 1712, married to Bertha Knutsdatter (daughter of Knut Olsen on farm no. 4, Austrheim). They lived on Osnes and farmed there. Among their children we know the following: Anna, married to Anbjorn Rasmussen Tuo and Gjoa, married to Elling Johannesen, Austrheim.

Petter is mentioned in the county records in 1698, when he is due his inheritance, and the last time in 1714, when he receives salvage money for the shipwreck of the vessel from Arendal.

9. **Jakob Torkelsen.** 1762 – 1771

The main road north from Skarshaugen with the pilot shelter on top of the hill. Photo was taken in the late 1930s.

Born in 1730, died Feb. 25, 1771, of unknown origin.

Married on Jan. 19, 1762 to **Malene Halvorsdatter,** born 1739, died May 22, 1825 on Steinsnes in Skåre, daughter of Torborg and Halvor Steinsnes.

Children:

a. Halvor, baptized Feb. 4, 1763, further information unknown.
b. Guro. baptized Sept. 28, 1766, married in 1798 to widower Bard Olsen, Steinsnes in Skåre.
c. Torborg, baptized Mar. 29, 1771, buried Nov. 23, 1771.

Jakob was a tenant at Skare. He and his neighbor Kornelius Johannesen perished at sea, and in April 1771 there was a settlement of his estate that was assessed at 23–0–6 rdl., while debt and expenses amounted to 11–1–18. His possessions were listed as follows:

> 1 cow and 1 calf 5–1–0, 1 pig 0–3–8, 2 spring herring fishing nets 0–3–16 and 1 cabin with a barn and laundry house 9–0–0.

Malene married again to Torbjorn Monsen, next tenant farmer.

Postcard picture from 1935 of Sørvågen (South Harbor) during mackerel fishing season.

10. **Torbjorn Monsen.** 1772 – 1785.
Born 1750, buried Nov. 28, 1789, son of Marthe Svendsdatter and Mons Johannesen, Rossbo in Skåre.

Married on June 26, 1772 to **Malene Halvorsdatter,** widow of previous tenant farmer.

Children:

a. Jakob, baptized Apr. 17, 1773, married in 1801 to Anna Olsdatter, farm no. 4 – 8, Austrheim.
b. Martha, baptized Nov. 23, 1775, twin, buried Mar. 31, 1776.
c. Torborg, baptized Nov. 23, 1775, twin.
d. Mons, baptized Mar. 6, 1779, buried Sept. 19, 1779.
e. Sven, buried June 24, 1781, 4 days old.

The family moved to Bakken (part of Moksheim?) around 1785.

Myhren, cotter property.

11. **Amund Paulsen.** 1774 – 1837.
Born 1749, buried July 4, 1802, son of Trua Olsdatter and Paul Bårdsen, tenant farmer no. 15 a, Hovland.

Married on Sept. 28, 1774 to **Malene Jonsdatter,** baptized Dec. 26, 1753, died June 6, 1837, daughter of Berta Andersdatter, and Jon Jørgensen, farm no. 1 – 6 b, Klovning.

Children:

a. Svend, baptized Dec. 16, 1774, buried Mar. 25, 1779.
b. Berta, baptized June 29, 1776, married in 1813 to Hagen Tollefsen in Skåre.
c. Anna, baptized June 9, 1778, she had a son Paul baptized Jan. 13, 1817 with Ole Olsen, "a traveling salesman."
d. Trua, baptized May 15, 1780, buried Apr. 4, 1813.
e. Malene, baptized May 5, 1782, buried Mar. 14, 1812.
f. Jorgine Olina, baptized June 1, 1784, buried Apr. 3, 1791
g. Andreas, baptized May 18, 1788, buried Feb. 8, 1789.
h. Jon, baptized Sept. 5, 1790. died Aug. 21, 1845. He had a daughter Elisabet, born June 4, 1820 with Berte Kristine, J.datter, Nordvik.
i. Paul, baptized Dec. 27, 1792, buried July 3, 1803.
j. Sven. baptized May 30, 1795, named godfather 1817–1827, further information unknown.

This place is incorrectly listed under Tuo in the 1801 census. In the settlement after John Jørgensen Klovning the same year, it is listed under Nordvik. The correct place should be somewhere on the property between Tuo and Nordvik. Originally it was the intention that Berta Ellingsdatter, widow of Thomas Johannsen, should take over the property, but she had already died in 1790. Annual rent for the property was listed in 1803 as 18 days of work plus 32 sk. in cash to the owner.

Ambores, cotter property.

12. **Tollef Gudmundsen.** 1831 – 1870.

Baptized Apr. 15, 1804, died Sept. 23, 1857, son of Berta Ambjornsdatter and Gudmund Thomassen, farm no. 3 – 2 n, Austrheim.

Married on June 27, 1830 to **Marta Serine Johannesdatter,** baptized May 1, 1803, died Oct. 13, 1870. daughter of Anna Karine Ådnesdatter and Johannes Ambjornsen, tenant farmer no. 13 e. Nordvik.

Children:

a. Johannes, born Oct. 22, 1830, died Apr. 4, 1837.

b. Berthe Gurine, born Apr. 25, 1833, married in 1868 to Oliver Knutsen, tenant farmer no. 18, Kvalvik.
c. Mette Karine, born Nov. 3, 1835, died July 11, 1859. She and 6 others from Utsira drowned on their way home from Bergen.
d. Tollef Johan, born May 30, 1839, next tenant farmer.
e. Anne Martha, born June 30, 1842, died Nov. 21, 1846.

Tollef was tenant farmer on farm no. 2 here in the period of 1831 – 36, before he got a lease contract dated Jan. 7, 1843 from J. Dahm on a piece of land at the northern part of Myre called "Ambores." This contract gave him the right to carve out 1 cord of peat from Naesset (the peninsula) at Nordvik and also the western part. Annual compensation to the owner was 2 ort.

In 1865 Marta Serine sowed 1 barrel of oats and 1/4 barrel of potatoes. The livestock consisted of 1 cow, 18 sheep and 1 pig.

13. **Tollef Johan Tollefsen.** 1862 – 1910

Born May 30, 1839, died Sept. 3, 1892, son of previous tenant farmer.

Married in 1st marriage on Oct. 5, 1862 to **Berthe Gurine Anbjornsdatter,** born Dec. 28, 1831, died Aug. 11, 1876, daughter of Anne Marte Larsdatter and Anbjorn Gudmundsen, farm no. 3 –4 d, Austrheim.

Married in 2nd marriage to **Marta Eline Rasmusdatter,** born Apr. 29, 1851, died Apr. 17, 1910, daughter of Berta Serine Larsdatter and Rasmus Knutsen, Osnes.

Children in 1st marriage:

a. Tollef, born Sept. 26, 1863, died Oct. 5, 1863.
b. Tollef Severin, born Feb. 23, 1865.
c. Anne Marthe, born Aug. 9, 1866, died May 24, 1898.
d. Mette Karine (Kaia), born May 10, 1868, married in 1889 to Knut T. Kvalvik, farm no. 1 – 5, Kvalvik.
e. Berthe Jonette, born Sept. 15, 1870.
f. Anbjor Elene (Lene), born May 10, 1874, married to Johannes Torkelsen, Hausken. Lene was raised by Karine and Lars Agsteberg, Austrheim.

Children in 2nd marriage:

g. Ludvig, born in 1878, died Sept. 24, 1897, fell overboard from a ship in the Baltic Sea.
h. Johannes, born Jan. 5, 1880.
i. Regine Berthea (Thea), born Sept. 23, 1881, married in 1904 to Ole Sjursen, farm no. 3 – 3, Kvalvik.
j. Jonette Marie, born Dec. 9, 1883, married in 1911 to Thomas Gudmundsen, farm no. 1 – 12, Klovning.

k. Hanne Tobia, born Dec. 22, 1886, married Osnes, emigrated to USA.
l. Peder Amandius, born Sept. 3, 1889, emigrated to USA 190x.
m. Berta Gurine, born Dec. 30, 1891.

The lease contract to Tollef from Mathias Ellingsen on the lot where his parents' house stood is dated May 8, 1871. He paid 4 Spd. annually in rent and contributed 6 working days per year.

Tollef is in 1875 listed as a tenant without acreage, bricklayer and fisherman.

14. **Johannes Rasmussen.** 1863 – 1866
See tenant farm no. 14, Klovning.

15. **Nils Thomassen.** 1865 – 1866
See under tenant farmer no. 18, Klovning.

16. **Soren Nilsen.** 1865 – 1902
Born Mar. 21, 1820, died Jan. 25, 1902. son outside marriage of Berthe Kristensdatter Nordvik and Nils Olsen Skjolingstad.

Unmarried.

Soren was a handyman. In the 1840s he worked on Klovning and at Hovland in 1851. In the years 1852 and 1858 he is not on the island, and in 1859–60 he worked at Kvalvik. In 1865 he is a handyman at the John Mathias Johnsen household, and in 1875 – 1900 he is with the household of Mathias Ellingsen, Skare.

Johannes Johannesen (1847 – 1890) and Thomasine Rasmusdatter Dalastein (1853 – 1929).

Postcard picture taken around 1907. The Dalastein home is in center.

17. **Johannes Johannesen Dalastein.** 1878 – 1929
Born Oct. 18, 1847, died Mar. 10, 1890, son of Berta Kristine Johannesdatter and Johannes Knutsen, farm no. 4 – 3 g, Klovning.

Married June 22, 1878 to **Thomasine Rasmusdatter,** born Mar. 16, 1853, died Dec. 31, 1929, daughter of Guri Johannesdatter and Rasmus Gudmundsen, farm no. 2 – 5 i, Skare.

Children:

a. Jon Kristian, born Oct. 28, 1878, emigrated to USA in 1898, married Christina in 1904, four children, lived in Modesto, Stanislaus Co., California.
b. Berthe Gurine, born June 25, 1880. tenant farmer no. 40, Skare.
c. Rasmus Gurinius, born Oct. 20, 1882.
d. Hans Tobias, born Aug. 6, 1884, died Aug. 16, 1884.
e. Hans Tobias, born Sept. 6, 1885, emigrated to USA.
f. *Jenny* Theresie, born Sept. 24, 1887, married 1921 to Gudmund G. Klovning, tenant farmer no. 42, Skare.
g. Johannes, born Sept. 15, 1890, died Dec. 15, 1890.
h. Thomasine, born Sept. 15, 1890, died Aug. 1, 1891.

Johannes was a sailor. In his last years before he passed away, he skippered on the vessels in the Harbor Authority's fleet. He and Nils

Marine pilots around turn of the century. From left: Nils Johan Eriksen, Bendiksen from Foyne, Erik Eriksen Skare, A. Bertel Helgesen Nordvik, Chief Pilot Ring, Elling Eriksen Skare, Senior Pilot Jensen, Rasmus Thomassen Nordvik and John Mathias Ellingsen Skare.

Olai Johannesen (son of Johannes Olsen, Hovland) drowned on their way to Haugesund with a load of herring.[55]

Johannes and Hans Knut Eriksen got a lease contract, signed on Apr. 3, 1889, for a piece of property from Erik Eriksen which included a boat shed, for 200 kr. and 6 days of work, 2 days in each season. The house was then already built.

18. **Nils Johan Eriksen.** 1875 – 1942

Born Feb. 27, 1848, died Aug. 26, 1924, son of Torborg and Erik Svendsen, farm no. 1 – 8 g, Skare.

Married on Aug. 18, 1880 to **Anne Kristine Larsdatter,** born Sept. 1, 1859, died Dec. 19, 1942, daughter of Ingeborg Katrine Asbjornsdatter and Lars Jakob Sivertsen, Torvestad.

Children:

a. Erik Torvald, born June 12, 1881, died Oct. 21, 1881.
b. Lovise Kathrine, born Oct. 25, 1882, died July 28, 1891.
c. Torborg, born June 12, 1884.
d. Bendikte Elisabeth, born July 25, 1886.
e. Nelly Kristine, born Aug. 26, 1888, lived in Denmark.
f. Lovise Kathrine, born Nov. 10, 1891, died June 29, 1949, also had a farm here.
g. Erna Åser, born Nov. 26, 1893, died Dec. 8, 1971. Erna also had a farm here.
h. Gudrun Marie, born Aug. 8, 1896, her son was: Bernhard Haugen, born Nov. 1, 1918. Gudrun also had a farm here.

---

[55] *Haugesunderen* newspaper, Mar. 14, 1890 (Note 23).

i. Erling, born Aug. 27, 1897, was a tailor in Bergen, married to Beate Bjordal from Haugesund.
j. Ruth, born May 5, 1899, married to Heiestad, lived in Oslo.
k. Lars, born June 7, 1902, died Dec. 13, 1918.

Nils Johan was a full–time marine pilot on Utsira in the period 1878 – 1908.[56]

The main dwelling here was built on leased land in 1875, it was assessed in 1879 at 1320 kroner. The house was 7.8 x 6.3 meters, built with logs with basement and tiled roof. Anne Kristine got the deed to this house, farm no. 17 in 1932. The estate was later taken over by Bernhard Haugen and others, and is now a summerhouse.

19. **Lars Peder Knoph Oppen.** 1885 – 1899
Born 1845, died July 23, 1898, son of Ingeborg Marie and Hans Otto Knoph Oppen, Utsira Lighthouse no. 14 c.

Married on Apr. 10, 1885 to **Karoline Rasmusdatter**, born Apr. 22, 1848, died Dec. 7, 1921, daughter of Guri Johannesdatter and Rasmus Gudmundsen, farm no. 2–5 f, Skare.

Karoline's son with Johan Nyman Mikalsen, Hovland.
a. Ole Johan, born July 27, 1874, married in 1903 to Lavine Kristine Trulsdatter, farm no. 21 – 5, Nordvik.

Children:
b. Othelie Marie, born Sept. 3, 1885.
c. Berthe Gurine, born Oct. 7, 1886.
d. Laura Kathrine, born Sept. 27, 1891, died Oct. 14, 1891.

Lars Peder was a commercial seaman, and from 1890 on, he was assistant lighthouse keeper at Utsira Lighthouse.

After her husband died, Karoline moved to Naesset with her children, farm no. 21, Nordvik.

20. Hans Knut Eriksen. 1883 – 1940
Born May 18, 1842, died June 19, 1925, son of Torborg and Erik Svendsen, farm no. 1 – 8 e, Skare.

Married on Apr. 1, 1883 to **Anne Marie Gudmundsdatter,** born Apr. 4, 1861, died May 2, 1940, daughter of Marthe Elisabet

[56] *Haugesund Avis* newspaper, Aug. 28, 1924 (Note 24).

Photo from 1918. From the left: Marie and Hans Knut Eriksen, Korner Hansen. In front: Erik Hansen and Anna Shuster.

Sjursdatter and Gudmund J. Rasmussen, tenant farmer no. 11 a, Austrheim.

Children:

a. Erik Tobias, born Jan. 22, 1884, died in 1928, emigrated to USA (San Bruno, California), married Anna Shuster Hansen.
b. Gudmund Martin, born Sept. 24, 1887, died Oct. 2, 1887.
c. *Gustav* Magnus, born July 17, 1890, married in 1915 to Lovise Tobiasdatter Sørhus, farm no. 1 – 6, Kvalvik.
d. Hanna Marie, born Oct. 4, 1893, married in 1919 to Ingvald Klovning, tenant farmer no. 26, Klovning.
e. Klara Constanse Kvalvik, born Aug. 30, 1897, died July 19, 1902.
f. Hans Knut Korner, born Feb. 1, 1904, emigrated to USA (Oakland, California), married in 1932 to Birgith N. Mortensen, Stavanger.

In 1889 Hans Knut received, together in part with Johannes Dalastein, a lease from his brother Erik on a lot for a combination house and boat shed at Kvarneset. The house was already built.

Hans Knut was a seaman before he took over the mail route Haugesund – Feoy – Utsira with his boat. He ran this route until the summer of 1905, when the route was taken over by the vessel H.D.S.' d/s "Karmøy." For further information see pictures and art by Nils Okland in *Haugesunds Avis* newspaper, dated Dec. 23, 1960.

Obituary:
"Hans Knut Eriksen, an old well-known man died Friday, 83 years old. He was the oldest inhabitant on Utsira.

He was born on Utsira, where his father was a marine pilot. In his younger days he sailed on commercial ships to faraway parts of the world, but later settled on Utsira as a fisherman. For 13 years he ran the postal route to Utsira from Haugesund. He later was a fisherman, and late in life until his death, he made fishing nets.

During his last years he suffered somewhat from arthritis. He was a stout and well-liked man. His wife, somewhat younger, is still living. They have 4 children, 2 live in America and 2 live on Utsira."
- from *Haugesunds Avis* newspaper, 23 June, 1925.

Obituary and photo in Haugesund Avis *newspaper, June 23, 1925.*

21. **Erik *Tobias* Eriksen.** 1894 – 1902
Born June 11, 1869, son of Anne Marthe and Erik Eriksen, farm no. 1 – 9 e, Skare.

Married to **Marie Kristine Bentsen,** born in 1871 in Kristiansand.

Children:
a. Martha Kristine, born June 2, 1894.
b. *Emma* Marie, born Mar. 10, 1896, married Johannes Rasmussen Beite, emigrated to USA.
c. Klare Cippora, born June 27, 1898.

Erik Tobias was a seaman. In 1900 they lived on farm no. 1 here.

They emigrated to the USA in 1902 and settled at Stuart Island, WA.

22. **Peder Jakob Johnsen Helgeland.** 1898 – 1909
Born in 1861 on Spannhelgeland, died in 1899 in USA.

Married Oct. 15, 1884 to **Hanna Katrine (Kaia) Eriksdatter,** born Mar. 24, 1865, died Dec. 25, 1952, daughter of Anne Marthe and Erik Eriksen, farm no. 1 – 9 c, Skare.

Children:

a. Johan Adolf, born Nov. 4, 1884, returned to USA in 1902 on SS *Campania.*
b. Elida Amanda *Louise*, born Sept. 1887 in Nebraska, USA, died Sept. 1928 in Seattle, WA, married first to Knut Wisnes, then to George Roscoe Bushnell.
c. Ernst, born Sept. 29, 1891 in S. Dakota, died Mar. 31, 1979 in Seattle, WA.
d.. Clarence Hjalmar, born in Apr. 4, 1896 in N. Dakota, died Mar. 31, 1979 in Seattle.
e. Petra Katrine, born Jan. 30, 1898 in S. Dakota, died Jun. 24, 1949 in Los Angeles, Calif., married William Shelton.

The Kaia (Hanna Katrine Eriksdatter) and Peder Jakob Helgeland family around 1889 (photo probably taken in USA).

Peder was a seaman, and they emigrated to Lead City, S. Dakota, USA in 1887. Hanna Katrine (Kaia) and the children moved back to Utsira after her husband died. She built a house here, farm no. 16, Krossen, in 1898, where she ran a general store. She sold her house to Adolf Ellingsen and returned to Lead City in 1904 on the SS *Baltic*. They later moved to Seattle, WA.

23. **Johan Mathias Bendiksen.** 1905 – 1958

Born May 14, 1878, died Apr. 13, 1938, son of Berthe Helgesine and John Bendik Mathiassen, farm no. 3 – 2 b, Skare.

Married Nov. 19, 1905 to **Anna Sofie Mikalsdatter,** born Mar. 7, 1880, daughter of Thala Sophie and Svend Mikael Larsen, farm no. 4 – 5 k, Klovning.

Children:

a. John Bernhard Stener, born Sept. 26, 1906, next tenant farmer.
b. Thala Sofie, born Feb. 24, 1908, married in 1933 to Thor Ånestad, Randaberg, lived in New Bedford. Mass., USA.
c. Mikael Klovning, born Dec. 21, 1910, married to Marion Nelson, lived in New Bedford.
d. John *Mathias*, born June 28, 1812, married in 1938 to Doris Gustavson, lived in New Bedford.
e. Judit *Magnhild Adeleide*, born May 21, 1915, married in 1940 to Bjarne Espeset, Utsira School no. 26.
f. Johan, born Sept. 4, 1919, married in 1945 to Solveig Martinsdatter Nordrehagen, Randaberg, lives in New Bedford, Mass., USA.

The main dwelling here, farm no. 4, Fjeldheim, was built in 1906.

John Mathias Bendiksen (1878 – 1938) and Anna Sofie Mikalsdatter (1880 – ?).

24. **John B. Stener Bendiksen.** 1931 – 1937.
Born Sept. 26, 1906, son of previous tenant farmer.

Married Mar. 11, 1931 to **Juline Nilsen.** born July 2, 1905, daughter of Jonette and Martin Nilsen, tenant farmer no. 20 d, Austrheim.

Children:

a. Johan Mathias, born Dec. 17, 1933.
b. Martin, born Nov. 23, 1936.
c. Solveig, born Mar. 7, 1943.
d. Mabel, born Dec. 20, 1946.

The family moved to Viken, Torvestad, and after that they emigrated to New Bedford, Mass, USA.

25. **Andreas Miljeteig.** 1940 – 1968

Born July 23, 1896, died Jan. 14, 1968, son of Margreta Olsdatter Miljeteig and Ørjan Aslaksen, Skålnes, in Skånevik.

Married on Oct. 25, 1924 to **Hjordis Valnumsdatter,** born May 12, 1904, died Feb. 8, 1950, daughter of Laura and Valnum Jørgensen, tenant farmer no. 21 – a, Klovning.

Children:

a. *Magnus* Oyvind, born Dec. 22, 1925, next tenant farmer.
b. *Aslaug* Valborg, born Apr. 26, 1928, married in 1952 to Mikal Nilsen, tenant farmer no. 75, Nordvik.

26. **Magnus Miljeteig.** 1940 – 1977

Born Dec. 22, 1925, died Dec. 30, 1977, son of previous tenant farmer.

Unmarried.

Magnus took over the farm here in the 1950s. He perished at sea during the M/S "Emly" shipwreck outside Akrehamn.

27. **Tor Kjell Torsdal.** 1985 –

Born Nov. 16, 1958, son of Ågot and Ole Torsdal, tenant farmer no. 29 b, Skare.

Married Nov. 6, 1992 to **Sissel Liadal**, born Sept. 9, 1969, daughter of Sigmund Liadal, Haugesund.

Children:

a. Ole Mikal, born June 21, 1991.
b. Siv Hilde, born Oct. 5, 1993.

Tor Kjell took over farm no. 4 here in 1985. He is chief engineer onboard M/S "Utsira."

28. **Kasper L. M. Bendiksen.** 1923 – 1970
Born Nov. 6, 1888, died Apr. 4, 1943, son of Berthe Helgesine and John Bendik Mathiassen, farm no. 3 – 2 c, Skare.

Married on July 8, 1923 to **Tilla T. Kvalvik,** born July 23, 1899, died May 9, 1978, daughter of Lisa and Bendik Tollefsen, farm no. 4 – 1 a, Kvalvik.

Children:

a. Ågot Elisabeth, born Oct. 25, 1925, next tenant farmer.

They built their main dwelling here on farm no. 20, Midtun, in 1935.

29. **Ole Torsdal.** 1954 – 1989
Born Oct. 3, 1920, died Jan. 7, 1986, from Vedavagen.

Married on May 27, 1954 to **Ågot Bendiksen,** born Oct. 25, 1925, died May 28, 1991, daughter of previous tenant farmer.

Children:

a. Margrete, born Aug. 12, 1957, married to Magne Hopland, lives in Stavanger.
b. Tor Kjell, born Nov. 16, 1958, married in 1992 to Sissel Liadal, tenant farmer 27, Skare.

The farm was in 1993 taken over by Utsira Municipality.

30. **Martine Ellingsen.** 1930 – 1970
Born Nov. 21, 1894, died Mar. 23, 1970, daughter of Malene Mikkeline and J. Mathias Ellingsen, farm no. 2 – 6 h, Skare.

She became engaged to **Knut Kristian Skåren,** born Mar. 6, 1904, died Apr. 11, 1930, son of Thomine and Johannes Gudmundsen, farm no. 22 – 3 g, Nordvik. Knut and his brother Lars perished at sea while fishing for lobster just prior to their wedding.

Children:

a. Kristian, born Aug. 4, 1930, next tenant farmer.

Martine arranged to have the old dwelling on farm no. 2 separated from her brother Mikal's farm in 1924. The house was built around 1875 and became farm no. 13, Brekke.

The southern part of Skare with Kvarkaneset, Rabben, Smauget and Staraberget in the background. Arial photo taken by Telemark Aircraft Co. in 1954

31. **Kristian Skåren.** 1955 – 1967

Born Aug. 4, 1930, died in 1975, son of previous tenant farmer.

Married in 1955 to **Birgit Malmin,** born in 1935.

Children:

a. Marit Karin, born Oct. 12, 1955.
b. Per Bjarne, born June 2, 1959.
c. Kjell Bjorn, born Aug. 22, 1962.
d. Tor Magne, born Mar. 17, 1964.
e. Kjetil, born Apr. 17, 1972.

Kristian took over the farm here in 1963. He was a radio operator. They moved to Stavanger.

32. **Åstein Thomassen.** 1931 – 1975

Born Aug. 18, 1906. died Sept. 18, 1957, son of Hanna and Thomas Eriksen, farm no. 6 – 1, Skare.

Married Nov. 19, 1931 to **Marthine Nilsen,** born July 2, 1905, daughter of Jonette and Martin Nilsen, tenant farmer no. 20 c, Austrheim.

Children:

a. Tordis *Hagny*, born Jan. 4, 1933, next tenant farmer.
b. Jorunn Margit, born Feb. 20, 1934, married in 1952 to Magnus Skare, tenant farmer no. 52, Hovland.
c. Sigurd, born Jan. 20, 1935, married to Edith Kristine Hettervik. He is a marine pilot and lives in Stavanger.
d. Åshild, born Aug. 30, 1948, married to Hakon Kleppe, lives in Bergen.

They built their home here on farm no. 19, Skarheim, in 1935. The farm was taken over by Jane Marit Skare Martinsen in 1993.

33. **Thore Thorsen.** 1954 – 1965

Born Apr. 30, 1934, died in 1995, son of Olga and Gaut Thorsen, next farmer.

Married May 15, 1954 to **Hagny Thomassen,** born Jan. 4, 1933, daughter of previous tenant farmer.

Children:

a. Grethe Jorun, born Apr. 27, 1956. married to Svein Kare Johansen, lives in Stavanger.
b. Astein Johan, born Nov. 20, 1959, died Sept. 4, 1973.
c. Thor Hallgeir, born Aug. 1, 1963, lives in Stavanger.

The family moved to Moksheim on May 10, 1965.

34. **Gaut Thorsen.** 1947 – 1969.

Born Sept. 16, 1900, died Apr. 5, 1994, son of Kristine and Thore Thorsen, Vibransoy.

Married in 1928 to **Olga Olsen,** born Oct. 10, 1902, died Dec. 30, 1984, daughter of Hansine and Johan Olsen in Drammen.

Children:

a. Martha *Kristine*, born May 28, 1929, married in 1949 to Elling Haugseth, tenant farmer no. 27, Austrheim.
b. Thore, born Apr. 30, 1934, previous tenant farmer.

Gaut was a marine pilot. They lived on Rovaer before they came to Utsira and built a house, farm no. 23, Solberg, in 1948. The family moved to Haugesund, and the farm was taken over by Harald Eriksen.

35. **Elling Haugseth,** 1949 – 1960
They lived here before they built their home at Austrheim and moved there.

36. **Harry Halvorsen.** 1991 –
Born Apr. 2, 1962 in Roan in South Trondelag.

Married in 1989 in Lebanon to **Miriam Boulos,** born Nov. 22, 1968, She was from Lebanon.

Children:

a. George Nicholaos, born Mar. 12, 1991.
b. Harald Johan, born Nov. 12, 1992.

Harry worked as an assistant nurse at Siratun from 1988. In 1989 he spent one–half year with the United Nations in Lebanon. They took over the farm here, farm no. 23, in 1991.

37. **Hjalmar Thomassen.** 1940 – 1988
Born Feb. 17, 1913, died Feb. 16, 1985, son of Hanna and Thomas Eriksen, farm no. 6 – 1 g, Skare.

Married Dec. 1, 1940 to **Jenny Sjursen,** born Oct. 28, 1916, died Aug. 31, 1988, daughter of Thea and Ole Sjursen, farm no. 3 – 3 f, Kvalvik.

Children:

a. *Harald* Torstein, born Apr. 4, 1944, next tenant farmer.
b. Tor Odd, born Apr. 7, 1951, married in 1988 to Kjellfrid Tveiterå, lives in Egersund.
c. John Henry, born Mar. 7, 1953, married in 1975 to Herborg Hansen, tenant farmer no. 38, Kvalvik.
d. Oyvind, born June 6, 1958.

They built their main dwelling here, farm no. 28, Nordhaug, in 1952.

39. **Harald Thomassen. 1984 – 1993**
Born Apr. 4, 1944, son of previous tenant farmer.

Married in 1991 to **Eva Ophaug,** born Jan. 12, 1941, from Skjervoy in Troms.

They moved to Arendal in 1994. Their farm here is taken over by Stian Thomassen.

39. **Knut M. L. Lervik.** 1909 – 1913

Born 1883, died 1927, from Haugesund.

Married to **Julie Kristine Austrheim,** born Jan. 20, 1887, daughter outside marriage of Elling Mathiassen and Jonette Kathrine Sjursdatter, Kvalvik.

Children:

a. Lindy Sofie, born Mar. 25, 1910, died in 1949, married to Sofus Nuland, Haugesund.
b. Jon Mikael, born Apr. 23, 1912, died in an accident onboard M/S "Erling Lindoe" in England, Sept. 13, 1939.
c. Casilie Evelyn, born Apr. 6, 1914, married in 1939 to Magne Styve, lives in Haugesund.
d. Magnhild Judith, born Oct. 2, 1916, married in 1939 to Martin Nilsen, lives in Haugesund.
e. Lars Gerhard, born Mar. 24, 1919, married in 1942 to Solveig Hansen, lives in Haugesund.
f. Sverre Aleksander, born Oct. 1, 1921, died in 1930.
g. Rolf Wilhelm, born Oct. 4, 1924, watchmaker in Haugesund, married in 1950 to Aslaug Jacobsen.
h. Kirsten Magdalene, born Dec. 10, 1926, married to Vagn Søndergård, lives in Copenhagen.

Knut Lervik was a shoemaker. They built their home here, farm no. 31, Nylund, in 1911 (expanded in 1949). They moved to Haugesund in 1913. They lived at Niels Skorpensgaten 7.

40. **Gurine J. Dalastein.** 1913 – 1930.
Born June 25, 1880. died Jan. 10, 1930, daughter of Thomasine and Johannes Dalastein, tenant farmer no. 17 b, Skare.

Unmarried.

Gurine took over the farm in 1913 after Knut Lervik, together with her cousin.

41. **Gurine G. Klovning.** 1913 – 1921
Born Dec. 23, 1881, daughter of Mette Kistine and Gudmund Jørgensen, farm no. 1 – 10 g, Klovning.

Unmarried.

They started a general store here under the name "Gurine J. Dalastein." Gurine G. Klovning moved in 1921 to Vaulen, Stavanger.

Outside their home "Hjemmet" around 1916. From left: Thea Tollefsen, Gurine Klovning, Kaia Klovning, Jenny Dalastein Gudmundsen, Gurine Dalastein, "Tysko" Agnes Geuer and Thomas Bendiksen.

42. **Gudmund G. Klovning.** 1921 – 1976
Born Oct. 23, 1889, died Apr. 1, 1967, son of Mette Kistine and Gudmund Jørgensen, farm no. 1 – 10 j, Klovning.

Married Oct. 8, 1921 to **Jenny Teresia Dalastein,** born Sept. 24, 1887, died Jan. 13, 1976, daughter of Thomasine and Johannes Dalastein, tenant farmer no. 17 f, Skare.

Children:

a. *Guttorm* Magne, born Jan. 23, 1927, died Jan. 8, 1977, married to Anbjorg Hausken, Torvestad.
b. *Johannes* Torfred, born June 15, 1929, took over and now run the business.
c. *John* Martin, born Feb. 24, 1931, died Feb. 27, 1978, was head of social services on Utsira. He worked enthusiastically for the Utsira historical book project in the 1970's. Also had a farm here.

Jenny and Gudmund took over the store from Gurine in January 1930 under the name Jenny Gudmundsen, commonly called "Hjemmet" (the "Home").

Gudmund became Mayor of Utsira in the period 1932 – 1940.

43. **Tobias Skare.** 1943 –
Born May 7, 1919. died Nov. 8, 1980, son of Åsa Oline and Adolf Ellingsen, farm no. 1–11 e, Skare.

Married Apr. 17, 1943 to **Hanna Eriksen**, born Feb. 25, 1917, daughter of Hanna and Thomas Eriksen, farm no. 6–1 i, Skare.

Children:

a. Jorunn *Ågot*, born Jan. 4, 1944, lives in Oslo.
b. Terje. born June 29, 1946, married to Kjersti, lives in at Melbu in Vesterålen. He was a teacher here in 1983 – 84.
c. Leif Sigurd, born July 29, 1949, died Dec. 19, 1950.
d. Leif Sigurd, born Sept. 30, 1951, died Jan. 13, 1952.
e. Aud *Torill*, born Feb. 11, 1953, lives in Stavanger.
f. Geir Oyvind, born July 12, 1954. Geir also had a farm here.
g. *Kjellaug* Oddgunn, born Dec. 18, 1957, married to Åge Pedersen from Moelven, lives in Stavanger. She was a teacher here in 1982 – 83.

They built their main dwelling here, farm no. 35, Skarheim, in 1953.

44. **Hans Klovning,** 1945 –
Born May 8, 1917, son of Laura and Valnum Jørgensen, tenant farmer no. 21 f, Klovning.

Married in 1945 to **Tordis Klovning,** born June 25, 1924, daughter of Anne Martha and Mikal Klovning, farm no. 4 – 7 d, Klovning.

Children:

a. Anne Lise, born Mar. 20, 1946, married to Anders Henriksen Jordal, lives on Voss.
b. *Jan* Trygve, born Sept. 15, 1948. lives in Bergen.
c. Tor Harald, born Apr. 17, 1952, married in 1972 to Mary-Ann Borresen, tenant farm no. 40, Kvalvik.
d. Ellinor, born June 20, 1960, married in 1979 to Inge Silden, tenant farm no. 39, Kvalvik.

They built their main dwelling here, farm no. 37, Solberg, in 1954.

45. **Adolf Skare,** 1953 –
Born July 5, 1921, son of Åsa Oline and Adolf Ellingsen, farm no. 1 – 11 f, Skare.

Married June 27, 1953 to **Reidun Jakobsen,** born Mar. 8, 1932, daughter of Laura and Jakob Jakobsen, tenant farm no. 33 a, Kvalvik.

Children:

a. Åse Audhild, born July 14, 1954, died July 11, 1957.
b. *Rolf* Arne, born Dec. 31, 1957. married in 1981 to May Britt Austrheim, tenant farm no. 51, Skare.
c. John Bjarne, born Oct. 15, 1959, died Dec. 30, 1977, perished during the M/S "Emly" shipwreck outside Åkrehamn.
d. *Audun* Åstein, born Sept. 22, 1963, lives in Oslo.

The main dwelling here, farm no 16, Krossen, was built by Hanna Helgeland (tenant farm no. 22, Skare) in 1898 – 99.

46. **Hans Knut Hansen.** 1954 –
Born Sept. 15, 1922, son of Lovisa and Gustav Hansen, farm no. 1 – 6 d, Kvalvik.

Married Apr. 3, 1954 to **Valborg Martinsen,** born Nov. 5, 1923. daughter of Serine and Martin Eriksen, farm no. 5 – 1 k, Skare.

Children:
a. Herborg, born July 1, 1954, married in 1975 to John Hensy Thomassen, tenant farm no. 38, Kvalvik.
b. Roald, born Nov. 27, 1956.
c. Modstein, born June 22, 1959, married to Torbjorg Overhus, lives in Haugesund.
d. *Arvid* Magne, born Apr. 15, 1962, twin, married to Helene Valnumsen, lives in Viken, Torvestad. They moved to Utsira in 1995.
e. Gunn Lovise, born Apr. 15,1962, twin, married in 1992 to Gaut Harald Gautesen, Rovaer. She was chief municipal treasurer in Utsira 1987 – 1992. They live on Rovaer.

They built their main dwelling here, farm no. 40, Solgar, in 1962.

47. **Olav Helgesen.** 1941 – 1952
Born July 10, 1913, son of Åsa and Sivert Helgesen, farm no. 32 – 1 d, Nordvik.

Married Apr. 10, 1941 to **Klara Hellvik,** born June 5, 1920, daughter of Inger and Peder Hellvik, Egersund.

Children:
a. Kirsten Olaug, born Jan. 28, 1944, married to Leif Karlsen.
b. Svein Arvid, born Feb. 14, 1950, married to Margunn Nornes.

The family moved to Torvestad in 1952.

Picnicking in 1940. From Left: Borgny Kvalvik, Ragna Solheim Enghaugen, Ragnar Nygård, Tor Kvalvik, Tordis Klovning, Målfrid Klovning and Sigrunn Hansen. It is Hans Knut Hansen in the back playing the accordion.

48. **Peter Jensen Enevold.** 1922 – 1924.
Born Mar. 12, 1878, son of Martha and Elling Jensen Dyrendal in Rissa, Sør-Trøndelag, died Sept. 1, 1925 in Alberta, Canada.

Married Oct. 21, 1916 in Canada to **Hanna Knutsen**, born Aug. 5, 1892, daughter of Thomine and Hans Gudmundsen, farm no. 1 – 9 c, Austrheim.

Children:

a. Maureen, born July 31, 1917, married in 1942 to George R. Owen, Alberta, Canada.
b. Evelyn, born Mar. 25, 1919, married in 1940 to Robert Tatham, Edmonton, Canada.
c. Kenneth, born Jan. 5, 1921, married in 1942 to Mona Roderick, BC., Canada and Arizona, USA.
d. Thomas, born Mar. 10, 1923, married in 1943 to Mary Alice Hayes of Amish, Alberta, Canada.

The family lived here for two years. They moved back to Canada in 1924.

49. **Torodd Nilsen.** 1976–
Born Jan. 2, 1952, son of Målfrid and Arne Nilsen, tenant farmer no. 33 b, Klovning.

Married May 29, 1976 to **Torill Hansen,** born May 29, 1955, daughter of Sigrunn and Alf Hansen, tenant farmer 40 a, Hovland.

Children:
- a. Anne, born July 13, 1977.
- b. Ingrid, born Dec. 21, 1979.
- c. Vidar, born Nov. 16, 1982.

They built a main dwelling here, farm no.50, Solvang, in 1978.

Torodd works for Utsira Municipality as head of technical services. Torill is a nurse assistant at Siratun nursing home.

50. **Finn Klovning.** 1980 –
Born Apr. 21, 1952, son of Sigfryda and Ole Klovning, tenant farmer no. 22 c, Klovning.

Married Oct. 31, 1980 to **Anne Margrethe Støle,** born Mar. 22, 1962, from Torvestad.

Children:
- a. Arnfinn, born Apr. 27, 1981.
- b. Marianne, born Feb. 22, 1983.
- c. Aleksander, born Aug. 26, 1987.

They built their main dwelling here, farm no. 47, Utsikten, in 1981.

Finn is a crew member on M/S "Utsira." Anne Margrethe works for Sildakongen Productions.

51. **Rolf A. Skare.** 1981 –
Born Dec. 31, 1957, son of Reidun and Adolf Skare, tenant farmer no. 45 b, Skare.

Married Dec. 31, 1981 to **May Britt Austrheim,** born Mar. 8, 1964, daughter of Inger and Johan Austrheim, tenant farmer no. 28 d, Austrheim.

Children:
- a. Espen, born Apr. 9, 1982.
- b. Asle, born June 25, 1987.
- c. Steffen, born July 23, 1989.
- d. Simen, born July 4, 1993.

The harbor in Sørvågen (South Bay) in 1954. Photo: Telemark Aircraft Co

They built their main dwelling here, farm no. 45, Krossen, in 1984–85.

Rolf worked in the technical department for Utsira Municipality. May Britt works as a nursery teacher.

52. **Lars Gudmundsen.** 1863 – 1875

Baptized June 30, 1799, died Nov. 8, 1875., son of Berta Ambjornsdatter and Gudmund Thomassen, farm no. 3 – 2 1, Austrheim.

Married Oct. 10, 1819 to **Ella Eline Knutsdatter,** baptized Mar. 14, 1784, died in 1862, daughter of Valborg Johannesdatter and Knut Håkonsen, Osnes.

No children.

Lars was a marine pilot and lived on Feoy. He moved back to Utsira when his wife died and built a house on his brother's leased farm at Myre on Skare.

A deed dated Apr. 29, 1863 for a lot 18 x 9 alen was issued to Lars and his brother Rasmus from Mathias Ellingsen. They paid 4 Spd. in a one–time payment and 1 Spd. in annual payments for this deed. The house was then already built. In 1915 this house was taken out of farm no. 2 and was designated farm no. 11, Grindheim. In the period 1929 to 1958, the place served as the telephone switchboard for the area and also as the island's post office from 1955 to 1958. The owner was then Anne Kristine Rasmussen and from 1977 it was owned by Utsira Municipality.

53. **Johan Liadal.** 1952 – 1960
Born Apr. 19, 1903, died Apr. 27, 1968, son of Anna O. Moe and Johannes O. Liadal, from Liadal in Ørsta.

Married to **Signe Jacobine Hetland,** born May 15, 1902, died Mar.18, 1995, daughter of Janne Severine Jakobsdatter and Bendik Svendsen, Hetland, in Tysvaer.

Children:

a. Magne, born Mar. 24, 1933, died Aug. 28, 1983, married in 1966 to Klara Thorsen, lived in Haugesund.
b. Birger, born Nov. 3, 1936, married in 1971 to Brita Solveig Kvalnes, lives on Karmøy.
c. Sigmund, born July 31, 1942, married to Hilgot Gjellestad, Haugesund.

Johan was general manager of Utsira Power Co. from 1952 until power came to the Island via cable in 1958. He built himself a house here on farm no. 38, Grindheim, in 1955. The farm was taken over by Utsira Municipality and became the teacher residence in 1961. The family moved to Haugesund in 1960.

54. **Ludolf Martinsen.** 1954 – 1986
Born Feb. 3, 1909, died Oct. 8, 1986, son of Serine and Martin Eriksen, farm no. 5 – 1 d, Skare.

Married Sept. 16, 1950 to **Brita Grindheim,** born June 30, 1920, died in April 1954, daughter of Maren Sivertsdatter and Johan Hansen Notland, Øvre–Grindheim on Moster.

They lived on Moster, and Ludolf built himself a new main dwelling here in 1960, farm no. 36, Holt. This farm was taken over by Gunn Lovise Hansen in 1985.

55. **Rune Solvåg.** 1992 –
Born Dec. 24, 1966, from Mauseidvåg on Sunnmøre. He is the chief municipal treasurer for Utsira from 1992.

56. **Tove Helen Eriksen.** 1990 –
Born Oct. 17, 1969, daughter of Turid and Harald Eriksen, farm no. 6 – 3 c, Skare.

Lives together with **Kjell Ove Sandmo,** from Roan in South Trøndelag.

Children:

a. Erik, born Apr. 18, 1995.

57. **Arvid Magne Hansen**,
Born Apr. 15, 1962, son of Hans Knut Hansen and Valborg Martinsen, farm no. 6–46, Skare.

Married to **Helene Valnumsen**, lived in Viken, Torvestad.

They moved to Utsira in 1995.

The farm Klovning and the harbor in the foreground in 1954. In the background are farms no. 1, 2 and 4. Photo: Telemark Aircraft Co.

Klovning

Before 1824:	Reg. no. 52, tax 1 v. dried fish.
1824 – 1851:	Reg. no. 58. serial no. 249–251b, tax 4–3–10 skd.
1851 – 1886:	Reg. no. 68, serial no. 350a–351b, tax 4–3–6 skd.
1886 –:	Farm no. 30, tax 9 mark 11 ore.

Klovning is among the youngest farms at Utsira. It was separated from the Kvalvik properties in 1637 and was tax assessed to 1 våg dried fish, and was consequently one of the smallest farms on the island.

The name is probably derived from the large split boulder situated in the middle of the farm, and today called Klopsteinane (the "Broken Rock"). The name Klovning has over the years been written in many ways: In the 1660's: *Kløffning, in 1723: Klofning* and in 1744: *Klofning*.

There was only one farm here until 1778, then two and from 1855, three farms, and from 1908 until today, four farms. On the farm there was a lot for tenants called "Naesset" (a peninsula suitable for a small house).

The farm was assessed and registered in 1905–07.

The listing in the Registry in 1668 is as follows:

> Kløffning (Klovning), 1 vog dried fish, with fields of little use for grain, although enough peat for fuel, sowing 1 barrel, enough feed for 4 cows, and good for tax equivalent of – 1 barrel feed – 2 calf hides for local defense, a bucket of grain for the church, and 2 sk. in miscellaneous contributions.

Table of planted and harvested grain and potatoes:

Year	Grain sown	Potatoes planted	Grain harvested	Potatoes harvested
1668	1	–	–	–
1703	2	–	–	–
1712	2	–	–	–
1723	1.5	–	7.5	–
1802	3	–	16	–
1822	–	–	44	13
1845	10.5	3.5	–	–
1866	14	7	87	60
1875	13.5	8.5	–	–
1945	7	6.5	–	–

The numbers for 1945 are in dekars, otherwise in barrels.

Table showing livestock, inhabitated homes and number of inhabitants:

Year	Horses	Cows	Sheep	Inhabited homes	Number of inhabitants
1668	–	4	–	–	–
1703	1	6	x	–	–
1712	1	6	x	–	–
1723	–	4	–	–	–
1758	–	–	–	3	10
1801–02	2	7	4	3	11
1822	2	11	14	–	–
1845	3	12	22	4	27
1866	3	12.5	50	6	41
1875	2	9	44	9	57
1900	–	–	–	9	49

Farmers

Farm no. 1

1. **Elling Arvesen.** 1637 –
Son of Arve Kvalvik, farmer no. 3, Kvalvik.

Elling was the first inhabitant who cleared and established the first settlement at Klovning, which originally was part of Kvalvik. In the county records of Hardanger and Halsnoy Cloister, one can read the following note written in 1637:

> Leased on Udtzirre (Utsira). to Elling Arffuesen (Arvesen), a deserted, uninhabited plot, which his mother had access to, called Klouffningen (Klovning), which is located in Qualuogh (Kvalvik), and which he will clear and build on and pay 5 rdl.

Elling is not otherwise mentioned as taxpayer in the county records during the years 1638 – 44. Possibly he had been given a few years to build up his farm before he was required to pay tax.

2. **(Anders**). – 1657
Married to **(Marta?) Saebjornsdatter,** daughter of Saebjorn Aslaksen, Nedre–Hauge, Torvestad.

Their daughter was:

a. Anna, married to Jon Hansen, farmer no. 4 here.

3. **Hans Ingebretsen.** 1658 – 1672
Born 1614, mentioned for the first time in Halsnoy Cloister's record book for 1659. In 1663 he is listed as an assistant to the priest.

His children may possibly be:

a. Olaf, born 1649.
b. Ingebret, born 1642, farm no. 1 – 3, Hovland.
c. Elling, born 1655, farm no. 2 – 1, Kvalvik.

Hans is also mentioned several times in the court records, the last time in 1668, when he and Simon Hovland had a violent argument using foul language. Simon allegedly called Hans a thief.

4. **Jon Hansen.** 1673 – 1716
Born 1651 (1659?), died sometime between 1703 and 1706, son of Hans Jonsen, farmer no. 7, Kvalvik, formerly of Stange, Torvestad.
Married to **Anna Andersdatter,** daughter of farmer no. 2 here.

Known children:

a. Jens, born 1678, moved to Stange, Torvestad.
b. Hans, born 1689.
c. Jørgen, born 1693, next farmer,
d. (Name unknown), married around 1700 to Villum Larsen, Landanes.

Jon is mentioned as farmer on Klovning in 1673. In 1675 he was among those on Utsira who came to the Cloister to claim some of the salvaged items from the German shipwreck near Spannholmen during Christmas the year before.[57]

Jon is mentioned a couple of times in the county records. In 1699 he took Johannes Salvesen Visnes to court for 6 rdl. for a fishing net he had not paid for. However, Johannes did not show up. Also he took his handyman, Anders Knutsen, to court, since he allegedly left his place of work without permission, and had received 4 ort of his pay in advance. Anders did not show up in court, but as he is listed as a servant at this farm in the 1701 census, they must have reconciled. The following year Jon appealed the agreement concerning the plot his mother–in–law,` (Marta) Saebjornsdatter owned at Nedre–Hauge, and which, according to the agreement with both his brothers–in–law, Jon Tolleivsen and Anders Rasmussen Landenes, was evenly exchanged with a farm at Undheim on Jaeren. However, Jon lost that case.

In 1703, Jon's financial condition was described as "good," and the houses were estimated to require 1 rdl. in repair. He sowed 2 barrels of oats and fed 4 cows, 2 calves and some sheep. He owned all the animals, and he *did not owe anything to Frimand nor anybody else.*

Nine years later, in 1712, his widow Anna ran the farm. The financial condition *appeared to be good,* while repair of the houses amounted to 2 rdl. Otherwise, everything remained as in 1703.

5. **Jørgen Jonsen.** 1717 – 1749

Born 1693, buried June 25, 1769, son of previous farmer.

Married to **Malene Larsdatter**, died in 1746, daughter of Berthe Anbjornsdatter and Lars Johannesen, farmer no. 1 – 3, Skare.

Children:

a. Jon, born 1722, next farmer.
b. Anne, born around 1722, married to Rasmus Johannesen, Storesund in Torvestad.
c. Randi, born 1729, buried July 10, 1785.
d. Berthe, born 1731, married in 1759 to Jon Rasmussen, tenant farmer no. 6, Klovning.

Jørgen renewed his lease contract amounting to 2 v dried fish on Dec. 23, 1720. (He pays annually 1 v. dried fish for the use of the field "Spanderøde" for his sheep.

[57] See Note 25.

During a survey of the farm in 1721, he was required to repair the house and the barn, costing him 1–2–0 rdl. The fields and the meadows were in good condition, and he owed 3 rdl. for the lease.

In the estate settlement after Malene in 1746, the children inherited 23–3–15 rdl.

6. **Jon Jørgensen.** 1749 – 1800

Born 1722, died Sept. 15, 1800, son of previous farmer.

Married first to **Berta Andersdatter**, born 1725, buried Sept. 21, 1783, daughter of Berta Svensdatter and Anders Larsen, Hausken, Torvestad.

Married the second time on Dec. 14, 1785 to **Eli Villumsdatter,** born 1751, died Apr. 2, 1835, daughter of Eli Knutsdatter and Villum Knutsen, Osnes, Torvestad.

Children in first marriage:

a. Anders, born 1751, married in 1778 to Gunhild Mortensdatter, farmer no. 4 – 1, Klovning.
b. Malene, baptized Dec. 26, 1753, married in 1774 to Amund Paulsen, tenant farmer no. 11, Skare.
c. Jørgen, baptized Apr. 8, 1756, buried July 2, 1756, 10 weeks old.
d. Jørgen, baptized Jan. 23, 1758, died in 1758.
e. Berta, baptized Apr. 28, 1762, married in 1805 to widower Amund Hansen, Skjollingstad, Torvestad.
f. Gundele, baptized May 31, 1764, married in 1806 to Håkon Hansen, Asaldal, Stangeland.
g. Hans, baptized Sept. 3, 1767, married in 1791 to Kari Anbjornsdatter, tenant farm no. 17, Hovland.
h. Jørgen, baptized Jan. 19, 1769, buried Nov. 23, 1771, 4 years old.
i. Jon, baptized July 26, 1770, died Dec. 19, 1800.

Children in second marriage:

j. Anders, baptized Oct. 26, 1786, buried Mar. 25, 1787.
k. Villum, baptized July 5, 1788, died May 31, 1826.
l. Jørgen, baptized Oct. 2, 1791, farmer no. 8 here.

Jon's lease contract in the amount of 2 v. dried fish (on "Spanderøde) is dated Nov. 23, 1749.

Jon is mentioned in the court records in 1750; see farm no. 15, Nordvik.

In 1778 Jon left half of farm no. 4 to his son Anders.

There was an estate settlement after Berta's death in 1783. The estate then amounted to 119 rdl., from which the marriage portion to

Table of farmers at Klovning, 1700 – 1900.

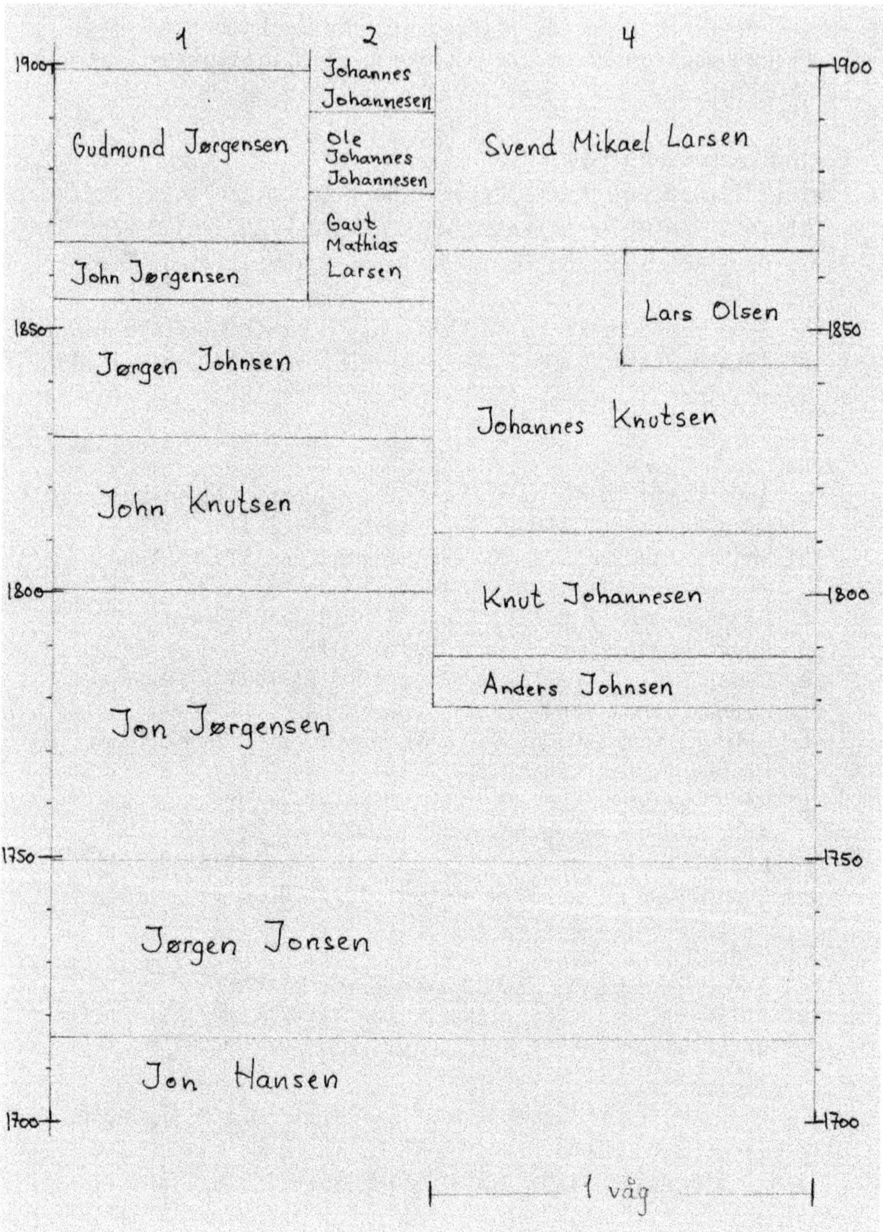

the unmarried children was subtracted amounting to 48 rdl., as well as 12 rdl. for the burial and miscellaneous expenses and deportment amounting to 8–2–16 rdl. Among the miscellaneous items left were:

> 1 mare 5–0–0, 2 cows and 2 calves 16–1–8, 1 fishing boat with sails 5–0–0, 1/3 ownership in fishing shed and boat without sail 6–0–0, 3 spring herring fishing nets 1–3–16, 20 lobster pots 1–2–16, 1 tiled heating stove 5–2–0, 2–1/2 barrels sowing grain 3–1–8, 1 small copper kettle weighing 1 bp. 12 mrk (approx. 9 kg.) 4–2–0, 6 silver spoons, 1 silver ring and 1 small silver drinking vessel 6–2–20, and miscellaneous clothing and bedding 21–1–11.

Jon was killed during an accident on a boat, and his son Jon was also injured in the same accident and died 6 to 7 weeks later. There was a settlement after both of them in 1801. There was 32–3–10 rdl. from the father and 55–1–3 from the son. Among the miscellaneous items mentioned are the following:

> 1 pair of gold buttons 7–0–0, 1 pair of silver pins 6–0–0, 2 four–oar boats 8–2–0, 3 fishing nets 1–2–0 and 1 optical viewing tube 0–3–8.

Eli married the second time in 1802 to John Knutsen, see below.

7. **John Knutsen.** 1801 – 1829
Baptized July 27, 1766, died Aug. 1, 1832, son of Ingeborg Olsdatter and Knut Hansen, Hasseloy. Knut Hansen was the son of Agnethe and Hans Pedersen, tenant farmer no.19, Nordvik. Ingeborg Olsdatter and the widow of the previous farmer here, Berta Andersdatter, were cousins. John Knutsen and Bård Bårdsen, Austrheim, were half–brothers.

Married Mar. 28, 1802 to **Eli Villumsdatter,** widow of previous farmer.

No children.

Lease contract to John in the amount of 1/2 v. dried fish was issued by Hans B. Forman on Oct. 12, 1801. He paid 30 rdl. for this lease.

In 1802 he sowed 1–1/2 barrels of grain and harvested 8 barrels. The livestock consisted of 1 horse, 2 cows, 1 calf and 2 sheep. The farm was valued at 70 rdl.

In 1822 the houses on the farm were described as follows:

> One cottage with half a kitchen under a roof together with Johannes Knudsen's house, covered with peat, 1 barn covered with a peat roof, of which half consists of stables for the cows, built with logs also covered

with peat, a second home with peat roof, 1 laundry house covered with peat. All of these buildings belonging to the farm are in usable condition.

Annual yield of the farm was then 20–22 barrels of grain and 4–6 barrels of potatoes. There was enough feed for 5 cows, 1 horse and 6 – 8 sheep. The farm was in 1823 assessed at 125 Spd.

In 1829 he turned the farm over to his stepson, Jørgen Johnsen, for an old age pension consisting of 5 barrels of oats, feed for 2 cows and 6 sheep, 2 cords of peat and free use of the field called "Skiftesflaekken." This pension was assessed at 50 Spd. for 5 years.

8. **Jørgen Johnsen.** 1829 – 1855
Baptized Oct. 2, 1791, died May 20, 1860, son of farmer no. 6 here.

Married Oct. 10, 1824 to **Valborg Gudmundsdatter,** baptized Feb. 10, 1802, died Jan. 17, 1886, daughter of Berta Ambjornsdatter and Gudmund Thomassen, farm no. 3 – 2 m, Austrheim.

Children:

a. Berta, born July 24, 1825, died Aug. 8, 1825.
b. John. born Apr. 4, 1827, next farmer.
c. Berte Eline, born Oct. 31, 1829, married in 1852 to Gaut Mathias Larsen, farm no. 2 – 1, Klovning.
d. Gudmund, born June 18, 1832, farmer no. 10 here.
e. Jørgen, born Feb. 22, 1835, married in 1871 to Berte Gurine Rasmusdatter, tenant farmer no. 20, Klovning.
f. Anna Martha, born Jan. 1, 1842, died July 11, 1859. She perished with six other people from Utsira when their boat capsized on their way home from Bergen.

The tenant farmer contract to Jørgen for 40 years from J. Dahm is dated Mar. 30, 1829. He has to pay an annual fee of 5 Spd. and 1 barrel of fish. Among other conditions, it is mentioned that: *he must allow the owner to dry as many barrels of oats as he may need for his own household.*

In 1841 Jørgen bought this farm, with a tax liability of 2–1–17 skdl., from J. Dahm for 300 Spd., and the deed is dated July 16, 1841. The deed includes a note saying that buyer and seller will split the fishing rights income as long as J. Dahm and his wife live. Also, Dahm reserves the right to let his geese feed on the property.

The livestock consisted in 1845 of 1 horse, 6 cows and 10 sheep.

In 1855 Jørgen divided the farm between his son John (2/3) and his son–in–law Gaut Mathias Larsen (1/3), farmer no. 2.

9. **John Jørgensen.** 1855 – 1866

Born Apr. 4, 1827, died Nov. 30, 1866, son of previous farmer.

Unmarried.

The deed to John on 2/3 of his father's farm, with a tax liability of 1–2–16 skdl., from the father in the amount of 333–1–16 Spd. is dated Sept. 26, 1855. He and his brother–in–law Gaut Mathias were required to provide the following to their parents:

> 5 barrels of oats and 1 barrel of barley, feed for 1 cow and 9 sheep and free use of the field "Abrahamsflaekken" including the "small boggy" area. This contract over 5 years was assessed at 137–2–12 Spd.

In 1865 there were 36 mål fields and pastures worth 365 Spd. There were meadows worth 74, peat for 30 and land rights for 26 Spd. Annual yield is 22 barrels of grain, 7 barrels of barley and 18 barrels of potatoes. The farm was valued at a total of 571 Spd.

The livestock consisted of 1 horse, 4 cows, 21 sheep and 1 pig.

10. **Gudmund Jørgensen** 1867 – 1899

Born June 18, 1832, died Apr. 24, 1900, son of farmer no. 8 here.

Married Oct. 4, 1868, to **Mette Kistine Rasmusdatter,** born Aug. 22, 1847, died June 11, 1921, daughter of Guri Johannesdatter and Rasmus Gudmundsen, farmer no. 2 – 5 e, Skare.

Mette Kistine Rasmusdatter (1847–1921).

Children:

a. Anne Marthe. born July 9, 1871, married in 1908 to Hans Mathias Gautesen, tenant farmer no. 25, Klovning.
b. *Jørgen* Johan, born Dec. 7, 1873, next farmer,
c. Ragla Gurine, born July 3, 1874, died Sept. 7, 1878.
d. *Thomas* Valnum, born May 4, 1876, next farmer no. 12 here.
e. Berthe Karine, born Mar. 3, 1878, unmarried, lived in Vaulen, Stavanger.
f. *Rasmus* Gurinius, born Nov. 7, 1879, married to Ellen Kyvik from Stord. He was a businessman in Stavanger.
g. Berthe *Gurine*. born Dec. 23, 1881, tenant farmer no. 41, Skare.

h. Laura Regine, born Apr. 20, 1884, unmarried, lived on Vaulen, Stavanger.
i. Martin Tobias, born July 10, 1887, emigrated to USA in 1907, unmarried, perished at sea.
j. Gudmund, born Oct. 23, 1889, married in 1921 to Jenny Johannesdatter Dalastein, tenant farm no. 42, Skare.
k. Ellen Kristine, born Jun 12, 1891, unmarried, lived on Vaulen, Stavanger.

Gudmund's son with Berthe Kristine Johannesdatter, Klovning:
l. Gudmund, born July 2, 1864.

The deed to Gudmund from John Jørgensen's heirs on this farm, indicating a tax liability of 1–2–16 skdl., in the amount of 330 Spd. is dated June 18, 1874.

In 1875 they are sowing 3 barrels of oats and 1 barrel of barley and planting 3 barrels of potatoes. The livestock consists of 1 horse, 3 cows and 10 sheep.

11. **Jørgen Gudmundsen.** 1899 – 1905
Born Dec. 7, 1873, died Oct. 3, 1905, son of previous farmer.
Unmarried.
The deed to Jørgen on this farm, with a tax liability of sk. 2.95, from the father in the amount of 1600 kroner is dated Apr. 15, 1899, and includes a contract for his father's old age worth 800 kr. consisting of:

> 200 kg. of oats, 100 kg. of barley and free use of the field, "the Southern Bog Meadow," feed for 1 cow and 3 sheep, and *permission to tie up the cow in the field in the fall*, 1/4 of the fishing rights income over 50 kr., use of 1 mål of birch wood forest and 25 hl. coal.

12. **Thomas V. Gudmundsen.** 1906 – 1940
Born May 4, 1876, died May 4, 1935, son of farmer no. 10 here.

Married Oct. 11, 1911 to **Jonette Marie Tollefsdatter,** born Dec. 9, 1883, died Apr. 17, 1962, daughter of Marta Eline Rasmusdatter and Tollef Johan Tollefsen, tenant farmer no. 13 j, Skare.

Children:
a. *Gudmund* Martin, born Aug. 7, 1912, died Dec. 8, 1928.
b. Thorleif, Oct. 23, 1913, next farmer.
c. Martha, born June 26, 1916, married in 1941 to Olav Sjursen Kvalvik, tenant farmer no. 32, Klovning.
d. *Jørgen* Magnus, born Dec. 4, 1918, died 1974, married to Edvarda Totsås, lived in Stavanger.

The Thomas Gudmundsen family in 1926. In front from left: Jørgen, born 1918, Målfrid, born 1923 and Sigmund, born 1920. In the back from the left: Martha, born 1916, Thomas (1876 – 1935), Jonette (1883 – 1962), Thorleif, born 1913 and Gudmund, born 1912.

e. Leif *Sigmund*, born Apr. 6, 1920, died May 16, 1946, he perished at sea during lobster fishing.
f. Målfrid, born Nov. 29, 1923, married in 1949 to Arne Nilsen, tenant farmer no. 33, Klovning.

The testament from his brother Jørgen deeding the farm to Thomas indicates a tax liability of sk.m. 2.91 and is dated Sept. 16, 1905. Thomas was in America when his brother died and he returned home to take over the farm.

13. **Thorleif Klovning.** 1940 – 1967
Born Oct. 23, 1913, died Apr. 19, 1967, son of previous farmer.

Married Dec. 28, 1956 to **Marie Kvalvik,** born Jan. 7, 1919, daughter of Thea and Ole Sjursen, farmer no. 3 – 3 g, Kvalvik.

No children.

Thorleif took over the estate here in 1956. When he died the farm continued to be used as an additional farm until sometime in the 1980s. The farm was taken over in 1974 by Odd Bjarne Kvalvik.

14. **Jostein Nilsen.** 1982 –
Born May 6, 1950, son of Målfrid and Arne Nilsen, tenant farmer no. 33 a, Klovning.

Married Aug. 4, 1973 to **Hanne *Mathea* Birkeland,** born Oct. 18, 1951, from Haugesund.

Children:

a. Ingvild, born Oct. 4, 1976.
b. Oystein. born Jan. 4, 1979.
c. Vegard. born Nov. 8, 1983.

Jostein is a teacher at Utsira Children and Youth School. Thea is a manager at the Social Security Services. They built their house here, farm no. 34, in 1975–76. They are now running the farm together with Torodd Nilsen.

Farm no. 2, From farm no. 1 in 1855

1. **Gaut Mathias Larsen.** 1855 – 1878.
Born Feb. 14, 1822, died Oct. 11, 1900, son of Martha Elisabeth Gautsdatter and Lars Hansen, farmer no. 17 – 3 g, Nordvik.

Married Apr. 4, 1852 to **Berthe Eline Jørgensdatter,** born Oct. 31, 1829, died Nov. 29, 1869, daughter of Valborg and Jørgen Johnsen, farm no. 1 – 8 c, Klovning.

Children:

a. Lars Johan, born June 13, 1852, died Mar. 11, 1870.
b. Jørgen, born Aug. 22, 1853, emigrated to USA in March 1884.
c. Hans Mathias, born July 21, 1856, married in 1908 to Anne Martha Gudmundsdatter, tenant farm no. 25, Klovning.
d. *Gudmund* Johan, born May 19, 1859. He was a patient at the Møllendal Asylum in Bergen.
e. Anne Martha, born Sept. 4, 1861, died Dec. 23, 1881.
f. Valborg Eline, born Dec. 25, 1863. She had a daughter Johanne Mathilde Valine, born Apr. 26, 1885, with Johan Mathias Olsen Lønning, Haugesund. And she had a daughter Bertha Amanda, born Mar. 3, 1888, with Nils Johan Gudmundsen Austrheim.

g. Marthe Elisabeth, born Feb. 28, 1866, died 1939, in the same place as her brother Gudmund, mentioned earlier. She had a daughter Gunda Elida, born Mar. 6, 1895, who married Kolbein Kolbeinsen, Imsland. She also had a daughter, Martea, born Mar. 5, 1911. Martea was adopted by Anne Martha Larsdatter Vikse.
h. Hansine, born July 2, 1868, died July 8, 1868.

The deed for the farm to Gaut Mathias from the father–in–law indicates a tax liability of sk.m. 3 ort 17 sk. and was valued at 166–3–8 Spd. It is dated Sept. 26, 1855, and contains 1/3 of the old age contract to the in–laws. See Farm no 1.

In 1865 the farm consisted of 24 mål of fields and meadows and is assessed at 170 Spd. There are additional pastures for 37, peat for 15 and fishing rights for another 13 Spd. The entire estate is assessed at 261 Spd. Annual yield is 12 barrels of oats, 2 barrels of barley and 12 barrels of potatoes.

The livestock consisted of 1 horse, 2 cows, 12 sheep and 1 pig.

Gaut Mathias had to abandon the farm in 1876 and the family settled on farm no. 4, Austrheim, in the house that Ole Andreas Olsen built.

2. **Ole Johannes Johannesen.** 1876 – 1891. See tenant farmer no. 29, Nordvik.

The deed from auction sale to Ole Johannes on this farm for 351 Spd is dated Apr. 24, 1876. Ole Johannes was a full–time marine pilot. They lived at "Varen" on farm no. 17, Nordvik. After he bought the farm here he moved the main dwelling from Nordvik and set it up at Klovning. The house, 11.6 x 5.2m, built with logs, clad with boards, covered with tiled roof and with basement, was in 1878 assessed at 1420 kr.

3. **Johannes Johannesen**. 1892 – 1939

Born Sept. 29, 1865, died Jan. 2, 1939, son of previous farmer.

Married Apr. 22, 1894 to **Thala Sofie Mikalsdatter,** born Dec. 27, 1867, died Oct. 13, 1954, daughter of Thala Sofie and Sven Mikael Larsen, farmer no. 4 – 5 f, Klovning, and widow of Martin Johannesen, Klovning.

Children:

a. Jenny Martine, born Sept. 17, 1894, died Dec. 4, 1935 at the hospital Betonia in Bergen.
b. Anna Martha, born May 26, 1897, married in 1920 to Isak Solheim, tenant farmer no. 24, Klovning.

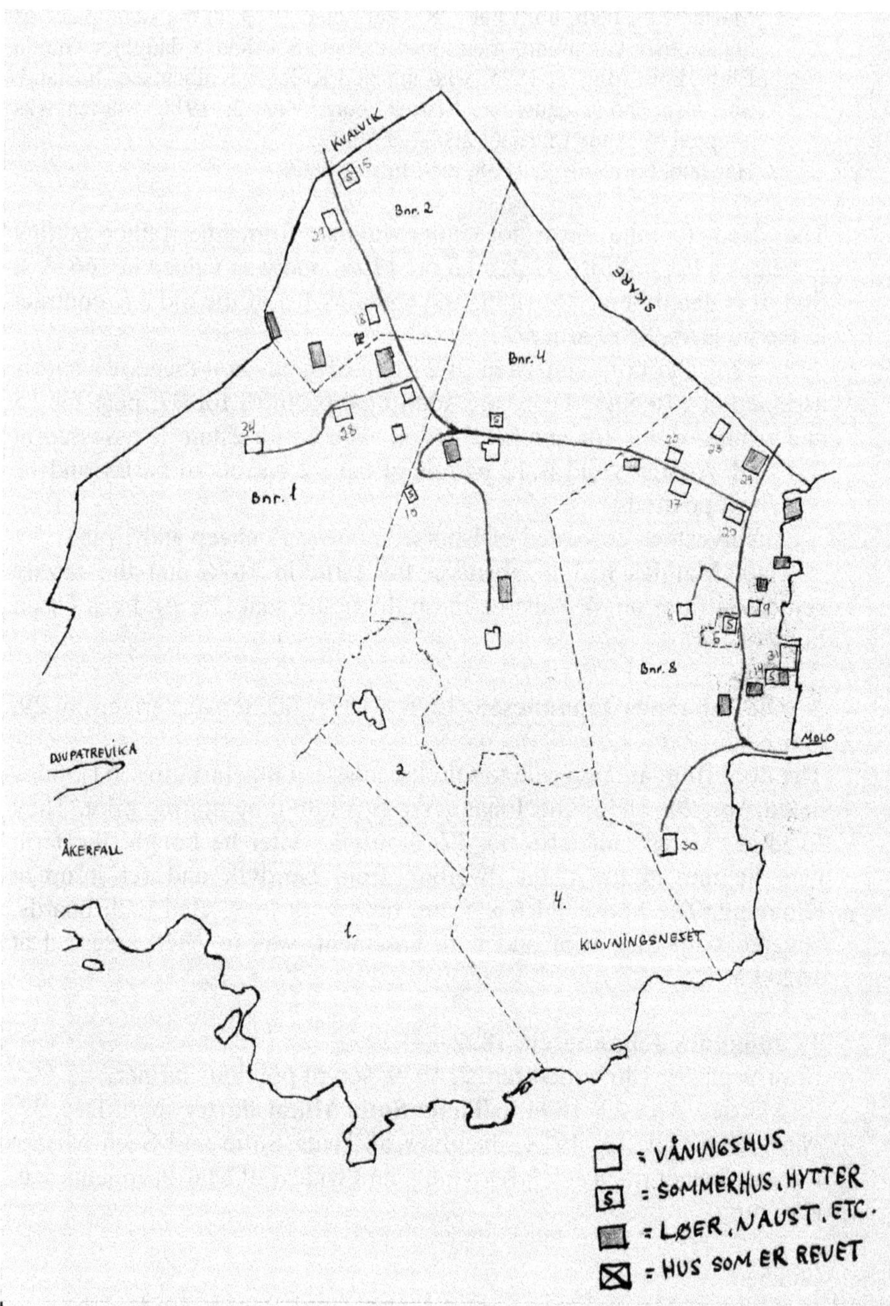

Map of Klovning. Key: 1 – Main dwelling 2 – Vacation homes, cabins 3 – Hay and misc. storage sheds. 4 –Houses that have been torn down. ("Bnr." translates as farm or farmer.)

Johannes Johanesen (1865 – 1939) and Thala Sofie Mikalsdatter Klovning (1867 – 1954). Photos from 1920.

c. *Thala* Sigfryda Marie, born Jan. 19, 1900, unmarried. She was a postal worker for many years at Utsira from 1919 to 1956; she also had a farm here.
d. *Laura Lovise,* born Apr. 8, 1902, married in 1931 to Valnum Klovning, tenant farmer no. 36, Hovland.
e. *Johannes* Trygve, born Jun 10, 1904, next farmer.
f. Åsa Oline, born Mar. 26, 1907, married in 1930 to Mathias Kvalvik, farmer no 4 – 2, Kvalvik.
g. Benny Amanda, born Aug. 26, 1910. twin., died Oct. 9, 1910.
h. Selma Otilia, born Aug. 26, 1910, twin., died Oct. 1, 1910.

The deed to Johannes from the other heirs to this farm, with a tax liability of sk.m. 1.31, in the amount of 1550 kroner is dated Aug. 28, 1906.

The main dwelling was separated from the farm in 1939 and was designated farm no. 18, Fredheim, and was eventually taken over by the daughter Thala. The post office was located here for many years.

4. **Johannes Klovning.** 1939 – 1960.
Born June 10, 1904, died June 27, 1954, son of previous farmer.

Married July 3, 1926 to **Marie Helgesen,** born Aug. 25, 1904, died Apr. 3, 1988, daughter of Gina and Johan Kristian Helgesen, tenant farmer no. 43 b, Nordvik.

Children:

a. *Judith* Marie, born Nov. 1, 1930, married in 1951 to Karsten Kvalvik, tenant farmer no. 72, Nordvik.
b. *Gerd* Kristense, born Dec. 2, 1932, married in 1956 to Johan George Johansen, farmer no. 18 – 10, Nordvik.
c. *Sigrunn* Johanna, born Aug. 14, 1934, married in 1954 to Alf Hansen, tenant farmer 40, Hovland.
d. Johannes, born Oct. 10, 1935, next farmer.
e. Arthur, born May 11, 1943, married in 1963 to Lilly Synnøve Solsvik, was separated and lives in Åkrehamn.

Johannes took over the Utsira ferry route in 1930 with the M/K "Telavaag." He bought a new boat in 1932, the "Sirafjord," which he sailed with until he died, except in the period 1940 – 47.

They built a new main dwelling here in 1933, farm no. 15, Solbakken, which was taken over in 1971 by Arthur Klovning.

There was a cow, a calf and 9 sheep on the farm in 1956.

5. **Johannes Klovning.** 1960 – 1978.
Born Oct. 10, 1935, died Feb. 10, 1995, son of previous farmer.

Married Aug. 13, 1960 to **Eldbjorg Hansen,** born Feb. 7, 1937, daughter of Karoline and Mathias Hansen, farm no. 4 – 13 b, Austrheim.

Children:

a. Irene, born June 19, 1961, married in 1979 to Toralf Austrheim, tenant farmer no. 35, Klovning.
b. Wenche, born Feb. 8, 1963, married in 1987 to Svein Inge Austrheim, lives on Hest, Førdesfjorden.
c. Johannes, born Oct. 17, 1966.
d. Lillian, born Sept. 12, 1968, married to Helge Naadland, lives in Stavanger.

They built a new main dwelling, farm no. 29, Solheim, in 1963.

Johannes took over the estate here in 1970. He also took over the ferry service to Utsira when his father died. He bought a new boat in 1958 that was also named "Sirafjord" and put in the same service. This boat was exchanged in 1968 with another new boat and got the same name. With this boat he ran the Utsira route until 1979, when Utsira Municipality took over the service with a new boat. The family moved to Haugesund in 1978.

The farm has since been utilized as an additional farm. It was taken over in 1992 by Irene Klovning Austrheim.

Farm no. 4. From farm no. 1 in 1778.

1. **Anders Johnsen.** 1778 – 1788

Born in 1751, buried on Mar. 25, 1786, son of Berta Andersdatter and John Jørgensen, farmer no. 1 – 6 a, Klovning.

Married July 5, 1778 to **Gunnhild Mortensdatter,** baptized Sept. 15, 1754, buried July 11, 1790, daughter of Synnøve Mikkelsdatter and Morten Bårdsen, Bergstøl in Skåre.

Children:

a. Berta, baptized Apr. 1, 1779, buried Aug. 30,1804.
b. Synnøve, baptized Dec. 28, 1780.
c. Jørgen, baptized Feb. 4, 1783, married in 1817 to Berta Ellingsdatter Austrheim. They lived on Storasund, Torvestad.

Lease contract to Anders for 1 v. dried fish (including 1/2 v. in "Spanderøde") is issued by A. W. Bredahl on Mar. 4, 1778. It is noted here:

> . . . Concerning the houses, the young ones shall build themselves a sufficient house to live in, but barn and laundry house should be divided in two equal parts which both will sufficiently maintain.

There was an estate settlement after Anders in 1786. The estate's cash holdings were 38–3–4 rdl., but beyond that there was not much left for the heirs after debt and expenses of 33–1–1 rdl. were paid. Among misc. items left the following are mentioned:

> 1 brown mare 3–2–0, 2 cows and 2 calves 11–1–0., 2 barrels of oats 3–0–0, 1 old cattle trough, capacity 2 bushels 1–2–0, 1 old four–oar boat 2–0–0, 12 lobster pots 1–0–0, 4 spring herring fishing nets 2–3–20 and silverware for 4–1–0.

Gunnhild was married a 2nd time in 1789 to Knut Johannesen (see below).

Travel communications on Utsira into a new era:
Some information on recent developments in the scheduled travel between Haugesund and the outer–most island in Norway.

As reported a few days ago a new boat was commissioned for the route Haugesund – Utsira. The new boat is called "Sirafjord" and is owned and operated by Captain Klovning. One of our associates was today on board the vessel and got a closer look. We met the master who informs us that the vessel (a classic fishing boat design with deck and pilothouse) was built in Sagvaag by Ottesen's Shipbuilding and is a 47 ton Brutto. The engine is a 60 HP Rubberstad engine. Both the hull and the engine are of rugged design and are approved and recommended by people in the industry and fishermen. The interior is comfortable and up to date. The crew quarters are aft and are well–suited also for passenger accommodations in case they may be required for overcrowded conditions. Further forward is a comfortable smoking saloon with leather upholstered furniture where the hours will pass quickly on the voyage out to the islands. All the way up forward is the largest saloon with room for around 80 passengers. The pleasantly furnished passenger accommodations will no doubt satisfy the most critical travelers. There is also plenty of deck space for passengers who prefer to walk around.

There is now substantial traffic on the route to Utsira. The ferry often carries close to 70 passengers, and in addition there is considerable cargo. The vessel also calls on Foyna and Rovaer, and then the trip takes 3 hours. The vessel can make 9 knots and the trip direct to Utsira is 1 ½ hrs. "Sirafjord" is a stable and safe boat, which is necessary on this often stormy route. The previous vessel was too small even though it was a good seagoing boat. During our visit onboard, we talked to an engineer who had worked on this route for 10 years and also sailed as master may times. He told us about the various vessels that have served this route over the years. The first master was Knut Eriksen who carried the mail with his boat built in Lista. In those years the mail service was sporadic for the Sira'ites. The sailings were often cancelled due to the weather or took several days out, or sometimes had to turn back.

The next vessel on the route was "Karmøy" and then came "Glygg", "Sagvaag", "Haugesund" and "Utsira," which eventually was not big enough and also lacked sufficient passenger accommodations for the number of passengers who traveled the route. The next vessels were "Herla", "Heim", "Televaag" and now finally "Sirafjord," which presents a suitable solution for this treacherous and difficult route. In 1918 when "Sagvaag" was decommissioned, explains Solheim, they often encountered loose mines and often had to sail south to Aakrahavn and from there west in order to avoid mined areas. There were many tough trips over the years between Haugesund and the outermost island, but there were never any accidents of any significance. Now when "Sirafjord" is serving this route, the voyage should be pure pleasure. There may be many people in Haugesund who have never been to Utsira, which is a beautiful and interesting island way out there in the ocean, and they may now have that opportunity to get there safely and comfortably. This new connection to the mainland should create conditions for renewed interest in the islands out west and tie them closer to our town.
– 4 Aug. 1931, *Haugesunds Avis.*

An old photo of Sørevågen dated July 1869. We can see that the breakwater is not finished. Also note all the sea sheds in the Tuevågen Bay. Photo: Riksantikvaren (State Historical Society).

2. **Knut Johannesen.** 1789 – 1812

Born 1768, died May 7, 1812, son of Tyrid Gautsdatter and Johannes Askildsen, Dale, Torvestad.

Married in 1st marriage on July 19, 1789 to **Gunnhild Mortensdatter,** widow of previous farmer.

Married in 2nd marriage on June 13, 1791 to **Ingeborg Tollefsdatter,** baptized July 16, 1758, died Feb. 5, 1818, daughter of Anna Olsdatter and Tollef Johannesen, Storesund, Torvestad.

Children in 2nd marriage:

a. Gundela, baptized July 7, 1793, buried Apr. 6, 1794.
b. Johannes, baptized Mar. 20, 1796, next farmer.
c. Ingeborg Oline, baptized Feb. 5, 1798, buried Oct. 27, 1799.

Ingeborg's daughter with Job Fredriksen, Lillesund:

d. Jobiane, baptized Jan. 27, 1788, married in 1810 to Rasmus Tollefsen, farm no. 7 – 7, Hovland.

Lease contract to Knut in the amount of 1 v. dried fish is issued by Borre Rosenkilde on Jan. 27, 1789.

In 1802 he sowed 1–1/2 barrels of grain and harvested 8 barrels. The livestock consisted of 1 horse, 2 cows, 1 calf, and 2 sheep. The farm was then assessed at 70 riksdalers.

In the settlement after Knut in 1813, the estate was worth 67 rdl. 72 sk. Left to be divided between Ingeborg and Johannes is 41 rdl. 4 sk. Among misc. items are the following:

> 1 brown mare 10–0–0, 2 cows ("Snorej"and "Plomrej") and a calf 27–2–12, 3 barrels of oats 8–0–0, 1 iron stove 2–0–0, 1 old four–oar boat with sail 2–0–0, 1/3 share in herring boat without sail 3–1–16, 3 large herring fishing nets 4–1–16 and 2 silver spoons 1–0–0.

3. **Johannes Knutsen**. 1812 – 1864
Baptized Mar. 20, 1796, died Sept. 8, 1864, son of previous farmer.

Married in 1st marriage Jan. 13, 1814 to **Guro Anbjornsdatter,** baptized Nov. 9, 1772, died Dec. 24, 1832, daughter of Anna Johannesdatter and Anbjorn Rasmussen, tenant farmer no. 7 – 5 i, Hovland.

Married in 2nd marriage Mar. 23, 1834 to **Berta Kristine Johannesdatter,** baptized July 23, 1808, died Apr. 11, 1887, daughter of Anna Karine Ådnesdatter and Johannes Ambjornsen, tenant farmer no. 13 g, Nordvik.

Children in 1st. marriage:

a. Knut, baptized Feb. 15, 1814, married in 1840 to Anne Lisbet Aliasdatter, Vikshåland. They farmed this place in the years 1842 – 1852. After that they lived on Feoy.

Children in 2nd. marriage:

b. Gurine, born Apr. 27, 1834, married in 1857 to Jakob Kristiansen, tenant farmer no. 11, Klovning.
c. Ingeborg Katrine (Karine), born July 6, 1835, tenant farmer no. 13, Klovning.
d. Berthe Kristine, born Mar. 15, 1838, married in 1872 to Bernt Tønnesen, tenant farmer no. 27, Hovland.
e. *Gunhilde* Oline Jorgine, born Nov. 5, 1840, married in 1863 to widower Kristoffer Danielsen, tenant farmer no. 9, Klovning.
f. Tyri *Hansine*, born Nov. 10, 1842, married in 1872 to Johannes Danielsen, Liknes in Åkra, brother of Kristoffer (see above).
g. Johannes, born Oct. 18, 1847, married in 1878 to Thomasine Rasmusdatter, tenant farm no. 17, Skare.

Lease contract on this farm is in the amount of 1 v. dried fish – *while underlying "Spanderoe" is left vacant* – from Hans B. Foreman dated Oct. 30, 1812 and an old age contract with Ingeborg as follows:

> One cow to be fed and milked daily, 3 barrels of oats to be provided yearly and also 1/2 barrel of pure grain. For sowing, 1/8 barrel of potatoes to be planted and harvested and 12 sheep also to be fed and cared for.

In 1822 the houses on the farm were described as follows:

> One cabin with half a kitchen under one roof together with the other tenants' house covered with peat. One barn with sod roof of which half is built with logs, 1 horse stable with sod roof, 1 brick laundry house. The houses are in fairly good condition.

The farm was in 1823 assessed at 125 Spd.

4. **Lars Olsen.** 1843 – 1864
Born in 1810, died Aug. 19, 1884, son of Astrid Helgesdatter and Ola Olsen, Tjernagel, Eikeland in Moster, lived on Hagland in Skåre.

Married June 29, 1835 to **Lisbeth Svendsdatter,** baptized May 11, 1809, died Nov. 21, 1889, daughter of Elisabeth Eliasdatter and Svend Eliassen, farmer no. 1 – 7 c, Skare.

Children:

a. Svend Michael, born Jan. 30, 1837, next farmer.
b. Ole Johan, born Mar. 11, 1841, married in 1869 to Inger Oline Larsdatter, lived on Vikshåland, Torvestad.
c. Gunela Aseline, born June 8, 1846, married in 1867 to Lars Henrik Hausken, Torvestad.

The deed to Lars on this farm with a tax liability of 1/2 v. dried fish, issued by J. Dahm in the amount of 300 Spd. is dated Dec. 24, 1838. In the deed it is mentioned that Johannes Knutsen was first offered a chance to buy this farm, but refused the offer.

Lars, who then was a tenant farmer at Skare, made an agreement in December 1842 with Johannes regarding access to half the farm. It is reasonable then to think that Lars at that time planned and built a new compound with the buildings and courtyard as it stands today.

5. **Svend Mikael Larsen.** 1864 – 1908
Born Jan. 30, 1837, died Feb. 14, 1914, son of previous farmer.

Married May 13, 1860 to **Thala Sophie Pedersdatter,** born July 25, 1834, died June 1, 1911, daughter of Anna Olsdatter and Peder Torbjornsen, Vikshåland, Torvestad.

Children:

a. Anna Sophie, born Sept. 25, 1860, died Jan. 18, 1874.

The family of Svend Mikael Larsen around 1903. Back row from left: Svend born 1874, Thala born 1867, Lars born 1866, Sofie born 1880, Peder born 1872 and Astrid born 1870. In front from the left: Lovise born 1862, Svend Mikael (1837 – 1914), Thala Sofie (1834–1911) and Synnøve born 1864.

b. Elida *Lovise*, born Jan. 19, 1862, married in 1883 to widower Hans Mathias Helgesen, farmer no. 15 – 3, Nordvik.
c. Lars Johannes, born Apr. 18, 1863, died Aug. 25, 1863.
d. Synnøve, born Apr. 22, 1864, married in 1890 to Severin Tollefsen, farmer no. 2 – 6, Austrheim.
e. *Lars* Martin, born Mar. 30, 1866, next farmer.
f. Thala Sophie, born Dec. 27, 1867, married in 1st marriage in 1891 to Martin Mikal Johannesen, tenant farmer no. 34, Klovning. Married in 2nd marriage in 1894 to Johannes Johannesen, farmer no. 2 – 3, Klovning.
g. *Astrid* Oline, born Jan. 20, 1870, married in 1891 to Elling Gudmundsen, farmer no. 3 – 7, Austrheim.
h. *Peder* Severin, born June 24, 1872, married in 1900 to Lisa Johannesdatter, tenant farmer no. 44, Nordvik.
i. *Svend* Edius, born Nov. 13, 1874, married in 1905 to Gurine Mathiasdatter, farm no. 8 – l, Klovning.
j. Ole, born Feb. 26, 1877, died Feb. 28, 1877.

k. Anna *Sofie*, born Mar. 7, 1880, married in 1905 to Johan M. Bendiksen, tenant farmer no. 23, Skare.

The deed to Mikal on this farm, with a tax liability of 2–1–15 sk.dl., from the father in the amount of 400 Spd. plus old age pension contract is dated Sept. 30, 1864. The old age pension contract is assessed at 100 Spd. for 5 years:

> 4 barrels of oats at 4 v., full use of the field called "Øvre Daleflaekket," including part of another field for growing potatoes either on the "Stor–åkeren" (main field) or "Dale–åkeren" (Dale field), and feed for 1–1/2 cows and 6 sheep.

He also was required to assist Berte Johannesdatter (farmer no. 3 here) with a contract consisting of:

> 2 barrels of oats, 1–1/2 potter with fresh milk in the period February 1st – November 1st, 1 cord of birch wood, use of the field "Sjaaflaekket," including *the use of the house which is still standing on the farm that she left as long as she does not sublease to married persons without my approval.*

In 1865 the farm consisted of 56 mål fields and meadows assessed at 462 Spd. There were meadows for 120, peat for 60 and fishing rights income for 95 Spd. Annual yield was reportedly 38 barrels of oats, 6 barrels of barley and 30 barrels of potatoes. The entire farm was assessed to 875 Spd.

The livestock consisted of 1 horse, 6 cows, 19 sheep and 1 pig.

The main dwelling here is 11.6 x 7.2 m., logged, with basement, lined with boards on the south and east side, covered with tiled roof and assessed at 570 Spd. The barn 17.9 x 6.3 m. is assessed at 100 Spd.

When in 1869 a telegraph switchboard was built on Utsira, Mikael rented out part of the main dwelling to the Telegraph Communication Authority. Two rooms downstairs, and 2 smaller rooms on the upper floors in the northern part of the house were made available to the Authority. The room toward the west became the general reception area with door and porch and an entrance with steps was constructed on the north side. The rent was established at 30 Spd. per year. The contract was dated Apr. 26, 1869.

Svend Mikael ran the telephone services from 1885 to 1910 and also the postal services from 1887 until his son took over in 1914.

In 1908 he let his son Lars take over two–thirds of the farm and Svend one–third, farm no. 8.

6. **Lars M. Klovning.** 1908 – 1930

Born Mar. 30, 1866, died May 1, 1940, son of previous farmer.

Married May 14, 1893 to **Mathilde Johansdatter,** born June 10, 1871, died Mar. 3, 1938, daughter of Karoline and Johan Helgesen, farmer no. 18 – 5 d, Nordvik.

Children:

a. *Hanna* Sofie, born Aug. 15, 1894, unmarried.
b. Minda *Lovise*. born Nov. 5, 1896, married in 1916 to Håkon Bådsvik, Skjoldastrumen.
c. Mikal Trygve. born Oct. 29, 1900, next farmer.
d. *Johan* Kristian. born June 10, 1903, married to Sølvi Steinsvik, (separated). He used the name Johan Teyler van der Hulst.
e. *Lars* Martin, born May 15, 1905, married to Erna from Horten, tenant farmer no. 16, Klovning.
f. Thomas, born Aug. 28, 1907. married to Elly, emigrated to New Bedford, (Mass.), USA.

The deed to Lars on this farm with tax liability of 2.87 sk.m. from the father in the amount of 4300 kroner plus old age contract valued at 610 kr. is dated Dec. 8, 1908.

Lars managed the postal services from 1914 until 1919.

7. **Mikal Klovning.** 1930 – 1978

Born Oct. 29, 1900, died Dec. 28, 1983, son of previous farmer.

Married Aug. 2, 1919 to **Martha Sørhus,** born Dec. 27, 1895, died Aug. 20, 1963, daughter of Anne Martha Laurine and Tobias Sørhus, tenant farmer no. 23 f, Klovning.

Children:

a. Mathilde, born Aug. 25, 1919, married in 1944 to Sverre Mortensen, Stavanger.
b. Laurine, born Jan. 19, 1921, married in 1946 to Lars Olafsen Bådsvik, Kolstø in Avaldsnes.
c. Lars Martin, born July 28, 1922, was a seaman and perished during the war with the S/S "Pollyanna," April 1st, 1941. He also had a farm here.
d. Tordis, born June 25, 1924, married in 1945 to Hans Klovning, tenant farmer no. 44, Skare.
e. *Martin* Mikal, born Mar. 17, 1926, died June 10, 1934, drowned.[58]
f. Else, born Jan. 26, 1929, married to Ansgar Finnesand, lives in Stavanger.

---

[58] *Haugesunds Avis* newspaper, June 11, 1934 (Note 26).

Mikal L. Klovning (1900 – 1983) around 1978.

g. Trygve *Martin*, born Mar. 30, 1934, married to Anne Heye, lived in Granvin.
h. *Bjarne* Leidulf, born July 26, 1935, married to Solveig Sverinsen, Moksheim.
i. *Reidar* Arnstein, born Nov. 19, 1937, next farmer.
j. Lars *Magne,* born Sept. 29, 1941, married to Eli Sjursen, lives in Porsgrunn.

The deed to Mikal from the parents on farm no. 4 and 7 is dated May 30, 1930.

The livestock in 1956 consisted of 3 cows, 2 calves, 1 horse and 7 sheep.

8. **Reidar Klovning.** 1981 –
Born Nov. 19, 1937, son of previous farmer.

Married in 1963 to **Johanne Birkeland,** born May 30, 1940 in Abelvaer, Naeroy county, North Trondelag.

Children:

a. Gerd Astrid, born June 13, 1958, married to Bjørn Sivertsen, lives in Hundvåg, Stavanger.

b. Trond, born Nov. 19, 1959, married to Inger Nilsen, divorced, lives on Utsira. Trond also has a farm here.
c. Reid Ståle, born Jan. 23, 1966, married in 1995 to Eldfrid Torunn Nordvik.

The family moved from Stavanger to Utsira in 1980. They built a new barn in 1983 and a new main dwelling in 1985. Reidar works in the offshore industry. He was district chairman on Utsira from 1992.

Farm no. 8. From Farm no. 4 in 1908

1. **Svend Klovning.** 1908 – 1948.
Born Nov. 13, 1874, died Sept. 18, 1961, son of Thala Sophie and Svend Mikael Larsen, farm no. 4 – 5 i, Klovning.

Married July 14, 1905 to **Gurine Mathiasdatter,** born Apr. 22, 1882, died July 4, 1969, daughter of Gunhilde and Mathias Jobsen, farm no. 10–2–d, Hovland.

Children:
a. Mikael *Trygve*, born May 9, 1906, next farmer.
b. *Mathias* George, born June 28, 1908, married to Astrid Tønnesen, Farsund.
c. *Svend* Edvind Gerhard, born June 1, 1910, married in 1935 to Åsa Oline Ellingsen, tenant farm no. 27, Klovning.
d. *Agnes* Sofie, born July 18, 1912, tenant farmer no. 30, Klovning.
e. *Lindy* Lovise, born Feb. 13, 1915, married in 1952 to John Hansen, tenant farmer no. 17, Klovning.
f. Gustav *Sverre*, born Sept. 20, 1917, tenant farmer no. 29, Klovning.
g. *John* Karsten, born Mar. 14, 1920, married in 1948 to Laurine Ellingsen, tenant farmer no. 28, Klovning.
h. Erling *Sigurd*, born Jan. 5, 1924, married to Randi Birkdal, Helle in Høgsfjord, lives in Sandnes.

The deed to Svend on one–third of the father's farm, with a tax liability of 44 sk.m., from his father in the amount of 800 kroner, plus old age contract, is dated Nov. 4, 1908.

Svend built a new main dwelling here in 1906. Besides the fishing activities, he together with his brother Peder traded in fish commodities. In 1936 he opened a general store in his house in Sørevågen. His son Sverre took over this store in 1948.

The Svend Klovning family in 1946. In the back row from left: Mathias, Svend, Sigurd, John, Sverre and Trygve. In front from left: Lindy, Gurine, Svend and Agnes.

2. **Trygve Klovning.** 1948 –

Born May 9, 1906, son of previous farmer.

Married Apr. 22, 1937 to **Sigrun Vestre,** born Apr. 10, 1910, died Nov. 16, 1980, daughter of Laura and Daniel Vestre, tenant farmer no. 48 a, Nordvik.

Children:

a. *Odd* Trygve, born Feb. 14, 1939, died Mar. 20, 1993, married to Ingunn Ludvigsen, moved to Haugesund. He was a ship owner.
b. Svein Gunnar, born May 9, 1940, died Oct. 7, 1982, married to Ruth Tove Hansen from Denmark, moved to Haugesund. He ran a shipping company with his brother.
c. *Laila* Dagmar, born Apr. 23, 1947.

Trygve was a seaman. He started a shipping company after the war. The first ship he owned he bought from England and was called M/S "United Boys." They built a new main dwelling on farm no. 20, Sentrum, in 1941.

This estate was taken over by Odd Trygve Klovning in 1974.

Tenant farmers

1. **Peder Olsen.** 1664
He is mentioned in the church census in 1664 under misc. persons and tenants.

2. **Abraham Olsen.** 1695 – 1705
Born in 1667 in Amsterdam, Holland.

Known Children:

a. Anna, born in 1695, buried July 2, 1767. In 1758 she is mentioned as a servant at the Johannes Ellingsen home, Kvalvik.
b. Ole, born in 1703, married to Anna Svendsdatter, tenant farm no. 11, Nordvik.
c. Rasmus, born in 1708, married to widow Karen Andresdatter, farm no. 1 – 5, Nordvik.
d. Abraham, born in 1712, he is mentioned in the military records in 1734.

We do not know how Abraham happened to come to Utsira, or if he actually is the brother of Petter Olsen, tenant farmer no. 8, Skare. According to Julie Ivers' (farm no. 4 – 2 e, Nordvik) research in the 1920s on the so–called "Dutch Inheritance," Abraham and Petter were supposed to have come from the Teyler family in Holland. According the Teyler family tree (developed by W.P.J. Overmeyer in 1901) it appears that there is a mistake, even though there may be several people named Abraham and Petter.

Abraham appears for the first time in the county records in 1698. He is then a tenant and owes some fees to the cloister.

Around 1706 the family moves to the rental property called "Backen," part of the Kvalvik farm. They appear to have exchanged places with the next tenant farmer.

3. **Gjertrud Kristoffersdatter,** 1706 –
Widow of Truls Hansen, see tenant farmer no. 8, Kvalvik.

She is mentioned as having a son and two stepsons in the census of 1706, but is not listed in the so–called "shoe tax" records in 1711.

4. **Andres Knutsen.** 1711 – 1730
Born in 1676, son of Knut Sjursen, farm no. 7 – 1 b, Hovland.

In 1711 he pays the "shoe tax" for himself, wife and 1 child:

a. Knut, born in 1711, next tenant farmer.

Andres is mentioned in the court records in 1727, when he together with Jon Hovland and Johannes Kvalvik found some items from a shipwreck.

5. **Knut Andersen.** 1735

Born 1711, son of previous tenant farmer.

In 1735 Knut was cited in court for having cohabited too early with his wife. He was possibly married to **Martha Hansdatter Hovland,** as he moved there. See tenant farmer no. 14, Hovland.

Naesset, tenant farm.

6. **Jon Rasmussen Klop**. 1759 – 1789.

Born 1732, buried Apr. 1, 1775, of unknown origin.

Married Apr. 8, 1759 to **Bertha Jørgensdatter,** born 1731, buried July 19, 1789, daughter of Malene and Jørgen Jonsen, farm no. 1 – 5 d, Klovning.

Children:

a. Malene, baptized Aug. 12, 1759, buried June 24, 1781.
b. Martha, baptized June 20, 1762, died Mar. 2, 1828. She had one son, Jon, baptized July 1, 1787 (see section 8 below) with Johannes Ambjornsen.
c. Knut, baptized Dec. 8, 1764, buried Nov. 23, 1771.

There was an estate settlement after Jon in 1775. He left items worth 39–1–20 rdl. Debt and expenses amounted to 19–2–12 rdl. The following miscellaneous items left are mentioned:

> 1 four–oar boat with sail 1–2–16, 1 old fishing boat with sail and equipment 1–2–0, 2 spring herring fishing nets 2–0–0, 1 *old cabin with kitchen and a small stable for farm animals* 8–0–0, 1 small cattle trough 2–0–0, one small shed 2–2–0, 1 hornless cow with red spot on side 4–0–0, 1 black heifer with horns 1–2–0, and 1 tiled heating stove 7–7–0.

Bertha was married a second time to Johannes Kristoffersen (See below.).

7. **Johannes Kristoffersen.** 1777 – 1807

Photo from 1869. Work on the breakwater project at full speed. Beiningen in the background. Photo provided by Historical Society.

Born 1748, buried Apr. 4, 1807, son of Elisabeth and Kristoffer Knutsen, tenant farmer no. 12 b, Nordvik.

Married Sept. 5, 1777 to **Bertha Jørgensdatter,** widow of previous farmer.

No children.

During their wedding, a brawl broke out among some of the guests. Kristen Monsen Hovland came out worst, and cited two of the guests in court. See farm no. 4 – 6, Hovland.

Johannes had to work nine days out of the year for each of the tenants on Klovning and in addition pay 32 sk. per year to the owner.

8. **Jon Johannesen.** 1819 – 1882

Baptized July 1, 1787, died Oct. 16, 1860. He was the son, outside marriage, of Martha Jonsdatter Klovning and Johannes Ambjornsen. Tuo later became Nordvik.

Married Apr. 25, 1818 to **Anne Andersdatter,** baptized July 8, 1792, died June 16, 1882, daughter of Martha Paulsdatter, and Anders Knutsen, tenant farmer no. 9 i, Austrheim, and later farm no. 1 – 8, Hovland.

Jon's son with Berthe Kristensdatter Nordvik.

a. Kristen, baptized May 30, 1813, tenant farmer no. 21, Kvalvik.

Children:

b. Berte Malene, born May 20, 1818, married in 1857 to widower Ole Karlsen, farm no. 3 – 1, Kvalvik.
c. Marta, born Sept. 14, 1819, died Mar. 30, 1832.
d. Anna, born May 24, 1821, married in 1843 to Svend Svendsen, Torvestad. They lived on Osnes, and later Hasseloy.
e. Andreas, born Mar. 15, 1824, died Dec. 5, 1824.
f. Johannes, born Sept. 28, 1825, married in 1850 to the widow Marthe Karine Larsdatter, farm no. 13 – 5, Nordvik, and farm no. 6 – 7, Austrheim.
g. Anne Marte, born Feb. 18, 1828, died Apr. 17, 1831.
h. Rasmus, born June 9, 1832, died Nov. 14, 1901, "Rasmussen Neset" was crippled and lived with his mother, went on relief.

The lease to Jon from Hans B. Forman on this farm is dated Nov. 18, 1819 and contains this clause:

> . . . is responsible to the landlord and agrees to pay rent and what is required to the church including half of normal work when required to each tenant farmer at Klovning, as is normally required by all cotters (tenant farmers) on Utsira.

The rental place here was in 1823 assessed at 12 Spd. It is listed that it could sustain 1 cow and able to yield 2 to 3 barrels of grain.

In 1865 there was nothing planted and no livestock on this property. Anne had a pension from all the farmers at Klovning.

9. **Kristoffer Danielsen.** 1863 – 1925

Born 1823, died Feb. 4, 1900, son of Kari Olsdatter, and Daniel Kristoffersen, Øvre–Liknes, Åkra.

Married first in 1849 to **Guri Olsdatter,** born 1828, died 1860, daughter of Ingeborg Guri and Ola Sebjornsen, Heggheim in Skudenes.

Married the second time Apr. 12, 1863 to ***Gunhilde*** **Oline Johannesdatter,** born Nov. 5, 1840, died Nov. 5, 1925, daughter of Berta Kristine Johannesdatter and Johannes Knutsen, farm no. 4 – 3 e, Klovning.

Children from first marriage:

a. *Daniel* Johan, born in 1850, died Feb. 12, 1887, was a shoemaker and perished at sea while fishing near Urter.[59]
b. Ola, born 1851, married in 1876 to Ingeborg Mettine Larsdatter, lived at Falnes parsonage, later at Aakra. Ola was a blacksmith, their daughter was Laura who married Valnum Jørgensen Klovning.
c. Kornelius, born 1853, married in 1899 to Johanne Elene Holgersdatter, lived in Vik, Skudenes.
d. Ingeborg Gurine, born 1854, married to Gudmund Didriksen, Hillesland, Skudenes.
e. *Kristian* Sigvald, born 1857, married in 1882 to Ingeborg Teodora Tønnesdatter, lived in Vik, Skudenes.
f. Govert, born and died in 1860.

Children from second marriage:

g. Berthe Gurine, born June 2, 1863, married in 1900 to Jakob Ommundsen, Haugesund, emigrated to USA.
h. Jobiane ("Janna"), born May 4, 1865, married in 1892 to Tore Torsen, Saevlandsvik.
i. Johan Andreas Martin, born July 13, 1867, moved to Åsgårdstrand, where he married Nilsine.
j. Sivert Andreas, born Apr. 2, 1870, emigrated to USA.
k. Kristine Thomine, born Sept. 13, 1872, married Peder S. Pedersen, a sailor from Hansted, Denmark and moved there.
l. Ånen *Severin*, born Sept. 12, 1875, next tenant farmer.
m. Gunhilde Katrine (Kaia), born Oct. 31, 1877, married in 1902 to Elling Mathiassen, Rabben, farm no. 10 – 3, Hovland.
n. Knut, born Apr. 6, 1881, emigrated to USA.
o. Thea Berntine, born Aug. 6, 1885, married in 1906 to Ole Kornelius Johannesen, Saevlandsvik.

The lease to Kristoffer on a house lot, 17 x 12 alen, from Svend Mikael Larsen is dated Sept. 8, 1867. It is noted in the contract that the house is already built. He paid 8 Spd. for this lease and an annual payment of 1 ort and 6 days work, 2 days in each season. He lived with his first wife at Heggheim in Skudenes Harbor. Kristoffer was a carpenter.

10. **Severin Klovning.** 1900 – 1956

Born Sept. 12, 1875, died Mar. 15, 1956, son of previous tenant farmer.

Unmarried.

---

[59] *Haugesunderen* newspaper, Feb. 16, 1887 (Note 27).

10b. **Marie J. Titland,** born October 1886, died July 5, 1980, came from Titland near Bergen. Worked for Severin Klovning for many years from 1927.

11. **Jakob Kristiansen.** 1857 – 1898
Born Mar. 25, 1819. died Jan. 29, 1884, son of Anne Kristine Jakobsdatter and Kristian Kaspersen, Glendrange, Flekkefjord.

Gurine Johannesdatter Klovning (1834–1898)

Married July 5, 1857 to **Gurine Johannesdatter,** born Apr. 27, 1834, died Apr. 20, 1898, daughter of Berta Kristine Johannesdatter and Johannes Knutsen, farm no. 4 – 3 b, Klovning.

Children:

a. Kristian, born Dec. 15, 1857, died Dec. 31, 1861.
b. Johannes, born Mar. 7, 1859, died Oct. 10, 1860.
c. Anna Kristine, born Dec. 25, 1861, died Jan. 28, 1877.
d. Berthe Kristine, born July 15, 1863, unmarried but had a daughter, Jenny Fosmark.
e. Kristian, born Sept. 12, 1865, married in 1900 to Anne Martha Larsdatter Vikse, farm no. 14 – 3, Nordvik.
f. Sara, born July 30, 1867, died Sept. 24, 1887.
g. Johanne, born Feb. 19, 1870, moved to Stavanger.
h. Andreas, born Sept. 10, 1872, married and lived in Stavanger.
i. Gudmund, born Feb. 21, 1878, died Apr. 1, 1878.
j. Jakob Johan, born May 12, 1880, died unmarried in USA.

Jakob got a lease contract to a house lot, 14 x 8 alen, near a place called "Thungar" from John Jørgensen in 1866.

Jakob was a log carpenter, and it is said that he came to Utsira the first time when they built the lighthouses. He is also associated with building the first schoolhouse on Utsira in 1859 – 61.

12. **Kristian Jakobsen.** 1890 – 1902
See Farm no. 14 – 3, Nordvik.

13. **Ingeborg Karine Johannesdatter,** 1859 – 1923.
Born July 6, 1835, died July 25, 1923, daughter of Berta Kristine Johannesdatter and Johannes Knutsen, farm no. 4 – 3 c, Klovning.
Unmarried.

Her son with Thore Mikal Thorsen, Nordvik:

a. Carl Johan, born July 5, 1859, died Dec. 28, 1924, married Elisabeth Jane Planciers in Cardiff (Wales). He was a sailor.

Her son with Hans Larsen Hage, Ferkingstad:

b. Knut, born May 27, 1867, emigrated to Portland, Maine, USA. He was a lighthouse keeper.

Her son with Johannes Johnsen, Austrheim:

c. Johan *Ingvald,* born Sept. 7, 1876, married in 1919 to Hanna Marie Hansen, tenant farmer no. 26, Klovning.

In 1900 she lived with her son Ingvald at the farm of the previous tenant, Kristian Jakobsen, and had her own household there.

Johannes Rasmussen (1841–1924)

14. **Johannes Rasmussen.** 1867 – 1924
Born July 16, 1841, died July 3, 1924, son of Guri Johannesdatter and Rasmus Gudmundsen, farm no. 2 – 5 c, Skare.

Married Jan. 23, 1863 to **Eli Kristine Ommundsdatter,** born Jan. 23, 1843, died May 1, 1902, daughter of Marta Olsdatter, and Ommund Helgesen, Nedre–Haug, Torvestad.

Children:

a. Lars Tobias, born Sept. 29, 1863, married in 1885 to Anne Marthe Laurine Johannesdatter, tenant farmer no. 23, Klovning.
b. Guriane (Janna), born Nov. 9, 1866, next tenant farmer.
c. Olga Mathilde, born Jan. 14, 1872, married in 1892 to Valnum Helgesen, farm no. 18 – 6, Nordvik.

The family lived on farm no. 1 here. In 1900 he is listed as storekeeper and fisherman. The main dwelling was built around 1870 and was named after the next tenant: "Trulsahuset." From here he operated a branch of his main store around 1920.

Truls Jobsen (1864 – 1941) and Janna Johannesdatter (1866 – 1936).

15. **Truls Jobsen.** 1814 – 1941
Born Mar. 20, 1864, died Mar. 22, 1941, son of Karoline Elisabeth Johnsdatter and Job Rasmussen, farm no. 7 – 9 j, Hovland.

Married to **Guriane (Janna) Johannesdatter,** born Nov. 9, 1866, died June 25, 1936, daughter of previous tenant farmer.

No children.

The deed to the farm, farm no. 9, Sorheim, issued to Janna from Thomas G. Klovning for 300 kr. is dated May 25, 1914.

Truls was chief municipal treasurer on Utsira from 1924 – 1933. The farm was taken over by Gurine and Svend Klovning in 1943. John Hansen took over the house in 1952.

16. **Lars Klovning.** 1978 – 1988
Born May 15, 1905, died Mar. 16, 1988, son of Mathilde and Lars Klovning, farm no. 4 – 6 e, Klovning.

Married to **Erna** from Horten.

Children:

a. Hanne, born Apr. 17, 1948.

Lars was a first mate and lived on Utsira after he retired. He took over farm no. 9 from John Hansen.

17. **John Hansen.** 1952 –
Born June 24, 1910, died July 3, 1994, son of Elisabeth and Severin Hansen, farm no. 4 – 12 b, Austrheim.

Married Sept. 27, 1952 to **Lindy Klovning,** born Feb. 13, 1915, daughter of Gurine and Svend Klovning, farm no. 8 – 1 e, Klovning.

No children.

John took over farm no. 9, Sørheim, in 1952. Lindy and John built a new main dwelling, farm no. 22, Urter, in 1968.

Lindy and John operated the central phone service on Utsira from 1964 until the phone service was automated in 1979.

18. **Nils Thomassen.** 1867 – 1874
Born 1837, son of Anna Johanna Tønnesdatter and Thomas Abrahamsen, Østhus in Åkra.

Married first on Apr. 2, 1865 to **Anne Serine Olsdatter,** born Jun. 8, 1839, died Feb. 26, 1874, daughter of Gurine Danielsdatter and Ole Karlsen, farm no. 3 – 1 b, Kvalvik.

Married the second time to **Berthe Kristine Sjursdatter,** born Mar. 22, 1835, daughter of Gurine Danielsdatter and Sjur Tollefsen, tenant farmer no. 30 a, Austrheim.

Children from first marriage:

a. Thomas, born July 21, 1865, died July 25, 1865.
b. Thomas, born Jan. 16, 1867, died Jan. 25, 1867.
c. Berthe Gurine, born Feb. 18, 1868.
d. *Thomas* Cornelius, born Mar. 8, 1872, twin, was a ship master, married to Antonette from Ålesund. Lived in Haugesund.
e. Ole Michal, born Mar. 8, 1872, twin, lived in Haugesund in 1900 as first mate on a ship, married Ellen Vilhelmine Vilhelmsen in Egersund in 1903.

The lease contract to Nils and his wife on a lot is dated Aug. 25, 1867 from Svend Mikael Larsen. On this contract there is a note that the house was already built, fees and other conditions as mentioned under Kristoffer Danielsen.

Nils was a builder and carpenter and was known as "Nils Snikker" (Nils the carpenter). The family moved to Hasseloy, Haugesund.

19. **Gudmund J. Rasmussen.** 1867 – 1874
See tenant farmer no. 11, Austrheim.

The lease to Gudmund and his wife on a lot, 16 x 14 alen, is dated Aug. 26, 1867 and is issued by Gaut Mathias Larsen. The lot was on the beach near "Naessepladset." Gudmund paid 8 Spd. for this and 3 days work per year. The house, 7.8 x 6.6 meters, framed, with basement, and clad with boards on 3 sides and covered with a tiled roof, was in 1869 assessed at 180 Spd.

The family lived on Austrheim before they leased here on Klovning. In 1875 they lived on farm no. 1, Kvalvik, and from 1881 on Skare. Gudmund Jørgensen Klovning took over the house here on Klovning.

20. **Jørgen Jørgensen.** 1870 – 1918
Born Feb. 22, 1835, died Apr. 20, 1918, son of Valborg Gudmundsdatter and Jørgen Johnsen, farm no. 1 – 8 e, Klovning.

Married Oct. 15, 1871 to **Berte Gurine Rasmusdatter,** born Sept. 10, 1849, died Sept. 3, 1878, daughter of Guri Johannesdatter and Rasmus Gudmundsen, farm no. 2 – 5 g, Skare.

Children:

a. Jørgen *Valnum*, born July 31, 1872, next tenant farmer.
b. Sevrine Elisabeth, born Nov. 8, 1875, died Apr. 12, 1876.

The deed to Jørgen on farm no. 6, "Fars Minde," from Svend Mikael Larsen for 50 kr. is dated Oct. 4, 1902.

21. **Valnum Jørgensen.** 1903 – 1960
Born July 31, 1872, died Aug. 11, 1960, son of previous tenant farmer. Married Aug. 16, 1903 to **Laura Kristoffersen,** born Apr. 9, 1882, died Oct. 18, 1960, daughter of Ingeborg and Ola Kristoffersen, Åkra.

Children:

a. *Hjordis* Birgitte, born May 12, 1904, married in 1924 to Andreas Miljeteig, tenant farmer no. 25, Skare.
b. *Olga* Mettine, born Mar. 13, 1906, married in 1934 to Helmer Håkonsen, Mannes, Åkra.
c. *Valnum* Ludolf, born July 5, 1908, married in 1931 to Lovise Klovning, tenant farm no. 36, Hovland.
d. *Gurine* Elisabeth, born June 29, 1911, married in 1934 to Nils Johannesen, Markhus, Åkrafjorden.

Jørgen Jørgensen (1835 – 1918) and Berte Gurine Rasmusdatter (1849 – 1878).

The Valnum Jørgensen family with Andreas Miljeteig around 1926.

Tobias Sørhus family in 1903. Back from left Åsa, Minda, Jenny, Lovise and Julie. In middle, Tobias and Laurine. Front from left, Gina, Martha and Ellen.

e. Ole, born Oct. 23, 1913, next tenant farmer.
f. *Hans* Alfred Magnus, born May 8, 1917, married in 1945 to Tordis Klovning, tenant farmer no. 44, Skare

Valnum leased the "Skolejorda," farm no. 6, Hovland, for many years.

22. **Ole Klovning.** 1944 –
Born Oct. 23, 1913, died Jan. 29, 1979, son of previous tenant farmer.

Married July 8, 1944 to **Sigfryda Skare,** born July 10, 1913, daughter of Åsa Oline and Adolf Ellingsen, farm no. 1 – 11 b, Skare.

Children:

a. *Lilly* Johanna, born May 16, 1945, married to Erling Karlsen, lives on Høllen in Søgne.

b. *Asta* Audny, born Nov. 13, 1947, married to Oystein Andersen, divorced, lives in Gjettum in Baerum. Asta has a farm here in Klovning.
c. *Finn* Oddvar, born Apr. 21, 1952, married in 1980 to Anne Margrethe Støle, tenant farmer no. 50, Skare.

23. **Tobias Sørhus.** 1885 – 1941
Born Sept. 29, 1863, died May 7, 1927, son of Eli Kristine Ommundsdatter and Johannes Rasmussen, tenant farmer no. 14 a, Klovning.

Married Dec. 18, 1885 to **Anne Martha *Laurine* Johannesdatter,** born Mar. 6, 1863, died Jan. 6, 1941, daughter of Anne Marthe Ådnesdatter and Ole Johannes Johannesen, tenant farmer no. 29 e, Nordvik, and later at farm no. 2 – 2, Klovning.

Children:

a. *Julia* Kristine, born July 22, 1886, married in 1907 to Konrad Knutsen, farmer no. 1 – 10, Austrheim.
b. *Åsa* Oline, born May 30, 1888, married in 1911 to Adolf Ellingsen, farmer no. 1 – 11, Skare.
c. *Jenny* Amalie, born July 13, 1890, died May 24, 1962. She also had a farm here.
d. *Minda* Marthea, born June 20, 1892, married in 1924 to Alfred Hansen, tenant farmer no. 35, Hovland.
e. Laura *Lovise*, born Nov. 26, 1893, married in 1915 to Gustav Hansen, farm no. 1 – 6, Kvalvik.
f. Anne *Martha*, born Dec. 17, 1895, married in 1919 to Mikal Klovning, farm no. 4 – 7, Klovning.
g. *Regine (Gina)* Gunhilde, born Aug. 4, 1898, died Sept. 10, 1989. Gina also had a farm here.
h. Benny Elisabeth, born Feb. 6, 1901. died Mar. 22, 1901.
i. *Ellen* Kristine, born June 2, 1902, married in 1921 to Tore J. Larsen, farm no. 15 – 11, Nordvik.
j. Thorvald Ludolf, born Oct. 23, 1907, died Jan 29, 1908.
k. Tordis Laurentse, born Mar. 7, 1909, died July 22, 1910

Gift certificate to Tobias on farm no. 5, from Ole Johannes Johannesen Klovning is dated May 4, 1890. The house was built the year before.

Tobias worked for the Port Authority and as a carpenter in addition to fishing. The farm was taken over in 1941 by Jenny Sørhus, and after her death it was taken over by her sister, Gina.

24. **Isak B. Pedersen Solheim.** 1920 – 1952
Born Apr. 9, 1894 on Folderoy, died Aug. 13, 1933, son of Ranveig Isaksdatter, Kuvik and Peder Olsen, Indre Saetre on Moster.

Married 1920 to **Anna Marta Johannesen,** born May 26, 1897, daughter of Thala Sofie and Johannes Johannesen, farm no. 2 – 3 b, Klovning.

Children:

a. *Johannes* Sverre, born July 5, 1920, chief engineer, lives in Bergen.
b. Ragna, born May 8, 1922, married to Martin Enghaugen, Onsoy near Fredrikstad.

Isaak was a seaman during WW1 and also master on the M/K "Haugesund" and "Sagvåg," sailing the route in Utsira and in Sunnhordaland. Later he was chief engineer on M/K "Sirafjord" on the Utsira ferry route[60].

25. **Hans Mathias Gautsen.** 1890 – 1905
Born July 21, 1856, died Dec. 17, 1916, son of Berthe Eline Jørgensdatter and Gaut Mathias Larsen, farm no. 2 – 1 c, Klovning.

Married July 30, 1908 to **Anne Marta Gudmundsdatter**, born July 9, 1871, daughter of Mette Kistine Rasmusdatter and Gudmund Jørgensen, farm no. 1 – 10 a, Klovning.

Anne Marta's children outside her marriage:

a. Valborg Gurine, born June 16, 1899, died May 29, 1905.

They took over the main dwelling after Berthe Gurine and Oliver Knutsen in 1906 and lived there. Anne Marta moved to Stavanger and sold it later (around 1930) to Åsa and Mathias Kvalvik.

26. **Ingvald Klovning.** 1919 – 1954
Born Sept. 7, 1876, died December 1954, son of Ingeborg Karine Johannesdatter, tenant farm no. 13 c, Klovning.

Married May 24, 1919 to ***Hanna*** **Marie Hansen,** born Oct. 4, 1893, died Nov. 4, 1947, daughter of Anne Marie Gudmundsdatter and Hans Knut Eriksen, tenant farmer no. 20 d, Skare.

Children:

a. Inga *Karine*, born Sept. 10, 1922, married in 1950 to Sigurd Kolstø, Avaldsnes.

---

[60] *Haugesund Avis* newspaper, Aug. 16, 1933 (Note 28).

From left, and Severin Klovning (1875-1956) and Ingvald Klovning (1876-1954).

b. Kristine *Marie*, born June 23, 1924, married to Kliford Jacobsen, Avaldsnes.
c. Hagny *Ingebjorg*, born July 4, 1927, married in 1951 to Nils Kristian H. Kolstø, Avaldsnes.

The deed to Ingvald on this property, farm no. 10, Vesterheim, from Lars Mikaelsen Klovning in the amount of 350 kroner is dated Apr. 6, 1915

27. **Svend Klovning.** 1935 – 1946

Born June 1, 1910, son of Gurine and Svend Klovning, farm no. 8 – 1 c, Klovning.

Married Oct. 4, 1935 to **Åsa Oline Ellingsen,** born Feb. 16, 1912, daughter of Åsa Oline and Adolf Ellingsen, farm no. 1 – 11 a, Skare.

Children:

a. Sigrid *Gunvor*, born June 5, 1937, married to Randolf Hoyvik, lives in Stavanger.

b. Aud Åsa, born May 15, 1943, married to Bjarne Knutsen, lives in Stavanger.
c. Svein Olav, born June 30, 1950, married to Eli, lives in Stavanger.

Svend built himself a main dwelling here, farm no. 17, "Utsikten," in 1938. Sven was a radio–telegraph operator and worked for Utsira Radio for a couple of years before the war. The family moved to Tjensvoll, Stavanger in 1947.

29. **John K. Klovning.** 1948 –
Born Mar. 14, 1920, died Jan. 23, 1984, son of Gurine and Svend Klovning, farm no. 8 – 1 g, Klovning.

Married May 15, 1948 to **Laurine Ellingsen,** born Feb. 27, 1923, daughter of Åsa Oline and Adolf Ellingsen, farm no. 1 – 11 g, Skare.

Children:
a. *Grete* Synnøve, born Sept. 30, 1949, married in 1973 to Tom Hansen, Tvedestrand.
b. Arne Olav, born Sept. 20, 1951, married in 1976 to Marit Eide, tenant farmer no. 42, Hovland.
c. Leif Karsten. born Mar. 27, 1955, married in 1980 to Kjellaug Eikeland, tenant farmer no. 31, Klovning.

John took over the property here after his brother Svend. John was general manager of the commercial refrigeration plant in Sørvågen.

29. **Sverre Klovning.** 1948 –
Born Sept. 20, 1917, son of Gurine and Svend Klovning,farm no. 8 – 1 f, Klovning.

Sverre took over the general store after his father in 1948. He built a new building for the business in 1952, farm no. 24, Sveingard. From here he ran the general store with his sister Agnes until 1980. Sverre was also active in the local county political life on Utsira from 1953. He was county chairman on Utsira for 16 years, from 1960 to 1975. In these years he also participated in the provincial government.

Sverre also participated for many years in the work to produce the Utsira book, and conducted seminars in genealogy for the general public. He was also chairman of the elderly council for Utsira

30. **Agnes Klovning.** 1948 –
Born July 18, 1912, sister of previous tenant farmer.

Agnes has been running the business with her brother Sverre since 1948, They took over farm no. 14, Solbakken, on Skare, in 1974.

Sverre Klovning on his 3–wheeler motorbike in 1950.

31. **Leif K. Klovning.** 1980 –
Born Mar. 27, 1955, son of Laurine and John Klovning, tenant farm no. 28 c, Klovning.

Married Nov. 1, 1980 to **Kjellaug Eikeland,** born Mar. 17, 1958, from Bryne.

Children:

a. Kjersti, born July 1, 1981.
b. Kjetil, born Apr. 15, 1984.
c. Katrine. born June 21, 1988.

Leif took over the general store after Sverre Klovning on Jan. 1, 1981, and has since upgraded and modernized the facilities. They built a new main dwelling, farm no. 23, Midgard, in 1981.

32. **Olav Kvalvik.** 1941 –

Born May 3, 1909, died June 15, 1952, son of Thea and Ole Sjursen, farm no. 3 – 3 d, Kvalvik.

Married Apr. 24, 1941 to **Martha Klovning.** born June 26, 1916, daughter of Jonette and Thomas G. Klovning, farm no. 1 – 12 c, Klovning.

Children:

a. *Turid* Marie, born June 11, 1942, married to Kjell Ingvald Nesse, lives in Hafrsfjord and Utsira.
b. *Odd* Bjarne, born Nov. 3, 1947, married to Berit Henriksen, lives in Moss.

33. **Arne Nilsen.** 1949 –

Born Sept. 9, 1918, son of Anna and Jørgen Nilsen, farm no. 14 – 4 c, Nordvik.

Married Apr. 23, 1949 to **Malfrid Klovning,** born Nov. 29, 1922, daughter of Jonette and Thomas G, Klovning, farm no. 1 – 12 f, Klovning.

Children:

a. *Jostein* Arvid, born May 6, 1950, married in 1973 to Thea Birkeland, farm no. 1 – 14, Klovning.
b. *Torodd* Johan, born Jan. 2, 1952, married in 1976 to Torill Hansen, tenant farmer no. 49, Skare.
c. John Magne, born May 23, 1954, married to Linda Bisset from Scotland, lives on Gausel, Sandnes.

They built a main dwelling here, farm no. 28, Soltun, in 1957 – 58.

Målfrid was a postal clerk on Utsira from 1978–84.

34. **Martin Johannesen.** 1891 – 1893.

Born Nov. 22, 1855, died Mar. 13, 1892, son of Anne Marthe Ådnesdatter and Ole Johannes Johannesen, tenant farmer no. 29 a, Nordvik, later farm no. 2 – 2, Klovning.

Married Aug. 2, 1891 to **Thala Sofie Mikalsdatter,** born Dec. 27, 1867, died Oct. 13, 1954. daughter of Thala Sofie and Svend Mikael Larsen, farm no. 4 – 5 f, Klovning.

No children.

Thala Sofie got married in 2nd marriage in 1894 to Johannes Johannesen, farm no. 2 – 3, Klovning, the brother of Martin.

35. **Toralf Austrheim.** 1990 –

Sørvågen with the pilot boat "Parat," owned by Thomas Eriksen, and the "Egerø" (right), owned by Hans Knut Eriksen, in background. Photo by Wilse in 1913. Norwegian Folk Museum

Born Apr. 29, 1957, son of Astrid and Elling Austrheim, farm no. 3 – 9 b, Austrheim.

Married Nov. 23, 1979 to **Irene Klovning,** born June 19, 1961, daughter of Eldbjorg and Johannes Klovning, farm no. 2 – 5 a, Klovning.

Children:

a. Monica, born May 21, 1980.
b. Tor Ingve, born June 10, 1981.
c. Synnøve, born May 27, 1987.
d. Terese, born Jan. 6, 1993.

Toralf was ship master of the ferry M/S "Utsira" since 1990. They lived at Visnes, Karmøy, before they moved to Utsira.

36. **Olav Bådsvik.** 1990 –

Born May 10, 1946, son of Laurine and Lars Olafsen Baadsvik, Avaldsnes.

Children:

a. Tyri Karoline, born Mar. 18, 1980.
b. Thor Mikael, born Jan. 28, 1984.

Olav took over farm no. 18, Fredheim, in 1994.

37. **Odd Rømteland.** 1978 – 1979
Odd was from Lindesnes. He was general manager of social services on Utsira from 1978 – 79.

38. **Hans Erik Lundberg.** 1988 – 1991
From Madla, Hafsfjord. He was hired as Manager of Technical Services for Utsira County from 1988 – 91.

39. **Vera Breitve.** 1989 – 1990
From Karmøy. She was General Manager of Utsira Nursing Home from 1989–90.

40. **Tove Line.** 1990 – 1992
From Jaeren. He was general manager of Utsira Nursing Home from 1990 – 1992.

41. **Karen Solem.** 1991 – 1993.
From Jøa, in Fosnes County, Nord Trøndelag. She was a Nurse Assistant at Siratun Nursing Home from 1991–93.

42. **Kirsti Storesund.** 1993 –
From Haugesund. She was general manager of Siratun Nursing Home from 1993.

43. **Ole Damm Kvilhaug.** 1992 –
Born Jan. 31, 1966, from Karmøy. He was general manager of Utsira Fishing Industry A/S from 1992.

44. **Turid Kvalvik Nesse.** 1999 -
Born June 11, 1942, on Utsira, daughter of Olav Kvalvik and Martha Klovning Kvalvik, tenant farmer no. 32, Klovning.

Married to **Kjell Ingvald Nesse**, born on Bømlo, Nov. 3, 1945.

Children:

a. Odd Ingve, born June 1, 1968, in Stavanger; married Josephine Bermeo, from Negros-Fillip; two children: Odd Joseph and Odin Jose.
b. Trude, born July 26, 1970, Stavanger; separated; one son, Troy Kyrre.
c. Irmelin, born Aug. 1, 1978, in Stavanger; married Morten Halvorsen, from Stavanger; two children: Othilia and Dennis.

Spanne

Spanne or Spande was a farm on the southwestern fields, in the flat, grassy area which today is called "Øygaren" (*Øydgarden*). The name probably comes from the Spanne Sound, which is nearby, or possibly Spanne Island (Spannholmane), which is also nearby.
The name "Spann," which means "bucket" in Norwegian and is also an old measuring unit of volume, may have been given to the island as an indication of fishing rights income due to the farmers, for fishing activities in the waters around Utsira.

Here are also some of the old historical sites from the Middle Ages, which were excavated by Jan Petersen in 1929 – 33, and that exposed remnants from the Migration Period in the years 400 – 600 AD.

From the records of Hardanger and Halsnoy Cloister we have the names of the early settlers on Spanne:

1. **Nils Jonsen.** 1612 – 1614

He paid 2 rdl. for a first lease in 1612, but things apparently did not work out too well for Nils, as already two years later it is:

2. **Helge Jensen.** 1615 – 1619

He paid 4 ort for a first lease on Spanne. We cannot see Helge either in the records after that. From 1620 it is Peder Austrheim who leases Spanne: *The deserted Spander – 1 v.*
However, there was still another man who attempted to lease this farm:

3. **Ivar Pedersen.** 1630 – 1631

He paid 3 rdl. for the first lease in 1630; however, already the following year it is Peder Austrheim who pays the taxes for Spanne.

In the following 200 years Spanne was farmed by the Klovning farmers who took responsibility for paying the taxes of 1 v. dried fish.

In the records of Halsnoy Cloister from 1659 we see, however, that Klaus Stange, Torvestad, is listed as a user of the farm. According to the Land Authority's records in 1661, it is the farmers on Kvalvik and Klovning who jointly farmed Spanne.

Kvalvik

Before 1824:	Reg. no. 50, tax 2 v.tf. (3 – 4 våger before 1637).
1824–1851:	Reg. no. 59, tax 4–3–10 skd., serial no. 252–254b.
1851–1886:	Reg. no. 69, tax 4–3–5 skd., serial no. 352–354.
1886:	Farm no. 31, tax assessment 8 mark 64 ore.

Kvalvik is situated in the middle of the island. It borders on Nordvik to the north, Skare to the east and Klovning to the south. It was listed as 4 v. dried fish in tax assessment before 1620, and after that, 3 våger until Klovning was separated from the estate in 1637, and 2 våger after that. The name of the farm ("Kvalvik") may come from the fact that a whale (kval) was beached there in the bay (vik) – or "Whalebay."

The name of the farm is spelled as follows in the various time periods. In 1521: Quauick, in 1610: Qualuoig, in 1614: Qualuig and in 1723: Qvalwig.

Kvalvik was, except for the period in the middle of the 1600s, farmed by one single farmer until 1815. In 1850 there were four farms, and from 1945 there have been five farms. Today there are no independent farms left at Kvalvik, but the area is utilized as additional or supplementary fields.

There were 2 unregistered farms at Kvalvik: "Backen," or "Kleven" (also called "Qvaligspladset"), was the largest one, and which became in 1838 farm no. 3, and "Jupatrae," or "Jupatrevik," which was somewhat smaller.

In the official Land Register in 1668 the following was recorded:

> Qualuig (Kvalvik), 2 våger fish, very poor grain fields, but sufficient to provide enough fuel (dried peat), potential for planting 2 barrels (grain), to provide sufficient feed for 9 head (of cattle), estimated 2 wetter (approx. 75 kg.) grain and 4 calf hides in tax for local defense, 2 spand (15 kg. of grain) to the church and 4 sk. in misc. contributions.

Kvalvik (the Bay) and Kvalvik village in the background. The small lake all the way to the left is "Laugarevatnet" (Lake Laugare). Photo: Telemark Aircraft Co.

Table showing planted and harvested grain and potatoes:

Year	Grain sown	Potatoes planted	Grain harvested	Potatoes harvested
1668	2	–	–	–
1703	3	–	–	–
1712	3	–	–	–
1723	3	–	14	–
1802	6.5	–	40	–
1822	–	–	53	14
1845	11	3.5	–	–
1866	15.3	6.7	84	56
1875	14.6	8.2	–	–
1945	9.4	7.6	–	–

All units are barrels except for year 1945, which indicates dekars.

Table showing livestock, inhabitated homes and no. of inhabitants:

Year	Horses	Cows	Sheep	Inhabitated Homes	Number of Inhabitants
1668	–	9	–	–	–
1703	1	6	x	–	–
1712	1	7	x	–	–
1723	1	6	x	–	–
1758	–	–	–	2	8
1801–02	3	9	8	3	15
1822	5	13	40	–	–
1845	4	10	56	5 (6)	34
1866	2	15	35	8	48
1875	2	12	39	7	45
1900	–	–	–	8	34

Farmers

1. **Thomas.** 1521
He is the first person known by name living on Kvalvik, according to the tax register in 1521.

2. **Olav.** 1563
He is mentioned in the tax register of 1563.

3. **Arve.** 1605 – 1641.

He is mentioned in the county records until 1633, after that only his widow is listed until 1641.

Their son:

a. Elling, he arranged for separation of Klovning as an independent farm in 1637.

4. **Jakob.** 1634 – 1638
He is mentioned in the local records during these years. He may have been married to a daughter of the previous farmer.

5. **Harald Knutsen.** 1639 – 1665
Born in 1608. He may have been married to the widow of the previous farmer. From the 1650's he ran the farm by himself.

Known children:

a. Sjur, born in 1643.

6. **Rasmus.** 1641 –
He is mentioned in the local records after the widow of Arve Kvalvik, and appears to have farmed half of the farm.

7. **(Hans Jonsen Stange).** 1665 – 1685
Born in 1631, son of Jon Hansen Lande in Avaldsnes.
Possibly married to **Elisabet Henriksdatter.**

Known children:

a. Jon, born in 1651 (1659) married to Anna Andresdatter, farm no. 1 – 4, Klovning.
b. Olav, born 1660.

Hans was a farmer at Stange, Torvestad, before he leased here at Kvalvik. We have no firm records of this other than what is written in the local records regarding the shipwreck of the German vessel on Spannholmen during Christmas, 1674. We learn from these records that in the period after the shipwreck, there was *tobacco for sale* both at the house of *Hans Kvalvik* and at the house of his son *Jon Klovning.*

8. **Peder.** 1673
He is only mentioned in a summary of all the farmers at Utsira in the military records for that year.

Farm no. 2.

1. **Elling Hansen.** 1685 – 1738

Born in 1655, died around 1725, possibly son of Hans Ingebretsen, farm no. 1 – 3 c, Klovning.

We do not know the name of Elling's wife. (Anna or Berta?), but the widow at Kvalvik is mentioned for the last time in the records in 1734, when it is listed that she is due 1–2–9 rdl. in royal assistance contribution.

Known children (they had 5 children in 1711):

a. Elling, born 1691, died sometime between 1701 and 1706.
b. Johannes, born 1693, tenant farmer no. 10, Kvalvik.
c. Berta, born 1704, next farmer.
d. Knut, born 1711, died 1733.
e. Hans, born 1714, died 1733, he was a marine pilot.
f. Gjoa, birthdate unknown, married to Knut Olsen, farmer no. 4 – 5, Austrheim.

Elling was leasing around 1685 and his lease contract of 2 v. dried fish is dated Dec. 23, 1720.

In 1703 his financial condition was described as "conditional." The buildings on the farm were in good condition with required repair estimated to 5 ort. He was planting 3 barrels of oats and feeding 4 cows, 2 calves, 1 horse and some sheep. He owned all the animals himself and had no debt to the Cloister proprietor, Mr. Friman. He owed 5 rdl. in tax.

In 1712 the planting and livestock were the same as in 1703, while repairs on his buildings were now assessed to 3 rdl. and 3 ort. It is recorded that Elling's financial situation was now described as follows:

> . . . in 1711 owing 1 rdl. in tax, besides also owing, here and there, 3 or 4 rdl. for grain products, particularly to a Michel Eeg – for stretching out payments – but how much is not possible to determine.

In 1721 there was once again a survey made of the farms on Utsira. It was determined that the buildings on Kvalvik were in need of repair at an estimated 1 rdl. 3 ort. Fields and meadows were in good condition, and Elling provided the information that he had borrowed 11 rdl. in order to pay his taxes and lease money.

In 1723 it is recorded about Kvalvik:

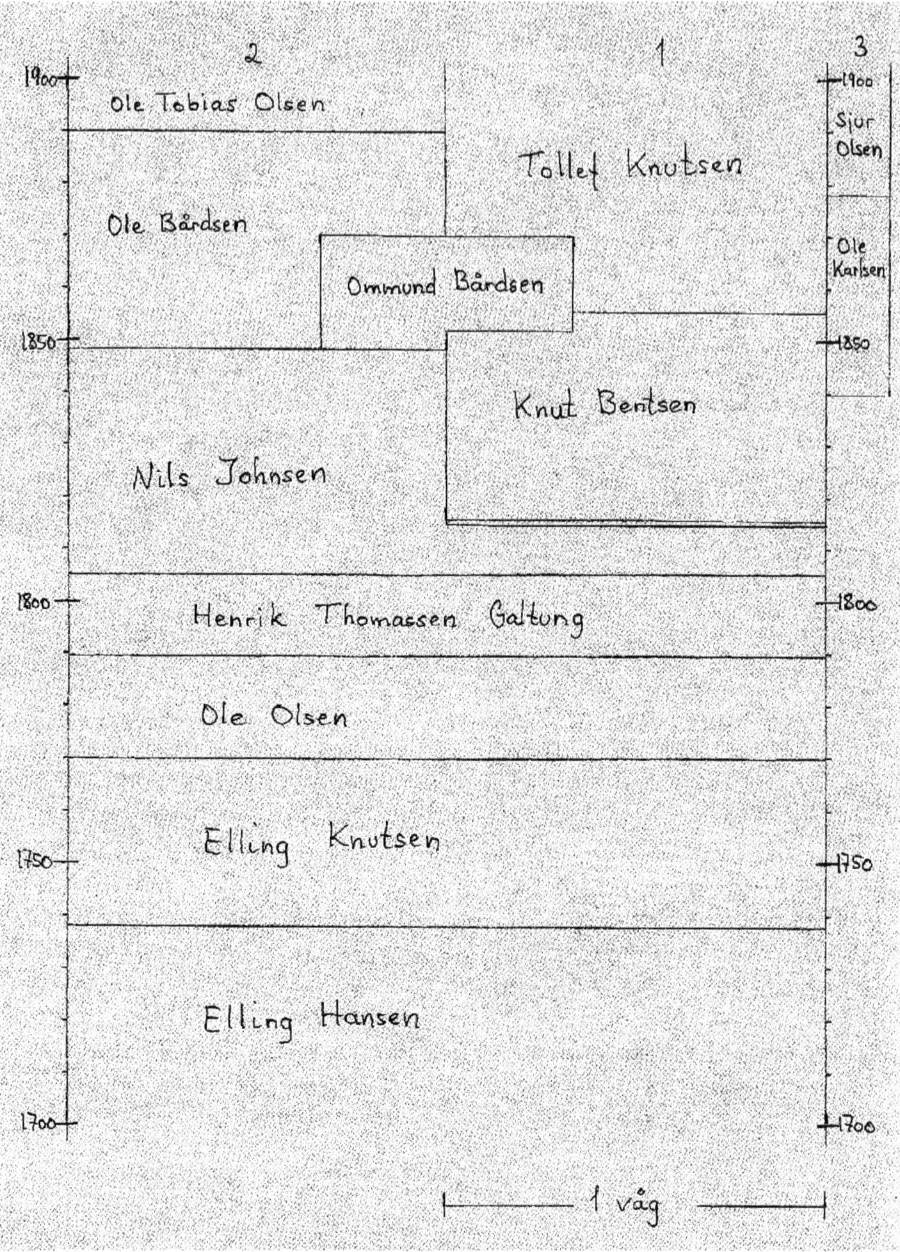

Table of farmers at Kvalvik 1700 – 1900.

2 v. dried fish (taxes). Concerning Utsira it appears Elling Hansen farms all (of Kvalvik); he was not available himself, but according to the local sheriff he sows 3 barrels and harvests 14 barrels, feeds 1 horse, and 6 cows.

2. **Elling Knutsen.** 1738 – 1770.
Born 1718, died Feb. 24, 1770. son of Knut Ellingsen, L.–Hagland in Skåre.

Married around 1738 to **Berta Ellingsdatter,** born in 1704, died Mar. 11, 1769, daughter of previous farmer.

Children:

a. Gunhild, born 1739, married in 1764 to Ivar Mathiassen, Vikse in Skåre.
b. Anna, born 1741, married in 1761 to Sven Mathiassen, farm no. 4 – 6, Austrheim.
c. Hans, born 1743, buried Sept. 29, 1763.
d. Berta, born 1747, married in 1770 to Thomas Johannesen, farmer no. 1 – 4, Skare.
e. Engelbret, born 1749, buried Mar. 12, 1769.

Lease contract to Elling for 2 v. dried fish is dated in 1738 without any actual date.

Elling was a full time marine pilot. Elling and Ole Knutsen Austrheim presented their pilot logs, dated Dec. 2, 1740, to the local council in 1741.

There was an estate settlement after Berta in May 1769. The estate contained misc. items worth 112–2–8 rdl. Debt and expenses amounted to 37–2–0 rdl. and a wedding gift to the youngest daughter of 30 rdl. Among the expenses, the entire amount of 12 rdl. is included for repair of the buildings, indicating that several of the buildings were in bad shape. Among misc. items left the following are mentioned.

> 5 cows 22–3–0, 4 heifers 12–3–0,, 3 oxen 6–2–0, 2 calves 2–3–0, 2 horses (mares) 9–0–0, 4 rams 3–0–0, 1 pig 1–0–0, 1/2 share in outside mill with housing and associated equipment 3–0–0, 3 kettles 5–2–16, 1 baking board 0–3–8, 4 barrels of oats 5–1–8, 1 tiled heating stove 6–0–0, 1/2 six–oar boat with sail 2–2–0, 1 old four–oar boat without sail 1–2–0, 4 spring herring fishing nets 2–2–0, 20 lobster pots 0–3–8, 1 brass candleholder 0–2–16, misc. silverware including a drinking cup, engraved with the initials E.K., 2–2–4.

In March the following year there is an estate sttlement after Elling. The value of the estate is then 57 rdl. and 37–1–22 was divided among the heirs.

3. **Ole Olsen.** 1770 – 1789

Born 1734, buried Oct. 16, 1787, son of Synnøve Mikkelsdatter and Ole Larsen, St. Hagland in Skåre.

Married June 30, 1771 to **Mari Knutsdatter,** born 1743, died Sept. 8, 1822, daughter of Berta Knutsdatter and Knut Sjursen, tenant farmer no. 15 a, Nordvik.

Children:

a. Ole, baptized May 31, 1773, buried Mar. 25, 1774.
b. Ole, baptized Mar. 15, 1775, buried Mar. 25, 1779.
c. Berta, baptized Oct. 5, 1777, buried Mar. 25, 1779.
d. Berta, baptized Nov. 16, 1779, married in 1802 to Jørgen Johnsen, farm no. 13 – 3, Nordvik.
e. Karen Oline, baptized May 16, 1783, farmer no. 5 here.

Lease contract to Ole for 2 v. dried fish, from Mrs. Vallentinsen is dated Feb. 28, 1770.

Ole and his brother, Mikkel Nordvik, drowned outside Røvaer. Ole left miscellaneous items worth 165–1–4 rdl, in addition he was owed 19 rdl. However, 145–2–12 rdl. was left to the heirs. Among misc. items the following are mentioned:

> 11 cows (Lovrej, Spangrej, Plomrej, Mørkrej, Brandsia, Lokrej, Roedsia, Sortsia and Brandrej at Klovning), 47–2–0, 1 calf and 2 oxen 5–0–0, 12 sheep with lamb 6–0–0, 8 rams 5–1–8, 1 small pig 0–2–16, 1 mare with foal 3–2–0, 1 small horse 4–0–0, 1 outside mill with housing and tools 4–0–0, 1/2 shed on the waterfront 1–0–0, 1 old four–oar boat with sail 2–0–0, 5 spring herring fishing nets 2–2–16, 24 lobster pots 1–2–0, 1 scale 1–1–0, 2 lockers one with and one without locks 0–3–16, 1 cast–iron stove *in the large living room* 6–0–0, 1 small stove 4–2–0, 2 cattle troughs 4–0–0, 16 barrels of oats 17–1–9, silver 9–1–16, 2 brass candle holders 1–1–12 and cash 10–3–14.

Mari was married in 2nd marriage in 1789 to Henrik Thomassen Galtung, see below.

4. **Henrik Thomassen Galtung.** 1789 – 1805.

Baptized Mar. 4, 1770. died Apr. 27, 1846, son Anna Torsdatter and Thomas Johannesen, Feoy.

The house that Henrik Thomassen Galtung built in 1805. To the right is Kaia and Knut Kvalvik's house. Both of these houses are now gone. Photo by Robert Kloster in 1932. Bergen Historic Museum.

Married in 1st. marriage July 19, 1789 to **Mari Knutsdatter,** widow of previous farmer.

Married in 2nd. marriage May 10, 1824 to **Anna Kristoffersdatter,** baptized Feb. 17, 1782, died Aug. 11, 1834, daughter of Anna Mikkelsdatter and Kristoffer Olsen, Torvestad.

No children.

Lease contract, 2 v. dried fish, to Henrik issued by Peder Valentinsen Forman on Feb. 2, 1789.

In 1802 he sowed 5 barrels and harvested 30 barrels of grain. The livestock consisted of 2 horses, 5 cows, 2 calves and 8 sheep and a mill also was on the farm, but *was not part of the house.* The farm was assessed to 240 rdl.

In 1805 he turned the farm over to Nils Johnsen against an old age contract consisting of:

> 9 barrels of oats and 1 barrel of pure grain, free use of 2 parcels, "Langflekket" (southeast of "Smørdusk"), 70 x 45 alen, and "Tarhaug" (northeast of Kleivane and north of Karl Asbjornsen's rental property), 104 x 48 alen, winter and summer feed for 4 cows and 40 sheep. Also 4 parcels, the entire Stora–trae (southwest of Jupatrae rental property), another field of 100 x 24 alen, southwest of Kalberg (Henrik was already

in the process of building a new house here), and also a field called "Grotlen," *which stretches from the Stem–farm to the Trae–farm, and finally a similar parcel of the Herberg property actually belonging to the Qualvik farm.* In addition Nils was required to provide all necessary fuel (peat) for heating the house.

This was a very comprehensive contract, which Nils Johnsen must have had his hands full to honor.

5. **Nils Johnsen.** 1805 – 1847.
Baptized July 23, 1780, died Nov. 29, 1840, son of Margrete Jørgensdatter and John Nilsen, farm no. 13 –2 c, Nordvik.

Married in 1st marriage on Mar. 23, 1806 to **Kari Oline Olsdatter,** baptized May 16, 1783, died May 13, 1824, daughter of farmer no. 3 here.

Married in 2nd marriage on July 3, 1825 to **Anne Marie Johnsdatter,** baptized Feb. 19, 1806, died Dec. 2, 1849, daughter of Oline Johannesdatter and John Larsen, Dale, Torvestad.

Children in 2nd marriage:

a. Kari Oline, born Oct. 22, 1825, married in 1845 to Gudmund Knutsen, farmer no. 1 – 8, Austrheim.
b. Johanne Margrete, born Dec. 28, 1827, died Feb. 28, 1828.
c. Johanne Margrete, born Apr. 6, 1829, died Dec. 25, 1850. She died two hours after she gave birth to a stillborn child. The father was Sjur Knutsen.
d. Jon, born in 1832, died Sept. 24, 1832, 2 weeks old.
e. Marta Oline, born Dec. 14, 1833, died June 21, 1834.
f. Nils, born Jan. 15, 1836, married in 1860 to Karen Juliane Hansdatter, tenant farmer no. 10, Austrheim.
g. Lars, born June 12, 1839, married to Elene Ånensdatter, Halseid. They lived on Vikse in Skåre. Their daughter was Anne Martha Vikse, farm no. 14 – 3, Nordvik.

Lease contract to Nils for 2 v. dried fish is issued by Hans B. Foreman and dated Oct. 22, 1805, including an old age contract to the previous farmer (see above). He paid 140 rdl. in lease money.

Nils farmed the entire Kvalvik farm until 1815, when he relinquished half the farm, farm no. 1, to Bernt Bentsen.

In 1822 the buildings on the farm were described as follows:

1 cabin with kitchen, under one roof and attached to Knud Bentsen's house, covered with a peat (turf) roof and with a peat shed at the end of the house. The western half of the house is under the same roof as the other

house on the farm, also covered with a peat roof. These houses are in fairly good condition. There is also a new cabin with an old log–built barn, also covered with peat turf.

There was also a mill on the farm. The quality of the soil is good and there is sufficient peat for their own consumption.

Annual yield is 25 barrels of grain and 6 – 8 barrels of potatoes, and the livestock consists of 5 cows, 1 calf, 2 horses and 20 sheep. The farm was in total assessed at 160 Spd.

J. Dahm sold this farm in 1840 to Bård Ommundsen Saebø for 325 Spd. He let his two sons, Ole and Ommund, lease this farm.

In the settlement after Nils in 1841, the value of the estate was assessed at 155 Spd., to be divided between the heirs there was left 63–3–0 Spd. From this amount payments of 19–2–23 Spd. were made to Mr. Hjortdahl in Bergen, 15 Spd. to Sjur Knutsen, 10 Spd. in repair of the houses on the property and 8 Spd. for the funeral. Misc. items left in the estate were:

1 four–man fishing boat with old main and jib 6–0–0, 2 old four–oar boats 3–0–0, 1 boat shed 5–0–0, 5 spring herring fishing nets 4–2–0, 2 pollock and 1 coalfish fishing nets 2–2–0, 40 lobster pots with ropes and floats 2–0–0, 1 lobster container 0–1–0, 26 fir barrels 6–2–12, 2 barrels of salt 2–1–0, 2 horses, 10 and 16 years–old, 15–0–0, 3 cows (*Tamrei, Fraerei and Dyrei*) 6 and 12 years–old 21–0–0, 3 sheep 3–0–0, 1 *wagon with iron reinforcements on the wheels* 0–3–0 2 carts with wheels 1–2–0, 1 outside mill with housing 10–0–0, 1 small stove 2–0–0, 1 painted– and 1 old oak locker with iron reinforcements and lock 3–0–0, silver 2–2–0, blue– and white–striped bedding with down fill 8–0–0 and *one small log cabin with two sets of windows with curtains, small additional rooms with 1/2–size windows, kitchen in the northern end, floor and attic, lined with boards and roof covered with tiles,* all estimated at 30–0–0.

In May 1847 Anne Marte secured herself the following old age pension from the new owner, Bård Ommundsen Saebø:

3–1/2 barrels of oats, 2 v. 36 mrk. barley, 2 cans of cod liver oil, 1 cord of peat, feed for 1 cow and 5 sheep, use of the field "Langeflaekket." She actually also had the full use of the field "Kolbergstykket" until her youngest child was 25 years old. The contract was assessed at 75 Spd. for 5 years.

Anne Marte was married in her second marriage to Sjur Knutsen Austrheim, tenant farmer no. 26, Hovland.

6. **Ole Bårdsen.** 1848 – 1888

Born Sept. 29, 1827, died May 6, 1889 in Bergen, son of Eli Olina Olavsdatter, and Bård Ommundsen, Saebø, Torvestad.

Married Mar. 30,1850 to **Torine Toresdatter,** born Mar. 19, 1826, died Feb. 7, 1900, daughter of Anne Kirstine Johannesdatter, and Thore Thorsen, farmer no. 15 – 8 c, Nordvik.

Children:

a. Bår *Mathias*, born July 11, 1850, married to Bertha Ombo from Jelsa. Mathias sailed for many years as first mate and skippered on the Great Lakes in the USA. They lived in Oakland, California, for 40 years. Both died in 1927.[61]

b. Thore Mikal, born Nov. 6, 1851, married in 1884 to Lovise Gurine Mathiasdatter, tenant farmer no. 27, Kvalvik.

c. Andreas *Bertel*, born Aug. 28, 1853, died May 9, 1885, married in 1882 to Bolla Elisabet Nilsdatter Osnes. He was a seaman, killed in an accident on harbor project in Sørvågen shortly before he was to leave for USA.[62] They had a son, Bertel Elias, born Sept. 17, 1883, who emigrated to USA, died in 1963 in Oakland, Calif.

d. Elen Kristine, born Apr. 29, 1856, died June 3, 1857.

e. Elias Thimann, born June 2, 1858, married to Arenstine Marie Jørgensen, Arendal. They emigrated to the USA around 1910.

f. Berthe Malene, born Sept. 29, 1860, married to Martin Hansen, Tønsberg. They emigrated to the USA in October 1887.

g. Johannes, born Dec. 5, 1862, married in 1894 to Berthe Karine Konradsdatter, tenant farm no. 32, Kvalvik.

h. Ole *Tobias*, born May 9, 1865, farmer no. 8 here.

i. Anne Marthe, born Feb. 17, 1869, died Nov. 28, 1893.

j. Elen Oline, born July 15, 1871, emigrated to the USA and got married there.

The lease contract from the father on two–thirds of the farm went to Ole (the rest of the farm went to his brother Ommund), in the amount of 2 bp dried fish and is dated Sept. 22, 1848. Bård kept a piece of land called "Stemmen," which Johannes Gudmundsen had been promised he could lease. In the declaration from Bård dated Nov. 24, 1858, it is stated that the use of "Stemmen," *including the field belonging to the rental property called Grutlene,* is returned to Ole and Ommund.

---

[61] *Haugesund Avis* newspaper, July 25, 1927 (Note 29).

[62] *Haugesunderen* newspaper, May 13, 1885 (Note 30).

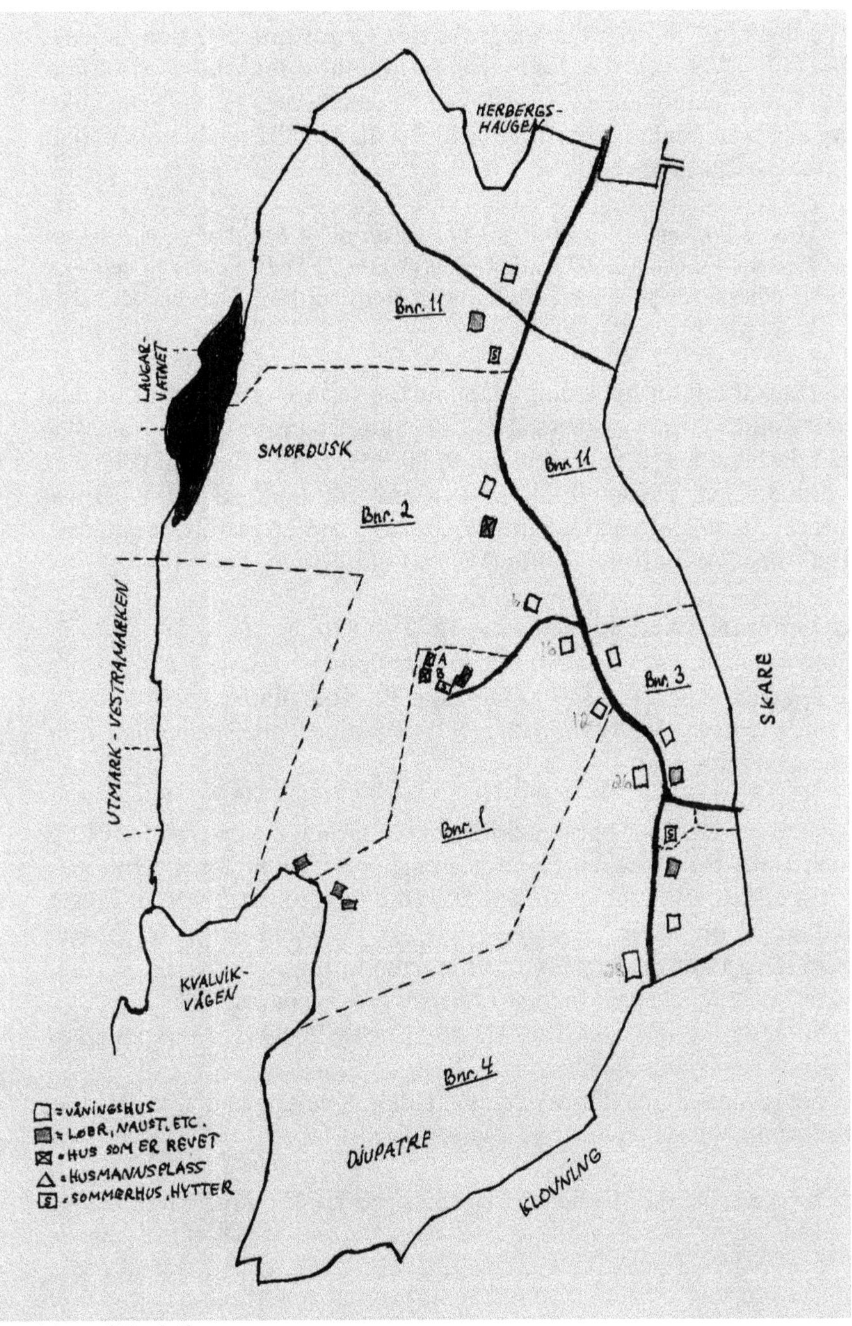

Map of Kvalvik.
Key: 1–Main dwelling, 2–Barns, sheds, etc., 3–Houses now torn down, 4–tenant houses, 5–Summer houses, vacation cabins.

The deed to Ole from the father for this farm worth 300 Spd. is dated Oct. 17, 1859, and the deed covering the third for which his brother still had a lease contract, for 150 rdl. is dated Aug. 1, 1860, including tax in the amount of 2 bp. dried fish or 2 dl. 16 sk. The old age contract to the parents at Saebø:

> 10 v. 2 bp. oats, 1 barrel of good cod liver oil, 1 barrel of good potatoes, feed for 4 sheep and 2/3 cord of peat (or 1–0–72 Spd. in cash) all delivered to either Oydegards Bay, Jensa Bay or Helganes Bay. The contract over 5 years was assessed to 50 Spd.

In 1865 the farm, including "Ommund's farm," consisted of 74 mål fields and meadows assessed at 508 Spd. There were open areas in addition worth 110 Spd., peat worth 60 Spd. and fishing rights income worth 33 Spd. The entire farm was worth 760 Spd.. Annual yield was then 29 barrels of oats, 9 barrels of barley, and 26 barrels of potatoes. The livestock consisted of 1 horse, 5 cows, 15 sheep and 1 pig.

7. **Ommund (Amund) Bårdsen.** 1849 – 1870
Born Sept. 26, 1823, brother of previous farmer.

Married Apr. 10, 1849 to **Hansine B. Knutsdatter,** born Feb. 19, 1818, died Jan. 30, 1892, daughter of Kristine Tollefsdatter and Knut Bentsen, farmer no. 1 – 2 a, Kvalvik.

No children.

Amund leased, for 2 bp.tf., a third of both farm no. 1 and farm no. 2, in such a way that these 3 each farmed equal parts of the entire farm.

The lease contract to Amund from the father for 1/3 v.tf. or in new skilling, 3 ort 18 sk., is dated Sept. 21, 1849 and the lease contract from Knut Bentsen for 1/3 v.tf. or in new skilling, 3 ort 13 sk., is dated May 14, 1852. He paid in total 120 Spd. in lease money.

In 1865 the livestock consisted of 1 horse, 5 cows, 13 sheep and 1 pig.

They turned the farm over to Tollef Knutsen and Ole Bårdsen against an old age contract from them consisting of:

> 8 v. oats, the use of a field which could provide 35 "skru,"[63] required soil and peat from *an area called "Nielsetorvskjaeren,"* 2 cans of fresh milk in

[63] Possibly refers to compost resulting from mule droppings, used in cutting peat, which they referred to as "peat–cutter" mules.

The family of Tobias Olsen Kvalvik in front of their home in 1915

the period Feb. 1 to Oct. 31, in addition to 2 cans in the period May 16 to July 15, if no one else under similar old age contract required it from them, winter and summer feed for 3 sheep and unlimited use of boat shed in "Kvalvikvågen." This contract was worth about 100 Spd for 5 years.

We do not know what happened to Amund, but it was reported that he disappeared around the time when they were planning to travel to the USA in 1871. In 1872 it is mentioned in the loan register that he was "out of town."

9. **Ole Tobias Olsen.** 1889 – 1934
Born May 9, 1865, died Nov. 17, 1946, son of farmer no. 6 here.

Married Apr. 19, 1890 to **Berthe *Malene* Larsdatter,** born June 10, 1867, died Feb. 13, 1944, daughter of Marthe Kristine Mathiasdatter and Lars Johan Thorsen, farm no. 15 – 9 c, Nordvik.

Photo from 1920. In back from left: Mildred Olsen and Torine Kvalvik.
In front from left: Methy Rasmussen and Karoline B. Hoff.

Children:

a. Martha *Karine* (Kaia), born May 14, 1890, died 1964, married in 1915 to Erik Bernhard Askelsen, Eide in Fjellberg, lived in Saebøvik.
b. Ole *Toralv*, born Sept. 1, 1891, married in 1922 to Gjertrud Bakke, farm no. 11 – 1, Kvalvik.
c. *Laura* Marie, born Sept. 1, 1891, married in 1916 to Mikal Mathiassen, farm no. 2 – 7, Skare.
d. *Amanda* Malene, born Mar. 25, 1896, married in 1925 to August Knutsen, farm no. 4 – 13, Hovland.
e. Ludolf Mikal Trygve, born Sept. 9, 1897, died July 6, 1903. He drowned in a well.
f. *Mathie* Bertea, born July 20, 1900, married in 1928 to Elling Rasmussen, farm no. 7 – 12, Hovland.
g. Torine, born Aug. 7, 1901, died Aug. 15, 1901.
h. Torine, born Nov. 6, 1902, married in 1936 to Edvard Kvalvik, tenant farmer no. 34, Kvalvik.
i. *Olga* Martine, born Sept. 3, 1904, died 1970, married to Rolf Eitland, Korshavn in Austad.
j. Ludolf *Mikael*, born June 6, 1906, next farmer.
k. Lars Johan, born Feb. 14, 1908, died Mar. 12, 1909.

The deed to Tobias from the mother on this farm, tax liability sk.m. 3.91, is dated Jan. 17, 1898 in the amount of 2000 kr. including a pension contract:

> 288 kg. of oats, 90 kg. of barley, 1–3/5 hl. (hundred liter) new potatoes, free use of the "Henrikstykket" field, winter feed for 1 cow and 8 sheep, 1–1/2 cord of birch wood, 10 liter petroleum and 1 liter milk daily, when her own cow did not give milk. The contract over 5 years was assessed at 730 kr.

Tobias sold part of the farm in 1914 to Utsira Municipality for a new church yard, farm no. 5, sk.m. 0.06.

His son Toralf got two–thirds of farm no. 11 in 1937.

9. **Mikal Kvalvik.** 1934 –

Born June 6, 1906, died Jan. 27, 1966, son of previous farmer.

Married Nov. 18, 1933 to **Karoline Helgesen,** born Jan. 11, 1909, daughter of Serine and Thomas Helgesen, farm no. 30 – 1 d, Nordvik.

Children:

a. *Brynhild* Torbjorg, born Oct. 15, 1934, married in 1963 to Roar Saebø; they live in Saebøvik on Halsnoy in Kvinnherad.
b. *Torfrid* Reidun, born Apr. 27, 1936, married in 1961 to Jakob Bernhard Bergeland, Finnoy; they live on Ålgaard.

c. Kåre Modolf, born Jan. 11, 1938, married to Ruth Sofie Wik, from Kilengrein in Telemark; they live on Sola.

The deed to Mikal from the father on this farm, 1.27 sk. m., is dated July 1, 1943.

Mikal worked some time as a carpenter besides fishing and running the farm. In the late 1940s he became ill and subsequently was incapacitated.

The farm around 1956 had 2 cows, some chickens and 3 sheep and was utilized in the later years as an additional farm. The estate was, in 1974, taken over by Kåre Kvalvik, Sola.

Farm no. 1. From farm no. 2 in 1815

1. **Bent Bentsen.** 1815 – 1816

Baptized May 5, 1793, died Apr. 16, 1816, son of Berte Knutsdatter and Bent Bentsen, Veste in Skåre. (Berta and Nils Johnsen were step–siblings).

Unmarried.

Lease contract to Bent on the southern half of Kvalvik, 1 v. dried fish, was issued by Hans B. Forman on Aug. 17, 1815.

During a visit by Hans B. Forman on Utsira in July 1815, a contract was written between Nils Johnsen and Bent regarding dividing the farm and the houses between them. Bent got the half located south of the courtyard and over to the Kvalvikvågen, while Nils kept the northern part, all the way over to Herberg. Bent took over the southern half of the main dwelling, and the eastern part of the barn including 2 small sheds south of the barn. Nils kept the other part of the main dwelling including the recently built stable. Bent also had to take responsibility for half of the pension contract to Henrik Thomassen and his wife. The contract was dated July 17, 1815.

Bent died the year after, and there was an estate settlement after him in 1817. He left items valued at 32 Spd., funeral expenses amounted to 13–1/2 Spd., and the rest was divided among the heirs. Among misc. items the following are mentioned:

> 1 old bay filly, 26 years old and blind in one eye, 2–0–0, 1 sheep with lamb, 1–1–0, 4 barrels oat cereal, 6–0–0, 600 pieces "ragede" (cured) herring, 1–1–0, some salted herring, 1–3–0, 1 spring herring net 1–0–0, 7 lobster pots 0–3–12, 1 psalm book 0–2–12 and 1 *tobacco pipe with decorative carving* 0–2–12.

2. **Knut Bentsen.** 1816 – 1856

Baptized Apr. 17, 1796, died Oct. 18, 1872, brother of last farmer.

Married on June 29, 1817 to **Kristine Tollefsdatter,** born 1794 at Kristinegård near Bergen, died Nov. 14, 1869.

Children:

a. Hansine Berentine, born Feb. 19, 1818, married in 1849 to Ommund Bårdsen, next farmer, and farm no. 2 – 7, Kvalvik.
b. *Petronelle*, born Oct. 5, 1820, married in 1843 to John Mathias Johnsen, farm 3 – 1, Skare.
c. Bendix, born Sept. 15, 1823, died Dec. 16, 1828.
d. Tollef, born Oct. 20, 1827, died Sept. 26, 1830.
e. Bendix, born Nov. 26, 1832, died Apr. 14, 1837.
f. Tollef, born Oct. 2, 1835, farmer no. 4 here.

The lease contract to Knut from Hans B. Forman on these farms in the amount 1 våger dried fish is dated June 27, 1816. The conditions are the same as for his brother Bent. In addition the following conditions had to be met:

> . . . in addition, the intention is that Knut Bentsen fulfills the loving commitment to our servant of more than 15 years, Christine Tollevsen, who, being without parents, may continue to enjoy the aforementioned farm, and without conditions legally benefit and share outfield and meadows, and half of the southern part and associated outhouses, including outfields adjacent to the farm Qvalviig, free without rent. Hence, due to this Christian promise at our engagement, I hereby lease the southern part of Qvalvig including the unregistered homestead "Jupetrae" to Knud Bentsen and his fiance Christine Tollevsdatter . . .

In 1822 the houses on the farm were described as follows:

> 1 living room and kitchen and 1 paneled chamber in the southern part under one roof and attached to another farmer's house here on this farm, covered with peat moss as is also the eastern half of the building belonging to Niels Johnsen's farm. The western part is the same. These buildings are old and in need of repair. One new framed barn is covered with planks and an old horse stall on the southern side of the building is also covered with peat.

Aerial photo from 1994. We can see Kvalvik in the background. Photo by: Hilmar Tollefsen Air Photos.

The annual yield of the farm is 18 barrels of grain and 6 – 8 barrels of potatoes, while the livestock consists of 2 horses, 5 cows and 20 sheep. The farm was assessed in 1823 to 130 Spd.

Knut purchased this farm from J. Dahm for 300 Spd., and paid 66 mrk. t.f. (merker torrfisk or dried fish) in taxes. The deed is dated Dec. 27, 1838. Not included is the half of Karl Asbjornsen's rental property that was sold to Ole Karlsen.

Knut was chairman of the first Utsira Parish Board, 1837 – 1840.

He had already sold the farm to his son Tollef in 1852, and 4 years later he and Kristine retired with an old age contract.

3. **Amund Bårdsen.** 1852 – 1870

He leased out 1/3 of this farm in addition to 1/3 of farm no. 2, see more about him there.

4. **Tollef Knutsen.** 1856 – 1919.
Born Oct. 2,1835, died Jan. 14, 1922, son of farmer no. 2 here.

Married Mar. 30, 1856 to **Torborg Eriksdatter,** born Nov. 18, 1833, died Apr. 13, 1915, daughter of Torborg and Erik Svendsen, farmer no. 1 – 8 b, Skare.

Tollef Knutsen (1835 – 1922) and Torborg Eriksdatter (1833–1915).

Children:

a. *Knut* Kristian, born June 27, 1857, next farmer.
b. Lovise Marie, born May 14, 1859, married in 1879 to Hans Mathias Helgesen, farmer no. 16 – 3, Nordvik.
c. *Edvard* Theodores, born May 11, 1861, emigrated to USA in 1888. He perished at sea. He had a son, Johan Gunvald, born June 29, 1886, who in 1900 lived in Haugesund and married Berthe Gurine Olsdatter Kvalvik.
d. Amund, born Nov. 4, 1863, emigrated to USA in 1887.
e. Hans Knut, born Jan. 16, 1866, emigrated to USA, perished at sea.
f. Elias, born Jan. 16, 1868, emigrated to USA. He and his brother perished at sea.
g. *Thomine* Cathrine, born July 23, 1871, married in 1893 to Johannes Gudmundsen, farmer no. 22 – 3, Nordvik.
h. Ånen Bendik, born July 16, 1874, married in 1898 to Elisabeth (Lisa) Mathiasdatter, farm no. 4 – 1, Kvalvik.

i. *Thomas* Mikal, born Sept. 23, 1877, married to Ingeborg Olsen, ran a clothing store in Stavanger.

The deed to Tollef from his father on this farm, 66 mrk. dried fish, or 2–0–16 sk. d., for 400 Spd. is dated May 14, 1852 (before Tollef became 17 years old). He took over the farm in 1856 against a pension to his parents that among other items consisted of:

> 5 barrels of oats, 1 barrel of barley, feed for 1–1/2 cows and 6 sheep, 1–1/2 cord of peat, 3 cans of cod liver oil, the field called "Torvhugget" and a smaller field next to it. Amund Bårdsen had to contribute 1/3 of this contract.

In 1865 the farm consisted of 60 mål fields and meadows (including the part which Amund Bårdsen farmed) and was assessed at 462 Spd. There were outfields for 110, peat for 60 and fishing rights income for 33 Spd. The entire farm was assessed at 752 Spd. Annual yield was 27 barrels of oats, 6 barrels of barley and 22 barrels of potatoes. The livestock consisted of 1 horse, 4 cows, 8 sheep and 1 pig.

A new main dwelling was built in 1869. In 1898 the farm was divided in two equal parts, farm no. 4 was separated out for his son Ånen Bendik, while Knut took over the remaining part. Torborg and Tollef then moved over to the old house, "Henriks–huset" as it was known, after Henrik Thomassen Galtung who built it around 1805.

5. **Knut Kvalvik.** 1898 – 1922
Born June 27, 1857, died Mar. 30, 1940, son of previous farmer.

Married May 30, 1889 to **Mette Karine (Kaia) Tollefsdatter,** born May 10, 1868, died Nov. 8, 1957, daughter of Berthe Gurine Anbjornsdatter and Tollef Johan Tollefsen, tenant farmer no. 13 d, Skare.

No children.

The deed to Knut from the father on this farm, sk. m 1.87, for 1400 kroner plus pension contract is dated July 12, 1919. Knut is listed in the 1900 census as a merchant, farmer and owner of the main building, while his parents live in the pension house. Five years later a new main building was built on the farm, the only building left standing today.
Knut worked for the federal harbor department, before he started his general store in Sørvågen in the mid 1880's. He ran this store with his wife until he died. He also ran a hostel from his home in Kvalvik.

Kaia was vice chairwoman of the women's municipal government from 1926–1928.

Knut Tollefsen Kvalvik (1857 – 1940) and his wife Kaia Tollefsdatter (1868 – 1957).

6. **Gustav Hansen.** 1922 – 1961.

Born July 17, 1890, died Oct. 11, 1961, son of Anne Marie and Hans Knut Eriksen, tenant farmer no. 23 c, Skare.

Married Nov. 17, 1915 to **Lovisa Tobiasdatter Sørhus,** born Nov. 26, 1893, died Nov. 17, 1960, daughter of Anne Martha Laurine Johannesdatter and Tobias Sørhus, tenant farmer no. 23 e, Klovning.

Children:

a. Hanna *Marie*, born Sept. 6, 1916, died May 16, 1940. Marie also had a farm here.
b. Lars Tobias. born June 13, 1918, died Nov. 24, 1918.
c. Tordis *Laurine*, born Nov. 1, 1919, died June 14, 1934.
d. Hans Knut, born Sept. 15, 1922, married in 1954 to Valborg Martinsen, next farmer.
e. Tobias, born Sept. 23, 1924, married in 1952 to Svanhild Klovning, tenant farm no. 37, Kvalvik.
f. Einar, born July 30, 1929, died June 26, 1943.
g. *Gudrun* Ludveig, born Jan. 9, 1934, married in 1963 to Robert Peter Tollefsen. They live in Oakland, California, USA.

The deed to Gustav on this farm, sk. m. 1.87, from Knut Kvalvik in the amount of 8000 kroner is dated Nov. 20, 1922. In 1956 the livestock consisted of 2 cows, 10 sheep and some chickens. The estate was taken over in 1963 by Gudrun Hansen.

7. **Hans Knut Hansen.** 1961 – 1985.

The Gustav Hansen family in 1953: From left: Gudrun, Tobias, Gustav, Hans Knut and Lovise.

See tenant farmer no. 46, Skare.

The farm has since been utilized as an additional farming area.

Farm no. 3. From farm no. 1 and 2 in 1838, earlier rental property

1. Ole Karlsen. 1841 – 1875.
Baptized Dec. 4, 1806, died May 1, 1876, son of Anna Olsdatter and Karl Asbjornsen, tenant farmer no. 13 e, Kvalvik.

Married in 1st marriage Dec. 16, 1838 to **Gurine Danielsdatter,** born 1807, died Nov. 1, 1855, daughter of Brita Kristendatter and Daniel Bårdsen, Tunge in Utvik, Avaldsnes, and widow of Sjur Tollefsen, Austrheim.

Married in 2nd marriage July 2, 1857 to **Berthe Malene Jonsdatter,** born May 20, 1818, died Jan. 4, 1904, daughter of Anne Andersdatter and Jon Johannesen, tenant farmer no. 8 b, Klovning.

Ole's daughter with Ingeborg Knutsdatter Austrheim:

a. Ingeborg, born May 20, 1832, married in 1860 to Ole Olsen Haga, Risoy.

Children in 1st marriage:

The vessel "Sira," pulling herring fishing net in 1948, owned by Gustav Hansen.

b. Anne Serine, born June 8, 1839, married in 1865 to Nils Thomassen Østhus, tenant farmer no. 18, Klovning.
c. Sjur, born Jan. 7, 1843, next farmer.

Children in 2nd marriage:

d. Karl Johan, born Sept. 24, 1857. died Oct. 4, 1857
e. Berthe *Gurine*, born July 19, 1859. In 1900 she lived in Haugesund and did laundry. She had a son Johan Gunvald, born June 29, 1886, with Edvard T. Tollefsen, Kvalvik.
f. Anne Malene, born Dec. 13, 1861, married Bikshavn, Haugesund.

Berthe Malene's daughter with Ådne Isaksen, N. Håland:

g. Anne Marthe, born June 18, 1841, next farmer.

The inheritance deed to Ole from J. Dahm on the rental property "Qvalvigspladset," sk. 12 mrk. dried fish, and amounting to 75 Spd. is dated Dec. 27, 1838.

He took over the farm in 1841 against a pension contract to his father, consisting of, among other items: 6 v. oats, feed for 2 sheep, free room, heat and light, estimated value 30 Spd. for 5 years.
The farm was assessed in 1865 to 140 Spd. and consisted of 13 mål fields and meadows. The entire estate including outfields for 25 and peat for 19 Spd. was estimated to be worth 190 Spd.

Annual yield was 10 barrels of oats, 3 barrels of barley and 8 barrels of potatoes. The livestock consisted of 1 horse, 2 cows, 10 sheep and 1 pig.

In the settlement after Gurine in 1857 there were assets worth 292 Spd., of which the farm itself made up for 200 Spd. From that amount 114 Spd. was subtracted to pay for debt, 12 Spd. for the funeral and 10 Spd. in settlement costs.

Sjur Olsen Kvalvik (1843–1914).

2. **Sjur Olsen.** 1875 – 1914. Born Jan. 7, 1843, died Aug. 29, 1914, son of previous farmer.

Married July 5, 1863 to **Anne Marthe Ådnesdatter,** born June 18, 1841, died Apr. 28, 1890, daughter of previous farmer.

Children:

a. Berthe Marie, born Mar. 26, 1862, had a daughter Berthe Kristine, (1884–1885) with Ole Kristoffersen, Liknes. She emigrated to USA in 1887 and married Olstad there.
b. *Jonette* Cathrine, born Mar. 19, 1865, married in 1900 to Martin Nilsen, tenant farmer no. 20, Austrheim.
c. Berthe Malene, born Feb. 20, 1868, emigrated to USA in 1893, married Kristian Disserud in 1897.

d. *Olava* Gurine, born Sept. 15, 1871, died in 1974, emigrated to USA in 1888, quarantined at Ellis Island for six months, lived in Wisconsin, married Benjamin Thompson in 1894, moved in S. Dakota, then Mahnomen, Minnesota, 7 children, died 103 yrs. old.
e. Anna *Serine*, born Aug. 6, 1875, married to Martin Johannesen, tenant farmer no. 28, Kvalvik.
f. Olga Mathilde, born Oct. 16, 1877, died Sept. 2, 1912.
g. Sofie Amalie, born Mar. 2, 1881, married to Karl Helgesen, Haugesund.
h. *Ole* Mikal, born July 14, 1883, next farmer.

The mortgage on the farm Sjur received in the settlement after his father, sk. m. 0.99, is dated May 29, 1879.

In 1875 Sjur is described in the records as a farmer, tenant farmer and fisherman. His father was then an invalid. The livestock consisted of 1 cow and 4 sheep.

Sjur was assistant lighthouse attendant for Utsira lighthouse from 1899 until he died.

3. **Ole Sjursen.** 1915 – 1955.
Born July 14, 1883, died Nov. 15, 1961, son of previous farmer.

Married Jan. 17, 1904 to **Regine Berthea (Thea) Tollefsen,** born Sept. 23, 1881, died Dec. 19, 1957, daughter of Marta Eline Rasmusdatter and Tollef Johan Tollefsen, tenant farmer no. 13 i, Skare.

Children:

a. Sigrid Marie, born May 15, 1904, died May 9, 1909.
b. *Laura* Birgitte, born Sept. 22, 1905, married in 1931 to Jakob Jakobsen, tenant farmer no.33, Kvalvik.
c. Jenny Malene, born Aug. 16, 1907, died Mar. 20, 1909.
d. *Olav* Bernhard, born May 3, 1909, married in 1941 to Martha Klovning, tenant farm no. 32, Klovning.
e. *Sigvald* Ludolf, born Sept. 13, 1912, next farmer.
f. *Jenny* Malene, born Oct. 28, 1916, married in 1940 to Hjalmar Thomassen, tenant farmer no. 37, Skare
g. Olga *Marie,* born Jan. 7, 1919, married in 1956 to Thorleif Klovning, farmer no. 1 – 13, Klovning.

The deed from the other heirs to Ole for this farm, with a tax burden of sk, m. 0.99, in the amount of 1365 kroner is dated Oct. 27, 1915.

A new main dwelling was built in 1916. In 1956 the farm had livestock consisting of 2 cows and 9 sheep.

Bendik Tollefsen (1874–1918) and Lisa Mathiasdatter (1876–1936).

4. **Sigvald Sjursen.** 1960 – 1980
Born Sept. 13, 1912, died Aug. 26, 1984, son of previous farmer.

Unmarried.

The farm has been farmed in recent years as an additional farm, and was taken over in 1990 by Marie Klovning.

Farm no 4. Espedalen. From farm no. 1 in 1898

1. **Bendik Tollefsen.** 1898 – 1935
Born July 16, 1874, died Feb. 20, 1918, son of Torborg Eline Eriksdatter and Tollef Knutsen, farm no. 1 – 4 h, Kvalvik.

Married July 12, 1898 to **Elisabeth (Lisa) Mathiasdatter,** born Aug. 2, 1876, died Apr. 17, 1936, daughter of Gunhilde Oline Ellingsdatter and Mathias Jobsen, farm no. 10 – 2 b, Hovland.

Children:

a. *Tilla* Teoline, born July 23, 1899, married in 1923 to Kasper Bendiksen, tenant farmer no. 28, Skare.

b. Mathias George, born May 8, 1901, died Feb. 27, 1903.
c. Marie Gunhilde, born Feb. 15, 1903, died May 1, 1903.
d. *Mathias* George, born Feb. 26, 1904, next farmer.
e. Edvard, born Oct. 31, 1905, married in 1936 to Torine Kvalvik, tenant farm no. 34, Kvalvik.
f. Elias, born July 27, 1907, married in 1935 to Marie Gunhilde Haugland, tenant farm no. 37, Hovland.
g. *Benny* Elisabet, born Jan. 14, 1911, married in 1935 to Nils Larsen, Stråtveit in Vats.

Bendik took over half the farm in 1898 according to the purchasing contract dated Mar. 29, 1898, and the deed from his father, with a recorded tax liability of sk. m. 1.87, was in the amount of 1400 kroner, plus an old age pension contract worth 500 kr., dated Dec. 17, 1906.

They built their main dwelling here in 1900. This was taken out of the estate in 1936 and became farm no. 9, Vestheim, and eventually taken over by his son Edvard. A new barn was built in 1905.

2. **Mathias Kvalvik.** 1935 – 1978.
Born Feb. 26, 1904, died Apr. 15, 1951, son of previous farmer.

Married Dec. 30, 1930 to **Åsa Klovning,** born Mar. 26, 1907, daughter of Thala and Johannes Klovning, farmer no. 2 – 2 c. Klovning.

Children:

a. *Tor* Johannes, born Oct. 15, 1931, married in 1955 to Ellinor Sofie Johannesen, was Harbor Master in Haugesund.
b. *Borgny* Elise, born Dec. 20, 1937, married in 1961 to Edvin Kvalvik, moved to Valevåg, Sveio.

The deed to Mathias for this farm from the other heirs is dated May 19, 1936. They bought the "Oliver House" from Ann Martha Gautsen around 1930. Mathias sailed as First Mate for a number of years before the war.

In 1956 the livestock consisted of 3 cows, 1 horse, some chickens and 4 sheep. The farm was eventually taken over by Reidar Klovning in 1986.

Farm no. 11. From Farm no. 2 in 1937

1. **Toralf Kvalvik.** 1937 – 1971

Born Sept. 1, 1891, died Mar. 19, 1971, son of Berthe Malene Larsdatter and Tobias Olsen, farm no. 2 – 8 b, Kvalvik.

Married July 2, 1922 to Gjertrud Bakke, born Jan. 16, 1898, died Jan. 13, 1990, daughter of Adrianne and Nils Bakke, Malangen in Troms.

Children:

a. Malmfrid, born Jan. 20, 1924, married in 1950 to Idar Havikbotn, Utsira School no. 28.
b. Arne, born Nov. 15, 1925, died 1983, married to Else Margrethe Molstad, lived in Kopervik.
c. Oddmund, born June 23, 1930, married to Elisabeth Dueland, lives in Haugesund.
d. Norunn, born May 7, 1937, married to Ottar Severin Andreassen, lives in Vikedal.
e. *Torbjorg* Gjertrud, born Aug. 31, 1942, married to Gunnar Håland, lives in Horpestad, Bryne.

Toralf took over 2/3 of the farm, inherited from his father in 1937, with a tax liability of sk. m. 2.55.

The main dwelling on the farm was built in 1930. The barn was built in 1942. The livestock consisted in 1956 of 8 cows, a horse, chickens and 12 sheep.

Toralf was chairman of the first history book committee, which was established on the island in 1952. He collected material for many years for the future Utsira farm history book.

Gjertrud was a teacher on Utsira in the years 1920 – 1963.

The farm here was in later years used as additional farmland, and in 1992 it was taken over by Torbjorn Rasmussen.

Tenant farmers

1. **Bjorn.** 1606 – 1612

He is mentioned in the county records during the above years.

2. **Elling.** 1629 – 1633

He is mentioned as an impoverished cotter. He is possibly Elling Arvesen, farmer no. 1 at Klovning.

3. **Torkel.** 1640 – 1644

He is mentioned in the county records during the above years.

Bridal couple in 1922. Toralf Kvalvik (1891–1971) and Gjertrud Bakke (1898–1990).

4. **Peder Johansen.** 1664
Born 1630. He is listed as a tenant in the 1664 census. It may possibly be the same Peder who is listed in 1673 as one of the farmers at Kvalvik.

5. **Sjur (Haraldsen).** 1675
He is mentioned in the court records of 1675 in connection with the shipwreck of a German vessel. He may be son of Harald Knutsen, farmer no. 5 here.

Harvesting at Kvalvik around 1920 west of Herbergshaugen. From left: Sina Dalastein, Methy Rasmussen, Kaia Olsen and Tobias Kvalvik.

6. **Elling Johannesen.** 1677
Born around 1660 and is mentioned in the military records in 1677, otherwise unknown. It is possible that a person called Johannes Ellingsen, born in 1685 and who was a farm hand on Skare in 1701, may have been a son of Elling.

7. **Peder Olsen.** 1692
He is mentioned in the military records in that year.

8. **Truls Hansen.** 1688 – 1705
Born in 1657, died sometime in the period 1701 to 1707. Origin is unknown.

Married in first marriage to (name unknown).

Married a second time to **Gjertrud Kristoffersdatter**, further history unknown.

Children in first marriage:

a. Hans. born 1688.
b. Bår, born 1690.

Children in 2nd marriage:

c. Kristoffer, born 1698.

They are listed as tenants here in 1701. Abraham Olsen is running the farm here in 1706, while Gjertrud and the children live at Klovning. The place here is called "Backen" at that time.

"Backen," cotter place

9. **Abraham Olsen.** 1706 – 1734
He took over this place after Gjertrud. See more about this family under tenant farmer no. 2, Klovning.

10. **Johannes Ellingsen.** 1735 – 1759
Born 1693, buried Mar. 31, 1765, son of Elling Hansen, farm no. 2 – 1, Kvalvik.

Possibly married to **Anna Abrahamsdatter,** born 1695, buried July 2, 1767, daughter of previous tenant farmer. She is listed in 1758 as servant here, and she (or her sister) may have been the wife of Johannes.

Known children:

a. Elling, born 1720, married in 1749 to Randi Larsdatter, farm no. 1 – 5, Austrheim.
b. Thomas, born 1724, married in 1749 to Ingeborg Larsdatter, farm no. 1 – 4, Skare.
c. Rasmus, born 1727, next tenant farmer.

11. **Rasmus Johannesen.** 1759 – 1766
Born 1727, buried Nov. 23, 1765, son of previous tenant farmer.

Married in 1st marriage on Jan. 23, 1759 to **Guri Knutdatter,** born 1720, buried Apr. 8, 1759, origin is unknown. (She may be daughter of Knut Olsen Austrheim on farm no. 4.)

Married in 2nd marriage Oct. 31, 1760 to **Kari Knutsdatter,** possibly sister of Guri (above). No children.

The following note is listed in the church records in 1763:

> Martha Simonsdatter committed adultery with the married man, Rasmus Johansen, on Udzire according to testimony and confessions of both her and Rasmus Johansen.

Rasmus perished at sea and Kari married the 2nd time on Mar. 22, 1767 to:

12. **Mats Torkelsen.** 1767 – 1794

Born 1743, buried Mar. 25, 1787, from Vikedal (Sigleskar or Skipevåg?).

They did not have any children.

There was an estate settlement after Mats in 1787. Among the estate assets of 84–2–17 rdl., there was 62–3–13 rdl. left for the widow and his relatives in Vikedal and Jelsa. Among misc. items the following are listed:

> Standing buildings on the farm 23–0–0, 2 cows 8–2–0, 1 small pig and one ram 1–2–0, 1 old tiled heating stove 4–2–0, 1 cattle trough of 12–can capacity 2–0–0, 1 baking board 0–3–8, 1 six–oar boat *with unusable sails* 3–0–0, 1 four–oar boat with sail 1–2–16, 5 spring herring fishing nets 2–2–0, 1 large, old herring fishing net 0–0–16, 12 lobster pots 0–3–0, 1 old fishing scoop 0–1–0, 1/2 of a boat shed 0–3–0, 4 silver spoons (engraved with M.T.S. and T.S.S.) 4–0–0, 2 silver drinking cups (engraved with T.S.K.K.D.) and a pair of silver buckles 3–2–8, 2 pillows, 1 feather-filled and one filled with straw 0–2–0, 1 clothing chest with lock and ornamental reinforcements 0–3–8, 1 main sail and jib for a six–oar boat 1–2–0.

13. **Karl Asbjørnsen.** 1793 – 1841

Baptized May 8, 1768, died Dec. 31, 1848, son of Marta Jørgensdatter and Asbjorn Olsen, Grønningen, Torvestad.

Married Dec. 6, 1794, to **Anna Olsdatter,** baptized Dec. 19, 1770, died May 13, 1837, daughter of Malene Knutsdatter and Ole Knutsen, farm no. 6 – 2 a, Austrheim.

Children:

a. Malene, baptized Jan. 15, 1795, buried June 30, 1816.
b. Marta, baptized Apr. 16, 1797, buried Oct. 1, 1797, 3 months old.
c. Oline, baptized Sept. 30, 1798, married in 1834 to Kristian Kristiansen, moved to Rossabø in Skåre.
d. Marta Serine, baptized Oct. 17, 1802, married in 1829 to Jakob Jonsen, tenant farmer no. 16, Kvalvik.
e. Ole, baptized Dec. 4, 1806, married in 1838 to Gurine Danielsdatter. He got the deed to the place here, farm no. 3.
f. Anne Marie, baptized July 11, 1813, died Apr. 17, 1862.
g. Malene, born Jan. 30, 1818, married in 1844 to Jon Olsen, Lillesund in Skåre. Emigrated to USA in 1855.

The farm was assessed to 30 Spd. in 1823, and was able to sustain 1 cow and a horse and yield 8 – 9 barrels of grain. The two tenants on Kvalvik each had to work 3 days each season.

View from Herbergshaugen southward toward Siradal. Kvalvik to the right, all the way to the left is the chapel. In the middle of the picture is the J. Dahm house. Photo by Robert Kloster, 1932, Historic Museum in Bergen.

Ole Karlsen inherited and got the deed to this rental place in 1838.

In the estate settlement after Anna in 1839 the place is referred to as "Qvalvigsnesset." The inventory and misc. items were auctioned off for 87–1–8 Spd. and only 11–2–16 Spd. was left to the heirs.

Jupatrevik, cotter place.

14. **Ole Olsen.** 1775 – 1820
Born 1749, died June 21, 1799, son of Valborg Knutsdatter and Ole Reiersen, farm no. 3 – 1 c, Austrheim.

Married July 9, 1775 to **Malene Oddsdatter,** baptized June 20, 1754, died Apr. 11, 1835, daughter of Helga Johannesdatter and Odd Danielsen, Ovrebo, Torvestad.

Children:

a. Valborg, baptized Nov. 2, 1775, died Sept. 12, 1867. She lived in 1865 with her brother Knut; was then blind.

b. Helga, baptized Feb. 2, 1780.
c. Ole, baptized July 20, 1783, buried Mar. 25, 1784.
d. Ole, baptized Apr. 3, 1785, married in 1809 to Maria Kristensdatter, farm no. 4 – 7, Hovland.
e. Anna, baptized May 18, 1788, married in 1814 to Jon Monsen, Skjøllingstad, Torvestad.
f. Odd, baptized Jan. 21, 1792, married in 1815 to Eli Ingebrigstdatter, Røvaer. Moved to Hausken, Torvestad.
g. Knut, born in 1796, married to Siri Iversdatter, tenant farmer no. 17, Kvalvik.

It must have been hard to manage to feed a family on this place. In 1822 – 23 it is indicated that the place could sustain 1 cow and yield only 1 barrel of grain per year. The place was then deserted but was used by Knut Bentsen. It was assessed to 10 Spd.

The settlement after Ole in 1799 indicates, however, that the situation here was not among the worst on the island. The estate's assets are worth 40–2–15 rdl. and left to the heirs are 29 rdl. Among the misc. items left are:

> 1 cabin with a barn 20–0–0, 1 iron stove 6–0–0, 1 *small boat shed with sod roof* 2–0–0, 1 cow "Drivrej" 4–0–0, 1 small foal 1–0–0, 1 old four–oar boat with sail 2–0–16 and 30 lobster pots 2–2–0.

15. **Anders Andersen.** 1800 – 1818

Baptized Sept. 9, 1780, died Aug. 11, 1818, son of Ingeborg Knutsdatter and Anders Pedersen, farmer no. 1 – 7 m, Hovland.

Unmarried.

Anders was a farmhand on Kvalvik, in 1801 with Henrik T. Galtung. There was an estate settlement after him in 1819. He left assets worth 20–4–2 Spd. His two sisters inherited 13–2–0 Spd. Misc. items left consisted mostly of the deceased's clothing as follows:

> 1 pair of gold collar buttons 4–0–0, 1 silver hat pin 0–4–0, silver buttons 0–3–0, silver coins 0–2–12 and a pair of new shoes 0–4–0.

16. **Jakob Jonsen.** 1829 – 1835

He was tradesman from Haraldseid in Skjold. He married Marta Serine Karlsdatter in 1829, see under tenant farmer no. 31, Austrheim.

17. **Knut Olsen.** 1834 – 1876

Born 1796, died Nov. 4, 1874, son of Malene and Ole Olsen, no. 14 here.

Herring fishing in Nordviksvagen around 1910. Photo by A. P. Wallevik, Hardanger Folk Museum in Utne.

Married Sept. 29, 1834 to **Siri Iversdatter,** baptized Mar. 26, 1797, died Nov. 6, 1876, daughter of Siri Johannesdatter and Iver Bårdsen, Bakken in Norheim, Torvestad.

Children:

a. Ole, born 1835, died Mar. 29, 1835, 2 weeks old.
b. Ole Iver (Oliver), born May 8, 1836, next tenant farmer.
c. Martha Malene, born Nov. 25, 1840, died Sept. 17, 1922, married to shoemaker Ole Salvesen from Sira in Bakke county. They lived in Brogade 75 in Haugesund (1885).

Knut is listed in 1865 as a cotter without farmland on farm no. 1. In 1875 Siri has three sheep and lives with her son and daughter in their household.

18. **Oliver Knutsen.** 1868 – 1905
Born May 8, 1836, died Mar. 12, 1902, son of previous tenant farmer.

Married Mar. 29, 1868 to **Berthe Gurine Tollefsdatter,** born Apr. 25, 1833, died Aug. 6, 1905, daughter of Marta Serine Johannesdatter and Tollef Gudmundsen, tenant farmer no. 12 b, Skare.

They had one stillborn daughter on Nov. 25, 1872.

The lease contract to Oliver from Tollef Knutsen on the house lot, 14 x 14 alen is dated May 14, 1869. The lot was located near the old road in Espedalen. He paid 7 Spd. in annual rent for this lease and 6 days of work. "The Oliver house" as it later was referred to, was taken over by Anna Martha and Hans Gautsen, before it was eventually taken over by Åsa and Mathias Kvalvik around 1930.

19. **Hans Hansen.** 1832 – 1851
Baptized Feb. 7, 1796, died Mar. 18, 1848, son of Anna Hansdatter and Hans Hansen, tenant farmer no. 20 i, Nordvik (later no. 18, Hovland).

Married in 1st marriage on Oct. 15, 1823 to **Barbro Olsdatter,** born 1767 (1775?), died Aug. 6, 1840. She is listed as Opheim in marriage documents.

Married in 2nd. marriage on Oct. 10, 1842 to **Ragnhild Larsdatter**, born in 1801, died in 1880 at Østhus, Åkra, daughter of Lars Olsen, Breim in Gloppen.

No children.

They received a lease for a house lot in Kvalvik from J. Dahm. The house was then already built in a field on the farm in Skare with the rights to cut peat in Vestramarka. The lease is dated Sept. 21, 1832 and is paid for with 5 days of work per year.

Ragnhild was married the 2nd time in 1851 to the widower Sjur Johannesen from Etne. They moved to Saevik, and later again to Østhus in Åkra.

20. **Sigbjorn Knutsen.** 1847 – 1850
Born 1822, son of Knut Knutsen Birkeland.

Married July 1, 1849 to **Anne Marthe Rasmusdatter,** born Feb. 21, 1827, daughter of Jobiane Jobsdatter and Rasmus Tollefsen, farmer no. 7 – 7 g, Hovland.

Sigbjorn was a ship carpenter. They moved to Bergen. They had children: Anna Cathrine, born in 1851, Jobiane, born in 1852, Rasmus Johan, born 1853, Severine, born 1858 and Andreas Martin, born in 1862.

21. **Kristen Johnsen.** 1848 – 1863.
Baptized May 30, 1813, died July 9, 1883 on Klovning. He was the son outside marriage of Berthe Kristinsdatter and John Johannesen Klovning.

Unmarried.

Kristen was a handyman. He was not on the island in 1865, but he worked for John Mathias Johnsen Skare in 1875.

From left: Jørgen Nilsen, Hersleb Helgesen and Tollef Tollefsen Kvalvik.

22. **Jakob Bentsen.** 1838 – 1869
Baptized June 3, 1804, died Mar. 6, 1869, son of Berte Knutsdatter and Bent Bentsen, Veste in Skåre.

Married June 26, 1830 to **Ingeborg Oline Rasmusdatter,** baptized Mar. 15, 1812, died Aug. 18, 1868, daughter of Jobiane Jobsdatter and Rasmus Tollefsen, farmer no. 7 – 7 a, Hovland.

Children:

a. Berta, born Jan. 10, 1831, married to Tollef Amundsen, tenant farmer no. 29, Kvalvik.
b. Rasmus, born Apr. 14, 1833, next tenant farmer.
c. Ånen Bendix, born Jan. 14, 1836. died Aug. 7, 1836.
d. Jobiane, born Aug. 2, 1838.
e. Ånen Bendix, born Aug. 2, 1842, married in 1862 to Anna Helene Jakobie Pedersdatter. Skeiseid, merchant in Haugesund.
f. Gunhilde Oline, born June 4, 1845. married in 1869 to Johannes Pedersen, tenant farmer no. 24, Kvalvik.

g. Gurine, born Nov. 24, 1848, married widower Johannes Pedersen in 1872.
h. Niels Johan, born Apr. 24, 1852, seaman, married in 1882 to Eli Karine Hansdatter, Veste, lived in Haugesund.

The family lived a few years as tenant farmers at farm no. 7 in Hovland before they moved to Kvalvik. They also lived at farm no. 2 and Jakob is listed in 1865 as fisherman and tenant without farmland.

23. **Rasmus Jakobsen.** 1855 – 1858
Born Apr. 14, 1833, son of previous tenant farmer.
Married on Apr. 10, 1855 to **Karen Elisabeth Israelsdatter,** born in 1829 in Bergen.

Children:
a. Hans Jakob, born Jan. 17, 1856; he was a seaman in 1885.
b. Elisabeth Wilhelmine, born Mar. 25, 1860 in Skåre; she was a dressmaker in 1885.

The family moved around 1858 to Storesund in Skåre. In 1885 the family lived in Haraldsgt. 179 in Haugesund. Rasmus at that time worked as a boathouse handyman for F. Eide.

24. **Johannes Pedersen.** 1869 – 1870
Born 1838 in Flatland in Jevnaker.
Married first on May 9, 1869 to **Gunhilde Oline Jakobsdatter,** born June 4, 1845, died May 23, 1871 in Haugesund, daughter of Ingeborg and Jakob Bentsen, tenant farm no. 22 above.
Remarried May 14, 1872 to **Gurine Jakobsdatter**, born Nov. 24, 1848, sister of Gunhilde, above.

Children born on Utsira:
a. Caroline, born Oct. 9, 1869, married Karl M. Karlstad, lived in Kristiana.

Johannes was a smith and worked on the harbor project on Utsira and other places in Norway. In 1872 he lived at Vanse, Vest-Agder.

25. **Margrethe Larsdatter.** 1844
She had a daughter with her fiancé, bachelor **Ole Hansen Østhus**, died June 29, 1845, 24 years old, lived at Hovland:

a. Oline, born Jan. 19, 1844.

Margrethe probably worked on Kvalvik, but it is not known where she originated or where she and her daughter moved later.

26. **Gudmund Tollefsen.** 1895 – 1897
Born Nov. 22, 1871, died April 24, 1928, son of Berthe Jakobsdatter and Tollef Amundsen, tenant farmer no. 29 f, Kvalvik.

Married to **Sina Larsdatter Nedrejordet**, born in 1870 in Fjellberg.

Children born on Utsira:

a. Larsine Gunhilde, born Mar. 2, 1895, died July 9, 1897.

Foster son:

b. Lauritz Carlsen, living in USA in 1928.

Gudmund was a seaman. In 1900 the family lived in Haugesund.

27. **Thore Mikal Olsen.** 1884 – 1887
Born Nov. 6, 1851, died July 31, 1887. son of Torine Toresdatter and Ole Bårdsen, farm no. 2 – 6 b, Kvalvik.

Married July 10, 1884 to **Lovise Gurine Mathiasdatter,** born Dec. 14, 1866, died Dec. 7, 1885, daughter of Martha Olava Mikkelsatter and J. Mathias Ellingsen, farm no. 2 – 4 a, Skare.

Children:

a. Martha Olava, born Dec. 26, 1884, worked as a nurse in Oakland, Calif., USA.

In the 1875 census Thore Mikal is not listed but assumed living in Helgoland – as a fisherman. When they got married in 1884 he is listed as a farmer and probably in line to take over after his parents, but both died at young age.

28. **Martin Johannesen.** 1904.
Born in 1878, died Sept. 29, 1940 in Osterøy. From Stamnes, Bruvik.

Married to **Serine Sjursdatter,** born Aug. 6, 1875, daughter of Anne Marthe Ådnesdatter and Sjur Olsen, farmer no. 3 – 2 e, Kvalvik.

Children born on Utsira:

a. Sofie Amanda, born Aug. 15, 1904, died 1983.

Martin was a seaman. He is listed as a work boat skipper in 1904. He moved to Stamnes, Nordaland.

29. **Tollef Amundsen.** 1857 – 1903
Born 1834 on Ramsvik in Etne, died Mar. 27, 1903.

Married Dec. 6, 1857 to **Berthe Jakobsdatter,** born Jan. 10, 1831, died Mar. 8, 1897, daughter of Ingeborg and Jakob Bentsen, tenant farmer no. 22 a, Kvalvik.

Children:

a. Ingeborg Oline, born Jan. 29, 1858, married in 1887 to Nils Johannes Nilsen, tenant farmer no. 19, Austrheim.
b. Martin Cornelius, born Apr. 8, 1860, died Apr. 20, 1872.
c. Job, born Jan. 25, 1864, next tenant farmer.
d. Gunhilde, born Feb. 6, 1867, died May 14, 1867.
e. Jakob Ingvald, born Oct. 11, 1868, married in 1895 to Eli Serine Nilsdatter, Veim, Førdefjorden. He died July 6, 1897 and Eli Serine and the daughter emigrated to USA.
f. Gudmund, born Nov. 22, 1871, married to Sina Larsdatter, tenant farm no. 26, Kvalvik.
g. Martin Cornelius, born Dec. 3, 1875, was a fisherman and lived with his father in 1900, married Sofie Mariane Jørgensen, Åsgårdstrand, Vestfold in 1901.

The lease contract to Tollef from Ole Bårdsen, Tollef Knutsen and Amund Bårdsen on a house lot, 96 x 96 alen, at Smørdusk is dated July 20, 1860. In compensation he pays with three work days per year, and furthermore it is noted: *He should not be allowed to have chickens.*

Tollef worked for many years for the Harbor Authority.

30. **Job Tollefsen.** 1885 – 1936
Born Jan. 25, 1864, died July 1, 1936, son of previous tenant farmer.

Married Nov. 10, 1885 to **Martha Ludvigsdatter,** born 1862 on Grip, Hitra, died Mar. 31, 1925.

Children:

a. Ludvig, born Aug. 1, 1886 in Kristiansund, next tenant farmer.
b. Tollef Kornelius, born Jan. 5, 1889, died Jan. 31, 1910.
c. Edvard. born Aug. 25, 1892, died Feb. 26, 1928 in Bergen. He was a tailor.
d. Jenny, born Apr. 24, 1898, twin, died Apr. 29, 1898.
e. Jenny, born and died Apr. 24, 1898, twin.

The lease contract to Job on the house lot from Tollef Knutsen is dated

Job Tollefsen (1864 – 1936) and Martha Ludvigsdatter Kvalvik (1862 – 1925).

Apr. 16, 1892. Compensation for the lot was an annual contribution of six days work. The house of Hansine Knutsdatter (widow of Amund Bårdsen) was on the lot and this house was bought by Job at an auction in the spring. It was separated from the farm in 1938 and was designated farm no. 12, "Fagerheim."

As his father did, Job worked for the Harbor Authority for many years. He was hired as a smith and machinist from 1881 to 1925.

31. **Ludvig J. Kvalvik.** 1936 – 1954

They built themselves a house in Nordvik and it is listed there as tenant farm no. 72 a.

32. **Johannes Olsen.** 1902 – 1920

Born Dec. 5, 1862, son of Torine Toresdatter and Ole Bårdsen, farmer no. 2 – 6 g, Kvalvik.

Married Oct. 14, 1894 to **Berthe Karine Konradsdatter** born June 5, 1875, daughter of Berthe Gurine Jobsdatter, and Konrad Severin Ånensen, tenant farmer no. 25 f, Hovland.

Children:

a. Andreasn Bertel, born Feb. 8, 1896.

Among those on the outermost island.
The man who for 44 years worked on harbor projects from Hammerfest to the Swedish Border.

By the crossroads where the road goes westward towards Kvalvik on Utsira lies a pretty, small, white–painted house. On the south side of the house on each side of the stone steps leading up to the front door, one can each summer find a richly blooming flower bed sheltered from the rough wind bearing down the island valley from the north. And inside behind the window panes in the living room on the south side of the house one can see healthy–looking potted plants in full bloom cared for by loving hands. There is a feeling of coziness and hominess about this well–kept little house, and I have spent many pleasant times under this roof. It is my old friend Job Tollefsen who lives there. He is now past 70, but is still going strong keeping up with everything that is going on through radio and newspapers. It is now 9 years since Job Tollefsen retired as a smithy and machinist with the Harbor Authority after 44 years of work there. He began working in 1881 and has since then worked without interruption until he retired in 1925.

It is an impressive number of harbor and breakwater projects that Job Tollefsen has worked on over the years. The first project was Svaeholt near Hammerfest, and Grip near Kristiansund, then Godoy near Alesund. In 1884 and 1885 he worked on Sørehavnen (the southern port) on Utsira, and the devastating accident that happened there is still fresh in his mind. Some explosives accidentally ignited and debris was thrown all over the place killing two workers, Gudmund Nakken and Bertel Kvalvik, both from Utsira. One of them was thrown high up in the air by the explosion.

After Utsira, Tollefsen came to the Ferkingstad project at Karmøy and from there to Flekkefjord for a dredging project and then on to Risoer and Hvaler Islands near Fredrikstad for a breakwater project. From there he moved on to Asgaardstrand, Hellesoy on Jaeren, Obrestad and Kvitsoy. Then it was off to Gyllestad and Baardsholmen on Lista followed by three years on the lock project in Skjold and dredging in Roeksundskanalen, and from there to Fedje and finally Statt where he spent two years on a breakwater and launching ramp project.

Job Tollefsen, as can be seen, worked on harbor and breakwater projects all the way from Finnmark to the Swedish border. He has put in many an arduous turn along our long, exposed coastline, and any time he now enjoys in his cozy little home out there – on Norway's outermost island – is well deserved.

—Ola Nordmann

from Haugesunds Avis, 5 Oct. 1934.

b. Konstanse Bertine, born Dec. 8, 1897.
c. Olav Torvald, born Mar. 8, 1901.
d. Jenny Charlotte, born Mar. 24, 1903.
e. Mildrid Marie, born Sept. 16, 1908.
f. Job, born Nov. 26, 1911.
g. Mathias Bernhard, born June 15, 1914.

The family lived on Kvarkaneset before they built their home in Kvalvik. This later became farm no. 6, Tunheim, which later was taken over by Svend Klovning.

Johannes was a fisherman and also sailed as a seaman, and from 1908 he sailed as first mate. The family emigrated to the USA in 1920.

33. **Jakob Jakobsen.** 1932 – 1972
Born June 21, 1904, died Apr. 11, 1983, son of Amanda and Knut Jakobsen, Haugesund.

Married in 1931 to **Laura Kvalvik,** born Sept. 22, 1905, died June 2, 1972, daughter of Thea and Ole Sjursen, farm no. 3 – 3 b, Kvalvik.

Children:
a. *Reidun* Olaug, born Mar. 8, 1932, married 1953 to Adolf Skare, tenant farmer no. 45, Skare.
b. *Kjell* Arnstein, born Oct. 23, 1934, married in 1960 to Misao Harada from Japan and moved to Haugesund.
c. Jon *Bjarne*, born Nov. 29, 1940, died Aug. 11, 1962, perished while whale hunting in the South Seas.

Jakob was a seaman. They lived on farm no. 3 with Ole Sjursen.

34. **Edvard Kvalvik.** 1936 – 1992
Born Oct. 31, 1905, died Jan. 6, 1991, son of Lisa and Bendik Tollefsen, farm no. 4 – 1 e, Kvalvik.

Married June 27, 1936 to **Torine Kvalvik,** born Nov. 6, 1902, died May 3, 1992, daughter of Berthe Malene and Tobias Olsen, farm no. 2 – 8 h, Kvalvik.

Children:
a. Eldbjorg, born Jan. 10, 1940, married to Aksel Olsen, Ohm in Vats.

Edvard took over the main dwelling from his parents in 1936, when it was separated and designated farm no. 9, Vestheim. In 1976 the estate was taken over by their daughter, Eldbjorg.

From the living room in Lisa and Bendik Kvalvik's home in 1926. From Left: Edvard Kvalvik, Kasper Bendiksen, Tilla Bendiksen, Lisa Kvalvik and Benny Stråtveit.

35. **John Larsen,** 1936 – 1955
See farm no. 75, Nordvik.

36. **John Klovning.** 1948 – 1952
See tenant farm no. 28, Klovning.

37. **Tobias Hansen** 1963 –
Born Sept. 23, 1924, died Nov. 7, 1968, son of Lovisa and Gustav Hansen, farm no. 1 – 6 e, Kvalvik.

Married Nov. 29, 1952 to **Svanhild Klovning**, born July 9, 1932, daughter of Lovise and Valnum Klovning, tenant farmer no. 36, Hovland.

Children:

a. *Gunnar* Leidulf, born Feb. 6, 1954, married to Marit Grande, lives in Baerum.
b. *Vigleik* Ludvig, born Apr. 1, 1955, married in 1983 to Hilde Skjevdal, lives in Asker.
c. Torstein, born Nov. 1, 1960, lives in Oslo.
d. Synnøve, born Apr. 9, 1964, married in 1994 to Frode Honsi, lives in Stavanger.

They built their main dwelling here, farm no. 16, Kleiva, in 1963.

Tobias was a teacher for a couple of years at Utsira School, 1961 – 63. Svanhild works for Siratun Nursing Home.

38. **John Henry Thomassen.** 1975 –
Born Mar. 7, 1953, son of Jenny and Hjalmar Thomassen, tenant farmer no. 37 c, Skare.

Married Aug. 23, 1975 to **Herborg Hansen,** born July 1, 1854, daughter of Valborg and Hans Knut Hansen, tenant farmer no. 46 a, at Skare.

Children:

a. Stian, born July 24, 1977.
b. Einar, born Nov. 13, 1979.
c. John Helge, born Jan. 29, 1985.
d. Martin, born July 12, 1988.
e. Vibeke, born Mar. 27, 1990.

They built their main dwelling here on farm no. 3 in 1976.

39. **Inge Silden.** 1979 –
Born Sept. 1, 1951, from Silden in Sogn.

Married 1979 to **Ellinor Klovning,** born June 20, 1960, daughter of Tordis and Hans Klovning, tenant farmer no. 44 d, Skare.

Divorced.

Children:

a. Roy Inge, born Aug. 19, 1979.
b. Vivian, born Apr. 7, 1981.
c. Stig Henning, born Sept. 9, 1986.
d. Tanita Elise, born July 7, 1991.

They built their main dwelling here on farm no. 26, in 1981. Inge works on the ferry M/S "Utsira."

40. **Tor Harald Klovning.** 1984 – 1992
Born Apr. 17, 1952, son of Tordis and Hans Klovning, tenant farmer no. 44 c, Skare.

Married in 1972 to **Mary–Ann Børresen.** born 1953, from Bryne.

Children:

a. Cecilie, born 1974.
b. Mette, born 1977.
c. Hege, born 1980.
d. Susanne, born Apr. 22, 1985.

Their adoptive daughter:

e. Tine Agnieszka, born Aug. 12, 1983.

They lived on Bryne before they moved to Utsira in 1984, when they built their main dwelling here on farm no. 28. Tor Harald is an electrician, and the family moved to Haugesund in December 1992.

41. **Egil Skare.** 1993 –
Born June 6, 1967, son of Sigrid and Odd Skare, farm no. 1 – 13 a, Skare.

Married Aug. 21, 1993 to **Norunn Hauge,** born July 7, 1968, from Morgedal in Telemark.

Children:

a. Sindre, born Dec. 6, 1994.

They took over this property. Egil is chief engineer on the ferry M/S "Utsira." Norunn is a teacher at Utsira Children and Youth School.

Utsira Lighthouse

1851 – 1886: Registration. no. 70, tax liability 0–1–13 skd.
1886– : Farm no. 32, tax 0.39 sk.m.

According to a proposal by the Marine Department (authorized by the King on Feb. 18, 1843), construction of the two lighthouses on Utsira was begun in the spring of 1843. With as many as 120 men working, the towers were finished in the fall that same year. The living quarters for the attendants, tool sheds, laundry house (including two rooms for the lighthouse keeper), and a boat shed with a road up to the lighthouses, were built the following year. The total cost of the project came to 37, 383 Spd. The lighthouses were commissioned and put into operation on Aug. 15, 1844.

The deed to the Marine Department on behalf of the Lighthouse Authority, issued by the local farmers of west Nordvik, Kvalvik, Skare and Klovning, in the amount of 245 Spd. is dated Sept. 1, 1843.

Lighthouse keepers

1. **Nikolai Hansen Smith.** 1844 – 1854

Born May 7, 1801, died June 13, 1887 in Egersund, son of ironworks owner Hans Sivertsen Smith and Magdalene Marie Classen, Froland.

Married July 4, 1833 to his brother's daughter, **Hanne Smith**, born Mar. 11, 1808. died Dec. 8, 1890 on Årstad in Egersund, daughter of ironworks owner Sivert Nicolai Smith and Birgitte Johanne Christiane Roosen, Froland.

Utsira Lighthouses in 1913. Photos by Wilse. Norwegian Folk Museum.

Children:

a. Maria, born in 1835 in Lillesand, died Apr. 21, 1902 on Årstad.
b. Juline Birgithe Smith, born Sept. 24, 1838, died young.
c. Antheanette Marie Smith, born Sept. 27, 1840, died unmarried in 1902 at Egersund.
d. Anna Catharina, born Apr. 29, 1843, married in 1869 in Egersund to Johan Eberhart Klepzig, a sea captain.
e. Peter Hersleb Classen, born Mar. 18, 1845, was a sailor in 1865, died before 1890.
f. Jakobine Jobine, born May 23, 1847, married in 1884 to first mate Johan Henrik Steinkopf, Stavanger.
g. Herman, born May 18, 1849, died Jan. 30, 1916, married and lived with his wife in Antwerp, Belgium. Later he was lighthouse keeper at Eigeroy, Egersund.

Nikolai was a ship captain before he was hired as the lighthouse keeper in the Terningen Lighthouse in South Trondelag in 1841. In 1844 he became the first lighthouse keeper at Utsira Lighthouse. He remained in this position until the fall of 1854, when he was appointed lighthouse keeper at the new lighthouse at Eigeroy near Egersund.

In 1844 Nikolai suggested to the lighthouse commissioner that farm no. 1 at Hovland, which was for sale at that time, should be purchased by the state for this purpose, but this was not acted upon and he ended up purchasing the farm himself for 1000 Spd. However, when he later moved away from the island, he sold the farm to the Lighthouse Authority for 820 Spd. Nikolai must have been interested in farming because in 1850 he became one of only two in the entire Torvestad Church District who signed up as a member of Stavanger County Farming Association (The other member was Haagen H. Bakken, Skåre.).

2. **Just Hammerich Haasted.** 1855 – 1863

Baptized May 22, 1803, died June 25, 1863 on Utsira, the son of ship captain Lars Nielsen Haasted and Birgithe Fredericha Hammerrich, Flekkefjord.

Unmarried.

Just Hammerich was a merchant in Flekkefjord, before he was hired as the lighthouse keeper on Utsira.

3. **Ole Johan Sundt Eyde.** 1863 – 1884

Born June 26, 1812 in Flekkefjord, and died there on Mar. 13, 1888, son of Christen Johnsen Eyde and Petrine Louise Wiborg, Flekkefjord.

Ole Johan Sundt Eyde (1812–1888) and Susanne Kirstine Evensen (1825–1888).

Married Oct. 20, 1844 on Bragernes to **Susanne Kirstine Evensen,** born June 2, 1825, died Mar. 13, 1888 in Kristiania, daughter of merchant Ole Evensen and Birthe Kirstine Nordbye.

Children:

a. Marie Eyde, born Nov. 16, 1847 in Drammen, married in 1869 on Utsira to Ole Amundsen Norshuus (1837–1913). He was a telegraph inspector in Bergen from 1892 – 1905.
b. Louise Eyde, born Nov. 3, 1849 in Drammen, married in 1872 to wholesaler Christoffer Nielsen Wiig, Drammen.
c. Olga Eyde, born Sept. 18, 1851 in Drammen, married in 1872 to Hans Peter Egede Bjerck, Drammen.

Ole Johan was a ship captain before he was hired as a lighthouse keeper on Slotteroy Lighthouse in 1859. He began working as the lighthouse keeper at the Utsira Lighthouse on Sept. 18, 1863.

4. **Ole Schavland.** 1884 – 1887

Born Oct. 16, 1824 on Talgje, died Mar. 17, 1887 on Utsira, son of police inspector Christopher C. Østebø and Elisabeth Schavland (daughter of the church minister Schavland in Strand).

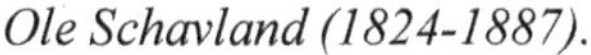

Ole Schavland (1824-1887).

Married in first marriage in 1843 to **Martha Thorsen** (born Nåden), from Judaberg, born 1813, died 1864, widow of hotel host Nils Thorsen.

Married the second time in 1865 to **Lovise Olsen,** born 1843, the daughter of Lavense Serine Larsdatter and Lars Olsen, Skudesneshavn.

Children from second marriage:

a. Christopher, born Aug. 27, 1866, died in 1909, married to Bolette Karine (Kaia) Thomasdatter Beite. They lived in Mobile, Alabama.
b. Lars, born Oct. 15, 1867, died Oct. 14, 1877.
c. Olaf, born Dec. 30, 1868. He and his brother Christopher accompanied George (Jørgen) Hovland back to the USA, after George was home visiting in the 1880's.
d. Martha, born Mar. 16, 1870, died Feb. 11, 1872.
e. Sigvald, born Aug. 19, 1871, married and settled in Portland, Oregon.
f. *Martha* Lovise, born Jan. 2, 1873, died in 1973, married in 1899 to ship captain Mathias Knutsen, Bergen. They lived in Mobile, Alabama.
g. Elisabeth, born Aug. 3, 1874, died Mar. 8, 1875.
h. Elisabeth, born Aug. 19, 1876, married to Boye, lived in Mobile, Alabama.
i. Laurentse, born Nov. 3, 1877, unmarried. She was a teacher and lived in Omaha, Nebraska.
j. Laura, born Apr. 13, 1879, married Anthony Parsons, Omaha, Nebraska in 1911.
k. Lars, born Aug. 28, 1880. died Apr. 3, 1881.
l. Lars, born Nov. 16, 1882, died July 24, 1890.

Ole ran a small hotel establishment and a general store on Judaberg, Finnoy. Later he ran a fish processing plant salting herring and operated a freighter trading in the North Sea. He was also part owner in several sailing ships out of Stavanger. He was the postmaster on Finnoy from 1853 until he moved to Utsira, and was the mayor on Finnoy during the period 1858 –1877 (with some brief interruptions).

Sørvågen 1949. Lighthouse Manager Aspen and Minister Karl Vaula.

In the early 1880's, his ship "Tolga" perished in a shipwreck and around the same time the sailing crisis in Stavanger occurred, so Ole went bankrupt and lost his properties on Judaberg.[64]

5. **Johannes Sørensen.** 1887 – 1902
Born in 1832 in Nevlunghavn, died Nov. 16, 1903 in Haugesund.

Married to **Jakobine Kristine Jakobsen,** born in 1841 in Fredriksvaern.

Children:

a. Carl Anton Severin, born 1866 in Lindås, emigrated to the USA in 1890.
b. Andreas Martin, born 1868 in Lindås.

---

[64] See Note 31.

c. Oline Gurine, born 1870 in Lindås, married in 1895 to school superintendent Erling Sorboen, Aurdal.
d. Thorvald, born Dec. 18, 1872, in Bjornor, died June 9, 1896.
e. Johanne, born 1875 in Bjornor, twin.
f. Jacobine Christine, born 1875 in Bjornor, twin, married in 1899 to bank teller Ferdinand Fredrik Hansen, Bergen.

Johannes was the assistant lighthouse keeper at the Hellesoy Lighthouse from 1862 into the 1870's, and then was hired at the Bjørnør Lighthouse, before becoming the lighthouse keeper at Utsira in 1887.

The family moved to Haugesund in 1902. When Johannes died, the family moved to Drammen.

6. **Paul Chr. Gärtner**. 1902 – 1907
Born 1848 in Trondheim, died Aug. 14, 1907 on Utsira.

7. **Bendix Roth.** 1908–1920
From Stavanger.

Bendix was the assistant at the Ekerø Lighthouse from 1892–1899, and became the lighthouse keeper on Røvaersholmen from 1899–1908. He received the King's Medal of Merit in silver when he retired in 1920.

8. **Fridtjof B. F. Aspen.** 1920 – 1947
Born in 1872 on Froya, South Trondelag, died in 1959.

Married to **Dagny,** born May 18, 1895,

Children:

a. Fritz, born Mar. 14, 1916, married in 1940 to Julia Helgesen, see no. 37 below.
b. Harry, born in 1918, married and lives in Haugesund.
c. Brit, birth date uncertain.

Fridtjov was a sailor before he was hired as the lighthouse keeper at the Agdenes Lighthouse in 1909. From 1912 until he took over the position as the lighthouse keeper at the Utsira Lighthouse, he was the lighthouse keeper on Feistein.

Fridtjov became the chairman of the Lighthouse Keeper Association in 1923, and in 1929 he founded *Norsk Fyrtidende* ("Norwegian Lighthouse Gazette") a Norwegian lighthouse publication, and was the chief editor until 1943.

Lighthousekeeper Severin Haugland at work in the lighthouse, 1950.

9. **Severin Haugland.** 1947 – 1964
Born June 17, 1895, died Dec. 31, 1970, son of Johanne and Anders Haugland, Stord.

Married in 1920 to **Benny Bendiksen,** born Feb. 19, 1899, died Jan. 18, 1983, daughter of Gina and Thomas Bendiksen, farmer no. 3 – 3 b, Skare.

Children:

a. *Gina* Theresia, born Sept. 19, 1920, married in 1942 to Thomas Helgesen, farmer no. 32 – 2, Nordvik.
b. *Anna* Johanna, born June 1, 1922, married to Edvin Hansen, Spydeberg in Østfold, lives in Oslo.
c. *Bjarne* Severin, born Mar. 27, 1924, married to Bjorg Helen Myrvold, lived on Nesodden, now in Askim. Bjarne perished during the M/S "Etnefjell" shipwreck on Oct. 31, 1968.
d. *Oystein* Reidar, born June 1, 1929, married in 1956 to Reidun Skåren, farm no. 11 and 29 below and tenant farmer no. 76, Nordvik.

Severin sailed as crew on the coastal ferries "Sagvåg" and "Haugesund" during the years 1916 – 1922. In 1922 he became chief mate on the "Karmsund," a position he held until 1925, when he started working as a lighthouse keeper on Marsteinen lighthouse. From 1931 to 1940 he served on Obrestad lighthouse on Jaeren and after that on Digrudgrunn lighthouse in the Oslo fjord. He worked here until 1947 when he became chief lighthouse keeper on Utsira.

They built their main dwelling in Nordvik, farm no. 63, Varden, in 1963, which was taken over by Reidun and Oystein Haugland in 1975.

10. **Arild Klefstad.** 1964 – 1977
Born 1912, Arild was a lighthouse keeper for 17 years on Skråva lighthouse near Svolvaer, then at Fruholmen lighthouse near Hammerfest, before he became chief lighthouse keeper in Utsira in 1964.

Married to **Darly.**

11. **Bernt Johan Morsund.** 1977–1990
Born in 1925 in Bud, Fraena.

Married 195x to **Nancy Lovise Drågen.** born June 29, 1930, from Bud, Fraena.

Children:

a. Helge, born in 1952 in Vardø.
b. Svein Egil, born in 1954 in Kirkenes.
c. Anne Grete, born in 1955 in Kirkenes.
d. Knut Jarle, born Sept. 26, 1966.

Bernt Johan started as a lighthouse attendant on Utsira lighthouse in October 1959. In 1977 he took over as chief lighthouse keeper after Arild Klefstad. Before he came to Utsira he served in Vardø during the years 1949 – 1954 and in Bøkefjord, Kirkenes from 1954–1959.

11 b. **Oystein Haugland.** 1990 – 1994
Oystein was chief lighthouse keeper after Bernt Morsund, see under tenant farmer no. 76, Nordvik.

Deputy lighthouse keepers 1844 – 1885

12. **Gabriel Edvard Lund.** 1844 – 1853
Married to **Anne.**

13. **Michal Jensen.** 1853 – 1862
Married to **Maren Kristine Christoffersdatter.**

Children born on Utsira:

a. Marius Michael, born Oct. 1, 1858.
b. Jens Osvald August, born Aug. 25, 1860.
c. Ole, born 1854.

In 1865 he is working at the lighthouse in Langoy, Bamble, Telemark.

14. **Hans Otto Knoph Oppen.** 1862 – 1885
Born in 1811 in Asker Church district.

Married to **Ingeborg Marie,** born 1811 in Drammen, died May 25, 1867.

Children, all born in Kragerø:

a. Laurine Josephine, born 1840.
b. Otilie Marie, born 1843.
c. Lars Peder Knoph, born 1845, married in 1885 to Karoline Rasmusdatter Skare, farm no. 32, see below.
d. Christian Borchmann, born 1848, he was an apprentice shoemaker in 1875. He emigrated to USA in 1889, married Christina, lived in Shell Creek, Madison County, Nebraska.
e. Olaus *Daniel.* born 1851.

The position of deputy-lighthouse keeper was changed after Hans Otto left the position and became first assistant lighthouse keeper. From 1890 staff was reduced to chief lighthouse keeper, first assistant and deputy assistant, the latter serving only during the winter season.

Lighthouse officers

15. **Chr. Steffens.** 1844 – 1847

16. **Kristian N. Paulsen.** 1844 – 1890
He and Mikkel Jørgensen Hovland are the ones with the longest service on Utsira lighthouse, see farm no. 4 – 10, Hovland.

17. **Hans K. Martens.** 1847 – 1853
Born in 1790 in Bergen (?).

Hans and the lighthouse keeper Mr. Smith did not get along. In 1851 Smith accused Hans of sleeping on his watch in the eastern tower during the night of June 9 – 10. However, the case was resolved amicably: *and both agreed to refrain from getting involved in each other's affairs.*

Published in Stavanger County Newspaper no. 1, 1843.

Public Notice.

For the new lighthouse project at Utsira not too far from Stavanger it is required to purchase the list of materials described below for delivery to the Marine Department before January 31 according to the sealed proposal and specifications for delivery and acceptance at the lowest possible price:

1. Received written proposals at the Marine department for delivery according to specifications for the afore mentioned Lighthouse Project will be opened February 1st in the coming month. The proposal with the lowest bid that meets the specifications and is accompanied with trustworthy assurances of complete fulfillment of the contract will be selected.
2. Proposals for deliveries are according to the numbers in the list of materials indicated below.
3. Proposals for bricks and rocks according to material list below must be proposed loaded onboard ships approved for public transportation at places of manufacture and specified in the proposal or delivered "free ashore" to preferred harbor in southern or northern Utsira. However, in either case the cargo must be first inspected and approved at a mutually agreed point and time.
   All other items may be delivered at any port on Utsira.
   If a delay is caused for any reason at the shipping point resulting in more than 6 days delay, not counting holydays, a compensation of 24 skilling per working day will be paid by the Lighthouse Authority. The cargo ships should be committed to load and unload night and day if required by the project manager.
   If the receiver of the brick and rocks can arrange for no further transport immediately, or there is a delay beyond normal shipment times, payments should proceed as agreed upon.
4. All materials must be delivered according to schedule agreed upon in the contract, and according paragraph 2 and 3.
5. The material quality will be determined by a committee consisting of the project manager and designated people at the site, and their ruling is final and binding.
6. If the material in the previous paragraph do not meet the specifications or is not delivered according to the agreed upon schedule, the vendor must accept that the project manager has the right to purchase the material at the vendor's cost and at the project manager's convenience from somewhere else.
7. The vendor must include a confirmation from appropriate officials that he is a responsible, solvent and fully capable in completing his accepted responsibilities. In case he is not able to provide such confirmation he must carry insurance to cover the same.
   Proposal for brick and rocks must be accompanied by samples with appropriate identifications, official name and seal and must be furnished at the vendor's cost and be comparable with the actual shipment.
8. Payment will be made when delivery is complete.
9. The vendors, whose proposals are accepted, should be so advised by the Marine Department by February 15th.

No .	Materials							Date of Delivery To Utsira
1	25,000 well–cured red bricks 81/2 "– 9" l, 4 – 41/2' w., 2't							June 15,1843
2	25,000 well–cured red bricks 81/2 "– 9" l, 4 – 41/2' w., 2't							July 15, 1843
3	25,000 well–cured red bricks 81/2 "– 9" l, 4 – 41/2' w., 2't							Aug. 31,1843
4	20,000 well–cured red bricks 12" long							June 30,1843
5	35 barrels lime							June 15,1843
6	90,000 4 in. nails							May 1, 1843
7	3,000 5 in. "							"
8	4,000 6 in. "							"
9	14,000 3 in. "							"
10	0 Dozen	10 pcs.	Fir lumber		7 ft. long		11" dia.	Month of May, 1843
11	0 "	3 "	"	"	7 "		7" "	"
12	0 "	4 "	"	"	9 "		10" "	"
13	0 "	5 "	"	"	13 "		10" "	"
14	0 "	9½ "	"	"	9½ "		9" "	"
15	0 "	6 "	"	"	12½ "		9 " "	"
16	1 "	2 "	"	"	6 "		8 " "	"
17	1 "	0 "	"	"	7 "		8" "	"
18	6 "	6 "	"	"	8 "		8" "	"
19	4 "	8 "	"	"	10 "		8" "	"
20	4 "	8 "	"	"	12 "		8" "	"
21	1 "	0 "	"	"	6 "		7" "	"
22	2 "	0 "	"	"	8½ "		7" "	"
23	1 "	0 "	"	"	8 "		7" "	"
24	2 "	0 "	"	"	11 "		7" "	"
25	3 "	8 "	"	"	14 "		8" "	"

Notes:

#1. If vendor delivers from his dock and not on Utsira, the delivery time must be 1 month earlier than indicated.

#2. Low quality brick will not be accepted.

#3. The lime must be well processed and must not contain moisture. Must be measured in barrels. Larger pieces must be crunched to smaller pieces. Large pieces which cannot be crunched will be taken out and returned and subtracted from shipment.

#4. The nails must be made in Norway. If any boxes are not full, supplement nails will be purchased at the cost of the vendor.

#5. All lumber must be straight and logged in winter.

No.	List of Materials (continued)	Delivery date
26	7 r 0 pcs. Fir lumber 16 ft. long, 7 in. diameter	26–38:
27	1 – 0 “ “ 7’ “ 7” “	May, 1843
28	1 – 8 “ Spruce 8’ “ 10” “	“
29	2 – 2 “ “ 7’ “ 8” “	“
30	5 – 0 “ “ 12’ “ 8” “	“
31	4 – 0 “ “ 13’ “ 8” “	“
32	1 – 5 “ “ 7’ “ 7” “	“
33	3 – 3 “ “ 16’ “ 7” “	“
34	1 – 4 “ “ 10’ “ 7” “	“
35	1 – 9 “ “ 16’ “ 7” “	“
36	24 – 0 ” “ 10 to12’ 7” “	“
37	200 – Tæffe Board 11 to12’ 1½” thick, 7 in. wide	“
38	18 – Good Fir Board 11 to12’ 1½” 7” “	“
39	400 – Tæffe Board 11 to12’ 1½” 7” “	39–56
40	3 Good Fir Board 24’ 1½” 6” w/sharp edges	July, 1843
41	19 – “ – 14’ 1½” “ 6” “	“
42	3 – “ – 12½’ 1½” “ 6” “	“
43	9 – “ – 11 to12’ 1½” “ 6” “	“
44	108½ “ – 11 to12’ 1½“ 8 or 9” “	“
45	70 – “ – 10 1½” 8 or 9” “	“
46	13 – “ – 9 1½” 8 or 9” “	“
47	45 – “ – 8 1½” 8 or 9” “	“
48	14 – “ – 9 1½“ 8 or 9” “	“
49	3 – Spruce Board 24’ 2” 6 “ “	“
50	9 – “ – 12½ 2” 6” “	“
51	3 “ – 11’ 2” 6” “	“
52	6 – “ – 10’ 2” 6” “	“
53	2½ – “ – 11 to 12’ 3” 9” “	“
54	2½ – “ – 11’ 3” 9” “	“
55	4 – “ – 12’ 3” 9” “	“
56	90 – Pre–cut Wood 11 to 12’ 2” wide 1½” thick	“
57	30 – Standard Wood 11 to 12’ 7 to 8” “ 3” “	57–63
58	40 – Lathe Planks 11 to 12’ alen 4 to 5“ top	May, 1843
59	15 – Pre–cut Wood 11 to 12’ ft. 2” wide 1½“ thick	“
60	2 Stpd. Sq. Iron Bars ¾”, 1” and 5/4” equal amt. of each	“
61	2 Flat Iron Bars	“
62	4 Barrels of Tar	“
63	6 Barges of Charcoal	“
64	1500 Barrels of Sand	Summer

#1: All lumber should be straight and logged in winter.
#2: All boards and planks should be dry and free of cracks.
#3: Sand should be good masonry sand and not beach sand.

The Marine Department of the Royal Norwegian Government, Christiania Dec. 13th. 1842.

18. **Mikkel Jørgensen** 1853 – 1898
See farm no. 2 – 1, Hovland.

19. **Lars Haasted.** 1885 – 1890

20. **Ove Broch.** 1885 – 1920
Born Oct. 5, 1850 in Bergen.
Married to **Trine Elise Pedersdatter,** born 1861 in Tromø.

Children:
- a. Konrad. born Apr. 4, 1899, died Apr. 11, 1903.
- b. Erling, born July 13, 1901.

21. **Rasmus Pettersen Hoydal.** 1920 – 1932
Born May 6, 1889 in Volda.
Married Oct. 23, 1921 to **Jenny Marie Larsen,** born Sept. 5, 1902, daughter of Thora Toresdatter and Mons Larsen, tenant farmer no. 40 e, Nordvik.

Children:
- a. Peder Ludolf, born Mar. 26, 1922.
- a. Turid Målfrid, born Feb. 7, 1926, died May 21, 1926.
- c. Ragnhild Jorunn, born Oct. 7, 1931.

Rasmus was employed by the Lighthouse Authority from 1908. In August 1932 he became lighthouse operator at Synnes lighthouse near Ålesund.

22. **Nicolai H. K. Fosse.** 1932 – 1950
He came from South Trøndelag and was married to **Sissi.**
Nicolai was hired in 1950 as chief lighthouse keeper at Hestholmen lighthouse on Hitra.

23. **Erling Lilleland.** 1950 – 1957.
Came from Jaeren and married **Karen.**

24. **Martin Valseth.** 1958–1965
From South–Trondelag. Married to Gjertrud.

25. **Bernt Johan Morsund.** 1959 – 1977
See no. 11 above.

26. **Johan Nilsen.** 1965 – 1969

See under tenant farmer no. 55, Nordvik.

27. **Roald Eriksen**. 1969 – 1971
He came from Tjøme in Vestfold and served on Faerder lighthouse before he came to Utsira.

28. **Gerhard Skåren.** 1968 –
See under farm no. 1 – 17, Hovland.

29. **Oystein Haugland.** 1971 – 1990
See under tenant farm no. 76, Nordvik.

30. **Torbjorn Rasmussen.** 1977
See farm no. 7 – 13, Hovland.

Deputy lighthouse attendants

31. **Iver Martin Unsgård.** 1885 – 1890

32. **L. Peder K. Oppen.** 1890 – 1898
See tenant farm no. 19, Skare.

33. **Ove Broch.** 1898
See item 20 above.

34. **P. Jacobsen.** 1898 – 1899

35. **Sjur Olsen.** 1899 – 1914
See farm no. 3 – 2, Kvalvik.

36. **Johannes G. Gudmundsen.** 1914 – 1934
See farm no. 22 – 3, Nordvik.

37. **Fritz Aspen.** 1934 – 1946
Born Mar. 14, 1916, son of Dagny and Fridtjov Aspen, no. 8 above.

Married Oct. 20, 1940 to **Julia Helgesen,** born Nov. 14, 1918, daughter of Julie and Hersleb Helgesen, tenant farmer no. 50 f, Nordvik.

Children:

a. Dagfinn, born Apr. 16, 1942, married to Torill Lindoe, now lives in Haugesund.
b. Inger Elise. born Jan. 16, 1947, married to Geir Ingebritsen.

Fritz later became employed at the Customs Dept. and the family moved to Haugesund.

38. **Johan Nilsen.** 1946 – 1965
See under tenant farm no. 55, Nordvik.

39. **Gerhard Skåren.** 1965 – 1967
See farm no. 1 – 17, Hovland.

Utsira Coastal Radio Station

Lot no. 27, Austerheim, farm no 9. Røvaretre. From farm no. 2 in 1914.

The Telegraph Authority bought this parcel with a tax liability of sk.m. 0.40, from Severin Tollefsen in 1914 for 4157.25 kroner. The construction was started the same year, but was not completed before the war ended in 1918 – 1919. It was in operation when WWII broke out in 1940, and was destroyed during a bombing raid by the British toward the end of the war and was never rebuilt.

Managers

1. **Wilhelm Pedersen.** 1919 – 1923.
Born in 1878, came from Trøndelag.
Married to **Anna Elise Marie,** died Jan. 15, 1921 on Utsira.

Children:
a. Ågot.

Wilhelm was hired in 1922 as manager of Tjøme Radio–Telegraph.

2. **Alv Heggstad.** 1922 – 1929
Born in 1823, married to **Robertine Sofie Osenbrock.**

Children born on Utsira:
a. Tormod, born July 3, 1925.
b. Marit, born May 18, 1928.

Above: Utsira Coastal Radio Station in 1930. Note fishing vessels in background. Below: Postcard of Utsira Radio from middle of 1920s. The old attenna tower in on the right.

From the Assistant's official residence in 1927. From left: Alma (their maid), Astrid, Bjørnulf and Thorleif Kristiansen.

In 1927 he was a temporary assistant on Svalbard.

3. **Aksel J. Høglund.** 1929 – 1940
Born in1898, came from Fauske in Nordland, married to **Solveig.**

Children:
a. Sonja.

Telegraph operators and others

4. **Oskar M. Stinessen.** 1922 – 1928
Born in 1897, came from Bessaker, married to **Ruth Enstad,** born in 1898.

Children born on Utsira:
a. Turid, born Oct. 8, 1926.
b. Grete, born Nov. 14, 1927.

They lived in the old Hoie house. In 1924 Oskar served as a temporary assistant on Spitsbergen.

5. **Thorleif Kristian Kristiansen.** 1924 – 193x
Born in Dec. 29, 1884, in Kristiania (Oslo), died Feb. 1959 in Droebak, Akershus.

Married in first marriage in 1910 to **Astrid Nilsen,** born in Apr. 1, 1884 in Kristiania, died Mar. 3, 1945 in Stavanger.

Children:

a. Bjørnulf Røst, born June 8, 1913 in Horten, Vestfold, died Jan. 14, 1971 in Forsand, Rogaland, married Karen Tjensvold (1911–1940) in 1932. Remarried Nansy Bentsdatter Ville (1915–2009) in 1943.
b. Thorleif Martin Røst, born Sept. 5, 1915 on Røst, Nordland, died Mar. 7, 1917 on Røst.

Kristiansen was one of the pioneer wireless operators in Norway. From 1910 he work at the Røst Radio. The wireless connection between the island Røst and Sørvågen Radio was the first in Norway and the second in the world (1906) to use the new invention from Marconi.

Married a second time to Dagmar Halvorsen, born 1890, died 1977.

6. **Reidar Nordaas.** 1923 – 1933
He came from Sandnessjoen.

Married to **Marie Skjelde,** born Nov. 24, 1899, daughter of Tomine Larsdatter and Olav Skjelde, farm no. 16 – 4 b, Nordvik.

Children:

a. Agnete, born Apr. 25, 1922, married in Kristiansand.
b. Tordis, born Oct. 31, 1923, died July 10, 1926.

Reidar sailed as a first mate until 1923 when he was hired as a temporary assistant at Utsira Radio. From 1930 he was a telegraph operator. In 1934 he took a leave of absence and worked for Notodden Broadcasting, and later at Askoy, Lille–Bergen.

7. **Ragnar Ingvald Olsen Beinnes.** 1931 – 1936
Born in 1900. Married to **Bergliot**.

8. **Ottar Engen Smith.** 1933 – 1934
Born Nov. 22, 1906 in Mo on Romerike.

Married Jan. 21, 1934 to **Marie Jakobine Bakke,** born Oct. 7, 1908 at Malangen in Troms (sister of Gjertrud Bakke Kvalvik).

9. **Petter Berg.** 1936 –
Came from Stavanger.

10. **Odd Johan Naeset.** 1938 – 1940
Born in 1910.

11. **Einar van der Fehr Schumann**. 1938 – 1940
Born in 1917.

12. **Steinar Olav Seland.** 1930 – 1937(?)
Born Feb. 15, 1906 in Haugesund.

Married June 26, 1935 to **Astrid Margrete Haltbak,** born Oct. 25, 1904 in Kristiansund.

No children born on Utsira.

Steinar was a telegraph operator assistant from 1930.

13. **Nils Kr. Fjellberg.** 1928 – 1945
He came from Stavanger.

Nils was a jack–of–all–trades and worked as a handyman and technician from July 1, 1928 until the station was closed.

14. **Svend Klovning.** 1937 – 1940
See under tenant farm no. 27, Klovning.

15. **Trygve Klovning.** 193x – 1940
See farm no. 8 – 2, Klovning.

The following persons have also worked for shorter periods at Utsira Radio:
Rolf Suleng, Agnes Svendsen, from Haugesund, **Leif Kleve, Groll, Tøgersen, Luth Hansen, Fiane Mø Olsen, Horverak, Mø.**

Class photo and key of students and staff in front of Utsira School. from 1924. Kneeling from left: 1. Mikal Klovning Bendiksen, 2. Birger Nilsen, 3. Mathias M. Rasmussen, 4. Mathias Bendiksen, 5. Fritz Aspen?, 6. Olav Skjelde, 7. Elmer Thomassen, 8. Johan S. Helgesen, 9. John Hansen, 10. Svend Klovning, 11. Tobias Austrheim, 12. John Larsen, 13. Andreas Skjelde, 14. Lars Skåren. Standing, from left: 15. Teacher Gjertrud Bakke Kvalvik, 16. Sigrunn Vestre Klovning, 17. Kaia (Kari) Skjelde, 18. Martha Skåren Vestre, 19. Hilma Eriksen Garberg, 20. Gurine Klovning Markhus, 21. Martha Helgesen Selvåg, 22. Karoline Helgesen Valler, 23. Hanna Helgesen Skåren, 24. Kristine Nilsen Bjelland, 25. Åsa Ellingsen Klovning, 26. Sofie Johannesen Landa, 27. Benny Kvalvik Stråtveit, 28. Methie Eriksen Fikstveit, 29. Emma Haugland Steinsvik, 30. Gurine Ellingsen Nilsen, 31. Solveig Helgesen Skjelde, 32. Rasmus Ellingsen (Lynghilder), 33. Thomas Austrheim, 34. Teacher Ola K. Fosså.

Utsira School

The task of building a permanent school was first taken up by the School Committee in 1853. Several years went by before the community became comfortable with the expenses they were facing to take on this project, but in 1859 construction was started on a lot provided on Mikkel Jørgensen's farm on Hovland, farm no. 3. Two years later it was in operation, and was used as both school house and living quarters for the teacher and his family until 1912, when a new larger schoolhouse was built. This is the building that today is called "The Old School."[65]

Before the island got its permanent schoolhouse, each farmer was required to provide lodging for teachers and students for a defined period of time each year (usually around 6 – 7 days) and it was known as an ambulatory school. The teacher or schoolmaster was usually one of the island's most accomplished readers or best writers or, as it is described in the school protocol in 1739: *. . . the best and most capable of the farmers, when no better persons can be found.*

The preacher Erik Ivarsen Leganger wrote in 1742 the following about Utsira:

> When the head schoolmaster goes to Utsira, which is 25 kilometers out in the ocean, I cannot see that he can get out there more than 3 times per year – as the priest does, and suggest that he gets out there 14 days ahead of the priest and travels back with him. The other year the schoolmaster we had out there died. He was a good schoolmaster and very good with the young people. His daughter, a young girl, is now the schoolmistress and who now does the guiding of the young ones and is assisting every other Sunday in the church and helps to gather the congregation together for reading of the scriptures and singing of psalms.

[65] "Case Journal for the Utisra County School System, 1845–89" (Note 32).

The church minister put forward a proposal to hire a schoolmaster, but nothing came of it. Who the people were, a father and a daughter, who got such a nice review by the priest we have not been able to find out.[66] The people we know who were schoolmasters on Utsira were:

1. **Ådne Helgesen Nordvik.** 1772 to around 1780
See under tenant farmer no. 23, Nordvik.

2. **Johannes Helgesen Nordvik.** around 1780 to 1789
See farm no. 15 – 7, Nordvik.

3. **Ole Jakobsen Austrheim.** 1790 to around 1794
See farm 6 – 4, Austrheim.

4. **John Helgesen Nordvik.** 1800 to 1808
See farm no. 1 – 10, Nordvik.

5. **Thore Thorsen Nordvik**. 1817 to 1821
See under farm no. 15 – 8, Nordvik.

6. **Sjur Tollefsen Austrheim.** 1829 to 1833
See tenant farm no. 30, Austrheim.

7. **L. S. Storesund.** 1834 – 1835

Ad in "Stavanger Amtstidende" newspaper" August 15, 1853.

The position as Church Lead Singer and Itinerant School Master is vacant and is desired to be filled soonest. The church singer position is anticipated to bring in an annual income of 10 to 15 Spd., and the teacher part of the position an additional income of 25 Spd. and until further notice 40 Spd. annually from the Governmental Information Services Fund. In addition, free food and shelter during the school session, 35 to 40 weeks annually. Applications for this position should be mailed in a properly stamped envelope to Karmsund Church Parish for the attention of the undersigned within 4 weeks of today.
Torvestad Parsonage, August 12, 1853.
J. Jensen, Parson.

8. **Ole Knutsen Austrheim.** 1836 – 1840
See tenant farm no. 29, Austrheim.

---

[66] See Note 33.

9. **Reinert Johannesen Ove.** 1841 (?) – 1846
He was from Vikebygd and was forced to quit as schoolmaster in Fjellberg in Nov. 1846 due to sickness. He arranged for a substitute the following year.

10. **Lars Andersen Selsaas.** 1847 – 1853
He had been acting headmaster of the itinerant school in Fjeldberg parish for four years before he came to Utsira. In the fall of 1851 he quit his position there, but when the Board did not find any suitable applicants for the position of church lead singer and schoolmaster, Lars agreed to continue as schoolmaster for the rest of 1853.

11. **Ole Reinertsen Agdesten.** 1854 – 1857
Born 1833, died Feb. 24, 1891 in Bergen, son of Madel Larsdatter Hetlesaeter and Reinert Agdesten from Stord.

Married on Apr. 6, 1858 on Finnoy to **Gundela Oline Jobsdatter,** born Oct. 11, 1839, died Dec. 30, 1882 in Bergen, daughter of Elisabeth Karoline and Job Rasmussen, farm no. 7 – 9 a, Hovland.

The family Ole Agdesten around 1868, Gunhilde (1839 – 1882) with Reinert Johan, born 1867, on her lap, Mathilde Jobiane, born 1858, Ole (1833 – 1891) with Elisabeth Karoline, born 1863, on his lap.

Their children:

a. Mathilde Jobiane, born 1858.
b. Thora Johanne, born 1861, died 1867.
c. Elisabeth Karoline, born 1863.
d. Reinert Johan, born 1867.
e. Toralf Johannes, born 1869.
f. Oscar Gunnerius, born 1872, died very young.

g. Oscar Gunnerius, born 1875.
h. Karl Konow, 1878.
i. Harald, born 1880.

Ole was married in his 2nd marriage in 1886 to **Kirsten Marie Westbø** from Finnoy.

They had 3 children:

j. Gunhilde Stefana, born 1887.
k. Elisabeth Marie, born 1889.
l. Ole Kristinius, born 1890.

Ole started out as the church lead singer and teacher on Utsira Mar. 21, 1854, and in the spring of 1857 he took the same position on Finnoy. From 1860 he was a teacher in Bergen. From May and until September 1857 the church minister arranged for a substitute, the then 15–year–old Tollef Thomassen Herberg.

Knut Knutsen Åsen (1828–1892).

12. **Knut Knutsen Åsen,** 1857 – 1887.
Born in 1828, died Sept. 6, 1892, son of Ingeborg Sorensdatter Bolset and Knut Kristensen Grepstad, Jølster in Sunnfjord.

Married in 1853 to **Helga Larsdatter,** born 1834, died Dec. 8, 1885, from Stord.

Children:

a. Knut, born 1853 on Stord, emigrated to USA.
b. Laurits Johan, born in 1855, died Apr. 14, 1858, drowned.
c. *Laurits* Johan, born Aug. 19, 1858, married in 1883 to Kristine Tollefsdatter, Austrheim. They lived in Haugesund before they emigrated to California in USA in 1887. Laurits was a skipper.
d. Ida Lovise, born Oct. 11, 1860. died Apr. 4, 1864.
e. Ole, born Aug. 14, 1862, died Mar. 31, 1864.
f. Ida Lovise, born May 10, 1864, died Mar. 9, 1867.
g. Ole Samuel Ludvig, born Apr. 1, 1866, died Feb. 3, 1884.
h. Ida Lovise, born Feb. 24, 1868, died Jan. 11, 1890.
i. Johan Marius, born Dec. 21, 1869, merchant seaman, emigrated to USA, perished at sea.
j. Antonette Elisa Katrine, born Feb. 12, 1872, died Sept. 5, 1881.

Golden Anniversary.

A Golden Anniversary is celebrated tomorrow, March 19th in Oakland, Ca for Ships Master Lauritz Aasen and his wife, Christine Elisabeth, born Oestrem. Aasen is son of a teacher who taught for a period at Utsira. His wife is daughter of Tollef Oestreim, Utsira. Lauritz Aasen started early at sea and sailed on many vessels out of Haugesund, among them as First Mate for the shipowners J. Thorsen and N. J. Hauge's "SS Ingeborg." In 1887 the couple sailed for America and settled in California. In 1897 they moved to Portland, Oregon. Aasen skippered a number of ships on the California coast as well as many in international trade out of Portland. He now lives in Oakland. Aasen is now 74 years old and his wife is somewhat younger. They have 3 children, 2 sons and 1 daughter who all live in California. Aasen is a respected Norwegian in Oakland and has been a good seaman.

From Haugesunds Avis newspaper, March 18, 1933.

k. Christine, born and died May 19, 1874, lived 20 min.
l. *Hanna* Kristine, born Sept. 15, 1875, emigrated to USA in 1887, married and lived in Oakland, CA.
m. Anne Theresie, born Feb. 20, 1879.
n. Antonette Elisa Kathrine (Trina), born Sept. 23, 1881, died in 1976, she was married and lived in Oakland, CA.

Knut was an itinerant schoolteacher in Jølster 1848 – 49, before he finished school at Stord Seminar in 1853. He was a home teacher in 1853–54, church lead singer and itinerant schoolteacher in Fusa in 1855–57 before he began the same position on Utsira on Sept. 7, 1857. The first years before the school was finished, it is said that the family lived in the house owned by Sjur Knutsen on Kvarkaneset.

Knut had to leave his position as teacher in October 1887 due to illness. The School Board gave this testimony to Knut, when he applied for leave of absence:

> The Utsire School Board takes this opportunity to confirm their appreciation and recommend that Mr. Åsen's application be approved, as Mr. Åsen has been an utmost skillful and conscientious teacher. His students have gained by his instruction and knowledge and have later excelled by his guidance and learned valuable lessons of independent thinking. With respect to the last, Mr. Åsen had an extraordinary ability to develop the children to be able to absorb new material and to become independent and knowledgeable human beings.

Seminarians, **Andreas Kolbeinsen Sydnes** from Fjeldberg and **K. Kristiansen** from Haugesund were both substitutes for Knut Åsen during two seasons in 1886.

Oystein Rullestad (1866 – 1936).

13. **Oystein Rullestad.** 1887 – 1891
Born Apr. 28, 1866, died Nov. 10, 1936, from Rullestad in Skånevik.

Married on Sept. 20, 1890 to **Helene Johansdatter,** born May 15, 1873, daughter of Karoline and Johan Helgesen, farm no. 18 – 5e, Nordvik.

Children:

a. Lars, born July 27, 1891, married in 1917 to Sigrid Sørensen.
b. Karoline, born Oct. 23, 1892, was a teacher in Stavanger
c. Hagbard, born Feb. 18, 1895, died in 1921. He was a dentist in Stavanger.
d. Hanna, born Mar. 12, 1897, married in 1927 to Kristian Gilje, Stavanger.
e. Oystein, born Dec. 25, 1902, married in 1930 to Sigrid Jespersen, was a dentist in Stavanger.
f. Helene, born Apr. 21, 1905, married in 1930 to Bernt A. Hansen, Stavanger.
g. Borghild Marie, born Sept. 25, 1907, married in 1938 to Arne Pedersen, Stavanger.

Oystein came to Utsira as a substitute teacher in November 1887, and was hired as a full–time teacher and church lead singer on Apr. 1, 1889. In October 1891 they moved to Kopervik and in January 1894 they moved to Stavanger. In May–June 1889 the seminarian Mr. Nils Olsen Hoiland became substitute teacher for Rullestad. That Rullestad was a popular teacher is shown by the following letter written to the school board by concerned citizens and attached to the school board's recommendation for hiring Rullestad as a permanent teacher in the district:

For the attention of the Kristiansand Church district School Board.
The undersigned Municipality Board members and property owners on Utsira are proud to recommend that the beloved Mr. Rullestad who has served so honorably as teacher and church lead singer be hired as full–time teacher here. We can confirm that the children's relationship to the teacher is such that their most prevalent desire is to go to school every day and learn, and where they consequently make great progress. The parents enjoy the loving relationship between students and the teacher and the progress they make in all the subjects. The students gather around the teacher as their benefactor in order to be instructed and taught, a fact which is much appreciated by the parents. Hoping that the honored School Board after being informed of our deep desire and sincere wish, will agree to our request to hire Mr. Rullestad as a full–time church lead singer and teacher, we remain

Signed: Utsire, 21 November 1888

Chairman Johan Heljesen, Rep. Rasmus Thomassen, Rep. Gudmund Jørgensen – Present: Mathias Jobsen, Tollef Heljesen, Knud Gudmundsen, Tobias Johannesen, Bendik Mathiassen (p.p.), Elling Gudmundsen, Tobias Olsen, Mathias Larsen, M. Ellingsen, Bertel Heljesen, Erik Eriksen.

Ingjald Jacob Baldersheim (1864 – 1896).

14. **Ingjald Jacob Baldersheim**. 1892 – 1896
Born 1864, died Apr. 8, 1896, from Baldersheim in Fusa parish.

Married to **Marta Malene,** born in 1869.

Children:

a. Hans Christian Bernhard, born Nov. 23, 1893, moved to Haugesund.
b. *Sigvat* Kristoffer Ingemann, born May 9, 1895, moved to Haugesund. He married Marta Gjerde, Haugesund in 1939.

Marta Malene and the two children moved to Haugesund after Ingjald died.

15. **Mathias Okland.** 1896 – 1902
Born Sept. 22, 1844, died in 1931, son of Anna Mathiasdatter and Lars Nilsen, Økland in Valestrand.

Married in 1872 to **Signe Nilsdatter Sundnes,** born Feb. 25, 1843, died in 1913, daughter of Marta Nilsdatter and Nils Kristoffersen, Eidsvåg.

Children:

a. Laura, born Oct. 28, 1875, died Sept. 18, 1883.
b. Nils Andreas, born June 10, 1882, married to Hanna Olava Johanesdatter, Bergstøl. Nils was Parish Clerk and teacher at Torvestad in 1914–1921, later, School Inspector in Rogaland County. They lived on Øvre–Hauge, Torvestad.
c. Laura, born Sept. 15, 1886, died in 1953. She was a teacher in Haugesund.

Mathias Okland was a teacher and church clerk in Valestrand before he was hired in 1896 by Utsira. In 1902 they moved to Torvestad, where he was teacher and church clerk from 1903 – 1914.

Hans Rasmus Ljoen (1871–)

16. **Hans Rasmus Ljoen.** 1902 – 1905
Born **Sept. 26,** 1871 in Sunnylven, Sunnmøre.

He was teacher at Utsira Primary School in 1903. In 1905 Hans was hired as a teacher in Åkra, Karmøy.

17. **Anders Jakobsen Kvamme.** 1906 – 1914
Born July 15, 1883 in Innvik in Sogn.

Married June 26, 1907 to **Andrine Larsdatter Bale,** born June 23, 1875 in Balestrand.

Anders Kvamme (1883–).

Children born on Utsira:

a. Jakob Anfinn, born Sept. 1, 1908.
b. Elias, born Feb. 13, 1910.
c. Andreas Georg, born Feb. 13, 1912.

Anders Kvamme was a teacher in Leikanger for 2 1/2 years before he began working as teacher and church lead singer on Utsira in the spring of 1906. The family moved to Sund in Hordaland in 1914, and after that to Brekke in Sogn.

18. **Louise M. Åmot.** 1912

Born Dec. 30, 1890 in Gular in Sunnfjord.

Louise Åmot was the first teacher at the new school that started operations that year. She graduated from Volda Teachers College in 1912 and worked in Utsira for a short period of time. Among other assignments she was a teacher in Skudesnes in 1919 – 24 and a lecturer at Voss High School from 1926.

Ragna Eliassen (1885–)

19. **Ragna S. Eliassen.** 1912 – 1920
Born Jan. 28, 1885 in Vikedal.

Ragna began teaching in Utsira in the spring of 1912 and left this position in the spring of 1920.

20. **Hans Øvrebø,** 1914 – 1917.
Born Dec. 1, 1882 in Solvorn, Hafslo in Sogn and Fjordene.

Married in 1911 to **Jenny Amalie Olaisdatter.**

Children born on Utsira:
a. Sigrun Klingenberg, born Feb. 24, 1915.

Hans Øvrebø (1882–)

Hans began teaching on Utsira in the fall of 1914, and he left that position in the spring of 1917, after which he became a teacher in Skjold.

21. **Peder Andreas Jonsson.** 1917 – 1920.
Born Dec. 12, 1884 in Fjell, Hordaland.

Married to **Anna Vika.**

Children born on Utsira:
a. Berit, born June 27, 1918, died Dec. 16, 1918.

1903 photo of Utsira Primary School students and teacher Hans Rasmus Ljeon, with graphic key underneath (names on opposite page).

See names next page.

Photo opposite: Utsira Primary School 1903. 1.Elen K. Gudmundsdatter, 2.Hanna K. Knutsdatter, 3. Hanna A. Johansdatter, 4. Pauline A. Tollefsdatter, 5. Milla O. L. Ellingsdatter, 6. Helvig A. Torkelsdatter, 7. Jenny A. Tobiasdatter, 8. Hanna S. Larsdatter, 9. Tilla B. N. Johansdatter, 10. Lovise K. N. Johansdatter, 11. Tilla G. Matiasdatter, 12. Marta K. Tobiasdatter, 13. Sigfrida O. Ellingsdatter, 14. Erna Aa. Nilsdatter, 15. Erling Nilsen, 16. Lars E. Monsen, 17. Nils C. Nilsen, 18. Gustav M. Hansen, 19. Sigvald Hansen, 20. Gudmund Gudmundsen, 21. Johan K. Valnumsen, 22. A.S.D. Tollefsdatter, 23. Sigfrida A. Hansdatter, 24. Julia A. Tollefsdatter, 25. Hans R. Ljoen, Schoolmaster, 26. Aasa B. Johannesdatter, 27. Eminda A. Ellingsdatter, 28. Johs. M. Johannesen, 29. Mikal J. Mathiassen, 30. Laura L. Tobiasdatter, 31. Kristine Rasmusdatter, 32. Minda M. Tobiasdatter, 33. Milla M. Elllingsdatter, 34. Anne M. Tobiasdatter, 35. Amanda M. Tobiasdatter, 36. Hanna M. Hans–Knutsdatter, 37. Berte K. Ellingsdatter, 38. Berte G. Tollefsdatter, 39. Jenny K. Valnumsdatter, 40. Peder A. Tollefsen, 41. Hersleb K. Johansen, 42. Thomas B. Knutsen, 43. Edvard Jobsen, 44. Sofie A. Ellingsdatter, 45. Jenny M. Johannesdatter, 46. Milla A. Rasmusdatter, 47. Julia M. Nilsdatter, 48. MindLa M. Larsdatter, 49. Laura M. Tobiasdatter, 50. Gunda Ellingsdatter, 51. Marthine Mathiasdatter, 52. Hanna V. Nilsdatter, 53. Nelly J. Knutsdatter, 54. Johs. Rasmussen, 55. Konrad B. Thomassen, 56. Svend M.T. Ellingsen, 57. Konrad A. Hansen, 58. Hjalmar P. Helgeland, 59. Gudmund Nilsen, 60. Ernst Helgeland, 61. Ole T. Olsen, 62. Andreas B. Olsen and 63. Gudrun Nilsdatter.

Peder was a teacher on Utsira from May 1917 until April 1920 when he moved to Vikebygd.

22. ***Johannes* Elias Havikebotn,** 1920 – 1921.

Born July 14, 1878, died in 1954. He came from Havikebotn near Florø.

Married to ***Ida* Marie Søreide,** born Jan. 2, 1886, died in 1971. She came from Solund in Ytre Sogn.

Johannes Havikebotn (1878–1954)

Children:

a. Reidar, born in March 1905, died in March 1906.
b. *Anfinn* Trygvard, born Aug. 22, 1906, died in 1967.
c. Solveig, born Apr. 24, 1911.
d. *Jardar* Søreide, born Dec. 11, 1914.
a. Eldbjorg, born Sept. 4, 1916, died in 1991.

b. Idar, born Oct. 30, 1919 in Solund, married in 1950 to Malmfrid Kvalvik, see no. 28 below.

Johannes was hired as a teacher in Utsira in May 1920 and resigned from that position in January the following year. After that he was a teacher in Reinli, South–Audnedal county in Valdres, before moving to Svelvik, south of Drammen.

23. **Gjertrud Bakke Kvalvik.** 1920 – 1963
With her 43 years as a teacher on Utsira, Gjertrud is the longest serving teacher here, see farm no. 11 – 1, Kvalvik.

Ola K. Fosså (1860–1932)

24. **Ola K. Fosså.** 1921 – 1925
Born Mar. 10, 1860. died in 1932, son of Ragnhild Eriksdatter and Knut Olsen, Fosså in Hjelmland.

Married in 1888 to **Berta Johanna,** born Nov. 24, 1864, died in 1939, daughter of Ranveig Henriksdatter and Josef Hadlesen, Ytre Ramsfjell, Hjelmel.

They had 8 children.

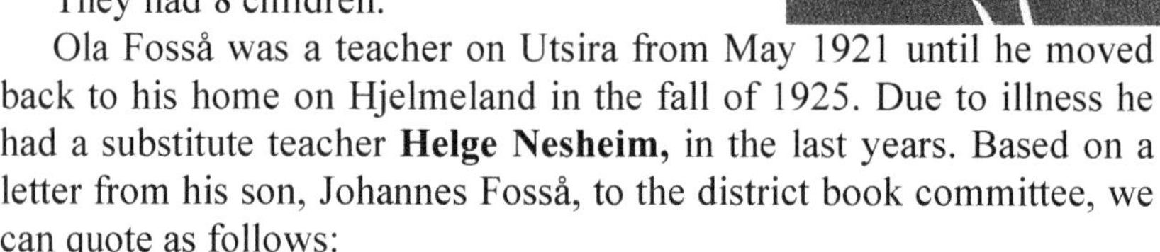

Ola Fosså was a teacher on Utsira from May 1921 until he moved back to his home on Hjelmeland in the fall of 1925. Due to illness he had a substitute teacher **Helge Nesheim,** in the last years. Based on a letter from his son, Johannes Fosså, to the district book committee, we can quote as follows:

> My father graduated from the teachers college in Koparvik in his youth. After several teaching positions as a young man, he left the teaching profession due to poor health. He took over the farm after my grandfather and worked this farm for many years. During the teacher shortage after WW I he took up teaching again, first in Åna–Sira, where he taught from the month of May in 1919 to around March in 1921. From March 1921 he was a teacher on Utsira. He lived on Utsira until the fall 1925, when he moved home again to Hjelmeland. He apparently had a substitute in the last period there due to poor health.

25. **Nils Hansen Fjon.** 1925 – 1938
Born Dec. 4, 1902. He came from Haugesund.

Married on Nov. 10, 1927 to **Alise Øritsland,** born in 1905 in Haugesund.

In 1937 **Magnus Remme, Jakob Ove Farsund and Oddveig Botnen** were substitute teachers on Utsira. In 1938: **Jakob Gre.**

26. **Bjarne Espeset.** 1938 – 1946
Born Feb. 24, 1912 in Vik, Gaular in Sunnfjord.
Married on Nov. 1, 1940 to **Magnhild Fjeldheim,** born May 21, 1915, daughter of Sofie and Johan Mathias Bendiksen, tenant farmer no. 23 e, Skare.

Children:
- a. Kjellaug, born Sept. 25, 1941.
- b. Jostein, born Feb. 27, 1943.
- c. Magne Kolbein, born Feb. 10, 1946.
- d. Asbjorn, born June 24, 1949.
- e. Berit, born July 23, 1951.
- f. Sigrid, born Oct. 14, 1954.

Bjarne began as teacher in Utsira in the fall of 1938. He moved to Torvestad in the spring of 1946.

26a. **Magne Kåre Sømming** was substitute teacher here in 1943, and in 1946 **Ingebjørg Traedal** was a substitute.

27. **Martinius Johan Skjold.** 1945 – 1947

28. **Idar Havikbotn.** 1947 – 1960
Born Oct. 30, 1919 in Solund, son of Ida and Johannes Havikbotn, see no. 22, above.
Married July 22, 1950 to **Malmfrid Kvalvik,** born Jan. 20, 1924, daughter of Gjertrud and Toralf Kvalvik, farm no. 11 a, Kvalvik.

Children:
- a. Malmfrid Ida, born Apr. 9, 1953, married to Terje Hiller, lives in Haugesund.
- b. Gjertrud Torunn, born Apr. 29, 1955, married to Jon Magne Waernes, lives in Suldalsosen.
- c. Jardar. born June 24, 1963, lives on Bokn.

Idar was a teacher at the "continuation school" (a more practical alternative to high school) in the first year and after that he taught in the public school system. He was a teacher in Nerstrand for two years, and after that in Haugesund.

29. **Hans Vrå,** 1949 – 1950, teacher at the continuation school.
30. **Arnold Eiken,** 1951 – 1952, teacher at the continuation school, from Karmøy.
31. **Ragnvald Jåsund,** 1954 – 1955. teacher at the continuation school.
32. **Karl Anundsen,** 1958 – 1959, teacher at the continuation school, from Stavanger.
33. **Magnus Svindal,** 1960.
34. **Hans Sund**, 1960, from Koppervik.
35. **Torkel Kaupang,** 1960 – 1961,
36. **Magne Johansen,** 1961 – 1967, from Haugesund.
37. **Gerd Pedersen,** 1962 – 1967, from Arendal, married to Harry Skare.
38. **Tobias Hansen,** 1961 – 1963, tenant farmer no. 37, Kvalvik.
39. **Liv Abelsnes,** 1964.
40. **Anne Kristine Fagerland,** 1964 – 1965, from Saevlandsvik.
41. **Ellen Tove Eie**, 1964 – 1965, from Kviteseid, teacher at the continuation school.
42. **Fred Anthonsen,** 1965 – 1966, teacher at the continuation school, from Fredrikstad.
43. **Bjarne Eldholm,** 1964 – 1965 and 1967 – 1975, from Stavanger, school principal, married to Oddny Myrvang, see no. 69 below.
44. **Anna Tjøsvoll,** 1965.
45. **Else Wallset,** 1965.
46. **Ole Johan Hovland,** 1965 – 1966, from Haugesund.
47. **Jonas Bjarne Hansen,** 1966 – 1967 and 1971 – 1972, from Sandnes, married in 1970 to Eli Skare.
48. **Eva Husby–Thorsen,** 1967. teacher at the continuation school, from Torvestad.
49. **Edvard Langkås,** 1967 – 1968, born in 1944, from Bø in Telemark, teacher at the continuation school.
50. **Thorvald Saehlie,** 1967 – 1968, from Vang near Hamar, married.
51. **Rønnaug Håve,** 1967 – 1969, from Sjåk in Gudbrandsdalen.
52. **Kari Skåren,** 1967 – until today, school principal from 1987, see farm no. 56 – 2, Nordvik.
53. **Alvhild Vassel,** 1968 – 1969, from Herand in Hardanger.
54. **Dag Magne Jakobsen,** 1969 – 1970, teacher at the continuation school.
55. **Marit Seljeflot,** 1969 – 1971, from Ørsta.
56. **Kai Erik Simensen,** 1970 – 1972, school principal, from Randaberg.

57. **Ingrid Helle Olsen,** 1970 – 1971, from Stavanger.
58. **Tor Stornes,** 1971 – 1972, from Oslo.
59. **Margareth Flåtnes,** 1971 – 1972, from Stokke, Tønsberg.
60. **Bjorg Skålnes,** 1971 – to date, see tenant farmer no. 81, Nordvik.
61. **Jorunn Nordvik,** 1971 – 1972, 1987 – 1992 and later, see farm no. 15 – 12, Nordvik
62. **Jon Iversen,** 1972 – 1973, from Oslo.
63. **Haldis Sagvold,** 1972 – 1973.
64. **Paul Tore Paulsen,** 1972 – 1974, school principal, from Arendal, married.
65. **Astri Jernquist,** 1972 – 1974.
66. **Osmund Thorsnes,** 1973.
67. **Gerd Hilde Neset,** 1973.
68. **Jone Oliversen,** 1973.
69. **Oddny Myrvang Eldholm,** 1973 – 1975, married to Bjarne, no. 43 here.
70. **Steinar Røssevold,** 1973 – 1975, from Ålesund.
71. **Per Breivigen,** 1973 – 1974, from Hovden, Setesdal.
72. **Jostein Nilsen**, 1974 to date, see farm no. 1 – 14, Klovn.
73. **Helene Daviksnes,** 1974 – 1975.
74. **Ole Førland,** 1974 – 1975.
75. **Enok Lauvås,** 1974 – 1977, School Principal, from Sandnes.
76. **Thorild Albrechtsen Løvoll,** 1975 – 1977, from Lunner, married to Terje, no. 77 here.
77. **Terje Løvoll,** 1975 – 1977.
78. **Inge Strømø,** 1977 – 1978.
79. **Walther Hansen,** 1977 – 1979, School Principal.
80. **Kjellaug Klovning,** 1978 – 1979 and later, married in 1980 to Leif K. Klovning, tenant farmer no. 31, Klovning.
81. **Marit Eide Klovning,** 1978 – to date, married in 1976 to Arne O. Klovning, tenant farmer no. 42, Hovland.
82. **Lars Kvalem,** 1979.
83. **Ragnhild Sveen,** 1979 – 1980, from Sveio.
84. **Oddmund Borlaug,** 1979 – 1985, School Principal, from Bergen.
85. **Heidi Katrine Bentsen,** 1980.
86. **Bodil Jensen,** 1982, married to Tor Leif Helgesen.
87. **Kjellaug Skare,** 1982 – 1983, daughter of Hanna and Tobias Skare, tenant farmer no. 43, Skare.
88. **Terje Skare,** 1983 – 1984, son of Hanna and Tobias Skare, tenant farmer no. 43, Skare.
89. **Anne Kvilhaug,** 1984, from Karmøy.
90. **Marit Søndenaa,** 1985 – 1986, from Haugesund.

91. **Odd Arne Birkelund,** 1985 – 1987, School Principal, from Tromsø.
92. **Lars Herman Kløcker,** 1986 – 1987, from Skien, living with Synnøve Tryggestad, from Hellesylt, public school teacher.
93. **Norunn Hauge,** 1987 to date, married in 1993 to Egil Skare, tenant farmer no. 41, Kvalvik.
94. **Embrik Kaslegard,** 1989 – 1994, born 1965, from Torpo in Hallingdal, married to:
95. **Gerd Line Roysi,** 1989 – 1994, born 1965, from Ål in Hallingdal. Their children are: Sondre, born Feb. 12, 1991 and Gaute, born July 7, 1993.
96. **Atle Blehr Patterson,** 1991 to date, born Dec. 18, 1966, from Odda, married May 8, 1993 to:
97. **Inger Johanne Slagnes,** 1991 to date, born Mar. 15, 1967, from Volda. Their daughter is: Anna, born Nov. 6, 1993.

In addition to the above, others have taught for Utsira on an hourly basis for shorter periods of time in crafts and carpentry.

NOTES

1. Information is from Jan Petersen's manuscripts in the *Bygdebok-Arkivet* (Local History Archives), Stavanger Museum, Stavanger, Norway. See see http://www.museumstavanger.no (in Norwegian).
2. From Nils Okland's article in "Yearbook from Karmsund," 1951–55, pages 83–85, Haugaland Museum, Haugaland, Norway. See website at http://www.haugalandmuseene.no (in Norwegian).
3. District Financial Records of 1646 for Stavanger, Norway.
4. Information from *Stamtavle over slekten Forman (*"Forman Family Genealogical Records"), Bergen – Copenhagen, 1917, by Anthon Mohr Wiesener and Vilh. H. Finsen.
5. It was perhaps Jens who was married to Tore Svendsbø. She was married on Utsira and had four daughters. One was married to Pål Berge, Sveio, one was the mother of Torstein Hagland, one possibly married on Mølstre in Sveio, and the last one was married on Utsira. For further information see *Gards og Ættesoge for Sveio* ("Farm and family history in Sveio"), Vol. 1, page 169 and Vol. 2, page 227.
6. Stavanger County Archives, Section 86, Supplements.
7. *Rogaland Fiskarsoga* ("Rogaland Fishing History"), 1933, page 303.
8. *Stavanger Amtstidende* (Stavanger County Gazette), August 1, 1859. According to the article, " . . . and yet another example of the sorry effects of hard liquor."
9. From *Haugesund Avis* newspaper, Sept. 15, 1904.
10. The information is taken from "The Ostrem–Simonsen Family History," 1957, written by Berentine and Kristian's granddaughter Bertina Skaret, and also from George B. Hovland's autobiography.
11. *Vestlandsposten* newspaper, Nov. 28, 1914 and "The Ostrem–Simonsen Family History," written by Amanda Nesvig and Bertina Skaret, 1959.
12. According to *Ifølge tingbok for Ryfylke* (Court Records of Ryfylke), C 1 1761–1766, p. 91b (Reg. Nov. 23, 1761): *Sheriff Andreas Stoer on behalf of Anbjorn Rasmussen Hovland is requesting the two men, John Olsen Houge and Elling Johannesen Østrem under oath to explain how closely Anbjorn Rasmussen and Anne Johansdatter Osnes are related in their marriage? The above–mentioned men testified under oath that Anbjorn Rasmussen's father and Anne Johansdatter's mother's father were half–brothers, consequently they had separate fathers and the same mother. Accordingly, the said persons are related once and twice removed, but not as in intermarriage.*

13. Article in *Skolehistorisk Årbok for Rogaland* ("School History Yearbook for Rogaland"), 1993, page 61.
14. The 82–year–old George B. Hovland wrote a brief review of his life, from his birth at Utsira until he lived as a pensioner with his daughter, Lavina Martha, in Ainsworth, Nebraska. It is 14–15 pages long and is in the possession of his grandchild Joy Brocker, Littleton, Colorado. Here George writes about the ships he sailed on before he in 1866 attended the Navigasjonskole (The School of Navigation) in Stavanger. The crossing with the ship *Undine* in 1871 is detailed and his decision to settle in Newman Grove, Nebraska, his "contact" with Knute Nelson, and how he became a successful farmer, merchant and hotel host. His Utsira visits in 1882 and 1885 are described and how after he was "swindled out of everything he owned" when the railroad came. His story ends like this (from a letter): . . . *"he is now 82 years old past is on his feet and looken efter his buisnes and alway looken for more..."*
15. Bergen newspaper *Bergen Stiftstidende*, 21 and 28 August and also, 29 Sept. 1842.
16. Haugesund newspaper *Haugesund Avis*, Nov. 18, 1933 and the Christmas issue in 1934.
17. Haugesund newspaper, Sept. 4, 1900.
18. The vessel *De Vrouw Alberdine* tore loose from anchor in Helgoland in the fall of 1808 after a trip to London. In the panic that must have ensued when the ship appeared to collide with another ship, the crew managed to climb over into another vessel, and *De Vrouw Alberdine* drifted empty without crew across the sea in the direction of Utsira. The ship was salvaged and this caused a huge excitement and a lot of activity in Utsira as well as Stavanger and also Kristiansand. (excerpt from letter of Egil Harald Grude, dated Jan. 14, 1987).

    According to records it was 16 men from Utsira who on Oct. 23 in 1808 salvaged this ship. These men where: Ole Jakobsen Austrheim, John Knudsen Klovning, Gaut Johannesen Nordvik, Bård Bårdsen Austrheim, Tormod Sorensen Nordvik, Ole Olsen Kvalvik, Anders Andersen Kvalvik, Jakob Torbjornsen Austrheim, Lars Hansen Nordvik, Nils Johnsen Kvalvik, Lars Thomassen Skare, Rasmus Thomassen Hovland, Knut Johannesen Klovning, John Johannesen Klovning, Ole Gudmundsen Austrheim and Thore Thorsen Nordvik. Johannes Helgesen Nordvik, Bård Bårdsen the younger Austrheim, and Anbjorn Gudmundsen Austrheim were not successful in their claim that they assisted in the salvage of the ship.

    Four of those 16 men — Tormod Sorensen Nordvik, Ole Kvalvik, Anders Andersen Kvalvik and Lars Thomassen Skare — sold their shares to ship captain Nomen Frereihs, Stavanger, for 90 rdl. each share, on Oct. 30, 1808. The cargo, which consisted of 27,136 lbs. of indigo, was sold at auction in August and October 1809. Natural indigo dye was at the time very expensive and was known as "Asia's Blue Gold."

    It is still not clear if all the people who salvaged this ship got their full share of the salvaging money, which was 5000 rdl. per person. Below is an excerpt from Joh. N. Tønnesen's *Kaperfart og skipsfart 1807-1814* ("Privateer Activities and Commercial Shipping 1807 – 1814"), published in 1955, page 112:

...It may also be of interest to know that this ship, salvaged by 16 men from Utsira -- when the ship and its cargo were sold -- the King (government) was awarded with 1/2 of the salvaging money, and the other 1/2 went to the men who salvaged the ship. Their part amounted to 80,000 rdl. at a time, August 1809, when the value of the rdl. was fairly good. One can easily understand how 5000 rdl. per person might change the financial conditions for many poor fishermen and marine pilots, particularly since many of the salvaging crew bore the same family name, and particularly if they had the sense to invest the money in real values before inflation made it worthless.

19. Stavanger newspaper *Amtstidende and Adresseavis*, Sept. 3, 1868.
20. *Stavangeren* newspaper, Aug. 21, 1880, and *Haugesund Avis* newspaper, Mar. 24, 1923.
21. *Haugesund Avis* newspaper, Mar. 18, 1927. Jan. 4, 1928 and Mar. 18, 1932.
22. Jonas Dahl's novel *Cargadør Sahl* from 1898 provides a good characterization of Dahm and Sira'ites, see also article in *Haugesund Avis*, Feb. 3, 1930 and Feb. 24, 1931.
23. *Haugesunderen* newspaper, Mar. 14, 1890.
24. *Haugesunds Avis* newspaper, Aug. 28, 1924.
25. See county records for Sunhordaland I.A. 16a, 1675, vol. 9b–10b, *Vårting holdt på Halsnøy Kloster* ("Meeting held at Halsnøy Cloister"), *April 30, 1675*. Also letter from the King of same year.
26. *Haugesund Avis*, June 11, 1934.
27. *Haugesunderen*, Feb. 16, 1887.
28. *Haugesunds Avis*, Aug. 16, 1933.
29. *Haugesunds Avis*, July 25, 1927.
30. *Haugesunderen*, May 13, 1885.
31. The information is for the most part taken from Nils Modstein Vestbø, Steinesvåg on Judaberg.
32. From *Forhandlingsprotokol for Udsire Sogns Skolevæsen* ("Case Journal for Utsira Parish School System"), 1845–89.
33. Article, *Klokkarættene Wegner og Bø i Torvestad* ("Parish Clerk Families of Wegner and Bø in Torvestad"), taken from the *Årbok for Karmsund* (Karmsund Yearbook), 1951–55, pages 93–94.
34. Two Scottish girls were saved from a shipwreck off the west coast of Norway and were brought ashore and cared for to the extent that they settled and established their families there. It appeared that they had a substantially rich brother in Holland who died without any dependants. His last will and testament apparently dedicated his estate to the sisters on the condition that the money should only be made available 150 years after he died. It was determined that the brother was identified as Pieter Teyler van der Holst, who the records showed died in Damstraat in 1778.

It was documented that on April 8, 1873, the courts ruled that even though proper relationship could be proven, all rights to the inheritance were void, if not claimed within 30 years after van der Holst's death. This ruling was confirmed in the Supreme Court in Haag in 1925.

It had been determined that a notarized copy of the testament of Pieter Teyler van der Holst dated May 1757 existed, identifying van der Holst's nephew, Willem van der Vooren and a niece Jacoba van der Vooren and other identified institutions, church organizations and servants as heirs, and there was no mention of any potential Norwegian heirs.

The Dutch government had also confirmed that no further funds from the estate were undisposed and further claims should be discouraged.

This also convinced Norwegian authorities that the case was closed, but it still did not convince everyone on the west coast of Norway in those hard times. As late as 1930, there are records of people moving to Bergen in efforts to establish a relationship to the Scottish girls. More at http://home.online.no/~fndbred/holl.htm (in Norwegian).

35. Ulvestad, Martin, *Nordmændene I Amerika – deres Historie og Rekord* ("Norwegians in America – their History and Record"), 1907, State Archives in Bergen University Library, digital copy at http://da2.uib.no/cgi-win/WebBok.exe?slag=lesbok&bokid=ulvestad.

INDEX

A

B

C

D

E

F

G

H

I

J

K

L

M

N

O

P

R

S

T

U

V

W

Jostein Austrheim

Born in 1953, Jostein Austrheim worked as a farmer on the family farm named Austrheim on the island of Utsira in Norway from 1974 until 2009. Since then, he has been spending most of his time working as a carpenter/caretaker and restructuring and modernizing his house. His greatest hobby is the history of Utsira. He had been collecting material since the beginning of the 1980s and the culmination of that research was *Utsira, Gard og Slekt* (Utsira, Farm and Family), by Jostein Austrheim, published in 1995, of which this book is a translation, and *Utsira fram til år 2000* (Utsira, to the year 2000), by Roar Svendsen and Bjørn Arild Hansen Ersland, with the assistance of Jostein Austreim, published in May, 2000.

Austrheim graduated from Rogaland Jordbruksskole (Rogaland Agricultural College) of Tveit (1972), at Nedstrand, Tysvær, Norway. He was planning graduate study when he was called back to Utsira to manage the farm due to his father's ill health. Like many other local history writers, there was an interest in the farmers and their families who were the driving force behind the present day.

The writer hopes this translation of his book will be well received among its readers.

Photo by Johannes Christoffersen, Sept. 2011

Johannes Christoffersen

Johannes Christoffersen, a native of Norway, was born in Kragero in 1931 and grew up in Skien. In 1964 he emigrated to the USA and moved with his family, wife and baby daughter, to New York where he worked for the Norwegian company, the Kvaerner Group, promoting Norwegian ship technology to the world shipbuilding market. In 1978 he moved to the West Coast, settled in Bellevue, WA, and started his own company. The main activity was in partnership with other Norwegian and American companies to retrofit ocean-going tankers during voyages world-wide with Inert Gas Systems and Performance and Condition Monitoring instrumentation.

Now retired, Christoffersen enjoys sailing and hiking along with his photo hobby and the good life in the great Northwest, with his wife, Ragnhild, and their daughter, Marianne, and her family consisting of husband and two children, who live near by.

Photo by Jostein Austrheim, Sept. 2011

Ferry leaving Utsira harbor, Sept. 2011. Photo by Johannes Christoffersen.

www.ingramcontent.com/pod-product-compliance
Lightning Source LLC
Chambersburg PA
CBHW071302310326
41914CB00118B/1933/J

* 9 7 8 0 6 1 5 5 9 8 3 7 6 *